PENGUIN BOOKS

THE ISRAEL-ARAB READER

WALTER LAQUEUR is director of the Institute of Contemporary History and the Wiener Library in London. He is coeditor (with George Mosse) of the *Journal of Contemporary History*. His books have been widely acclaimed and have been translated into many languages. These works include: *Young Germany, Russia and Germany: A Century of Conflict, The Road to War, The Fate of the Revolution, Struggle for the Middle East, Europe Reborn, Out of the Ruins of Europe, A History of Zionism, Weimar: A Cultural History 1918–1933, Confrontation: The Middle East and World Politics, The Terrible Secret,* and two novels, *The Missing Years* and *Farewell to Europe.* His latest historical work is *Europe In Our Time.*

BARRY RUBIN is a senior fellow in Middle East studies at the Georgetown University Center for Strategic and International Studies and a professorial lecturer at the Georgetown University School of Foreign Service. He is the author of *Paved with Good Intentions: The American Experience and Iran, The Arab States and the Palestine Conflict,* and *Secrets of State: The State Department in U.S. Foreign Policy,* among other works.

THE
ISRAEL-ARAB
READER

A Documentary History
of the Middle East Conflict

REVISED AND UPDATED

Walter Laqueur and Barry Rubin, editors

PENGUIN BOOKS

PENGUIN BOOKS

Viking Penguin, a division of Penguin Books USA Inc.,
375 Hudson Street, New York, New York 10014, U.S.A.
Penguin Books Ltd, 27 Wrights Lane,
London W8 5TZ, England
Penguin Books Australia Ltd, Ringwood,
Victoria, Australia
Penguin Books Canada Ltd, 10 Alcorn Avenue, Suite 300,
Toronto, Ontario, Canada M4V 3B2
Penguin Books (N.Z.) Ltd, 182–190 Wairau Road,
Auckland 10, New Zealand

Penguin Books Ltd. Registered Offices:
Harmondsworth, Middlesex, England

First published 1969
Revised edition published 1970
Third revised edition published 1976
This fourth revised and updated edition first published in
Pelican Books 1984
Penguin Books 1991
Published simultaneously in Canada

1 3 5 7 9 10 8 6 4 2

LIBRARY OF CONGRESS CATALOGING IN PUBLICATION DATA
Main entry under title:
The Israel-Arab reader.
  Bibliography: p.
  1. Jewish-Arab relations—1917–   —Sources.
I. Laqueur, Walter, 1921–   . II. Rubin, Barry M.
DS119.7.I8256   1984b   956   84-10992
ISBN 0 14 01.6990 3

Grateful acknowledgment is made to The New York Times
Company for permission to reprint the maps on pages 580
and 581. Copyright © 1975 by The New York Times
Company.

Map on page xv by David Lindroth

Printed in the United States of America
Set in Times Roman

Contents

PART III: *ISRAEL AND THE ARAB WORLD 1948-1967*

PART IV: *VIEWS AND COMMENTS: THE ARAB-ISRAELI CONFLICT TODAY AND TOMORROW*

Gamal Abdel Nasser: "The Most Severe Crisis"

PART V: *FROM WAR TO WAR*

PART VI: *THE YOM KIPPUR WAR AND AFTER*

PART VII: *CAMP DAVID AND WAR IN LEBANON*

Introduction

This collection of documents and commentary aims to provide a better understanding of the background and contemporary direction of the Arab-Israeli conflict. The story of the unfolding crisis is traced on the basis of Zionist and Arab declarations, the findings and recommendations of the various commissions of inquiry during the 1930s and 1940s, and the statements of Arab, Zionist, and other involved leaders. Following this, the events surrounding the 1967 and 1973 wars and their aftermath are analyzed by participants, as are events leading to the negotiation of the Camp David accords and the positions of Israel, the Arab states, the PLO, the United States, the USSR, and Europeans concerning possible settlements of the conflict and the future of the West Bank and of the Palestinians.

We would like to record our gratitude to the Middle Eastern Document Section at the Institute of Contemporary History (the Wiener Library) in London and, in particular, to Mrs. Christa Wichmann and Mr. Ze'ev Ben Shlomo for assisting in the collection of documents and to Mr. Eric Fredell for helping in the preparation of Part VII.

Walter Laqueur
Barry Rubin

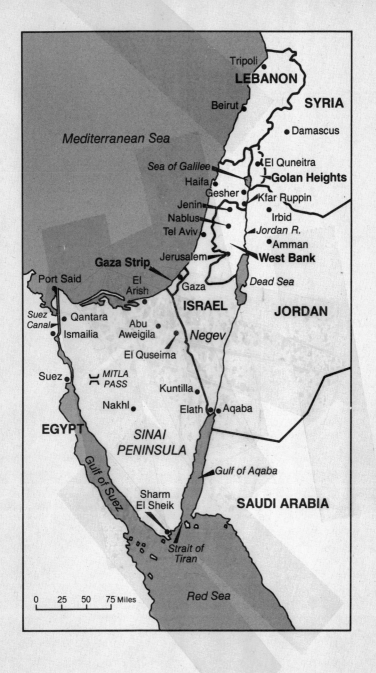

PART I

From the Bilu to the British Mandate

Part I of the Reader covers the period from the first stirrings of the Jewish and Arab national movements to 1917, the date of the Balfour Declaration. The tie between the Jewish communities in what was still commonly defined as the diaspora had been submerged but never entirely severed; it survived, for instance, in the traditional prayer ("Next year in Jerusalem") and found its political expression in the emergence of the Zionist movement in the last decade of the nineteenth century. There was no specific Arab Palestinian national consciousness, but among the leaders of the Arab population of the Ottoman Empire the demand for national self-determination gained ground. After the defeat of the Turks in 1918, this movement quickly gathered momentum.

Document 1

The Manifesto of the Bilu

Bilu are the first letters of a passage in Isaiah, Chapter 2, Verse 5: "House of Jacob, come let us go." The Biluim, about five hundred young people mainly from the Kharkov region. were part of the wider movement of the "Lovers of Zion" (*Hovevei Zion*) which had developed in Russia in the early eighteen-eighties mainly under the impact of the pogroms of 1881. This manifesto was issued by a Bilu group in Constantinople in 1882.

To our brothers and sisters in Exile!
'If I help not myself, who will help me?'
Nearly two thousand years have elapsed since, in an evil hour, after a heroic struggle, the glory of our Temple vanished in fire and our kings and chieftains changed their crowns and diadems for the chains of exile. We lost our country where dwelt our beloved sires. Into the Exile we took with us, of all our glories, only a spark of the fire by which our Temple, the abode of our Great One, was engirdled, and this little spark kept us alive while the towers of our enemies crumbled into dust, and this spark leapt into celestial flame and shed light on the heroes of our race and inspired them to endure the horrors of the dance of death and the tortures of the *autos-da-fé*. And this spark is again kindling and will shine for us, a true pillar of fire going before us on the road to Zion, while behind us is a pillar of cloud, the pillar of oppression threatening to destroy us. Sleepest thou, O our nation? What hast thou been doing until 1882? Sleeping, and dreaming the false dream of Assimilation. Now, thank God, thou art awak-

ened from thy slothful slumber. The Pogroms have awakened thee from thy charmed sleep. Thine eyes are open to recognise the cloudy delusive hopes. Canst thou listen silently to the taunts and mockeries of thine enemies? . . . Where is thy ancient pride, thine olden spirit? Remember that thou wast a nation possessing a wise religion, a law, a constitution, a celestial Temple whose wall* is still a silent witness to the glories of the past; that thy sons dwelt in palaces and towers, and thy cities flourished in the splendour of civilisation, while these enemies of thine dwelt like beasts in the muddy marshes of their dark woods. While thy children were clad in purple and fine linen, they wore the rough skins of the wolf and the bear. Art thou not ashamed?

Hopeless is your state in the West; the star of your future is gleaming in the East. Deeply conscious of all this, and inspired by the true teaching of our great master, Hillel, 'If I help not myself, who will help me?' we propose to form the following society for national ends.

1. The Society will be named 'BILU', according to the motto 'House of Jacob, come, let us go'. It will be divided into local branches according to the numbers of its members.

2. The seat of the Committee shall be Jerusalem.

3. Donations and contributions shall be unfixed and unlimited.

WE WANT:

1. A home in our country. It was given us by the mercy of God; it is ours as registered in the archives of history.

2. To beg it of the Sultan himself, and if it be impossible to obtain this, to beg that we may at least possess it as a state within a larger state; the internal administration to be ours, to have our civil and political rights, and to act with the Turkish Empire only in foreign affairs, so as to help our brother Ishmael in the time of his need.

We hope that the interests of our glorious nation will rouse the national spirit in rich and powerful men, and that everyone, rich or poor, will give his best labours to the holy cause.

Greetings, dear brothers and sisters!

HEAR, O ISRAEL! The Lord our God, the Lord is one, and our land Zion is our one hope.

GOD be with us! THE PIONEERS OF BILU.

---

* The Wailing Wall.

Document 2

Negib Azouri: Program of the League of the Arab Fatherland*

N. Azouri, a Christian Arab, edited the journal *L'Indé-pendance Arabe* in Paris before the first world war. His *"Réveil de la Nation Arabe dans l'Asie Turque . . ."* (1905) from which this excerpt is drawn was the "first open demand for the secession of the Arab lands from the Ottoman Empire." (Sylvia G. Haim: *Arab Nationalism*)

. . . There is nothing more liberal than the league's program. The league wants, before anything else, to separate the civil and the religious power, in the interest of Islam and the Arab nation, and to form an Arab empire stretching from the Tigris and the Euphrates to the Suez Isthmus, and from the Mediterranean to the Arabian Sea.

The mode of government will be a constitutional sultanate based on the freedom of all the religions and the equality of all the citizens before the law. It will respect the interests of Europe, all the concessions and all the privileges which had been granted to her up to now by the Turks. It will also respect the autonomy of the Lebanon, and the independence of the principalities of Yemen, Nejd, and Iraq.

The league offers the throne of the Arab Empire to that prince of the Khedivial family of Egypt who will openly declare himself in its favor and who will devote his energy and his resources to this end.

It rejects the idea of unifying Egypt and the Arab Empire under the same monarchy, because the Egyptians do not belong to the Arab race; they are of the African Berber family and the language which they spoke before Islam bears no similarity to Arabic. There exists, moreover, between Egypt and the Arab Empire a natural frontier which must be respected in order to avoid the introduction, in the new state, of the germs of discord and destruction. Never, as a matter of fact, have the ancient Arab caliphs succeeded for any length of time in controlling the two countries at the same time. . . .

* Translated by Sylvia G. Haim.

Document 3

Theodor Herzl: The Jewish State

Theodor Herzl (1860-1904) was the founder of modern political Zionism. In the preface to *Der Judenstaat* (published in 1896) he says: "The Idea which I have developed in this pamphlet is a very old one: it is the restoration of the Jewish State."

. . . The Jewish question still exists. It would be foolish to deny it. It is a remnant of the Middle Ages, which civilized nations do not even yet seem able to shake off, try as they will. They certainly showed a generous desire to do so when they emancipated us. The Jewish question exists wherever Jews live in perceptible numbers. Where it does not exist, it is carried by Jews in the course of their migrations. We naturally move to those places where we are not persecuted, and there our presence produces persecution. This is the case in every country, and will remain so, even in those highly civilized—for instance, France—until the Jewish question finds a solution on a political basis. The unfortunate Jews are now carrying the seeds of Anti-Semitism into England; they have already introduced it into America.

I believe that I understand Anti-Semitism, which is really a highly complex movement. I consider it from a Jewish standpoint, yet without fear or hatred. I believe that I can see what elements there are in it of vulgar sport, of common trade jealousy, of inherited prejudice, of religious intolerance, and also of pretended self-defence. I think the Jewish question is no more a social than a religious one, notwithstanding that it sometimes takes these and other forms. It is a national question, which can only be solved by making it a political world-question to be discussed and settled by the civilized nations of the world in council.

We are a people—one people.

We have honestly endeavored everywhere to merge ourselves in the social life of surrounding communities and to preserve the faith of our fathers. We are not permitted to do so. In vain are we loyal patriots, our loyalty in some places running to extremes; in vain do we make the same sacrifices of life and property as our fellow-citizens; in vain do we strive to increase the fame of our native land in science and art, or her wealth by trade and commerce. In countries where we have lived for centuries we are still cried down as strangers, and often by those whose ancestors were not yet domiciled in the land where Jews had already had experience of suffering. The majority may decide which are the strangers; for this, as indeed every point which arises in the relations between nations, is a question of might. I do not here surrender any portion of our prescriptive right, when I make this statement merely in my own name as an individual. In the world as it now is and for an indefinite period will probably remain, might precedes right. It is useless, therefore, for us to be loyal patriots, as were the Huguenots who were forced to emigrate. If we could only be left in peace. . . .

But I think we shall not be left in peace.

Oppression and persecution cannot exterminate us. No nation on earth has survived such struggles and sufferings as we have gone through. Jew-baiting has merely stripped off our weaklings; the strong among us were invariably true to their race when persecution broke out against them. This attitude was most clearly apparent in the period immediately following the emancipation of the Jews. Those Jews who were advanced intellectually and materially entirely lost the feeling of belonging to their race. Wherever our political well-being has lasted for any length of time, we have assimilated with our surroundings. I think this is not discreditable. Hence, the statesman who would wish to see a Jewish strain in his nation would have to provide for the duration of our political well-being; and even a Bismarck could not do that.

For old prejudices against us still lie deep in the hearts of the people. He who would have proofs of this need only listen to the people where they speak with frankness and simplicity: proverb and fairy-tale are both Anti-Semitic. A nation is everywhere a great child, which can certainly be educated; but its education would, even in most favorable circumstances, occupy such a vast amount of time that we could, as already mentioned, remove our own difficulties by other means long before the process was accomplished.

Assimilation, by which I understood not only external conformity in dress, habits, customs, and language, but also identity of feeling and manner—assimilation of Jews could be effected only by intermarriage. But the need for mixed marriages would have to be felt by the majority; their mere recognition by law would certainly not suffice. . . .

No one can deny the gravity of the situation of the Jews. Wherever they live in perceptible numbers, they are more or less persecuted. Their equality before the law, granted by statute, has become practically a dead letter. They are debarred from filling even moderately high positions, either in the army, or in any public or private capacity. And attempts are made to thrust them out of business also: "Don't buy from Jews!"

Attacks in Parliaments, in assemblies, in the press, in the pulpit, in the street, on journeys—for example, their exclusion from certain hotels—even in places of recreation, become daily more numerous. The forms of persecutions varying according to the countries and social circles in which they occur. In Russia, imposts are levied on Jewish villages; in Rumania, a few persons are put to death; in Germany, they get a good beating occasionally; in Austria, Anti-Semites exercise terrorism over all public life; in Algeria, there are travelling agitators; in Paris, the Jews are shut out of the so-called best social circles and excluded from clubs. Shades of anti-Jewish feeling are innumerable. But this is not to be an attempt to make out a doleful category of Jewish hardships.

I do not intend to arouse sympathetic emotions on our behalf. That would be foolish, futile, and undignified proceeding. I shall content myself with putting the following questions to the Jews: Is it not true that, in countries where we live in perceptible numbers, the position of Jewish lawyers, doctors, technicians, teachers, and employees of all descriptions becomes daily more intolerable? Is it not true, that the Jewish middle classes are seriously threatened? Is it not true, that the passions of the mob are incited against our wealthy people? Is it not true, that our poor endure greater sufferings than any other proletariat? I think that this external pressure makes itself felt everywhere. In our economically upper classes it causes discomfort, in our middle classes continual and grave anxieties, in our lower classes absolute despair.

Everything tends, in fact, to one and the same conclusion, which is clearly enunciated in that classic Berlin phrase: "*Juden Raus!*" (Out with the Jews!)

I shall now put the Question in the briefest possible form: Are we to "get out" now and where to?

Or, may we yet remain? And, how long?

Let us first settle the point of staying where we are. Can we hope for better days, can we possess our souls in patience, can we wait in pious resignation till the princes and peoples of this earth are more mercifully disposed towards us? I say that we cannot hope for a change in the current of feeling. And why not? Even if we were as near to the hearts of princes as are their other subjects, they could not protect us. They would only feel popular hatred by showing us too much favor. By "too much," I really mean less than is claimed as a right by every ordinary citizen, or by every race. The nations in whose midst Jews live are all either covertly or openly Anti-Semitic.

The common people have not, and indeed cannot have, any historic comprehension. They do not know that the sins of the Middle Ages are now being visited on the nations of Europe. We are what the Ghetto made us. We have attained pre-eminence in finance, because mediaeval conditions drove us to it. The same process is now being repeated. We are again being forced into finance, now it is the stock exchange, by being kept out of other branches of economic activity. Being on the stock exchange, we are consequently exposed afresh to contempt. At the same time we continue to produce an abundance of mediocre intellects who find no outlet, and this endangers our social position as much as does our increasing wealth. Educated Jews without means are now rapidly becoming Socialists. Hence we are certain to suffer very severely in the struggle between classes, because we stand in the most exposed position in the camps of both Socialists and capitalists. . . .

The Plan

The whole plan is in its essence perfectly simple, as it must necessarily be if it is to come within the comprehension of all.

Let the sovereignty be granted us over a portion of the globe large enough to satisfy the rightful requirements of a nation; the rest we shall manage for ourselves.

The creation of a new State is neither ridiculous nor impossible. We have in our day witnessed the process in connection with nations which were not largely members of the middle class, but poorer, less educated, and consequently weaker than ourselves. The Governments of all countries scourged by Anti-Semitism will be keenly interested in assisting us to obtain the sovereignty we want.

The plan, simple in design, but complicated in execution, will be carried out by two agencies: The Society of Jews and the Jewish Company.

The Society of Jews will do the preparatory work in the

domains of science and politics, which the Jewish Company will afterwards apply practically.

The Jewish Company will be the liquidating agent of the business interests of departing Jews, and will organize commerce and trade in the new country.

We must not imagine the departure of the Jews to be a sudden one. It will be gradual, continuous, and will cover many decades. The poorest will go first to cultivate the soil. In accordance with a preconceived plan, they will construct roads, bridges, railways and telegraph installations; regulate rivers; and build their own dwellings; their labor will create trade, trade will create markets and markets will attract new settlers, for every man will go voluntarily, at his own expense and his own risk. The labor expended on the land will enhance its value, and the Jews will soon perceive that a new and permanent sphere of operation is opening here for that spirit of enterprise which has heretofore met only with hatred and obloquy.

If we wish to found a State today, we shall not do it in the way which would have been the only possible one a thousand years ago. It is foolish to revert to old stages of civilization, as many Zionists would like to do. Supposing, for example, we were obliged to clear a country of wild beasts, we should not set about the task in the fashion of Europeans of the fifth century. We should not take spear and lance and go out singly in pursuit of bears; we would organize a large and active hunting party, drive the animals together, and throw a melinite bomb into their midst.

If we wish to conduct building operations, we shall not plant a mass of stakes and piles on the shore of a lake, but we shall build as men build now. Indeed, we shall build in a bolder and more stately style than was ever adopted before, for we now possess means which men never yet possessed.

The emigrants standing lowest in the economic scale will be slowly followed by those of a higher grade. Those who at this moment are living in despair will go first. They will be led by the mediocre intellects which we produce so superabundantly and which are persecuted everywhere.

This pamphlet will open a general discussion on the Jewish Question, but that does not mean that there will be any voting on it. Such a result would ruin the cause from the outset, and dissidents must remember that allegiance or opposition is entirely voluntary. He who will not come with us should remain behind.

Let all who are willing to join us, fall in behind our banner and fight for our cause with voice and pen and deed.

Those Jews who agree with our idea of a State will attach themselves to the Society, which will thereby be authorized to confer and treat with Governments in the name of our people. The Society will thus be acknowledged in its relations with Governments as a State-creating power. This acknowledgment will practically create the State.

Should the Powers declare themselves willing to admit our sovereignty over a neutral piece of land, then the Society will enter into negotiations for the possession of this land. Here two territories come under consideration, Palestine and Argentine. In both countries important experiments in colonization have been made, though on the mistaken principle of a gradual infiltration of Jews. An infiltration is bound to end badly. It continues till the inevitable moment when the native population feels itself threatened, and forces the Government to stop a further influx of Jews. Immigration is consequently futile unless we have the sovereign right to continue such immigration.

The Society of Jews will treat with the present masters of the land, putting itself under the protectorate of the European Powers, if they prove friendly to the plan. We could offer the present possessors of the land enormous advantages, assume part of the public debt, build new roads for traffic, which our presence in the country would render necessary, and do many other things. The creation of our State would be beneficial to adjacent countries, because the cultivation of a strip of land increases the value of its surrounding districts in innumerable ways.

Document 4

The Basle Declaration

This official statement of Zionist purpose was adopted by the first Zionist Congress in Basle in August 1897.

The aim of Zionism is to create for the Jewish people a home in Palestine secured by public law.

The Congress contemplates the following means to the attainment of this end:

1. The promotion, on suitable lines, of the colonization of Palestine by Jewish agricultural and industrial workers.

2. The organization and binding together of the whole of Jewry by means of appropriate institutions, local and international, in accordance with the laws of each country.

3. The strengthening and fostering of Jewish national sentiment and consciousness.

4. Preparatory steps towards obtaining government consent, where necessary, to the attainment of the aim of Zionism.

Document 5

The Sykes–Picot Agreement

Sir Mark Sykes (1873-1919), a distinguished British orientalist, and Charles Georges-Picot, formerly French Consul in Beirut, prepared a draft agreement in 1915–16 about the post-war division of the Middle East, which was also approved in principle by Russia.

1.   Sir Edward Grey to Paul Cambon, 15 May 1916

I shall have the honour to reply fully in a further note to your Excellency's note of the 9th instant, relative to the creation of an Arab State, but I should meanwhile be grateful if your Excellency could assure me that in those regions which, under the conditions recorded in that communication, become entirely French, or in which French interests are recognised as predominant, any existing British concessions, rights of navigation or development, and the rights and privileges of any British religious, scholastic, or medical institutions will be maintained.

His Majesty's Government are, of course, ready to give a reciprocal assurance in regard to the British area.

2.   Grey to Cambon, 16 May 1916

I have the honour to acknowledge the receipt of your Excellency's note of the 9th instant, stating that the French Government accept the limits of a future Arab State, or Confederation of States, and of those parts of Syria where French interests predominate, together with certain conditions attached thereto, such as they result from recent discussions in London and Petrograd on the subject.

I have the honour to inform your Excellency in reply that the acceptance of the whole project, as it now stands, will involve the abdication of considerable British interests, but, since His Majesty's Government recognise the advantage to the general cause of the Allies entailed in producing a more favourable internal political situation in Turkey, they are ready to accept the arrangement now arrived at, provided that the co-operation of the Arabs is secured, and that the Arabs fulfil the conditions and obtain the towns of Homs, Hama, Damascus, and Aleppo.

It is accordingly understood between the French and British Governments—

1. That France and Great Britain are prepared to recognize and protect an independent Arab State or a Confederation of Arab States in the areas (A) and (B) marked on the annexed map (*map not reproduced: Ed.*), under the suzerainty of an Arab chief. That in area (A) France, and in area (B) Great Britain, shall have priority of right of enterprise and local loans. That in area (A) France, and in area (B) Great Britain, shall alone supply advisers or foreign functionaries at the request of the Arab State or Confederation of Arab States.

2. That in the blue area France, and in the red area Great Britain, shall be allowed to establish such direct or indirect administration or control as they desire and as they may think fit to arrange with the Arab State or Confederation of Arab States.

3. That in the brown area there shall be established an international administration, the form of which is to be decided upon after consultation with Russia, and subsequently in consultation with the other Allies, and the representatives of the Shereef of Mecca.

4. That Great Britain be accorded (1) the ports of Haifa and Acre, (2) guarantee of a given supply of water from the Tigris and Euphrates in area (A) for area (B). His Majesty's Government, on their part, undertake that they will at no time enter into negotiations for the cession of Cyprus to any third Power without the previous consent of the French Government.

5. That Alexandretta shall be a free port as regards the trade of the British Empire, and that there shall be no discrimination in port charges or facilities as regards British shipping and British goods; that there shall be freedom of transit for British goods through Alexandretta and by railway through the blue area, whether those goods are intended for or originate in the red area, or (B) area, or area (A); and there shall be no discrimination, direct or indirect against British

goods on any railway or against British goods or ships at any port serving the areas mentioned.

That Haifa shall be a free port as regards the trade of France, her dominions and protectorates, and there shall be no discrimination in port charges or facilities as regards French shipping and French goods. There shall be freedom of transit for French goods through Haifa and by the British railway through the brown area, whether those goods are intended for or originate in the blue area, area (A), or area (B), and there shall be no discrimination, direct or indirect, against French goods on any railway, or against French goods or ships at any port serving the areas mentioned.

6. That in area (A) the Bagdad Railway shall not be extended southwards beyond Mosul, and in area (B) northwards beyond Samarra, until a railway connecting Baghdad with Aleppo via the Euphrates Valley has been completed, and then only with the concurrence of the two Governments.

7. That Great Britain has the right to build, administer, and be sole owner of a railway connecting Haifa with area (B), and shall have a perpetual right to transport troops along such a line at all times.

It is to be understood by both Governments that this railway is to facilitate the connexion of Baghdad with Haifa by rail, and it is further understood that, if the engineering difficulties and expense entailed by keeping this connecting line in the brown area only make the project unfeasible, that the French Government shall be prepared to consider that the line in question may also traverse the polygon Banias-Keis Marib-Salkhab Tell Otsda-Mesmie before reaching area (B).

8. For a period of twenty years the existing Turkish customs tariff shall remain in force throughout the whole of the blue and red areas, as well as in areas (A) and (B), and no increase in the rates of duty or conversion from *ad valorem* to specific rates shall be made except by agreement between the two Powers.

There shall be no interior customs barriers between any of the above-mentioned areas. The customs duties leviable on goods destined for the interior shall be collected at the port of entry and handed over to the administration of the area of destination.

9. It shall be agreed that the French Government will at no time enter into any negotiations for the cession of their rights and will not cede such rights in the blue area to any third Power, except the Arab State or Confederation of Arab States

without the previous agreement of His Majesty's Government, who, on their part, will give a similar undertaking to the French Government regarding the red area.

10. The British and French Governments, as the protectors of the Arab State, shall agree that they will not themselves acquire and will not consent to a third Power acquiring territorial possessions in the Arabian peninsula, nor consent to a third Power installing a naval base either on the east coast, or on the islands, of the Red Sea. This, however, shall not prevent such adjustment of the Aden frontier as may be necessary in consequence of recent Turkish aggression.

11. The negotiations with the Arabs as to the boundaries of the Arab State or Confederation of Arab States shall be continued through the same channel as heretofore on behalf of the two Powers.

12. It is agreed that measures to control the importation of arms into the Arab territories will be considered by the two Governments.

I have further the honour to state that, in order to make the agreement complete, His Majesty's Government are proposing to the Russian Government to exchange notes analogous to those exchanged by the latter and your Excellency's Government on the 26th April last. Copies of these notes will be communicated to your Excellency as soon as exchanged.

I would also venture to remind your Excellency that the conclusion of the present agreement raises, for practical consideration, the question of the claims of Italy to a share in any partition or rearrangement of Turkey in Asia, as formulated in article 9 of the agreement of the 26th April, 1915, between Italy and the Allies.

His Majesty's Government further consider that the Japanese Government should be informed of the arrangement now concluded.

Document 6

The McMahon Letter

Sir Henry McMahon (1862–1949), British High Commissioner in Cairo, negotiated in 1915–16 with Husain Ibn Ali, the Sherif of Mecca. The British government promised to support his bid for the restoration of the Caliphate (and leadership in the Arab world) if Husain supported the British war effort against Turkey. Palestine was not mentioned by name in this exchange: the Arabs subsequently claimed that it had been included in the promise of an independent Arab state. The British denied this—as evidenced by McMahon's letter published in the London *Times* in 1937.

October 24, 1915.

I have received your letter of the 29th Shawal, 1333, with much pleasure and your expression of friendliness and sincerity have given me the greatest satisfaction.

I regret that you should have received from my last letter the impression that I regarded the question of limits and boundaries with coldness and hesitation; such was not the case, but it appeared to me that the time had not yet come when that question could be discussed in a conclusive manner.

I have realised, however, from your last letter that you regard this question as one of vital and urgent importance. I have, therefore, lost no time in informing the Government of Great Britain of the contents of your letter, and it is with great pleasure that I communicate to you on their behalf the following statement, which I am confident you will receive with satisfaction.

The two districts of Mersina and Alexandretta and portions of Syria lying to the west of the districts of Damascus, Homs, Hama and Aleppo cannot be said to be purely Arab, and should be excluded from the limits demanded.

With the above modification, and without prejudice to our existing treaties with Arab chiefs, we accept those limits.

As for those regions lying within those frontiers wherein Great Britain is free to act without detriment to the interests of her ally, France, I am empowered in the name of the Government of Great Britain to give the following assurances and make the following reply to your letter:

(1) Subject to the above modifications, Great Britain is prepared to recognise and support the independence of the Arabs in all the regions within the limits demanded by the Sherif of Mecca.

(2) Great Britain will guarantee the Holy Places against all external aggression and will recognise their inviolability.

(3) When the situation admits, Great Britain will give to the Arabs her advice and will assist them to establish what may appear to be the most suitable forms of government in those various territories.

(4) On the other hand, it is understood that the Arabs have decided to seek the advice and guidance of Great Britain only, and that such European advisers and officials as may be required for the formation of a sound form of administration will be British.

(5) With regard to the *vilayets* of Bagdad and Basra, the Arabs will recognise that the established position and interests of Great Britain necessitate special administrative arrangements in order to secure these territories from foreign aggression to promote the welfare of the local populations and to safeguard our mutual economic interests.

I am convinced that this declaration will assure you beyond all possible doubt of the sympathy of Great Britain towards the aspirations of her friends the Arabs and will result in a firm and lasting alliance, the immediate results of which will be the expulsion of the Turks from the Arab countries and the freeing of the Arab peoples from the Turkish yoke, which for so many years has pressed heavily upon them.

I have confined myself in this letter to the more vital and important questions, and if there are any other matters dealt with in your letters which I have omitted to mention, we may discuss them at some convenient date in the future.

It was with very great relief and satisfaction that I heard of the safe arrival of the Holy Carpet and the accompanying offerings which, thanks to the clearness of your directions and the excellence of your arrangements, were landed without trouble or mishap in spite of the dangers and difficulties occasioned by the present sad war. May God soon bring a lasting peace and freedom of all peoples.

I am sending this letter by the hand of your trusted and excellent messenger, Sheikh Mohammed ibn Arif ibn Uraifan, and he will inform you of the various matters of interest, but of less vital importance, which I have not mentioned in this letter.

(Compliments).

(Signed): A. HENRY McMAHON.

Document 7

The Balfour Declaration

British policy during the war years became gradually committed to the idea of the establishment of a Jewish home in Palestine. After discussions on cabinet level and consultation with Jewish leaders, the decision was made known in the form of a letter by Arthur James Lord Balfour (1848-1930) to Lord Rothschild.

Foreign Office
November 2nd, 1917.

Dear Lord Rothschild,

I have much pleasure in conveying to you, on behalf of His Majesty's Government, the following declaration of sympathy with Jewish Zionist aspirations which has been submitted to, and approved by, the Cabinet.

"His Majesty's Government view with favour the establishment in Palestine of a national home for the Jewish people, and will use their best endeavours to facilitate the achievement of this object, it being clearly understood that nothing shall be done which may prejudice the civil and religious rights of existing non-Jewish communities in Palestine, or the rights and political status enjoyed by Jews in any other country."

I should be grateful if you would bring this declaration to the knowledge of the Zionist Federation.

Yours sincerely,
ARTHUR JAMES BALFOUR.

Document 8

The Feisal–Weizmann agreement and Feisal–Frankfurter letters

During the peace conference Emir Feisal (1855-1933), the son of Husain, the Sherif of Mecca, met various Jewish leaders and signed an agreement with Dr. Chaim Weizmann (1877-1952), leader of the Zionist movement. Feisal, who in 1921 became King of Iraq, had it announced ten years later that "His Majesty does not remember having written anything of that kind with his knowledge."

Agreement Between Emir Feisal and Dr. Weizmann January 3, 1919

His Royal Highness the Emir Feisal, representing and acting on behalf of the Arab Kingdom of Hedjaz, and Dr. Chaim

Weizmann, representing and acting on behalf of the Zionist Organisation, mindful of the racial kinship and ancient bonds existing between the Arabs and the Jewish people, and realising that the surest means of working out the consummation of their national aspirations is through the closest possible collaboration in the development of the Arab State and Palestine, and being desirous further of confirming the good understanding which exists between them, have agreed upon the following Articles:

ARTICLE I

The Arab State and Palestine in all their relations and undertakings shall be controlled by the most cordial goodwill and understanding, and to this end Arab and Jewish duly accredited agents shall be established and maintained in the respective territories.

ARTICLE II

Immediately following the completion of the deliberations of the Peace Conference, the definite boundaries between the Arab State and Palestine shall be determined by a Commission to be agreed upon by the parties hereto.

ARTICLE III

In the establishment of the Constitution and Administration of Palestine all such measures shall be adopted as will afford the fullest guarantees for carrying into effect the British Government's Declaration of the 2d of November, 1917.

ARTICLE IV

All necessary measures shall be taken to encourage and stimulate immigration of Jews into Palestine on a large scale, and as quickly as possible to settle Jewish immigrants upon the land through closer settlement and intensive cultivation of the soil. In taking such measures the Arab peasant and tenant farmers shall be protected in their rights, and shall be assisted in forwarding their economic development.

ARTICLE V

No regulation nor law shall be made prohibiting or interfering in any way with the free exercise of religion; and further the free exercise and enjoyment of religious profession and worship without discrimination or reference shall forever be allowed. No religious test shall ever be required for the exercise of civil or political rights.

ARTICLE VI

The Mohammedan Holy Places shall be under Mohammedan control.

ARTICLE VII

The Zionist Organisation proposes to send to Palestine a Commission of experts to make a survey of the economic possibilities of the country, and to report upon the best means for its development. The Zionist Organisation will place the aforementioned Commission at the disposal of the Arab State for the purpose of a survey of the economic possibilities of the Arab State and to report upon the best means for its development. The Zionist Organisation will use its best efforts to assist the Arab State in providing the means for developing the natural resources and economic possibilities thereof.

ARTICLE VIII

The parties hereto agree to act in complete accord and harmony on all matters embraced herein before the Peace Congress.

ARTICLE IX

Any matters of dispute which may arise between the contracting parties shall be referred to the British Government for arbitration.

Given under our hand at London, England, the third day of January, one thousand nine hundred and nineteen.

CHAIM WEIZMANN.
FEISAL IBN-HUSSEIN.

RESERVATION BY THE EMIR FEISAL

If the Arabs are established as I have asked in my manifesto of January 4th addressed to the British Secretary of State for Foreign Affairs, I will carry out what is written in this agreement. If changes are made, I cannot be answerable for failing to carry out this agreement.

FEISAL IBN-HUSSEIN.

Feisal-Frankfurter Correspondence

DELEGATION HEDJAZIENNE, *Paris, March 3, 1919.*
DEAR MR. FRANKFURTER: I want to take this opportunity of my first contact with American Zionists to tell you what I have often been able to say to Dr. Weizmann in Arabia and Europe.

We feel that the Arabs and Jews are cousins in race, having suffered similar oppressions at the hands of powers stronger than themselves, and by a happy coincidence have been able to take the first step towards the attainment of their national ideals together.

We Arabs, especially the educated among us, look with the deepest sympathy on the Zionist movement. Our deputation here in Paris is fully acquainted with the proposals submitted yesterday by the Zionist Organization to the Peace Conference, and we regard them as moderate and proper. We will do our best, in so far as we are concerned, to help them through: we will wish the Jews a most hearty welcome home.

With the chiefs of your movement, especially with Dr. Weizmann, we have had and continue to have the closest relations. He has been a great helper of our cause, and I hope the Arabs may soon be in a position to make the Jews some return for their kindness. We are working together for a reformed and revived Near East, and our two movements complete one another. The Jewish movement is national and not imperialist. Our movement is national and not imperialist, and there is room in Syria for us both. Indeed I think that neither can be a real success without the other.

People less informed and less responsible than our leaders and yours, ignoring the need for cooperation of the Arabs and Zionists have been trying to exploit the local difficulties that must necessarily arise in Palestine in the early stages of our movements. Some of them have, I am afraid, misrepresented your aims to the Arab peasantry, and our aims to the Jewish peasantry, with the result that interested parties have been able to make capital out of what they call our differences.

I wish to give you my firm conviction that these differences are not on questions of principle, but on matters of detail such as must inevitably occur in every contact of neighbouring peoples, and as are easily adjusted by mutual goodwill. Indeed nearly all of them will disappear with fuller knowledge.

I look forward, and my people with me look forward, to a future in which we will help you and you will help us, so that the countries in which we are mutually interested may once again take their places in the community of civilised peoples of the world.

Believe me,

Yours sincerely,

(*Sgd.*) FEISAL.
5TH MARCH, 1919.

ROYAL HIGHNESS:

Allow me, on behalf of the Zionist Organisation, to acknowledge your recent letter with deep appreciation.

Those of us who come from the United States have already been gratified by the friendly relations and the active cooperation maintained between you and the Zionist leaders, particularly Dr. Weizmann. We knew it could not be otherwise; we knew that the aspirations of the Arab and the Jewish peoples were parallel, that each aspired to reestablish its nationality in its own homeland, each making its own distinctive contribution to civilisation, each seeking its own peaceful mode of life.

The Zionist leaders and the Jewish people for whom they speak have watched with satisfaction the spiritual vigour of the Arab movement. Themselves seeking justice, they are anxious that the just national aims of the Arab people be confirmed and safeguarded by the Peace Conference.

We knew from your acts and your past utterances that the Zionist movement—in other words the national aims of the Jewish people—had your support and the support of the Arab people for whom you speak. These aims are now before the Peace Conference as definite proposals by the Zionist Organisation. We are happy indeed that you consider these proposals "moderate and proper," and that we have in you a staunch supporter for their realisation. For both the Arab and the Jewish peoples there are difficulties ahead—difficulties that challenge the united statesmanship of Arab and Jewish leaders. For it is no easy task to rebuild two great civilisations that have been suffering oppression and misrule for centuries. We each have our difficulties we shall work out as friends, friends who are animated by similar purposes, seeking a free and full development for the two neighbouring peoples. The Arabs and Jews are neighbours in territory; we cannot but live side by side as friends.

Very respectfully,

(Sgd.) FELIX FRANKFURTER.

Document 9

Recommendations of the King–Crane Commission

The King–Crane Commission was appointed by President Wilson, following a suggestion by Dr. Howard Bliss, President of the American University in Beirut and a sympathizer with the Arab cause. Its main function was to determine which of the Western nations should act as the mandatory power for Palestine.

August 28, 1919

The Commissioners make to the Peace Conference the following recommendations for the treatment of Syria:

1. We recommend, as most important of all, and in strict harmony with our instructions, that whatever foreign administration (whether of one or more powers) is brought into Syria, should come in, not at all as a colonization Power in the old sense of that term, but as a Mandatory under the League of Nations, with the clear consciousness that "the well-being and development" of the Syrian people form for it a "sacred trust".

(1) To this end the mandate should have a limited term, the time of expiration to be determined by the League of Nations, in the light of all the facts as brought out from year to year, in the annual reports of the Mandatory to the League or in other ways.

(2) The Mandatory Administration should have, however, a period and power sufficient to ensure the success of the new State; and especially to make possible carrying through important educational and economic undertakings, essential to secure founding of the State.

(3) The Mandatory Administration should be characterized from the beginning by a strong and vital educational emphasis in clear recognition of the imperative necessity of education for the citizens of a democratic state, and the development of a sound national spirit. This systematic cultivation of national spirit is particularly required in a country like Syria, which has only recently come to self-consciousness.

(4) The Mandatory should definitely seek, from the beginning of its trusteeship, to train the Syrian people to independent self-government as rapidly as conditions allow, by

setting up all the institutions of a democratic state, and by sharing with them increasingly the work of administration and so forming gradually an intelligent citizenship, interested unselfishly in the progress of the country, and forming at the same time a large group of disciplined civil servants.

(5) The period of "tutelage" should not be unduly prolonged, but independent self-government should be granted as soon as it can safely be done; remembering that the primary business of government is not the accomplishment of certain things, but the development of citizens.

(6) It is peculiarly the duty of the Mandatory in a country like Syria, and in this modern age, to see that complete religious liberty is ensured, both in the constitution and in the practice of the state, and that a jealous care is exercised for the rights of all minorities. Nothing is more vital than this for the enduring success of the new Arab State.

(7) In the economic development of Syria, a dangerous amount of indebtedness on the part of the new State should be avoided, as well as any entanglements financially with the affairs of the Mandatory Power. On the other hand the legitimate established privileges of foreigners such as rights to maintain schools, commercial concessions, etc., should be preserved, but subject to review and modification under the authority of the League of Nations in the interest of Syria. The Mandatory Power should not take advantage of its position to force a monopolistic control at any point to the detriment either of Syria or of other nations; but it should seek to bring the new State as rapidly as possible to economic independence as well as to political independence. Whatever is done concerning the further recommendations of the Commission, the fulfillment of at least the conditions now named should be assured, if the Peace Conference and the League of Nations are true to the policy of mandatories already embodied in "The Covenant of the League of Nations". This should effectively guard the most essential interests of Syria, however the machinery of administration is finally organized. The Damascus Congress betrayed in many ways their intense fear that their country would become, though under some other name, simply a colonial possession of some other Power. That fear must be completely allayed.

2. We recommend, in the second place that the unity of Syria be preserved, in accordance with the earnest petition of the great majority of the people of Syria.

(1) The territory concerned is too limited, the population

too small, and the economic, geographic, racial and language unity too manifest to make the setting up of independent states within its boundaries desirable, if such division can possibly be avoided. The country is very largely Arab in language, culture, traditions, and customs.

(2) This recommendation is in line with important "general considerations" already urged, and with the principles of the League of Nations, as well as in answer to the desires of the majority of the population concerned.

(3) The precise boundaries of Syria should be determined by a special commission on boundaries, after the Syrian territory has been in general allotted. The Commissioners believe, however, that the claim of the Damascus Conference to include Cilicia in Syria is not justified, either historically or by commercial or language relations. The line between the Arabic-speaking and the Turkish-speaking populations would quite certainly class Cilicia with Asia Minor rather than with Syria. Syria, too, has no such need of further sea coast as the large interior sections of Asia Minor.

(4) In standing thus for the recognition of the unity of Syria, the natural desires of regions like the Lebanon, which have already had a measure of independence, should not be forgotten. It will make for real unity, undoubtedly, to give a large measure of local autonomy, and especially in the case of strongly unified groups. Even the "Damascus Program" which presses so earnestly the unity of Syria, itself urges a government "on broad decentralization principles".

Lebanon has achieved a considerable degree of prosperity and autonomy within the Turkish Empire. She certainly should not find her legitimate aspirations less possible within a Syrian national State. On the contrary, it may be confidently expected that both her economic and political relations with the rest of Syria would be better if she were a constituent member of the State, rather than entirely independent of it.

As a predominantly Christian country, too, Lebanon naturally fears Moslem domination in a unified Syria. But against such domination she would have a four-fold safeguard: her own large autonomy; the presence of a strong Mandatory for the considerable period in which the constitution and practice of the new State would be forming; the oversight of the League of Nations, with its insistence upon religious liberty and the rights of minorities; and the certainty that the Arab Government would feel the necessity of such a state, if it were to commend itself to the League of Nations. Moreover, there would be less danger of reactionary Moslem attitude, if Christians were present in the state in considerable numbers, rather than largely segregated outside the state, as experience of the relations of different religious faiths in India suggests.

As a predominantly Christian country, it is also to be noted that Lebanon would be in a position to exert a stronger and more helpful influence if she were within the Syrian State, feeling its problems and needs, and sharing all its life, instead of outside it, absorbed simply in her own narrow concerns. For the sake of the larger interests, both of Lebanon and of Syria, then, the unity of Syria is to be urged. It is certain that many of the more thoughtful Lebanese themselves hold this view. A similar statement might be made for Palestine; though, as "the Holy Land" for Jews and Christians and Moslems alike, its situation is unique, and might more readily justify unique treatment, if such treatment were justified anywhere. This will be discussed more particularly in connection with the recommendation concerning Zionism.

3. We recommend, in the third place, that Syria be placed under an (e) Mandatory Power, as the natural way to secure real and efficient unity.

(1) To divide the administration of the provinces of Syria among several mandatories, even if existing national unity were recognized; or to attempt a joint mandatory of the whole on the commission plan:—neither of these courses would be naturally suggested as the best way to secure and promote the unity of the new State, or even the general unity of the whole people. It is conceivable that circumstances might drive the Peace Conference to some such form of divided mandate; but it is not a solution to be voluntarily chosen, from the point of view of the larger interests of the people, as considerations already urged indicate.

(2) It is not to be forgotten, either, that, however they are handled politically, the people of Syria are there, forced to get on together in some fashion. They are obliged to live with one another—the Arabs of the East and the people of the Coast, the Moslems and the Christians. Will they be helped or hindered, in establishing tolerable and finally cordial relations, by a single mandatory? No doubt the quick mechanical solution of the problem of different relations is to split the people up into little independent fragments. And sometimes, undoubtedly, as in the case of the Turks and Armenians, the relations are so intolerable as to make some division impera-

tive and inevitable. But in general, to attempt complete separation only accentuates the differences and increases the antagonism. The whole lesson of the modern social consciousness points to the necessity of understanding "the other half", as it can be understood only by close and living relations. Granting reasonable local autonomy to reduce friction among groups, a single mandatory ought to form a constant and increasingly effective help to unity of feeling throughout the state, and ought to steadily improve group relations.

The people of Syria, in our hearings, have themselves often insisted that, so far as unpleasant relations have hitherto prevailed among various groups, it has been very largely due to the direct instigation of the Turkish Government. When justice is done impartially to all; when it becomes plain that the aim of the common government is the service of all classes alike, not their exploitation, decent human relations are pretty certain to prevail, and a permanent foundation for such relations to be secured—a foundation which could not be obtained by dividing men off from one another in antagonistic groups.

The Commissioners urge, therefore, for the largest future good of all groups and regions alike, the placing of the whole of Syria under a single mandate.

4. We recommend, in the fourth place, that Emir Feisal be made the head of the new united Syrian State.

(1) This is expressly and unanimously asked for by the representative Damascus Congress in the name of the Syrian people, and there seems to be no reason to doubt that the great majority of the population of Syria sincerely desire to have Emir Feisal as ruler.

(2) A constitutional monarchy along democratic lines, seems naturally adapted to the Arabs, with their long training under tribal conditions, and with their traditional respect for their chiefs. They seem to need, more than most people, a King as the personal symbol of the power of the State.

(3) Emir Feisal has come, too, naturally into his present place of power, and there is no one else who could well replace him. He had the great advantage of being the son of the Sherif of Mecca, and as such honored throughout the Moslem world. He was one of the prominent Arab leaders who assumed responsibility for the Arab uprising against the Turks, and so shared in the complete deliverance of the Arab-speaking portions of the Turkish Empire. He was consequently hailed by the "Damascus Congress" as having "merited their full confidence and entire reliance". He was taken up and

supported by the British as the most promising candidate for the headship of the new Arab State—as Arab of the Arabs, but with a position of wide appeal through his Sherifian connection, and through his broad sympathies with the best in the Occident. His relations with the Arabs to the east of Syria are friendly, and his kingdom would not be threatened from that side. He undoubtedly does not make so strong an appeal to the Christians of the West Coast, as to the Arabs of the East; but no man can be named who would have a stronger general appeal. He is tolerant and wise, skilful in dealing with men, winning in manner, a man of sincerity, insight, and power. Whether he has the full strength needed for his difficult task it is too early to say; but certainly no other Arab leader combines so many elements of power as he, and he will have invaluable help throughout the mandatory period.

The Peace Conference may take genuine satisfaction in the fact that an Arab of such qualities is available for the headship of this new state in the Near East.

5. We recommend, in the fifth place, serious modification of the extreme Zionist program for Palestine of unlimited immigration of Jews, looking finally to making Palestine distinctly a Jewish State.

(1) The Commissioners began their study of Zionism with minds predisposed in its favor, but the actual facts in Palestine, coupled with the force of the general principles proclaimed by the Allies and accepted by the Syrians have driven them to the recommendation here made.

(2) The Commission was abundantly supplied with literature on the Zionist program by the Zionist Commission to Palestine; heard in conferences much concerning the Zionist colonies and their claims and personally saw something of what had been accomplished. They found much to approve in the aspirations and plans of the Zionists, and had warm appreciation for the devotion of many of the colonists, and for their success, by modern methods, in overcoming great natural obstacles.

(3) The Commission recognized also that definite encouragement had been given to the Zionists by the Allies in Mr. Balfour's often quoted statement, in its approval by other representatives of the Allies. If, however, the strict terms of the Balfour Statement are adhered to—favoring "the establishment in Palestine of a national home for the Jewish people," "it being clearly understood that nothing shall be done which may prejudice the civil and religious rights of existing non-

Jewish communities in Palestine"—it can hardly be doubted that the extreme Zionist Program must be greatly modified. For "a national home for the Jewish people" is not equivalent to making Palestine into a Jewish State; nor can the erection of such a Jewish State be accomplished without the gravest trespass upon the "civil and religious rights of existing non-Jewish communities in Palestine". The fact came out repeatedly in the Commission's conference with Jewish representatives, that the Zionists looked forward to a practically complete dispossession of the present non-Jewish inhabitants of Palestine, by various forms of purchase.

In his address of July 4, 1918, President Wilson laid down the following principle as one of the four great "ends for which the associated peoples of the world were fighting": "The settlement of every question, whether of territory, of sovereignty, of economic arrangement, or of political relationship upon the basis of the free acceptance of that settlement by the people immediately concerned, and not upon the basis of the material interest or advantage of any other nation or people which may desire a different settlement for the sake of its own exterior influence or mastery". If that principle is to rule, and so the wishes of Palestine's population are to be decisive as to what is to be done with Palestine, then it is to be remembered that the non-Jewish population of Palestine—nearly nine-tenths of the whole—are emphatically against the entire Zionist program. The tables show that there was no one thing upon which the population of Palestine were more agreed than upon this. To subject a people so minded to unlimited Jewish immigration, and to steady financial and social pressure to surrender the land, would be a gross violation of the principle just quoted, and of the peoples' rights, though it kept within the forms of law.

It is to be noted also that the feeling against the Zionist program is not confined to Palestine, but shared very generally by the people throughout Syria, as our conferences clearly showed. More than 72 per cent—1350 in all—of all the petitions in the whole of Syria were directed against the Zionist program. Only two requests—those for a united Syria and for independence—had a larger support. This general feeling was only voiced by the "General Syrian Congress," in the seventh, eighth and tenth resolutions of their statement.

The Peace Conference should not shut its eyes to the fact that the anti-Zionist feeling in Palestine and Syria is intense and not lightly to be flouted. No British officer, consulted by the Commissioners, believed that the Zionist program could be carried out except by force of arms. The officers generally thought that a force of not less than fifty thousand soldiers would be required even to initiate the program. That of itself is evidence of a strong sense of the injustice of the Zionist program, on the part of the non-Jewish populations of Palestine and Syria. Decisions, requiring armies to carry them out, are sometimes necessary, but they are surely not gratuitously to be taken in the interests of a serious injustice. For the initial claim, often submitted by Zionist representatives, that they have a "right" to Palestine, based on an occupation of two thousand years ago, can hardly be seriously considered.

There is a further consideration that cannot justly be ignored, if the world is to look forward to Palestine becoming a definitely Jewish state, however gradually that may take place. That consideration grows out of the fact that Palestine is "the Holy Land" for Jews, Christians, and Moslems alike. Millions of Christians and Moslems all over the world are quite as much concerned as the Jews with conditions in Palestine, especially with those conditions which touch upon religious feelings and rights. The relations in these matters in Palestine are most delicate and difficult. With the best possible intentions, it may be doubted whether the Jews could possibly seem to either Christians or Moslems proper guardians of the holy places, or custodians of the Holy Land as a whole. The reason is this: the places which are most sacred to Christians—those having to do with Jesus—and which are also sacred to Moslems, are not only not sacred to Jews, but abhorrent to them. It is simply impossible, under those circumstances, for Moslems and Christians to feel satisfied to have these places in Jewish hands, or under the custody of Jews. There are still other places about which Moslems must have the same feeling. In fact, from this point of view, the Moslems, just because the sacred places of all three religions are sacred to them, have made very naturally much more satisfactory custodians of the holy places than the Jews could be. It must be believed that the precise meaning, in this respect, of the complete Jewish occupation of Palestine has not been fully sensed by those who urge the extreme Zionist program. For it would intensify, with a certainty like fate, the anti-Jewish feeling both in Palestine and in all other portions of the world which look to Palestine as "the Holy Land".

In view of all these considerations, and with a deep sense of sympathy for the Jewish cause, the Commissioners feel bound to recommend that only a greatly reduced Zionist program be attempted by the Peace Conference and even that, only very gradually initiated. This would have to mean that Jewish immigration should be definitely limited, and that the project for making Palestine distinctly a Jewish common-wealth should be given up.

There would then be no reason why Palestine could not be included in a united Syrian State, just as other portions of the country, the holy places being cared for by an International and Inter-religious Commission, somewhat as at present, under the oversight and approval of the Mandatory and of the League of Nations. The Jews, of course, would have represen-tation upon this Commission.

[The remaining part of this document recommended that the United States be asked to undertake the single Mandate for all Syria. Ed.]

Document 10

Memorandum Presented to the King–Crane Commission by the General Syrian Congress

This is one of the first Arab statements on record opposing Jewish migration to Palestine.

July 2, 1919

We the undersigned members of the General Syrian Congress, meeting in Damascus on Wednesday, July 2nd, 1919, made up of representatives from the three Zones, viz., the Southern, Eastern, and Western, provided with credentials and authorizations by the inhabitants of our various districts, Moslems, Christians, and Jews, have agreed upon the following statement of the desires of the people of the country who have elected us to present them to the American Section of the International Com-mission; the fifth article was passed by a very large majority; all the other articles were accepted unanimously.

1.   We ask absolutely complete political independence for Syria within these boundaries: the Taurus System on the North; Rafah and a line running from Al Jauf to the south of the Syrian and the Hejazian line to Akaba on the south; the Euphrates and Khabur Rivers and a line extending east of Abu Kamal to the east of Al Jauf on the east; and the Mediterranean on the west.

2.   We ask that the Government of this Syrian country should be a democratic civil constitutional Monarchy on broad decentralization principles, safeguarding the rights of minorities, and that the King be the Emir Feisal, who carried on a glorious struggle in the cause of our liberation and merited our full confidence and entire reliance.

3.   Considering the fact that the Arabs inhabiting the Syrian area are not naturally less gifted than other more advanced races and that they are by no means less developed than the Bulgarians, Serbians, Greeks, and Roumanians at the beginning of their independence, we protest against Article 22 of the Covenant of the League of Nations, placing us among the nations in their middle stage of development which stand in need of a mandatory power.

4.   In the event of the rejection by the Peace Conference of this just protest for certain considerations that we may not understand, we, relying on the declarations of President Wilson that his object in waging war was to put an end to the ambition of conquest and colonization, can only regard the mandate mentioned in the Covenant of the League of Nations as equivalent to the rendering of economical and technical assistance that does not prejudice our complete independence. And desiring that our country should not fall a prey to colonization is farthest from any thought of colonization and has no political ambition in our country, we will seek the technical and economical assistance from the United States of America, provided that such assistance does not exceed 20 years.

5.   In the event of America not finding herself in a position to accept our desire for assistance, we will seek this assistance from Great Britain, also provided that such assistance does not infringe the complete independence and unity of our country and that the duration of such assistance does not exceed that mentioned in the previous article.

6.   We do not acknowledge any right claimed by the French Government in any part whatever of our Syrian country and refuse that she should assist us or have a hand in our country under any circumstances and in any place.

7.   We oppose the pretensions of the Zionists to create a Jewish commonwealth in the southern part of Syria,

known as Palestine, and oppose Zionist migration to any part of our country; for we do not acknowledge their title but consider them a grave peril to our people from the national, economical, and political points of view. Our Jewish compatriots shall enjoy our common rights and assume the common responsibilities.

8.   We ask that there should be no separation of the southern part of Syria, known as Palestine, nor of the littoral western zone, which includes Lebanon, from the Syrian country. We desire that the unity of the country should be guaranteed against partition under whatever circumstances.

9.   We ask complete independence for emancipated Mesopotamia and that there should be no economical barriers between the two countries.

10.   The fundamental principles laid down by President Wilson in condemnation of secret treaties impel us to protest most emphatically against any treaty that stipulates the partition of our Syrian country and against any private engagement aiming at the establishment of Zionism in the southern part of Syria; therefore we ask the complete annulment of these conventions and agreements.

The noble principles enunciated by President Wilson strengthen our confidence that our desires emanating from the depths of our hearts, shall be the decisive factor in determining our future; and that President Wilson and the free American people will be our supporters for the realization of our hopes thereby proving their sincerity and noble sympathy with the aspiration of the weaker nations in general and our Arab people in particular.

We also have the fullest confidence that the Peace Conference will realize that we would not have risen against the Turks, with whom we had participated in all civil, political, and representative privileges, but for their violation of our national rights, and so will grant us our desires in full in order that our political rights may not be less after the war than they were before, since we have shed so much blood in the cause of our liberty and independence.

We request to be allowed to send a delegation to represent us at the Peace Conference to defend our rights and secure the realization of our aspirations.

Document 11

The British Mandate

The San Remo Conference decided on April 24, 1920 to assign the Mandate under the League of Nations to Britain. The terms of the Mandate were also discussed with the United States which was not a member of the League. An agreed text was confirmed by the Council of the League of Nations on July 24, 1922, and it came into operation in September 1923.

"The Council of the League of Nations:

Whereas the Principal Allied Powers have agreed, for the purpose of giving effect to the provisions of Article 22 of the Covenant of the League of Nations, to entrust to a Mandatory selected by the said Powers the administration of the territory of Palestine, which formerly belonged to the Turkish Empire, within such boundaries as may be fixed by them; and

Whereas the Principal Allied Powers have also agreed that the Mandatory should be responsible for putting into effect the declaration originally made on November 2nd, 1917, by the Government of His Britannic Majesty, and adopted by the said Powers, in favour of the establishment in Palestine of a national home for the Jewish people, it being clearly understood that nothing should be done which might prejudice the civil and religious rights of existing non-Jewish communities in Palestine, or the rights and political status enjoyed by Jews in any other country; and

Whereas recognition has thereby been given to the historical connexion of the Jewish people with Palestine and to the grounds for reconstituting their national home in that country; and

Whereas the Principal Allied Powers have selected His Britannic Majesty as the Mandatory for Palestine; and

Whereas the mandate in respect of Palestine has been formulated in the following terms and submitted to the Council of the League for approval; and

Whereas His Britannic Majesty has accepted the mandate in respect of Palestine and undertaken to exercise it on behalf of the League of Nations in conformity with the following provisions; and

Whereas by the aforementioned Article 22 (paragraph 8), it is provided that the degree of authority, control or administration to be exercised by the Mandatory, not having been previously agreed upon by the Members of the League, shall be explicitly defined by the Council of the League of Nations;

Confirming the said Mandate, defines its terms as follows:

ARTICLE 1.

The Mandatory shall have full powers of legislation and of administration, save as they may be limited by the terms of this mandate.

ARTICLE 2.

The Mandatory shall be responsible for placing the country under such political, administrative and economic conditions as will secure the establishment of the Jewish national home, as laid down in the preamble, and the development of self-governing institutions, and also for safeguarding the civil and religious rights of all the inhabitants of Palestine, irrespective of race and religion.

ARTICLE 3.

The Mandatory shall, so far as circumstances permit, encourage local autonomy.

ARTICLE 4.

An appropriate Jewish agency shall be recognized as a public body for the purpose of advising and cooperating with the Administration of Palestine in such economic, social and other matters as may affect the establishment of the Jewish national home and the interests of the Jewish population in Palestine, and, subject always to the control of the Administration, to assist and take part in the development of the country.

The Zionist Organization, so long as its organization and constitution are in the opinion of the Mandatory appropriate, shall be recognized as such agency. It shall take steps in consultation with His Britannic Majesty's Government to secure the cooperation of all Jews who are willing to assist in the establishment of the Jewish national home.

ARTICLE 5.

The Mandatory shall be responsible for seeing that no Palestine territory shall be ceded or leased to, or in any way placed under the control of, the Government of any foreign Power.

ARTICLE 6.

The Administration of Palestine, while ensuring that the rights and position of other sections of the population are not prejudiced, shall facilitate Jewish immigration under suitable conditions and shall encourage, in co-operation with the Jewish agency referred to in Article 4, close settlement by Jews on the land, including State lands and waste lands not required for public purposes.

ARTICLE 7.

The Administration of Palestine shall be responsible for enacting a nationality law. There shall be included in this law provisions framed so as to facilitate the acquisition of Palestinian citizenship by Jews who take up their permanent residence in Palestine.

ARTICLE 8.

The privileges and immunities of foreigners, including the benefits of consular jurisdiction and protection as formerly enjoyed by Capitulation or usage in the Ottoman Empire, shall not be applicable in Palestine.

Unless the Powers whose nationals enjoyed the aforementioned privileges and immunities on August 1st, 1914, shall have previously renounced the right to their re-establishment, or shall have agreed to their non-application for a specified period, these privileges and immunities shall, at the expiration of the mandate, be immediately re-established in their entirety or with such modifications as may have been agreed upon between the Powers concerned.

ARTICLE 9.

The Mandatory shall be responsible for seeing that the judicial system established in Palestine shall assure to foreigners, as well as to natives, a complete guarantee of their rights.

Respect for the personal status of the various peoples and communities and for their religious interests shall be fully guaranteed. In particular, the control and administration of Waqfs shall be exercised in accordance with religious law and the dispositions of the founders.

ARTICLE 10.

Pending the making of special extradition agreements relating to Palestine, the extradition treaties in force between the Mandatory and other foreign Powers shall apply to Palestine.

ARTICLE 11.

The Administration of Palestine shall take all necessary measures to safeguard the interests of the community in connection with the development of the country, and, subject to any international obligations accepted by the Mandatory, shall have full power to provide for public ownership or control of any of the natural resources of the country or of the public works, services and utilities established or to be established therein. It shall introduce a land system appropriate to the needs of the country having regard, among other things, to the desirability of promoting the close settlement and intensive cultivation of the land.

The Administration may arrange with the Jewish agency mentioned in Article 4 to construct or operate, upon fair and equitable terms, any public works, services and utilities, and to develop any of the natural resources of the country, in so far as these matters are not directly undertaken by the Administration. Any such arrangements shall provide that no profits distributed by such agency, directly or indirectly, shall exceed a reasonable rate of interest on the capital, and any further profits shall be utilized by it for the benefit of the country in a manner approved by the Administration.

ARTICLE 12.

The Mandatory shall be entrusted with the control of the foreign relations of Palestine, and the right to issue exequaturs to consuls appointed by foreign Powers. He shall also be entitled to afford diplomatic and consular protection to citizens of Palestine when outside its territorial limits.

ARTICLE 13.

All responsibility in connexion with the Holy Places and religious buildings or sites in Palestine, including that of preserving existing rights and of securing free access to the Holy Places, religious buildings and sites and the free exercise of worship, while ensuring the requirements of public order and decorum, is assumed by the Mandatory, who shall be responsible solely to the League of Nations in all matters connected herewith, provided that nothing in this article shall prevent the Mandatory from entering into such arrangements as he may deem reasonable with the Administration for the purpose of carrying the provisions of this article into effect; and provided also that nothing in this Mandate shall be construed as conferring upon the Mandatory authority to interfere with the fabric or the management of purely Moslem sacred shrines, the immunities of which are guaranteed.

ARTICLE 14.

A special Commission shall be appointed by the Mandatory to study, define and determine the rights and claims in connection with the Holy Places and the rights and claims relating to the different religious communities in Palestine. The method of nomination, the composition and the functions of this Commission shall be submitted to the Council of the League for its approval, and the Commission shall not be appointed or enter upon its functions without the approval of the Council.

ARTICLE 15.

The Mandatory shall see that complete freedom of conscience and the free exercise of all forms of worship, subject only to the maintenance of public order and morals, are ensured to all. No discrimination of any kind shall be made between the inhabitants of Palestine on the ground of race, religion or language. No person shall be excluded from Palestine on the sole ground of his religious belief.

The right of each community to maintain its own schools for the education of its own members in its own language, while conforming to such educational requirements of a general nature as the Administration may impose, shall not be denied or impaired.

ARTICLE 16.

The Mandatory shall be responsible for exercising such supervision over religious or eleemosynary bodies of all faiths in Palestine as may be required for the maintenance of public order and good government. Subject to such supervision, no measures shall be taken in Palestine to obstruct or interfere with the enterprise of such bodies or to discriminate against any representative or member of them on the ground of his religion or nationality.

ARTICLE 17.

The Administration of Palestine may organize on a voluntary basis the forces necessary for the preservation of peace and order, and also for the defence of the country, subject, however, to the supervision of the Mandatory, but shall not use them for purposes other than those above specified save with the consent of the Mandatory. Except for such purposes, no military, naval or air forces shall be raised or maintained by the Administration of Palestine.

Nothing in this article shall preclude the Administration of Palestine from contributing to the cost of the maintenance of the forces of the Mandatory in Palestine.

The Mandatory shall be entitled at all times to use the roads, railways and ports of Palestine for the movement of armed forces and the carriage of fuel and supplies.

ARTICLE 18.

The Mandatory shall see that there is no discrimination in Palestine against the nationals of any State Member of the League of Nations (including companies incorporated under its laws) as compared with those of the Mandatory or of any foreign State in matters concerning taxation, commerce or navigation, the exercise of industries or professions, or in the treatment of merchant vessels or civil aircraft. Similarly, there shall be no discrimination in Palestine against goods originating in or destined for any of the said States, and there shall be freedom of transit under equitable conditions across the mandated area.

Subject as aforesaid and to the other provisions of this mandate, the Administration of Palestine may, on the advice of the Mandatory, impose such taxes and customs duties as it may consider necessary, and take such steps as it may think best to promote the development of the natural resources of the country and to safeguard the interests of the population. It may also, on the advice of the Mandatory, conclude a special customs agreement with any State the territory of which in 1914 was wholly included in Asiatic Turkey or Arabia.

ARTICLE 19.

The Mandatory shall adhere on behalf of the Administration of Palestine to any general international conventions already existing, or which may be concluded hereafter with the approval of the League of Nations, respecting the slave traffic, the traffic in arms and ammunition, or the traffic in drugs, or relating to commercial equality, freedom of transit and navigation, aerial navigation and postal, telegraphic and wireless communication or literary, artistic or industrial property.

ARTICLE 20.

The Mandatory shall co-operate on behalf of the Administration of Palestine, so far as religious, social and other conditions may permit, in the execution of any common policy adopted by the League of Nations for preventing and combating disease, including diseases of plants and animals.

ARTICLE 21.

The Mandatory shall secure the enactment within twelve months from this date, and shall ensure the execution of a Law of Antiquities based on the following rules. This law shall ensure equality of treatment in the matter of excavations and archaeological research to the nationals of all States Members of the League of Nations. . . .

ARTICLE 22.

English, Arabic and Hebrew shall be the official languages of Palestine. Any statement or inscription in Arabic on stamps or money in Palestine shall be repeated in Hebrew and any statement or inscription in Hebrew shall be repeated in Arabic.

ARTICLE 23.

The Administration of Palestine shall recognize the holy days of the respective communities in Palestine as legal days of rest for the members of such communities.

ARTICLE 24.

The Mandatory shall make to the Council of the League of Nations an annual report to the satisfaction of the Council as to the measures taken during the year to carry out the provisions of the mandate. Copies of all laws and regulations promulgated or issued during the year shall be communicated with the report.

ARTICLE 25.

In the territories lying between the Jordan and the eastern boundary of Palestine as ultimately determined, the Mandatory shall be entitled, with the consent of the Council of the League of Nations, to postpone or withhold application of such provisions of this mandate as he may consider inapplicable to the existing local conditions, and to make such provision for the administration of the territories as he may consider suitable to those conditions, provided that no action shall be taken which is inconsistent with the provisions of Articles 15, 16 and 18.

ARTICLE 26.

The Mandatory agrees that if any dispute whatever should arise between the Mandatory and another Member of the League of Nations relating to the interpretation or the application of the provisions of the mandate, such dispute, if it cannot be settled by negotiation, shall be submitted to the Permanent Court of International Justice provided for by Article 14 of the Covenant of the League of Nations.

ARTICLE 27.

The consent of the Council of the League of Nations is required for any modification of the terms of this mandate.

ARTICLE 28.

In the event of the termination of the mandate hereby conferred upon the Mandatory, the Council of the League of Nations shall make such arrangements as may be deemed necessary for safeguarding in perpetuity, under guarantee of the League, the rights secured by Articles 13 and 14, and shall use its influence for securing, under the guarantee of the League, that the Government of Palestine will fully honour the financial obligations legitimately incurred by the Administration of Palestine during the period of the mandate, including the rights of public servants to pensions or gratuities.

The present instrument shall be deposited in original in the archives of the League of Nations and certified copies shall be forwarded by the Secretary General of the League of Nations to all Members of the League.

DONE AT LONDON the twenty-fourth day of July, one thousand nine hundred and twenty-two."

PART II

Palestine 1920-1947

Part II of the Reader deals with the unhappy history of the British Mandate, from the Balfour Declaration promising the establishment of a Jewish Home in Palestine to the British decision to return the Mandate to the United Nations, and the U.N. resolution about partition and the establishment of an Arab and a Jewish state in Palestine. During this period Arab opposition grew against Jewish colonization and immigration; there was frequent unrest (in 1920–21, 1928, 1933, 1936–39) and the various suggestions for a solution to the conflict were rejected as impractical.

The Churchill White Paper—1922

In view of growing opposition to Zionism, a new statement of policy was drafted in 1922 by the then British Colonial Secretary, which, while not explicitly opposing the idea of a Jewish state, "redeemed the Balfour promise in depreciated currency" to quote a contemporary British source.

STATEMENT OF BRITISH POLICY
IN PALESTINE ISSUED BY
MR. CHURCHILL IN JUNE, 1922.

The Secretary of State for the Colonies has given renewed consideration to the existing political situation in Palestine, with a very earnest desire to arrive at a settlement of the outstanding questions which have given rise to uncertainty and unrest among certain sections of the population. After consultation with the High Commissioner for Palestine the following statement has been drawn up. It summarizes the essential parts of the correspondence that has already taken place between the Secretary of State and a Delegation from the Moslem Christian Society of Palestine, which has been for some time in England, and it states the further conclusions which have since been reached.

The tension which has prevailed from time to time in Palestine is mainly due to apprehensions, which are entertained both by sections of the Arab and by sections of the Jewish population. These apprehensions, so far as the Arabs are concerned, are partly based upon exaggerated interpretations of the meaning of the Declaration favouring the establishment of a Jewish National Home in Palestine, made on behalf of His Majesty's Government on 2nd November, 1917. Unauthorized statements have been made to the effect that the purpose in view is to create a wholly Jewish Palestine. Phrases have been used such as that Palestine is to become "as Jewish as England is English." His Majesty's Government regard any such expectation as impracticable and have no such aim in view. Nor have they at any time contemplated, as appears to be feared by the Arab Delegation, the disappearance or the subordination of the Arabic population, language, or culture in Palestine. They would draw attention to the fact that the terms of the Declaration referred to do not contemplate that Palestine as a whole should be converted into a Jewish National Home, but that such a Home should be founded *in Palestine*. In this connection it has been observed with satisfaction that at the meeting of the Zionist Congress, the supreme governing body of the Zionist Organization, held at Carlsbad in September, 1921, a resolution was passed expressing as the official statement of Zionist aims "the determination of the Jewish people to live with the Arab people on terms of unity and mutual respect, and together with them to make the common home into a flourishing community, the upbuilding of which may assure to each of its peoples an undisturbed national development."

It is also necessary to point out that the Zionist Commission in Palestine, now termed the Palestine Zionist Executive, has not desired to possess, and does not possess, any share in the general administration of the country. Nor does the special position assigned to the Zionist Organization in Article IV of the Draft Mandate for Palestine imply any such functions. That special position relates to the measures to be taken in Palestine affecting the Jewish population, and contemplates that the Organization may assist in the general development of the country, but does not entitle it to share in any degree in its Government.

Further, it is contemplated that the status of all citizens of Palestine in the eyes of the law shall be Palestinian, and it has never been intended that they, or any section of them, should possess any other juridical status.

So far as the Jewish population of Palestine are concerned it appears that some among them are apprehensive that His Majesty's Government may depart from the policy embodied in the Declaration of 1917. It is necessary, therefore, once more to affirm that these fears are unfounded, and that that

Declaration, re-affirmed by the Conference of the Principal Allied Powers at San Remo and again in the Treaty of Sèvres, is not susceptible of change.

During the last two or three generations the Jews have recreated in Palestine a community, now numbering 80,000, of whom about one-fourth are farmers or workers upon the land. This community has its own political organs; an elected assembly for the direction of its domestic concerns; elected councils in the towns; and an organization for the control of its schools. It has its elected Chief Rabbinate and Rabbinical Council for the direction of its religious affairs. Its business is conducted in Hebrew as a vernacular language, and a Hebrew Press serves its needs. It has its distinctive intellectual life and displays considerable economic activity. This community, then, with its town and country population, its political, religious, and social organizations, its own language, its own customs, its own life, has in fact "national" characteristics. When it is asked what is meant by the development of the Jewish National Home in Palestine, it may be answered that it is not the imposition of a Jewish nationality upon the inhabitants of Palestine as a whole, but the further development of the existing Jewish community, with the assistance of Jews in other parts of the world, in order that it may become a centre in which the Jewish people as a whole may take, on grounds of religion and race, an interest and a pride. But in order that this community should have the best prospect of free development and provide a full opportunity for the Jewish people to display its capacities, it is essential that it should know that it is in Palestine as of right and not on sufferance. That is the reason why it is necessary that the existence of a Jewish National Home in Palestine should be internationally guaranteed, and that it should be formally recognized to rest upon ancient historic connection.

This, then, is the interpretation which His Majesty's Government place upon the Declaration of 1917, and, so understood, the Secretary of State is of opinion that it does not contain or imply anything which need cause either alarm to the Arab population of Palestine or disappointment to the Jews.

For the fulfilment of this policy it is necessary that the Jewish community in Palestine should be able to increase its numbers by immigration. This immigration cannot be so great in volume as to exceed whatever may be the economic capacity of the country at the time to absorb new arrivals. It is essential to ensure that the immigrants should not be a burden upon the people of Palestine as a whole, and that they should not deprive any section of the present population of their employment. Hitherto the immigration has fulfilled these conditions. The number of immigrants since the British occupation has been about 25,000.

It is necessary also to ensure that persons who are politically undesirable are excluded from Palestine, and every precaution has been and will be taken by the Administration to that end.

It is intended that a special committee should be established in Palestine, consisting entirely of members of the new Legislative Council elected by the people, to confer with the administration upon matters relating to the regulation of immigration. Should any difference of opinion arise between this committee and the Administration the matter will be referred to His Majesty's Government, who will give it special consideration. In addition, under Article 81 of the draft Palestine Order in Council, any religious community or considerable section of the population of Palestine will have a general right to appeal, through the High Commissioner and the Secretary of State, to the League of Nations on any matter on which they may consider that the terms of the Mandate are not being fulfilled by the Government of Palestine.

With reference to the Constitution which it is now intended to establish in Palestine, the draft of which has already been published, it is desirable to make certain points clear. In the first place, it is not the case, as has been represented by the Arab Delegation, that during the war His Majesty's Government gave an undertaking that an independent national government should be at once established in Palestine. This representation mainly rests upon a letter dated the 24th October, 1915, from Sir Henry McMahon, then His Majesty's High Commissioner in Egypt, to the Sherif of Mecca, now King Hussein of the Kingdom of the Hejaz. That letter is quoted as conveying the promise to the Sherif of Mecca to recognise and support the independence of the Arabs within the territories proposed by him. But this promise was given subject to a reservation made in the same letter, which excluded from its scope, among other territories, the portions of Syria lying to the west of the district of Damascus. This reservation has always been regarded by His Majesty's Government as covering the vilayet of Beirut and the independent Sanjak of Jerusalem. The whole of Palestine west of the Jordan was thus excluded from Sir H. McMahon's pledge.

Nevertheless, it is the intention of His Majesty's Government to foster the establishment of a full measure of self-government in Palestine. But they are of opinion that, in the special circumstances of that country, this should be accomplished by gradual stages and not suddenly. The first step was taken when, on the institution of a Civil Administration, the nominated Advisory Council, which now exists, was established. It was stated at the time by the High Commissioner that this was the first step in the development of self-governing institutions, and it is now proposed to take a second step by the establishment of a Legislative Council containing a large proportion of members elected on a wide franchise. It was proposed in the published draft that three of the members of this Council should be non-official persons nominated by the High Commissioner, but representations having been made in opposition to this provision, based on cogent considerations, the Secretary of State is prepared to omit it. The Legislative Council would then consist of the High Commissioner as President and twelve elected and ten official members. The Secretary of State is of opinion that before a further measure of self-government is extended to Palestine and the Assembly placed in control over the Executive, it would be wise to allow some time to elapse. During this period the institutions of the country will have become well established; its financial credit will be based on firm foundations, and the Palestinian officials will have been enabled to gain experience of sound methods of government. After a few years the situation will be again reviewed, and if the experience of the working of the constitution now to be established so warranted, a larger share of authority would then be extended to the elected representatives of the people.

The Secretary of State would point out that already the present Administration has transferred to a Supreme Council elected by the Moslem community of Palestine the entire control of Moslem religious endowments (Wakfs), and of the Moslem religious Courts. To this Council the Administration has also voluntarily restored considerable revenues derived from ancient endowments which had been sequestrated by the Turkish Government. The Education Department is also advised by a committee representative of all sections of the population, and the Department of Commerce and Industry has the benefit of the co-operation of the Chambers of Commerce which have been established in the principal centres.

It is the intention of the Administration to associate in an increased degree similar representative committees with the various Departments of the Government.

The Secretary of State believes that a policy upon these lines, coupled with the maintenance of the fullest religious liberty in Palestine and with scrupulous regard for the rights of each community with reference to its Holy Places, cannot but commend itself to the various sections of the population, and that upon this basis may be built up that spirit of co-operation upon which the future progress and prosperity of the Holy Land must largely depend.

Document 13

The MacDonald Letter

Following the Arab riots of 1929, the British Labor government published a new statement of policy (the Passfield White Paper), which urged the restriction of immigration and of land sales to Jews. It was bitterly denounced by Zionist leaders as a violation of the letter and the spirit of the Mandate. The MacDonald letter, while not openly repudiating the Passfield report, gave assurances that the terms of the Mandate would be fulfilled. It was rejected by the Arabs as the "Black Letter". James Ramsay MacDonald (1866-1937) was Prime Minister in 1931; Lord Passfield (Sidney Webb, 1859-1947) was Colonial Secretary in the Labor cabinet.

Premier MacDonald's Letter
Addressed to Dr. Chaim Weizmann
February 13, 1931

DEAR DR. WEIZMANN:

In order to remove certain misconceptions and misunderstandings which have arisen as to the policy of his Majesty's Government with regard to Palestine, as set forth in the White Paper of October, 1930, and which were the subject of a debate in the House of Commons on Nov. 17, and also to meet certain criticisms put forward by the Jewish Agency, I have pleasure in forwarding you the following statement of our position, which will fall to be read as the authoritative interpretation of the White Paper on the matters with which this letter deals.

It has been said that the policy of his Majesty's Government involves a serious departure from the obligations of the mandate as hitherto understood; that it misconceives the mandatory obligations, and that it foreshadows a policy which is inconsistent with the obligations of the mandatory to the Jewish people.

His Majesty's Government did not regard it as necessary to quote in extenso the declarations of policy which have been previously made, but attention is drawn to the fact that, not only does the White Paper of 1930 refer to and endorse the White Paper of 1922, which has been accepted by the Jewish Agency, but it recognizes that the undertaking of the mandate is an undertaking to the Jewish people and not only to the Jewish population of Palestine. The White Paper places in the foreground of its statement my speech in the House of Commons on the 3d of April, 1930, in which I announced, in words that could not have been made more plain, that it was the intention of his Majesty's Government to continue to administer Palestine in accordance with the terms of the mandate as approved by the Council of the League of Nations. That position has been reaffirmed and again made plain by my speech in the House of Commons on the 17th of November. In my speech on the 3d of April I used the following language:

> His Majesty's Government will continue to administer Palestine in accordance with the terms of the mandate as approved by the Council of the League of Nations. This is an international obligation from which there can be no question of receding.
>
> Under the terms of the mandate his Majesty's Government are responsible for promoting the establishment of a national home for the Jewish people, it being clearly understood that nothing shall be done which might prejudice the civil and religious rights of existing non-Jewish communities in Palestine or the rights and political status enjoyed by Jews in any other country.
>
> A double undertaking is involved, to the Jewish people on the one hand and to the non-Jewish population of Palestine on the other; and it is the firm resolve of his Majesty's Government to give effect, in equal measure, to both parts of the declaration and to do equal justice to all sections of the population of Palestine. That is a duty from which they will not shrink and to discharge of which they will apply all the resources at their command.

That declaration is in conformity not only with the articles but also with the preamble of the mandate, which is hereby explicitly reaffirmed.

In carrying out the policy of the mandate the mandatory cannot ignore the existence of the differing interests and viewpoints. These, indeed, are not in themselves irreconcilable, but they can only be reconciled if there is a proper realization that the full solution of the problem depends upon an understanding between the Jews and the Arabs. Until that is reached, considerations of balance must inevitably enter into the definition of policy.

A good deal of criticism has been directed to the White Paper upon the assertion that it contains injurious allegations against the Jewish people and Jewish labor organizations. Any such intention on the part of his Majesty's Government is expressly disavowed. It is recognized that the Jewish Agency have all along given willing cooperation in carrying out the policy of the mandate and that the constructive work done by the Jewish people in Palestine has had beneficial effects on the development and well-being of the country as a whole. His Majesty's Government also recognizes the value of the services of labor and trades union organizations in Palestine, to which they desire to give every encouragement.

A question has arisen as to the meaning to be attached to the words 'safeguarding the civil and religious rights of all inhabitants of Palestine irrespective of race and religion' occurring in Article II, and the words 'insuring that the rights and position of other sections of the population are not prejudiced' occurring in Article VI of the mandate. The words 'safeguarding the civil and religious rights' occurring in Article II cannot be read as meaning that the civil and religious rights of individual citizens are unalterable. In the case of Suleiman Murra, to which reference has been made, the Privy Council, in construing these words of Article II said 'It does not mean . . . that all the civil rights of every inhabitant of Palestine which existed at the date of the mandate are to remain unaltered throughout its duration; for if that were to be a condition of the mandatory jurisdiction, no effective legislation would be possible.' The words, accordingly, must be read in another sense, and the key to the true purpose and meaning of the sentence is to be found in the concluding words of the article, 'irrespective of race and religion.' These words indicate that in respect of civil and religious rights the mandatory is not to discriminate between persons on the ground of religion or race, and this protective provision applies equally to Jews, Arabs and all sections of the population.

The words 'rights and position of other sections of the population,' occurring in Article VI, plainly refer to the non-Jewish community. These rights and position are not TO BE prejudiced; that is, are not to be impaired or made worse. The effect of the policy of immigration and settlement on the economic position of the non-Jewish community cannot be excluded from consideration. But the words are not to be read as implying that existing economic conditions in Palestine should be crystallized. On the contrary, the obligation to facilitate Jewish immigration and to encourage close settlement by Jews on the land remains a positive obligation of the mandate and it can be fulfilled without prejudice to the rights and position of other sections of the population of Palestine.

We may proceed to the contention that the mandate has been interpreted in a manner highly prejudicial to Jewish interests in the vital matters of land settlement and immigration. It has been said that the policy of the White Paper would place an embargo on immigration and would suspend, if not indeed terminate, the close settlement of the Jews on the land, which is a primary purpose of the mandate. In support of this contention particular stress has been laid upon the passage referring to State lands in the White Paper, which says that 'it would not be possible to make available for Jewish settlement in view of their actual occupation by Arab cultivators and of the importance of making available suitable land on which to place the Arab cultivators who are now landless.'

The language of this passage needs to be read in the light of the policy as a whole. It is desirable to make it clear that the landless Arabs, to whom it was intended to refer in the passage quoted, were such Arabs as can be shown to have been displaced from the lands which they occupied in consequence of the land passing into Jewish hands, and who have not obtained other holdings on which they can establish themselves, or other equally satisfactory occupation. The number of such displaced Arabs must be a matter for careful inquiry. It is to landless Arabs within this category that his Majesty's Government feels itself under an obligation to facilitate their settlement upon the land. The recognition of this obligation in no way detracts from the larger purposes of development which his Majesty's Government regards as the most effectual means of furthering the establishment of a national home for the Jews. . . .

Further, the statement of policy of his Majesty's Government did not imply a prohibition of acquisition of additional land by Jews. It contains no such prohibition, nor is any such intended. What it does contemplate is such temporary control of land disposition and transfers as may be necessary not to impair the harmony and effectiveness of the scheme of land settlement to be undertaken. His Majesty's Government feels bound to point out that it alone of the governments which have been responsible for the administration of Palestine since the acceptance of the mandate has declared its definite intention to initiate an active policy of development, which it is believed will result in a substantial and lasting benefit to both Jews and Arabs.

Cognate to this question is the control of immigration. It must first of all be pointed out that such control is not in any sense a departure from previous policy. From 1920 onward, when the original immigration ordinance came into force, regulations for the control of immigration have been issued from time to time, directed to prevent illicit entry and to define and facilitate authorized entry. This right of regulation has at no time been challenged.

But the intention of his Majesty's Government appears to have been represented as being that 'no further immigration of Jews is to be permitted so long as it might prevent any Arab from obtaining employment.' His Majesty's Government never proposed to pursue such a policy. They were concerned to state that, in the regulation of Jewish immigration, the following principles should apply: viz., that 'it is essential to insure that the immigrants should not be a burden on the people of Palestine as a whole, and that they should not deprive any section of the present population as a whole, and that they should not deprive any section of the present population of their employment.' (White Paper 1922.)

In one aspect, his Majesty's Government have to be mindful of their obligations to facilitate Jewish immigration under suitable conditions, and to encourage close settlement by Jews on the land; in the other aspect, they have to be equally mindful of their duty to insure that no prejudice results to the rights and position of the non-Jewish community. It is because of this apparent conflict of obligations that his Majesty's Government have felt bound to emphasize the necessity of the proper application of the absorptive principle.

That principle is vital to any scheme of development, the primary purpose of which must be the settlement both of Jews and of displaced Arabs on the land. It is for that reason that his Majesty's Government have insisted, and are compelled to insist, that government immigration regulations must be properly applied. The considerations relevant to the limits of absorptive capacity are purely economic considerations.

His Majesty's Government did not prescribe and do not contemplate any stoppage or prohibition of Jewish immigration in any of its categories. The practice of sanctioning a labor schedule of wage-earning immigrants will continue. In each case consideration will be given to anticipated labor requirements for works which, being dependent upon Jewish or mainly Jewish capital, would not be or would not have been undertaken unless Jewish labor was available. With regard to public and municipal works failing to be financed out of public funds, the claim of Jewish labor to a due share of the employment available, taking into account Jewish contributions to public revenue, shall be taken into consideration. As regards other kinds of employment, it will be necessary in each case to take into account the factors bearing upon the demand for labor, including the factor of unemployment among both the Jews and the Arabs.

Immigrants with prospects of employment other than employment of a purely ephemeral character will not be excluded on the sole ground that the employment cannot be guaranteed to be of unlimited duration.

In determining the extent to which immigration at any time may be permitted it is necessary also to have regard to the declared policy of the Jewish Agency to the effect that 'in all the works or undertakings carried out or furthered by the Agency it shall be deemed to be a matter of principle that Jewish labor shall be employed.' His Majesty's Government do not in any way challenge the right of the Agency to formulate or approve and endorse this policy. The principle of preferential, and indeed exclusive, employment of Jewish labor by Jewish organizations is a principle which the Jewish Agency are entitled to affirm. But it must be pointed out that if in consequence of this policy Arab labor is displaced or existing unemployment becomes aggravated, that is a factor in the situation to which the mandatory is bound to have regard.

His Majesty's Government desire to say, finally, as they have repeatedly and unequivocally affirmed, that the obligations imposed upon the mandatory by its acceptance of the mandate are solemn international obligations from which there is not now, nor has there been at any time, any intention to depart. To the tasks imposed by the mandate, his Majesty's Government have set their hand, and they will not withdraw it. But if their efforts are to be successful, there is need for coöperation, confidence, readiness on all sides to appreciate the difficulties and complexities of the problem, and, above all, there must be a full and unqualified recognition that no solution can be satisfactory or permanent which is not based upon justice, both to the Jewish people and to the non-Jewish communities of Palestine.

RAMSAY MACDONALD

Document 14

From the Report of the Palestine Royal Commission (Peel Commission)—1937

A Royal Commission headed by Lord Peel was appointed in 1936, following the outbreak of fresh Arab riots earlier that year. Its report, published in July 1937, stated that the desire of the Arabs for national independence and their hatred and fear of the establishment of the Jewish National Home were the underlying causes of the disturbances. It found that Arab and Jewish interests could not be reconciled under the Mandate and it suggested, therefore, the partition of Palestine. The Jewish state was to comprise Galilee, the Yezreel Valley and the Coastal Plain to a point midway between Gaza and Jaffe, altogether about twenty per cent of the area of the country. The rest, Arab Palestine, was to be united with Transjordan. Jerusalem, Bethlehem, a corridor linking them to the Sea, and, possibly, Nazareth and the Sea of Genezareth would remain a British mandatory zone. The Arab leadership rejected the plan, the Zionist Congress accepted it with qualifications—against the wish of a substantial minority. The British government which had initially favored partition eventually rejected it in November 1938. (Document 16)

. . . To foster Jewish immigration in the hope that it might ultimately lead to the creation of a Jewish majority and the establishment of a Jewish State with the consent or at least the acquiescence of the Arabs was one thing. It was quite another to contemplate, however remotely, the forcible conversion of Palestine into a Jewish State against the will of the Arabs. For that would clearly violate the spirit and intention of the Mandate System. It would mean that national self-determination had been withheld when the Arabs were a majority in Palestine and only conceded when the Jews were a majority. It would mean that the Arabs had been denied the opportunity of standing by themselves: that they had, in fact, after an interval of conflict, been bartered about from Turkish sovereignty to Jewish sovereignty. It is true that in the light of history Jewish rule over Palestine could not be regarded as foreign rule in the same sense as Turkish; but the international recognition of the right of the Jews to return to their old homeland did not involve the recognition of the right of the Jews to govern the Arabs in it against their will. The case stated by Lord Milner against an Arab control of Palestine applies equally to a Jewish control. . . .

An irrepressible conflict has arisen between two national communities within the narrow bounds of one small country. About 1,000,000 Arabs are in strife, open or latent, with some 400,000 Jews. There is no common ground between them. The Arab community is predominantly Asiatic in character, the Jewish community predominantly European. They differ in religion and in language. Their cultural and social life, their ways of thought and conduct, are as incompatible as their national aspirations. These last are the greatest bar to peace. Arabs and Jews might possibly learn to live and work together in Palestine if they would make a genuine effort to reconcile and combine their national ideals and so build up in time a joint or dual nationality. But this they cannot do. The War and its sequel have inspired all Arabs with the hope of reviving in a free and united Arab world the traditions of the Arab golden age. The Jews similarly are inspired by their historic past. They mean to show what the Jewish nation can achieve when restored to the land of its birth. National assimilation between Arabs and Jews is thus ruled out. In the Arab picture the Jews could only occupy the place they occupied in Arab Egypt or Arab Spain. The Arabs would be as much outside the Jewish picture as the Canaanites in the old land of Israel. The National Home, as we have

said before, cannot be half-national. In these circumstances
to maintain that Palestinian citizenship has any moral meaning is a mischievous pretense. Neither Arab nor Jew has any
sense of service to a single State. . . .

Document 15

V. Jabotinsky: A Jewish State Now: Evidence Submitted to the Palestine Royal Commission*

Vladimir Ze'ev Jabotinsky (1880-1940) was the leader
of the Zionist–Revisionists advocating the establishment of
a Jewish state in its historic borders.

The conception of Zionism which I have the honour to represent here is based on what I should call the humanitarian
aspect. By that I do not mean to say that we do not respect
the other, the purely spiritual aspects of Jewish nationalism,
such as the desire for self-expression, the rebuilding of a
Hebrew culture, or creating some "model community of
which the Jewish people could be proud." All that, of course,
is most important; but as compared with our actual needs and
our real position in the world to-day, all that has rather the
character of luxury. The Commission have already heard a
description of the situation of World Jewry especially in Eastern Europe, and I am not going to repeat any details, but you
will allow me to quote a recent reference in *The New York
Times* describing the position of Jewry in Eastern Europe as
"a disaster of historic magnitude." I only wish to add that it
would be very naïve, and although many Jews make this mistake I disapprove of it—it would be very naïve to ascribe
that state of disaster, permanent disaster, only to the guilt of
men, whether it be crowds and multitudes, or whether it be
Governments. The thing goes much deeper than that. I am
very much afraid that what I am going to say will not be
popular with many among my co-religionists, and I regret
that, but the truth is the truth. We are facing an elemental
calamity, a kind of social earthquake. Three generations of
Jewish thinkers and Zionists among whom there were many
great minds—I am not going to fatigue you by quoting them

* V. Jabotinsky, House of Lords, London: February 11, 1937.

—three generations have given much thought to analysing the Jewish position and have come to the conclusion that the cause of our suffering is the very fact of the "Diaspora," the bedrock fact that we are everywhere a minority. It is not the anti-Semitism of men; it is, above all, the anti-Semitism of things, the inherent xenophobia of the body social or the body economic under which we suffer. Of course, there are ups and downs; but there are moments, there are whole periods in history when this "xenophobia of Life itself" takes dimensions which no people can stand, and that is what we are facing now. I do not mean to suggest that I would recognise that all the Governments concerned have done all they ought to have done; I would be the last man to concede that. I think many Governments, East and West, ought to do much more to protect the Jews than they do; but the best of Governments could perhaps only soften the calamity to quite an insignificant extent, but the core of the calamity is an earthquake which stands and remains. I want to mention here that, since one of those Governments (the Polish Government) has recently tried what amounts to bringing to the notice of the League of Nations and the whole of humanity that it is humanity's duty to provide the Jews with an area where they could build up their own body social undisturbed by anyone, I think the sincerity of the Polish Government, and of any other Governments who, I hope, will follow, should not be suspected, but on the contrary it should be recognised and acknowledged with due gratitude.—Perhaps the greatest gap in all I am going to say and in all the Commission have heard up to now is the impossibility of really going to the root of the problem, really bringing before you a picture of what that Jewish hell looks like, and I feel I cannot do it. I do hope that the day may come when some Jewish representative may be allowed to appear at the Bar of one of these two Houses just to tell them what it really is, and to ask the English people: "What are you going to advise us? Where is the way out? Or, standing up and facing God, say that there is no way out and that we Jews have just to go under." But unfortunately I cannot do it, so I will simply assume that the Royal Commission are sufficiently informed of all this situation, and then I want you to realise this: the phenomenon called Zionism may include all kinds of dreams—a "model community", Hebrew culture, perhaps even a second edition of the Bible—but all this longing for wonderful toys of velvet and silver is nothing in comparison with that tangible momentum of irresistible distress and need by which we are propelled and borne. We are not free agents. We cannot "concede" anything. Whenever I hear the Zionist, most often my own Party, accused of asking for too much—Gentlemen, I really cannot understand it. Yes, we do want a State; every nation on earth, every normal nation, beginning with the smallest and the humblest who do not claim any merit, any role in humanity's development, they all have States of their own. That is the normal condition for a people. Yet, when we, the most abnormal of peoples and therefore the most unfortunate, ask only for the same condition as the Albanians enjoy, to say nothing of the French and the English, then it is called too much. I should understand it if the answer were, "It is impossible," but when the answer is, "It is too much" I cannot understand it. I would remind you (excuse me for quoting an example known to every one of you) of the commotion which was produced in that famous institution when Oliver Twist came and asked for "more." He said "more" because he did not know how to express it; what Oliver Twist really meant was this: "Will you just give me that normal portion which is necessary for a boy of my age to be able to live." I assure you that you face here to-day, in the Jewish people with its demands, an Oliver Twist who has, unfortunately, no concessions to make. What can be the concessions? We have got to save millions, many *millions*. I do not know whether it is a question of re-housing one-third of the Jewish race, half of the Jewish race, or a quarter of the Jewish race; I do not know; but it is a question of millions. Certainly the way out is to evacuate those portions of the Diaspora which have become no good, which hold no promise of any possibility of a livelihood, and to concentrate all those refugees in some place which should *not* be Diaspora, not a repetition of the position where the Jews are an unabsorbed minority within a foreign social, or economic, or political organism. Naturally, if that process of evacuation is allowed to develop, as it ought to be allowed to develop, there will very soon be reached a moment when the Jews will become a majority in Palestine. I am going to make a "terrible" confession. Our demand for a Jewish majority is not our maximum—it is our minimum: it is just an inevitable stage if only we are allowed to go on salvaging our people. The point when the Jews will reach a majority in that country will not be the point of saturation yet—because with 1,000,000 more Jews in Palestine to-day you could already have a Jewish majority, but there are certainly 3,000,000 or 4,000,000 in the East who are virtually knocking at the door asking for admission, i.e., for salvation.

I have the profoundest feeling for the Arab case, in so far as that Arab case is not exaggerated. This Commission have already been able to make up their minds as to whether there is any individual hardship to the Arabs of Palestine as men, deriving from the Jewish colonisation. We maintain unanimously that the economic position of the Palestinian Arabs, under the Jewish colonisation and owing to the Jewish colonisation, has become the object of envy in all the surrounding Arab countries, so that the Arabs from those countries show a clear tendency to immigrate into Palestine. I have also shown to you already that, in our submission, there is no question of ousting the Arabs. On the contrary, the idea is that Palestine on both sides of the Jordan should hold the Arabs, their progeny, *and* many millions of Jews. What I do not deny is that in that process the Arabs of Palestine will necessarily become a minority in the country of Palestine. What I do deny is that *that* is a hardship. It is not a hardship on any race, any nation, possessing so many National States now and so many more National States in the future. One fraction, one branch of that race, and not a big one, will have to live in someone else's State: well, that is the case with all the mightiest nations of the world. I could hardly mention one of the big nations, having their States, mighty and powerful, who had not one branch living in someone else's State. That is only normal and there is no "hardship" attached to that. So when we hear the Arab claim confronted with the Jewish claim; I fully understand that any minority would prefer to be a majority, it is quite understandable that the Arabs of Palestine would also prefer Palestine to be the Arab State No. 4, No. 5, or No. 6—that I quite understand; but when the Arab claim is confronted with our Jewish demand to be saved, it is like the claims of appetite versus the claims of starvation. No tribunal has ever had the luck of trying a case where all the justice was on the side of one Party and the other Party had no case whatsoever. Usually in human affairs any tribunal, including this tribunal, in trying two cases, has to concede that both sides have a case on their side and, in order to do justice, they must take into consideration what should constitute the basic justification of all human demands, individual or mass demands—the decisive terrible balance of Need. I think it is clear.

Document 16

Against Partition: British Statement of Policy—November, 1938

. . . 3. His Majesty's Government have now received the report of the Palestine Partition Commission who have carried out their investigations with great thoroughness and efficiency, and have collected material which will be very valuable in the further consideration of policy. Their report is now published, together with a summary of their conclusions. It will be noted that the four members of the Commission advise unanimously against the adoption of the scheme of partition outlined by the Royal Commission. In addition to the Royal Commission's scheme, two other schemes described as plans B and C are examined in the report. One member prefers plan B. Two other members, including the Chairman, consider that plan C is the best scheme of partition which, under the terms of reference, can be devised. A fourth member, while agreeing that plan C is the best that can be devised under the terms of reference, regards both plans as impracticable. The report points out that under either plan, while the budget of the Jewish State is likely to show a substantial surplus, the budgets of the Arab State (including Trans-Jordan) and of the Mandated Territories are likely to show substantial deficits. The Commission reject as impracticable the Royal Commission's recommendation for a direct subvention from the Jewish State to the Arab State. They think that, on economic grounds, a customs union between the States and the Mandated Territories is essential and they examine the possibility of finding the solution for the financial and economic problems of partition by means of a scheme based upon such a union. They consider that any such scheme would be inconsistent with the grant of fiscal independence to the Arab and Jewish States. Their conclusion is that, on a strict interpretation of their terms of reference, they have no alternative but to report that they are unable to recommend boundaries for the proposed areas which will afford a reasonable prospect of the eventual establishment of self-supporting Arab and Jewish States.

4. His Majesty's Government, after careful study of the Partition Commission's report, have reached the conclusion that this further examination has shown that the political, administrative and financial difficulties involved in the pro-

posal to create independent Arab and Jewish States inside Palestine are so great that this solution of the problem is impracticable.

5. His Majesty's Government will therefore continue their responsibility for the government of the whole of Palestine. They are now faced with the problem of finding alternative means of meeting the needs of the difficult situation described by the Royal Commission which will be consistent with their obligations to the Arabs and the Jews. His Majesty's Government believe that it is possible to find these alternative means. They have already given much thought to the problem in the light of the reports of the Royal Commission and of the Partition Commission. It is clear that the surest foundation for peace and progress in Palestine would be an understanding between the Arabs and the Jews, and His Majesty's Government are prepared in the first instance to make a determined effort to promote such an understanding. With this end in view, they propose immediately to invite representatives of the Palestinian Arabs and of neighbouring States on the one hand and of the Jewish Agency on the other, to confer with them as soon as possible in London regarding future policy, including the question of immigration into Palestine. As regards the representation of the Palestinian Arabs, His Majesty's Government must reserve the right to refuse to receive those leaders whom they regard as responsible for the campaign of assassination and violence.

6. His Majesty's Government hope that these discussions in London may help to promote agreement as to future policy regarding Palestine. They attach great importance, however, to a decision being reached at an early date. Therefore, if the London discussions should not produce agreement within a reasonable period of time, they will take their own decision in the light of their examination of the problem and of the discussions in London, and announce the policy which they propose to pursue.

7. In considering and settling their policy His Majesty's Government will keep constantly in mind the international character of the Mandate with which they have been entrusted and their obligations in that respect.

Document 17

The White Paper of 1939

After the failure of the partition scheme and a subsequent attempt to work out an agreed solution at a Conference in London (February–March, 1939), the British government announced its new policy in a White Paper published on May 17, 1939. The Arab demands were largely met: Jewish immigration was to continue at a maximum rate of 15,000 for another five years. After that it was to cease altogether unless the Arabs would accept it. Purchase of land by Jews would be prohibited in some areas, restricted in others. Jewish reaction was bitterly hostile (Document 18), but the Arab leaders also rejected the White Paper: according to their demands, Palestine was to become an Arab state immediately, no more Jewish immigrants were to enter the country, the status of every Jew who had immigrated since 1918 was to be reviewed.

May 17, 1939

In the Statement on Palestine, issued on 9th November, 1938, His Majesty's Government announced their intention to invite representatives of the Arabs of Palestine, of certain neighbouring countries and of the Jewish Agency to confer with them in London regarding future policy. It was their sincere hope that, as a result of full, free and frank discussion, some understanding might be reached. Conferences recently took place with Arab and Jewish delegations, lasting for a period of several weeks, and served the purpose of a complete exchange of views between British Ministers and the Arab and Jewish representatives. In the light of the discussions as well as of the situation in Palestine and of the Reports of the Royal Commission and the Partition Commission, certain proposals were formulated by His Majesty's Government and were laid before the Arab and Jewish delegations as the basis of an agreed settlement. Neither the Arab nor the Jewish delegation felt able to accept these proposals, and the conferences therefore did not result in an agreement. Accordingly His Majesty's Government are free to formulate their own policy, and after careful consideration they have decided to adhere generally to the proposals which were finally submitted to, and discussed with, the Arab and Jewish delegations.

2. The Mandate for Palestine, the terms of which were confirmed by the Council of the League of Nations in 1922, has governed the policy of successive British Governments for nearly 20 years. It embodies the Balfour Declaration and imposes on the Mandatory four main obligations. These obligations are set out in Article 2, 6 and 13 of the Mandate. There is no dispute regarding the interpretation of one of these obligations, that touching the protection of and access to the Holy Places and religious building or sites. The other three main obligations are generally as follows:—

(i) To place the country under such political, administrative and economic conditions as will secure the establishment in Palestine of a national home for the Jewish people, to facilitate Jewish immigration under suitable conditions, and to encourage, in co-operation with the Jewish Agency, close settlement by Jews on the land.

(ii) To safeguard the civil and religious rights of all the inhabitants of Palestine irrespective of race and religion, and, whilst facilitating Jewish immigration and settlement, to ensure that the rights and position of other sections of the population are not prejudiced.

(iii) To place the country under such political, administrative and economic conditions as will secure the development of self-governing institutions.

3. The Royal Commission and previous Commissions of Enquiry have drawn attention to the ambiguity of certain expressions in the Mandate, such as the expression "a national home for the Jewish people", and they have found in this ambiguity and the resulting uncertainty as to the objectives of policy a fundamental cause of unrest and hostility between Arabs and Jews. His Majesty's Government are convinced that in the interests of the peace and well-being of the whole people of Palestine a clear definition of policy and objectives is essential. The proposal of partition recommended by the Royal Commission would have afforded such clarity, but the establishment of self-supporting independent Arab and Jewish States within Palestine has been found to be impracticable. It has therefore been necessary for His Majesty's Government to devise an alternative policy which will, consistently with their obligations to Arabs and Jews, meet the needs of the situation in Palestine. Their views and proposals are set forth below under the three heads, (I) The Constitution, (II) Immigration, and (III) Land.

I.—THE CONSTITUTION

4. It has been urged that the expression "a national home for the Jewish people" offered a prospect that Palestine might in due course become a Jewish State or Commonwealth. His Majesty's Government do not wish to contest the view, which was expressed by the Royal Commission, that the Zionist leaders at the time of the issue of the Balfour Declaration recognised that an ultimate Jewish State was not precluded by the terms of the Declaration. But, with the Royal Commission, His Majesty's Government believe that the framers of the Mandate in which the Balfour Declaration was embodied could not have intended that Palestine should be converted into a Jewish State against the will of the Arab population of the country. That Palestine was not to be converted into a Jewish State might be held to be implied in the passage from the Command Paper of 1922 which reads as follows:—

"Unauthorized statements have been made to the effect that the purpose in view is to create a wholly Jewish Palestine. Phrases have been used such as that 'Palestine is to become as Jewish as England is English.' His Majesty's Government regard any such expectation as impracticable and have no such aim in view. Nor have they at any time contemplated . . . . the disappearance or the subordination of the Arabic population, language or culture in Palestine. They would draw attention to the fact that the terms of the (Balfour) Declaration referred to do not contemplate that Palestine as a whole should be converted into a Jewish National Home, but that such a Home should be founded *in Palestine*."

But this statement has not removed doubts, and His Majesty's Government therefore now declare unequivocally that it is not part of their policy that Palestine should become a Jewish State. They would indeed regard it as contrary to their obligations to the Arabs under the Mandate, as well as to the assurances which have been given to the Arab people in the past, that the Arab population of Palestine should be made the subjects of a Jewish State against their will.

5. The nature of the Jewish National Home in Palestine was further described in the Command Paper of 1922 as follows:

"During the last two or three generations the Jews have re-created in Palestine a community, now numbering 80,000, of whom about one-fourth are farmers or workers upon the land. This community has its own political organs; an elected assembly for the direction of its domestic concerns; elected councils in the towns; and an organisation for the control of its schools. It has its elected Chief Rabbinate and Rabbinical Council for the direction of its religious affairs. Its business is conducted in Hebrew as a vernacular language, and a Hebrew press serves its needs. It has its distinctive intellectual life and displays considerable economic activity. This community, then, with its town and country population, its political, religious and social organisations, its own language, its own customs, its own life, has in fact 'national' characteristics. When it is asked what is meant by the development of the Jewish National Home in Palestine, it may be answered that it is not the imposition of a Jewish nationality upon the inhabitants of Palestine as a whole, but the further development of the existing Jewish community, with the assistance of Jews in other parts of the world, in order that it may become a centre in which the Jewish people as a whole may take, on grounds of religion and race, an interest and a pride. But in order that this community should have the best prospect of free development and provide a full opportunity for the Jewish people to display its capacities, it is essential that it should know that it is in Palestine as of right and not on sufferance. That is the reason why it is necessary that the existence of a Jewish National Home in Palestine should be internationally guaranteed, and that it should be formally recognised to rest upon ancient historic connection."

6. His Majesty's Government adhere to this interpretation of the Declaration of 1917 and regard it as an authoritative and comprehensive description of the character of the Jewish National Home in Palestine. It envisaged the further development of the existing Jewish community with the assistance of Jews in other parts of the world. Evidence that His Majesty's Government have been carrying out their obligation in this respect is to be found in the facts that, since the statement of 1922 was published, more than 300,000 Jews have immigrated to Palestine, and that the population of the National Home has risen to some 450,000, or approaching a third of the entire population of the country. Nor has the Jewish community failed to take full advantage of the opportunities given to it. The growth of the Jewish National Home and its achievements in many fields are a remarkable constructive effort which must command the admiration of the world and must be, in particular, a source of pride to the Jewish people.

7. In the recent discussions the Arab delegations have re-

peated the contention that Palestine was included within the area in which Sir Henry McMahon, on behalf of the British Government, in October, 1915, undertook to recognise and support Arab independence. The validity of this claim, based on the terms of the correspondence which passed between Sir Henry McMahon and the Sharif of Mecca, was thoroughly and carefully investigated by British and Arab representatives during the recent conferences in London. Their Report, which has been published, states that both the Arab and the British representatives endeavoured to understand the point of view of the other party but that they were unable to reach agreement upon an interpretation of the correspondence. There is no need to summarize here the arguments presented by each side. His Majesty's Government regret the misunderstandings which have arisen as regards some of the phrases used. For their part they can only adhere, for the reasons given by their representatives in the Report, to the view that the whole of Palestine west of Jordan was excluded from Sir Henry McMahon's pledge, and they therefore cannot agree that the McMahon correspondence forms a just basis for the claim that Palestine should be converted into an Arab State.

8. His Majesty's Government are charged as the Mandatory authority "to secure the development of self-governing institutions" in Palestine. Apart from this specific obligation, they would regard it as contrary to the whole spirit of the Mandate system that the population of Palestine should remain forever under Mandatory tutelage. It is proper that the people of the country should as early as possible enjoy the rights of self-government which are exercised by the people of neighbouring countries. His Majesty's Government are unable at present to foresee the exact constitutional forms which government in Palestine will eventually take, but their objective is self-government, and they desire to see established ultimately an independent Palestine State. It should be a State in which the two peoples in Palestine, Arabs and Jews, share authority in government in such a way that the essential interests of each are secured.

9. The establishment of an independent State and the complete relinquishment of Mandatory control in Palestine would require such relations between the Arabs and the Jews as would make good government possible. Moreover, the growth of self-governing institutions in Palestine, as in other countries, must be an evolutionary process. A transitional period will be required before independence is achieved, throughout

which ultimate responsibility for the Government of the country will be retained by His Majesty's Government as the Mandatory authority, while the people of the country are taking an increasing share in the Government, and understanding and co-operation amongst them are growing. It will be the constant endeavour of His Majesty's Government to promote good relations between the Arabs and the Jews.

10. In the light of these considerations His Majesty's Government make the following declaration of their intentions regarding the future government of Palestine:—

(1) The objective of His Majesty's Government is the establishment within ten years of an independent Palestine State in such treaty relations with the United Kingdom as will provide satisfactorily for the commercial and strategic requirements of both countries in the future. The proposal for the establishment of the independent State would involve consultation with the Council of the League of Nations with a view to the termination of the Mandate.

(2) The independent State should be one in which Arabs and Jews share in government in such a way as to ensure that the essential interests of each community are safeguarded.

(3) The establishment of the independent State will be preceded by a transitional period throughout which His Majesty's Government will retain responsibility for the government of the country. During the transitional period the people of Palestine will be given an increasing part in the government of their country. Both sections of the population will have an opportunity to participate in the machinery of government, and the process will be carried on whether or not they both avail themselves of it.

(4) As soon as peace and order have been sufficiently restored in Palestine steps will be taken to carry out this policy of giving the people of Palestine as increasing part in the government of their country, the objective being to place Palestinians in charge of all the Departments of Government, with the assistance of British advisers and subject to the control of the High Commissioner. With this object in view His Majesty's Government will be prepared immediately to arrange that Palestinians shall be placed in charge of certain Departments, with British advisers. The Palestinian heads of Departments will sit on the Executive Council which advises the High Commissioner. Arab and Jewish representatives will be invited to serve as heads of Departments approximately in proportion to their respective populations. The number of

Palestinians in charge of Departments will be increased as circumstances permit until all heads of Departments are Palestinians, exercising the administrative and advisory functions which are at present performed by British officials. When that stage is reached consideration will be given to the question of converting the Executive Council into a Council of Ministers with a consequential change in the status and functions of the Palestinian heads of Departments.

(5) His Majesty's Government make no proposals at this stage regarding the establishment of an elective legislature. Nevertheless they would regard this as an appropriate constitutional development, and, should public opinion in Palestine hereafter show itself in favour of such a development, they will be prepared, provided that local conditions permit, to establish the necessary machinery.

(6) At the end of five years from the restoration of peace and order, an appropriate body representative of the people of Palestine and of His Majesty's Government will be set up to review the working of the constitutional arrangements during the transitional period and to consider and make recommendations regarding the constitution of the independent Palestine State.

(7) His Majesty's Government will require to be satisfied that in the treaty contemplated by sub-paragraph (1) or in the constitution contemplated by sub-paragraph (6) adequate provision has been made for:—

(*a*) the security of, and freedom of access to, the Holy Places, and the protection of the interests and property of the various religious bodies.

(*b*) the protection of the different communities in Palestine in accordance with the obligations of His Majesty's Government to both Arabs and Jews and for the special position in Palestine of the Jewish National Home.

(*c*) such requirements to meet the strategic situation as may be regarded as necessary by His Majesty's Government in the light of the circumstances then existing.

His Majesty's Government will also require to be satisfied that the interests of certain foreign countries in Palestine, for the preservation of which they are at present responsible, are adequately safeguarded.

(8) His Majesty's Government will do everything in their power to create conditions which will enable the independent Palestine State to come into being within ten years. If, at the end of ten years, it appears to His Majesty's Government that,

contrary to their hope, circumstances require the postponement of the establishment of the independent State, they will
consult with representatives of the people of Palestine, the
Council of the League of Nations and the neighbouring Arab
States before deciding on such a postponement. If His Majesty's Government come to the conclusion that postponement
is unavoidable, they will invite the co-operation of these
parties in framing plans for the future with a view to achieving the desired objective at the earliest possible date.

11. During the transitional period steps will be taken to
increase the powers and responsibilities of municipal corpora-
tions and local councils.

II.—IMMIGRATION

12. Under Article 6 of the Mandate, the Administration of
Palestine, "while ensuring that the rights and position of other
sections of the population are not prejudiced," is required to
"facilitate Jewish immigration under suitable conditions." Beyond this, the extent to which Jewish immigration into Palestine is to be permitted is nowhere defined in the Mandate.
But in the Command Paper of 1922 it was laid down that for
the fulfilment of the policy of establishing a Jewish National
Home

"it is necessary that the Jewish community in Palestine
should be able to increase its numbers by immigration. This
immigration cannot be so great in volume as to exceed whatever may be the economic capacity of the country at the time
to absorb new arrivals. It is essential to ensure that the immigrants should not be a burden upon the people of Palestine
as a whole, and that they should not deprive any section of
the present population of their employment."

In practice, from that date onwards until recent times, the
economic absorptive capacity of the country has been treated
as the sole limiting factor, and in the letter which Mr. Ramsay
MacDonald, as Prime Minister, sent to Dr. Weizmann in
February 1931 it was laid down as a matter of policy that
economic absorptive capacity was the sole criterion. This interpretation has been supported by resolutions of the Permanent Mandates Commission. But His Majesty's Government
do not read either the Statement of Policy of 1922 or the
letter of 1931 as implying that the Mandate requires them,
for all time and in all circumstances, to facilitate the immigration of Jews into Palestine subject only to consideration of the
country's economic absorptive capacity. Nor do they find any-

thing in the Mandate or in subsequent Statements of Policy to support the view that the establishment of a Jewish National Home in Palestine cannot be effected unless immigration is allowed to continue indefinitely. If immigration has an adverse effect on the economic position in the country, it should clearly be restricted; and equally, if it has a seriously damaging effect on the political position in the country, that is a factor that should not be ignored. Although it is not difficult to contend that the large number of Jewish immigrants who have been admitted so far have been absorbed economically, the fear of the Arabs that this influx will continue indefinitely until the Jewish population is in a position to dominate them has produced consequences which are extremely grave for Jews and Arabs alike and for the peace and prosperity of Palestine. The lamentable disturbances of the past three years are only the latest and most sustained manifestation of this intense Arab apprehension. The methods employed by Arab terrorists against fellow-Arabs and Jews alike must receive unqualified condemnation. But it cannot be denied that fear of indefinite Jewish immigration is widespread amongst the Arab population and that this fear has made possible disturbances which have given a serious setback to economic progress, depleted the Palestine exchequer, rendered life and property insecure, and produced a bitterness between the Arab and Jewish populations which is deplorable between citizens of the same country. If in these circumstances immigration is continued up to the economic absorptive capacity of the country, regardless of all other considerations, a fatal enmity between the two peoples will be perpetuated, and the situation in Palestine may become a permanent source of friction amongst all peoples in the Near and Middle East. His Majesty's Government cannot take the view that either their obligations under the Mandate, or considerations of common sense and justice, require that they should ignore these circumstances in framing immigration policy.

13. In the view of the Royal Commission the association of the policy of the Balfour Declaration with the Mandate system implied the belief that Arab hostility to the former would sooner or later be overcome. It has been the hope of British Governments ever since the Balfour Declaration was issued that in time the Arab population, recognizing the advantages to be derived from Jewish settlement and development in Palestine, would become reconciled to the further growth of the Jewish National Home. This hope has not been

fulfilled. The alternatives before His Majesty's Government are either (i) to seek to expand the Jewish National Home indefinitely by immigration, against the strongly expressed will of the Arab people of the country; or (ii) to permit further expansion of the Jewish National Home by immigration only if the Arabs are prepared to acquiesce in it. The former policy means rule by force. Apart from other considerations, such a policy seems to His Majesty's Government to be contrary to the whole spirit of Article 22 of the Covenant of the League of Nations, as well as to their specific obligations to the Arabs in the Palestine Mandate. Moreover, the relations between the Arabs and the Jews in Palestine must be based sooner or later on mutual tolerance and goodwill; the peace, security and progress of the Jewish National Home itself require this. Therefore His Majesty's Government, after earnest consideration, and taking into account the extent to which the growth of the Jewish National Home has been facilitated over the last twenty years, have decided that the time has come to adopt in principle the second of the alternatives referred to above.

14. It has been urged that all further Jewish immigration into Palestine should be stopped forthwith. His Majesty's Government cannot accept such a proposal. It would damage the whole of the financial and economic system of Palestine and thus affect adversely the interests of Arabs and Jews alike. Moreover, in the view of His Majesty's Government, abruptly to stop further immigration would be unjust to the Jewish National Home. But, above all, His Majesty's Government are conscious of the present unhappy plight of large numbers of Jews who seek a refuge from certain European countries, and they believe that Palestine can and should make a further contribution to the solution of this pressing world problem. In all these circumstances, they believe that they will be acting consistently with their Mandatory obligations to both Arabs and Jews, and in the manner best calculated to serve the interests of the whole people of Palestine, by adopting the following proposals regarding immigration:—

(1) Jewish immigration during the next five years will be at a rate which, if economic absorptive capacity permits, will bring the Jewish population up to approximately one-third of the total population of the country. Taking into account the expected natural increase of the Arab and Jewish populations, and the number of illegal Jewish immigrants now in the country, this would allow of the admission, as from the beginning of April this year, of some 75,000 immigrants over the next

five years. These immigrants would, subject to the criterion of
economic absorptive capacity, be admitted as follows:—

(*a*) For each of the next five years a quota of 10,000 Jewish immigrants will be allowed on the understanding that a
shortage in any one year may be added to the quotas for subsequent years, within the five-year period, if economic absorptive capacity permits.

(*b*) In addition, as a contribution towards the solution of
the Jewish refugee problem, 25,000 refugees will be admitted
as soon as the High Commissioner is satisfied that adequate
provision for their maintenance is ensured, special consideration being given to refugee children and dependants.

(2) The existing machinery for ascertaining economic absorptive capacity will be retained, and the High Commissioner
will have the ultimate responsibility for deciding the limits of
economic capacity. Before each periodic decision is taken,
Jewish and Arab representatives will be consulted.

(3) After the period of five years no further Jewish immigration will be permitted unless the Arabs of Palestine are
prepared to acquiesce in it.

(4) His Majesty's Government are determined to check
illegal immigration, and further preventive measures are being
adopted. The numbers of any Jewish illegal immigrants who,
despite these measures, may succeed in coming into the country and cannot be deported will be deducted from the yearly
quotas.

15. His Majesty's Government are satisfied that, when the
immigration over five years which is now contemplated has
taken place, they will not be justified in facilitating, nor will
they be under any obligation to facilitate, the further development of the Jewish National Home by immigration
regardless of the wishes of the Arab population.

III.—LAND

16. The Administration of Palestine is required, under
Article 6 of the Mandate, "while ensuring that the rights and
position of other sections of the population are not prejudiced," to encourage "close settlement by Jews on the land,"
and no restriction has been imposed hitherto on the transfer
of land from Arabs to Jews. The Reports of several expert
Commissions have indicated that, owing to the natural growth
of the Arab population and the steady sale in recent years of
Arab land to Jews, there is now in certain areas no room for

further transfers of Arab land, whilst in some other areas such transfers of land must be restricted if Arab cultivators are to maintain their existing standard of life and a considerable landless Arab population is not soon to be created. In these circumstances, the High Commissioner will be given general powers to prohibit and regulate transfers of land. These powers will date from the publication of this statement of policy and the High Commissioner will retain them throughout the transitional period.

17. The policy of the Government will be directed towards the development of the land and the improvement, where possible, of methods of cultivation. In the light of such development it will be open to the High Commissioner, should he be satisfied that the "rights and position" of the Arab population will be duly preserved, to review and modify any orders passed relating to the prohibition or restriction of the transfer of land.

18. In framing these proposals His Majesty's Government have sincerely endeavoured to act in strict accordance with their obligations under the Mandate to both the Arabs and the Jews. The vagueness of the phrases employed in some instances to describe these obligations has led to controversy and has made the task of interpretation difficult. His Majesty's Government cannot hope to satisfy the partisans of one party or the other in such controversy as the Mandate has aroused. Their purpose is to be just as between the two peoples in Palestine whose destinies in that country have been affected by the great events of recent years, and who, since they live side by side, must learn to practice mutual tolerance, goodwill and co-operation. In looking to the future, His Majesty's Government are not blind to the fact that some events of the past make the task of creating these relations difficult; but they are encouraged by the knowledge that at many times and in many places in Palestine during recent years the Arab and Jewish inhabitants have lived in friendship together. Each community has much to contribute to the welfare of their common land, and each must earnestly desire peace in which to assist in increasing the well-being of the whole people of the country. The responsibility which falls on them, no less than upon His Majesty's Government, to co-operate together to ensure peace is all the more solemn because their country is revered by many millions of Moslems, Jews and Christians throughout the world who pray for peace in Palestine and for the happiness of her people.

Document 18

The Zionist Reaction to the White Paper

*Statement by the Jewish Agency
for Palestine (1939)*

1. The new policy for Palestine laid down by the Mandatory in the White Paper now issued denies to the Jewish people the right to rebuild their national home in their ancestral country. It transfers the authority over Palestine to the present Arab majority and puts the Jewish population at the mercy of that majority. It decrees the stoppage of Jewish immigration as soon as the Jews form a third of the total population. It puts up a territorial ghetto for Jews in their own homeland.

2. The Jewish people regard this policy as a breach of faith and a surrender to Arab terrorism. It delivers Britain's friends into the hands of those who are biting her and must lead to a complete breach between Jews and Arabs which will banish every prospect of peace in Palestine. It is a policy in which the Jewish people will not acquiesce. The new regime now announced will be devoid of any moral basis and contrary to international law. Such a regime can only be established and maintained by force.

3. The Royal Commission invoked by the White Paper indicated the perils of such a policy, saying it was convinced that an Arab Government would mean the frustration of all their (Jews') efforts and ideals and would convert the national home into one more cramped and dangerous ghetto. It seems only too probable that the Jews would fight rather than submit to Arab rule. And repressing a Jewish rebellion against British policy would be as unpleasant a task as the repression of the Arab rebellion has been. The Government has disregarded this warning.

4. The Jewish people have no quarrel with the Arab people. Jewish work in Palestine has not had an adverse effect upon the life and progress of the Arab people. The Arabs are not landless or homeless as are the Jews. They are not in need of emigration. Jewish colonization has benefited Palestine and all its inhabitants. Insofar as the Balfour Declaration contributed to British victory in the Great War, it contributed also, as was pointed out by the Royal Commission, to the liberation of the Arab peoples. The Jewish people has shown

its will to peace even during the years of disturbances. It has not given way to temptation and has not retaliated to Arab violence. But neither have the Jews submitted to terror nor will they submit to it even after the Mandatory has decided to reward the terrorists by surrendering the Jewish National Home.

5. It is in the darkest hour of Jewish history that the British Government proposes to deprive the Jews of their last hope and to close the road back to their Homeland. It is a cruel blow, doubly cruel because it comes from the government of a great nation which has extended a helping hand to the Jews, and whose position must rest on foundations of moral authority and international good faith. This blow will not subdue the Jewish people. The historic bond between the people and the land of Israel cannot be broken. The Jews will never accept the closing to them of the gates of Palestine nor let their national home be converted into a ghetto. The Jewish pioneers who, during the past three generations, have shown their strength in the upbuilding of a derelict country, will from now on display the same strength in defending Jewish immigration, the Jewish home and Jewish freedom.

Document 19

Towards a Jewish State: The Biltmore Program (1942)

During a visit to the United States by David Ben Gurion, Chairman of the Executive of the Jewish Agency, Zionist policy was reformulated. At a conference at the Biltmore Hotel in New York, in May 1942, the establishment of a Jewish state was envisaged to open the doors of Palestine to Jewish refugees escaping from Nazi terror and to lay the foundations for the establishment of a Jewish majority.

Declaration Adopted by the Extraordinary Zionist Conference, Biltmore Hotel, New York City, May 11, 1942

1. American Zionists assembled in this Extraordinary Conference reaffirm their unequivocal devotion to the cause of democratic freedom and international justice to which the people of the United States, allied with the other United

Nations, have dedicated themselves, and give expression to their faith in the ultimate victory of humanity and justice over lawlessness and brute force.

2. This Conference offers a message of hope and encouragement to their fellow Jews in the Ghettos and concentration camps of Hitler-dominated Europe and prays that their hour of liberation may not be far distant.

3. The Conference sends its warmest greetings to the Jewish Agency Executive in Jerusalem, to the Va'ad Leumi, and to the whole Yishuv in Palestine, and expresses its profound admiration for their steadfastness and achievements in the face of peril and great difficulties. The Jewish men and women in field and factory, and the thousands of Jewish soldiers of Palestine in the Near East who have acquitted themselves with honor and distinction in Greece, Ethiopia, Syria, Libya and on other battlefields, have shown themselves worthy of their people and ready to assume the rights and responsibilities of nationhood.

4. In our generation, and in particular in the course of the past twenty years, the Jewish people have awakened and transformed their ancient homeland; from 50,000 at the end of the last war their numbers have increased to more than 500,000. They have made the waste places to bear fruit and the desert to blossom. Their pioneering achievements in agriculture and in industry, embodying new patterns of cooperative endeavor, have written a notable page in the history of colonization.

5. In the new values thus created, their Arab neighbors in Palestine have shared. The Jewish people in its own work of national redemption welcomes the economic, agricultural and national development of the Arab peoples and states. The Conference reaffirms the stand previously adopted at Congresses of the World Zionist Organization, expressing the readiness and the desire of the Jewish people for full cooperation with their Arab neighbors.

6. The Conference calls for the fulfilment of the original purpose of the Balfour Declaration and the Mandate which *"recognizing the historical connection of the Jewish people with Palestine"* was to afford them the opportunity, as stated by President Wilson, to found there a Jewish Commonwealth.

The Conference affirms its unalterable rejection of the White Paper of May 1939 and denies its moral or legal validity. The White Paper seeks to limit, and in fact to nullify

Jewish rights to immigration and settlement in Palestine, and, as stated by Mr. Winston Churchill in the House of Commons in May 1939, constitutes "a breach and repudiation of the Balfour Declaration." The policy of the White Paper is cruel and indefensible in its denial of sanctuary to Jews fleeing from Nazi persecution; and at a time when Palestine has become a focal point in the war front of the United Nations, and Palestine Jewry must provide all available manpower for farm and factory and camp, it is in direct conflict with the interests of the allied war effort.

7. In the struggle against the forces of aggression and tyranny, of which Jews were the earliest victims, and which now menace the Jewish National Home, recognition must be given to the right of the Jews of Palestine to play their full part in the war effort and in the defense of their country, through a Jewish military force fighting under its own flag and under the high command of the United Nations.

8. The Conference declares that the new world order that will follow victory cannot be established on foundations of peace, justice and equality, unless the problem of Jewish homelessness is finally solved.

The Conference urges that the gates of Palestine be opened; that the Jewish Agency be vested with control of immigration into Palestine and with the necessary authority for upbuilding the country, including the development of its unoccupied and uncultivated lands; and that Palestine be established as a Jewish Commonwealth integrated in the structure of the new democratic world.

Then and only then will the age-old wrong to the Jewish people be righted.

Document 20

Adolf Hitler, Zionism and the Arab Cause*

Haj Amin al Husaini, the most influential leader of Palestinian Arabs, lived in Germany during the Second World War. He met Hitler, Ribbentrop and other Nazi leaders on various occasions and attempted to coordinate Nazi and Arab policies in the Middle East.

* *Documents on German Foreign Policy 1918-45*, Series D, Vol. XIII, London, 1964, pp. 881 ff.

BERLIN, NOVEMBER 30, 1941.

Record of the Conversation Between the Führer and the Grand Mufti of Jerusalem on November 28, 1941, in the Presence of Reich Foreign Minister and Minister Grobba in Berlin

The Grand Mufti began by thanking the Führer for the great honor he had bestowed by receiving him. He wished to seize the opportunity to convey to the Führer of the Greater German Reich, admired by the entire Arab world, his thanks for the sympathy which he had always shown for the Arab and especially the Palestinian cause, and to which he had given clear expression in his public speeches. The Arab countries were firmly convinced that Germany would win the war and that the Arab cause would then prosper. The Arabs were Germany's natural friends because they had the same enemies as had Germany, namely the English, the Jews, and the Communists. They were therefore prepared to cooperate with Germany with all their hearts and stood ready to participate in the war, not only negatively by the commission of acts of sabotage and the instigation of revolutions, but also positively by the formation of an Arab Legion. The Arabs could be more useful to Germany as allies than might be apparent at first glance, both for geographical reasons and because of the suffering inflicted upon them by the English and the Jews. Furthermore, they had had close relations with all Moslem nations, of which they could make use in behalf of the common cause. The Arab Legion would be quite easy to raise. An appeal by the Mufti to the Arab countries and the prisoners of Arab, Algerian, Tunisian, and Moroccan nationality in Germany would produce a great number of volunteers eager to fight. Of Germany's victory the Arab world was firmly convinced, not only because the Reich possessed a large army, brave soldiers, and military leaders of genius, but also because the Almighty could never award the victory to an unjust cause.

In this struggle, the Arabs were striving for the independence and unity of Palestine, Syria, and Iraq. They had the fullest confidence in the Führer and looked to his hand for the balm on their wounds which had been inflicted upon them by the enemies of Germany.

The Mufti then mentioned the letter he had received from Germany, which stated that Germany was holding no Arab territories and understood and recognized the aspirations to independence and freedom of the Arabs, just as she supported the elimination of the Jewish national home.

A public declaration in this sense would be very useful for its propagandistic effect on the Arab peoples at this moment. It would rouse the Arabs from their momentary lethargy and give them new courage. It would also ease the Mufti's work of secretly organizing the Arabs against the moment when they could strike. At the same time, he could give the assurance that the Arabs would in strict discipline patiently wait for the right moment and only strike upon an order from Berlin.

With regard to the events in Iraq, the Mufti observed that the Arabs in that country certainly had by no means been incited by Germany to attack England, but solely had acted in reaction to a direct English assault upon their honor.

The Turks, he believed, would welcome the establishment of an Arab government in the neighboring territories because they would prefer weaker Arab to strong European governments in the neighboring countries, and, being themselves a nation of 7 millions, they had moreover nothing to fear from the 1,700,000 Arabs inhabiting Syria, Transjordan, Iraq, and Palestine.

France likewise would have no objections to the unification plan because she had conceded independence to Syria as early as 1936 and had given her approval to the unification of Iraq and Syria under King Faisal as early as 1933.

In these circumstances he was renewing his request that the Führer make a public declaration so that the Arabs would not lose hope, which is so powerful a force in the life of nations. With such hope in their hearts the Arabs, as he had said, were willing to wait. They were not pressing for immediate realization of their aspirations; they could easily wait half a year or a whole year. But if they were not inspired with such a hope by a declaration of this sort, it could be expected that the English would be the gainers from it.

The Führer replied that Germany's fundamental attitude on these questions, as the Mufti himself had already stated, was clear. Germany stood for uncompromising war against the Jews. That naturally included active opposition to the Jewish national home in Palestine, which was nothing other than a center, in the form of a state, for the exercise of destructive influence by Jewish interests. Germany was also aware that the assertion that the Jews were carrying out the function of economic pioneers in Palestine was a lie. The work there was done only by the Arabs, not by the Jews. Germany was resolved, step by step, to ask one European nation after the other to solve its Jewish problem, and at the proper time direct a similar appeal to non-European nations as well.

Germany was at the present time engaged in a life and death struggle with two citadels of Jewish power: Great Britain and Soviet Russia. Theoretically there was a difference between England's capitalism and Soviet Russia's communism; actually, however, the Jews in both countries were pursuing a common goal. This was the decisive struggle; on the political plane, it presented itself in the main as a conflict between Germany and England, but ideologically it was a battle between National Socialism and the Jews. It went without saying that Germany would furnish positive and practical aid to the Arabs involved in the same struggle, because platonic promises were useless in a war for survival or destruction in which the Jews were able to mobilize all of England's power for their ends.

The aid to the Arabs would have to be material aid. Of how little help sympathies alone were in such a battle had been demonstrated plainly by the operation in Iraq, where circumstances had not permitted the rendering of really effective, practical aid. In spite of all the sympathies, German aid had not been sufficient and Iraq was overcome by the power of Britain, that is, the guardian of the Jews.

The Mufti could not but be aware, however, that the outcome of the struggle going on at present would also decide the fate of the Arab world. The Führer therefore had to think and speak coolly and deliberately, as a rational man and primarily as a soldier, as the leader of the German and allied armies. Everything of a nature to help in this titanic battle for the common cause, and thus also for the Arabs, would have to be done. Anything, however, that might contribute to weakening the military situation must be put aside, no matter how unpopular this move might be.

Germany was now engaged in very severe battles to force the gateway to the northern Caucasus region. The difficulties were mainly with regard to maintaining the supply, which was most difficult as a result of the destruction of railroads and highways as well as of the oncoming winter. If at such a moment, the Führer were to raise the problem of Syria in a declaration, those elements in France which were under de Gaulle's influence would receive new strength. They would interpret the Führer's declaration as an intention to break up France's colonial empire and appeal to their fellow country-men that they should rather make common cause with the English to try to save what still could be saved. A German declaration regarding Syria would in France be understood to refer to the French colonies in general, and that would at the present time create new troubles in western Europe, which means that a portion of the German armed forces would be immobilized in the west and no longer be available for the campaign in the east.

The Führer then made the following statement to the Mufti, enjoining him to lock it in the uttermost depths of his heart:

1. He (the Führer) would carry on the battle to the total destruction of the Judeo-Communist empire in Europe.

2. At some moment which was impossible to set exactly today but which in any event was not distant, the German armies would in the course of this struggle reach the southern exit from Caucasia.

3. As soon as this had happened, the Führer would on his own give the Arab world the assurance that its hour of liberation had arrived. Germany's objective would then be solely the destruction of the Jewish element residing in the Arab sphere under the protection of British power. In that hour the Mufti would be the most authoritative spokesman for the Arab world. It would then be his task to set off the Arab operations which he had secretly prepared. When that time had come, Germany could also be indifferent to French reaction to such a declaration.

Once Germany had forced open the road to Iran and Iraq through Rostov, it would be also the beginning of the end of the British world empire. He (the Führer) hoped that the coming year would make it possible for Germany to thrust open the Caucasian gate to the Middle East. For the good of their common cause, it would be better if the Arab proclamation were put off for a few more months than if Germany were to create difficulties for herself without being able thereby to help the Arabs.

He (the Führer) fully appreciated the eagerness of the Arabs for a public declaration of the sort requested by the Grand Mufti. But he would beg him to consider that he (the Führer) himself was the Chief of State of the German Reich for 5 long years during which he was unable to make to his own homeland the announcement of its liberation. He had to wait with that until the announcement could be made on the basis of a situation brought about by the force of arms that the Anschluss had been carried out.

The moment that Germany's tank divisions and air squadrons had made their appearance south of the Caucasus, the public appeal requested by the Grand Mufti could go out to the Arab world.

The Grand Mufti replied that it was his view that everything would come to pass just as the Führer had indicated. He was fully reassured and satisfied by the words which he had heard from the Chief of the German State. He asked, however, whether it would not be possible, secretly at least, to enter into an agreement with Germany of the kind he had just outlined for the Führer.

The Führer replied that he had just now given the Grand Mufti precisely that confidential declaration.

The Grand Mufti thanked him for it and stated in conclusion that he was taking his leave from the Führer in full confidence and with reiterated thanks for the interest shown in the Arab cause.

SCHMIDT

Documents 21–23

The Anglo–American Committee of Inquiry—1946

An Anglo-American Inquiry Committee was appointed in November, 1945, to examine the status of the Jews in former Axis-occupied countries and to find out how many were impelled by their conditions to migrate. Britain, weakened by the war, found itself under growing pressure from Jews and Arabs alike and the Labor Government decided, therefore, to invite the United States to participate in finding a solution. The Report of the Committee was published on May 1, 1945 (Document 21). President Truman welcomed its recommendation that the immigration and land laws of the 1939 White Paper were to be rescinded. Prime Minister Attlee, on the other hand, declared that the report would have to be "considered as a whole in all its implications." Arab reaction was hostile

(Document 22); the Arab League announced that Arabs would not stand by with their arms folded. The Ihud (Association) group led by Dr. J. L. Magnes and Professor M. Buber (who submitted Document 23 to the Committee), favored a bi-national solution, equal political rights for Arabs and Jews, and a Federative Union of Palestine and the neighboring countries. Ihud found little support among the Jewish Community. It had, in the beginning, a few Arab sympathizers, but some of them were assassinated by supporters of the Mufti and the others dropped out.

Document 21

Recommendations and Comments

THE EUROPEAN PROBLEM

Recommendation No. 1. We have to report that such information as we received about countries other than Palestine gave no hope of substantial assistance in finding homes for Jews wishing or impelled to leave Europe.

But Palestine alone cannot meet the emigration needs of the Jewish victims of Nazi and Fascist persecution; the whole world shares responsibility for them and indeed for the resettlement of all "displaced persons."

We therefore recommend that our Governments together, and in association with other countries, should endeavor immediately to find new homes for all such "displaced persons," irrespective of creed or nationality, whose ties with their former communities have been irreparably broken.

Though emigration will solve the problems of some victims of persecution, the overwhelming majority, including a considerable number of Jews, will continue to live in Europe. We recommend therefore that our Governments endeavor to secure that immediate effect is given to the provision of the United Nations Charter calling for "universal respect for, and observation of, human rights and fundamental freedoms for all without distinction as to race, sex, language or religion."
Comment. In recommending that our Governments, in association with other countries, should endeavor to find new homes for "displaced persons," we do not suggest that any country should be asked to make a permanent change in its

immigration policy. The conditions which we have seen in Europe are unprecedented and so unlikely to arise again that we are convinced that special provision could and should be made in existing immigration laws to meet this unique and peculiarly distressing situation. Furthermore, we believe that much could be accomplished—particularly in regard to those "displaced persons," including Jews, who have relatives in countries outside Europe—by a relaxation of administrative regulations.

Our investigations have led us to believe that a considerable number of Jews will continue to live in most European countries. In our view the mass emigration of all European Jews would be of service neither to the Jews themselves nor to Europe. Every effort should be made to enable the Jews to rebuild their shattered communities, while permitting those Jews who wish to do so to emigrate. In order to achieve this, restitution of Jewish property should be effected as soon as possible. Our investigations showed us that the Governments chiefly concerned had for the most part already passed legislation to this end. A real obstacle, however, to individual restitution is that the attempt to give effect to this legislation is frequently a cause of active anti-Semitism. We suggest that, for the reconstruction of the Jewish communities, restitution of their corporate property, either through reparations payments or through other means, is of the first importance.

Nazi occupation has left behind it a legacy of anti-Semitism. This cannot be combatted by legislation alone. The only really effective antidotes are the enforcement by each Government of guaranteed civil liberties and equal rights, a program of education in the positive principles of democracy, the sanction of a strong world public opinion—combined with economic recovery and stability.

REFUGEE IMMIGRATION INTO PALESTINE

Recommendation No. 2. We recommend (a) that 100,000 certificates be authorized immediately for the admission into Palestine of Jews who have been the victims of Nazi and Fascist persecution; (b) that these certificates be awarded as far as possible in 1946 and that actual immigration be pushed forward as rapidly as conditions will permit.

Comment. The number of Jewish survivors of Nazi and Fascist persecution with whom we have to deal far exceeds 100,000: indeed there are more than that number in Germany,

Austria and Italy alone. Although nearly a year has passed since their liberation, the majority of those in Germany and Austria are still living in assembly centers, the so-called "camps," island communities in the midst of those at whose hands they suffered so much.

In their interests and in the interests of Europe, the centers should be closed and their camp life ended. Most of them have cogent reasons for wishing to leave Europe. Many are the sole survivors of their families and few have any ties binding them to the countries in which they used to live.

Since the end of hostilities, little has been done to provide for their resettlement elsewhere. Immigration laws and restrictions bar their entry to most countries and much time must pass before such laws and restrictions can be altered and effect given to the alterations.

Some can go to countries where they have relatives; others may secure inclusion in certain quotas. Their number is comparatively small.

We know of no country to which the great majority can go in the immediate future other than Palestine. Furthermore, that is where almost all of them want to go. There they are sure that they will receive a welcome denied them elsewhere. There they hope to enjoy peace and rebuild their lives.

We believe it is essential that they should be given an opportunity to do so at the earliest possible time. Furthermore, we have the assurances of the leaders of the Jewish Agency that they will be supported and cared for.

We recommend the authorization and issue of 100,000 certificates for these reasons and because we feel that their immediate issue will have a most salutary effect upon the whole situation.

In the awarding of these certificates priority should, as far as possible, be given to those in the centers and to those liberated in Germany and Austria who are no longer in the centers but remain in those countries. We do not desire that other Jewish victims who wish or will be impelled by their circumstances to leave the countries where they now are or that those who fled from persecution before the outbreak of war should be excluded. We appreciate that there will be difficulty in deciding questions of priority, but none the less we urge that so far as possible such a system should be adhered to, and that, in applying it, primary consideration should be given to the aged and infirm, to the very young and also to skilled workmen whose services will be needed for many months on work rendered necessary by the large influx.

It should be made clear that no advantage in the obtaining of a certificate is to be gained by migrating from one country to another or by entering Palestine illegally.

Receiving so large a number will be a heavy burden on Palestine. We feel sure that the authorities will shoulder it and that they will have the full cooperation of the Jewish Agency.

Difficult problems will confront those responsible for organizing and carrying out the movement. The many organizations —public and private—working in Europe will certainly render all the aid they can; we mention UNRRA especially. Cooperation by all throughout is necessary.

We are sure that the Government of the United States, which has shown such keen interest in this matter, will participate vigorously and generously with the Government of Great Britain in its fulfillment. There are many ways in which help can be given.

Those who have opposed the admission of these unfortunate people into Palestine should know that we have fully considered all that they have put before us. We hope that they will look upon the situation again, that they will appreciate the considerations which have led us to our conclusion, and that above all, if they cannot see their way to help, at least they will not make the position of these sufferers more difficult.

PRINCIPLES OF GOVERNMENT:
NO ARAB, NO JEWISH STATE

Recommendation No. 3. In order to dispose, once and for all, of the exclusive claims of Jews and Arabs to Palestine, we regard it as essential that a clear statement of the following principles should be made:

(I) That Jew shall not dominate Arab and Arab shall not dominate Jew in Palestine. (II) That Palestine shall be neither a Jewish state nor an Arab state. (III) That the form of government ultimately to be established, shall, under international guarantees, fully protect and preserve the interests in the Holy Land of Christendom and of the Moslem and Jewish faiths.

Thus Palestine must ultimately become a state which guards the rights and interests of Moslems, Jews and Christians alike and accords to the inhabitants, as a whole, the fullest measure of self-government consistent with the three paramount principles set forth above.

Comment. Throughout the long and bloody struggle of Jew and Arab for dominance in Palestine, each crying fiercely: "This land is mine"—except for the brief reference in the Report of the Royal Commission (Hereinafter referred to as the Peel Report) and the little evidence, written and oral, that we received on this point—the great interest of the Christian world in Palestine has been completely overlooked, glossed over or brushed aside.

We therefore emphatically declare that Palestine is a Holy Land, sacred to Christian, to Jew and to Moslem alike; and because it is a Holy Land, Palestine is not, and can never become, a land which any race or religion can justly claim as its very own.

We further, in the same emphatic way, affirm that the fact that it is the Holy Land sets Palestine completely apart from other lands and dedicates it to the precepts and practices of the brotherhood of man, not those of narrow nationalism.

For another reason, in the light of its long history, and particularly its history of the last thirty years, Palestine cannot be regarded as either a purely Arab or a purely Jewish land.

The Jews have a historic connection with the country. The Jewish National Home, though embodying a minority of the population, is today a reality established under international guarantee. It has a right to continued existence, protection and development.

Yet Palestine is not, and never can be a purely Jewish land. It lies at the crossroads of the Arab world. Its Arab population, descended from long-time inhabitants of the area, rightly look upon Palestine as their homeland.

It is, therefore, neither just nor practicable that Palestine should become either an Arab state, in which an Arab majority would control the destiny of a Jewish minority, or a Jewish state, in which a Jewish majority would control that of an Arab minority. In neither case would minority guarantees afford adequate protection for the subordinated group.

A Palestinian put the matter thus: "In the hearts of us Jews there has always been a fear that some day this country would be turned into an Arab state and the Arabs would rule over us. This fear has at times reached the proportions of terror . . . Now this same feeling of fear has started up in the hearts of Arabs . . . fear lest the Jews acquire the ascendancy and rule over them."

Palestine, then, must be established as a country in which the legitimate national aspirations of both Jews and Arabs can be reconciled without either side fearing the ascendancy of the other. In our view this cannot be done under any form of constitution in which a mere numerical majority is decisive, since it is precisely the struggle for a numerical majority which bedevils Arab-Jewish relations. To ensure genuine self-government for both the Arab and the Jewish communities, this struggle must be made purposeless by the constitution itself.

MANDATE AND UNITED NATIONS TRUSTEESHIP

Recommendation No. 4. We have reached the conclusion that the hostility between Jews and Arabs and, in particular, the determination of each to achieve domination, if necessary by violence, make it almost certain that, now and for some time to come, any attempt to establish either an independent Palestinian state or independent Palestinian states would result in civil strife such as might threaten the peace of the world. We therefore recommend that, until this hostility disappears, the Government of Palestine be continued as at present under mandate pending the execution of a trusteeship agreement under the United Nations.

Comment. We recognize that in view of the powerful forces both Arab and Jewish, operating from outside Palestine, the task of Great Britain, as mandatory, has not been easy. The Peel Commission declared in 1937 that the mandate was unworkable, and the Permanent Mandates Commission of the League of Nations thereupon pointed out that it became almost unworkable once it was publicly declared to be so by such a body. Two years later the British Government, having come to the conclusion that the alternative of partition proposed by the Peel Commission was also unworkable, announced their intention of taking steps to terminate the mandate by establishment of an independent Palestine state.

Our recommendations are based on what we believe at this stage to be as fair a measure of justice to all as we can find in view of what has gone before and of all that has been done. We recognize that they are not in accord with the claims of either party, and furthermore that they involve a departure from the recent policy of the mandatory.

We recognize that, if they are adopted, they will involve a long period of trusteeship, which will mean a very heavy burden for any single Government to undertake, a burden which would be lightened if the difficulties were appreciated and the trustee had the support of other members of the United Nations.

EQUALITY OF STANDARDS

Recommendation No. 5. Looking toward a form of ultimate self-government consistent with the three principles laid down in Recommendation No. 3, we recommend that the mandatory or trustee should proclaim the principle that Arab economic, educational and political advancement in Palestine is of equal importance with that of the Jews; and should at once prepare measures designed to bridge the gap which now exists and raise the Arab standard of living to that of the Jews; and to bring the two peoples to a full appreciation of their common interest and common destiny in the land where both belong.

Comment. Our examination of conditions in Palestine led us to the conclusion that one of the chief causes of friction is the great disparity between the Jewish and Arab standards of living. Even under conditions of war, which brought considerable financial benefits to the Arabs, this disparity has not been appreciably reduced. Only by a deliberate and carefully planned policy on the part of the mandatory can the Arab standard of living be raised to that of the Jews. In stressing the need for such a policy we would particularly call attention to the discrepancies between the social services, including hospitals, available in Palestine for Jews and Arabs.

SOCIAL AID

We fully recognize that the Jewish social services are financed to a very great extent by the Jewish community in Palestine, with the assistance of outside Jewish organizations; and we would stress that nothing should be done which would bring these social services down to the level of those provided for the Arabs, or halt the constant improvements now being made in them.

We suggest that consideration be given to the advisability of encouraging the formation by the Arabs of an Arab community on the lines of the Jewish community which now largely controls and finances Jewish social services. The Arabs will have to rely, to a far greater extent than the Jews, on financial aid from the Government. But the Jews of Palestine should accept the necessity that taxation, raised from both Jews and Arabs, will have to be spent very largely on the Arabs in order to bridge the gap which now exists between the standard of living of the two peoples.

FURTHER IMMIGRATION POLICY

Recommendation No. 6. We recommend that pending the early reference to the United Nations and the execution of a trusteeship agreement, the mandatory should administer Palestine according to the mandate, which declares, with regard to immigration, that "the administration of Palestine, while insuring that the rights and position of other sections of the population are not prejudiced, shall facilitate Jewish immigration under suitable conditions."

Comment. We have recommended the admission of 100,000 immigrants, victims of Nazi persecution, as soon as possible. We now deal with the position after the admission of that number. We cannot look far into the future. We cannot construct a yardstick for annual immigration. Until a trusteeship agreement is executed it is our clear opinion that Palestine should be administered in accordance with the terms of the mandate quoted above.

Further than that we cannot go in the form of a recommendation. In this disordered world speculation as to the economic position of any country a few years ahead would be a hazardous proceeding. It is particularly difficult to predict what, after a few years have passed, will be the economic and political condition of Palestine. We hope that the present friction and turbulence will soon die away and be replaced by an era of peace, absent so long from the Holy Land; that the Jew and Arab will soon realize that collaboration is to their mutual advantage, but no one can say how long this will take.

The possibility of the country sustaining a largely increased population at a decent standard of living depends largely on whether or not plans referred to in Recommendation No. 8 can be brought to fruition.

The Peel Commission stated that political as well as economic considerations have to be taken into account in regard to immigration, and recommended a "political high level" of 12,000 a year. We cannot recommend the fixing of a minimum or of a maximum for annual immigration in the future. There are too many uncertain factors.

We desire, however, to state certain considerations which

we agree should be taken into account in determining what number of immigrants there should be in any period. It is the right of every independent nation to determine in the interests of its people the number of immigrants to be admitted to its lands. Similarly it must, we think, be conceded that it should be the right of the Government of Palestine to decide, having regard to the well-being of all the people of Palestine, the number of immigrants to be admitted within any given period.

In Palestine there is the Jewish National Home, created in consequence of the Balfour Declaration. Some may think that that declaration was wrong and should not have been made; some that it was a conception on a grand scale and that effect can be given to one of the most daring and significant colonization plans in history. Controversy as to which view is right is fruitless. The national home is there. Its roots are deep in the soil of Palestine. It cannot be argued out of existence; neither can the achievements of the Jewish pioneers.

The Government of Palestine in having regard to the well-being of all the people of Palestine cannot ignore the interests of so large a section of the population. It cannot ignore the achievements of the last quarter of a century. No Government of Palestine doing its duty to the people of that land can fail to do its best not only to maintain the national home but also to foster its proper development and such development must, in our view, involve immigration.

The well-being of all the people of Palestine, be they Jews, Arabs or neither, must be the governing consideration. We reject the view that there shall be no further Jewish immigration into Palestine without Arab acquiescence, a view which would result in the Arab dominating the Jew. We also reject the insistent Jewish demand that forced Jewish immigration must proceed apace in order to produce as quickly as possible a Jewish majority and a Jewish State. The well-being of the Jews must not be subordinated to that of the Arabs; nor that of the Arabs to the Jews. The well-being of both, the economic situation of Palestine as a whole, the degree of execution of plans for further development, all have to be carefully considered in deciding the number of immigrants for any particular period.

Palestine is a land sacred to three faiths and must not become the land of any one of them to the exclusion of the others, and Jewish immigration for the development of the national home must not become a policy of discrimination against other immigrants. Any person, therefore, who desires and is qualified under applicable laws to enter Palestine must not be refused admission or subjected to discrimination on the ground that he is not a Jew. All provisions respecting immigration must be drawn, executed and applied with that principle always firmly in mind.

Further, while we recognize that any Jew who enters Palestine in accordance with its laws is there of right, we expressly disapprove of the position taken in some Jewish quarters that Palestine has in some way been ceded or granted as their state to the Jews of the world, that every Jew everywhere is, merely because he is a Jew, a citizen of Palestine and therefore can enter Palestine as of right without regard to conditions imposed by the Government upon entry and that therefore there can be no illegal immigration of Jews into Palestine. We declare and affirm that any immigrant Jew who enters Palestine contrary to its laws is an illegal immigrant.

[Recommendations 7-9 deal with land policy, economic development, and education. Ed.]

Document 22

*The Arab Case for Palestine: Evidence Submitted
by the Arab Office, Jerusalem, to the
Anglo–American Committee of Inquiry,
March, 1946*

The Problem of Palestine

1. The whole Arab people is unalterably opposed to the attempt to impose Jewish immigration and settlement upon it, and ultimately to establish a Jewish State in Palestine. Its opposition is based primarily upon right. The Arabs of Palestine are descendants of the indigenous inhabitants of the country, who have been in occupation of it since the beginning of history; they cannot agree that it is right to subject an indigenous population against its will to alien immigrants, whose claim is based upon a historical connection which ceased effectively many centuries ago. Moreover they form the majority of the population; as such they cannot submit to a policy of immigration which if pursued for long will turn them from a majority into a minority in an alien state; and they claim the democratic right of a majority to make its own decisions in matters of urgent national concern. . . .

2. In addition to the question of right, the Arabs oppose the

claims of political Zionism because of the effects which Zionist settlement has already had upon their situation and is likely to have to an even greater extent in the future. Negatively, it has diverted the whole course of their national development. Geographically Palestine is part of Syria; its indigenous inhabitants belong to the Syrian branch of the Arab family of nations; all their culture and tradition link them to the other Arab peoples; and until 1917 Palestine formed part of the Ottoman Empire which included also several of the other Arab countries. The presence and claims of the Zionists, and the support given them by certain Western Powers have resulted in Palestine being cut off from the other Arab countries and subjected to a regime, administrative, legal, fiscal and educational, different from that of the sister-countries. Quite apart from the inconvenience to individuals and the dislocation of trade which this separation has caused, it has prevented Palestine participating fully in the general development of the Arab world.

First, while the other Arab countries have attained or are near to the attainment of self-government and full membership of the U.N.O., Palestine is still under Mandate and has taken no step towards self-government; not only are there no representative institutions, but no Palestinian can rise to the higher ranks of the administration. This is inacceptable on grounds of principle, and also because of its evil consequence. It is a hardship to individual Palestinians whose opportunities of responsibility are thus curtailed; and it is demoralizing to the population to live under a government which has no basis in their consent and to which they can feel no attachment or loyalty.

Secondly, while the other Arab countries are working through the Arab League to strengthen their ties and coordinate their policies, Palestine (although her Arab inhabitants are formally represented in the League's Council) cannot participate fully in this movement so long as she has no indigenous government; thus the chasm between the administrative system and the institutions of Palestine and those of the neighbouring countries is growing, and her traditional Arab character is being weakened.

Thirdly, while the other Arab countries have succeeded in or are on the way to achieving a satisfactory definition of their relations with the Western Powers and with the world-community, expressed in their treaties with Great Britain and other Powers and their membership of the United Nations

Organization, Palestine has not yet been able to establish any definite status for herself in the world, and her international destiny is still obscure.

3. All these evils are due entirely to the presence of the Zionists and the support given to them by certain of the Powers; there is no doubt that had it not been for that, Arab Palestine would by now be a self-governing member of the U.N.O. and the Arab League. Moreover, in addition to the obstacles which Zionism has thus placed in the way of Palestine's development, the presence of the Zionists gives rise to various positive evils which will increase if Zionist immigration continues.

The entry of incessant waves of immigrants prevents normal economic and social development and causes constant dislocation of the country's life; in so far as it reacts upon prices and values and makes the whole economy dependent upon the constant inflow of capital from abroad it may even in certain circumstances lead to economic disaster. It is bound moreover to arouse continuous political unrest and prevent the establishment of that political stability on which the prosperity and health of the country depend. This unrest is likely to increase in frequency and violence as the Jews come nearer to being the majority and the Arabs a minority.

Even if economic and social equilibrium is re-established, it will be to the detriment of the Arabs. The superior capital resources at the disposal of the Jews, their greater experience of modern economic technique and the existence of a deliberate policy of expansion and domination have already gone far toward giving them the economic mastery of Palestine. The biggest concessionary companies are in their hands; they possess a large proportion of the total cultivable land, and an even larger one of the land in the highest category of fertility; and the land they possess is mostly inalienable to non-Jews. The continuance of land-purchase and immigration, taken together with the refusal of Jews to employ Arabs on their lands or in their enterprises and the great increase in the Arab population, will create a situation in which the Arab population is pushed to the margin of cultivation and a landless proletariat, rural and urban, comes into existence. This evil can be palliated but not cured by attempts at increasing the absorptive capacity or the industrial production of Palestine; the possibility of such improvements is limited, they would take a long time to carry out, and would scarcely do more than keep pace with the rapid growth of the Arab population; moreover in present circumstances they would be used primarily for the benefit of the Jews and thus might increase the disparity between the two communities.

Nor is the evil economic only. Zionism is essentially a political movement, aiming at the creation of a state: immigration, land-purchase and economic expansion are only aspects of a general political strategy. If Zionism succeeds in its aim, the Arabs will become a minority in their own country; a minority which can hope for no more than a minor share in the government, for the state is to be a Jewish state, and which will find itself not only deprived of that international status which the other Arab countries possess but cut off from living contact with the Arab world of which it is an integral part.

It should not be forgotten too that Palestine contains places holy to Moslems and Christians, and neither Arab Moslems nor Arab Christians would willingly see such places subjected to the ultimate control of a Jewish Government.

4. These dangers would be serious enough at any time, but are particularly so in this age, when the first task of the awakening Arab nation is to come to terms with the West; to define its relationship with the Western Powers and with the westernized world community on a basis of equality and mutual respect, and to adapt what is best in Western civilization to the needs of its own genius. Zionist policy is one of the greatest obstacles to the achievement of this task: both because Zionism represents to the Arabs one side of the Western spirit and because of the support given to it by some of the Western Powers. In fact Zionism has became in Arab eyes a test of Western intentions towards them. So long as the attempt of the Zionists to impose a Jewish state upon the inhabitants of Palestine is supported by some or all of the Western Governments, so long will it be difficult if not impossible for the Arabs to establish a satisfactory relationship with the Western world and its civilization, and they will tend to turn away from the West in political hostility and spiritual isolation; this will be disastrous both for the Arabs themselves and for those Western nations which have dealings with them.

5. There are no benefits obtained or to be expected from Zionism commensurate with its evils and its dangers. The alleged social and economic benefits are much less than is claimed. The increase in the Arab population is not primarily due to Zionist immigration, and in any case would not neces-

sarily be a sign of prosperity. The rise in money wages and earnings is largely illusory, being offset by the rise in the cost of living. In so far as real wages and the standard of living have risen, this is primarily an expression of a general trend common to all Middle Eastern countries. The inflow of capital has gone largely to raising money prices and real estate values. The whole economy is dangerously dependent upon the citrus industry. The benefits derived from the establishment of industries and the exploitation of the country's few natural resources have been largely neutralized by the failure of Jewish enterprises to employ Arabs.

The Zionist contention that their social organizations provide health and social services for the Arab population is exaggerated; only a minute proportion of the Arabs, for example, are looked after by Jewish health organizations. Even if true it would prove nothing except that the Government was neglecting its responsibilities in regard to the welfare of the population. Arab voluntary social organizations have grown up independently of Jewish bodies and without help from them. Even in so far as social and economic benefits have come to the Arabs from Zionist settlement, it remains true on the one hand that they are more than counter-balanced by the dangers of that settlement, and on the other that they are only incidental and are in no way necessary for the progress of the Arab people. The main stimulus to Arab economic and social progress does not come from the example or assistance of the Zionists but from the natural tendency of the whole Middle Eastern areas, from the work of the Government and above all from the newly awakened will to progress of the Arabs themselves. The Arabs may have started later than the Jews on the road of modern social and economic organization, but they are now fully awake and are progressing fast. This is shown in the economic sphere for example by the continued development of the Arab citrus industry and financial organizations, in the social sphere by the growth of the labour movement and the new Land Development Scheme.

If any proof were needed of this, it could be found in the progress made during the last three decades by the neighbouring countries. None of the Arab countries is stagnant today: even without the example and capital of the Zionists, they are building up industries, improving methods and extending the scope of agriculture, establishing systems of public education and increasing the amenities of life. In some countries and spheres the progress has been greater than among the Arabs of Palestine, and in all of them it is healthier and more normal.

The Zionists claim further that they are acting as mediators of Western civilization to the Middle East. Even if their claim were true, the services they were rendering would be incidental only: the Arab world has been in direct touch with the West for a hundred years, and has its own reawakened cultural movement, and thus it has no need of a mediator. Moreover the claim is untrue: so long as Jewish cultural life in Palestine expresses itself through the medium of the Hebrew language, its influence on the surrounding world is bound to be negligible; in fact, Arab culture today is almost wholly uninfluenced by the Jews, and practically no Arabs take part in the work of Jewish cultural or educational institutions. In a deeper sense the presence of the Zionists is even an obstacle to the understanding of Western civilization, in so far as it more than any other factor is tending to induce in the Arabs an unsympathetic attitude towards the West and all its works.

6. Opposition to the policy of the Zionists is shared by all sections of the Palestinian Arab people. It is not confined to the towns people but is universal among the rural population, who stand to suffer most from the gradual alienation of the most fertile land to the Jewish National Fund. It is felt not only by the landowners and middle class but by the working population, both for national reasons and for reasons of their own. It is not an invention of the educated class; if that class have seen the danger more clearly and sooner than others, and if they have assumed the leadership of the opposition, that is no more than their duty and function.

Moreover not only the Arab Moslem majority are opposed to Zionism but also and equally the Arab Christian minority who reject Zionism both because they share to the full in the national sentiments of other Arabs and because as Christians they cannot accept that their Holy Places should be subject to Jewish control, and cannot understand how any Christian nation could accept it.

7. The sentiments of the Palestinian Arabs are fully shared by the other Arab countries, both by their Government and their peoples. Their support has shown itself in many ways: in Pan-Arab Conferences, in the moral and material support given by the whole Arab world to the revolt of 1936-39, in the diplomatic activities of Arab Governments, and most recently in the formation of the Arab League, which has

taken the defense of Palestine as one of its main objectives. The members of the Arab League are now taking active measures to prevent the alienation of Arab lands to the Zionists and Jewish domination of the economic life of the Middle East. . . .

8. In the Arab view, any solution of the problem created by Zionist aspirations must satisfy certain conditions:

(i) It must recognize the right of the indigenous inhabitants of Palestine to continue in occupation of the country and to preserve its traditional character.

(ii) It must recognize that questions like immigration which affect the whole nature and destiny of the country, should be decided in accordance with democratic principles by the will of the population.

(iii) It must accept the principle that the only way by which the will of the population can be expressed is through the establishment of responsible representative government. (The Arabs find something inconsistent in the attitude of Zionists who demand the establishment of a free democratic commonwealth in Palestine and then hasten to add that this should not take place until the Jews are in a majority.)

(iv) This representative Government should be based upon the principle of absolute equality of all citizens irrespective of race and religion.

(v) The form of Government should be such as to make possible the development of a spirit of loyalty and cohesion among all elements of the community, which will override all sectional attachments. In other words it should be a Government which the whole community could regard as their own, which should be rooted in their consent and have a moral claim upon their obedience.

(vi) The settlement should recognize the fact that by geography and history Palestine is inescapably part of the Arab world; that the only alternative to its being part of the Arab world and accepting the implications of its position is complete isolation, which would be disastrous from every point of view; and that whether they like it or not the Jews in Palestine are dependent upon the goodwill of the Arabs.

(vii) The settlement should be such as to make possible a satisfactory definition within the framework of U.N.O. of the relations between Palestine and the Western Powers who possess interests in the country.

(viii) The settlement should take into account that Zionism is essentially a political movement aiming at the creation of a

Jewish state and should therefore avoid making any concession which might encourage Zionists in the hope that this aim can be achieved in any circumstances.

9. In accordance with these principles, the Arabs urge the establishment in Palestine of a democratic government representative of all sections of the population on a level of absolute equality; the termination of the Mandate once the Government has been established; and the entry of Palestine into the United Nations Organization as a full member of the working community.

Pending the establishment of a representative Government, all further Jewish immigration should be stopped, in pursuance of the principle that a decision on so important a matter should only be taken with the consent of the inhabitants of the country and that until representative institutions are established there is no way of determining consent. Strict measures should also continue to be taken to check illegal immigration. Once a Palestinian state has come into existence, if any section of the population favours a policy of further immigration it will be able to press its case in accordance with normal democratic procedure; but in this as in other matters the minority must abide by the decision of the majority.

Similarly, all further transfer of land from Arabs to Jews should be prohibited prior to the creation of self-governing institutions. The Land Transfer Regulations should be made more stringent and extended to the whole area of the country, and severer measures be taken to prevent infringement of them. Here again once self-government exists matters concerning land will be decided in the normal democratic manner.

10. The Arabs are irrevocably opposed to political Zionism, but in no way hostile to the Jews as such nor to their Jewish fellow-citizens of Palestine. Those Jews who have already entered Palestine, and who have obtained or shall obtain Palestinian citizenship by due legal process will be full citizens of the Palestinian state, enjoying full civil and political rights and a fair share in government and administration. There is no question of their being thrust into the position of a "minority" in the bad sense of a closed community, which dwells apart from the main stream of the State's life and which exists by sufferance of the majority. They will be given the opportunity of belonging to and helping to mould the full community of the Palestinian state, joined to the Arabs by links of interest and goodwill, not the goodwill of the strong to the powerless, but of one citizen to another.

It is to be hoped that in course of time the exclusiveness of the Jews will be neutralized by the development of loyalty to the state and the emergence of new groupings which cut across communal divisions. This however will take time; and during the transitional period the Arabs recognize the need for giving special consideration to the peculiar position and the needs of the Jews. No attempt would be made to interfere with their communal organization, their personal status or their religious observances. Their schools and cultural institutions would be left to operate unchecked except for that general control which all governments exercise over education. In the districts in which they are most closely settled they would possess municipal autonomy and Hebrew would be an official language of administration, justice and education.

11. The Palestinian State would be an Arab state not (as should be clear from the preceding paragraph) in any narrow racial sense, nor in the sense that non-Arabs should be placed in a position of inferiority, but because the form and policy of its government would be based on a recognition of two facts: first that the majority of the citizens are Arabs, and secondly that Palestine is part of the Arab world and has no future except through close co-operation with the other Arab states. Thus among the main objects of the Government would be to preserve and enrich the country's Arab heritage, and to draw closer the relations between Palestine and the other Arab countries. The Cairo Pact of March, 1945, provided for the representation of Palestine on the Council of the Arab League even before its independence should be a reality; once it was really self-governing, it would participate fully in all the work of the League, in the cultural and economic no less than the political sphere. This would be of benefit to the Jewish no less than the Arab citizens of Palestine, since it would ensure those good relations with the Arab world without which their economic development would be impossible.

12. The state would apply as soon as possible for admission into U.N.O., and would of course be prepared to bear its full share of the burdens of establishing a world security-system. It would willingly place at the disposal of the Security Council whatever bases or other facilities were required, provided those bases were really used for the purpose for which they were intended and not in order to interfere in the internal affairs of the country, and provided also Palestine and the other Arab states were adequately represented on the controlling body.

The state would recognize also the world's interest in the maintenance of a satisfactory regime for the Moslem, Christian and Jewish Holy Places. In the Arab view however the need for such a regime does not involve foreign interference in or control of Palestine; no opportunity should be given to Great Powers to use the Holy Places as instruments of policy. The Holy Places can be most satisfactorily and appropriately guarded by a Government representative of the inhabitants, who include adherents of all three faiths and have every interest in preserving the holy character of their country.

Nor in the Arab view would any sort of foreign interference or control be justified by the need to protect the Christian minorities. The Christians are Arabs, who belong fully to the national community and share fully in its struggle. They would have all the rights and duties of citizens of a Palestinian state, and would continue to have their own communal organizations and institutions. They themselves would ask for no more, having learnt from the example of other Middle Eastern countries the dangers of an illusory foreign "protection" of minorities.

13. In economic and social matters the Government of Palestine would follow a progressive policy with the aim of raising the standard of living and increasing the welfare of all sections of the population, and using the country's natural resources in the way most beneficial to all. Its first task naturally would be to improve the condition of the Arab peasants and thus to bridge the economic and social gulf which at present divides the two communities. Industry would be encouraged, but only in so far as its economic basis was sound and as part of a general policy of economic development for the whole Arab world; commercial and financial ties with the other Arab countries would so far as possible be strengthened, and tariffs decreased or abolished.

14. The Arabs believe that no other proposals would satisfy the conditions of a just and lasting settlement. In their view there are insuperable objections of principle or of practice to all other suggested solutions of the problem.

(1) The idea of partition and the establishment of a Jewish state in a part of Palestine is inadmissible for the same reasons of principle as the idea of establishing a Jewish state in the whole country. If it is unjust to the Arabs to impose a Jewish state on the whole of Palestine, it is equally unjust to impose it in any part of the country. Moreover, as the Wood-

head Commission showed, there are grave practical difficulties
in the way of partition; commerce would be strangled, communications dislocated and the public finances upset. It would
also be impossible to devise frontiers which did not leave
a large Arab minority in the Jewish state. This minority would
not willingly accept its subjection to the Zionists, and it would
not allow itself to be transferred to the Arab state. Moreover,
partition would not satisfy the Zionists. It cannot be too
often repeated that Zionism is a political movement aiming
at the domination at least of the whole of Palestine; to give
it a foothold in part of Palestine would be to encourage it
to press for more and to provide it with a base for its activities.
Because of this, because of the pressure of population and
in order to escape from its isolation it would inevitably be
thrown into enmity with the surrounding Arab states and this
enmity would disturb the stability of the whole Middle East.

(2) Another proposal is for the establishment of a bi-
national state, based upon political parity, in Palestine and
its incorporation into a Syrian or Arab Federation. The Arabs
would reject this as denying the majority its normal position
and rights. There are also serious practical objections to the
idea of a bi-national state, which cannot exist unless there
is a strong sense of unity and common interest overriding the
differences between the two parties. Morover, the point made
in regard to the previous suggestion may be repeated here:
this scheme would in no way satisfy the Zionists, it would
simply encourage them to hope for more and improve their
chances of obtaining it. . . .

Document 23

*The Case for a Bi-national State**

The Arab Contention

The Arabs say that "the existence of the Jewish National
Home, whatever its size, bars the way to the attainment by
the Arabs of Palestine of the same national status as that
attained, or soon to be attained, by all the other Arabs of
Asia" (Royal Commission, p. 307). That is so. And they ask
if they are not as fit for self-government as the Arabs of other
countries. They are.

* Reprinted from M. Buber and J. L. Magnes, *Arab-Jewish Unity*. London:
Victor Gollancz Ltd., 1947.

Arab Concessions

But the whole history of Palestine shows that it just has not been made for uni-national sovereign independence. This is an inescapable fact which no one can disregard. Although the Arabs cannot have a uni-national independent Arab Palestine, they can enjoy independence in a bi-national Palestine together with their Jewish fellow-citizens. This will afford them a maximum of national freedom. What the bi-national State will take away from them is sovereign independence in Palestine. There are other Arab States with sovereign independence. But we contend that the sovereign independence of tiny Palestine, whether it be Jewish sovereignty or Arab sovereignty, is a questionable good in this post-war period, when even great States must relinquish something of their sovereignty and seek union, if the world is not to perish. We contend that for this Holy Land the idea of a bi-national Palestine is at least as inspiring as that of an Arab sovereign Palestine or a Jewish sovereign Palestine.

Jewish Concessions

On the other hand, the bi-national Palestine would deprive the Jews of their one chance of a Jewish State. But this bi-national Palestine would be the one State in the world where they would be a constituent nation, i.e. an equal nationality within the body politic, and not a minority as everywhere else. The absence of a Jewish State would make more difficult direct access by the Jewish people to U.N.O. To compensate for this, some form should be devised for giving the Jewish people a recognised place within the structure of the United Nations Organisation.

Nevertheless, the concessions the Jews would have to make on these matters are, we think, more far-reaching than the concessions the Arabs of Palestine would have to make. But the hard facts of the situation are that this is not a Jewish land and it is not an Arab land—it is the Holy Land, a bi-national country—and it is in the light of such hard facts that the problem must be approached.

The Advantages of a Bi-national Palestine

Before proceeding to outline our suggestions as to the political structure of the bi-national Palestine, we should like finally to point out some of the advantages of bi-nationalism based on parity in a country which has two nationalities.

FAILURE OF MINORITY GUARANTEES

1. The breakdown of the minority guarantees provided for in the Versailles Peace treaties is proof that in a bi-national country the only safeguard for a minority is equality with the majority. There is no prospect of peace in a country where there is a dominant people and a subordinate people. The single nation-State is a proper form for a country where there is but one legally recognised nationality, as, for example, the United States. But in countries with more than one recognised nationality—and they are numerous in Europe and in Asia—bitterness is engendered among the minority because the civil service, the military, the economic key positions, foreign affairs, are in the hands of the ruling class of the majority nation. Parity in a multi-national country is the only just relationship between the peoples.

SWITZERLAND

2. The multi-national state is an effective method of affording full protection for the national languages, cultures and institutions of each nationality. That there can be full cultural autonomy combined with full allegiance to the multi-national political state is proven in Switzerland's history for more than 100 years. The Swiss are divided by language, religion and culture; nor do the linguistic and religious groupings coincide in the various cantons. Yet all of these divergencies have not been obstacles to political unity. This is a newer form of democracy which is as important for multi-national states as the more familiar form of democracy is for uni-national states. The Swiss example is most relevant to Palestine, although there are, of course, many points of difference.

OTHER MULTI-NATIONAL COUNTRIES

The Soviet Union is a newer example of a multi-national State. The new Yugoslav State is an attempt at multi-national federalism. Professor Seton Watson outlines a bi-national solution of the age-long problem of Transylvania. Roumanian domination, Hungarian domination, partition had all been tried without success.

BI-NATIONALISM A HIGH IDEAL

3. In many senses the multi-national state represents a higher, more modern and more hopeful ideal than the uni-national sovereign independent State. The old way of having a major people and a minor people in a State of various nationalities is reactionary. The progressive conception is parity among the peoples of the multi-national State. The way of peace in the world to-day and tomorrow is through federation, union. Dividing up the world into tiny nationalistic sovereign units has not been the success the advocates of self-determination had hoped for at the end of the First World War. (Cobban, *National Self-Determination*.) The peoples who have been placed by fate or by history in the same country have warred with one another for domination throughout the centuries. The majority have tried to make the State homogeneous through keeping down the minority nationalities. The federal multi-national State, based on the parity of the nationalities, is a most hopeful way of enabling them to retain their national identity, and yet of coalescing in a larger political framework. It results in separate nationalities, yet a single citizenship. This is a noble goal to which the youth of multi-national countries can be taught to give their enthusiasm and their energies. It is a modern challenge to the intelligence and the moral qualities of the peoples constituting multi-national lands.

Documents 24–25

The United Nations Takes Over

British Foreign Secretary Ernest Bevin announced on February 14, 1947, that His Majesty's Government had decided to refer the Palestine problem to the United Nations. Tension inside Palestine had risen, illegal Jewish immigration continued, there was growing restiveness in the Arab countries: Palestine, Bevin said, could not be so divided as to create two viable states, since the Arabs would never agree to it, the Mandate could not be administered in its present form, and Britain was going to ask the United Nations how it could be amended.

The United Nations set up a U.N. Special Committee on Palestine (U.N.S.C.O.P.) composed of representatives of eleven member states. Its report and recommendations were published on August 31, 1947 (Document 24). The Jewish Agency occepted the partition plan as the "indispensable minimum," the Arab governments and the Arab Higher Executive rejected it. On November 29, 1947, the U.N. General Assembly endorsed the partition plan by a vote of thirty-three to thirteen (Document 25). The two-thirds majority included the United States and the Soviet Union but not Britain.

Document 24

Summary of the Report of U.N.S.C.O.P. (U.N. Special Committee on Palestine)

August 31, 1947

(a) GENERAL RECOMMENDATIONS OF THE COMMITTEE

The eleven unanimously-adopted resolutions of the Committee were:

That the Mandate should be terminated and Palestine granted independence at the earliest practicable date (recommendations I and II);

That there should be a short transitional period preceding the granting of independence to Palestine during which the authority responsible for administering Palestine should be responsible to the United Nations (recommendations III and IV);

That the sacred character of the Holy Places and the rights of religious communities in Palestine should be preserved and stipulations concerning them inserted in the constitution of any state or states to be created and that a system should be found for settling impartially any disputes involving religious rights (recommendation V);

That the General Assembly should take steps to see that the problem of distressed European Jews should be dealt with as a matter of urgency so as to alleviate their plight and the Palestine problem (recommendation VI);

That the constitution of the new state or states should be fundamentally democratic and should contain guarantees for the respect of human rights and fundamental freedoms and for the protection of minorities (recommendation VII);

That the undertakings contained in the Charter whereby states are to settle their disputes by peaceful means and to refrain from the threat or use of force in international relations in any way inconsistent with the purposes of the United Nations should be incorporated in the constitutional provisions applying to Palestine (recommendation VIII);

That the economic unity of Palestine should be preserved (recommendation IX);

That states whose nationals had enjoyed in Palestine privileges and immunities of foreigners, including those formerly enjoyed by capitulation or usage in the Ottoman Empire, should be invited to renounce any rights pertaining to them (recommendation X);

That the General Assembly should appeal to the peoples of Palestine to cooperate with the United Nations in its efforts to settle the situation there and exert every effort to put an end to acts of violence (recommendation XI);

In addition to these eleven unanimously approved recommendations, the Special Committee, with two members (Uruguay and Guatemala) dissenting, and one member recording no opinion, also approved the following twelfth recommendation:

"*Recommendation XII. The Jewish Problem in General*
"It is recommended that
"In the appraisal of the Palestine question, it be accepted as incontrovertible that any solution for Palestine cannot be considered as a solution of the Jewish problem in general."

(b)   MAJORITY PROPOSAL: PLAN OF PARTITION WITH ECONOMIC UNION

According to the plan of the majority (the representatives of Canada, Czechoslovakia, Guatemala, Netherlands, Peru, Sweden and Uruguay), Palestine was to be constituted into an Arab State, a Jewish State and the City of Jerusalem. The Arab and the Jewish States would become independent after a transitional period of two years beginning on September 1, 1947. Before their independence could be recognized, however, they must adopt a constitution in line with the pertinent recommendations of the Committee and make to the United Nations a declaration containing certain guarantees, and sign a treaty by which a system of economic collaboration would be established and the economic union of Palestine created.

The plan provided, *inter alia,* that during the transitional period, the United Kingdom would carry on the administration of Palestine under the auspices of the United Nations and on such conditions and under such supervision as the United Kingdom and the United Nations might agree upon. During this period a stated number of Jewish immigrants was to be admitted. Constituent Assemblies were to be elected by the populations of the areas which were to comprise the Arab and Jewish States, respectively, and were to draw up the constitutions of the States.

These constitutions were to provide for the establishment in each State of a legislative body elected by universal suffrage and by secret ballot on the basis of proportional representation and an executive body responsible to the legislature. They would also contain various guarantees, e.g., for the protection of the Holy Places and religious buildings and sites, and of religious and minority rights.

The Constituent Assembly in each State would appoint a provisional government empowered to make the declaration and sign the Treaty of Economic Union, after which the independence of the State would be recognized. The Declaration would contain provisions for the protection of the Holy Places and religious buildings and sites and for religious and minority rights. It would also contain provisions regarding citizenship.

A treaty would be entered into between the two States, which would contain provisions to establish the economic union of Palestine and to provide for other matters of common interest. A Joint Economic Board would be established consisting of representatives of the two States and members appointed by the Economic and Social Council of the United Nations to organize and administer the objectives of the Economic Union.

The City of Jerusalem would be placed, after the transitional period, under the International Trusteeship System by means of a Trusteeship Agreement, which would designate the United Nations as the Administering Authority. The plan contained recommended boundaries for the city and provisions concerning the governor and the police force.

The plan also proposed boundaries for both the Arab and Jewish States.

(c) MINORITY PROPOSAL:
PLAN OF A FEDERAL STATE

Three U.N.S.C.O.P. members (the representatives of India, Iran and Yugoslavia) proposed an independent federal state. This plan provided, *inter alia*, that an independent federal state of Palestine would be created following a transitional period not exceeding three years, during which responsibility for administering Palestine and preparing it for independence would be entrusted to an authority to be decided by the General Assembly.

The independent federal state would comprise an Arab State and a Jewish State. Jerusalem would be its capital.

During the transitional period a Constituent Assembly would be elected by popular vote and convened by the administering authority on the basis of electoral provisions which would ensure the fullest representation of the population.

The Constituent Assembly would draw up the constitution of the federal state, which was to contain, *inter alia*, the following provisions:

The federal state would comprise a federal government and governments of the Arab and Jewish States, respectively.

Full authority would be vested in the federal government with regard to national defence, foreign relations, immigration, currency, taxation for federal purposes, foreign and inter-state waterways, transport and communications, copyrights and patents.

The Arab and Jewish States would enjoy full powers of local self-government and would have authority over education, taxation for local purposes, the right of residence, commercial licenses, land permits, grazing rights, inter-state migration, settlement, police, punishment of crime, social institutions and services, public housing, public health, local roads, agriculture and local industries.

The organs of government would include a head of state, an executive body, a representative federal legislative body composed of two chambers, and a federal court. The executive would be responsible to the legislative body.

Election to one chamber of the federal legislative body would be on the basis of proportional representation of the population as a whole, and to the other on the basis of equal representation of the Arab and Jewish citizens of Palestine. Legislation would be enacted when approved by majority votes in both chambers; in the event of disagreement between the two chambers, the issue would be submitted to an arbitral body of five members including not less than two Arabs and two Jews.

The federal court would be the final court of appeal regarding constitutional matters. Its members who would include not less than four Arabs and three Jews, would be elected by both chambers of the federal legislative body.

The constitution was to guarantee equal rights for all minorities and fundamental human rights and freedoms. It would guarantee, *inter alia,* free access to the Holy Places and protect religious interests.

The constitution would provide for an undertaking to settle international disputes by peaceful means.

There would be a single Palestinian nationality and citizenship.

The constitution would provide for equitable participation of representatives of both communities in delegations to international conferences.

A permanent international body was to be set up for the supervision and protection of the Holy Places, to be composed of three representatives designated by the United Nations and one representative of each of the recognized faiths having an interest in the matter, as might be determined by the United Nations.

For a period of three years from the beginning of the transitional period Jewish immigration would be permitted into the Jewish State in such numbers as not to exceed its absorptive capacity, and having due regard for the rights of the existing population within that State and their anticipated natural rate of increase. An international commission, composed of three Arab, three Jewish and three United Nations representatives, would be appointed to estimate the absorptive capacity of the Jewish State. The commission would cease to exist at the end of the three-year period mentioned above.

The minority plan also laid down the boundaries of the proposed Arab and Jewish areas of the federal state.

Document 25

U.N. General Assembly Resolution on the Future Government of Palestine (Partition Resolution)

November 29, 1947

The General Assembly,

Having met in special session at the request of the mandatory Power to constitute and instruct a special committee to prepare for the consideration of the question of the future government of Palestine at the second regular session;

Having constituted a Special Committee and instructed it to investigate all questions and issues relevant to the problem of Palestine, and to prepare proposals for the solution of the problem, and

Having received and examined the report of the Special Committee (document A/364) including a number of unanimous recommendations and a plan of partition with economic union approved by the majority of the Special Committee,

Considers that the present situation in Palestine is one which is likely to impair the general welfare and friendly relations among nations;

Takes note of the declaration by the mandatory Power that it plans to complete its evacuation of Palestine by 1 August 1948;

Recommends to the United Kingdom, as the mandatory Power for Palestine, and to all other Members of the United Nations the adoption and implementation, with regard to the future government of Palestine, of the Plan of Partition with Economic Union set out below;

Requests that

(a) The Security Council take the necessary measures as provided for in the plan for its implementation;

(b) The Security Council consider, if circumstances during the transitional period require such consideration, whether the situation in Palestine constitutes a threat to the peace. If it decides that such a threat exists, and in order to maintain international peace and security, the Security Council should supplement the authorization of the General Assembly by taking measures, under Article 39 and 41 of the Charter, to empower the United Nations Commission, as provided in this resolution, to exercise in Palestine the functions which are assigned to it by this resolution;

(c) The Security Council determine as a threat to the peace, breach of the peace or act of aggression, in accordance with Article 39 of the Charter, any attempt to alter by force the settlement envisaged by this resolution;

(d) The Trusteeship Council be informed of the responsibilities envisaged for it in this plan;

Calls upon the inhabitants of Palestine to take such steps as may be necessary on their part to put this plan into effect;

Appeals to all Governments and all peoples to refrain from taking any action which might hamper or delay the carrying out of these recommendations, and

Authorizes the Secretary-General to reimburse travel and subsistence expenses of the members of the commission referred to in Part I, Section B, paragraph 1 below, on such basis and in such form as he may determine most appropriate in the circumstances, and to provide the Commission with the necessary staff to assist in carrying out the functions assigned to the Commission by the General Assembly.

Plan of Partition with Economic Union
Part I—Future Constitution and
Government of Palestine

A. TERMINATION OF MANDATE
PARTITION AND INDEPENDENCE

1. The Mandate for Palestine shall terminate as soon as possible but in any case not later than 1 August 1948.

2. The armed forces of the mandatory Power shall be progressively withdrawn from Palestine, the withdrawal to be completed as soon as possible but in any case not later than 1 August 1948.

The mandatory Power shall advise the Commission, as far in advance as possible, of its intention to terminate the Mandate and to evacuate each area.

The mandatory Power shall use its best endeavours to ensure that an area situated in the territory of the Jewish State, including a seaport and hinterland adequate to provide facilities for a substantial immigration, shall be evacuated at the earliest possible date and in any event not later than 1 February 1948.

3. Independent Arab and Jewish States and the Special International Regime for the City of Jerusalem, set forth in part III of this plan, shall come into existence in Palestine two months after the evacuation of the armed forces of the mandatory Power has been completed but in any case not later than 1 October 1948. The boundaries of the Arab State, the Jewish State, and the City of Jerusalem shall be described in parts II and III below.

4. The period between the adoption by the General Assembly of its recommendation on the question of Palestine and the establishment of the independence of the Arab and Jewish States shall be a transitional period.

B. Steps Preparatory to Independence

1. A Commission shall be set up consisting of one representative of each of five Member States. The Members represented on the Commission shall be elected by the General Assembly on as broad a basis, geographically and otherwise, as possible.

2. The administration of Palestine shall, as the mandatory Power withdraws its armed forces, be progressively turned over to the Commission, which shall act in conformity with the recommendations of the General Assembly, under the guidance of the Security Council. The mandatory Power shall to the fullest possible extent co-ordinate its plans for withdrawal with the plans of the Commission to take over and administer areas which have been evacuated.

In the discharge of this administrative responsibility the Commission shall have authority to issue necessary regulations and take other measures as required.

The mandatory Power shall not take any action to prevent, obstruct or delay the implementation by the Commission of the measures recommended by the General Assembly.

3. On its arrival in Palestine the Commission shall proceed to carry out measures for the establishment of the frontiers of the Arab and Jewish States and the City of Jerusalem in accordance with the general lines of the recommendations of the General Assembly on the partition of Palestine. Nevertheless, the boundaries as described in part II of this plan are to be modified in such a way that village areas as a rule will not be divided by state boundaries unless pressing reasons make that necessary.

4. The Commission, after consultation with the democratic parties and other public organizations of the Arab and Jewish

States, shall select and establish in each State as rapidly as possible a Provisional Council of Government. The activities of both the Arab and Jewish Provisional Councils of Government shall be carried out under the general direction of the Commission.

If by 1 April 1948 a Provisional Council of Government cannot be selected for either of the States, or, if selected, cannot carry out its functions, the Commission shall communicate that fact to the Security Council for such action with respect to that State as the Security Council may deem proper, and to the Secretary-General for communication to the Members of the United Nations.

5. Subject to the provisions of these recommendations, during the transitional period the Provisional Councils of Government, acting under the Commission, shall have full authority in the areas under their control, including authority over matters of immigration and land regulation.

6. The Provisional Council of Government of each State, acting under the Commission, shall progressively receive from the Commission full responsibility for the administration of that State in the period between the termination of the Mandate and the establishment of the State's independence.

7. The Commission shall instruct the Provisional Councils of Government of both the Arab and Jewish States, after their formation, to proceed to the establishment of administrative organs of government, central and local.

8. The Provisional Council of Government of each State shall, within the shortest time possible, recruit an armed militia from the residents of that State, sufficient in number to maintain internal order and to prevent frontier clashes.

This armed militia in each State shall, for operational purposes, be under the command of Jewish or Arab officers resident in that State, but general political and military control, including the choice of the militia's High Command, shall be exercised by the Commission.

9. The Provisional Council of Government of each State shall, not later than two months after the withdrawal of the armed forces of the mandatory Power, hold elections to the Constituent Assembly which shall be conducted on democratic lines.

The election regulations in each State shall be drawn up by the Provisional Council of Government and approved by the Commission.

Qualified voters for each State for this election shall be

persons over eighteen years of age who are: (*a*) Palestinian citizens residing in that State and (*b*) Arabs and Jews residing in the State, although not Palestinian citizens, who, before voting, have signed a notice of intention to become citizens of such State.

Arabs and Jews residing in the City of Jerusalem who have signed a notice of intention to become citizens, the Arabs of the Arab State and the Jews of the Jewish State, shall be entitled to vote in the Arab and Jewish States respectively.

Women may vote and be elected to the Constituent Assemblies.

During the transitional period no Jew shall be permitted to establish residence in the area of the proposed Arab State, and no Arab shall be permitted to establish residence in the area of the proposed Jewish State, except by special leave of the Commission.

10. The Constituent Assembly of each State shall draft a democratic constitution for its State and choose a provisional government to succeed the Provisional Council of Government appointed by the Commission. The constitutions of the States shall embody chapters 1 and 2 of the Declaration provided for in section C below and include *inter alia* provisions for:

(*a*) Establishing in each State a legislative body elected by universal suffrage and by secret ballot on the basis of proportional representation, and an executive body responsible to the legislature;

(*b*) Settling all international disputes in which the State may be involved by peaceful means in such a manner that international peace and security, and justice, are not endangered;

(*c*) Accepting the obligation of the State to refrain in its international relations from the threat or use of force against the territorial integrity or political independence of any State, or in any other manner inconsistent with the purposes of the United Nations;

(*d*) Guaranteeing to all persons equal and non-discriminatory rights in civil, political, economic and religious matters and the enjoyment of human rights and fundamental freedoms, including freedom of religion, language, speech and publication, education, assembly and association;

(*e*) Preserving freedom of transit and visit for all residents and citizens of the other State in Palestine and the City of Jerusalem, subject to considerations of national security, provided that each State shall control residence within its borders.

11. The Commission shall appoint a preparatory economic commission of three members to make whatever arrangements are possible for economic co-operation, with a view to establishing, as soon as practicable, the Economic Union and the Joint Economic Board, as provided in section D below.

12. During the period between the adoption of the recommendations on the question of Palestine by the General Assembly and the termination of the Mandate, the mandatory Power in Palestine shall maintain full responsibility for administration in areas from which it has not withdrawn its armed forces. The Commission shall assist the mandatory Power in the carrying out of these functions. Similarly the mandatory Power shall co-operate with the Commission in the execution of its functions.

13. With a view to ensuring that there shall be continuity in the functioning of administrative services and that, on the withdrawal of the armed forces of the mandatory Power, the whole administration shall be in charge of the Provisional Councils and the Joint Economic Board, respectively, acting under the Commission, there shall be a progressive transfer, from the mandatory Power to the Commission, of responsibility for all the functions of government, including that of maintaining law and order in the areas from which the forces of the mandatory Power have been withdrawn.

14. The Commission shall be guided in its activities by the recommendations of the General Assembly and by such instructions as the Security Council may consider necessary to issue.

The measures taken by the Commission, within the recommendations of the General Assembly, shall become immediately effective unless the Commission has previously received contrary instructions from the Security Council.

The Commission shall render periodic monthly progress reports, or more frequently if desirable, to the Security Council.

15. The Commission shall make its final report to the next regular session of the General Assembly and to the Security Council simultaneously.

C. Declaration

A declaration shall be made to the United Nations by the provisional government of each proposed State before independence. It shall contain *inter alia* the following clauses:

General Provision

The stipulations contained in the declaration are recognized as fundamental laws of the State and no law, regulation or official action shall conflict or interfere with these stipulations, nor shall any law, regulation or official action prevail over them.

Chapter 1.—Holy Places, Religious Buildings and Sites

1. Existing rights in respect of Holy Places and religious buildings or sites shall not be denied or impaired.

2. In so far as Holy Places are concerned, the liberty of access, visit and transit shall be guaranteed, in conformity with existing rights, to all residents and citizens of the other State and of the City of Jerusalem, as well as to aliens, without distinction as to nationality, subject to requirements of national security, public order and decorum.

Similarly, freedom of worship shall be guaranteed in conformity with existing rights, subject to the maintenance of public order and decorum.

3. Holy Places and religious buildings or sites shall be preserved. No act shall be permitted which may in any way impair their sacred character. If at any time it appears to the Government that any particular Holy Place, religious building or site is in need of urgent repair, the Government may call upon the community or communities concerned to carry out such repair. The Government may carry it out itself at the expense of the community or communities concerned if no action is taken within a reasonable time.

4. No taxation shall be levied in respect of any Holy Place, religious building or site which was exempt from taxation on the date of the creation of the State.

No change in the incidence of such taxation shall be made which would either discriminate between the owners or occupiers of Holy Places, religious buildings or sites, or would place such owners or occupiers in a position less favourable in relation to the general incidence of taxation than existed at the time of the adoption of the Assembly's recommendation.

5. The Governor of the City of Jerusalem shall have the right to determine whether the provisions of the Constitution of the State in relation to Holy Places, religious buildings and sits within the borders of the State and the religious rights appertaining thereto, are being properly applied and respected,

and to make decisions on the basis of existing rights in cases of disputes which may arise between the different religious communities or the rites of a religious community with respect to such places, buildings and sites. He shall receive full co-operation and such privileges and immunities as are necessary for the exercise of his functions in the State.

Chapter 2.—Religious and Minority Rights

1. Freedom of conscience and the free exercise of all forms of worship, subject only to the maintenance of public order and morals, shall be ensured to all.

2. No discrimination of any kind shall be made between the inhabitants on the ground of race, religion, language or sex.

3. All persons within the jurisdiction of the State shall be entitled to equal protection of the laws.

4. The family law and personal status of the various minorities and their religious interests, including endowments, shall be respected.

5. Except as may be required for the maintenance of public order and good government, no measure shall be taken to obstruct or interfere with the enterprise of religious or charitable bodies of all faiths or to discriminate against any representative or member of these bodies on the ground of his religion or nationality.

6. The State shall ensure adequate primary and secondary education for the Arab and Jewish minority, respectively, in its own language and its cultural traditions.

The right of each community to maintain its own schools for the education of its own members in its own language, while conforming to such educational requirements of a general nature as the State may impose, shall not be denied or impaired. Foreign educational establishments shall continue their activity on the basis of their existing rights.

7. No restriction shall be imposed on the free use by any citizen of the State of any language in private intercourse, in commerce, in religion, in the Press or in publications of any kind, or at public meetings.[1]

8. No expropriation of land owned by an Arab in the Jew-

---

[1] The following stipulation shall be added to the declaration concerning the Jewish State: "In the Jewish State adequate facilities shall be given to Arabic-speaking citizens for the use of their language, either orally or in writing, in the legislature, before the Courts and in the administration."

ish State (by a Jew in the Arab State) [2] shall be allowed except for public purposes. In all cases of expropriation full compensation as fixed by the Supreme Court shall be paid previous to dispossession.

Chapter 3.—*Citizenship, International Conventions and Financial Obligations*

1. *Citizenship.* Palestinian citizens residing in Palestine outside the City of Jerusalem, as well as Arabs and Jews who, not holding Palestinian citizenship, reside in Palestine outside the City of Jerusalem shall, upon the recognition of independence, become citizens of the State in which they are resident and enjoy full civil and political rights. Persons over the age of eighteen years may opt, within one year from the date of recognition of independence of the State in which they reside, for citizenship of the other State, providing that no Arab residing in the area of the proposed Arab State shall have the right to opt for citizenship in the proposed Jewish State and no Jews residing in the proposed Jewish State shall have the right to opt for citizenship in the proposed Arab State. The exercise of this right of option will be taken to include the wives and children under eighteen years of age of persons so opting.

Arabs residing in the area of the proposed Jewish State and Jews residing in the area of the proposed Arab State who have signed a notice of intention to opt for citizenship of the other State shall be eligible to vote in the elections to the Constituent Assembly of that State, but not in the elections to the Constituent Assembly of the State in which they reside.

2. *International conventions.* (a) The State shall be bound by all the international agreements and conventions, both general and special, to which Palestine has become a party. Subject to any right of denunciation provided for therein, such agreements and conventions shall be respected by the State throughout the period for which they were concluded.

(b) Any dispute about the applicability and continued validity of international conventions or treaties signed or adhered to by the mandatory Power on behalf of Palestine shall be referred to the International Court of Justice in accordance with the provisions of the Statute of the Court.

3. *Financial obligations.* (a) The State shall respect and fulfil all financial obligations of whatever nature assumed on

[2] In the declaration concerning the Arab State, the words "by an Arab in the Jewish State" should be replaced by the words "by a Jew in the Arab State."

behalf of Palestine by the mandatory Power during the exercise of the Mandate and recognized by the State. This provision includes the right of public servants to pensions, compensation or gratuities.

(*b*) These obligations shall be fulfilled through participation in the Joint Economic Board in respect of those obligations applicable to Palestine as a whole, and individually in respect of those applicable to, and fairly apportionable between, the States.

(*c*) A Court of Claims, affiliated with the Joint Economic Board, and composed of one member appointed by the United Nations, one representative of the United Kingdom and one representative of the State concerned, should be established. Any dispute between the United Kingdom and the States respecting claims not recognized by the latter should be referred to that Court.

(*d*) Commercial concessions granted in respect of any part of Palestine prior to the adoption of the resolution by the General Assembly shall continue to be valid according to their terms, unless modified by agreement between the concession-holder and the State.

[Section D has been deleted: "Economic Union and Transit." Part II of the Resolution deals with the borders of the new State; Part III with "Capitulations." Ed.]

PART III

Israel and the Arab World
1948-1967

Part III of the Reader extends from the establishment of the State of Israel in May, 1948 to the aftermath of the third Arab–Israeli war in 1967. The United Nations resolution about the partition of Palestine was bitterly resented by the Palestinian Arabs and their supporters in the neighboring countries who tried to prevent with the force of arms the establishment of a Zionist state by the "Jewish usurpers." This attempt failed and Israel, as a result, seized areas beyond those defined in the U.N. resolution. The armistice of 1949 did not restore peace; an Arab refugee problem came into being, guerrilla attacks, Israel retaliation and Arab blockage of the Suez Canal and the Gulf of Aqaba led to the second and third Arab–Israeli Wars.

State of Israel Proclamation of Independence

The Proclamation of Independence was published by the Provisional State Council in Tel Aviv on May 14, 1948. The Provisional State Council was the forerunner of the Knesset, the Israeli parliament. The British Mandate was terminated the following day and regular armed forces of Transjordan, Egypt, Syria and other Arab countries entered Palestine.

The Land of Israel was the birthplace of the Jewish people. Here their spiritual, religious and national identity was formed. Here they achieved independence and created a culture of national and universal significance. Here they wrote and gave the Bible to the world.

Exiled from the Land of Israel the Jewish people remained faithful to it in all the countries of their dispersion, never ceasing to pray and hope for their return and the restoration of their national freedom.

Impelled by this historic association, Jews strove throughout the centuries to go back to the land of their fathers and regain their statehood. In recent decades they returned in their masses. They reclaimed the wilderness, revived their language, built cities and villages, and established a vigorous and ever-growing community, with its own economic and cultural life. They sought peace, yet were prepared to defend themselves. They brought the blessings of progress to all inhabitants of the country and looked forward to sovereign independence.

In the year 1897 the First Zionist Congress, inspired by

Theodor Herzl's vision of the Jewish State, proclaimed the right of the Jewish people to national revival in their own country.

This right was acknowledged by the Balfour Declaration of November 2, 1917, and re-affirmed by the Mandate of the League of Nations, which gave explicit international recognition to the historic connection of the Jewish people with Palestine and their right to reconstitute their National Home.

The recent holocaust, which engulfed millions of Jews in Europe, proved anew the need to solve the problem of the homelessness and lack of independence of the Jewish people by means of the re-establishment of the Jewish State, which would open the gates to all Jews and endow the Jewish people with equality of status among the family of nations.

The survivors of the disastrous slaughter in Europe, and also Jews from other lands, have not desisted from their efforts to reach Eretz-Yisrael, in face of difficulties, obstacles and perils; and have not ceased to urge their right to a life of dignity, freedom and honest toil in their ancestral land.

In the second World War the Jewish people in Palestine made their full contribution to the struggle of the freedom-loving nations against the Nazi evil. The sacrifices of their soldiers and their war effort gained them the right to rank with the nations which founded the United Nations.

On November 29, 1947, the General Assembly of the United Nations adopted a Resolution requiring the establishment of a Jewish State in Palestine. The General Assembly called upon the inhabitants of the country to take all the necessary steps on their part to put the plan into effect. This recognition by the United Nations of the right of the Jewish people to establish their independent State is unassailable.

It is the natural right of the Jewish people to lead, as do all other nations, an independent existence in its sovereign State.

ACCORDINGLY WE, the members of the National Council, representing the Jewish people in Palestine and the World Zionist Movement, are met together in solemn assembly today, the day of termination of the British Mandate for Palestine; and by virtue of the natural and historic right of the Jewish people and of the Resolution of the General Assembly of the United Nations.

WE HEREBY PROCLAIM the establishment of the Jewish State in Palestine, to be called Medinath Yisrael (The State of Israel).

WE HEREBY DECLARE that, as from the termination of the Mandate at midnight, the 14th-15th May, 1948, and pending the setting up of the duly elected bodies of the State in accordance with a Constitution, to be drawn up by the Constituent Assembly not later than the 1st October, 1948, the National Council shall act as the Provisional State Council, and that the National Administration shall constitute the Provisional Government of the Jewish State, which shall be known as Israel.

THE STATE OF ISRAEL will be open to the immigration of Jews from all countries of their dispersion; will promote the development of the country for the benefit of all its inhabitants; will be based on the principles of liberty, justice and peace as conceived by the Prophets of Israel; will uphold the full social and political equality of all its citizens, without distinction of religion, race, or sex; will guarantee freedom of religion, conscience, education and culture; will safeguard the Holy Places of all religions; and will loyally uphold the principles of the United Nations Charter.

THE STATE OF ISRAEL will be ready to co-operate with the organs and representatives of the United Nations in the implementation of the Resolution of the Assembly of November 29, 1947, and will take steps to bring about the Economic Union over the whole of Palestine.

We appeal to the United Nations to assist the Jewish people in the building of its State and to admit Israel into the family of nations.

In the midst of wanton aggression, we yet call upon the Arab inhabitants of the State of Israel to preserve the ways of peace and play their part in the development of the State, on the basis of full and equal citizenship and due representation in all its bodies and institutions—provisional and permanent.

We extend our hand in peace and neighbourliness to all the neighbouring states and their peoples, and invite them to co-operate with the independent Jewish nation for the common good of all. The State of Israel is prepared to make its contribution to the progress of the Middle East as a whole.

Our call goes out to the Jewish people all over the world to rally to our side in the task of immigration and development, and to stand by us in the great struggle for the fulfilment of the dream of generations for the redemption of Israel.

With trust in the Rock of Israel, we set our hand to this Declaration, at this Session of the Provisional State Council, on the soil of the Homeland, in the city of Tel-Aviv, on this Sabbath eve, the fifth of Iyar, 5708, the fourteenth of May, 1948.

Document 27

The Law of Return

The "Law of Return" was passed unanimously by the Knesset on July 5, 1950 and written into the State Legislation.

The Law of Return states:
1. Every Jew has the right to immigrate to the country.
2. (*a*) Immigration shall be on the basis of immigration visas.
   (*b*) Immigrant visas shall be issued to any Jew expressing a desire to settle in Israel, except if the Minister of Immigration is satisfied that the applicant:
   (i) acts against the Jewish nation; or
   (ii) may threaten the public health or State security.
3. (*a*) A Jew who comes to Israel and after his arrival expresses a desire to settle there may, while in Israel, obtain an immigrant certificate.
   (*b*) The exceptions listed in Article 2 (*b*) shall apply also with respect to the issue of an immigrant certificate, but a person shall not be regarded as a threat to public health as a result of an illness that he contracts after his arrival in Israel.
4. Every Jew who migrated to the country before this law goes into effect, and every Jew who was born in the country either before or after the law is effective enjoys the same status as any person who migrated on the basis of this law.
5. The Minister of Immigration is delegated to enforce this law and he may enact regulations in connection with its implementation and for the issue of immigrant visas and immigrant certificates.

Document 28

The Manifesto of the United Arab
Republic (Preamble)

The manifesto concerning the principles to govern the new
Federal State of the United Arab Republic was published
in April 1963. It was prepared in connection with an
abortive attempt to establish federal union in the Arab
world. Signed by Gamal Abdel Nasser and the presidents
of Iraq and Syria, it is of interest mainly in view of the
reference to Palestine.

In the name of the Merciful Compassionate God,
In the name of the Almighty God,
The three delegations representing the United Arab Republic, Syria and Iraq met in Cairo and in response to the
will of the Arab people in the three regions and the great
Arab fatherland, brotherly talks began between the three delegations on Saturday, April 6, and ended on Wednesday, April
17, 1963.
The delegations in all their discussions were inspired by
faith that Arab unity was an inevitable aim deriving its principles from the oneness of language bearing culture and
thought, common history-making sentiment and conscience,
common national struggle deciding and defining destiny, common spiritual values stemming from Divine messages and
common social and economic understanding based on liberty
and socialism.
The delegations were guided by the will of the masses
of the Arab peoples, demanding unity, struggling to attain
it and sacrificing in its defence, and realising that the
hard core of the union is to be formed by the unification of
the parts of the homeland which have acquired their freedom
and independence and in which nationalist, progressive governments have emerged with the determination to destroy the
alliance of feudalism, capital, reaction and imperialism, and
to liberate the working forces of the people in order to join
them in alliance and to express their genuine will.
The revolution of July 23 was a historical turning point at
which the Arab people in Egypt, discovering their identity
and regaining their free will, set out on their quest for free-

dom, Arabism and union. The revolution of the 14th of Ramadan (February 8) illuminated the true Arab face of Iraq, and the path leading it to the horizons of unity, envisaged by the zealous elements of the July 14 revolution. The revolution of March 8 put Syria back into the line of the union destroyed by the setback of reactionary secession, having destroyed all the obstacles which the reactionaries and imperialism had determinedly put up in the path of union.

The three Revolutions thus met which affirmed again that unity is a revolutionary action deriving its conceptions from the people's faith, its power from their will, and its objectives from their aspirations for freedom and socialism.

Unity is a revolution—a revolution because it is popular, a revolution because it is progressive, and a revolution because it is a powerful tide in the current of civilisation.

Unity is especially a revolution because it is profoundly connected with the Palestine cause and with the national duty to liberate that country. It was the disaster of Palestine that revealed the conspiracy of the reactionary classes and exposed the treacheries of the hired regional parties and their denial of the people's objectives and aspirations. It was the disaster of Palestine that showed the weakness and backwardness of the economic and social systems that prevailed in the country, released the revolutionary energies of our people and awakened the spirit of revolt against imperialism, injustice, poverty and underdevelopment. It was the disaster of Palestine that clearly indicated the path of salvation, the path of unity, freedom and socialism. This was kept in mind by the delegations during their talks. If unity is a sacred objective, it is also the instrument of the popular struggle and its means to achieve its major objectives of freedom and security in liberating all the parts of the Arab homeland and in establishing a society of sufficiency and justice, a society of socialism, in continuing the revolutionary tide without deviation or relapse and its extension to embrace the greater Arab homeland, and in contributing to the progress of human civilisation and consolidation of world peace.

It was unanimously agreed that unity between the three regions would be based, as required by the Arab people, on the principles of democracy and socialism, would be a real and strong unity which would consider the regional circumstances to consolidate the ties of unity on a basis of practical understanding, not ignore the reasons for partitioning and separation, and make the power of each region a power for

the Federal State of the Arab Nation, and make the Federal
State a power for each of its regions as well as for the whole
Arab Nation.

Document 29

The Draft Constitution of the
"Palestine Liberation Organisation"

The charter of the Palestine Liberation Organisation
(PLO) was prepared under Egyptian auspices following
an agreement at the Arab Summit Conference in 1963 by
Ahmed Shukairy, a lawyer born in Palestine who represented Saudi Arabia and later Syria in the U.N. and ultimately became President of the PLO. The role of the PLO
on the eve of the Arab-Israeli war was later criticized in
the Arab capitals and Shukairy forced to resign in December 1967.

1. In accordance with this constitution, an organisation
known as "The Palestine Liberation Organisation" shall be
formed, and shall launch its responsibilities in accordance with
the principles of the National Charter and clauses of this constitution.

2. All the Palestinians are natural members in the Liberation Organisation exercising their duty in the liberation of
their homeland in accordance with their abilities and efficiency.

3. The Palestinian people shall form the larger base for
this Organisation; and the Organisation, after its creation,
shall work closely and constantly with the Palestine people
for the sake of their organisation and mobilisation so they
may be able to assume their responsibility in the liberation
of their country.

4. Until suitable conditions are available for holding free
general elections among all the Palestinians and in all the countries in which they reside, the Liberation Organisation shall
be set up in accordance with the rules set in this constitution.

5. Measures listed in this constitution shall be taken for the
convocation of a Palestinian General Assembly in which shall
be represented all Palestinian factions, emigrants and residents, including organisations, societies, unions, trade unions
and representatives of (Palestinian) public opinions of various

ideological trends; this assembly shall be called The National Assembly of the Palestine Liberation Organisation.'

6. In preparation and facilitation of work of the assembly, the Palestinian representative at the Arab League (i.e., Ahmed Shukairy), shall, after holding consultations with various Palestinian factions, form:

a)—A Preparatory Committee in every Arab country hosting a minimum of 10,000 Palestinians; the mission of each one of these committees is to prepare lists according to which Palestinian candidates in the respective Arab country will be chosen as members of the assembly; these committees shall also prepare studies and proposals which may help the assembly carry out its work; these studies and proposals shall be presented to the Coordination Committee listed below.

b)—A Coordination Committee, with headquarters in Jerusalem; the mission of this committee shall be to issue invitations to the assembly, adopt all necessary measures for the holding of the assembly, and coordinate all proposals and studies as well as lists of candidates to the assembly, as specified in the clause above; also the committee shall prepare a provisional agenda—or as a whole, undertake all that is required for the holding and success of the assembly in the execution of its mission.

7. The National Assembly shall be held once every two years; its venue rotates between Jerusalem and Gaza; the National Assembly shall meet for the first time on May 14, 1964, in the city of Jerusalem.

8. To facilitate its work, the Assembly shall form the following committees:

a)—The Political Committee: shall be in charge of studying the political sides of the Palestine question in the Arab and international fields.

b)—The Charter By-laws and Lists Committee: shall consider the National Charter as well as the various by-laws and lists required by the Organisation in the execution of its duties.

c)—The Financial Committee: shall formulate a complete plan for the National Palestinian Fund required for financing the Organisation.

d)—Information Committee: shall work out a complete scheme for information and offices to be established in various parts of the world.

e)—The Juridical Committee: shall study the various legal aspects of the Palestine question, be it in relation to principles of International Law, U.N. Charter, or international documents pertaining to the Palestine question.

f)—Proposals and Nomination Committee: shall coordinate proposals and nominations submitted to the Assembly.

g)—Awakening Committee: shall study ways and means for the up-bringing of the new generations both ideologically and spiritually so they may serve their country and work for the liberation of their homeland.

h)—The National Organisation Committee: shall lay down general plans pertaining to trade unions, federations, sports organisations and scouts groups; this is in accordance with rules and laws in effect in Arab countries.

9. The National Assembly shall have a Presidency Office composed of the president, two vice presidents, a secretary, and a secretary general; these officers shall be elected by the National Assembly when it meets.

10. These (above-listed eight committees) shall submit their reports and recommendations to the National Assembly which, in turn, shall discuss them and issue the necessary resolutions.

11. The National Assembly shall have an executive apparatus to be called 'The Executive Committee of the Liberation Organisation' which shall practice all responsibilities of the Liberation Organisation in accordance with the general plans and resolutions issued by the National Assembly.

12. The Executive Committee shall be formed of fifteen members elected by the National Assembly; the Committee shall in its turn elect a President, two Vice Presidents and a Secretary General.

13. The Executive Committee can be called to a meeting in the time and place decided by the President, or by a proposal submitted by five members of the Committee.

14. The President of the Executive Committee shall represent the Palestinians at the Arab League; therefore, his office shall be in Cairo since the Arab League Headquarters is there.

15. The Executive Committee shall establish the following departments:

a)—Department of Political and Information Affairs.

b)—Department of the National Fund.

c)—Department of General Affairs.

Each one of these departments shall have a Director General and the needed number of employees. Duties of each one of these departments shall be defined by special by-laws prepared by the Executive Committee.

16. The Executive Committee has the right of calling the National Assembly to meet in a place and time it specifies; it has the right also to call to a meeting any committee of the National Assembly to study certain subjects.

17. The Executive Committee shall have a consultative council to be known as 'The Shura (Consultative) Council'; the Executive Committee shall select the president and members of this council from people of opinion and prestige among the Palestinians; prerogatives of the Consultative Council are in matters proposed to it by the Executive Committee.

18. The Arab states shall avail the sons of Palestine the opportunity of enlisting in their regular armies on the widest scale possible.

19. Private Palestinian contingents shall be formed in accordance with the military needs and plans decided by the Unified Arab Military Command in agreement and cooperation with the concerned Arab states.

20. A Fund, to be known as 'The National Palestinian Fund', shall be established to finance operations of the Executive Committee: the Fund shall have a Board of Directors whose members shall be elected by the National Assembly.

21. Sources of the Fund are to be from:

a)—Fixed taxes levied on Palestinians and collected in accordance with special laws.

b)—Financial assistance offered by the Arab governments and people.

c)—A 'Liberation Stamp' to be issued by the Arab states and be used in postal and other transactions.

d)—Donations on national occasions.

e)—Loans and assistance given by the Arabs or by friendly nations.

22. Committees, to be known as 'Support Palestine Committees', shall be established in Arab and friendly countries to collect donations and to support the Liberation Organisation.

23. The Executive Committee shall have the right to issue by-laws for fulfillment of provisions of this constitution.

24. This draft constitution shall be submitted to the National Assembly for consideration; what is ratified of it cannot be changed except by a two-thirds majority of the National Assembly.

Document 30

United Nations General Assembly Resolution on the Internationalization of Jerusalem

This U.N. Resolution (No. 303[IV]) and the following one (Document 31—Resolution 619[VII]) are among those most frequently quoted in the discussions about the Arab-Israeli conflict.

December 9, 1949

The General Assembly,

Having regard to its resolution 181 (II) of 29 November 1947 and 194 (III) of 11 December 1948,

Having studied the reports of the United Nations Conciliation Commission for Palestine set up under the latter resolution,

I. Decides

In relation to Jerusalem,

Believing that the principles underlying its previous resolutions concerning this matter, and in particular its resolution of 29 November 1947, represent a just and equitable settlement of the question,

1. To restate, therefore, its intention that Jerusalem should be placed under a permanent international regime, which should envisage appropriate guarantees for the protection of the Holy Places, both within and outside Jerusalem and to confirm specifically the following provisions of General Assembly resolution 181 (II):

(1) The City of Jerusalem shall be established as a *corpus separatum* under a special international régime and shall be administered by the United Nations; (2) The Trusteeship Council shall be designated to discharge the responsibilities of the Administering Authority . . . ; and (3) The City of Jerusalem shall include the present municipality of Jerusalem plus the surrounding villages and towns, the most eastern of which shall be Abu Dis; the most southern, Bethlehem; the most western, Ein Karim (including also the built-up area of Motsa); and the most northern, Shu'fat, as indicated on the attached sketch-map; (*map not reproduced: Ed.*)

2. To request for this purpose that the Trusteeship Council at its next session, whether special or regular, complete the

preparation of the Statute of Jerusalem, omitting the now in-applicable provisions, such as articles 32 and 39, and, without prejudice to the fundamental principles of the international régime for Jerusalem set forth in General Assembly resolution 181 (II) introducing therein amendments in the direction of its greater democratization, approve the Statute, and proceed immediately with its implementation. The Trusteeship Council shall not allow any actions taken by any interested Government or Governments to divert it from adopting and implementing the Statute of Jerusalem;

II. Calls upon the States concerned, to make formal under-takings, at an early date and in the light of their obligations as Members of the United Nations, that they will approach these matters with good will, and be guided by the terms of the present resolution.

Document 31

U.N. Security Council Resolution Concerning Restrictions on the Passage of Ships through the Suez Canal

September 1, 1951

THE SECURITY COUNCIL

1. *Recalling* that in its resolution of 11 August 1949 (S/1376) relating to the conclusion of Armistice Agreements between Israel and the neighbouring Arab States, it drew attention to the pledges, in these Agreements "against any further acts of hostility between the Parties";

2. *Recalling* further that in its resolution of 17 November 1950 (S/1907) it reminded the States concerned that the Armistice Agreements to which they were parties contemplated "the return of permanent peace in Palestine," and therefore urged them and the other States in the area to take all such steps as would lead to the settlement of the issues between them;

3. *Noting* the report of the Chief of Staff of the Truce Supervision Organization to the Security Council of 12 June 1951 (S/2194);

4. *Further noting* that the Chief of Staff of the Truce Supervision Organization recalled the statement of the senior Egyptian delegate in Rhodes on 13 January 1949, to the effect that his delegation was "inspired with every spirit of co-operation, conciliation and a sincere desire to restore peace

in Palestine," and that the Egyptian Government has not complied with the earnest plea of the Chief of Staff made to the Egyptian delegate on 12 June 1951, that it desist from the present practice of interfering with the passage through the Suez Canal of goods destined for Israel;

5. *Considering* that since the Armistice regime, which has been in existence for nearly two and a half years, is of a permanent character, neither party can reasonably assert that it is actively a belligerent or requires to exercise the right of visit, search, and seizure for any legitimate purpose of self-defence;

6. *Finds* that the maintenance of the practice mentioned in paragraph 4 above is inconsistent with the objectives of a peaceful settlement between the parties and the establishment of a permanent peace in Palestine set forth in the Armistice Agreement;

7. *Finds further* that such practice is an abuse of the exercise of the right of visit, search and seizure;

8. *Further finds* that that practice cannot in the prevailing circumstances be justified on the ground that it is necessary for self-defence;

9. *And further noting* that the restrictions on the passage of goods through the Suez Canal to Israel ports are denying to nations at no time connected with the conflict in Palestine valuable supplies required for their economic reconstruction, and that these restrictions together with sanctions applied by Egypt to certain ships which have visited Israel ports represent unjustified interference with the rights of nations to navigate the seas and to trade freely with one another, including the Arab States and Israel;

10. *Calls upon* Egypt to terminate the restrictions on the passage of international commercial shipping and goods through the Suez Canal wherever bound and to cease all interference with such shipping beyond that essential to the safety of shipping in the Canal itself and to the observance of international conventions in force.

Document 32

President Nasser on Zionism and Israel

The following excerpts are from Nasser's "The Philosophy of the Revolution," and speeches on various occasions between 1960 and 1963. Nasser served as an army officer in the Palestine War of 1948. The liberation of Palestine has been one of the chief planks of his political program, but there have been conflicting statements as to whether there was a definitive plan for the liberation. On several occasions, he announced that his army would soon be ready to enter Palestine on "a carpet of blood," on others that the time was not ripe yet.

As far as I am concerned I remember that the first elements of Arab consciousness began to filter into my mind as a student in secondary schools, wherefrom I went out with my fellow schoolboys on strike on December 2nd of every year as a protest against the Balfour Declaration whereby England gave the Jews a national home usurped unjustly from its legal owners.

When I asked myself at that time why I left my school enthusiastically and why I was angry for this land which I never saw I could not find an answer except the echoes of sentiment. Later a form of comprehension of this subject began when I was a cadet in the Military College studying the Palestine campaigns in particular and the history and conditions of this region in general which rendered it, throughout the last century, an easy prey ravaged by the claws of a pack of hungry beasts.

My comprehension began to be clearer as the foundation of its facts stood out when I began to study, as a student in the Staff College, the Palestine campaign and the problems of the Mediterranean in greater detail.

And when the Palestine crisis loomed on the horizon I was firmly convinced that the fighting in Palestine was not fighting on foreign territory. Nor was it inspired by sentiment. It was a duty imposed by self-defense.

Address by President
Gamal Abdel Nasser in Aleppo
(February 17, 1960)

Yesterday, the elderly Foreign Minister of Israel threatened the U.A.R. and said that Israel would not tolerate the ban on Israeli ships transiting the Suez Canal.

I would like to tell her and her master, Ben Gurion, as well as the Israeli people, that Israeli ships and cargoes will not, under any circumstances, transit the Canal.

Once these cargoes arrive in Port-Said or in any other port in the U.A.R. they become the property of the people of Palestine against whom Zionism and imperialism have conspired.

Eleven years after this tragedy, the people of Palestine have not changed. They, and we, are working for the restoration of their rights in their homeland. The rights of the people of Palestine are Arab rights above all. We feel it is our sacred duty to regain those rights for the people of Palestine.

By this unity which is binding you and the power of Arab unity and Arab nationalism, we can march along the road of freedom and liberation in order to get back the usurped rights of the Palestine Arabs.

Speech by President Gamal Abdel Nasser at a Mass Rally of the Youth Organisations in Damascus (October 18, 1960)

Now for the Palestinian issue. Wherever I have been in this or the Southern Region I hear the strong call for the liberation of this Arab territory of Palestine, and I would like to tell you, Brethren, that all that we are now doing is just a part of the battle for Palestine. Once we are fully emancipated from the shackles of colonialism and the intrigues of colonialist agents, we shall take a further step forward towards the liberation of Palestine.

When we have brought our armed forces to full strength and made our own armaments we will take another step forward towards the liberation of Palestine, and when we have manufactured jet aircraft and tanks we will embark upon the final stage of this liberation.

Address by President Gamal Abdel Nasser on the 11th Anniversary of the Revolution at the Republican Square, Cairo (July 22, 1963)

Work and readiness are the only means to protect the Arab's right in Palestine.

Arab unity is our hope of liberating Palestine and restoring the rights of the people of Palestine.

Arab unity is a sort of preparation, a human and national preparation as well as a preparation with weapons and plans in all fields. It is not enough to deliver speeches declaring that we would liberate Palestine and liberate it just on paper for political consumption. As I said before, we do not have any defined plan for the liberation of Palestine. I mention this because I find it my duty to say it. But we have a plan to be implemented in case of any Israeli aggression against us or against any Arab country.

In this case, we know well what to do. We have to be prepared. We have a plan for this preparation and for the unification of the Arab world which is the only means to protect the Arab land and safeguard Arab Nationalism.

God be with you and may his peace and mercy be upon you.

Speech Delivered by President Gamal Abdel Nasser at Alexandria on the Return of Another Contingent of U.A.R. Troops in Yemen (August 11, 1963)

The Armed Forces are getting ready for the restoration of the rights of the Palestine people because the Palestine battle was a smear on the entire Arab nation. No one can forget the shame brought by the battle of 1948. The rights of the Palestine people must be restored. Therefore, we must get ready to face Israel and Zionism as well as Imperialism which stands behind them.

Document 33

Ahmed Shukairy: The Palestine Refugees

Excerpts from a speech at the United Nations by Shukairy in 1958 when serving as a member of the Saudi Arabian mission.

The Five Principles

Having portrayed the refugees' problem against its lengthy background of United Nations' action, of the Conciliation Commission and the relief Agency, we come to the crucial question. What is next? What is the solution?

In my submission, this is the question which must engage our attention and call for our action; and I shall endeavor to answer the question in a manner devoid of any decoration.

For when the destiny of a whole people is involved, when the fundamental human rights are in question, and lastly when the peace of the world is at stake, there should be no fineness in our approach. The need calls for plain talking characterized with frankness, and sharp frankness indeed.

It is for these reasons that it becomes our duty to answer the question in all the candour under our command. In this spirit, Mr. Chairman, I propose now to deal with three matters: The solution of the problem, the fundamental principles of the solution, and the measures and sanctions to implement the solution.

Beginning with the fundamental principle of the solution, I must reiterate, even to the point of redundance, that these fundamental principles constitute the only basis for the solution to the refugee question. No matter how we view the problem, no solution can offer a chance for a peaceful settlement unless it takes full cognizance of the following five principles:

FIRST: The *de facto* situation created by Israel is entirely unacceptable as a basis for the solution of the Palestine problem in general, or the refugee question in particular. This *de facto* situation is the *fait accompli* of military action that does not vest rights non existing, or divest rights already existing.

SECOND: The rights of the refugees to their homes and homeland are not related to, or in any way dependent upon, the consent or refusal of Israel. These rights are natural, inherent and self-existing. They are not bestowed even by the United Nations, let alone Israel. They cannot be denied even by the United Nations, let alone Israel. They are vested in the refugees; they reside with the refugees. Thus, consent or no consent, these rights are theirs imprescriptible, irresistible and indivisible.

THIRD: Resettlement, reintegration, rehabilitation or any similar projects, no matter what their connotation may be, are not a solution by themselves. They should be planned or implemented not as aims, but merely as a means to meet the legitimate aspirations of the refugees and to the extent of giving effect to their inherent right to their homeland.

FOURTH: The relief program of the refugees is no solution to the problem, neither is it a substitute, no matter for how long it is continued. It is a humanitarian measure having no political implications.

FIFTH: Works projects, and self-support programs are not a solution; nor a solution to avoid the solution. Self-supporting or dependent, a refugee remains a refugee and his status remains an international problem until it is finally and satisfactorily solved.

To recast such a background has become the more necessary after we heard yesterday the statement on behalf of the United States. The Distinguished Representative of the United States, in his outline of the background of the refugee question, has omitted certain truths entirely, related half truths on certain aspects and finally arrived at wrongful conclusions on the substance of the problem.

As to the termination of the mandate of the Agency in favor of a better system as implied in the statement of the United States, we have serious misgivings of paramount nature. I must assure the Distinguished Representative of the United States that no Arab State, and no refugee, to use the words of the Distinguished Representative of the United States, feels it "best to let matters ride as in the past." To the refugees, continuation of relief is a source of great humiliation. To the Arab Governments it is a source of distress. If "some" feel differently, I assure the Distinguished Representative of the United States, it is not the Arabs anyhow. These refugees who are costing you 7 cents a day per head, have properties, revenues, fortunes in their homeland. The minute they lay hand on their properties they will be the first to thank you and plead the discontinuation of relief. It is only then that the U. N. responsibility ends, but not before.

I must, therefore, make it quite clear to the Committee in general and to the Distinguished Representative of the United States in particular, that we shall resist any attempt which directly or indirectly reduces in any degree the right of the refugees to repatriation. At a later stage of the debate, I will show the flaw in the reasoning underlying the position of the United States on the question. I simply wish to say here and now that any measure that might be in the direction of even scratching the right to repatriation or absolving the United Nations from its responsibility will be resisted in the Committee and in the Arab World.

With these five principles in mind, I can turn now to the solution of the problem. Here I would say that we need not look for a solution. The solution is there. It is repatriation and nothing but repatriation. It is the only solution that does not dishonour, but certainly does honour the Charter. It is the only solution that does not defeat, but rather does endorse the resolution of the United Nations. It is the only solution

that does not defame the bill of human rights, but surely gives
it a worthy fame. Lastly, it is the only solution that constitutes
an investment of peace, and an asset of confidence in this
organization.

After all, repatriation is one of those principles that cannot
be questioned by the United Nations. It does not stand by
our acceptance, nor does it lapse by our non-acceptance. To
borrow a legal term, repatriation is a right *In Rem,* that can
be exercised against the whole world, if need be. It springs
from the right to a homeland, which is not subject to waiver,
surrender, or compensation. Compensation is one remedy
open for individual property rights, but a homeland does not
submit to compensation even for the most precious possessions
of this planet, and indeed the whole universe with all its fabulous riches. This is no exaggeration, unless I exaggerate your
feelings towards your respective homelands.

Document 34

Erskine Childers: The Other Exodus*

Erskine Childers, an Irish journalist has published articles
bitterly critical of Israeli policies. The present article was
originally published in the London weekly *The Spectator*
(May 12, 1961) and provoked a great deal of controversy.
Childers, the grandson of a well known Irish patriot and
writer, also worked for the British Broadcasting Corpora-
tion and subsequently became a leading official in Irish
television.

The Palestine Arab refugees wait, and multiply, and are
debated at the United Nations. In thirteen years, their numbers have increased from 650,000 to 1,145,000. Most of them
survive only on rations from the U.N. agency, UNRWA.
Their subsistence has already cost L.S. 110,000,000. Each
year, UNRWA has to plead at New York for the funds
to carry on, against widespread and especially Western lack
of sympathy. There is one reason for this impatience: the
attitude created towards these refugees by Israeli argument.
For over ten years, Israeli spokesmen have claimed that:

Unless we understand how this problem was caused we
cannot rightly judge how it should be solved. . . . The re-

* Reprinted by permission of *The Spectator* Limited.

sponsibility of the Arab Governments is threefold. Theirs is the initiative for its creation. Theirs is the onus for its endurance. Above all—theirs is the capacity for its solution.

(Abba Eban to the U.N. 1957).

In this inquiry, I propose only briefly to examine the last two of these three claims. The last, about a "solution," is that if the Arab host governments were willing, they could resettle the refugees quite easily outside Palestine—where, as Israel claims and as President Kennedy's 1960 election platform also had it, "there is room and opportunity for them." This is not even remotely true. UNRWA's new chief, Dr. John Davis, has now bluntly and bravely warned against "facile assumptions that it rests with the host governments to solve the problem . . . the simple truth is that the jobs . . . do not exist today within the host countries." Nor can the jobs be created, Dr. Davis reports, because most of the refugees are unskilled peasants—precisely the host countries' worst problem among their own rapidly expanding populations.

These Arabs, in short, are displaced persons in the fullest, most tragic meaning of the term—an economic truth cruelly different from the myth. But there is also the political myth, and it too has been soothing our highly pragmatic Western conscience for thirteen years. This is the Israeli charge, solemnly made every year and then reproduced around the world, that these refugees are—to quote a character in Leon Uris's *Exodus*—"kept caged like animals in suffering as a deliberate political weapon."

This, again, Dr. Davis has now bravely called a "misconception." The reality here is that the refugees themselves fanatically oppose any resettlement outside Palestine. UNRWA even had to persuade them that concrete huts, even in the U.N. camps, replacing their squalid tents and hovels, would not be the thin end of a resettlement wedge. Unlike other refugees, these refuse to move; they insist on going home.

Why? The answer, I believe, lies in the third of the three issues Israel argues—in the cause itself of the mass exodus. The very fact that cause is argued by both sides is significant. Israel claims that the Arabs left because they were ordered to, and deliberately incited into panic, by their own leaders who wanted the field cleared for the 1948 war. It is also argued that there would today be no Arab refugees if the Arab States had not attacked the new Jewish State on May 15, 1948 (though 800,000 had already fled before that date).

The Arabs charge that their people were evicted at bayonet-point and by panic deliberately incited by the Zionists.

Examining every official Israeli statement about the Arab exodus, I was struck by the fact that no primary evidence of evacuation orders was ever produced. The charge, Israel claimed, was "documented"; but where were the documents? There had allegedly been Arab radio broadcasts ordering the evacuation; but no dates, names of stations, or texts of messages were ever cited. In Israel in 1958, as a guest of the Foreign Office and therefore doubly hopeful of serious assistance, I asked to be shown the proofs, I was assured they existed, and was promised them. None had been offered when I left, but I was again assured. I asked to have the material sent on to me. I am still waiting.

While in Israel, however, I met Dr. Leo Kohn, professor of political science at Hebrew University and an ambassador-rank adviser to the Israeli Foreign Office. He had written one of the first official pamphlets on the Arab refugees. I asked him for concrete evidence of the Arab evacuation orders. Agitatedly, Dr. Kohn replied: "Evidence? Evidence? What more could you want than this?" and he took up his own pamphlet. "Look at this 'Economist' report," and he pointed to a quotation. "You will surely not suggest that the 'Economist' is a Zionist journal?"

The quotation is one of about five that appear in every Israeli speech and pamphlet, and are in turn used by every sympathetic analysis. It seemed very impressive: it referred to the exodus from Haifa, and to an Arab broadcast order as one major reason for that exodus.

I decided to turn up the relevant (October 2) 1948 issue of the 'Economist.' The passage that has literally gone around the world was certainly there, but I had already noticed one curious word in it. This was a description of the massacre at Deir Yassin as an "incident." No impartial observer of Palestine in 1948 calls what happened at this avowedly non-belligerent, unarmed Arab village in April, 1948, an "incident"—any more than Lidice is called an "incident." Over 250 old men, women and children were deliberately butchered, stripped and mutilated or thrown into a well, by men of the Zionist Irgun Zvai Leumi.

Seen in its place in the full 'Economist' article, it was at once clear that Dr. Kohn's quotation was a second-hand account, inserted as that of an eye-witness at Haifa, by the journal's own correspondent who had not been in that city at the time. And in the rest of the same article, written by the Economist correspondent himself, but never quoted by Israel, the second great wave of refugees were described as "all destitute, as the Jewish troops gave them an hour in which to quit, but simultaneously requisitioned all transport."

It was now essential to check all other, even secondary, Israeli "evidence." Another stock quotation down the years has been that, supposedly, of the Greek-Catholic Archbishop of Galilee. For example, Israel's Abba Eban told the U.N. Special Political Committee in 1957 that the Archbishop had "fully confirmed" that the Arabs were urged to flee by their own leaders.

I wrote to His Grace, asking for his evidence of such orders. I hold signed letters from him, with permission to publish, in which he has categorically denied ever alleging Arab evacuation orders; he states that no such orders were ever given. He says that his name has been abused for years; and that the Arabs fled through panic and forcible eviction by Jewish troops.

As none of the other stock quotations in Israeli propaganda are worth comment, I next decided to test the undocumented charge that the Arab evacuation orders were broadcast by Arab radio—which could be done thoroughly because the BBC monitored all Middle Eastern broadcasts throughout 1948. The records, and companion ones by a U.S. monitoring unit, can be seen at the British Museum.

There was not a single order, or appeal, or suggestion about evacuation from Palestine from any Arab radio station, inside or outside Palestine, in 1948. There is repeated monitored record of Arab appeals, even flat orders, to the civilians of Palestine to stay put. To select only two examples: on April 4, as the first great wave of flight began, Damascus Radio broadcast an appeal to everyone to stay at their homes and jobs. On April 24, with the exodus now a flood, Palestine Arab leaders warned that:

> Certain elements and Jewish agents are spreading defeatist news to creats chaos and panic among the peaceful population. Some cowards are deserting their houses, villages or cities. . . . Zionist agents and corrupt cowards will be severely punished (Al-Inqaz, the Arab Liberation Radio, at 12.00 hours).

Even Jewish broadcasts (in Hebrew) mentioned such Arab appeals to stay put. Zionist newspapers in Palestine reported the same: none so much as hinted at any Arab evacuation orders.

The fact is that Israel's official charges, which have vitally influenced the last ten years of Western thought about the refugees, are demonstrably and totally hollow. And from this alone, suspicion is justified. Why make such charges at all? On the face of it, this mass exodus might have been entirely the result of "normal" panic and wartime dislocation.

We need not even touch upon Arab evidence that panic was quite deliberately incited. The evidence is there, on the Zionist record. For example, on March 27, four days before the big offensive against Arab centres by the official Zionist (Haganah) forces, the Irgun's radio unit broadcast in Arabic. Irgun, a terrorist organisation like the Stern Gang, was officially disowned by Ben Gurion and the Haganah. Yet just four days before the Haganah offensive Irgun warned "Arabs in urban agglomerations" that typhus, cholera and similar diseases would break out "heavily" among them "in April and May."

The effect may be imagined. Two weeks later, it was this same Irgun, apparently so solicitous of Arab welfare, that butchered the people of Deir Yassin. Irgun then called a press conference to announce the deed; paraded other captured Arabs through Jewish quarters of Jerusalem to be spat upon; then released them to tell their kin of the experience. Arthur Koestler called the "bloodbath" of Deir Yassin "the psychologically decisive factor in this spectacular exodus." But this was only Irgun, it may be said. Is there evidence that official Zionist forces—the Haganah under Ben Gurion and the Jewish Agency—were inciting panic? An Israeli Government pamphlet of 1958 states that "the Jews tried, by every means open to them, to stop the Arab evacuation" (this same 1958 pamphlet has diluted Deir Yassin to "the one and only instance of Jewish high-handed (sic) action in this war").

There is one recorded instance of such an appeal. It is beyond dispute even by Arabs, that in Haifa the late gentle Mayor, Shabeitai Levi, with the tears streaming down his face, implored the city's Arabs to stay. But elsewhere in Haifa, Arthur Koestler wrote in his book that Haganah loudspeaker vans and the Haganah radio promised that city's Arabs escort to "Arab territory," and "hinted at terrible consequences if their warning were disregarded." There are many witnesses of this loudspeaker method elsewhere. In Jerusalem the Arabic warning from the vans was, "The road to Jericho is open!

Fly from Jerusalem before you are all killed!" (Meyer Levin in *Jerusalem Embattled*). Bertha Vester, a Christian missionary, reported that another theme was, "Unless you leave your homes, the fate of Deir Yassin will be your fate." The Haganah radio station also broadcast, in Arabic, repeated news of Arabs fleeing "in terror and fear" from named places.

Still, however, we have plumbed this exodus only so far as panic is concerned. There are U.N. and Economist reports of forcible expulsion, which is something else. How much evidence is there for this? And were only the "unofficial" Irgun and Stern forces responsible? This is what Nathan Chofshi, one of the original Jewish pioneers in Palestine, wrote in an ashamed rebuttal of an American Zionist rabbi's charges of evacuation orders:

> If Rabbi Kaplan really wanted to know what happened, we old Jewish settlers in Palestine who witnessed the fight could tell him how and in what manner we, Jews, forced the Arabs to leave cities and villages . . . some of them were driven out by force of arms; others were made to leave by deceit, lying and false promises. It is enough to cite the cities of Jaffa, Lydda, Ramleh, Beersheba, Acre from among numberless others. (in 'Jewish Newsletter,' New York, February 9, 1959).

Were official Zionist troops involved at any of these places? I propose to select, for the sake of brevity, only the Lydda-Ramleh area. It was about the exodus from this area, among others, that the Economist reported. "Jewish troops gave them an hour to quit."

In their latest book, which has been publicly endorsed by Ben Gurion, Jon Kimche and his brother devoted considerable detail to the Zionist offensive against Lydda and Ramleh. It was undertaken by official Israeli forces under Yigael Alon. And the immediately responsible officer was Moshe Dayan, commander of the 1956 Sinai attack, now a Cabinet Minister. Kimche has described how, on July 11, 1948, Dayan with his columns:

> . . . drove at full speed into Lydda, shooting up the town and creating confusion and a degree of terror among the population . . . its Arab population of 30,000 either fled or were herded on the road to Ramallah. The next day Ramleh also surrendered and its Arab population suffered the same fate. Both towns were sacked by the victorious Israelis.

Ramallah, on the road to which these particular Arabs— numbering over 60,000 from this one area alone—were

herded, was up in the Judean hills, outside Zionist-held territory. The "road to Jericho," which Arabs in Jerusalem were
warned to take, brought them into the Jordan Valley. Some
85,000 are still there in one U.N. camp alone, under the
Mount of Temptation. The Arab population of Acre, mentioned by Chofshi, exceeded 45,000: Acre was attacked by
official Zionist troops.

From this analysis of only some of the sources of the Arab
exodus, then, it is clear beyond all doubt that official Zionist
forces were responsible for expulsion of thousands upon
thousands of Arabs, and for deliberate incitement to panic.
Seen from the viewpoint of the Arab refugees themselves,
little more would need to be said. And needless to say, even
those Arabs expelled or who fled through "unofficially" incited panic can hardly be asked to look differently on the
Israeli Government today. It pays former Irgunists and Stern-
ists the same war pensions as former Haganah troops; its
denial of expulsion is total.

But is it conceivable that Ben Gurion and his colleagues
could have deliberately contemplated an "emptying" of Palestine? That a motive existed is beyond doubt. The U.N. partition scheme had in no way solved the "Arab problem" that
a Jewish State would face. It would have given Zionism what
its leaders publicly called the "irreducible minimum" of
territory in a Palestine they claimed should entirely belong
to them. And we know that the official Zionist movement had
in fact no intention of accepting the U.N. territorial award.
Six weeks before the British Mandate ended, before the Israeli
State was proclaimed, and before the Arab States sent in their
armies, an all-out Zionist military offensive was launched.
Later, Ben Gurion publicly said of this offensive:

> As fighting spread, the (Arab) exodus was joined by
> Bedouin and fellahin (peasants), but not the remotest Jewish
> homestead was abandoned and nothing a tottering (British)
> administration could unkindly do stopped us from reaching
> our goal on May 14, 1948, in a State made larger and Jewish
> by the Haganah (cf. Rebirth and Destiny of Israel).

The Jewish State envisaged by the U.N. would have contained a 45 per cent Arab population: the extra territory
attacked by the Zionists before May 14 would have increased
that ratio—for example, by more than 80,000 Arabs in Jaffa
alone. But it was not just a question of numbers. The Arabs
owned and occupied far too much of the territory's productive

and social facilities to enable anything like the mass Jewish immigration of which Zionists dreamed.

What this meant in terms of motive can be seen in the statistics that followed the Arab exodus. More than 80 per cent, of the entire land area of Israel is land abandoned by the Arab refugees. Nearly a quarter of all the standing buildings in Israel had been occupied by those Arabs. Ten thousand shops, stores and other firms inside new Israel had been Arab. Half of all the citrus fruit holdings in the new State had belonged to the Arabs now made refugees. By 1954, more than one-third of the entire Jewish population of Israel was living on "absentee property"—most of it now "absorbed" into the Israeli economy, and unilaterally sequestered by Israeli legislation against a "global" compensation offer.

It is, then, little wonder that old Chaim Weizmann, Israel's first President, described the Arab exodus as a "miraculous simplification of Israel's tasks." But was it "miraculous"? Unexpected? In no way part of combined military and economic planning of nascent Israel's leaders?

We come to perhaps the most grave evidence of all. The mass exodus began in April, 1948. By June, the U.N. Mediator was fully seized of it. He formally demanded a statement of policy from the new Israeli Government about the refugees. At first, he could get no satisfaction. Then, in an official letter dated: August 1, 1948, Israeli's Foreign Minister replied.

It was only four months since the first waves of flight; only eleven weeks since Israel had been proclaimed, ostensibly calling on the Arabs to "play their part in the development of the State." And it was at this time that a Government since claiming that this whole exodus was unexpected and despite its implorings, formally denied the refugees the right of return. Israel did not merely plead "security," but told the United Nations:

> On the economic side, the reintegration of the returning Arabs into normal life, and even their mere sustenance, would present an insuperable problem. The difficulties of accommodation, employment, and ordinary livelihood would be insuperable.

The case rests. This is not the place to discuss a "solution," and no summary conclusion is needed, save perhaps to recall the words of an official Israeli spokesman, though in rather different import:

Unless we understand how this problem was caused, we cannot rightly judge how it should be solved.

The Arabs of Palestine now enter their fourteenth year of exile. If you go among them in the hills of Judea, they will take you by the arm to a crest of land and point downwards, across the rusty skeins of barbed wire. "Can you see it—over there beside those trees? That is my home."

It is shaming beyond all brief descriptions to move among these million people, as a Westerner. It is shaming for many Jews, and some speak out as Nathan Chofshi has bravely done:

> We came and turned the native Arabs into tragic refugees. And still we dare to slander and malign them, to besmirch their name. Instead of being deeply ashamed of what we did and trying to undo some of the evil we committed . . . we justify our terrible acts and even attempt to glorify them.

Document 35

Abba Eban: The Refugee Problem

Excerpts from a speech (Nov. 17, 1958) by the Chief Israeli representative to the United Nations who subsequently became Foreign Minister of Israel.

How Was the Refugee Problem Caused?

AGGRESSION BY ARAB STATES CREATED REFUGEE PROBLEM

The Arab refugee problem was caused by a war of aggression, launched by the Arab States against Israel in 1947 and 1948. Let there be no mistake. If there had been no war against Israel, with its consequent harvest of bloodshed, misery, panic and flight, there would be no problem of Arab refugees today. Once you determine the responsibility for that war, you have determined the responsibility for the refugee problem. Nothing in the history of our generation is clearer or less controversial than the initiative of Arab governments for the conflict out of which the refugee tragedy emerged. The historic origins of that conflict are clearly defined by the confessions of Arab governments themselves:

"This will be a war of extermination," declared the Secretary General of the Arab League speaking for the governments of six Arab States; "It will be a momentous massacre to be spoken of like the Mongolian massacre and the Crusades."

PALESTINE ARABS URGED TO FLEE
BY ARAB LEADERS

The assault began on the last day of November 1947. From then until the expiration of the British Mandate in May 1948 the Arab States, in concert with Palestine Arab leaders, plunged the land into turmoil and chaos. On the day of Israel's Declaration of Independence, on May 14, 1948, the armed forces of Egypt, Jordan, Syria, Lebanon and Iraq, supported by contingents from Saudi Arabia and the Yemen, crossed their frontiers and marched against Israel. The perils which then confronted our community; the danger which darkened every life and home; the successful repulse of the assault and the emergence of Israel into the life of the world community are all chapters of past history, gone but not forgotten. But the traces of that conflict still remain deeply inscribed upon our region's life. Caught up in the havoc and tension of war; demoralized by the flight of their leaders; urged on by irresponsible promises that they would return to inherit the spoils of Israel's destruction—hundreds of thousands of Arabs sought the shelter of Arab lands. A survey by an international body in 1957 described these violent events in the following terms:

"As early as the first months of 1948 the Arab League issued orders exhorting the people to seek a temporary refuge in neighboring countries, later to return to their abodes in the wake of the victorious Arab armies and obtain their share of abandoned Jewish property" (Research Group for European Migration Problems Bulletin, Vol. V—No. 1, 1957, p. 10).

Contemporary statements by Arab leaders fully confirm this version. On 16 August 1948 Msgr. George Hakim, the Greek Catholic Archbishop of Galilee, recalled:

"The refugees had been confident that their absence from Palestine would not last long; that they would return within a few days—within a week or two; their leaders had promised them that the Arab armies would crush the 'Zionist gangs' very quickly and that there would be no need for panic or fear of a long exile."

A month later on September 15, 1948, Mr. Emile Ghoury who had been the Secretary of the Arab Higher Committee at the time of the Arab invasion of Israel declared:

"I do not want to impugn anyone but only to help the refugees. The fact that there are these refugees is the direct consequence of the action of the Arab States in opposing partition and the Jewish State. The Arab States agreed upon this policy unanimously and they must share in the solution of the problem."

MISERY IS RESULT OF UNLAWFUL RESORT TO FORCE BY ARABS

No less compelling than these avowals by Arab leaders are the judgments of United Nations organs. In April 1948, when the flight of the refugees was in full swing, the United Nations Palestine Commission inscribed its verdict on the tablets of history:

"Arab opposition to the plan of the Assembly of 29 November 1947 has taken the form of organized efforts by strong Arab elements, both inside and outside Palestine, to prevent its implementation and to thwart its objectives by threats and acts of violence, including repeated armed incursions into Palestine territory. The Commission has had to report to the Security Council that powerful Arab interests, both inside and outside Palestine, are defying the resolution of the General Assembly and are engaged in a deliberate effort to alter by force the settlement envisaged therein."

This is a description of the events between November 1947 and May 1948 when the Arab exodus began. Months later, when the tide of battle rolled away, its consequences of bereavement, devastation and panic were left behind. At the General Assembly meetings in 1948 the United Nations Acting Mediator recorded a grave international judgment:

"The Arab States had forcibly opposed the existence of the Jewish State in Palestine in direct opposition to the wishes of two-thirds of the members of the Assembly. Nevertheless their armed intervention proved useless. The (Mediator's) report was based solely on the fact that the Arab States had no right to resort to force and that the United Nations should exert its authority to prevent such a use of force."

The significance of the Arab assault upon Israel by five neighboring States had been reflected in a letter addressed by the Secretary General of the United Nations to representatives of the permanent members of the Security Council on 16 May 1948:—

"The Egyptian Government," wrote the Secretary-General, "has declared in a cablegram to the President of the Security Council on 15 May that Egyptian armed forces have entered Palestine and it has engaged in 'armed intervention' in that country. On 16 May I received a cablegram from the Arab League making similar statements on behalf of the Arab States. I consider it my duty to emphasize to you that *this is the first time since the adoption of the Charter that Member States have openly declared that they have engaged in armed intervention outside their own territory*."

Arab Governments Must Accept Responsibility

These are only a few of the documents which set out the responsibility of the Arab Governments for the warfare of which the refugees are the main surviving victims. Even after a full decade it is difficult to sit here with equanimity and listen to Arab representatives disengaging themselves from any responsibility for the travail and anguish which they caused. I recall this history not for the purpose of recrimination, but because of its direct bearing on the Committee's discussion. Should not the representatives of Arab States, as the authors of this tragedy, come here in a mood of humility and repentance rather than in shrill and negative indignation? Since these governments have, by acts of policy, created this tragic problem, *does it not follow that the world community has an unimpeachable right to claim their full assistance in its solution?* How can governments create a vast humanitarian problem by their action—then wash their hands of all responsibility for its alleviation? The claim of the world community on the cooperation of Arab governments is all the more compelling when we reflect that these States, in their vast lands, command all the resources and conditions which would enable them to liberate the refugees from their plight, in full dignity and freedom.

With this history in mind the Committee should not find it difficult to reject the assertion that the guilt for the refugee problem lies with the United Nations itself. The refugee problem was not created by the General Assembly's recommendation for the establishment of Israel. It was created by the attempts of Arab governments to destroy that recommendation by force. The crisis arose not as Arab spokesmen have said because the United Nations adopted a resolution eleven years ago; it arose because Arab governments attacked that resolution by force. If the United Nations proposal had been peacefully accepted, there would be no refugee problem to-day hanging as a cloud upon the tense horizons of the Middle East.

The next question is—why has the problem endured?

Why Does the Refugee Problem Endure?

REFUGEE PROBLEM CANNOT BE SOLVED BY REPATRIATION

In his statement to the Committee on November 10, 1958, the representative of the United States said:

> "In our view it is not good enough consciously to perpetuate for over a decade the dependent status of nearly a million refugees."

Other speakers in this debate have echoed a similar sense of frustration.

Apart from the question of its origin, the perpetuation of this refugee problem is an unnatural event, running against the whole course of experience and precedent. Since the end of the Second World War, problems affecting forty million refugees have confronted Governments in various parts of the world. In no case, except that of the Arab refugees, amounting to less than two percent of the whole, has the international community shown constant responsibility and provided lavish aid. In every other case a solution has been found by the integration of refugees into their host countries. Nine million Koreans; 900,000 refugees from the conflict in Viet Nam; 8½ million Hindus and Sikhs leaving Pakistan for India; 6½ million Moslems fleeing India to Pakistan; 700,000 Chinese refugees in Hong Kong; 13 million Germans from the Sudetenland, Poland and other East European States reaching West and East Germany; thousands of Turkish refugees from Bulgaria; 440,000 Finns separated from their homeland by a change of frontier; 450,000 refugees from Arab lands arrived destitute in Israel; and an equal number converging on Israel from the remnants of the Jewish holocaust in Europe—these form the tragic procession of the world's refugee population in the past two decades. *In every case but that of the Arab refugees now in Arab lands the countries in which the refugees sought shelter have facilitated their integration.* In this case alone has integration been obstructed.

The paradox is the more astonishing when we reflect that the kinship of language, religion, social background and national sentiment existing between the Arab refugees and their Arab host countries has been at least as intimate as those existing between any other host countries and any other refugee groups. It is impossible to escape the conclusion that the integration of Arab refugees into the life of the Arab world is an objectively feasible process which has been resisted for political reasons.

In a learned study on refugee problems published by the Carnegie Endowment for International Peace in November 1957 under the title "Century of the Homeless Man" Dr. Elfan Rees, Advisor on Refugees to the World Council of Churches, sums up the international experience in the following terms:

> "No large scale refugee problem has ever been solved by repatriation, and there are certainly no grounds for believing that this particular problem can be so solved. Nothing can bring it about except wars which in our time would leave nothing to go back to. War has never solved a refugee problem and it is not in the books that a modern war would."

ARAB LEADERS BLOCK SOLUTION FOR POLITICAL REASONS

Those words should be compared with Mr. Shukairy's peroration, in which he seems to look forward to a settlement of the refugee problem by a war launched for the extinction of Israel's independence. Such a war, whose result would not be that envisaged by Mr. Shukairy, would be more likely to create new refugee problems than to solve the existing ones.

Dr. Rees' Report continues:

> "This then is not a case of a refugee rejecting a particular solution but of the international community having to reject it as dangerous and impossible. It is time this was done with more frankness and force than has been used hitherto. Until it is—real danger remains, and these refugee problems will be unnecessarily perpetuated by the rejection of other and viable solutions."

The Carnegie Endowment publication concludes:

> "The facts we must face force us to the conclusion that for most of the world refugees the only solution is integration where they are."

Another important study on refugee problems carried out last year has been published by the Research Group for European Migration. This study reaches the following grave conclusion:

> "The official attitude of the (Arab) host countries is well known. It is one of seeking to prevent any sort of adaptation and integration because the refugees are seen as a political means of pressure to get Israel wiped off the map or to get the greatest possible number of concessions."

It is painfully evident that this refugee problem has been artificially maintained for political motives against all the economic, social and cultural forces which, had they been allowed free play, would have brought about a solution.

Recent years have witnessed a great expansion of economic potentialities in the Middle East. The revenues of the oil bearing countries have opened up great opportunities of work and development, into which the refugees by virtue of their linguistic and national background could fit without any sense of dislocation. The expansion in the areas of Arab sovereignty has also created opportunities of employment which did not exist in the days of colonial tutelage. There cannot be any doubt that if free movement had been granted to the refugees there would have been a spontaneous absorption of thousands of them into these expanded Arab economies. It is precisely this that Arab Governments have obstructed. In his report to the Eighth session of the General Assembly the Director of UNRWA describes Arab policies on free movement in a highly significant passage:

> "The full benefit of the spread of this large capital investment (in Arab countries) will be felt only if restrictions on the movement of refugees are withdrawn. This is a measure which was proposed in the original three-year plan but little has been done so far to give effect to it. Such freedom of movement would enable refugees to take full advantage of the opportunities for work arising in countries such as Iraq, Saudi Arabia and the Persian Gulf Sheikhdoms where economic development has already taken place."

There has, of course, been some movement of refugees into the new labor opportunities of the region. The force of economic attraction has sometimes prevailed. But these potentialities can only be fully realized if political resistance to integration is overcome. There are broad opportunities in the Arab world for refugees to build new lives; but the governments concerned have so far sought to debar refugees from using them. In the survey published by the Carnegie Endowment the obstructive record of Arab governments is set out in graphic words:

> "The history of UNRWA has been a clinical study in frustration. No Agency has been better led or more devoutly served but the organized intransigence of the refugees and the calculated indifference of the Arab States concerned have brought all its plans to nought. By chicanery it is feeding the dead, by political pressure it is feeding non-refugees, its relief supplies have been subjected in some instances to import duty, its personnel policies are grossly interfered with and its 'constructive measures,' necessarily requiring the concurrence of governments, have been pigeon-holed. The net result is that relief is being provided in 1957 to refugees who could have been rehabilitated in 1951 with 'home and jobs,' without prejudice to their just claims."

In a survey on "Social Forces in the Middle East 1956," Dr. Channing B. Richardson of Hamilton University writes:

> "Towards UNRWA the attitudes of the Arab Governments vary between suspicion and obstruction. It cannot be denied that the outside observer gains the impression that the Arab governments have no great desire to solve the refugee problem."

In June, 1957 the Chairman of the Near Eastern Sub-Committee of the United States Senate Foreign Relations Committee reported at the end of an illuminating survey:

> "The fact is that the Arab States have for ten years used the Palestine refugees as political hostages in their struggle with Israel. While Arab delegates in the United Nations have condemned the plight of their brothers in the refugee camps nothing has been done to assist them in a practical way lest political leverage against Israel be lost."

450,000 JEWISH REFUGEES FROM ARAB LANDS ABSORBED BY ISRAEL

The failure or refusal of Arab governments to achieve a permanent economic integration of refugees in their huge lands appears all the more remarkable when we contrast it with the achievements of other countries when confronted by the challenge and opportunity of absorbing their kinsmen into their midst. Israel with her small territory, her meager water resources and her hardpressed finances, has found homes, work and citizenship in the past ten years for nearly a million newcomers arriving in destitution no less acute than those of Arab refugees. These refugees from Arab lands left their homes, property and jobs behind. Their standards of physique and nutrition were in many cases pathetically low. They have had to undergo processes of adaptation to a social, linguistic and national ethos far removed from any that they had known before. Thus, integration in this case has been far more arduous than it would be for Arab refugees in Arab lands, where no such differences exist between the society and culture of the host country and those with which the refugees are already familiar. If Israel in these conditions could assimilate nearly one million refugees—450,000 of them from Arab lands—how much more easily could the vast Arab world find a home for a similar number of Arab refugees if only the same impulse of kinship asserted itself.

This is concisely described in the report published by the Carnegie Endowment:

"There is another aspect of the Middle East refugee problem that is also frequently ignored. It is necessary to remember that concurrently with the perpetuation of the Arab refugee problem more than 400,000 Jews have been forced to leave their homes in Iraq, the Yemen, and North Africa. They have not been counted as refugees because they were readily and immediately received as new immigrants into Israel. Nevertheless they were forced to leave their traditional homes against their will and to abandon, in the process, all that they possessed. The latest addition to their number are the 20,000 Jews for whom life has become impossible in Egypt. Fifteen thousand of them have sought asylum in Israel while the remainder are in Europe seeking other solutions to their problem."

Nor is this an isolated example of what can be achieved by Governments in circumstances much less favorable than those which the Arab States command. Less than two weeks ago the representative of Finland, in the Third Committee of this Assembly, gave the following moving account of what a small country can achieve in refugee integration:

"In 1944 the 3,300,000 people who lived within the present boundaries of Finland had to receive in a couple of weeks' time around 440,000 displaced persons, all Finnish citizens who had left their homesteads after the new frontier line had cut off some 13 percent of our territory from the rest of Finland. . . .

As in 1944 practically no emigration of the displaced persons was possible and none of them could be sent back to their earlier home region, complete integration was the only solution. It was an extremely heavy economic burden taking into consideration that there was no international aid, that the reparation of war destruction and the payment of war indemnities all came simultaneously and that the displaced persons came practically empty handed."

I will not ask the Committee to consider the other numerous precedents. Enough has been said to prove the crucial point that there is no objective difficulty in solving such problems provided the will for a solution exists.

Indeed, compared with other problems, the Arab refugee problem is one of the easiest to solve.

REFUGEES CLOSELY AKIN TO ARABS IN HOST COUNTRIES

The Research Group for European Migration points out in its report (pps. 25-26) that

"The Palestine refugees have the closest possible affinities of national sentiment, language, religion and social organization with the Arab host countries and the standard of living of the majority of the refugee population is little different from those of the inhabitants of the countries that have given them refuge or will do so in the future."

The same point is made in the report of a Special Study Commission to the Near East and Africa despatched by the Committee on Foreign Affairs of the United States House of Representatives, the source of a great proportion of U.N. relief funds:

"Unlike refugees in other parts of the world the Palestine refugees are no different in language and social organization from the other Arabs. Resettlement therefore would be in familiar environment. If the local governments are unwilling to tackle the problem except on their own terms there is little incentive for outside governments to continue financial support. Original humanitarian impulse which led to the creation and perpetuation of UNRWA is gradually being perverted into a political weapon." (May 19, 1958).

REGIONAL ECONOMIC DEVELOPMENT BLOCKED BY ARAB GOVERNMENTS

Most of the recent literature describes Arab resistance to integration by two methods—political opposition to integration; and careful scrutiny of UNRWA's activities to ensure that they do not develop into permanent solutions. The policy of obstruction however also has a third heading. I refer to the rejection of economic development proposals which seemed to hold the promise of a refugee solution. The thinking behind these plans was simple but imaginative. The international community was willing to create special opportunities of livelihood by irrigating new areas of land, establishing new farms or, in some cases, new village communities with industrial as well as agricultural activity. Refugees were to be placed into these newly created labor opportunities. The result would be a reduction of the number of refugees receiving relief and progress towards lightening the international burden.

None of these schemes has won Arab acceptance. Many of them have been rejected precisely because their implementation would help solve the refugee problem. A typical and spectacular instance is to be found in the long negotiations conducted between 1953 and 1956 on a project for the co-ordinated use of the Jordan and Yarmuk Rivers. Israel was prepared, despite certain disavowal—indeed is still prepared— to cooperate in this plan. Ambassador Eric Johnston has summed up his experience in the following words:

> "Between 1953 and 1956, at the request of President Eisenhower, I undertook to negotiate with these States a comprehensive Jordan Valley development plan that would have provided for the irrigation of some 225,000 acres. . . . After two years of discussion, technical experts of Israel, Jordan, Lebanon and Syria agreed upon every important detail of a unified Jordan plan. But in October 1956 it was rejected for political reasons at a meeting of the Arab League. . . . Three years have passed and no agreement has yet been reached on developing the Jordan. Every year a billion cubic meters of precious water still roll down the ancient stream, wasted, to the Dead Sea."

ARAB GOVERMENTS PREFER REFUGEE STATUS QUO

In the light of these experiences it cannot be doubted that Arab Governments have been determined that the refugees shall remain refugees; and that the aim of wrecking any alternative to "repatriation" has been pursued by these governments with an ingenuity worthy of a better cause. With an international agency working for integration; with millions of dollars expended every year to move refugees away from a life of dependence, the Arab governments have brought us to a point where there are more refugees on United Nations rolls than ever before.

How to Solve the Arab Refugee Problem

RESETTLEMENT AMONG HOST COUNTRIES THE ONLY SOLUTION

Any discussion of this problem revolves around the two themes of resettlement, and what is called "repatriation." There is a growing skepticism about the feasibility of repatriation. These hundreds of thousands of Arab refugees are now in Arab lands on the soil of their kinsmen. They have been nourished for ten years on one single theme—hatred of Israel; refusal to recognize Israel's sovereignty; resentment against Israel's existence; the dream of securing Israel's extinction. All these implacable sentiments found expression in the address by the representative of Saudi Arabia.

REPATRIATION A THREAT TO SECURITY

Repatriation would mean that hundreds of thousands of people would be introduced into a State whose existence they oppose, whose flag they despise and whose destruction they are resolved to seek. The refugees are all Arabs; and the countries in which they find themselves are Arab countries. Yet the advocates of repatriation contend that these Arab refugees should be settled in a non-Arab country, in the only social and cultural environment which is alien to their background and tradition. The Arab refugees are to be uprooted from the soil of nations to which they are akin and loyal—and placed in a State to which they are alien and hostile. Israel, whose sovereignty and safety are already assailed by the States surrounding her, is invited to add to its perils by the influx from hostile territories of masses of people steeped in the hatred of her existence. All this is to happen in a region where the Arab nations possess unlimited opportunities for resettling their kinsmen, and in which Israel has already contributed to a solution of the refugee problems of Asia and Africa by receiving 450,000 refugees from Arab lands among its immigrants.

Surely the Committee will not find it difficult to understand why this solution finds such little favor. In discussing the rights and duties of individuals let us not forget the rights and duties of States. Israel is a small sovereign State whose pri-

mary preoccupation is that of its safety. It cannot in conscience entertain a solution which would involve its own
disruption, and bring misery and disillusionment to refugees
who have surely suffered enough from false hopes and vain
illusions. While every State is entitled to respect for its
security needs, Israel is surely unique in the acuteness of the
threats which surround her. No other State on the face of the
globe is surrounded, as we are, by hostile neighbors who
openly avow its destruction. To suggest that in addition to
facing external perils from the north, south and east, we
should import a massive quantity of hatred and rancor into
our midst is to demand something beyond prudence or reason.

Arab Countries True 'Patria' for Arab Refugees

There are three other considerations which must be placed
on the scale against repatriation. First the word itself is not
accurately used in this context. Transplanting an Arab refugee
from an Arab land to a non-Arab land is not really "repatria·
tion." "Patria" is not a mere geographical concept. Resettlement of a refugee in Israel would be not repatriation, but
alienation from Arab society; a true repatriation of an Arab
refugee would be a process which brought him into union
with people who share his conditions of language and heritage,
his impulses of national loyalty and cultural identity.

Second, the validity of the "repatriation" concept is further
undermined when we examine the structure of the refugee
population. More than 50% of the Arab refugees are under
15 years of age. This means that at the time of Israel's establishment many of those, if born at all at that time, were under
5 years of age. We thus reach the striking fact that a majority
of the refugee population can have no conscious memory of
Israel at all.

Thirdly those who speak of repatriation to Israel might not
always be aware of the measure of existing integration of
refugees into countries of their present residence. In the Kingdom of Jordan, refugees have full citizenship and participate
fully in the Government of the country. They are entitled to
vote and be elected to the Jordanian parliament. Indeed
many of them hold high rank in the government of the kingdom. Thousands of refugees are enrolled in the Jordanian
army and its National Guard. It is, to say the least, eccentric
to suggest that people who are citizens of another land and
are. actually or potentially enrolled in the armed forces of a

country at war with Israel are simultaneously endowed with an optional right of Israel citizenship.

In the Syrian region of Egypt refugees have not been granted citizenship; but by virtue of a law of July 1956, their status is, to a large degree, assimilated to that of citizens. This is especially so in respect of the right to work and to establish commercial enterprises. According to the law of July 1956, refugees are subject to compulsory military service in the Syrian army. Here again, to adduce an unconditional right "repatriation" would signify that those who are citizens of a state foreign and hostile to Israel have a simultaneous right to be regarded as Israel citizens! Is there any state represented here which would acknowledge a right of entry to those who having left its shores have become the citizens of a foreign and hostile state, and have taken military service under Governments which proclaim a state of war against it?

This is merely a striking example of the sharp paradox which we enter if we try to reconcile the slogan of "repatriation" with the actual context, the hard facts of Arab Israel relations.

I do not believe it necessary to speak at any length on the point that resettlement in Arab countries is free from all the disadvantages which adhere to "repatriation." Every condition which has ever contributed to a solution of refugee problems by integration is present in this case. With its expanse of territory, its great rivers, its resources of mineral wealth, its accessibility to international aid, the Arab world is easily capable of absorbing an additional population, not only without danger to itself, but with actual reinforcement of its security and welfare. . . .

Document 36

Golda Meir: A Call for Disarmament

From an address by the then Israeli Foreign Minister before the U.N. General Assembly on October 9, 1962.

The small and new countries, emerging into a world of armed camps, suffer twofold. Our immediate aim is rapid development, but since the danger of war still looms over every dispute, we are constantly burdened with defense expenditures to the detriment of our development needs. We too quickly learn the bitter lesson that those who threaten others must be deterred by some equilibrium, and let not those whose declared policy is to attack their neighbour cry out in mock indignation when the latter seeks some means of defense.

My Government rejects war as a means of settling disputes. From the day that the State of Israel was established, my Government has called for settling all outstanding differences by direct negotiations.

We do not rest content with calling upon the Great Powers to find a way to disarmament, and to settle outstanding problems by negotiation and conciliation between them. We are prepared to put this into practice in the dispute in which we are involved with our neighbours. As we have done in the past, we call again upon the Arab States to agree to complete disarmament with mutual inspection, covering all types of weapons, and to accept that method of direct negotiations as the only means for solving all differences between them and Israel . . .

There are many that are misled by two fallacies regarding the Middle East. The first is that it is an Arab region. In fact there are in it more non-Arabs than Arabs—Moslems, Christians and Jews. This composite pattern of peoples of various faiths and cultures has always been the pattern of the Middle East, each people with its historic continuity, past, present and future.

The second fallacy is that all would be well in that region if it were not for the tension between the Arab States and Israel. I would be the last to underrate the difficulties and dangers which arise from that conflict. But this is only one source of tension in a part of the world which is, unhappily, the scene of so much political instability, economic and social backwardness, rivalry and friction between different countries and regions and the pressures of the cold war. Anyone who follows the affairs of the Middle East knows that during this last year the focus of trouble in the area has been the bitter struggles within the Arab world which have made of the Arab League no longer even a façade of unity.

Israel longs for the day when the political independence and territorial integrity of every single State in the area—Arab and non-Arab—will be assured and when we can all concentrate on the welfare of our people. When I refer to the turmoil in the Arab world, it is because we are a Middle Eastern country and therefore affected by all that affects the peace of our area.

As far as the Israel-Arab dispute itself is concerned, it is well to see clearly what is the basic problem. It is the denial by the Arab States of Israel's right to exist. If this attitude were to change, and if the Arab States and Israel were to discuss their differences at the conference table in a frank and open manner, I am positive that solutions could be found on all the specific issues.

Year after year Israel has come on this rostrum with one demand—peace between it and its Arab neighbours. May I say here that we were grateful to the distinguished Deputy Foreign Minister of Ghana when he drew our attention again to the important statement of President Nkrumah during the 15th General Assembly, in which he called for recognition of the political realities in the Middle East and for insurance against non-aggression. We are entirely in agreement with that view.

The Arab denial of Israel's right of existence has a direct bearing on the distressing refugee problem. We are willing, and always have been willing, to discuss with the Arab Governments what can best be done to secure the future of the refugees in the light of the political and economic realities in the region. But a natural solution to the problem is frustrated by the Arab dream of destroying Israel and openly-proclaimed Arab intention of using the refugees for this purpose.

This design has been openly propagated even from the rostrum of this Assembly. This small spot of land, in which the Jewish people have revived their ancient home and nationhood, must again be wrested from them and they again be scattered to the four corners of the earth. Our neighbours have tried to achieve this by various means, open or guerilla warfare, economic boycott, propaganda and threats.

Negotiations and conciliation are proclaimed from this rostrum as the method to solve all other problems in the world except this one, which must, according to these spokesmen, be resolved by force. For every other nation, they claim co-existence, practised in peace. For Israel, non-existence, to be achieved by war. This doctrine not only runs counter to the basic principles of the United Nations Charter; its acceptance strikes at the very roots of our organization.

The world of today is overwhelmed by ideological disputes, international conflicts and economic controversies. In face of this situation, the basic concepts of the Charter, on the eschewing of force, on the unremitting search for peace, on international co-operation, on negotiation as the means to solve problems, have gained a new depth and significance. As long as negotiation is sought, there is hope. Those who rule out negotiation in the Middle East, those who year after year engage in sterile and stereotyped speeches of hostility, should know that their attitude is irrelevant to the basic theme of the international community and can have no echo in an organization which has proclaimed peace to be synonymous with human survival: that they are assaulting the foundations of human progress.

The policy of the Israel Government has been and continues to be peace. It is peace, not only for the world, but also between us and our neighbours. We believe in co-existence and co-operation everywhere and we shall do everything in our power towards that end . . .

Despite all the speeches which we have heard from Arab representatives, we are convinced that for us and for our neighbours the day must come when we shall live in amity and co-operation. Then will the entire Middle East become a region where the tens of millions of people will dwell in peace and then will its economic potentialities and rich cultural heritage achieve fulfilment. This Israel believes and towards this end we shall devote all our efforts.

Document 37

Fayez A. Sayegh: Zionist Colonialism in Palestine

This statement is from a booklet published in Beirut in 1965 by a leading spokesman of the Palestinian refugees maintaining that the Liberation of Palestine from the Zionist usurpers was the only possible solution of the problem.

In 1948, the Palestinian Arab people was forcibly dispossessed. Most Palestinians were evicted from their country. Their unyielding resistance and their costly sacrifices over three decades had failed to avert the national catastrophe.

But those sacrifices were not in vain. For they safeguarded the Palestinian national rights and underscored the legitimacy of the Arabs' claim to their national heritage. Rights undefended are rights surrendered. Unopposed and acquiesced in, usurpation is legitimized by default. For forfeiture of its patrimony, the Palestinian generation of the Inter-War era will

be indicted by the Palestinian generations to come. It lost indeed—but not without fighting. It was dislodged indeed—but
not for want of the will to defend its heritage.

Nor has the people of Palestine retroactively bestowed un-
deserved legitimacy upon the Zionist colonization of Palestine
by recognizing the *fait accompli* after the fact. Many have
been the self-appointed counselors of "realism", urging upon
Palestinians acknowledgement of the new *status quo* in Palestine and acceptance of their exile "in good grace"; and many
have been the lucrative offers of economic aid for "resettlement" and "rehabilitation" outside Palestine. But the people
which had remained for thirty years undaunted by the combined power of British Imperialism and Zionist Colonialism,
and which subsequently refused to allow the seizure of its land
and the dispersal of its body to conquer its soul also, knew
very well how to resist those siren-calls.

The Zionist settler-state, therefore, has remained a usurper,
lacking even the semblance of legitimacy—because the people
of Palestine has remained loyal to its heritage and faithful to
its rights . . .

The people of Palestine, notwithstanding all its travails and
misfortunes, still has undiminished faith in its future.

And the people of Palestine knows that the pathway to that
future is the liberation of its homeland.

It was in this belief that the Palestinian people—after
sixteen years of dispersion and exile, during which it had
reposed its faith in its return to its country in world conscience and international public opinion, in the United Nations, and/or in the Arab states—chose at last to seize the
initiative. In 1964, it reasserted its corporate personality by
creating the Palestine Liberation Organization.

Only in the liberation of Palestine, spearheaded by Palestinians prepared to pay the price, can the supreme sacrifices
of past generations of Palestinians be vindicated, and the
visions and hopes of living Palestinians be transformed into
reality.

Documents 38–42

Towards the Third Round

The Arab-Israeli conflict again escalated with the Egyptian
decision in mid-May, 1967 to concentrate troops in Sinai
and the announcement that the Straits of Tiran would be

closed to Israeli shipping. In his speech on May 25, Nasser said that "under no circumstances" would he allow the Israeli flag to pass the Straits. On the day after: "Recently we felt we are strong enough, that if we were to enter a battle with Israel, with God's help, we could triumph" (Document 39). On the 29th: "The issue now at hand is not the Gulf of Aqabah but the rights of the Palestinian people" (Document 41). Meanwhile Hassanain Haykal, Egypt's leading spokesman, had explained (on May 26— Document 40) why a war with Israel was inevitable. On June 9, after the Egyptian defeat, Nasser announced his resignation (Document 42), but several hours after, following demonstrations in Cairo, withdrew it. The summing up of the war and its pre-history as Nasser saw it, appears in Part IV of this Reader (page 197).

Document 38

Nasser's Speech at UAR Advanced Air Headquarters, May 25, 1967

The entire country looks up to you today. The entire Arab nation supports you. It is clear that in these circumstances the entire people support you completely and consider the armed forces as their hope today. It is also a fact that the entire Arab nation supports our armed forces in the current situation through which the entire Arab nation is passing.

What I wish to say is that we are now in 1967 and not in 1956 after the tripartite aggression. A great deal was said then and all the secrets revealed had a double interpretation. Israel, its commanders and rulers, boasted a great deal after 1956. I have read every word written about the 1956 events and I also know exactly what happened in 1956.

On the night of 29th October 1956 the Israeli aggression against us began. Fighting began on 30th October. We received the Anglo-Frenoh ultimatum which asked us to withdraw several miles west of the Suez Canal. On 31st October the Anglo-French attack on us began. The air raids began at sunset on 31st October. At the same time all our forces in Sinai were withdrawn completely to inside Egypt.

Thus in 1956 we did not have an opportunity to fight Israel. We decided to withdraw before the actual fighting with Israel began. Despite our decision to withdraw Israel was unable to occupy any of our positions except after we left them. Yet Israel created a major uproar, boasted and said a great deal about the Sinai campaign and the Sinai battle. Everyone of you knows all the rubbish that was said. They probably believed what they said themselves.

Today, more than 10 years after Suez all the secrets have been exposed. The most important secret concerns when they brought Ben Gurion to France to employ him as a dog for imperialism, to begin the operation. Ben Gurion refused to undertake anything unless he was given a written guarantee that they would protect him from the Egyptian bombers and the Egyptian Air Force. All this is now no longer secret. The entire world knows. It was on this basis that France sent fighter aircraft to Ben Gurion, and it was also on this basis that Britain pledged to Ben Gurion to bomb Egyptian airfields within 24 hours after the aggression began.

This goes to show how much they took into account the Egyptian forces. Ben Gurion himself said he had to think about the Haifa-Jerusalem-Tel Aviv triangle, which holds one-third of Israel's population. He could not attack Egypt out of fear of the Egyptian air force and bombers. At that time we had a few Ilyushin bombers. We had just acquired them to arm ourselves. Today we have many Ilyushins and other aircraft. There is a great difference between yesterday and today, between 1956 and 1967. Why do I say all this? I say it because we are in a confrontation with Israel. Israel today is not backed by Britain and France as was the case in 1956. It has the United States supporting it and supplying it with arms. But the world cannot again accept the plotting which took place in 1956.

Israel has been clamouring since 1956. They spoke of Israel's competence and high standard of training. It was backed in this by the West and the Western press. They capitalised on the Sinai campaign where no fighting actually took place because we withdrew to confront Britain and France.

Today we have a chance to prove the fact. We have, indeed, a chance to make the world see matters in their true perspective. We are now face to face with Israel. In recent days Israel has been making aggressive threats and boasting. On 12th May a very impertinent statement was made. Anyone reading this statement must believe that these people are so boastful and deceitful that one simply cannot remain silent.

The statement said that the Israeli commanders announced they would carry out military operations against Syria in order to occupy Damascus and overthrow the Syrian Government. On the same day the Israeli Premier, Eshkol, made a very threatening statement against Syria. At the same time the commentaries said that Israel believed that Egypt could not make a move because it was bogged down in Yemen.

Of course they say that we are bogged down in Yemen and have problems there. We are in Yemen but they seem to have believed the lies they have been saying all these years about our being in Yemen. It is very possible that the Israelis themselves believed such lies. We are capable of carrying out our duties in Yemen and at the same time doing our national duty here in Egypt, both in defending our borders and in attacking if Israel attacks any Arab country.

On 13th May we received accurate information that Israel was concentrating on the Syrian border huge armed forces of about 11 to 13 brigades. These forces were divided into two fronts, one south of Lake Tiberias and the other north of the Lake. The decision made by Israel at this time was to carry out an attack against Syria starting on 17th May. On 14th May we took action, discussed the matter and contacted our Syrian brothers. The Syrians also had this information. Based on the information Lt-Gen. Mahmud Fawzi left for Syria to co-ordinate matters. We told them that we had decided that if Syria was attacked Egypt would enter the battle right from the start. This was the situation on 14th May; forces began to move in the direction of Sinai to take up their normal positions.

News agencies reported yesterday that these military movements must have been the result of a previously well laid plan. I say that the sequence of events determined the plan. We had no plan prior to 13th May because we believed that Israel would not have dared to make such an impertinent statement.

On 16th May we requested the withdrawal of the United Nations Emergency Force [UNEF] in a letter from Lt-Gen. Mahmud Fawzi. We requested the complete withdrawal of the UNEF. A major world wide campaign, led by the United States, Britain and Canada, began opposing the withdrawal of the UNEF from Egypt. Thus we felt that attempts were being made to turn the UNEF into a force serving neo-imperialism. It is obvious that the UNEF entered Egypt with our approval and therefore cannot continue to stay in Egypt except with our approval. Until yesterday a great deal was said about the UNEF. A campaign is also being mounted against the UN Secretary-General because he made a faithful and honest decision and could not surrender to the pressure brought to bear upon him by the United States, Britain and Canada to make the UNEF an instrument for implementing imperialism's plans.

It is quite natural, and I say this quite frankly, that had the UNEF ignored its basic task and turned to working for the aims of imperialism we would have regarded it as a hostile force and forcibly disarmed it. We are definitely capable of doing such a job. I say this now not to discredit the UNEF but to those who have neo-imperialist ideas and who want the UN to achieve their neo-imperialist aims—that there is not a single nation which respects itself and enjoys full sovereignty which could accept these methods in any shape or form. At the same time I say that the UNEF has honourably and faithfully carried out its duties. The UN Secretary-General refused to succumb to pressure. He issued immediate orders to the UNEF to withdraw. Consequently we praise the UNEF which has stayed 10 years in our country serving peace. And when they left—at a time when we found that the neo-imperialist force wanted to divert them from their basic task—we gave them a cheerful send-off and saluted them.

Our forces are now in Sinai and we are fully mobilised both in Gaza and Sinai. We notice that there is a great deal of talk about peace these days. Peace, peace, international peace, international security, UN intervention, and so on and so forth, all appears daily in the press. Why is it that no one spoke about peace, the UN and security when on 12th May the Israeli premier and the Israeli commanders made their statements that they would occupy Damascus, overthrow the Syrian regime, strike vigorously at Syria, and occupy a part of Syria? It was obvious that the press approved of the statements made by the Israeli premier and commanders.

There is talk about peace now. What peace? If there is a true desire for peace we say that we also work for peace. But does peace mean ignoring the rights of the Palestinian people because of the passage of time? Does peace mean that we should concede our rights because of the passage of time? Nowadays they speak about a UN presence in the region for the sake of peace. Does a UN presence in the region for peace mean that we should close our eyes to everything? The UN has adopted a number of resolutions in favour of the Palestinian people. Israel has implemented none of these resolutions. This brought no reaction from the UN.

Today US Senators, members of the House of Representatives, the press and the entire world speak in favour of Israel, of the Jews. But nothing is said in the Arabs' favour. The UN resolutions which favour the Arabs have not been implemented. What does this mean? No one is speaking in the Arabs' favour. How does the UN stand with regard to the Palestinian people? How does it stand with regard to the rights of the Palestinian people? How does it stand with regard to the tragedy which has continued since 1948? Talk of peace is heard only when Israel is in danger. But when Arab rights and the rights of the Palestinian people are lost, no one speaks about peace, rights, or anything like this.

It is clear, therefore, than an alliance exists between the Western powers, chiefly represented by the United States and Britain, with Israel. There is a political alliance. This political alliance prompts the Western powers to give military equipment to Israel. Yesterday and the day before yesterday the entire world was speaking about Sharm ash-Shaykh, navigation in the Gulf of Aqabah, and Eilat Port. This morning I heard the BBC say that in 1956 Abd an-Nasir promised to open the Gulf of Aqabah.

Of course, this is not true. It was copied from a British paper called the 'Daily Mail.' No such thing happened. Abd an-Nasir would never forfeit any UAR right. As I said, we would never give away a grain of sand from our soil or our country.

The armed forces' responsibility is now yours. The armed forces yesterday occupied Sharm ash-Shaykh. What does this mean? It is affirmation of our rights and our sovereignty over the Gulf of Aqabah which constitutes Egyptian territorial waters. Under no circumstances will we allow the Israeli flag to pass through the Gulf of Aqabah.

The Jews threaten war. We tell them you are welcome, we are ready for war. Our armed forces and all our people are ready for war, but under no circumstances will we abandon any of our rights. This water is ours. War might be an opportunity for the Jews, for Israel and Rabin, to test their forces against ours and to see that what they wrote about the 1956 battle and the occupation of Sinai was all a lot of nonsense.

With all this there is imperialism, Israel and reaction. Reaction casts doubt on everything and so does the Islamic alliance. We all know that the Islamic alliance is now represented by three states: the Kingdom of Saudi Arabia, the Kingdom of Jordan and Iran. They are saying that the purpose of the Islamic alliance is to reunite the Muslim against Israel. I would like the Islamic alliance to serve the Palestine question in only one way—by preventing the supply of oil to Israel. The oil which now reaches Israel, which reaches Eilat, comes from some of the Islamic alliance states. It goes to Eilat from Iran. Who then is supplying Israel with oil? The Islamic alliance—Iran, an Islamic alliance state. Such is the Islamic alliance. It is an imperialist alliance and this means it sides with Zionism because Zionism is the main ally of imperialism.

The Arab world, which is now mobilised to the highest degree, knows all this. It knows how to deal with the imperialist agents, the allies of Zionism and the fifth column.

They say they want to co-ordinate their plans with us. We cannot co-ordinate our plans in any way with Islamic alliance members because it would mean giving our plans to the Jews and to Israel. This is a vital battle. When we said that we were ready for the battle we meant that we would surely fight if Syria or any other Arab state was subjected to aggression.

The armed forces are now everywhere. The army and all the forces are now mobilised and so are the people. They are all behind you, praying for you day and night and believing that you are the pride of their nation, of the Arab nation. This is the feeling of the Arab people in Egypt and outside Egypt. We are confident that you will honour the trust. Everyone of us is ready to die and not give away a grain of his country's sand. This for us is the greatest honour. It is the greatest honour for us to defend our country. We are not scared by the imperialist, Zionist or reactionary campaigns. We are independent and we know the taste of freedom. We have built a strong national army and achieved our aims. We are building our country. There is currently a propaganda campaign, a psychological campaign, and a campaign of doubt against us. We leave all this behind us and follow the course of duty and victory. May God be with you.

Document 39

Nasser's Speech to Arab Trade Unionists, May 26, 1967

Thank you for this initiative. You have provided me with an opportunity to see you. I have actually heard your speeches and resolutions, there is nothing to add during this meeting to what you have already said. You, the Arab workers' federation, represent the biggest force in the Arab world.

We can achieve much by Arab actions, which is a main part of our battle. We must develop and build our countries to face the challenge of our enemies. The Arab world now is very different from what it was 10 days ago. Israel is also different from what it was 10 days ago. Despair has never found its way into Arab hearts and never will. The Arabs insist on their rights and are determined to regain the rights of the Palestinian people. The Arabs must accomplish this set intention and this aim. The first elements of this aim appeared in the test of Syria and Egypt in facing the Israeli threat. I believe that this test was a major starting point and basis from which to achieve complete cohesion in the Arab world. What we see today in the masses of the Arab people everywhere is their desire to fight. The Arab people want to regain the rights of the people of Palestine.

For several years, many people have raised doubts about our intentions towards Palestine. But talk is easy and action is difficult, very difficult. We emerged wounded from the 1956 battle. Britain, Israel and France attacked us then. We sustained heavy losses in 1956. Later, union was achieved. The 1961 secession occurred when we had only just got completely together and had barely begun to stand firmly on our feet.

Later the Yemeni revolution broke out. We considered it our duty to rescue our brothers, simply because of the principles and ideals which we advocated and still advocate.

We were waiting for the day when we would be fully prepared and confident of being able to adopt strong measures if we were to enter the battle with Israel. I say nothing aimlessly. One day two years ago, I stood up to say that we have no plan to liberate Palestine and that revolutionary action is our only course to liberate Palestine. I spoke at the summit conferences. The summit conferences were meant to prepare the Arab states to defend themselves.

Recently we felt we are strong enough, that if we were to enter a battle with Israel, with God's help, we could triumph. On this basis, we decided to take actual steps.

A great deal has been said in the past about the UN Emergency Force (UNEF). Many people blamed us for UNEF's presence. We were not strong enough. Should we have listened to them, or rather built and trained our Army while UNEF still existed? I said once that we could tell UNEF to leave within half an hour. Once we were fully prepared we could ask UNEF to leave. And this is what actually happened.

The same thing happened with regard to Sharm al Shaykh. We were also attacked on this score by some Arabs. Taking Sharm al Shaykh meant confrontation with Israel. Taking such action also meant that we were ready to enter a general war with Israel. It was not a separate operation. Therefore we had to take this fact into consideration when moving to Sharm al Shaykh. The present operation was mounted on this basis.

Actually I was authorised by the [Arab Socialist Union's] Supreme Executive Committee to implement this plan at the right time. The right time came when Syria was threatened with aggression. We sent reconnaissance aircraft over Israel. Not a single brigade was stationed opposite us on the Israeli side of the border. All Israeli brigades were confronting Syria. All but four brigades have now moved south to confront Egypt. Those four are still on the border with Syria. We are confident that once we have entered the battle we will triumph, God willing.

With regard to military plans, there is complete co-ordination of military action between us and Syria. We will operate as one army fighting a single battle for the sake of a common objective—the objective of the Arab nation.

The problem today is not just Israel, but also those behind it. If Israel embarks on an aggression against Syria or Egypt the battle against Israel will be a general one and not confined to one spot on the Syrian or Egyptian borders. The battle will be a general one and our basic objective will be to destroy Israel. I probably could not have said such things five or even three years ago. If I had said such things and had been unable to carry them out my words would have been empty and worthless.

Today, some 11 years after 1956, I say such things because I am confident. I know what we have here in Egypt and what

Syria has. I also know that other states—Iraq, for instance, has sent its troops to Syria; Algeria will send troops; Kuwait also will send troops. They will send armoured and infantry units. This is Arab power. This is the true resurrection of the Arab nation, which at one time was probably in despair.

Today people must know the reality of the Arab world. What is Israel? Israel today is the United States. The United States is the chief defender of Israel. As for Britain, I consider it America's lackey. Britain does not have an independent policy. Wilson always follows Johnson's steps and says what he wants him to say. All Western countries take Israel's view.

The Gulf of Aqabah was a closed waterway prior to 1956. We used to search British, US, French and all other ships. After the tripartite aggression—and we all know the tripartite plot—we left the area to UNEF which came here under a UN resolution to make possible the withdrawal of Britain, France and Israel. The Israelis say they opened the maritime route. I say they told lies and believed their own lies. We withdrew because the British and the French attacked us. This battle was never between us and Israel alone.

I have recently been with the armed forces. All the armed forces are ready for a battle face to face between the Arabs and Israel. Those behind Israel are also welcome.

We must know and learn a big lesson today. We must actually see that in its hypocrisy and in its talks with the Arabs, the United States sides with Israel 100 per cent and is partial in favour of Israel. Why is Britain biased towards Israel? The West is on Israel's side. Gen. de Gaulle's personality caused him to remain impartial on this question and not to toe the US or the British line; France therefore did not take sides with Israel.

The Soviet Union's attitude was great and splendid. It supported the Arabs and the Arab nation. It went to the extent of stating that, together with the Arabs and the Arab nation, it would resist any interference or aggression.

Today every Arab knows foes and friends. If we do not learn who our enemies and our friends are, Israel will always be able to benefit from this behaviour. It is clear that the United States is an enemy of the Arab because it is completely biased in favour of Israel. It is also clear that Britain is an enemy of the Arabs because she, too, is completely biased in favour of Israel. On this basis we must treat our enemies and those who side with our enemies as our actual enemies. We can accord them such treatment. In fact we are not states without status. We are states of status, occupying an important place in the world. Our states have thousands of years of civilisation behind them—7,000 years of civilisation. Indeed, we can do much; we can expose the hypocrisy—the hypocrisy of our enemies if they try to persuade us that they wish to serve our interests. The United States seeks to serve only Israel's interests. Britain also seeks to serve only Israel's interests.

The question is not one of international law. Why all this uproar because of the closure of the Gulf of Aqabah? When Eshkol and Rabin threatened Syria, nobody spoke about peace or threats to peace. They actually hate the progressive regime in Syria. The United States, Britain and reaction—which is the friend of the United States and Britain—do not favour the national progressive regime in Syria. Israel, of course, shares their feelings. Israel is an ally of the United States and Britain. When Israel threatened Syria, they kept quiet and accepted what it said. But when we exercise one of our legitimate rights, as we always do, they turn the world upside down and speak about threats to peace and about a crisis in the Middle East. They fabricate these matters and threaten us with war.

We shall not relinquish our rights. We shall not concede our right in the Gulf of Aqabah. Today, the people of Egypt, the Syrian Army, and the Egyptian Army comprise one front. We want the entire front surrounding Israel to become one front. We want this. Naturally there are obstacles at present. Of course, Wasfi at-Tall is a spy for the Americans and the British. We cannot co-operate with these spies in any form, because the battle is one of destiny and the spies have no place in this battle. We want the front to become one united front around Israel. We will not relinquish the rights of the people of Palestine, as I have said before. I was told at the time that I might have to wait 70 years. During the crusader's occupation, the Arabs waited 70 years before a suitable opportunity arose and they drove away the crusaders. Some people commented that Abd an-Nasir said we should shelve the Palestinian question for 70 years. I do not mean exactly 70 years, but I say that as a people with an ancient civilisation, as an Arab people, we are determined that the Palestine question will not be liquidated or forgotten. The whole question then, is the proper time to achieve our aims. We are preparing ourselves constantly.

You are the hope of the Arab nation and its vanguard. As workers, you are actually building the Arab nation. The quicker we build, the quicker we will be able to achieve our aim. I thank you for your visit and wish you every success. Please convey my greetings and best wishes to the Arab workers in every Arab country.

Document 40

Hassanain Haykal: An Armed Clash with Israel Is Inevitable—Why?

Al Ahram, May 26, 1967.

It is extremely difficult to write about current events, particularly when such events are as swift and violent as a hurricane. But it is easy to write about what has already happened, to give an account and analysis of facts. It is also safe to write about what could take place in the future, because the future is boundless. Tomorrow never comes because every day has a tomorrow. The real problem is to speak about what is taking place while it happens. Then every interpretation may endure only a few minutes or even seconds.

There are two considerations which make the problem even more difficult: the topic is one of destiny and life, and there is the need for rational, intelligent writing without indulging in a long composition or platitudes.

What I am going to say after this introduction will in fact be no more than a collection of observations which I think are important at present. The first observation is that I believe an armed clash between the UAR and Israel is inevitable. This armed clash could occur at any moment, at any place along the line of confrontation between the Egyptian forces and the enemy Israeli forces—on land, air or sea along the area extending from Gaza in the North to the Gulf of Aqabah at Sharm ash-Shaykh in the South. But why do I emphasise this in such a manner? There are many reasons, particularly the psychological factor and its effect on the balance of power in the Middle East.

Passage through the Gulf of Aqabah is economically important to Israel at a time when it is suffering the symptoms a man has on waking up after a long, boisterous and drunken party. The fountains of German reparations are drying up. Israel has also drained the sources of contributions and gifts. Although emergency sources will emerge as a result of the present crisis, particularly with the help of Western propaganda trumpets, people in the West, at least many of them, are getting tired of an entity which has been unable to lead a normal life, like a child who does not want to grow up, who cannot depend on himself and does not want to take on any responsibility. Israel is suffering from an economic crisis. There are over 100,000 unemployed, nearly one quarter of Israel's manpower. The new blow had added to the economic plight. Israel attached great importance to its trade with East Africa and Asia. This trade depended on one route: the Red Sea via the Gulf of Aqabah, to Eilat. There were many projects for enlarging the port of Eilat, which at present can handle 400,000 tons a year. In addition, there were the oil lines. Israel has built two pipelines to carry Iranian oil from Eilat to the Haifa oil refinery. Israel has also dreamed of digging a canal from Eilat to Ashdod to compete with or replace the Suez Canal.

In my personal opinion all these important economic matters and questions are not the decisive factor which will influence or dictate the Israeli reaction to the closure of the Gulf of Aqabah. The decisive factor in my opinion is the psychological factor. The economic aspect swings back and forth between yes and no. From this aspect the challenge of war can be either accepted or put off. But the psychological factor cannot swing back and forth. From this aspect there is one answer: Yes. It is in the light of the compelling psychological factor that the needs of security, of survival itself, make acceptance of the challenge of war inevitable.

One thing is clear: The closure of the Gulf of Aqabah to Israeli navigation and the ban on the import of strategic goods, even when carried by non-Israeli ships, means first and last that the Arab nation represented by the UAR has succeeded for the first time, *vis-à-vis* Israel, in changing by force a *fait accompli* imposed on it by force. This is the essence of the problem, regardless of the complications surrounding it and future contingencies.

As for the complications, we can find in the past ample justification for Arab resistance. We could say that the British mandate in Palestine had sold Palestine to Zionism in accordance with a resolution adopted by the League of Nations. This is true. We could say that the UN betrayed Palestine, and this is true. We could say Arab reaction from the Jordanian King Abdullah to the Saudi King Faysal connived at the plot against Palestine, and this is true. We could say about the Gulf of Aqabah that in 1956 imperialism, represented by the British and French forces, imposed a *fait accompli* during this period from autumn 1956 to spring 1967. It was imperialist not Israeli arms which imposed this *fait accompli*. We could say all this is seeking to justify Arab resistance. But the naked and rocky truth which remains after all this is that the accomplished fact was aggressively imposed by force. The Arabs did not have the force to resist the accomplished fact, let alone to change it by force and to impose a substitute consistent with their rights and interests.

As for the contingencies which may be precipitated by this new development, I do not think I need go into detail.

Israel has built its existence, security and future on force. The prevalent philosophy of its rulers has been that the Arab quakes before the forbidding glance, and that nothing deters him but fear. Thus Israeli intimidation reached its peak. Provocation went beyond tolerable bounds. But all of this, from the Israeli point of view, had the psychological aim of convincing the Arabs that Israel could do anything and that the Arabs could do nothing; that Israel was omnipotent and could impose any accomplished fact, while the Arabs were weak and had to accept any accomplished fact. Despite the error and danger in this Israeli philosophy—because two or even three million Israelis cannot by military force or by myth dominate a sea of 80 million Arabs—this philosophy remained a conviction deeply embedded in Israeli thinking, planning and action for many disturbing years, without any Arab challenge capable of restoring matters to their proper perspective.

Now this is the first time the Arabs have challenged Israel in an attempt to change an accomplished fact by force and to replace it by force with an alternative accomplished fact consistent with their rights and interests. The opening of the Gulf of Aqabah to Israel was an accomplished fact imposed by the force of imperialist arms. This week the closure of the Gulf of Aqabah to Israel was an alternative accomplished fact imposed and now being protected by the force of Arab arms. To Israel this is the most dangerous aspect of the current situation . . . Therefore it is not a matter of the Gulf of Aqabah but of something bigger. It is the whole philosophy of Israeli security. It is the philosophy on which Israeli existence has pivoted since its birth and on which it will pivot in the future.

Hence I say that Israel must resort to arms. Therefore I

say that an armed clash between UAR and the Israeli enemy is inevitable.

As from now, we must expect the enemy to deal us the first blow in the battle. But as we wait for that first blow, we should try to minimise its effect as much as possible. The second blow will then follow. But this will be the blow we will deliver against the enemy in retaliation and deterrence. It will be the most effective blow we can possibly deal. Why do I say this now? My point of view is as follows:

When one studies the strategy of the Egyptian action of the 10 great days from 14th to 23rd May in which the positions and balance in the Middle East changed, one will immediately perceive two factors which at first sight may appear contradictory: The first factor: Egypt was ready and prepared. The second factor: the Egyptian action was a complete surprise, even to Egypt in so far as it was a reaction to a specific situation, namely, Israel's threat to and readiness to invade Syria.

By analysing the first factor in the strategy of the Egyptian action during the 10 great days which changed the positions and balance in the Middle East we find that there are roots extending from the spring of 1967 back to the time when the UAR called for the Arab summit conferences. The first summit conference was convened in January 1964. The first item submitted by the UAR to that conference was the Jordan headwaters. At that time the anti-Egyptian Western propaganda which was backed by the reactionary elements sought, discreetly at times but most of the time shamelessly, to hamper Egyptian policy at that time by two propaganda themes: (1) that Egypt's whole aim in the summit conferences policy was to settle the Yemeni issue with Saudi Arabia; (2) that when Egypt called for the summit conferences it wanted to abandon the responsibility of action for Palestine, in accordance with the traditional method which says that when you face a problem for which you cannot find a solution the only way to bury and get rid of it is to form a commission to discuss and study it. All this, of course, was untrue, since Egypt at the time imagined that the Arab summit conferences could draw up the policy of the liberation battle and could prepare for it. Egypt wanted unified action to be the front of a broad movement which might have world-wide political influence serving the strategy of battle. Besides, unified Arab action might be beneficial in providing possibilities for defending Arab countries which at that time did not have reassuring defences. At

the same time Egypt believed that when the time came for
earnest action, loyalty and fidelity to the trust dictated that
it should primarily depend on itself.

Accordingly the summit conferences were a broad front
suitable for world-wide political influence. It was also possible
for them to help strengthen the defence of Arab countries surrounding Israel. Behind this broad front and the consolidation
of the other Arab countries surrounding Israel Egypt could
prepare and mobilise its own effective forces.

The remainder of the story of the summit conferences is
known and I do not propose to repeat it. It ended in utter
failure because of Arab reactionary rancour, and because
reaction had greater hatred for Arab social progress than for
the Israeli enemy, which wants to humiliate all the Arabs
whatever their social views. The broad front for unified Arab
action therefore collapsed with the failure of the summit
conferences. The possibilities of strengthening the defence of
the other Arab countries surrounding Israel did not sufficiently
materialise as they should have done. Egypt was unable to
control all those circumstances but it was able to control
the third objective, namely, to prepare and mobilise its
effective forces.

Anti-Egyptian Western propaganda, backed by the Arab
reactionary elements, continued to attack Egypt fiercely. The
attack went to the length of spreading the belief that the
entire Egyptian Army had perished in Yemen, had been
scattered into aimless groups, and that the remainder had
been killed, wounded or captured. Similarly it was said that
the Egyptian economy was collapsing and could not stand on
its feet, let alone bear the weight of any bold venture and
carry on with it. But Egypt knew the truth and was confident
that the truth would appear to the entire Arab nation one day
when the time was ripe for serious action.

Egypt, then, was prepared and ready. This is the first fact
about the strategy of Egyptian action during the 10 great days.

I will now come to the second factor in the crisis. This
factor is that the Egyptian action was a complete surprise.
It appears, and it is now almost certain, that the forces hostile
to Egypt, that is imperialism, Arab reaction and Israel, had
come in the end to believe their own propaganda. People
sometimes fall prey to the lies they themselves fabricate.
Something of that sort must certainly have happened, otherwise Israel would not have persisted in its threats against
Syria and gone to the length of the cry of 'March on Damas-

cus.' It must have felt certain that there would be no decisive Egyptian reaction, because there were insufficient forces for any initiative or retaliatory action.

It was this Israeli threat to Syria and information confirming it concerning intentions and plans that precipitated the emergency situation to which Egypt had to react immediately, even though it came as a surprise to it. There was preparation and mobilisation of the effective Egyptian forces. There was national consciousness and abidance by its principles. There was creative leadership. What I mean to say is that Egypt was not prepared for this specific contingency but was prepared for all contingencies including such a one.

Now, to turn to the march of events during the 10 great days which changed the situation and the balance of the Middle East. Events began to move. One calculated and effective step followed another: the decision was taken to implement the joint defence agreement with Syria—this is the decision which Lt-Gen. Muhammad Fawzi, the Chief of Staff of the Egyptian Armed Forces, carried on the five-hour visit to Damascus. Then followed the message addressed by Lt-Gen. Muhammad Fawzi to the Commander of the UN Emergency Force to withdraw his forces from the Egyptian borders with Israel. The Egyptian Armed Forces then, without waiting, actually began occupying all the border positions. The Foreign Minister Mahmud Riyad then sent his message to the UN Secretary-General U Thant on the withdrawal and evacuation of the Emergency Forces in the UAR and Gaza. Then followed the advance on Sharm al Shaykh, the entrance to the Gulf of Aqabah; the order was issued to close the Gulf of Aqabah to Israeli shipping and to strategic goods for Israel even if transported aboard non-Israeli ships; and all the US initiatives were rejected. All these actions were backed by a massive, ready force enjoying a morale brimming over with a fighting spirit the like of which the Middle East has never seen.

Two results were thus achieved, that is to say: (1) The plan against Syria collapsed; the invasion of Syria became impossible because all of the enemy forces streamed into the South to confront the Egyptian concentration. (2) The accomplished fact which the British-French invasion, and not the Israeli Army, had imposed in 1956 to the benefit of Israel, was changed.

In other words the strategy of this stage achieved its first objective by frustrating the plot to invade Syria, and moreɔver, it achieved another longed-for and precious objective: the return of the armed forces to direct confrontation with Israel and the closing once again of the door to the Gulf of Aqabah in Israel's face.

Is this, then, the end of the matter? I would answer that I have explained—or rather tried to explain—with the first observation in this inquiry that the problem has not ended but rather has hardly begun. This is because I am confident that for many reasons, chiefly the psychological, Israel cannot accept or remain indifferent to what has taken place. In my opinion it simply cannot do so. This means, and that is what I intend to say in the second observation of this inquiry that the next move is up to Israel. Israel has to reply now. It has to deal a blow. We have to be ready for it, as I said, to minimise its effect as much as possible. Then it will be our turn to deal the second blow, which we will deliver with the utmost possible effectiveness.

In short, Egypt has exercised its power and achieved the objectives of this stage without resorting to arms so far. But Israel has no alternative but to use arms if it wants to exercise power. This means that the logic of the fearful confrontation now taking place between Egypt, which is fortified by the might of the masses of the Arab nation, and Israel, which is fortified by the illusion of American might, dictates that Egypt, after all it has now succeeded in achieving must wait, even though it has to wait for a blow. This is necessitated also by the sound conduct of the battle, particularly from the international point of view. Let Israel begin. Let our second blow then be ready. Let it be a knockout.

Document 41

Nasser's Speech to National Assembly Members on May 29, 1967

Brothers, when Brother Anwar as Sadat informed me of your decision to meet me I told him that I myself was prepared to call on you at the National Assembly, but he said you were determined to come. I therefore responded to this and I thank you heartily for your consideration.

I was naturally not surprised by the law which Brother Anwar as Sadat read because I was notified of it before I came here. However, I wish to thank you very much for your feelings and for the powers given me. I did not ask for such powers because I felt that you and I were as one, that we could co-operate and work for the sublime interest of this country giving a great example of unselfishness and of work for the welfare of all. Thanks be to God, for four years now the National Assembly has been working and has given great examples. We have given great examples in co-operation and unselfishness and in placing before us the sublime and highest objective—the interest of this nation.

I am proud of this resolution and law. I promise you that I will use it only when necessary. I will, however, send all the laws to you. Thank you once again. The great gesture of moral support represented by this law is very valuable to my spirit and heart. I heartily thank you for this feeling and this initiative.

The circumstances through which we are now passing are in fact difficult ones because we are not only confronting Israel but also those who created Israel and who are behind Israel. We are confronting Israel and the West as well—the West, which created Israel and which despised us Arabs and which ignored us before and since 1948. They had no regard whatsoever for our feelings, our hopes in life, or our rights. The West completely ignored us, and the Arab nation was unable to check the West's course.

Then came the events of 1956—the Suez battle. We all know what happened in 1956. When we rose to demand our rights. Britain, France and Israel opposed us, and we were faced with the tripartite aggression. We resisted, however, and proclaimed that we would fight to the last drop of our blood. God gave us success and God's victory was great.

Subsequently we were able to rise and to build. Now, 11 years after 1956, we are restoring things to what they were in 1956. This is from the material aspect. In my opinion this material aspect is only a small part, whereas the spiritual aspect is the great side of the issue. The spiritual aspect involves the renaissance of the Arab nation, the revival of the Palestine question, and the restoration of confidence to every Arab and to every Palestinian. This is on the basis that if we are able to restore conditions to what they were before 1956 God will surely help and urge us to restore the situation to what it was in 1948 [prolonged applause].

Brothers, the revolt, upheaval and commotion which we now see taking place in every Arab country are not only because we have returned to the Gulf of Aqabah or rid ourselves of the UNEF, but because we have restored Arab honour and renewed Arab hopes.

Israel used to boast a great deal, and the Western powers, headed by the United States and Britain, used to ignore and even despise us and consider us of no value. But now that the time has come—and I have already said in the past that we will decide the time and place and not allow them to decide—we must be ready for triumph and not for a recurrence of the 1948 comedies. We shall triumph, God willing.

Preparations have already been made. We are now ready to confront Israel. They have claimed many things about the 1956 Suez war, but no one believed them after the secrets of the 1956 collusion were uncovered—that mean collusion in which Israel took part. Now we are ready for the confrontation. We are now ready to deal with the entire Palestine question.

The issue now at hand is not the Gulf of Aqabah, the Straits of Tiran, or the withdrawal of the UNEF, but the rights of the Palestine people. It is the aggression which took place in Palestine in 1948 with the collaboration of Britain and the United States. It is the expulsion of the Arabs from Palestine, the usurpation of their rights, and the plunder of their property. It is the disavowal of all the UN resolutions in favour of the Palestinian people.

The issue today is far more serious than they say. They want to confine the issue to the Straits of Tiran, the UNEF and the right of passage. We demand the full rights of the Palestinian people. We say this out of our belief that Arab rights cannot be squandered because the Arabs throughout the Arab world are demanding these Arab rights.

We are not afraid of the United States and its threats, of Britain and her threats, or of the entire Western world and its partiality to Israel. The United States and Britain are partial to Israel and give no consideration to the Arabs, to the entire Arab nation. Why? Because we have made them believe that we cannot distinguish between friend and foe. We must make them know that we know who our foes are and who our friends are and treat them accordingly.

If the United States and Britain are partial to Israel, we must say that our enemy is not only Israel but also the United States and Britain and treat them as such. If the Western Powers disavow our rights and ridicule and despise us, we Arabs must teach them to respect us and take us seriously. Otherwise all our talk about Palestine, the Palestine people, and Palestinian rights will be null and void and of no consequence. We must treat enemies as enemies and friends as friends.

I said yesterday that the States that champion freedom and peace have supported us. I spoke of the support given us by India, Pakistan, Afghanistan, Yugoslavia, Malaysia, the Chinese People's Republic and the Asian and African States.

After my statements yesterday I met the War Minister Shams Badran and learned from him what took place in Moscow. I wish to tell you today that the Soviet Union is a friendly Power and stands by us as a friend. In all our dealings with the Soviet Union—and I have been dealing with the USSR since 1955—it has not made a single request of us. The USSR has never interfered in our policy or internal affairs. This is the USSR as we have always known it. In fact, it is we who have made urgent requests of the USSR. Last year we asked for wheat and they sent it to us. When I also asked for all kinds of arms they gave them to us. When I met Shams Badran yesterday he handed me a message from the Soviet Premier Kosygin saying that the USSR supported us in this battle and would not allow any Power to intervene until matters were restored to what they were in 1956.

Brothers, we must distinguish between friend and foe, friend and hypocrite. We must be able to tell who is making requests, who has ulterior motives, and who is applying economic pressure. We must also know those who offer their friendship to us for no other reason than a desire for freedom and peace.

In the name of the UAR people, I thank the people of the USSR for their great attitude, which is the attitude of a real friend. This is the kind of attitude we expect. I said yesterday that we had not requested the USSR or any other state to intervene, because we really want to avoid any confrontation which might lead to a world war and also because we really work for peace and advocate world peace. When we voiced the policy of non-alignment, our chief aim was world peace.

Brothers, we will work for world peace with all the power at our disposal, but we will also hold tenaciously to our rights with all the power at our disposal. This is our course. On this occasion, I address myself to our brothers in Aden and say: Although occupied with this battle, we have not forgotten you. We are with you. We have not forgotten the struggle of Aden and the occupied South for liberation. Aden and the occupied South must be liberated and colonialism

must end. We are with them; present matters have not taken
our minds from Aden.

I thank you for taking the trouble to pay this visit. Moreover, your presence is an honour to the Qubbah Palace, and I
am pleased to have met you. Peace be with you.

Document 42

Nasser's Resignation Broadcast, June 9, 1967

Brothers, at times of triumph and tribulation, in the sweet
hours and bitter hours, we have become accustomed to sit
together to discuss things, to speak frankly of facts, believing
that only in this way can we always find the right path however difficult circumstances may be.

We cannot hide from ourselves the fact that we have met
with a grave setback in the last few days, but I am confident
that we all can and, in a short time, will overcome our
difficult situation, although this calls for much patience and
wisdom as well as moral courage and ability to work on our
part. Before that, brothers, we need to cast a glance back
over past events so that we shall be able to follow developments and the line of our march leading to the present conditions.

All of us know how the crisis started in the Middle East.
At the beginning of last May there was an enemy plan for
the invasion of Syria and the statements by his politicians and
all his military leaders openly said so. There was plenty of
evidence concerning the plan. Sources of our Syrian brothers
were categorical on this and our own reliable information
confirmed it. Add to this the fact that our friends in the Soviet
Union warned the parliamentary delegation, which was on
a visit to Moscow, at the beginning of last month, that there
was a premeditated plan against Syria. We considered it our
duty not to accept this silently. This was the duty of Arab
brotherhood, it was also the duty of national security. Whoever starts with Syria will finish with Egypt.

Our armed forces moved to our frontiers with a competence
which the enemy acknowledged even before our friends.
Several steps followed. There was the withdrawal of the
United Nations Emergency Force and the return of our forces
to the Sharm al Shaykh post, the controlling point in the
Straits of Tiran, which had been used by the Israeli enemy
as one of the after-effects of the tripartite aggression against

us in 1956. The enemy's flag passing in front of our forces was intolerable, apart from other reasons connected with the dearest aspirations of the Arab nation.

Accurate calculations were made of the enemy's strength and showed us that our armed forces, at the level of equipment and training which they had reached, were capable of repelling the enemy and deterring him. We realised that the possibility of an armed clash existed and accepted the risk.

Before us were several factors—national, Arab and international. A message from the US President Lyndon Johnson was handed to our Ambassador in Washington 26th May asking us to show self-restraint and not to be the first to fire, or else we should have to face grave consequences. On the very same night, the Soviet Ambassador asked to have an urgent meeting with me at 05.30 [as broadcast] after midnight. He informed me of an urgent request from the Soviet Government not to be the first to open fire.

In the morning of last Monday, 5th June, the enemy struck. If we say now it was a stronger blow than we had expected, we must say at the same time, and with complete certainty that it was bigger than the potential at his disposal. It became very clear from the first moment that there were other powers behind the enemy—they came to settle their accounts with the Arab national movement. Indeed, there were surprises worthy of note:

(1) The enemy, whom we were expecting from the east and north, came from the west—a fact which clearly showed that facilities exceeding his own capacity and his calculated strength had been made available to him.

(2) The enemy covered at one go all military and civilian airfields in the UAR. This means that he was relying on some force other than his own normal strength to protect his skies against any retaliatory action from our side. The enemy was also leaving other Arab fronts to be tackled with outside assistance which he had been able to obtain.

(3) There is clear evidence of imperialist collusion with the enemy—an imperialist collusion, trying to benefit from the lesson of the open collusion of 1956, by resorting this time to abject and wicked concealment. Nevertheless, what is now established is that American and British aircraft carriers were off the shores of the enemy helping his war effort. Also, British aircraft raided, in broad daylight, positions on the Syrian and Egyptian fronts, in addition to operations by a

number of American aircraft reconnoitering some of our positions. The inevitable result of this was that our land forces, fighting most violent and brave battles in the open desert, found themselves at the difficult time without adequate air cover in face of the decisive superiority of the enemy air forces. Indeed it can be said without emotion or exaggeration, that the enemy was operating with an air force three times stronger than his normal force.

The same conditions were faced by the forces of the Jordanian Army, fighting a brave battle under the leadership of King Husayn who—let me say for the sake of truth and honesty—adopted an excellent stand; and I admit that my heart was bleeding while I was following the battles of his heroic Arab Army in Jerusalem and other parts of the West Bank on the night when the enemy and his plotting forces massed no less than 400 aircraft over the Jordanian front.

There were other honourable and marvellous efforts. The Algerian people, under their great leader Hawwari Bumedien, gave without reservation and without stinting for the battle. The people of Iraq and their faithful leader Abd ar-Rahman Arif gave without reservation or stinting for the battle. The Syrian Army fought heroically, consolidated by the forces of the great Syrian people and under the leadership of their national Government. The peoples and governments of Sudan, Kuwait, Yemen, Lebanon, Tunisia and Morocco adopted honourable stands. All the peoples of the Arab nation, without exception, adopted a stand of manhood and dignity all along the Arab homeland; a stand of resolution and determination that Arab right shall not be lost, shall not be humiliated, and that the war in its defence is advancing, regardless of sacrifice and setbacks, on the road of the sure and inevitable victory. There were also great nations outside the Arab homeland who gave us invaluable moral support.

But the plot, and we must say this with the courage of men, was bigger and fiercer. The enemy's main concentration was on the Egyptian front which he attacked with all his main force of armoured vehicles and infantry, supported by air supremacy the dimensions of which I have outlined for you. The nature of the desert did not permit a full defence especially, in face of the enemy's air supremacy. I realised that the armed battle might not go in our favour. I, with others, tried to use all sources of Arab strength. Arab oil came in to play its part. The Suez Canal came in to play its part. A great role is still reserved for general Arab action. I am fully confident that it will measure up to its task. Our Armed Forces in Sinai were obliged to evacuate the first line of defence. They fought fearful tank and air battles on the second line of defence.

We then responded to the cease-fire resolution, in view of assurances contained in the latest Soviet draft resolution, to the Security Council, as well as French statements to the effect that no one must reap any territorial expansion from the recent aggression, and in view of world public opinion, especially in Asia and Africa, which appreciates our position and feels the ugliness of the forces of international domination which pounced on us.

We now have several urgent tasks before us. The first is to remove the traces of this aggression against us and to stand by the Arab nation resolutely and firmly; despite the setback, the Arab nation, with all its potential and resources, is in a position to insist on the removal of the traces of the aggression.

The second task is to learn the lesson of the setback. In this connection there are three vital facts, (1) The elimination of imperialism in the Arab world will leave Israel with its own intrinsic power; yet, whatever the circumstances, however long it may take, the Arab intrinsic power is greater and more effective. (2) Redirecting Arab interests in the service of Arab rights is an essential safeguard: the American Sixth Fleet moved with Arab oil, and there are Arab bases, placed forcibly and against the will of the peoples, in the service of aggression. (3) The situation now demands a united word from the entire Arab nation; this, in the present circumstances, is irreplaceable guarantee.

Now we arrive at an important point in this heartsearching by asking ourselves: does this mean that we do not bear responsibility for the consequences of the setback? I tell you truthfully and despite any factors on which I might have based my attitude during the crisis, that I am ready to bear the whole responsibility. I have taken a decision in which I want you all to help me. I have decided to give up completely and finally every official post and every political role and return to the ranks of the masses and do my duty with them like every other citizen.

The forces of imperialism imagine that Jamal Abd al-Nasser is their enemy. I want it to be clear to them that their enemy is the entire Arab nation, not just Jamal Abd al-Nasser. The forces hostile to the Arab national movement try to portray this movement as an empire of Abd al-Nasser. This is not true, because the aspiration for Arab unity began before Abd al-Nasser and will remain after Abd al-Nasser. I always used to tell you that the nation remains, and that the individual—whatever his role and however great his contribution to the causes of his homeland—is only a tool of the popular will, and not its creator.

In accordance with Article 110 of the Provisional Constitution promulgated in March 1964 I have entrusted my colleague, friend and brother Zakariya Muhiedin with taking over the point of President and carrying out the constitutional provisions on this point. After this decision, I place all I have at his disposal in dealing with the grave situation through which our people are passing.

In doing this I am not liquidating the revolution—indeed the revolution is not the monopoly of any one generation of revolutionaries. I take pride in the brothers of this generation of revolutionaries. It has brought to pass the evacuation of British imperialism, has won the independence of Egypt and defined its Arab personality, and has combated the policy of spheres of influence in the Arab world; it has led the social revolution and created a deep transformation in the Egyptian reality by establishing the people's control over the sources of their wealth and the result of Arab action; it recovered the Suez Canal and laid down the foundation of industrial upsurge in Egypt; it built the High Dam to bring fertile greenness to the barren desert; it laid down a power network over the whole of the north of the Nile Valley; it made oil resources gush out after a long wait. More important still, it gave the leadership of political action to the alliance of the people's working forces, the constant source of renewed leaderships carrying the banners of Egyptian and Arab struggle through its successive stages, building socialism, succeeding and triumphing.

I have unlimited faith in this alliance as the leader of national action: the peasants, the workers, the soldiers, the intellectuals and national capital. Its unity and cohesion and creative response within the framework of this unity are capable of creating—through work, serious work, difficult work, as I have said more than once—colossal miracles for this country in order to be a strength for itself, for its Arab nation, for the movement of national revolution and for world peace based on justice.

The sacrifices made by our people and their burning spirit

during the crisis and the glorious pages of heroism written by the officers and soldiers of our armed forces with their blood will remain an unquenchable torch in our history and a great inspiration for the future and its great hopes. The people were splendid as usual, noble as their nature, believing, sincere and loyal. The members of our armed forces were an honourable example of Arab man in every age and every place. They defended the grains of sand in the desert to the last drop of their blood. In the air, they were, despite enemy supremacy, legends of dedication and sacrifice, of courage and willingness to perform the duty in the best way.

This is an hour for action; not an hour for sorrow. It is a situation calling for ideals and not for selfishness or personal feelings. All my heart is with you, and I want all your hearts to be with me. May God be with us all, a hope in our hearts, a light and guidance. Peace and the blessing of God be with you.

PART IV

Views and Comments:
The Arab-Israeli Conflict
Today and Tomorrow

This section of the Reader presents a selection of Israeli and Arab views about the prospects of war and peace in the Middle East as expressed since the war of 1967, as well as the analysis and/or the opinions of outside observers. Three wars in twenty years have not brought a solution of the conflict any nearer; a renewal of fighting at some future date is again thought likely as no substantial progress has been made in the attempts to mediate between the two sides. There is, moreover, the distinct danger of big power involvement, and, as a result, the transformation of a local conflict into a world crisis.

"The Most Severe Crisis"

Nasser's Revolution Anniversary Speech at Cairo University, July 23, 1967.*

Brother compatriots, the 15th anniversary of the revolution of 23rd July 1952 comes while we are living through a crisis. We will not be exaggerating if we say that this is the most severe crisis we have faced in the history of our revolutionary work.

At no time has our work been easy. We have always had to face all kinds of political, economic, and military dangers. Every victory we have achieved came after difficulties and hardships which we bore patiently.

To carry out the revolution of 23rd July was not an easy job for our people after 70 years of British occupation. For 70 years the British, in collaboration with the feudalists and the capitalists, ruled this country with the backing of 80,000 British soldiers in the Suez Canal zone. Nor was our people's resistance to the policy of pacts and zones of influence which others tried to impose on us an easy job at a time when the national liberation movement had not attained the present level of independence and non-subservience.

Moreover, our people's acceptance of the challenge to build the High Dam was not an easy job in the face of the arrogance of the United States, which thought that by withdrawing a Western offer to finance the High Dam it could harm the Egyptian economy and reveal our people as incapable of assuming the responsibility of executing such a project, which is unequalled anywhere in the world. In fact by its arrogance

* This speech was delivered on the fifteenth anniversary of the Egyptian revolution, on July 23, 1967 at Cairo University It is the most detailed survey from the Arab point of view of the events leading to the Arab–Israeli war.

the United States wanted our people to lose confidence in themselves and to overthrow our revolutionary regime.

Nor was our people's endurance of the horrors of the Suez war an easy job. In 1956 our people were attacked by three states, two of which were big Powers. The aggression has utilised the base that imperialism had established in the heart of the Arab homeland to threaten and terrorise this homeland, once overtly and the second time covertly.

Our people's progress in the field of socialist reconstruction, self-reliance and justice and their attempt to increase national wealth through the enormous process of industrialisation; reclamation of vast lands; electrification of the entire country; restoration of all foreign interests; elimination of monopolism, capitalism, and feudalism; redistribution of land; provision for education, health and social security services; and the participation of the workers in the profits and administration of firms —all this, brothers, was not an easy job in this country where foreign and feudalist interests once dominated the national resources. It was not an easy job in the heart of this Arab world which was dominated by foreign and feudalist interests. Whatever happens in our country has its repercussions in our entire Arab world whether we like it or not.

Our people's acceptance of the responsibilities of Arab solidarity, the common struggle and of destiny was not an easy job. In exercising these responsibilities we resisted the attempt to invade Syria in 1957, accepted the consequences of unity and secession, supported the revolution in Iraq in 1958, supported the Algerian revolution from 1954 to 1962, and backed the Yemeni revolution and the revolution in South Arabia. The latest problem we have confronted and are still confronting is the attempt to invade Syria.

Brothers, our work has never been easy. The road of the struggle is strewn with dangers, the way to glory with sacrifices, and the way to great hopes with great sacrifices. Should the peoples fail to take this course they would face rigidity and backwardness. They would take no chances and would not face life—the sweet and bitter. Those who do not shoulder responsibilities have no right to entertain hopes. Those who do not take chances become the prisoner of fear itself because of their fear. This is not the quality of vigorous peoples; it is not their nature or their course.

I have said that the crisis we now face is one of the severest we have faced in the history of our revolutionary action for more than one reason. For one thing, this crisis which we are confronting, although it is not the gravest and most difficult we have faced, certainly marks the highest degree of hypocrisy and meanness we have encountered. Imperialism—we must admit this—has benefited from all its encounters with us and with the other peoples who have frequently been exposed to its assaults. This time imperialism did not face us overtly as it did in 1956. But imperialism made an effort—and we must admit that it was skilful—to conceal its role and hide its collusion. In the end perhaps imperialism left nothing to incriminate it but its fingerprints. But this is one thing and catching imperialism redhanded as we did in 1956 is something else.

For another thing, this is perhaps the first revolution anniversary that has found our homeland in the midst of a savage conspiracy. Despite their courage and insistence on confronting it, our people undoubtedly at the same time are experiencing deep sorrow and severe pain.

Brothers, perhaps Almighty God wanted to test us to judge whether we deserve what we have achieved, whether we are able to protect our achievements, and whether we have the courage to be patient and stand firm against affliction. Brothers, perhaps Almighty God also wanted to give us a lesson to teach us what we had not learned, to remind us of some things we might have forgotten, and to cleanse our souls of the blemishes that have affected us and the shortcomings that we must avoid [applause] as we build our new society. Whatever the Almighty's will may be, we accept His test as our destiny. We are fully confident that He is with us: He will protect our struggle should we set out to struggle; grant us victory if we be determined to triumph and open the road to justice to us; endow us with victory if we be determined to be the victor; and open the road of justice to us if we be able to place ourselves on His right path.

Brother compatriots, I do not want to take you back to the circumstances which paved the way to this crisis. I explained some of these circumstances to you in my address to the nation on 9th June right after the setback. Also I realise, and we must all realise, that what happened has happened and there is no use wailing over the debris. Now it is more important to learn the lesson, overcome the setback, rise above it, and proceed triumphantly on our road towards the achievement of our aspirations.

But I do believe that we must ponder certain important matters so that we may all be able to achieve the highest degree of clarity. The first thing which should be clear to us all is that it was not we who started the crisis in the Middle East. We all know that this crisis began with Israel's attempt to invade Syria. It is quite clear to us all that in that attempt Israel was not working for itself alone but also for the forces which had got impatient with the Arab revolutionary movement.

The information we received about the invasion of Syria came from many sources. Our Syrian brothers had information that Israel had mobilised 18 brigades on their front. We confirmed this information. It became evident to us that Israel had mobilised no less than 13 brigades on the Syrian front. Our parliamentary delegation headed by Anwar as-Sadat was on a visit to Moscow, and our Soviet friends informed Anwar as-Sadat at that time that the invasion of Syria was imminent.

What were we to do? We could have remained silent, we could have waited, or we could have just issued statements and cables of support. But if this homeland had accepted such behaviour it would have meant that it was deserting its mission, its role and even its personality. There was a joint defence agreement between us and Syria. We do not consider our agreements with the peoples of our Arab nation or others merely ink on paper. To us these agreements are sacred, an honour and an obligation. Between us and Syria, between us and all Arab peoples there was and always will be something far greater and more lasting than agreements and treaties: faith in the common struggle and the common fate. Therefore it was imperative that we take concrete steps to face the danger threatening Syria, especially since the statements of Israeli political and military leaders at the time and their open threats to Syria—as reported in the press and frankly noted at the UN—left no room for anyone to doubt any information or to wait or hesitate.

The second question: when we decided to move, our actions led to certain practical results. First we asked for the withdrawal of the UN Emergency Force. Then we restored Egyptian sovereignty rights in the Gulf of Aqabah. This was one of the things our Arab brothers had always insisted on. It was natural that such steps had a great impact on the area and the world.

The third question: by moving and taking the initiative to repel the danger to Syria, we realised—particularly from an international point of view—that the question was whether we should strike first in an armed battle. Had we done this we would have exposed ourselves to very serious consequences, greater than we would have been able to tolerate. First we would have faced direct US military action against us on the pretext that we had fired the first bullet in the battle.

Here I should like to draw your attention to certain important points. The first is the US warnings. Perhaps you have read about these US warnings. President Johnson's adviser summoned our Ambassador in Washington at a late hour at night and told him that Israel had information that we were going to attack. The adviser said this would put us in a serious situation and urged us to exercise self-restraint. They also said they were telling Israel the same thing so that it would also exercise self-restraint. We also received messages from President Johnson referring to the UN and urging us to exercise self-restraint.

The second point—which perhaps I have discussed before —is that on the following day the Russian Ambassador asked to see me and conveyed to me a message from the Soviet Premier urging self-restraint. He informed me about a message he had sent to the Israeli Premier and said that any action on our part would expose the world to great danger.

The third point is that the entire international community was against the outbreak of war. President de Gaulle was clear when he said France would define its attitude on the basis of who fired the first shot.

The fourth point is that we were the victims of a diplomatic trick, a political deception in which we had not imagined a major Power would involve itself. This political trick was played by the United States. It was represented in the US President's speech, his appeals, his request that we co-operate with the UN Secretary-General, and his offer to send the Vice-President to discuss with us ways to save the entire world from this crisis. The UN Secretary-General came here and we co-operated with him to the maximum. The Secretary-General asked for a breathing-space with regard to the Gulf of Aqabah and we agreed to this. He said he wanted this breathing-space so that all concerned would have time to pause and deal with matters. The first thing we pointed out to him was that no Israeli ships would be allowed to pass through the Canal [sic], that no strategic shipments would be allowed to pass, and, in the meantime, we would not search any ships. We accepted this and considered it a proposal by the Secretary-General of the UN, providing a breathing-space for all to discuss the matter.

After that an envoy of the US President arrived here. The emissary suggested that a Vice-President go to the United States. I approved the idea on the understanding that the Vice-President would meet President Johnson and explain our attitude to him. Then I sent a letter to the US President telling him: We welcome the visit of the US Vice-President but at the same time I am prepared to send Vice-President Zakariya Muhiedin to Washington to meet you and explain the Arab view to you. Naturally, the next day I received the reply that they welcomed Zakariya Muhiedin's trip to Washington to meet the American President and they requested that we set a date. We set it for Tuesday 6th June, and we all know that the aggression began on 5th June.

What does this mean? It means that large-scale political and diplomatic activities were going on and it was right in the light of these activities to think that the explosion would not occur soon.

The fifth point: in spite of all this, we were not reassured about all these things. We knew that something was in the making and that it would not be long in coming. It was obvious that something was being planned against us. In fact, I had felt for two years that something would be prepared against us, since the cessation of US aid and America's warnings to us not to arm or enlarge our army, nor to follow a course of technical development, nor to seek military development.

When we concentrated our forces I estimated that the likelihood of war breaking out was 20 per cent. Before we closed the Gulf of Aqabah, we convened a meeting of the Higher Executive Committee at my home. We discussed the closure of the Gulf of Aqabah. That meeting took place on 22nd May. At that meeting I told them that the possibility of war was 50 per cent. At another meeting I said that the likelihood of war was 80 per cent. At our meeting of the Higher Executive Committee it was obvious that our action would be defensive, that we would attack only if aggression was launched against Syria, and that we would be on the alert. At that meeting no one spoke at all of attacking Israel. There was no intention at all that we would launch an offensive against Israel. As I explained earlier it was clear from all our analyses that any attack on Israel would expose us to great dangers. The foremost of these dangers would be an American attack on us in view of the statements America made saying that it guaranteed the borders of the states in this area. It was obvious to us that when America said it guaranteed the borders of the states in this area and would not tolerate any changes in this area, America did not at all mean the Arab states, but by this it meant Israel. It meant that if an aggression was carried out against Israel, America would implement the statement made by President Kennedy that America guaranteed all the borders in this area.

On these grounds there was no discussion at all of launching an attack on Israel. But our entire operation at the Joint Command was defensive. As we estimated at that time, our concentrations were a deterrent action so that Israel would not commit aggression against Syria.

On 23rd May we announced the closure of the Gulf of Aqabah to Israeli ships. Then came the political changes in Israel at the beginning of June. As we followed what was going on there, the probability of war became 100 per cent.

What does this mean? It means that we did not trust in the least all the political and diplomatic activities of the United States. We realised that something was being planned and that it would not take long.

On Friday 2nd June I personally went to the Armed Forces Supreme Command HQ. I participated at a meeting which was attended by all senior officers of the armed forces. At that meeting I gave my view before listening to theirs. I said at that meeting on Friday 2nd June that we must expect the enemy to strike a blow within 48 to 72 hours and no later on the basis of the indications of events and developments. I also said at that meeting that I expected the aggression to take place on Monday 5th June and the first blow to be struck at our Air Force. The Air Force commander was present at the meeting.

What does this mean? It means that we did not underestimate the situation as a result of all the diplomatic contacts, the dispatch of the UN Secretary-General, and Johnson's approval of a visit by Zakariya Muhiedin. It was quite clear on any political calculation that Israel was bound to take military action, especially after Iraqi forces had moved and Jordan had joined the joint defence agreements.

Question No. 6: After what has happened, we must faithfully and honourably admit that the military battle did not go as we had expected and hoped. It confirmed the proverb that precaution does not deter fate.

I do not wish now to talk about the causes, nor will I permit myself or this people, while the battle continues, to apportion blame. This is a matter for history and the struggle of our people. But I can say with satisfaction, good will and a conscience ready to give an account at any time that first and last the responsibility was mine. I said this in my address to the nation on 9th June, and I say it now and will continue to say it, bearing all the consequences and accepting any judgment of it. Actually this was why I decided to resign on 9th June. I wanted to take the responsibility and step down, and I wanted the enemies of the Egyptian people and the Arab nation to know that the issue is not Abd al-Nasser or Abd al-Nasser's ambitions, as they said. The Egyptian people's struggle began before Abd al-Nasser and will go on after Abd al-Nasser. The Arab nation sought its unity before Abd al-Nasser. I have said and will always say that I am not the leader of this people. The greatest honour I desire is to be their representative at a particular stage in their continuous struggle, a struggle not dependent on any individual.

Question No. 7, concerns the US role. A large part of the part played by the United States is still vague. We know only a little about this part. The secrets of the 1956 Suez war became known only last year—exactly 10 years after the war. Therefore, we shall not know the secrets of the 1967 war now. It will be some years before we know everything.

A large part of the US role in the recent aggression is still vague. But we already know a few things. We have already found the answers to several questions. What was behind the political and diplomatic part which the United States played before the battle? This role included the call for self-restraint, the threat that any action taken by us would expose the entire region to dangers, the proposal to send the US Vice-President to confer with us on the subject, the approval of Zakariya Muhiedin's trip to Washington to meet Johnson to confer on the subject and to try to reach a solution. All this took place before the aggression, before the battle.

It was a deception. We must ask: in whose interest was this deception? Certainly, it was in the interest of the imperialist-Israeli aggression. The deception was part of a US plan drawn up two years ago. The aim of this plan was to overthrow the free revolutionary regimes, which do not heed the words of the big Powers and refuse to be under anyone's influence.

What was behind the part played by the Sixth Fleet near our shores a few days before the war? How many arms were transported to Israel in the period from the outset of the crisis to the day of the aggression? How many aircraft reached Israel? How many volunteer pilots? How do we explain the huge air power which the enemy used on all Arab fronts? They attacked the Egyptian, Jordanian and Syrian fronts simultaneously. They also sent aircraft to attack Iraqi airports. On the evening of 7th June just before dawn, King Husayn contacted me by telephone saying that 400 aircraft were attacking the Jordanian front and were seen on his radar equipment. Where did these aircraft come from?

How do we explain the role of the US espionage ship *Liberty?* You have all read in the papers that an American ship named *Liberty* was near our territorial waters—probably in these waters—and that the Israelis thought it was an Egyptian warship and attacked it with torpedo boats. Some 34 officers and crew of this US ship were killed in this incident. For whom was the US ship with all its scientific equipment working? It was said that the ship was there to decode operational messages. It was also said that those messages were sent to the United States. Later it was said that the messages were sent to Israel. Messages can be radioed very rapidly. It was also said that those messages were sent to US Embassies in the area. What did the Americans do? When the Israelis hit them they pulled themselves together, hushed up the story, and went to Malta to repair the ship. Had we attacked the US ship, the Americans would have given us an ultimatum because we are neither an American colony nor an imperialist bridgehead. Nor are we in the US sphere of influence.

There is another question: why were there US aircraft over our front lines? On Wednesday 7th June two aircraft bearing US markings were seen over our lines. At first I did not believe it, but the information was certain. We then issued a statement saying that American aircraft had flown over our lines and over the front. We also said that we, therefore, believed the Americans were participating in the operation. We also spoke of the aircraft that were attacking Jordan and said that there had been a non-Israeli air attack on Jordan. We broadcast a statement including details about the two aircraft we had observed in flight.

In the evening I received a letter from President Johnson. He contacted the Soviet Head of State and requested him to send us a letter because at that time we did not have relations with him. He said it was true that there were two US aircraft over our lines, but they were going to the aid of the USS *Liberty* the spy ship.

The question arises: were there other US aircraft? A second question is: would they have made their admission had we not broadcast the statement? In fact, one asks oneself such questions about the things one knows.

What is the explanation of the US attitude at the UN and after the end of the operations? The US attitude at the UN after the operations was fully to endorse Israel's point of view. The US position at the UN was for unconditional surrender by the Arabs. This was the US position at the UN after the operations had ended. What does this mean?

There is an appalling difference between the two US attitudes—the attitude in 1956 when America was surprised by the tripartite aggression against us and the attitude in 1967 when America was not taken by surprise. In 1956 America was surprised by the tripartite aggression against us. In 1967, despite the letters and the agreement to send Zakariya Muhiedin, America was not surprised by the Israeli aggression against us. When America was surprised it stood steadfast against the aggression and demanded that it be halted and that the aggressive forces withdraw. But when America was not taken by surprise, it supported the aggression and brought pressure to bear on any State which America could influence in any way. The result was the failure of the UN as we have seen.

It is certain that America was not taken by surprise. Stories began to be told. These days American papers abound in news reports saying that the issue has provoked discussions at the highest levels in America. US papers and the American *Life* magazine said that Israel submitted to the US President the view that it should launch an attack, saying that it felt superior. US newspapers also say that the US President sought the views of the US Chief of Staff and the US Intelligence Director and that they agreed. Accordingly, Israel was allowed to launch the offensive and to perpetrate aggression. At the same time Israel obtained guarantees from the United States that should the Arabs enter Israel, the Sixth Fleet would intercept them and if Israel entered the Arab countries, America would support Israel. These stories were published in newspapers. The Israeli Premier Eshkol has thanked the US President for telling him: The Sixth Fleet is there for you and to help you. Eshkol replied in a soothing manner to the US President and told him: I am afraid that when we become exposed to danger, you will be busy with Vietnam or you may be spending the weekend at your Texas ranch. But the US President emphatically assured him that the Sixth Fleet would protect him should the Arabs cross the borders into Israel. These articles, statements and all these stories were published in the papers. Therefore, the USA was not surprised by the aggression. . . .

[The second part of the speech, which has been deleted here, was devoted to domestic problems. Ed.]

The Six Days War:

Abba Eban's Speech at the Special Assembly of the United Nations, June 19, 1967.*

Our Watchword Is 'Forward to Peace'

The subject of our discussion is the Middle East, its past agony and its future hope. We speak of a region whose destiny has profoundly affected the entire human experience. In the heart of that region, at the very centre of its geography and history, lives a very small nation called Israel. This nation gave birth to the currents of thought which have fashioned the life of the Mediterranean world and of vast regions beyond. It has now been re-established as the home and sanctuary of a people which has seen six million of its sons exterminated in the greatest catastrophe ever endured by a family of the human race.

In recent weeks the Middle East has passed through a crisis whose shadows darken the world. This crisis has many consequences but only one cause. Israel's rights to peace, security, sovereignty, economic development and maritime freedom—indeed its very right to exist—has been forcibly denied and aggressively attacked. This is the true origin of the tension which torments the Middle East. All the other elements of the conflict are the consequences of this single cause. There has been danger, there is still peril in the Middle East because Israel's existence, sovereignty and vital interests have been and are violently assailed.

The threat to Israel's existence, its peace, security, sovereignty and development has been directed against her in the

* Reprinted from *The Jerusalem Post*.

first instance by the neighbouring Arab states. But all the conditions of tension, all the impulses of aggression in the Middle East have been aggravated by the policy of one of the Great Powers which under our Charter bear primary responsibilities for the maintenance of international peace and security. I shall show how the Soviet Union has been unfaithful to that trust. The burden of responsibility lies heavy upon her.

I come to this rostrum to speak for a united people which, having faced danger to the national survival, is unshakably resolved to resist any course which would renew the perils from which it has emerged.

The General Assembly is chiefly pre-occupied by the situation against which Israel defended itself on the morning of June 5. I shall invite every peace-loving state represented here to ask itself how it woud have acted on that day if it faced similar dangers. But if our discussion is to have any weight or depth, we must understand that great events are not born in a single instant of time. It is beyond all honest doubt that between May 14 and June 5, Arab governments led and directed by President Nasser, methodically prepared and mounted an aggressive assault designed to bring about Israel's immediate and total destruction. My authority for that conviction rests on the statements and actions of Arab governments themselves. There is every reason to believe what they say and to observe what they do.

The Pattern of Aggression 1957–1967

During Israel's first decade, the intention to work for her destruction by physical violence has always been part of the official doctrine and policy of Arab states. But many members of the United Nations hoped and believed that relative stability would ensure from the arrangements discussed in the General Assembly in March 1957. An attempt has been made to inaugurate a period of non-belligerency and co-existence in the relations between the UAR and Israel. A United Nations emergency force was to separate the armies in Sinai and Gaza. The Maritime Powers were to exercise free and innocent passage in the Gulf of Akaba and the Straits of Tiran. Terrorist attacks against Israel were to cease. The Suez Canal was to be opened to Israel shipping, as the Security Council had decided six years before.

In March 1957, these hopes and expectations were endorsed in the General Assembly by the United States, France, the

United Kingdom, Canada and other states in Europe, the Americas, Africa, Asia and Australia. These assurances, expressed with special solemnity by the four governments which I have mentioned, induced Israel to give up positions which she then held at Gaza and at the entrance to the Straits of Tiran and in Sinai. Non-belligerency, maritime freedom and immunity from terrorist attack were henceforth to be secured, not by Israel's own pressure but by the concerted will of the international community. Egypt expressed no opposition to these arrangements. Bright hopes for the future illuminated this hall ten years ago.

There were times during the past decade when it really seemed that a certain stability had been achieved. As we look back it becomes plain that the Arab governments regarded the 1957 arrangements merely as a breathing space enabling them to gather strength for a later assault. At the end of 1962, President Nasser began to prepare Arab opinion for an armed attack that was to take place within a few brief years. As his armaments grew his aggressive designs came more into light. On December 23, 1962, Nasser said:

> 'We feel that the soil of Palestine is the soil of Egypt, and of the whole Arab world. Why do we all mobilize? Because we feel that the land of Palestine is part of our land, and are ready to sacrifice ourselves for it.'

The present Foreign Minister of Egypt, Mahmoud Riad, echoed his master's voice:

> 'The sacred Arab struggle will not come to an end until Palestine is restored to its owners.'

In March 1963, the official Cairo radio continued the campaign of menace:

> 'Arab unity is taking shape towards the great goal—i.e. the triumphant return to Palestine with the banner of unity flying high in front of the holy Arab march.'

The newspaper Al-Gumhuriya published an official announcement on the same day:

> 'The noose around Israel's neck is tightening gradually . . . Israel is mightier than the empires which were vanquished in the Arab East and West . . . The Arab people will take possession of their full rights in their united homeland.'

Egypt is not a country in which the press utters views and opinions independently of the official will. There is thus significance in the statement of Al-Akhbar on April 4, 1963:

'The liquidation of Israel will not be realized through a declaration of war against Israel by Arab states, but *Arab unity and inter-Arab understanding will serve as a hangman's rope for Israel.*'

The Assembly will note that the imagery of a hangman's rope or of a tightening noose occurs frequently in the macabre vocabulary of Nasserism. He sees himself perpetually presiding over a scaffold. In June 1967 the metaphor of encirclement and strangulation was to come vividly to life, in Israel's hour of solitude and danger.

In February 1964 Nasser enunciated in simple terms what was to become his country's policy during the period of preparation:

'The possibilities of the future will be war with Israel. It is we who will dictate the time. It is we who will dictate the place.'

A similar chorus of threats arose during this period from other Arab capitals. President Aref of Iraq and President Ben-Bella of Algeria was especially emphatic and repetitive in their threat to liquidate Israel. The Syrian attitude was more ominous because it affected a neighbouring frontier. Syrian war propaganda has been particularly intense in the past few years. In 1964 the Syrian Defence Minister, General Abdulla Ziada, announced:

'The Syrian army stands as a mountain to crush Israel and demolish her. This army knows how to crush its enemies.'

Early last year Syria began to proclaim and carry out what it called a 'popular war' against Israel. The Syrian concept of 'popular war' expressed itself in the dispatch of trained terrorist groups into Israel territory to blow up installations and communication centres, to kill, maim, cripple and terrorise civilians in peaceful homes and farms. Sometimes the terrorists, trained in Syria, were dispatched through Jordan or Lebanon. The terrorist war was formally declared by President Al-Atassi on May 22, 1966, when he addressed soldiers on the Israel-Syrian front:

'We raise the slogan of the people's liberation war. We want total war with no limits, a war that will destroy the Zionist base.'

The Syrian Defence Minister, Hafiz Asad, said two days later:

> 'We say: We shall never call for, nor accept peace. We shall only accept war and the restoration of the usurped land. We have resolved to drench this land with our blood, to oust you, aggressors, and throw you into the sea for good. We must meet as soon as possible and fight a single liberation war on the level of the whole area against Israel, Imperialism and all the enemies of the people.'

Mr. President, from that day to this, not a week passed without Syrian officials adding to this turgid stream of invective and hate. From that day to this, there has not been a single month without terrorist acts, offensive to every impulse of human compassion and international civility, being directed from Syria against Israel citizens and territory. I would have no difficulty in filling the General Assembly's records with a thousand official statements by Arab leaders in the past two years announcing their intention to destroy Israel by diverse forms of organized physical violence. The Arab populations have been conditioned by their leaders to the anticipation of a total war, preceded by the constant harassment of the prospective victim.

Israel's Policy 1957–1967

From 1948 to this very day there has not been one statement by any Arab representative of a neighbouring Arab state indicating readiness to respect existing agreements or the permanent renunciation of force to recognize Israel's sovereign right of existence or to apply to Israel any of the central provisions of the United Nations Charter.

For some time Israel showed a stoic patience in her reaction to these words of menace. This was because the threats were not accompanied by a capacity to carry them into effect. But the inevitable result of this campaign of menace was the burden of a heavy race of arms. We strove to maintain an adequate deterrent strength and the decade beginning in March 1957 was not monopolized by security considerations alone. Behind the wall of a strong defence, with eyes vigilantly fixed on dangerous borders, we embarked on a constructive era in the national enterprise. These were years of swift expansion in our agriculture and industry, of intensive progress in the sciences and arts, of a widening international vocation, symbolized in the growth of strong links with the developing world. At the end of this first decade, Israel had established relations of commerce and culture with all the Americas, and with most of the countries of Western, Central and Eastern Europe. In her second decade she built constructive links with the emerging countries of the developing world with whom we are tied by a common aspiration to translate national freedom into creative economic growth and progress.

Fortified by friendships in all five continents, inspired by its role in the great drama of developments, intensely preoccupied by tasks of spiritual cooperation with kindred communities in various parts of the world, and in the efforts to assure the Jewish survival after the disastrous blows of Nazi oppressions, tenaciously involved in the development of original social ideas, Israel went on with its work. We could not concern ourselves exclusively with the torrent of hatred pouring in upon us from Arab governments. In the era of modern communication a nation is not entirely dependent on its regional context. The wide world is open to the voice of friendship. Arab hostility towards Israel became increasingly isolated, while our position in the international family became more deeply entrenched. Many in the world drew confidence from the fact that a very small nation could, by its exertion and example, rise to respected levels in social progress, scientific progress and the human arts, and so our policy was to deter the aggression of our neighbours so long as it was endurable, to resist it only when failure to resist would have invited its intensified renewal, to withstand Arab violence without being obsessed by it, and even to search patiently here and there for any glimmer of moderation and realism in the Arab mind. We also pursued the hope of bringing all the great powers to a harmonious policy in support of the security and sovereignty of Middle Eastern states. It was not easy to take this course. The sacrifice imposed upon our population by Arab violence was cumulative in its effects, but as it piled up month by month the toll of death and bereavement was heavy and in the last few years it was evident that this organized murder was directed by a central hand.

We were able to limit our response to this aggression so long as its own scope appeared to be limited. President Nasser seemed for some years to be accumulating inflammable material without an immediate desire to set it alight. He was heavily engaged in domination and conquest elsewhere. His speeches were strong against Israel, but his bullets, guns and poison gases were for the time being used to intimidate other

Arab states and to maintain a colonial war against the villagers of the Yemen and the peoples of the Arabian Peninsula.

But Israel's danger was great. The military build-up in Egypt proceeded at an intensive rate. It was designed to enable Egypt to press its war plans against Israel while maintaining its violent adventures elsewhere. In the face of these developments, Israel was forced to devote an increasing part of its resources to self-defence. With the declaration by Syria of the doctrine of a 'day by day military confrontation,' the situation in the Middle East grew darker. The Palestine Liberation Organization, the Palestine Liberation Army, the Unified Arab Command, the intensified expansion of military forces and equipment in Egypt, Syria, Lebanon, Jordan and more remote parts of the Arab continent—these were the signals of a growing danger to which we sought to alert the mind and conscience of the world.

The War Design, 1967

In three tense weeks between May 14, and June 5, Egypt, Syria and Jordan, assisted and incited by more distant Arab states, embarked on a policy of immediate and total aggression.

June 1967 was to be the month of decision. The 'final solution' was at hand.

There was no convincing motive for the aggressive design which was now unfolded. Egyptian and Soviet sources had claimed that a concentrated Israeli invasion of Syria was expected during the second or third week in May. No claim could be more frivolous or far-fetched. It is true that Syria was sending terrorists into Israel to lay mines on public roads and, on one occasion, to bombard the Israeli settlement at Manara from the Lebanese border. The accumulation of such actions had sometimes evoked Israeli responses always limited in scope and time. All that Syria had to do to ensure perfect tranquility on her frontier with Israel was to discourage the terrorist war. Not only did she not discourage these actions— she encouraged them, she gave them every moral and practical support. But the picture of Israeli troop concentrations in strength for an invasion of Syria was a monstrous fiction. Twice Syria refused to cooperate with suggestions by the U.N. authorities, and accepted by Israel, for a simultaneous and reciprocal inspection of the Israel-Syrian frontier. On one occasion the Soviet Ambassador complained to my Prime

Minister of heavy troop concentrations in the North of Israel. When invited to join the Prime Minister that very moment in a visit to any part of Israel which he would like to see, the distinguished envoy brusquely refused. The prospect of finding out the truth at first hand seemed to fill him with a profound disquiet. But by May 9, the Secretary-General of the United Nations from his own sources on the ground had ascertained that no Israeli troop concentration existed. This fact had been directly communicated to the Syrian and Egyptian Governments. The excuse had been shattered, but the allegations still remained. The steps which I now describe could not possibly have any motive or justification if an Israeli troop concentration, as both Egypt and Syria knew, did not exist. Indeed the Egyptian build-up ceased to be described by its authors as the result of any threat to Syria.

On May 14, Egyptian forces began to move into Sinai.

On May 16, the Egyptian Command ordered the United Nations Emergency Force to leave the border. The following morning the reason became clear. For on May 17, 1967, at 6 in the morning, Radio Cairo broadcast that Field-Marshal Amer had issued alert orders to the Egyptian armed forces. Nor did he mention Syria as the excuse. This announcement reads:

'1. The state of preparedness of the Egyptian armed forces will increase to the full level of preparedness for war, beginning 14.30 hours last Sunday.

2. Formations and units allocated in accordance with the operational plans will advance from their present locations to the designated positions.

3. The armed forces are to be in full preparedness to carry out any combat tasks on the Israel front in accordance with developments.'

On May 18, Egypt called for the total removal of the United Nations Emergency Force. The Secretary-General of the United Nations acceded to this request and moved to carry out, without reference to the Security Council or the General Assembly, without carrying out the procedures indicated by Secretary-General Hammerskjold in the event of a request for a withdrawal being made, without heeding the protesting voices of some of the permanent members of the Security Council and of the government at whose initiative the force had been established, without consulting Israel on the consequent prejudice to her military security and her vital maritime freedom, and without seeking such delay as would enable alternative measures to be concerted for preventing belligerency by sea and a dangerous confrontation of forces by land.

It is often said that United Nations procedures are painfully slow. This decision was disastrously swift. Its effect was to make Sinai safe for belligerency from North to South, to create a sudden disruption of the local security balance, and to leave an international maritime interest exposed to almost certain threat. I have already said that Israel's attitude to the peace-keeping functions of the United Nations has been traumatically affected by its experience. What is the use of a fire brigade which vanishes from the scene as soon as the first smoke and flames appear? Is it surprising that we are firmly resolved never again to allow a vital Israel interest and our very security to rest on such a fragile foundation?

The clouds now gathered thick and fast. Between May 14 and May 23, Egyptian concentrations in Sinai increased day by day. Israel took corresponding measures. In the absence of an agreement to the contrary it is, of course, legal for any state to place its armies wherever it chooses in its territory. It is equally true that nothing could be more uncongenial to the prospect of peace than to have large armies facing each other across a narrow space, with one of them clearly bent on an early assault. For the purpose of the concentration was not in doubt. On May 18, at 24.00 hours, the Cairo radio, Saut el-Arab, published the following order of the day by Abdul Mushin Murtagi, the General then commanding Sinai:

'The Egyptian forces have taken up positions in accordance with a definite plan.

'Our forces are definitely ready to carry the battle beyond the borders of Egypt.

'Morale is very high among the members of our armed forces because this is the day for which they have been waiting—to make a holy war in order to return the plundered land to its owners.

'In many meetings with army personnel they asked when the holy war would begin—the time has come to give them their wish.'

On May 21 General Amer gave the order to mobilize reserves. Now came the decisive step. All doubt that Egypt had decided upon immediate or early war was now dispelled. Appearing at an Air Force Base at 6 o'clock in the morning, President Nasser announced that he would blockade the Gulf of Akaba to Israeli ships, adding: 'The Jews threaten war and we say: by all means, we are ready for war.'

But the Jews were not threatening war. Prime Minister Eshkol was calling for a de-escalation of forces. Nasser treated this as a sign of weakness.

On May 25, Cairo Radio announced:

> 'The Arab people is firmly resolved to wipe Israel off the map and to restore the honour of the Arabs of Palestine.'

On the following day, May 26, Nasser spoke again:

> 'The Arab people wants to fight. We have been waiting for the right time when we will be completely ready. Recently we have felt that our strength has been sufficient and that if we make battle with Israel we shall be able, with the help of God, to conquer. Sharm e-Sheikh implies a confrontation with Israel. Taking this step makes it imperative that we be ready to undertake a total war with Israel.'

Writing in Al-Ahram, on May 26, Nasser's mouthpiece, Hasanein Heikal, wrote, with engaging realism:

> 'I consider that there is no alternative to armed conflict between the United Arab Republic and the Israeli enemy. This is the first time that the Arab challenge to Israel attempts to change an existing fact in order to impose a different fact in its place.'

On May 28, Nasser had a press conference. He was having them every day. He said:

> 'We will not accept any possibility of co-existence with Israel.'

And on the following day:

> 'If we have succeeded to restore the situation to what it was before 1956, there is no doubt that God will help us and will inspire us to restore the situation to what it was prior to 1948.'

There are various ways of threatening Israel's liquidation. Few ways could be clearer than this.

The troop concentrations and blockade were now to be accompanied by encirclement. The noose was to be fitted around the victim's neck. Other Arab states were closing the ring. On May 30 Nasser signed the Defence Agreement with Jordan, and described its purpose in these terms:

'The armies of Egypt, Jordan, Syria and Lebanon are stationed on the borders of Israel in order to face the challenge. Behind them stand the armies of Iraq, Algeria, Kuwait, Sudan and the whole of the Arab nation.

'This deed will astound the world. Today they will know that the Arabs are ready for the fray. The hour of decision has arrived.'

On June 4 Nasser made a statement on Cairo Radio after signing the protocol associating Iraq with the Egyptian-Jordanian Defence Pact. Here are his words:

'. . . We are facing you in the battle and are burning with desire for it to start, in order to obtain revenge. This will make the world realize what the Arabs are and what Israel is . . .'

Mr. President, Nothing has been more startling in recent weeks than to read discussions about who planned, who organized, who initiated, who wanted and who launched this war. Here we have a series of statements, mounting in crescendo from vague warning through open threat, to precise intention.

Here we have the vast mass of the Egyptian armies in Sinai with seven infantry and two armoured divisions, the greatest force ever assembled in that Peninsula in all its history. Here we have 40,000 regular Syrian troops poised to strike at the Jordan Valley from advantageous positions in the hills. Here we have the mobilized forces of Jordan, with their artillery and mortars trained on Israel's population centres in Jerusalem and along the vulnerable narrow coastal plain. Troops from Iraq, Kuwait and Algeria converge towards the battle-front at Egypt's behest. 900 tanks face Israel on the Sinai border, while 200 more are poised to strike the isolated town of Eilat at Israel's southern tip. The military dispositions tell their own story. The Northern Negev was to be invaded by armour and bombarded from the Gaza Strip. From May 27 onward, Egyptian air squadrons in Sinai were equipped with operation orders instructing them in detail on the manner in which Israeli airfields, pathetically few in number, were to be bombarded, thus exposing Israel's crowded cities to easy and merciless assault. Egyptian air sorties came in and out of Israel's southern desert to reconnoitre, inspect and prepare for the asault. An illicit blockade had cut Israel off from all her commerce with the eastern half of the world.

Blockade on Tiran Straits

Those who write this story in years to come will give a special place in their narrative to Nasser's blatant decision to close the Straits of Tiran in Israel's face. It is not difficult to understand why this outrage had a drastic impact. In 1957 the maritime nations, within the framework of the United Nations General Assembly, correctly enunciated the doctrine of free and innocent passage to the Straits. When that doctrine was proclaimed—and incidentally, not challenged by the Egyptian Representative at that time—it was little more than an abstract principle for the maritime world. For Israel it was a great but still unfulfilled prospect, it was not yet a reality. But during the ten years in which we and the other states of the maritime community have relied upon that doctrine and upon established usage, the principle had become a reality consecrated by hundreds of sailings under dozens of flags and the establishment of a whole complex of commerce and industry and communication. A new dimension has been added to the map of the world's communication. And on that dimension we have constructed Israel's bridge towards the friendly states of Asia and Africa, a network of relationships which is the chief pride of Israel in the second decade of its independence and on which its economic future depends.

All this, then, had grown up as an effective usage under the United Nations' flag. Does Mr. Nasser really think that he can come upon the scene in ten minutes and cancel the established legal usage and interests of ten years?

There was in his wanton act a quality of malice. For surely the closing of the Straits of Tiran gave no benefit whatever to Egypt except the perverse joy of inflicting injury on others. It was an anarchic act, because it showed a total disregard for the law of nations, the application of which in this specific case had not been challenged for ten years. And it was, in the literal sense, an act of arrogance, because there are other nations in Asia and East Africa that trade with the port of Eilat, as they have every right to do, through the Straits of Tiran and across the Gulf of Akaba. Other sovereign states from Japan to Ethiopia, from Thailand to Uganda, from Cambodia to Madagascar, have a sovereign right to decide for themselves whether they wish or do not wish to trade with Israel. These countries are not colonies of Cairo. They can trade with Israel or not trade with Israel as they wish, and

President Nasser is not the policeman of other African and Asian States.

Here then was a wanton intervention in the sovereign rights of other states in the eastern half of the world to decide for themselves whether or not they wish to establish trade relations with either or both of the two ports at the head of the Gulf of Akaba.

An Act of War

When we examine, then, the implications of this act, we have no cause to wonder that the international shock was great. There was another reason, too, for that shock. Blockades have traditionally been regarded, in the pre-Charter parlance, as acts of war. To blockade, after all, is to attempt strangulation—and sovereign states are entitled not to have their State strangled.

The blockade is by definition an act of war, imposed and enforced through violence.

Never in history have blockade and peace existed side by side. From May 24 onward, the question of who started the war or who fired the first shot became momentously irrelevant. There is no difference in civil law between murdering a man by slow strangulation or killing him by a shot in the head. From the moment at which the blockade was imposed, active hostilities had commenced and Israel owed Egypt nothing of her Charter rights. If a foreign power sought to close Odessa, or Copenhagen or Marseilles or New York Harbour by the use of force, what would happen? Would there be any discussion about who had fired the first shot? Would anyone ask whether aggression had begun? Less than a decade ago the Soviet Union proposed a draft resolution in the General Assembly on the question of defining aggression. The resolution reads:

'In an international conflict, that State shall be declared an attacker which first commits one of the following acts:
a. Naval blockade of the coastal ports of another State.'

This act constituted in the Soviet view aggression as distinguished from other specific acts designated in the Soviet draft as indirect aggression. In this particular case the consequences of Nasser's action had been fully announced in advance. On March 1, 1967, my predecessor announced that:

'Interference, by armed force, with ships of the Israel flag exercising free and innocent passage in the Gulf of Akaba and through the Straits of Tiran, will be regarded by Israel as an attack entitling it to exercise its inherent right of self-defence under Article 51 of the United Nations Charter and to take all such measures as are necessary to ensure the free and innocent passage of its ships in the Gulf and in the Straits.'

The representative of France declared that any obstruction of free passage in the Straits or Gulf was contrary to international law 'entailing a possible resort to the measures authorized by Article 51 of the Charter.'

The United States, inside and outside of the United Nations, gave specific endorsement to Israel's right to invoke her inherent right of self-defence against any attempt to blockade the Gulf. Nasser was speaking with acute precision when he stated that Israel now faced the choice either between being choked to death in her southern maritime approaches or to await the death blow from Northern Sinai.

Nobody who lived through those days in Israel, between May 23 and June 5, will ever forget the air of doom that hovered over our country. Hemmed in by hostile armies ready to strike, affronted and beset by a flagrant act of war, bombarded day and night by predictions of her approaching extinction, forced into a total mobilization of all her manpower, her economy and commerce beating with feeble pulse, her main supplies of vital fuel choked by a belligerent act, Israel faced the greatest peril of her existence that she had known since her resistance against aggression 19 years before, at the hour of her birth. There was peril wherever she looked and she faced it in deepening solitude. On May 24 and on succeeding days, the Security Council conducted a desultory debate which sometimes reached a point of levity. The Soviet Representative asserted that he saw no reason for discussing the Middle Eastern situation at all. The Bulgarian delegate uttered these unbelievable words.

'At the present moment there is really no need for an urgent meeting of the Security Council.'

A crushing siege bore down upon us. Multitudes throughout the world trembled for Israel's fate. The single consolation lay in the surge of public opinion which rose up in Israel's defence. From Paris to Montevideo, from New York to Amsterdam, tens of thousands of persons of all ages, peoples and affiliations marched in horrified protest at the approaching stage of genocide. Writers and scientists, religious leaders, trade union movements and even the Communist parties in France, Holland, Switzerland, Norway, Austria and Finland asserted their view that Israel was a peace-loving State, whose peace was being wantonly denied. In the history of our generation it is difficult to think of any other hour in which progressive world opinion rallied in such tension and agony of spirit.

To understand the full depth of pain and shock, it is necessary to grasp the full significance of what Israel's danger meant. A small sovereign State had its existence threatened by lawless violence. The threat to Israel was a menace to the very foundations of the international order. The State thus threatened bore a name which stirred the deepest memories of civilized mankind and the people of the remnant of millions, who, in living memory had been wiped out by a dictatorship more powerful, through scarcely more malicious, than Nasser's Egypt. What Nasser had predicted, what he had worked for with undeflecting purpose, had come to pass—the noose was tightly drawn.

On the fateful morning of June 5, when Egyptian forces moved by air and land against Israel's western coast and southern territory, our country's choice was plain. The choice was to live or perish, to defend the national existence or to forfeit it for all time.

From these dire moments Israel emerged in five heroic days from awful peril to successful and glorious resistance. Alone, unaided, neither seeking nor receiving help, our nation rose in self-defence. So long as men cherish freedom, so long as small states strive for the dignity of existence, the exploits of Israel's armies will be told from one generation to another with the deepest pride. The Soviet Union has described our resistance as aggression and sought to have it condemned. We reject this accusation with all our might. Here was armed force employed in a just and righteous cause, as righteous as the defenders at Valley Forge, as just as the expulsion of Hitler's bombers from the British skies, as noble as the protection of Stalingrad against the Nazi hordes, so was the defence of Israel's security and existence against those who sought our nation's destruction.

What should be condemned is not Israel's action, but the attempt to condemn it. Never have freedom, honour, justice, national interest and international morality been so righteously protected. While fighting raged on the Egyptian-Israel frontier and on the Syrian front, we still hoped to contain the conflict. Jordan was given every chance to remain outside the struggle. Even after Jordan had bombarded and bombed Israel territory at several points we still proposed to the Jordanian monarch that he abstain from general hostilities. A message to this effect reached him several hours after the outbreak of hostilities on the southern front on June 5.

Jordan answered not with words but with shells. Artillery opened fire fiercely along the whole front with special emphasis on the Jerusalem area. Thus Jordan's responsibility for the second phase of the concerted aggression is established beyond doubt. This responsibility cannot fail to have its consequences in the peace settlement. As death and injury rained on the city, Jordan had become the source and origin of Jerusalem's fierce ordeal. The inhabitants of the city can never forget this fact, or fail to draw its conclusions.

Soviet Role in the Middle East Crisis

Mr. President, I have spoken of Israel's defence against the assaults of neighbouring states. This is not the entire story. Whatever happens in the Middle East for good or ill, for peace or conflict, is powerfully affected by what the Great Powers do or omit to do. When the Soviet Union initiates a discussion here, our gaze is inexorably drawn to the story of its role in recent Middle Eastern history. It is a sad and shocking story, it must be frankly told.

Since 1955 the Soviet Union has supplied the Arab States with 2,000 tanks, of which more than 1,000 have gone to Egypt. The Soviet Union has supplied the Arab States with 700 modern fighter aircraft and bombers, more recently with ground missiles, and Egypt alone has received from the U.S.S.R. 540 field guns, 130 medium guns, 200 120 mm mortars, anti-aircraft guns, 175 rocket launchers, 650 anti-tank guns, seven destroyers, a number of Luna M and SPKA 2 ground-to-ground missiles, 14 submarines and 46 torpedo boats of various types including missile-carrying boats. The Egyptian Army has been trained by Soviet experts. This has been attested to by Egyptian officers captured by Israel. Most of this equipment was supplied to the Arab States after the Cairo Summit Conference of Arab leaders in January 1964 had agreed on a specific programme for the destruction of Israel, after they had announced and hastened to fulfil this plan by accelerating their arms purchases from the Soviet

Union. The proportions of Soviet assistance are attested to by the startling fact that in Sinai alone the Egyptians abandoned equipment and offensive weapons of Soviet manufacture whose value is estimated at two billion dollars.

Together with the supply of offensive weapons, the Soviet Union has encouraged the military preparations of the Arab States.

Since 1961, the Soviet Union has assisted Egypt in its desire to conquer Israel. The great amount of offensive equipment supplied to the Arab States strengthens this assessment.

A Great Power which professes its devotion to peaceful settlement and the rights of states has for 14 years afflicted the Middle East with a headlong armaments race, with the paralysis of the United Nations as an instrument of security and against those who defend it.

The constant increase and escalation of Soviet armaments in Arab countries has driven Israel to a corresponding, though far smaller, procurement programme. Israel's arms purchases were precisely geared to the successive phases of Arab, and especially Egyptian, rearmament. On many occasions in recent months we and others have vainly sought to secure Soviet agreement for a reciprocal reduction of arms supplies in our region. These efforts have borne no fruit. The expenditure on social and economic progress of one half of what has been put into the purchase of Soviet arms would have been sufficient to redeem Egypt from its social and economic ills. A corresponding diversion of resources from military to social expenditure would have taken place in Israel. A viable balance of forces could have been achieved at a lower level of armaments, while our region could have moved forward to higher standards of human and social welfare. For Israel's attitude is clear. We should like to see the arms race slowed down. But if the race is joined, we are determined not to lose it. A fearful waste of economic energy in the Middle East is the direct result of the Soviet role in the constant stimulation of the race in arms.

It is clear from Arab sources that the Soviet Union has played a provocative role in spreading alarmist and incendiary reports of Israel intentions amongst Arab Governments.

On June 9 President Nasser said:

'Our friends in the U.S.S.R. warned the visiting parliamentary delegation in Moscow at the beginning of last month, that there exists a plan of attack against Syria.'

Similarly an announcement by Tass of May 23 states:

'The Foreign Affairs and Security Committee of the Knesset have accorded the Cabinet special powers to carry out war operations against Syria. Israeli forces concentrating on the Syrian border have been put in a state of alert for war. General mobilization has also been proclaimed in the country . . .'

There was not one word of truth in this story. But its diffusion in the Arab countries could only have an incendiary result.

Cairo Radio broadcast on May 28 (0500 hours) an address by Marshal Gretchko at a farewell party in honour of the former Egyptian Minister of Defence, Shams ed-Din Badran:

'The U.S.S.R., her armed forces, her people and Government will stand by the Arabs and will continue to encourage and support them. We are your faithful friends and we shall continue aiding you because this is the policy of the Soviet nation, its Party and Government. On behalf of the Ministry of Defence and in the name of the Soviet nation we wish you success and victory.'

This promise of military support came less than a week after the illicit closing of the Tiran Straits, an act which the U.S.S.R. has done nothing to condemn.

U.S.S.R. Attitudes at the U.N.

The U.S.S.R. has exercised her veto right in the Security Council five times. Each time a just and constructive judgment has been frustrated. On January 22, 1964, France, the United Kingdom and the United States presented a Draft Resolution to facilitate work on the West Bank of the River Jordan in the B'not Ya'akov Canal Project. The Soviet veto held up regional water development for several years. On March 29, 1954, a New Zealand resolution simply reiterating U.N. policy on blockade along the Suez Canal was frustrated by Soviet dissent. On August 19, 1963, a United Kingdom and United States Resolution on the murder of two Israelis at Almagor was denied adoption by Soviet opposition. On December 21, 1964, the U.S.S.R. vetoed a United Kingdom and United States Resolution on incidents at Tel Dan, including the shelling of Dan, Dafna and Sha'ar Yashuv. On November 2, 1966, Argentina, Japan, the Netherlands, New Zealand and Nigeria joined to express regret at 'infiltration from Syria and loss of human life caused by the incidents in October and November 1966.' This was one of the few resolutions sponsored by member-States from five continents.

The Soviet use of veto has had a dual effect. First, it prevented any resolution which an Arab State has opposed, from being adopted by the Council. Secondly, it has inhibited the Security Council from taking constructive action in disputes between an Arab State and Israel because of the certain knowledge that the veto would be applied in what was deemed to be the Arab interest. The consequences of the Soviet veto policy have been to deny Israel any possibility of just and equitable treatment in the Security Council, and to nullify the Council as a constructive factor in the affairs of the Middle East.

Does all this really add up to a constructive intervention by the U.S.S.R. in the Arab-Israel tension? The position becomes graver when we recall the unbridled invective against the Permanent Representative of Israel in the Security Council. In its words and in the letter to the Israel Government, the U.S.S.R. has formulated an obscene comparison between the Israel Defence Forces and the Hitlerite hordes which overran Europe in the Second World War. There is a flagrant breach of international morality and human decency in this comparison. Our nation never compromised with Hitler Germany. It never signed a pact with it as did the U.S.S.R. in 1939.

To associate the name of Israel with the accursed tyrant who engulfed the Jewish people in a tidal wave of slaughter is to violate every canon of elementary taste and fundamental truth.

In the light of this history, the General Assembly will easily understand Israel's reaction to the Soviet initiative in convening this Special Session for the purpose of condemning our country and recommending a withdrawal to the position that existed before June 5.

Your (the Soviet) Government's record in the stimulation of the arms race, in the paralysis of the Security Council, in the encouragement throughout the Arab World of unfounded suspicion concerning Israel's intentions, your constant refusal to say a single word of criticism at any time of declarations threatening the violent overthrow of Israel's sovereignty and existence—all this gravely undermines your claims to objectivity. You come here in our eyes not as a judge or as a prosecutor, but rather as a legitimate object of international

criticism for the part that you have played in the sombre
events which have brought our region to a point of explosive
tension.

If the Soviet Union had made an equal distribution of the
friendship amongst the peoples of the Middle East, if it had
refrained from exploiting regional rancours and tensions for
the purpose of its own global policy, if it had stood in even-
handed devotion to the legitimate interests of all states, the
crisis which now commands our attention and anxiety would
never have occurred. To the charge of aggression I answer
that Israel's resistance at the lowest ebb of its fortunes will
resound across history, together with the uprising of our bat-
tered remnants in the Warsaw Ghetto, as a triumphant assertion of human freedom. From the dawn of its history the
people now rebuilding a State in Israel has struggled often in
desperate conditions against tyranny and aggression. Our action on June 5 falls nobly within that tradition. We have tried
to show that even a small state and a small people have the
right to live. I believe that we shall not be found alone in the
assertion of that right, which is the very essence of the Charter
of the United Nations. Similarly, the suggestion that everything goes back to where it was before the 5th of June is
totally unacceptable. The General Assembly cannot ignore
the fact that the Security Council, where the primary responsibility lay, has emphatically rejected such a course. It was not
Israel, but Syria, Egypt and Jordan, who violently shattered
the previous situation to smithereens. It cannot be recaptured.
It is a fact of technology that it is easier to fly to the moon
than to reconstruct a broken egg. The Security Council acted
wisely in rejecting the backward step, advocated by the Soviet
Union. To go back to the situation out of which the conflict
arose would mean that all the conditions for renewed hostilities would be brought together again. I repeat what I said
to the Security Council. Our watchword is not 'backward to
belligerency' but 'forward to peace'.

What the Assembly should prescribe is not a formula for
renewed hostilities, but a series of principles for the construction of a new future in the Middle East. With the cease-fire
established, our progress must be not backward to an armistice
regime which has collapsed under the weight of years and the
brunt of hostility. History summons us forward to permanent
peace and the peace that we envisage can only be elaborated
in frank and lucid dialogue between Israel and each of the

states which have participated in the attempt to overthrow her sovereignty and undermine her existence. We dare not be satisfied with intermediate arrangements which are neither war nor peace. Such patchwork ideas carry within themselves the seeds of future tragedy. Free from external pressures and interventions, imbued with a common love for a region which they are destined to share, the Arab and Jewish nations must now transcend their conflicts in dedication to a new Mediterranean future in concert with a renascent Europe and an Africa and Asia which have emerged at last to their independent role on the stage of history.

The Vision of Peace

In free negotiation with each of our neighbours we shall offer durable and just solutions redounding to our mutual advantage and honour. The Arab states can no longer be permitted to recognize Israel's existence only for the purpose of plotting its elimination. They have come face to face with us in conflict. Let them now come face to face with us in peace.

In peaceful conditions we could imagine communications running from Haifa to Beirut and Damascus in the north, to Amman and beyond in the east, and to Cairo in the south. The opening of these blocked arteries would stimulate the life, thought and commerce in the region beyond any level otherwise conceivable. Across the southern Negev, communication between the Nile Valley and the fertile crescent could be resumed without any change in political jurisdiction. What is now often described as a wedge between Arab lands would become a bridge. The Kingdom of Jordan, now cut off from its maritime outlet, could freely import and export its goods on the Israeli coast. On the Red Sea, cooperative action could expedite the port developments at Eilat and Akaba, which give Israel and Jordan their contact with a resurgent East Africa and a developing Asia.

The Middle East, lying athwart three continents, could become a busy centre of air communications, which are now impeded by boycotts and the necessity to take circuitous routes. Radio, telephone and postal communications, which now end abruptly in mid-air, would unite a divided region. The Middle East, with its historic monuments and scenic beauty, could attract a vast movement of travellers and pilgrims if existing impediments were removed. Resources which lie across national frontiers—the minerals of the Dead Sea and the phosphates of the Negev and the Arava—could be developed in mutual interchange of technical knowledge. Economic cooperation in agricultural and industrial development could lead to supranational arrangements like those which mark the European community. The United Nations could establish an economic commission for the Middle East, similar to the commissions now at work in Europe, Latin America and the Far East. The specialized agencies could intensify their support of health and educational development with greater efficiency if a regional harmony were attained. The development of arid zones, the desalination of water and the conquest of tropical disease are common interests of the entire region, congenial to a sharing of knowledge and experience.

In the institutions of scientific research and higher education of both sides of the frontiers, young Israelis and Arabs could join in a mutual discourse of learning. The old prejudices could be replaced by a new comprehension and respect, born of a reciprocal dialogue in the intellectual domain. In such a Middle East, military budgets would spontaneously find a less exacting point of equilibrium. Excessive sums devoted to security could be diverted to development projects.

Thus, in full respect of the region's diversity, an entirely new story, never known or told before, would unfold across the Eastern Mediterranean. For the first time in history, no Mediterranean nation is in subjection. All are endowed with sovereign freedom. The challenge now is to use this freedom for creative growth. There is only one road to that end. It is the road of recognition, of direct contact, of true cooperation. It is the road of peaceful co-existence. This road, as the ancient prophets of Israel foretold, leads to Jerusalem.

Jerusalem, now united after her tragic division, is no longer an arena for gun emplacements and barbed wire. In our nation's long history there have been few hours more intensely moving than the hour of our reunion with the Western Wall. A people had come back to the cradle of its birth. It has renewed its link with the memories which that reunion evokes. For 20 years there has not been free access by men of all faiths to the shrines which they hold in unique reverence. This access now exists. Israel is resolved to give effective expression, in cooperation with the world's great religions, to the immunity and sanctity of all the Holy Places. The prospect of a negotiated peace is less remote than it may seem. Israel waged her defensive struggle in pursuit of two objectives—security and peace. Peace and security, with their territorial, economic and demographic implications, can only be built by the free negotiation which is the true essence of sovereign responsibility. A call to the recent combatants to negotiate the conditions of their future co-existence is the only constructive course which this Assembly could take.

We ask the great powers to remove our tormented region from the scope of global rivalries, to summon its governments to build their common future themselves, to assist it, if they will, to develop social and cultural levels worthy of its past.

We ask the developing countries to support a dynamic and forward-looking policy and not to drag the new future back into the out-worn past.

To the small nations, which form the bulk of the international family, we offer the experience which teaches us that small communities can best secure their interests by maximal self-reliance. Nobody will help those who will not help themselves; we ask the small nations in the solidarity of our smallness, to help us stand firm against intimidation and threat such as those by which we are now assailed. We ask world opinion, which rallied to us in our plight, to accompany us faithfully in our new opportunity. We ask the United Nations, which was prevented from offering us security in our recent peril, to respect our independent quest for the peace and security which are the Charter's higher ends. We shall do what the Security Council decided should be done—and reject the course which the Security Council emphatically and wisely rejected. It may seem that Israel stands alone against numerous and powerful adversaries. But we have faith in the undying forces in our nation's history which have so often given the final victory to spirit over matter, to inner truth over mere quantity. We believe in the vigilance of history which has guarded our steps. The Guardian of Israel neither slumbers nor sleeps.

The Middle East, tired of wars, is ripe for a new emergence of human vitality. Let the opportunity not fall again from our hands.

The Right of Israel

By Yizhak Rabin*

Your Excellency, President of the State, Mr. Prime Minister, President of the Hebrew University, Rector of the University; Governors, Teachers, Ladies and Gentlemen:

I stand in awe before you, leaders of the generation, here in this venerable and impressive place overlooking Israel's eternal capital and the birth-place of our Nation's earliest history.

Together with other distinguished personalities who are no doubt worthy of this honour, you have chosen to do me great honour in conferring upon me the title of Doctor of Philosophy. Permit me to express to you here my feelings on this occasion. I regard myself, at this time, as a representative of the entire Israel Forces, of its thousands of officers and tens of thousands of soldiers who brought the State of Israel its victory in the six-day war. It may be asked why the University saw fit to grant the title of Honorary Doctor of Philosophy to a soldier in recognition of his martial activities. What is there in common to military activity and the academic world which represents civilisation and culture? What is there in common between those whose profession is violence and spiritual values? I, however, am honoured that through me you are expressing such deep appreciation to my comrades in arms and to the uniqueness of the Israel Defence Forces, which is no more than extension of the unique spirit of the entire Jewish People.

The world has recognised the fact that the Israel Defence Forces are different from other armies. Although its first task is the military task of ensuring security, the Israel Defence Forces undertakes numerous tasks of peace, tasks not of destruction but of construction and of the strengthening of the Nation's cultural and moral resources.

Our educational work has been praised widely and was given national recognition, when in 1966 it was granted the Israel Prize for Education, The Nahal, which combines military training and agricultural settlement, teachers in border villages contributing to social and cultural enrichment, these

---

* The text of an address by Rabin, formerly Israeli chief of staff and at present Israeli Ambassador in the United States, on the occasion of receiving an honorary doctorate from the Hebrew University, June 28, 1967.

are but a few small examples of the Israel Defence Forces'
uniqueness in this sphere.

However, today, the University has conferred this honorary
title on us in recognition of our Army's superiority of spirit
and morals as it was revealed in the heat of war, for we are
standing in this place by virtue of battle which though forced
upon us was forged into a victory astounding the world.

War is intrinsically harsh and cruel, bloody and tear-stained,
but particularly this war, which we have just undergone,
brought forth rare and magnificent instances of heroism and
courage, together with humane expressions of brotherhood,
comradeship, and spiritual greatness.

Whoever has not seen a tank crew continue its attack with
its commander killed and its vehicle badly damaged, whoever
has not seen sappers endangering their lives to extricate
wounded comrades from a minefield, whoever has not seen
the anxiety and the effort of the entire Air Force devoted to
rescuing a pilot who has fallen in enemy territory, cannot
know the meaning of devotion between comrades in arms.

The entire Nation was exalted and many wept upon hearing
the news of the capture of the Old City. Our Sabra Youth and
most certainly our soldiers do not tend to sentimentality and
shy away from revealing it in public. However, the strain of
battle, the anxiety which preceded it, and the sense of salvation and of direct participation of every soldier in the forging
of the heart of Jewish history cracked the shell of hardness
and shyness and released well-springs of excitement and spiritual emotion. The paratroopers, who conquered the Wailing
Wall, leaned on its stones and wept, and as a symbol this was
a rare occasion, almost unparalleled in human history. Such
phrases and cliches are not generally used in our Army but
this scene on the Temple Mount beyond the power of verbal
description revealed as though by a lightning flash deep truths.
And more than this, the joy of triumph seized the whole nation. Nevertheless we find more and more and more a strange
phenomenon among our fighters. Their joy is incomplete, and
more than a small portion of sorrow and shock prevails in
their festivities. And there are those who abstain from all cele-
bration. The warriors in the front lines saw with their own
eyes not only the glory of victory but the price of victory.
Their comrades who fell beside them bleeding. And I know
that even the terrible price which our enemies paid touched
the hearts of many of our men. It may be that the Jewish
People never learned and never accustomed itself to feel the

triumph of conquest and victory and therefore we receive it with mixed feelings.

The six-day war revealed many instances of heroism far beyond the single attack which dashes unthinkingly forward. In many places desperate and lengthy battles raged. In Rafiah, in El Arish, in Um Kataf, in Jerusalem, and in Ramat Hagollan, there, and in many other places, the soldiers of Israel were revealed as heroic in spirit, in courage, and in persistence which cannot leave anyone indifferent once he has seen this great and exalting human revelation. We speak a great deal of the few against the many. In this war perhaps for the first time since the Arab invasions of the spring of 1948 and the battles of Negba and Degania, units of the Israel Forces stood in all sectors, few against many. This means that relatively small units of our soldiers, often entered seemingly endless networks of fortification, surrounded by hundreds and thousands of enemy troops and faced with the task of forcing their way, hour after hour, in this jungle of dangers, even after the momentum of the first attack has passed and all that remains is the necessity of belief in our strength, the lack of alternative and the goal for which we are fighting, to summon up every spiritual resource in order to continue the fight to its very end.

Thus our armoured Forces broke through on all fronts, our paratroopers fought their way into Rafiah and Jerusalem, our sappers cleared minefields under enemy fire. The units which broke the enemy lines and came to their objectives after hours upon hours of struggle continuing on and on, while their comrades fell right and left and they continued forward, only forward. These soldiers were carried forward by spiritual values, by deep spiritual resources, far more than by their weapons or the technique of warfare.

We have always demanded the cream of our youth for the Israel Defence Forces when we coined the slogan 'Hatovim l'Tayis'—The Best to Flying, and this was a phrase which became a value. We meant not only technical and manual skills. We meant that if our airmen were to be capable of defeating the forces of four enemy countries within a few short hours, they must have moral values and human values.

Our airmen, who struck the enemies' planes so accurately that no one in the world understands how it was done and people seek technological explanations of secret weapons; our armoured troops who stood and beat the enemy even when their equipment was inferior to his; our soldiers in all various branches of the Israel Defence Forces who overcame our enemies everywhere, despite their superior numbers and fortifications; all these revealed not only coolness and courage in battle but a burning faith in their righteousness, an understanding that only their personal stand against the greatest of dangers could bring to their country and to their families victory, and that if the victory was not theirs the alternative was destruction.

Furthermore, in every sector our Forces' commanders, of all ranks far outshone the enemies' commanders. Their understanding, their will, their ability to improvise, their care for soldiers and above all, their leading troops into battle, these are not matters of material or of technique. They have no rational explanation, except in terms of a deep consciousness of the moral justice of their fight.

All of this springs from the soul and leads back to the spirit. Our warriors prevailed not by their weapons but by the consciousness of a mission, by a consciousness of righteousness, by a deep love for their homeland and an understanding of the difficult task laid upon them; to ensure the existence of our people in its homeland, to protect, even at the price of their lives, the right of the Nation of Israel to live in its own State, free, independent and peaceful.

This Army, which I had the privilege of commanding through these battles, came from the people and returns to the people, to the people which rises in its hour of crisis and overcomes all enemies by virtue of its moral values, its spiritual readiness in the hour of need.

As the representative of the Israel Defence Forces, and in the name of everyone of its soldiers, I accept with pride your recognition.

"We Shall Triumph"

President Nasser's speech at the National Congress of the Arab Socialist Union at Cairo University, Cairo, July 23, 1968. (The first part of the speech, which is omitted, was devoted to questions of domestic policy.)

The Middle East crisis: I do not want to go back to the circumstances which led to the Middle East crisis. All the details are known, starting with the premeditated aggression against Arab territory, to the imperialist collusion with the Israeli enemy, to the 5th June setback and its serious and sad results for our Arab nation. As you know, we lost the major part of our military power. We accepted the political solution experiment for several reasons. At that time we had no alternative to talking about a political solution; we had no armed forces to depend on. At the same time we are not advocates of war for the sake of war—not at all. If we can obtain our rights through political action, as happened in 1957, fine; if not, we have no alternative but to struggle for our rights and to liberate our land.

Furthermore, we want world public opinion to be on our side and really to know our position. At the same time, we must consider our present friends and our possible friends before we consider our enemies. A major part of the battle is taking place on an international level and under the eyes of public opinion throughout the entire world, which wants to live in peace.

We realised from the beginning, as we were trying a political solution, that it was a difficult and thorny road because the enemy was drunk with victory. We know that the principle that what has been taken by force cannot be regained by anything but force is a sound and correct principle in all circumstances. But we tried sincerely and are still trying sincerely on a basis from which we do not deviate. This basis is clear and definite in UAR policy: no negotiations with Israel, no peace with Israel, no recognition of Israel, and no deals at the expense of Palestinian soil or the Palestinian people.

These are the foundations on which we proceeded in regard to solving the Middle East crisis peacefully. However, since 23rd November and until now, give and take has been going on with the UN representative. Have we achieved anything? We have achieved nothing. We co-operated to the maximum with the UN Secretary-General's representative. We accepted the Security Council resolution, but Israel did not.

No projects exist now for a peaceful solution, and it does not seem to me that there will be any in the future. We hear what the representative of the UN Secretary-General says, and we express our opinion on what we hear. So far our opinion has been clear.

With regard to a political solution, we will not in any way agree to give away one inch of Arab territory in any Arab country.

It is clear that Israel, which rejected the Security Council resolution, has many aims. The first is to achieve a political objective, because it won a military victory but did not achieve a political gain. Israel wants direct negotiations and wants a peace treaty signed. We reject this. Israel thus won a military victory but has so far been unable to achieve the political objective—signing a peace treaty with any of the Arab States surrounding it.

Therefore Israel will not withdraw. Why should it withdraw from the territory it occupied after achieving a crushing military victory? Israel, as they say, will remain in this territory hoping that conditions or regimes will be changed and replaced by regimes which will agree to the conclusion of a peace treaty with Israel [shouts of "God forbid" from audience].

How would the conditions change? Israel knows that the occupation burdens the hearts of all the sons of the Arab nation. Occupation represents fragmentation. Occupation is something out of the ordinary and is like a nightmare to all of us. Israel and the imperialist forces working behind it would be able to influence the domestic fronts and might be able to change the regimes and replace them with others which would agree to the conclusion of peace with Israel. As long as Israel knows that we have not yet attained a crushing offensive military strength, it will remain where it is, hoping to achieve political victory through a changing of regimes.

Israel continues to refuse the Security Council resolution. Israel refuses to discuss the Security Council resolution. Israel says: We will remain in our places along the cease-fire lines until you agree to negotiate with us and conclude a peace treaty. Naturally we counter this by rebuilding our armed forces. A year ago after the defeat, we had no armed forces. We now have armed forces which may be greater than those existing before the battle. We are working for the development of the armed forces in order to attain supremacy because our enemy is a cunning enemy backed by a force which gives him everything—money and arms.

After this, we shall discuss the possibilities of the military and political solutions. Because of its nature, the crisis cannot last long. We have been waiting for one year. Our area is a sensitive one. The status quo cannot be accepted. This status quo is against nature and creates a situation conducive to quick ignition and explosion at any time.

There exists a basic and principal commitment which is a question of life or death: the liberation of the land inch by inch if necessary even if one martyr must fall on every inch of land. That is clear. A war to regain a right is a legal war. However, we shall allow no one to provoke us. We shall decide, prepare and arrange things. This is a lengthy matter which demands our patience and endurance. We must be patient and stand fast in order to triumph and attain supremacy. Having attained supremacy, we shall triumph.

Life will be meaningless and worthless to us however, until every inch of Arab soil is liberated. To us the liberation of Arab soil represents an indivisible whole. In no circumstances is there an alternative to the departure of the occupation forces from all occupied territory. Prior to this departure, there can be no peace in the Middle East in any circumstances. If there is no peace in the Middle East, it is very doubtful that the repercussions will be restricted to borders of the Middle East.

We do not address ourselves to Israel alone but to the whole world. We have nothing to say as far as Israel is concerned. Israel's role has been exposed. Its role as a stooge of world imperialism and colonialism has been fully exposed. However, our talk today is addressed to the world, which is anxious for peace and adheres to peace. We add that peace in this part of the world will not be achieved by the mere elimination of the consequences of the 5th June aggression. Real peace should take into consideration the legal rights of the Palestinian people.

The third subject is the armed forces. When we study the causes of the defeat—I have studied the causes of the defeat and attended command meetings which discussed everything that took place—when we study the causes of the defeat, it becomes clear to us that there was no deficiency among the officers and soldiers. We must know this well. A mistake was made and it is painful to go back over its details.

Four-fifths of our forces did not encounter the enemy and had no opportunity to fight. They were placed in extremely bad conditions. It is not advantageous to talk now about the past except within the limits necessary to reassess matters and to benefit from the lessons of the battle. Our soldiers and officers who entered the battles proved that they could stand firm and die. The Egyptian soldier is a fighting soldier who does not fear death. I fought with the Egyptian peasant soldier in 1948 and saw how he welcomes death.

We should therefore be doing our soldiers and officers an injustice if we looked at them on the basis of what has taken place. The fact is that a very large part of the army did not enter battle. Each of us knows that during the withdrawal operation the hostile forces were finally able to inflict the heaviest losses on us. We have now learned and benefited from the lessons of the battle. We have compensated for much of the loss our armed forces suffered last year. As I said before, we have attained defence capability. We shall now strive to transform our army into a strong offensive army supplied with the most up-to-date weapons.

I witnessed an exercise before leaving for the Soviet Union. I saw our armed forces that participated in it. I can say that in the past year they achieved as much as five years of work. One can say that we now have capable armed forces. However it is all-essential that we understand that the officers and soldiers are doing a very difficult job. They are now working day and night. Every officer and NCO feels that the whole country is watching him and assigning him a duty which will determine our fate and future. Each of them feels that the nation is giving him the responsibility. They are therefore carrying out this duty. However, our armed forces must bide their time and be ready to take the opportunity to achieve what they are duty bound to achieve.

We, as a people, fully support our armed forces and have full faith in them because when the people lose confidence in their armed forces, they also lose confidence in themselves and in their destiny. The people must give to their armed forces because there is no alternative. It is my duty to say that the people have given. What have they given? They have given their sons. The best of their sons are now members of the armed forces. The soldiers and officers of the armed forces are our sons. The people feel and live with them constantly. The people feel that the armed forces are living under difficult psychological and physical conditions as a result of their hard work, great efforts, training and exhausting conditions. To live under such conditions day after day is painful to the soul and to our armed forces, who see the enemy on the other bank of the Canal.

The fourth question is my recent visit to the Soviet Union and to Yugoslavia. Brothers, I mainly went to thank the leaders and people of the Soviet Union for everything they have given us and to discuss the situation. However, there is a fact which we must realise and know: Had it not been for the Soviet Union, we would now find ourselves facing the enemy without any weapons and compelled to accept his conditions. The United States would not have given us a single round of ammunition. It has given us and will give us nothing, but it gives Israel everything from guns to aircraft and missiles.

In reality, we have so far paid not one millieme for the arms we obtained from the Soviet Union to equip our armed forces. Actually, were it a question of payment, we have no money to buy arms. We all know the situation. We took part of the Soviet weapons as a gift and concluded a contract for the remainder for which we shall pay in the future in long-term installments. Had it not been for the Soviet Union and its agreement to supply us with arms, we should now be in a position similar to our position a year ago. We should have no weapons and should be compelled to accept Israel's condition under its threat.

At the same time, there exists a question which we must fully realise and understand: Why does the Soviet Union give us all these things? Why? We have one common aim with the Soviet Union—to resist imperialism. We do not want foreign influence in our part of the world. For its part, the Soviet Union is most anxious to oppose imperialism and to liquidate the imperialist concentrations to the south of its borders. Our ideological and national interest is against imperialism; the Soviet Union's ideological interest and strategy are against imperialism. I wish to tell you frankly and clearly that the Soviet Union has never tried, not even in our most crucial times, to dictate conditions to us or to ask anything of us. On the contrary, it has always been we who have asked.

Naturally, I did not pay my recent visit to the Soviet Union to express gratitude only, but to ask for things as well. After expressing my gratitude, I asked for things and after asking, I told them that I was ashamed. Do you not want anything from us? We ask you for things. But they answered: We have nothing to ask of you. I am actually telling this to you and to history so we may know who our friends and enemies are.

We went on asking for hours but they did not make one request of us. Even when I told them I felt ashamed that we were making many demands while they had asked nothing of us—I wish they had a request which we could fulfil—I asked if they had nothing to ask of us. They told us: We take this stand on the basis of our ideology—the ideology of national liberation and the peoples' struggle. We have nothing to ask.

The Soviet Union did not try to dictate any conditions to us. In our constant dealings with it, the Soviet Union has not tried to dictate any conditions—not even when we differed and we differed with the Soviet Union in 1959. At that time there was agreement on the first stage of the High Dam, the first industrialisation agreement and the arms deal agreement. Despite this, despite the difference which reached such extent that it was published in the newspapers, no attempt was made to apply pressure and no word of threat was uttered by the Soviet Union. Sincerity prompts me to say this.

There is another point. This is the element of the Soviet Navy and its appearance in the Mediterranean. I say that the States of the region, all the liberated States in the region, welcome the appearance of the Soviet Navy in the Mediterranean Sea as an element to balance the US Sixth Fleet, which sought to turn the Mediterranean into an American sea. The Soviet Navy did not threaten us. The Sixth Fleet is a strategic reserve for Israel, according to the Israel Premier himself. When the US Navy leaves the Mediterranean, then those who wonder about the danger of the presence of the Soviet Navy will be able to speak and be heard.

On this occasion, I may make a quick reference to our attitude towards the United States. US policy has failed rapidly in this region. No one other than an obvious agent can openly declare friendship for the United States. The entire Arab world is aware of what the United States has done. We expected something different from the United States, or at least we did not expect all that has happened. However, that is the United States' business.

Giving arms to Israel while it is occupying Arab territory means that the United States supports Israel in the occupation of the Arab territory. Giving aircraft to Israel while it is occupying Arab territory means that the United States supports Israel in the occupation of the Arab territory. The complete US support for Israel at the United Nations and the adoption and defence of the Israeli point of view means that the United States supports Israel's occupation of the Arab territory. The US refusal to make a statement stipulating the need for the withdrawal of the Israeli forces to the positions they occupied before 5th June is proof that the United States supports Israel and, indeed, colludes with Israel in what it has done and is doing. Every member of the Arab nation is aware of this.

This matter is not confined to the Arab nation but also includes other States. Last year, it appeared that some CENTO member-States wanted to absolve themselves of CENTO, which was formerly called the Baghdad Pact. Yesterday we read that the Turkish students were throwing Sixth Fleet crews into the sea. Why? No sensible man in the United States asks himself why this has happened in the Arab world and in other States.

The United States, which possesses means of power that no other State has had the chance to possess throughout history or in our era, should really ask itself what the people want of it. The people want the United States to adopt an attitude based on justice, an attitude based on equality, for as a great Power the United States should also have great principles which reject aggression and occupation and in no circumstances agree to support the aggressor and give him arms.

I shall now refer to my visit to Yugoslavia. I visited Yugoslavia for a short time. Maybe we stayed two nights there. The purpose of the visit was to prove our appreciation for President Tito's visit to us last August. He decided to come in August, the warmest time, last year. Such a gesture on his part deserves great appreciation. President Tito is our friend. After the setback, he actually played a very great role everywhere and in all States against aggression, occupation and Israel's methods. At the same time we discussed the new conference of non-aligned States.

We shall now speak about the economic situation. Despite all the conditions of war, the Egyptian economic situation is sound in its entirety. Industry has obtained investments, new factories are being opened daily, and agricultural products are setting records. This does not mean that we have no economic problems. No. We have economic problems. We have problems in respect of hard currency, the balance of payments and investments required for development. We want to employ the largest number of people and therefore we need a large amount of money. However, despite these problems, the economy is proceeding on its course. There were hopes that economic pressure would make us hungry and would place us in a situation so that we could not import wheat or food. Now, one year later, we are able to stand fast. There is wheat, flour and corn. There are no crises involving supplies, all this despite the fact that we have made an unprecedented allocation for the defence budget this year—over £E300 million.

The next point I wish to discuss concerns youth and its role. Concern about youth is one of the most important phenomena in our homeland. We must develop this concern.

The worst thing that can happen to any country is to have its youth feel indifferent. We want our youth to be interested in everything. The condition of youth must be one of our most important subjects, because youth is the hope of the homeland. Young people participating in public affairs is a healthy sign and a guarantee of hope for the future. This is the reason for the concern about the representation of youth at this Congress.

We also believe that the university's positive participation in forming concepts is necessary. I have spoken, perhaps in this very hall, of this many times in past years. The university must be the stronghold protecting national social development and opening the way before it. I never cease to say that the guarantees for the future are the universities, concern about the universities, and democracy.

The next point is Arab action. The battle against the enemy must have priority over everything else. The battle demands a single Arab nation. Up to now we have been trying by all means to attain this aim.

A meeting was held at Khartoum. I have spoken previously about the Khartoum meeting and its importance. We called for another summit conference but did not insist on it and substituted bilateral co-ordination instead. We are not about to be side-tracked. Some have tried to drag us along, but we are not prepared to be dragged.

There is one battle which is absorbing all our efforts in preparing for it; we have no time for anything else. It is the battle against the enemy. Our attitude towards any Arab State depends on that State's attitude towards the battle. Naturally, some states have sent us forces, Sudan and Algeria for instance. Their forces are with us. Other Arab countries such as Iraq and Kuwait have forces with us too. Some States have helped us to resist economically and have adhered to the Arab support agreement such as Saudi Arabia, Libya and Kuwait. I believe that Arab action can progress day after day in spite of the slow rate of progress.

The next point concerns Palestinian fida'i activity. We are fully committed to offering all help to the Palestinian fida'i action. We consider that the Palestinian struggle last year was a big sign of change in the whole Arab situation. Not only we but the entire world senses this indication that the Palestinian people have risen to champion their own cause by themselves and to defend their rights by themselves.

The ninth point concerns psychological warfare. Psychological warfare means an attempt to arouse doubt about everything. Its aim is to strike at the domestic front. But attempts to cast suspicion are not new to us. As we have said, in 1957 there were 11 clandestine radios broadcasting against us. Attempts to arouse suspicions are useless so far as the masses of the Arab nation are concerned.

Suspicion campaigns act in various directions. Firstly, they try to distort the essential widescale diplomatic activity of the UAR and to depict it as accepting suspect plans. Of course, it is our duty to launch a diplomatic offensive and expose Israel throughout the world. Of course, psychological warfare is being used in an effort to depict this diplomatic offensive as acceptance of suspicious plans.

Psychological warfare also seeks to speak of the Soviet Union and holds that our relations with the USSR have expanded and become closer and that this will drive us into communism and embroil us in subservience. All of us know these points and I do not have to repeat them.

There is a big difference between co-operation and subservience. When we concluded the 1955 arms deal with the Soviet Union they said there was danger in the arms deal because it would drag us into subservience. They cited examples. When we began to conclude the High Dam agreement with the Soviet Union, they said Soviet experts would come to work at the High Dam and that this would lead to some sort of subservience. More than 5,000 Soviet experts came to the High Dam, but none of them interfered in our domestic affairs and none of them tried to convert any of the people of Aswan to communism. Nothing of the sort happened.

Today they are saying the same thing. For example, they say the Soviet experts in the Army mean domination of the army and subservience. I have said before that we asked the Soviet Union for these experts and that the Soviet Union was not receptive to giving us experts, saying it would expose us to attack. But in fact, after the 5th June events, anyone with insight who could evaluate things felt that we needed training and that we had a great deal to learn about war. Thus we asked for and got the military experts. They are helping us. We have, in fact, benefited from them; we have benefited from them in all fields.

What the psychological warfare suggested when we received arms in 1955 and when we concluded the High Dam agreement in 1960 may again be suggested this time.

Brothers, we feel that the entire Arab nation must feel

grateful to the Soviet Union. Had it not been for the Soviet Union, as I have already said, we should now find ourselves with no arms in the face of the Israeli militarism, which has been blinded by its victory of June 1967. Egypt's independence—and I say this to all people—is not for sale, is not for anyone to buy and is not for mortgage. This will continue to be the case. It is this attitude that has placed us in the difficult situations we are experiencing. Had we agreed to subservience, such as that represented by the Baghdad Pact which we were asked under threats to join, we should have accepted subservience some years ago, long ago and there would have been no need for us to wage all these battles. We have not accepted subservience, we will never accept it and for this reason we have been struggling and fighting for freedom, independence and the building of a free homeland and free citizens.

There has also been the psychological war—poisoned news. It was reported in recent dispatches that demonstrations had been started in Alexandria and that travellers were the source of this information. Our country is an open, not a closed, country. Our country is not a closed country—people can come and go. Thousands of people enter and leave our country every hour. These reports reflect a form of psychological war involving false reports to influence us and to prove that the domestic front is not strong and is not steadfast and, at the same time, to influence the domestic front and shake it so that imperialism, Israel and those who stand behind Israel can achieve their purpose.

Our enemies have succeeded in winning a military victory, but our country has not fallen, has not accepted defeat, but has decided to stand fast. They have applied economic pressure to us and, despite this pressure, we have not surrendered but have marched on. We have imposed restrictions on ourselves and have accepted these restrictions. Our enemies have failed to destroy us economically. Hence, there remains one thing for them to do—to strike at the domestic front and to break up the alliance of the people's working forces because if the domestic front collapses the hostile imperialist forces and Israel will achieve the aims they have so far been unable to achieve.

The 10th and last point is the inevitability of victory and the conditions for victory. Brothers, there is no alternative to victory for our nation. The nation is capable of achieving victory provided it mobilises its forces and benefits properly from its energy and conditions, and also if we can build up and safeguard our domestic front according to the needs of the battle. The domestic front is the pillar of the fighting front. We must expose, defeat and crush all enemy attempts to influence the domestic front.

Now comes your role, brothers, comrades in the struggle, and members of the ASU National Congress. You are the command of the alliance of the people's working forces. You are the more capable of cohesion with these forces. You are the more capable of guiding them through work, struggle, clarity and truth. The battle is all the people's battle. It is the battle for the people's lives, and all the people must participate in it. It must be a victory for life and for the people. May God grant you success. Peace be with you.

The Moment of Truth

Towards a Middle East Dialogue

By Cecil Hourani*

This essay is addressed to the educated classes in the Arab countries: to those who still participate actively in the political, social, and intellectual life of their countries, and to those who have been excluded forcibly or by their own free will. To all I trust it will have a message of hope. Destructive as much of my argument is, my aim is positive and constructive. On the understanding of our errors in the past may be built the new society of the future. I have no recrimination against states or individuals. Time and history will provide their own judgment. The moment is one for solidarity and mutual tolerance, and above all for a free discussion among ourselves. In a climate of honest self-criticism and free expression those truths may emerge which can lead us from our present disarray to a new vision of ourselves and the world we would like to build.

At this moment when the destiny of the Arab nation is being decided, it is the duty of every Arab thinker to witness to the truth as he sees it, without fear and without dissimulation.

* Cecil Hourani, who was for ten years an adviser to President Bourguiba of Tunisia, lives now in Beirut. His essay was originally published in *El Nahar*, Beirut, and appeared in English in *Encounter*, November, 1967.

For too long has the field of publicity and expression been left in the hands of professional demagogues, blackmailers, and semi-educated fanatics. Our silence on the one hand, their vociferation on the other, have led the Arab nation not merely to disaster, but to the brink of disintegration.

The primary condition of a redressment of this situation is to see things as they are, in all their brutal clarity: then to take action to change them in the light of the ideals and objectives we set ourselves. A victory over ourselves is more important than a physical defeat on the battlefield. Governments, states, régimes, frontiers, are all transient things, subject to fluctuations and fortune. What is important is that a people should survive, not as a mere agglomeration of individuals, but as a living, creative force in history. We can only survive by acting positively ourselves, not by reacting negatively to what others may do, or seek to do, to us.

History has given to the Arab nation in the 20th century a unique chance to return to the community of living creative forces in the world: a conjunction of international affairs which made possible the independence of all our territories; and the discovery of enormous wealth which with almost no effort on our part gives us the means to accomplish all we need to refashion our society and to raise it to prosperity and progress.

This unique chance we are now in danger of losing. Our sovereign and political liberty gives us the means to bring about our own destruction more easily than we can construct our future. Our very freedom implies dangers greater than existed when we were dependent. No one will now save us from the consequences of our own mistakes and follies, except ourselves. The fact that we inhabit certain territories in this world of strategic importance or material wealth is not a sufficient guarantee of our safety or survival. We can be driven from these territories, or lose control of these riches. We can commit suicide as a nation. And history will then judge us as a people who did not know how to use the chances which had been offered them, and condemn us to the fate we shall have deserved.

The most dramatic, but not the only, example of our weakness, and of our failure to recognise both our weakness and our strength, lies in our relationship with the Zionist movement and with the State of Israel.

We have been able neither to come to terms with them: nor to destroy them: nor even to contain them.

As a result of our failure to decide what position to adopt, or to take the necessary measures of self-defence, we have allowed Israel to usurp the whole of Palestine, and to occupy the most important strategic positions in the Near East.

While it is true that the Zionist movement did not develop wholly in relationship to the Arab world, but also in an international climate outside our control, nevertheless since the establishment of Israel in 1948, against our will, our struggle against that State has taken place within the framework of the international community, and largely within the United Nations Organisation. The frontiers established in 1948 as a result of the cease-fire were not wholly advantageous to Israel, because they set a territorial limit to Zionism.

The Arab objective, therefore, if we had thought clearly and calmly, should have been the *containment of Israel* within its boundaries as limited by *de facto* arrangements arrived at after two wars we had lost, rather than its conquest and destruction.

That we were unable to distinguish clearly between containment and conquest was due primarily to a psychological weakness in us: *that which we do not like we pretend does not exist*. Because we refused to recognise a situation which was distasteful to us, we were unable to define our own relationship to that situation, or to distinguish between what we would have liked ideally, and what we were capable of achieving in practice.

As a policy of containment, the moves of the U.A.R. until 5 June 1967 could have been successful. But it had implicit dangers, the greatest of which was that in the minds of those who were practising it, it could be at any moment transformed successfully into a policy of conquest. By this confusion in their own minds about their aims, and by their misjudgment of their own strength, the Arab Governments brought about the disaster of June 5. They also lost the battle of public opinion. By foolish and irresponsible statements they allowed themselves to appear as the aggressor instead of the victims. While they talked of war and conquest, Israel prepared it.

For years Israel had cultivated the image of herself as a small defenceless State surrounded by heavily-armed neighbours bent on destroying her. While in fact we were trying to contain her, some of our spokesmen, for home consumption, were exaggerating our military capacities and promising our people conquests. This gave Israel a pretext for arming to the teeth. The balance of power which Israel was trying to maintain was not one between Israel and Egypt, but between Israel and all her neighbours combined. The higher technical skills of the Israelis, and the integration of her armed forces into her civilian population, combined with supplies of arms qualitatively at least equal to those of the Arabs, in fact gave her an advantage which we should have foreseen.

The greatest defeat, however, was not that on the battlefield or in propaganda and public opinion, but that which our Governments inflicted on their own people: countless lives lost uselessly; a great new exodus of refugees from their homes; economic losses and misery not yet calculable; a new despair and a new humiliation.

What greater proof of our capacities for self-deception and moral cowardice than that Ahmed Shouqairi still sits with our responsible leaders, or the claims of one Arab Head of State that we were not defeated because we did not use our full strength? Does not all this make one suspect that the "final victory" of which some talk would be nothing less than a *coup de grâce* delivered to the Arabs?

This is indeed our moment of truth: but some of our leaders cannot make up their minds whether they want to be Torero or Bull!

Another consequence of our unwillingness to accept as real what we do not like is that *when reality catches up with us, it is always too late*. At every *débâcle* we regret that we did not accept a situation which no longer exists. In 1948 we regretted that we had not accepted the 1947 U.N. plea for partition. In May 1967 we were trying to go back to pre-Suez. Today we would be happy—and are actually demanding the U.N.—to go back to things as they were before 5 June. From every defeat we reap a new regret and a new nostalgia, but never seem to learn a new lesson.

Yet every human situation—except annihilation—contains within it the seeds of its final reversal. Take for example the creation of Israel in 1948. It is true that in relation to our right to the total possession of Palestine this represented an Arab loss: but there were also gains to us in what happened in 1948. We won independence for part of Palestine in place of total dependence on the Mandatory Power before. Under the Mandatory Régime, Jewish immigration and the expansion of Zionism could have continued in the whole of Palestine: after 1948 Zionism was confined to a tiny territory which was strategically weak and scarcely viable economically. Had we consolidated the independence we had gained, we could have contained Israel, and with it World Zionism, for fifty years, after which Israel itself would have ceased to be a threat to us, and become just another Levantine state, part Jewish, part Arab, but overwhelmingly Oriental.

Instead of which, twenty years later, we have not only lost what remained of Arab Palestine: we have also helped Zionism to leap forward yet another stage in its dynamic progress towards full Jewish nationalism. The enormous material and moral support which the State of Israel received from Jewish citizens of other countries in the recent crisis shows that what extreme Zionists have always hoped, and moderate Jews always feared, is happening: namely the polarisation of Jewish nationalism around the State of Israel, and the progressive alienation of Jews from the societies in which they have been assimilated or at least accepted. The potential population of Israel is thus not the unborn generations in that country alone, but Jews from everywhere in the world.

Shall we in one, or ten, or twenty years, seek another "victory" like the one we have just gained, and lose the other side of the Jordan, the fertile plains of Jaulan and Hauran in Syria, and the Litani and Hasbani rivers in Lebanon? And shall we still have Ahmed Shouqairi with us to consecrate the final victory of stupidity over intelligence, of fanaticism over common sense, of dishonesty over truth?

The answer lies with us. What we do in reaction to the events of the last few weeks will determine the future of our people not for ten or twenty years, but for centuries. This time there can be no second chance. Either we continue on the same road that has led us to our present state, defeats, retreats, *débâcles,* and the rapid transformation of our settled urban and peasant populations in the Near East into a new nomadism: or we take positive measures to stop the process of disintegration, to limit the collapse, and to transform our military defeat into a political and a psychological victory.

What are these positive measures, and what are the psychological victories we may hope to gain?

We must first of all ask ourselves the question, what does victory mean in terms of our actual situation and our real strength? Does it mean victory over others—Israel, or the Anglo-Americans, or Western imperialism or international indifference, or all together? Does it mean we can impose our terms on others, draw frontiers as we want, dictate the conditions on which we agree to live with the rest of the world, and make others see us as we would like to see ourselves?

Our first effort must surely be to win a victory over ourselves: over defeatism on the one hand, extremism on the other. These two dangers are in fact intimately linked together. The real defeatists are not those who look facts in the face, accept them, and try to remedy the situation which brought them about, but those who refuse to do this, who deny facts, and who are thus preparing for new defeats.

The extremists are those who argue that our concepts were correct, but that we did not implement them seriously: and that therefore we should continue along the same path, but use more violent methods.

If however, our concepts were wrong, the use of the same methods even in a more violent form can only lead us to another defeat. It is therefore essential to re-think our basic ideas in terms of *reality,* rather than of wishes. What could we realistically hope to achieve?

Ourselves and Israel

I have pointed out the disastrous effects of not having formulated clearly in our minds the distinction between the containment and the conquest of Israel. The principal reason why we did not make this distinction, and imagined that we could at any moment switch from one to the other, was our failure to appreciate our own strength and weakness relatively to Israel and the rest of the world. We must therefore examine this question honestly and fearlessly.

1. The first basic truth we must face is that the Arabs as a whole do not yet have the scientific and technological skills, nor the general level of education among the masses, which make possible the waging of large-scale modern warfare. This is not merely a deduction from recent events: it is a statistically demonstrable fact. We do not have the educational facilities or standards at home, nor enough students abroad, to provide the General Staff, the officers, and the men capable of using modern weapons and modern methods. Nor do we have civilian populations sufficiently disciplined and educated

to collaborate with the armed forces and the civil authorities to the degree which modern warfare demands.

By not recognising this fact, our military leaders tried to fight the wrong kind of war. It is a classical accusation made against General Staffs that they use methods appropriate to the previous war. Our military thinkers and planners were trying to fight the next one. As a result our soldiers were not only unable to use the modern weapons that were placed in their hands: they were actually handicapped by them. Trapped in the tanks they could not manoeuvre, relying on the air support that never came, they fell easy victims to their enemies. And the material they had to abandon will be incorporated into the army of Israel, so that in fact we have helped to arm our opponents.

2. The second truth is that the rate of technological and scientific advance is so rapid in the modern world that even if in twenty years we can catch up with the military standards of today, we shall still be outdistanced by the Israelis, whose technological and scientific skills are the product not only of their own schools and research institutes, but of Jewish—and non-Jewish—talent throughout the world.

3. The third truth is that even if we had been able to defeat Israel militarily, we would have been deprived of the fruit of that victory by some of the Great Powers, who would have intervened to save Israel's political existence.

4. The fourth truth is that in twenty years, or even less, even if we succeed in bringing our scientific and technological skills to a point where we could wage a modern war, warfare itself will have taken on quite another aspect. The possession of nuclear weapons by smaller powers—including the Arab States and Israel—will offer a choice either of mutual annihilation or of international control: and in neither case shall we be able to get our own way on our own terms.

It is evident, therefore, that if we think primarily in terms of military power we shall be making a fundamental error. This does not mean that we should disarm. It does mean that we must re-appraise our own strength, and find a new relationship between military power on the one hand, and our political, economic, and geopolitical assets on the other.

What are the conclusions we should draw from these facts about our relationship to Israel? We must first of all realise that the immediate consequence of the present war has been to modify the strategic situation in favour of Israel, which has now reached more natural frontiers than she had before both for defence and attack. If therefore we try to rectify this situation by military force, we shall be in an even weaker position than we were in 1948, in 1956, or before 5 June 1967. And not only are we in a weaker position to attack: we are also less able to defend ourselves.

The conclusions to be drawn are two: in the first place, the resort to military force as a basic element in Arab policy towards Israel is an error. In the second place, our best chance of containing Israel lies in international pressures either within or outside the United Nations. These international pressures, of whatever nature, have, however, a price. What is the price we are prepared to pay, is a question I leave to later on.

If the balance of military power has now been seriously upset in favour of Israel, there are other aspects of the balance of power which remain in our favour. Some of these have always existed, though we have not used them properly: others spring from the defeat of 5 June itself, for in all situations lie the seeds of their reversal. In the first place, Israel's military victory was a limited one—limited by those territorial, geopolitical factors which make the physical conquest of the Arab world impossible. Military occupation is one thing, permanent conquest and domination quite another. In the second place, Israel's military victory was not a political one: it has not led her any nearer to that peace on her terms which she would like, or any nearer to the negotiating table with the Arabs. It has on the contrary brought against her a coalition of international pressures which never existed before, and liquidated the fruit of twenty years' work to win friends in Africa and Asia.

If military force is not the Arabs' best card, neither is it Israel's. By a military action far out of proportion to the immediate situation it had to face, Israel has brought into play other factors which in the long run may modify the situation within Israel in ways which their present leaders had never envisaged.

Firstly, let us suppose that international pressures do not succeed in forcing Israel to withdraw to her pre-5 June frontiers. By incorporating the Gaza Strip and the West Bank into her territory, the proportion of Arabs to Jews in Israel will be radically changed. The higher birth-rate of the Arabs will give them equality in numbers, then a majority, in a few years. And as the proportion of "Arab" Jews to European

Jews is also changing, the total population of Palestine will eventually, and before long, take on an oriental character. As we acquire some of their virtues, and they acquire some of our defects, the gap between Arab and Jew will narrow, and in fifty years could almost disappear.

Secondly, it is clear that the Zionist movement as a whole, and the Israeli leaders in particular, must now face a dramatic dilemma as a result of their *blitzkrieg* of 5 June. This dilemma is the following: If the Israeli Government accepts the Arabs within the territories she controls as full Israeli citizens, with equal civil and political rights, the concept of Israel which has hitherto been incorporated into her laws will have to be changed. Israel will no longer be a Jewish State, in which, as it does now, full citizenship requires not only membership of the Jewish religion, but Jewish ancestry. It will become a Jewish-Arab State in which nationality will be a function of residence or citizenship. Israel, in other words, as she has been since 1948, will no longer exist, and Palestine, with Arabs and Jews living together, will have been restored.

If, on the other hand, the Israeli authorities refuse to accept the Arabs as full citizens with equal civil and political rights, she will have on her hands a large population which she will be unable to liquidate or to govern.

It is the perception of this dilemma which is now leading some of the Israeli leaders to force the hands of the others and to try to have it both ways: to keep the territories they have conquered, and try to reduce the Arab population in numbers by encouraging their exodus across the Jordan. It is not difficult to foresee that the next step will be to encourage a new wave of Jewish immigration into Israel, to replace as many Arabs as possible in as short a period as possible.

If the extremists within Israel succeed in forcing the hand of the more reasonable, and getting the World Zionist movement to follow, then they will in fact make forever impossible their dream of an Arab-Jewish *rapprochement*. For the way in which the Arabs are ultimately going to judge the advantages of peace or war in their relations with Israel will depend on the way Israel treats the Arabs within its borders. If there is a genuine attempt to live together with the Arabs on terms of complete equality and within the same juropolitical framework, the way to an eventual conciliation between Israel, or Palestine, and the rest of the Arab world will have been opened. But if the Arabs are excluded from full citizenship, and reduced to the status of a colonised, dependent population, no peace will ever be possible, either inside or outside Palestine.

It is not difficult to draw logical conclusions about what Arab policy should be in the light of this situation, and of this dilemma which faces Israel. If the goals of Arab policy should be, as I have suggested, (1) the containment of Israel within whatever boundaries we can get international pressure to agree to and to stabilise, (2) the gradual transformation of Israel from a European-dominated "exclusive" Jewish State into a predominantly oriental Arab-Jewish State, then the problem of whether or not to make a formal "peace" becomes a secondary one. It will no longer be a question of principle on which no Arab leader can compromise: it becomes a question of expediency and efficacy. But there is no reason why we should accept the Israeli argument that peace can only be obtained by direct negotiations with them. Since the United Nations, or some other international group, will have to be a party to any attempt to stabilise frontiers, all our efforts to obtain a setlement can be canalised through that organisation. What we cannot afford is to have no policy at all: to be unable to support the conditions of war, and incapable of profiting from the advantages of peace.

The formulation of a consistent Arab policy towards Israel within the framework of the international community is thus perfectly possible and not difficult if we define both our aims and our methods. I have stated what these aims could be. As for the methods, a few are obvious, although others may also be found, and the way these methods are used will be up to the Arab negotiators to determine.

1. We should do all we can to secure the return to the frontiers as they were before 5 June 1967, not indeed as a final settlement but as a first step towards an arrangement in which the questions of frontiers, the rights of the refugees to return, and compensation will find a solution. The means we adopt to bring pressure on other powers to accept our point of view should be realistic, however: that is to say they should be capable of success, and they should not do us more harm than they can bring us benefits.

It is unlikely that we shall be able to achieve our objective without making some concessions. What these concessions might be, it is up to those governments who would have to make them to decide. But we should hope and insist that these governments would not act unilaterally, and thereby prejudice the outcome of any compromise they may accept.

2. In the event of our being unable to accept the terms on which a withdrawal from occupied territories is offered us, our second line of policy should be based on the principle that the forcible occupation of a territory involves a responsibility towards the inhabitants of that territory. We should not only bring the maximum international pressure to prevent Israel from expelling Arabs and expropriating their possessions in favour of new Jewish immigrants: we should bring the same international pressure on Israel to accord full political and civil rights to her Arab population, as well as the right of the Arab refugees to return. If all Palestine is re-united, there is no reason why any Palestinian should be prevented from returning to his country: not only the refugee masses now living in camps (old and new) should return: in addition all those Palestinians who have been able to find work and prosperity in the Arab countries should go back and help to rebuild the Palestine Arab community, and play their proper role in re-establishing the rights of the Arabs in their own country. The returning Arabs will not be a fifth column: one cannot be a fifth column in one's own country. The relations which the Palestinian Arabs within Palestine are then able or willing to establish with the Jews will be their own responsibility. The other Arab countries must help them by all means in their struggle to restore their rights and their human dignity: but the primary responsibility for their future will lie with the Palestinians themselves.

There remains one more question perhaps more important than any I have yet discussed, because in the long run it will determine our relations with the Jews and their relations with us. *The fate and the peace of the Near East should not be left to the initiative of Israel alone*. Even if Israel opts for the closed, exclusive type of society, and rejects the Arabs as fellow-citizens, *we should not do the same*. If there is no room in Israeli society for the Arabs, we should show that there is room in Arab society for the Jews. This has always been the pattern of our society, and the greatest victory of militant Zionism would be to get us to abandon it and to adopt their concept of the State. For in their hearts they know that a closed, exclusive, fanatic Israel can never co-exist with an open, liberal, and tolerant Arab society. There are Jews, however, in Israel and throughout the world who also reject the narrow vision and fanatical aims of some of their leaders, and who can be our allies in combating the introduction of racial nationalism into the Near East. Our greatest victory will be the day when the Jews in Palestine will prefer to live in an Arab society rather than in an Israeli one. It is up to us to make that possible.

Ourselves and the World

I have suggested that we formulate and try to implement a consistent Arab policy towards Israel within the framework of the international community, which means in effect the United Nations. But it is not only in the problem of Israel that the international community can be of service to us. In many of our foreign relations our numbers and our potential strength make the U.N. a suitable instrument of action. This implies, however, a correct appraisal of our strength and our weakness in the world.

Our greatest mistake in the past has been to overestimate our actual and to underestimate our potential strength. From this combination of misjudgments spring almost all the errors of our international behaviour. We have formulated and pursued policies we could not implement: we have neglected to practise policies which might have succeeded.

Nothing illustrates this truth better than the international policies we have adopted towards Israel. All our attempts to find military solutions have ended in failure, and led to subsequent political and diplomatic failures. On the other hand, our diplomatic, political and economic efforts have often met with success until we lost our advantages by pushing them too far, or not realising what these advantages were.

For example, the St. James's Conference in London in 1939 between the British Government and some of the Arab Governments led to the White Paper, which was in our favour, but which we rejected. In 1948 we secured the evacuation of British civil and military authorities from Palestine, but we did not take the necessary steps to take their place. In 1948 again, after our first unsuccessful war, we could have turned our military defeat into a limited political victory and confined Israel to an insignificant territory. Instead, we preferred our theoretical rights and principles to our real advantages. By

1967—and this was the basic cause of Israel's aggression on 5 June—we had succeeded in building up an economic situation in Jordan and most of the other Arab countries to a point where foreign investors were beginning to have serious doubts about putting money in Israel if that meant exclusion from Arab markets. We had also isolated Israel diplomatically in wide areas of international life. We lost all these advantages by failing to analyse the situation correctly. We did not perceive that the disparity between Israel's growing economic and diplomatic difficulties and her military strength would inevitably tempt her to restore the balance by a generalised rather than a localised military action. Instead of removing all possible pretexts for such an action we provided the pretexts they had difficulty in inventing themselves. . . .

The Arab Régimes

The greatest sources of weakness in the last twenty years has been the introduction into Arab political life of methods of government and of ideological slogans which are unsuitable and irrelevant to the actual conditions of the Arab countries. These methods and slogans have not only poisoned the relations between different Arab countries, they have also blinded some of their régimes to their real problems and their real interests.

The military régimes, for example, which have installed themselves in certain Arab countries since 1949 had their only justification in terms of the necessity of meeting external dangers. They have now given a public demonstration of their incompetence in war. What reason do we have to suppose that they are likely to be more successful in economic planning and development, in education, foreign affairs, finance, or culture?

Among the most harmful consequences of military régimes to the political, economic and social structure of the countries they have tried to govern is the exclusion from public life which they have deliberately or indirectly effected of vast numbers of educated and skilled citizens, who now languish idle either in their own countries, or in exile in others. This fact represents an enormous loss in terms of an investment in human resources going back at least forty years. The resulting poverty of technicians is felt not only in civilian affairs, but even in the armies themselves, so that it can reasonably be argued that the military régimes instead of strengthening their armed forces have in reality weakened them.

The introduction of ideological slogans and political and economic doctrines which derive from contexts radically different from those of the Arab countries has done even more harm to these countries both in their relations with each other and in their internal affairs. They have divided the Arab world into camps on issues which are not really relevant or along lines which do not make sense.

First of all, that between the so-called "progressive" or "revolutionary" and the "reactionary" or "conservative" régimes. It is interesting and significant that all those régimes which call themselves "progressive" are, in fact, military. What has led some of our leaders to adopt the language and imitate the style of movements and régimes with which they really have nothing in common? There are two basic reasons: the desire to find foreign allies and friends, and the need to seek popular support. Since most of the Arab countries have only recently emerged from Western domination or colonisation, it was natural for leaders seeking an easy popularity among the masses to align themselves with the enemies of the West in foreign policy, and to promise them economic and social welfare through "land reforms," "nationalisation," and other elements of the programme of certain socialist countries.

Except in Egypt, however, the "progressive" military régimes have not only failed to implement socialist programmes: they have actually lowered gross national products and seriously damaged the economic welfare of some sections of the population without improving that of others. Nor have they been able, or willing, to take those social and juridical measures which would have given a progressive character to their régimes, at least on paper. Not one of the "progressive" régimes, for example, has abolished polygamy. On the contrary, some of them have been trying to reintroduce a conservative interpretation of Islam·into public life. And certain of the régimes which have been classified as "conservative" or "reactionary" have done much for their populations in terms of economic progress and social legislation.

Secondly, the attempt to identify Arab nationalism with the "progressive" as opposed to the "reactionary" régimes has led to a senseless and dangerous conflict between some of the

Arab Governments, just as it has inflamed and divided public opinion all over the Arab world. We must reject and resist the claim that any one régime or party or leader has a monopoly on Arab nationalism, and refuse to accept that differences of opinion or of interests provide an adequate basis for classifying régimes or individuals as genuine nationalists or traitors. The poisonous campaigns waged by the radio stations and the press in certain countries should be condemned, ignored, or ridiculed, and every pressure should be brought on those governments which utilise or permit them to put an end to this scandal of the Arab world.

The Real Problem

The introduction into Arab life of political and social doctrines which are not relevant to it at its present stage not only weakens the Arab countries by dividing them on irrelevant issues; it also diverts their attention from their real problems. The only valid distinction at this time between the Arab countries lies in the degree of their economic and social development, and in the resources they possess to promote their progress. The real difference is between the less- and the more-underdeveloped, and between the rich and the poor. There is no reason why we should anticipate the problems of more highly developed societies before we have reached the stage where these problems become real and demand solutions. There is no reason why we should adopt the language and the political forms of social and economic conflicts which are not relevant to our societies.

The most immediate and urgent problems which face nearly all the Arab countries are those involved in establishing the minimum conditions on which a modern society may eventually be built. While the nature of that society, and the social and economic content of the measures to be taken to bring it into existence must certainly be studied and discussed, and will certainly provide eventually the grounds for divergent opinions and political movements, we have not yet reached that stage. There is a wide area for action where interests are common and basic enough for us to ignore or at least to postpone questions which may divide us at a moment when we need to be united.

For some of the under-developed countries of the world the necessity of finding an outside source for the capital investments and the technical skills they lack forces them to an involvement in the ideological conflict and divisions of the more-developed world. No such necessity exists for the Arab world, which has all the material, and many of the human resources, which it needs. There is sufficient capital and liquidity to make us independent of outside financial help, and to promote our own economic and social progress provided we use our resources intelligently, and take a broad view of both the existing and the future needs of the Arab world as a whole. We have vast territories, enormous natural resources, and vital strategic positions. What we need is to exploit them in terms of today's and tomorrow's needs. Countries which are rich today may not be always: others which are poor today possess potentialities which may one day make them rich. The total human and natural resources of the Arab world must be studied and then exploited in the light of a general plan, a moving idea.

It is this great responsibility which now faces the educated classes in the Arab countries. They have a unique chance which is not given to many of the educated classes of more developed countries and societies, weighed down as they often are by traditions and already established patterns of life which do not give much scope to originality or to individual initiative. It is our good fortune to be born at a time when not only great tasks await us, but when the possibility of action is also present.

Instead of the sterile and irrelevant discussions, the bitter divisions and mutual suspicions which dominate our political and intellectual life, we should try to establish among ourselves an understanding, an agreement on principles, a mutual confidence which will make possible the action which must now be undertaken if the Arab world is to be saved from a rapid decline.

The Argument between Arabs and Jews

An Exchange between Arnold Toynbee and J. L. Talmon*

London, 3 July, 1967

Dear Professor Talmon,

I have just been staying with my son Philip and I have read your paper "For Total Peace in the Middle East" which Isaiah Berlin passed on to him. I believe, like you, that this is the moment for everyone of good will and good sense to make an all-out effort to get total, genuine, and lasting peace there. I believe there is a real opportunity for this, if we seize it now. I am just back from the United States, and, three weeks ago, I stuck my neck out by writing, for the United Press International, an article saying this, and making some concrete proposals for bringing it about. The United Press tell me that my article has been reproduced pretty widely in the U.S. press, so a copy of it may come into your hands some time, but, as there is no time to lose, I am writing to you now direct.

I feel a responsibility for doing anything I can to help towards getting a permanent peace now. I have a number of reasons. (1) I am British, so I have a share of responsibility for my country's past actions. (2) As a young man during the First World War, I was working as a "temporary Foreign Office clerk" on Middle Eastern affairs, particularly on British war-time commitments in the Middle East, so I know the history of these from the inside. (3) I am known as a Western spokesman for the Arab cause, and it is therefore just possible that what I say in public now might have some influence in the Arab World, though it is perhaps more likely that the Arabs might write me off with the verdict that I am no friend of theirs after all. Anyway, I believe that the truest act of friendship that any friend of either the Arabs or the Israelis can do for them at this moment is to try to help them to see that the facts make genuine peace a prime interest for both parties. (4) Being now an old man, with grandchildren, I feel what Johnson and Kosygin seem to have felt when they

---

* This exchange of letters between Professors Toynbee and Talmon, dated July 1967, appeared in *Encounter*, October 1967. PROFESSOR ARNOLD TOYNBEE, who refers to himself as "a Western spokesman for the Arab cause," is the author of many studies of Islamic history, politics, and culture. J. L. TAL-MON is Professor of Modern History at the Hebrew University of Jerusalem.

met. One's grandchildren symbolise for me, in a concrete way, all the future generations of the human race—70 million unborn generations who might be deprived, by our generation, of their right to life if we, in our time, were to stumble into an atomic third world war. (5) Thinking also in terms of the present, I want to see something done now which, besides saving the world from an enormous catastrophe, will reduce present human suffering in the Middle East to a minimum. I should have been as much horrified at genocide of Jews in the Middle East as I was horrified at it in Europe. I also think it very wrong to treat any people, living or unborn, as political pawns, instead of treating them as suffering human beings whose alleviation ought to have priority over any political considerations. In discussing the Arab states' policy with my Arab friends, I have always pointed out to them that West Germany's post-war policy towards refugees from Eastern Germany and from east of the Oder-Neisse line has not only been humane, but has paid dividends to Western Germany, economically and therefore also politically. Israelis should look ahead for their grandchildren.

Now about the facts that each side has to face and about practical possibilities for a settlement.

In your paper, you yourself, have put your finger on the fact that Israel has to face. A series of more and more sensational victories in successive wars does not, in itself, give Israel the vital thing that she wants and needs: that is, real peace with her Arab neighbours. So long as Israel has not mutually-agreed permanent frontiers, but only a military front, always smouldering and periodically flaring up into full-blown hostilities, Israel has to stay constantly on the alert and cannot concentrate her energies on her own internal development, which is, and always has been, her real objective. She has demonstrated now conclusively that, in war, she can always conquer more Arab territory without any foreign military aid; but, the more of this that she occupies, the more she will become militarily over-extended, and the larger the proportion of her limited and precious man-power she will have to keep unprofitably mobilised. The Arab World has the same passive military advantage as Russia and China have: there is virtually no end to it. So Israel's overriding interest is genuine peace; even the greatest military victories will be fruitless unless they can be converted into that.

The Arabs have to face the fact that Israel has come to

stay; that a three-times repeated experience has shown that they cannot defeat her; that the Soviet Union is not going to war with the United States for the Arabs' sake; and that, in the unlikely event of the Arabs becoming, one day, able to destroy Israel, the United States would not let this happen.

I need not dwell on your psychological analysis of the present-day Arab state of mind. It is masterly; you have shown a power of sympathetic understanding by which you have entered into it imaginatively. This is very important and very encouraging, because Israel, as the present victor, holds the initiative. The party that has suffered injustice and has been humiliated is the one that is the more sensitive and that therefore needs the more delicate handling. The Palestinian Arabs have suffered injustice. To put it simply, they have been made to pay for the genocide of Jews in Europe which was committed by Germans, not by Arabs. The Arabs as a whole have been humiliated, because, in the establishment, first of the Jewish National Home and then of the State of Israel, the Arabs have, as you point out, never been consulted. It has all been done over their heads. They have been treated as "natives," with no more than sub-human rights. For a people with a great, but no longer actual, historic past, this is infuriating. The present Arab and present Chinese states of mind have the same explanation.

So I would plead with Israel to make the first move towards achieving the total genuine and lasting peace which is the supreme common interest of Israel, the Palestinian Arab refugees, and the Arab states. For Israel publicly to make the first move would be magnanimous as well as far-sighted. I suggest that Israel should now propose that the two sides should make the following simultaneous declaration:

> "The Arab states and the Palestinian Arab people pledge themselves to recognise, *bona fide*, the existence of Israel with the intention of making a permanent peace with her, and they also guarantee to negotiate permanent frontiers with Israel on approximately the 1948 armistice lines. Israel pledges herself to accept these agreed frontiers *bona fide*, with the intention, on her side, of making permanent peace, and she also undertakes to take the initiative in bringing about a satisfactory permanent settlement of the problem of the 1948 refugees."[1]

[1] The repatriation of the 1967 refugees was taken for granted in this letter. Ed.

If both sides would give these reciprocal pledges in a formal agreement of the kind that used to be called "preliminaries of peace," this would open the way for a negotiated treaty about details, and then things that have so far been impossible would become possible, *e.g.*:

1. In the conversion of the 1948 armistice lines into permanent frontiers, there could be minor rectifications, so long as these offset each other fairly on balance.

2. There could be a mutual opening up of communications that are vital to both parties. Israel could be assured of a right of way not only through the Straits of Tiran but through the Suez Canal too. Egypt could be assured of a right of way, across Israel, to Lebanon, Syria, Jordan, and Saudi Arabia, thus removing the "Polish corridor" irritant of Israel's having split the Arab World in two by extending from the Mediterranean coast to the Gulf of Aqaba. Syria and Jordan could be given a free port at Haifa, with a right of way to it, and Jordan could be given a second one at Jaffa.

3. The 1948 Palestinian Arab refugees could (a) be given monetary compensation for the loss of their property situated in Israel; (b) be given an extra indemnity for having been forced, as innocent victims of the conflict between Israel and the Arab states, to spend twenty years as refugees; (c) be given the option of either returning to their former homes on condition of becoming loyal citizens of Israel (as the Galilaean Arabs have been during the present crisis) or else being settled on good land outside Israel; (d) a fund could be raised for the refugees' resettlement, whether inside Israel or outside it. I am sure the majority will opt for resettlement *outside* Israel; but for Israel to offer the choice of returning home (on condition of their becoming *bona fide* loyal Israeli citizens) is psychologically very important for producing a change of heart among the refugees. If Israel appealed to the world to help her raise a fund for these four purposes, money would pour in.

4. Water for irrigation: in the London *Times* a few days ago, there was an important letter from Edmund de Rothschild about this, followed up next day by a long and constructive article by a desalination expert. They make the point that, even though desalination has not yet been made possible at an economic price, it would pay the world to subsidise it for the use of Israel and Jordan. This would (a) make it no longer necessary to pay a pittance to the refugees; (b) in combination with the Jordan water, it would supply abundant water for *both* Israel *and* Jordan, and would therefore make it unnecessary for them to contend with each other over their respective shares of Jordan water.

The future of the Old City of Jerusalem is a question of special urgency and danger. It is of crucial importance that

Israel should not take unilateral action for annexing it. This would not be valid in international law; it could not be accepted by the United Nations; it would make genuine peace between Israel and the Arabs impossible; and it would arouse the whole Muslim World, and probably a large part of the Christian World too, not only against Israel, but against the Jews in general. It might seriously prejudice the diaspora's position in many countries.

Moreover, possession of the Temple area (the Muslims' Haram ash-Sherif) would be an embarrassment for Israel. She would have either to refrain from rebuilding the Temple or else she would have to demolish the Dome of the Rock and the Al Aksa Mosque, which would really be unthinkable. Of course, Israelis and all other Jews must have free access to the Wailing Wall. I like the Pope's proposal for an international trusteeship for the holy places of *all* religions in Palestine. But any change of sovereignty here would be most provocative unless it were freely negotiated in exchange for some equivalent *quid pro quo*. For instance, Jordan might conceivably say to Israel: "Cede to us the fields, now in Israel, that belong to villages on the Jordan side of the frontier, and then we will cede to you the south-west corner of the Old City of Jerusalem, up to the western face of the Wailing Wall." A bargain on these lines would be all right, but unilateral action by Israel would be disastrous.

Well, I am writing this to you, and am sending copies to Isaiah Berlin and to a friend of mine in Baltimore, Maryland, Rabbi Agus.

I am now an old man, and most of my treasure is therefore in future generations. This is why I care so much, and why I am writing this letter to you.

Please make any use of my letter that you think useful. I am not marking it "confidential."

Yours sincerely,
Arnold Toynbee

Jerusalem, 18 July 1967

Dear Professor Toynbee,

I expressed to you by wire my first deeply felt reaction to your letter as soon as I finished reading it. I wish to apologise to you now for the ten days delay in sending you the detailed reply which I promised in my telegram. This was the last week of term at our University, teaching having been resumed at the end of June, after the interruption caused by mobilisation and war. I had also wished to show your letter to friends at the University and to a few persons in government circles for their comments. Finally, I needed time to ponder over what you say and sort out my own thoughts in the light of the feelings and ideas which animate the people of Israel at this moment.

May I say at the outset that I have reason to claim that I voice the sentiments of most Israelis in the appreciation of the moral fervour and sense of urgency which motivate your letter. I speak however only for myself when I deal with your concrete proposals and offer my own suggestions. All the same, I know for certain that a very strong volume of Israeli opinion shares my views on the practical prospects of an Arab-Israeli settlement; and I do not think I exaggerate if I add that, given the proper response from the other side, the suggestions voiced in the second part of this letter may easily become acceptable to the vast majority of the people of Israel, and—Israel being a genuine democracy—to its government.

You list a number of reasons for your feeling of "responsibility for doing anything [you] can to help towards getting a permanent peace now." I would add one reason which you do not mention, but which to me outweighs perhaps all those enumerated by you, for in a sense it contains them all. I seemed to hear in your letter the voice of Arnold Toynbee who in the *Study of History* had been speaking to me not just as the architect of a colossal edifice, but, if I may say so, as a prophet who stands in awe before the mystery of Time and is engaged in a passionate quest for overriding purpose and redeeming significance in History. Some of us who are living in "permanent and anguished intimacy with the mystery of Jewish martyrdom and survival" could not help responding to these "Judaic" ingredients in your work, and therefore felt especially pained by what to us, Jews and Zionists, appeared as a failure to accord to Judaism and its contemporary mutation, Israel, their due place in your scheme of civilisations merging and falling, vast spiritual forces shaping and dissolving them, all that supposedly leading to some salvationist denouement in the end, but now suddenly faced by the mortal danger of total and meaningless destruction.

I welcome, therefore, most heartily your letter as some kind of opening to a friendly and fruitful dialogue. And it is not in any spirit of polemic or out of a wish to put into your mouth things which you did not say in your letter, but out of deep respect and genuine inner need, that I feel compelled to make these few, general comments before I come to your suggestions.

Zionism did not start with Hitler, and to us, therefore, the emergence of Israel could not be summed up in the statement that the Arabs "have been made to pay for the genocide of Jews in Europe which was commited by Germans, not by Arabs."

Just as we would not base our right to exist as an independent state in the Middle East solely on our right of conquest and demand of the Arabs simply to bow to that fact of nature (or history), so we could not possibly subordinate the immemorial aspiration of the Jewish people, admittedly much quickened by the rise of nationalism in the world at large, and made unbearably urgent by murderous persecution, to the exclusive resolve of the Arabs. Whatever the degree of our imaginative understanding of Arab resentment at not having been consulted on the Balfour Declaration and the Palestine Mandate and for having had their objections overridden by the UN and their armed resistance to partition (the solution contrived to meet a clash of rights) overpowered by the Jews in 1948; and whatever the measure of our embarrassed sympathy for the terrible plight of the Palestine refugees, we could not put into question the very basis of our existence.

It is probably too much to ask—in this fallen state of mankind—of a nationalist movement to see the point of the other side and to make concessions to it readily and altruistically. Many as may have been the Zionist sins of commission or omission in this respect, every one of their attempts at a compromise had all along been met by Arabs with the absolute and implacable refusal to recognise any Jewish claim. This was bound to lead to the half-despairing, half-defiant reaction that since nothing could be done with them, it had to be done in spite of and even against them. Arab intransigence has proved a disastrous policy to the Arab interests. Every crisis culminating in armed clash cost the Arabs more and more, and weakened their position still further, which again deepened Arab neurosis on the point of Israel.

Wounded pride of a race with glorious memories is not an ignoble feeling. But an obsessive sense of injury and self-pity are conducive to sterile self-centredness and stultifying misanthropy. Where would we Jews have been today, had we never ceased to remember all the scores and been reliving all the humiliations we had suffered at the hand of every possible nation with which we had come into contact throughout our long history? What would have happened to the persecuted and maltreated of our race, had we behaved like the Arab States towards the Arab refugees: "May they suffer and rot, for it is all the doing of the Jews, and we must not make it easier for the enemy, but should on the contrary keep that sore running." Is there any hope of breaking this vicious circle —the source of so much misery to the peoples of the Middle East, and now threatening to engulf the whole world in an unspeakable catastrophe?

A man greatly revered by both of us, my late teacher R. H. Tawney, wrote:

> It is the tragedy of a world where man must walk by sight that the discovery of the reconciling formula is always left to future generations, in which passion has cooled into curiosity, and the agonies of peoples have become the exercise in the schools. The devil who builds bridges does not span such chasms till much that is precious to mankind has vanished down them for ever.

Surely enough blood has flowed down the chasms for the reconciling formula to be evolved and accepted at last. It is infinitely sad that *homo sapiens* should be so slow-witted, and that his reason should be so dominated and twisted by irrational drives and intractable aversions that only an overwhelming shock and inexorable *faits accomplis* are able to make the sweet voice of reason heard.

I entirely agree with you that on the morrow of the third Arab-Israel war in twenty years, the most self-absorbed nationalists on both sides should be ripe for the acceptance of the fact that galling as it is not to be able to attain one's supreme goal in its undiminished totality, that is the way the jealous gods will it. It may be hard upon the Arabs impelled by a vision of a pan-Arab Empire from Iran to the Atlantic to find the Jews planted on the Eastern shore of the Mediterranean. But the war to the bitter end advocated by the extremists, while most unlikely to wipe out Israel, is sure to bring, at once, the Arab States under Soviet domination, with Russian "advisers" and "technicians" in every office and regiment: a strange consummation of the dream of an Islamic renaissance. Even those no longer very numerous Jews who are still capable of becoming intoxicated with verses on the vastness of the Kingdom promised by the Almighty to His children have to wake up to the fact that God has played them an unfair trick in putting so many Arabs on the banks of the Jordan and scattering so many more in the countries around. The Israelis may defeat them again and again, but only to find the promised "rest and inheritance" removed further and further, and themselves condemned to live by the sword instead of walking by the spirit, to be a Sparta and not the combination of Jerusalem and Athens—the fondest dream of the noblest among the prospects of Zionism.

There is in fact no need to persuade Israel of the desirability and necessity of peace. All the effort is required on the other side. As to the actual terms envisaged by Israel, these would be a function of Arab readiness to recognise Israel and make a genuine peace with her. The graver our fears, the stiffer the guarantees we think necessary for our survival and security; the greater the confidence the Arabs are able to inspire, the more lenient are our terms likely to be.

You single out two items as all-important and indeed all-embracing: refugees and frontiers.

Only yesterday I was deeply impressed by a person whom I was always inclined to consider something of an extremist exclaiming with heat, "But we should pawn all we have to the tenth generation to solve this terrible problem of Arab refugees!"

I feel sure that, on this, all but one of your suggestions would be met: monetary compensation, extra-indemnity, participation in an international fund for resettlement. The difficulty would frankly be the suggestion of an Israeli offer to the Arab refugees of 1948 of the choice of returning home. You consider this as more important for its symbolic significance by expressing the certainty that the "majority will opt for resettlement outside Israel." As you know, we have made such an offer to the 1967 refugees who, seized by panic (out of implacable hostility to Israel or out of a desire to be with their own next of kin) crossed to the East Bank of the Jordan during and since the recent hostilities. We do not know yet how many will avail themselves of the offer to return to the West Bank. While I can see the human and symbolic significance, indeed the duty, of allowing such an option to the recent refugees, I doubt whether there is a case for doing the same in regard to the refugees of twenty years ago. It would not only create very grave problems for Israel. It would also impose upon the refugees, transplanted into realities quite different from those they knew a generation ago, strains and stresses which they would be spared if resettled in an Arab land or overseas. This does not mean that we shall not be prepared, as we have been in the past, to allow reunion of families or make special consideration where warranted.

This world should become one and a fit place for men and women of different races and religions to live together. Yet I cannot help remembering to what extent precisely régimes which claim to be inspired by a universal creed, which subordinates racial peculiarity and national self-assertion to proletarian solidarity and universal brotherhood, have found no other solution to their nationalities problem but in the expulsion of millions of women and children, and in the annexation of vast territories to which their historic claim bears no comparison at all to the strength of the Jewish claim to Palestine. Even in such advanced and rich countries like Belgium and Canada racial conflict is assuming a virulence which baffles all observers. Incidentally, in absorbing some hundreds of thousands of Jewish immigrants or refugees from the Arab countries, Israel has carried out something of an exchange of populations.

As to the territorial terms, again, I and many like me hold the realistic opinion that territory densely populated by Arabs is not only not an asset to Israel, but a liability which even from the strategic point of view outweighs the supposed strategic advantages of what is called "more defensible frontiers." But there are reservations. Israel is entitled to security, and while I do not wish to be an annexationist, I could not consider the 1949 (you say by mistake 1948) armistice frontiers as sacrosanct, and would think rectifications for which you make an allowance in your letter to be justified and indeed indispensable on those trouble spots like the Syrian ridge, the Sinai border, the Straits of Tiran. But I hasten to add that if other effective guarantees for our security could be devised—by way of demilitarisation, international force (not one always exposed to be sent unilaterally packing), international government—I dare say there would not be any insistent pressure for far-reaching territorial changes. The Gaza strip cannot remain an Egyptian enclave.

Israel has repeatedly offered Jordan free access to Israeli ports on the Mediterranean, and although I cannot see the necessity for Syria, which has good ports of her own, of free access to Haifa, surely in an atmosphere of good neighbourly relations this request, like the question of a right of way for Egypt through Israeli Arab territory to the other Arab States, would not present an insurmountable obstacle. But for this, free passage for Israeli shipping through the Suez canal is a precondition.

The question of Jerusalem is a point *sui generis,* and on this our opinions are likely to differ. Of one thing I can assure you: there is no person or group of persons, of any standing in Israel, even among the ultra-orthodox, who would dream of rebuilding the Temple and destroying Muslim or other sanctuaries. The whole matter is not worth a moment of your anxiety. At the same time, public opinion in Israel is so unanimous and determined on the retention of Jerusalem that no government would survive a week if it showed signs of giving in on that. I invite the historian Arnold Toynbee to weigh the pros and cons of this issue in historical perspective and with the historian's detachment, difficult as it is to treat this loaded problem in that way.

If Israel is prepared, and indeed is most anxious, to submit all holy places to international administration and supervision exercised by the accredited representatives of the various religions, Christian and Muslim, with extra-territoriality guaranteed, why should there be all that fuss about sovereignty over the areas which do not contain any holy places? In what way was the Hashemite dynasty of Jordan, whose rule over Jordan resulted from a pure post-World War I accident and indeed a British embarrassment, a more trustworthy guardian than an Israeli government, which (as you hint) has hostages in all the Christian nations? The Jordanians have not left a single synagogue standing in Old Jerusalem and paved the road with tombstones from the ancient cemetery on the Mount of Olives. Are we not faced here with a residue of that unhappy, age-long special attitude to the nation of deicides, whose inferiority to Christendom (and Islam) must be made especially manifest, and the members of which must never be allowed to rule or command the members of the true and triumphant faith? Internationalisation? I seem to detect signs that the Vatican has by no means made up its mind on the desirability of a Jerusalem run by the UN, in which pagan, communist-atheist and Muslim, not to speak of Protestant powers, constitute the vast majority. Finally, may I recall the tremendous agitation against the incorporation of Rome, the capital of Christendom, the seat of the Holy See, into the Kingdom of Italy in the 19th century. It requires an effort of imagination today to visualise a situation in which Rome is not the capital of Italy, but the free state of the Pope or an international city.

This brings me to my last and most immediately practical point: how to go about getting peace.

Like very many Israelis I fervently desire an early arrangement with King Hussein of Jordan. In order not to lose myself in too sanguine illustrations I would say no more than that this solution appears to me to be the least impossible of all solutions talked of. The Israelis have genuine respect and a sneaking affection for the brave little King, and one can hear expressions of almost sympathetic regret that he should have made the terrible blunder he did. Incidentally, the total absence in Israel of any hatred or contempt for the Arabs as such is best illustrated by the fact that the spate of songs and poems of war and victory has not produced a single hate hymn; and never has any note of abuse crept into radio or press. There have been only minor cases of plunder which received prompt punishment, although in the heat of firing and sniping there seems to have been some unnecessary destruction of houses. The people left homeless were soon provided with shelter. I believe it is our interest to come to terms with Jordan and that Hussein stands to gain no less than we from such a settlement which would return to him most of the West Bank, except Jerusalem, its immediate vicinity and a few strategic points elsewhere, while ensuring to Jordanians some form of free access to Jerusalem and the Holy places of Islam. I believe, like you, that the international community, especially the West, would be enthusiastically ready to offer very large sums and sponsor a joint international venture, with Israel and Jordan as partners, designed to resettle the refugees, execute those public works of irrigation and desalination you mention, solving thereby not only the refugee problem, but restoring Hussein to his former position. A common stake in joint prosperity would thus be created. Would Hussein dare to take such a step alone? Objectively speaking, Egypt and Syria can afford not to conclude any arrangement with Israel and play the part of the intransigent patriots; Jordan just cannot exist without it. Hussein had been for so long cruelly vilified and ill-used by the more powerful Arab States. In the war he and his army have acquitted themselves very honourably and the sacrifices made by them have been infinitely greater than those by other Arab States. So he has done more than his share to fight for Arab honour.

It is quite possible that once the shouting against Hussein for having come to terms with Israel had died down, the other Arab States would tire of their excitement and get down to their internal affairs and gradually slide into some modus vivendi, or even follow Hussein's example fairly soon.

Now I am going to stick out my neck with a good many Jews just as you in your words stuck out your neck with your Arabs. I dislike the idea of a separate little autonomous Arab State on the West Bank of Jordan which would be a camouflaged Israeli protectorate. Not only because I doubt its economic viability, am apprehensive of the crushing financial and administrative burden it is sure to impose upon Israel, fear its irredentism, and the grave security problems arising out of it. I recoil from the idea of Jews lording it over others. It is at variance with the image of Judaism I cherish, and the example of other nations makes me fear the dangers to the moral fibre, the psychological balance, and spiritual values lying in wait for a master race.

I pray that we shall not be compelled to assume that role, which may happen if an arrangement with Jordan proves impossible and the other Arab States refuse to establish peace with Israel.

You speak movingly of your grandchildren. I understand you well. I am a younger man and I have two small children. When I look into their eyes, I think of the million Jewish children whom the Nazis separated from their parents, starved to death and killed in the gas chambers. At such moments my heart goes out to all the children of the world, Arab, Vietnamese, and all others, and I feel like crying aloud: "Never, never again."

Yours sincerely,
J. L. Talmon

Palestine and Israel

By Albert Hourani*

At the heart of the Middle Eastern problem lies the problem of Palestine: the struggle of Palestinian Arabs and Jewish settlers for possession and mastery of the land. Now that the Powers have been drawn in and a local crisis has become a world-wide one, it is easy to forget the local causes of it; but it is dangerous, for unless they are treated the crisis may return.

The struggle of Arabs and Jews for Palestine cannot be explained by ancient religious hostility. Jews (and Christians) had always lived among the mainly Arab Muslim population of Palestine, and relations between them had usually been correct. But in the 1880s a new type of Jewish immigration began, mainly from Eastern Europe, inspired by the Zionist idea of a Jewish national home: this soon aroused the hostility of Ottoman officials and part of the population.

During its 30 years of rule, 1917-47, Britain bound itself by the Balfour Declaration and the Mandate to encourage the Jewish national home, subject to the rights of the existing population; immigration increased, particularly after the rise of Hitler, and Arab opposition became almost universal and drew in the surrounding Arab States.

This hostility sprang from the attempt to implant a new society in a land already occupied by an old one. When the settlers came they found a complete society already there: farmers, craftsmen and merchants, ancient towns and villages, religious institutions, a culture expressed in Arabic, a leadership which formed part of the Arab Ottoman *élite*. The aim of the newcomers was not to be absorbed into it but to create their own society with its farms and cities, institutions, Hebrew culture and political leaders.

In the age of European expansion, other such attempts were made to plant new societies amidst old ones. They always caused strain, but Zionist settlement in Palestine had special features. The new Jewish society, by the nature of the Zionist idea, was to be a complete and exclusive one. Its aim

* Albert Hourani is Director of the Middle Eastern Centre and fellow of St. Antony's College in Oxford. His article was first published in the *Observer*, (London), September 3, 1967. (Reprinted by permission of the *Observer* Foreign News Service.)

was to create a wholly Jewish economy: land bought by the Jewish National Fund became the inalienable property of the Jewish people and no non-Jew could ever be employed on it.

Zionist Idea

It is true, the Zionists bought their land. But in the Middle East political power and ownership of land have always gone together, and the Arabs were convinced that if the Jews had power they would seize the greater part of the land. That the Jews *would* take power became first a danger, then a certainty, as the Jewish population grew. Because of the nature of the Zionist idea, the new Jewish society was an expanding society, open to all who wished to come in. In 1922 Jews formed 13 per cent of the population of Palestine; in 1935, 28 per cent; in 1947, 33 per cent.

As numbers grew, the idea of a Jewish national home turned into that of a Jewish State, and this was unacceptable to the Arabs, not only because by the 1930s most of them were moved by the idea of an Arab State of which Palestine would be part, but because in a Jewish State they would have no choice (whatever guarantee the Mandate might contain) except between being a powerless minority and leaving their country.

Some Zionist leaders did indeed talk of a 'bi-national State,' but attempts at political agreement broke on the question of immigration. The Arabs wanted to preserve the Arab character of Palestine, and so wanted little or no Jewish immigration. The Zionists wanted to keep the doors of Palestine open, no matter what the form of government.

Here lay the dilemma of their policy: they wanted agreement with the Arabs and they wanted unlimited immigration, but they could not have both, and if forced to choose most of them would choose immigration.

The British, who were politically responsible, had no clear or stable policy on this matter. They had obligations to the Arabs and so opposed the idea of a Jewish State: they had obligations to the Zionists and so permitted immigration, not as much as the Jews wanted but enough to make a Jewish State possible. In 1948, unable to reach agreement with the two parties, they withdrew in circumstances which made fighting inevitable, and there happened what the Arabs had feared for so long.

The dynamic, exclusive, alien society which had grown up

among them seized power in the greater part of Palestine, with encouragement and help from some Western States, secured control of the land and brought in immigrants on a large scale; and two-thirds of the Arab inhabitants lost their lands and homes.

All wars create refugees, and after the armies have departed the peasants and merchants return to take up their lives again. Civilised Governments accept that they have a responsibility for those who live in the land they rule. But after the armistice agreements of 1949 Israel refused—with limited exceptions— to allow the Arab refugees to return. In a situation like this everything becomes political, and the Israelis made political use of the refugees.

Conquered Land

By refusing to consider the refugee problem except in the framework of a peace settlement with the surrounding Arab States, they linked together two matters which had no moral connection; for the return of the refugees was an obligation which they owed not to the surrounding Arab States but to the Palestinian Arabs themselves, as inhabitants of the land they had conquered. To make such a connection was the more tempting because Israel did not really wish the refugees to return. Even at a peace settlement it would only have offered to take back a small number; for what it wanted was to have the land without its inhabitants, so as to settle its own immigrants.

(This policy was made morally acceptable to Israelis and the outside world by the 'myth' that the Arabs left willingly under orders from their leaders. No more than the most tenuous evidence was produced for this, and, in fact, the flight of the Arabs presents no mystery. Some left for reasons of prudence, some from panic during the fighting, some were forced to go by the Israeli Army. What has happened this year throws some light on this. It is clear that no Arab Government ordered the Palestinians to leave this year, but a quarter of the inhabitants of the West Bank left in two months —and for the same reasons.)

Nothing could show more clearly that the basic dilemma of Zionist policy was still there. If it wanted land for immigrants, it was sensible to stop the return of the refugees. But if it wanted peace with the Arabs, then it was fatal.

After 1948, the first step to peace was that Israel should

recognise its responsibility to the Arabs who lived in its territory but had been displaced by the fighting. Only this could have set in motion a train of events leading towards peace; and only Israel, as victor and beneficiary of the war, could have taken the step. Israel never did so, and its attitude was accepted by the Western Powers. Every year the United Nations passed a resolution calling for the return or compensation of the refugees, but no one tried seriously to carry it out.

Shock of Exile

The assumption which underlay the attitude of Israel and the Western Powers was that sooner or later the refugees would melt away, absorbed into the surrounding Arab peoples, and then the problem of Palestine would cease to exist. But this was a false assumption. It was not a mass of individuals who fled in 1948, it was the greater part of a society. A common land and language, a common political fate, and the shock of exile created a Palestine Arab nation. After 1948 it lived scattered.

Allowing for natural increase, by the beginning of this year there must have been rather more than two million Palestinian Arabs: almost 400,000 in the Gaza Strip, 300,000 in Israel, 1,300,000 in Jordan, 150,000 each in Lebanon and Syria. About two-thirds of them were still registered refugees. Many of these had become wholly or partly self-supporting; if more had not, it was not (as was often said) because the host-countries did not wish them to be settled, but because the absorption of refugees depended on the pace of economic development, and this was bound to be slow in the early stages. In no country was their position satisfactory.

In Jordan they had full citizenship, but Palestinians and Transjordanians had not yet been welded into a complete unity, and positions of real power remained in Transjordanian hands; an intelligent policy of development created an economy into which some of them were absorbed, but the refugees formed a third of the whole population, and a country with such limited resources could not absorb so large a number in 20 years.

In Israel, their position was tolerable: they had civil and political rights, but fewer opportunities of higher education and skilled employment than Jews, they lived under a strict military control (until a relaxation in recent months), and were virtually shut out of the political community.

Thus the Palestinian Arabs remained in being as a nation which had lost almost everything but was determined to continue to exist: that is to say, to live with one another, and to live in Palestine. After 1948 this was the heart of the 'Palestine problem'; the *de facto* existence of Israel was not in serious danger, but what remained to be assured was the existence of the Palestinian nation. Its attitude to Israel was shared by the other Arab nations, for many reasons. The individual losses of the refugees were felt throughout Jordan, Syria and Lebanon, which belonged to the same geographical and historical unit as Palestine, and where almost every family had Palestinian connections.

More widespread still was a sense of human indignity, a feeling that in the eyes of Israel and the West the Arabs were surplus human beings, to be removed and dumped elsewhere to redress a wrong not they but Europe had done to the Jews. It seemed to most Arabs that Western Governments talked in one way about the rights of the Jews and in another about those of the Arabs. They often said that Israel was here to stay; they never said that the Palestinian Arab nation was here to stay. They talked in language of high principles and threats about Israel's right to free navigation; they used a milder language about the right of the refugees to return or compensation. Unwise statements by Arab spokesmen about throwing Israel into the sea were widely quoted and condemned; no one seemed to care that Israel had, in fact, thrown a large number of Arabs into the desert.

Together with this went an almost universal fear. So long as Israel remained open to all Jews who wished to immigrate, so long as it could maintain Western standards of technology and hope for wide support in Europe and America, there would be a danger of its expanding into the territory of the surrounding States. Sooner or later, most Arabs believed, Israel would absorb the rest of Palestine, and perhaps parts of southern Syria and Lebanon as well; for a second time the Palestinians would have to move out, and would find themselves walking down the road to Jericho or scrambling across the Jordan bridges.

Self-defeating

Whatever their differences on other matters, the Arab States were united in their attitude to Israel, and attracted the support—within limits—of most Afro-Asian and communist

States. But coalitions are fragile, in particular if they include States of unequal strength. The common object which brings them together becomes entangled with the separate interests and claims of each, and it was this which led the Arabs into statements and acts which were self-defeating. The essential point of their propaganda was justice for the Palestinian Arabs.

Before 1948 it had been possible to argue that a Jewish State should not be set up because this would be unjust to the Arabs; but once Israel had become a member of the UN, to talk in terms of its disappearance as a State was to embarrass allies and touch a sensitive spot in the European conscience. The official policy of the Arab States was not to destroy Israel but to return to the settlement of 1947-48 and a fulfilment of all the UN resolutions; but at the same time they insisted they were still in a state of active belligerence.

Extreme Terms

This was a dangerous policy for a weaker party to adopt towards a stronger: it gave Israel a license to attack whenever it could claim that its interests were in danger. Israel indeed always remained balanced between two policies: it wanted peace with the Arabs if it could obtain it on its own terms; but war with the Arabs might give it better frontiers.

An Arab policy based on inferior power but expressed in extreme terms played into Israel's hands. This was shown clearly in the events of May and June. For 10 years Egypt and Jordan had kept their frontiers with Israel quiet, and there is no reason to think they wanted a change. But the Syrian frontier was disturbed because of the difficult problem of the demilitarised zone.

Syria began supporting Palestinian activist groups; Israel replied, first by an unprovoked attack on Jordan, not Syria, then by threats which constituted a challenge to Egypt. Egypt replied by sending its Army to the frontier. In so doing Egypt acted as prisoner of the hopes it had aroused, but clearly it did not expect to fight. Egypt's acts were directed towards a political settlement, and its mistake was to think not that the Russians would support it more than they did, but that the Americans would restrain Israel more than they did —that the United States could or would force Israel to give Egypt a victory which might lead to further demands.

Israel called the Egyptian bluff in circumstances which

brought it the greatest possible support in the Western world, not only because of Egypt's bad relations with the US and Britain but because of foolish statements by Arab leaders skilfully used by Zionist propaganda.

The frightening wave of anti-Arab feeling which swept Europe and America in June is not the subject of this article. Ordinary people, Jews and non-Jews, certainly felt that Israel was threatened with destruction. It is more difficult to believe that the Israel Government thought so, knowing its own military strength and that it had a guarantee (implicit or formal) from the strongest Power in the world. However that may be, the defensive war soon became a 'defensive-offensive' one, and once more what the Palestinians had feared came true.

More Refugees

The Israeli victory has changed many things in the Middle East, but it has not changed the problem of Palestine. The Palestinian Arab people are still there, still in ruin and exile, still determined to exist. Perhaps two-thirds of them are now under Israeli rule; many more refugees have been created, and it is not certain that Israel will allow most of them to return; many who are not refugees have been ruined by the occupation of half Jordan; every individual Palestinian has now suffered or lost something because of Israel.

The attitude of the Palestinians towards Jordan may well have changed, and if the West Bank is returned Jordan may become a more solid and united State. But in spite of Israeli hopes and efforts, there is no reason to believe that the attitude of Palestinian Arabs towards Israel has changed, except to be hardened by new losses. The Arab States have more and not less reason to think of Israel as an expansionist State which, with the help or acquiescence of the US, may dominate politically and economically the region lying between Nile and Euphrates.

It seems not impossible that the Arab States will be persuaded to make a declaration of non-belligerence and the Israelis to withdraw from the conquered lands. Even so, the basic dilemma of Israeli policy remains. The Palestinian Arabs are the estranged neighbours with whom Israel must be reconciled if it is to become 'like all nations'; and it remains true, as it has been since 1948, that the first step towards a stable *modus vivendi* is one which only Israel can take—to accept its responsibility towards the indigenous people of the land it controls, and to grant the refugees the right of return or compensation.

In the long run it may be in Israel's interest to do this: only as a mixed State has it a chance of being accepted by its neighbours. But in the short run, the desire for security and for further immigration works against it. It seems more likely than not that Israel will do nothing. If so, it may stay in Gaza and the West Bank; part of the Arab population may be squeezed out; the rump of Jordan may be absorbed into some other State; and in a few more years the Palestinian Arab nation may rise once more to haunt Israel, this time inside as well as outside its frontiers.

Israel and the Arabs

By J. L. Talmon*

The Arab-Israeli dispute has become a world issue. This time the world has had a lucky escape, possibly thanks to the swiftness and completeness of the Israeli victory. No one can be sure of such good luck in the case of another round.

Who are the parties to the Israel-Arab conflict? Clearly not only the Jews of Israel on the one side, and the Palestine Arabs on the other. They are Israel—representing in some way world Jewry—and the Arab world acting on behalf of the Palestine Arabs.

To me, after reading Dr Hourani's article 'Palestine and Israel' in the *Observer* last week, the conflict illustrates that the view one takes on the particular rights and wrongs is determined by one's disposition towards the general case—recognition or non-recognition of an overriding right, a will to war or a will to peace.

But no one who believes and claims for his own people the right of national liberation and self-determination may decry Zionist settlement as 'imperialist invasion.' Nor must its significance be reduced to the dimensions of an asylum for a mob of refugees driven out by Hitler and then thrown upon the Arabs, who had no share in the persecution. It was only

* J. L. Talmon is Professor of Modern History at the Hebrew University, Jerusalem. His answer to Albert Hourani was published in the *Observer* (London), September 10, 1967 (Reprinted by permission of The Observer Foreign News Service.)

natural, once the urge for corporate self-expression in conditions of sovereign mastery over their own fate—the most
potent and universal impulse in modern times—had seized
the heirs of one of the most ancient peoples on earth, that
the aspiration should rivet itself to their ancient home, where
their identity was first evolved and where their distinct and
so significant contribution to mankind's heritage was shaped.

Persecution

Millions of Europe's Jews were then overtaken by a wave
of murderous persecutions without precedent. Literally hunted
for their lives, they had no Government to appeal to for
protection, no tribunal to turn to for redress—delivered into
the hands of assassins on the sole condition that they would
be put to death. This traumatic experience fired the Israelis
with the desperate resolve to gain, in one place in the world,
political sovereignty, without having to rely on the protection
or help of others, and to fight for it to death.

On the plane of lesser urgency, the annihilation of that
compact and vital Jewish civilisation in central and eastern
Europe, coupled with the loss of cohesion in Jewish life in
the remaining Diaspora, has left Israel as sole guarantor of
the survival of the corporate identity of the Jews as a people.
This explains the recent upsurge of first anguished and then
proud solidarity with Israel in all parts of Jewry.

But what about the Arab rights and claims? I would
classify myself as one of those Zionists who, though passionately convinced of the rightness of the Jewish case, are nevertheless made acutely uneasy by the thought of the Arabs. They
can find no sustenance in ascribing to the Arabs some special
dose of original sin and selfish greed, let alone inferiority.
Dr Weizmann aptly described our position when he spoke of
the Jewish-Arab conflict as a clash of rights, for which a
solution could be found only on the lines of least injustice, and
where no perfect justice was possible.

Dr Hourani seems to make the distinction between the
Palestine Arabs as a mass of human beings and Palestinian
Arab nationhood. On the sufferings of the former, I must
confess I have no answer, no more than to the bafflingly cruel
mystery why innocent people suffer and die when States
engage in wars, nor to the chilling fact that there has not
been a nation in history, including the mightiest Powers and

richest civilisations on earth, which has not established itself through invading, subjugating, expelling, or indeed annihilating vast native populations. Dr Hourani himself admits that the situation of the Arabs under Israeli jurisdiction has been tolerable.

Identity

Just as there is no justification for the claim that Israel is in any way an obstacle to the flowering of an Arab renaissance in the vast territories around Palestine, there is no ground for maintaining that Palestinian Arab national identity and culture have suffered mortal injury from the encroachment of the Jews. The Arabs themselves had until recently been vehemently denying the existence of such an entity as Palestine, insisting that the Holy Land was nothing but southern Syria, as administratively it was under the Turks. There has never been a distinct Arab-Palestinian culture, literature, dialect or national consciousness. Although it is one of the holy Muslim cities, Jerusalem has never played any role comparable to Cairo, Damascus or Baghdad in Arab history. And so, while the obliteration of Jewish Israel would make the survival of the Jewish entity very problematic, even a complete de-Arabisation of Palestine—which is hardly at stake—would have no vital effect on the Arab totality nor, in the last analysis, on even the aspiration towards permanent Arab unity.

Admittedly, not much thought was given to the Palestine Arabs before or at the end of the First World War. Britain, which issued the Balfour Declaration of 1917, and the countries which endorsed the Mandate on Palestine in 1921, had all been nurtured on biblical reminiscences of the eternal bond between the children of Israel and their promised land. They knew next to nothing of the Arabs, nor were they particularly worried about the rights of the native populations of the partitioned Ottoman Empire—especially since the Arabs had emerged after the First World War from centuries of Turkish bondage with large self-governing territories, in comparison with which what was promised to the Jews seemed so little.

For a fleeting moment it seemed also as if the Weizmann-Faisal agreement might ensure a *modus vivendi* between the diverse aspirations of the two races. Addicted to their idealistic endeavour, so pathetically eager to turn the desert into garden, the Jews would at first meet any argument about the Arabs with vague expressions of benevolence, quite sincerely disclaiming any wish to hurt them. They were passionately anxious to build up a normal integrated Jewish society and to disprove the slander of their detractors that they were made only for usury and commerce and not for labour and toil. They were also afraid of being put in the position of European planters in Asia and Africa, and so they insisted on employing only Jewish labour on the Jewish national land.

Then, in 1937, when the clash between Arabs and Jews became too acute, the Jews accepted the Royal (or Peel) Commission plan for partition, although by then the need for a refuge from antisemitic persecution was already desperately urgent. It was rejected uncompromisingly by the Arabs. The same happened in 1947—when the United Nations, with the United States and Russia acting as sponsors, resolved upon partition. The Arabs have never since tired of proclaiming a state of war against Israel. In violent and bloodcurdling language they continued to voice their intention to wipe out Israel, and indeed its inhabitants. Survivors of Auschwitz could not be expected to treat such threats as mere rhetoric or figures of speech. Nor could they be blamed if they resolved to acts of war, when day in and day out it was not only dinned into their ears that a state of siege was on, but demonstrated to them in the form of infiltration, sabotage, murder and arson.

Intransigent

It was as if God had hardened the heart of Pharaoh: the more intransigent the form of Arab enmity toward Israel, the worse were the consequences for the Arabs themselves. The armed resistance of the Arab States to the UN plan created the refugee problem; the resumption of fighting after the first cease-fire resulted in the loss of more Arab territory; Arab sabotage on the one hand and alliance with Russia on the other only led to a strengthening of Israel's might; finally, this year, the attempt to strangle Israel brought the Arabs a most humiliating *débâcle*.

The armistice agreements concluded in 1949 between the new State of Israel and the Arab countries contained *prima facie* all the guarantees for peace, if not in form, at least in substance. They forbade hostile propaganda, acts of sabotage, operations by military or paramilitary formations, above all armed intrusions or incursions by Army detachments.

In a state of war no points of contact are possible. Hence the irrelevance of the empirical approach, so dear to Anglo-Saxon statesmanship, which sets its hopes on gradual, imperceptible sliding from a state of half-war, half-peace into a state of full peace, from contact and cooperation in small things—such as sharing the waters of the Jordan—to sustained neighbourly give-and-take in all spheres.

This is the context of the question of refugees. Acute as the problem is in terms of human suffering, and few Jews, sons of a nation of exiles and refugees, can be callously indifferent to this aspect of the problem, the state of war makes its solution quite impossible. The world is understandably deeply exercised by the plight of hundreds of thousands of refugees wasting away their lives in camps in pitiable conditions.

One often hears the well-intentioned opinion that this is the most serious obstacle to peace, and that if this tragedy were to be put out of the way, peace could easily be established. The Arabs themselves have never said that the return of the Arab refugees to Palestine was their condition for peace; quite the reverse. In October 1949 the Egyptian Foreign Minister said: 'It should be known and well understood that in demanding the return of the refugees to Palestine the Arabs mean their return as masters of their country and not as slaves. More clearly, they envisage the liquidation of Israel.' In a speech in 1964 President Nasser stated: 'There have been attempts to separate the issues and present them in an imaginary way, as if the question of Israel is just the problem of refugees, and that once this problem is solved the Palestine question would be solved and no trace would be left of it. The Israeli danger lies in the very existence of Israel and in what this State represents.'

If war was the objective, no one could blame the Israelis for believing that the demand for the readmission of refugees, or compensation for them, was motivated not just by the wish to see them restored to their homes, but by the desire to use them as an instrument, a Trojan horse, to disrupt Israel. Besides, the way to solve the refugee problem is surely not by revanchism. What Pandora's boxes would be opened if all nations whose members had been driven from their homes by armed hostilities were to resort to war to right the wrong or merely to wreak vengeance.

Immigrants

Israel has already absorbed in the last 20 years about 600,000 Jewish immigrants from the Arab countries. The Arab refugee problem is intractable, not because no solution can be found through their resettlement and absorption elsewhere in the Arab countries, but because of the implacable Arab refusal even to consider such a possibility lest this blunt the edge of the refugee issue as a political weapon. In fact, the refugee problem is not the sole or even the main obstacle to peace: it is the state of war that is the chief obstacle to the solution of the refugee problem. But Arabs would not, and perhaps could not, see that, because Israel has become to them an obsession, indeed a neurosis.

The Arabs are a proud race enamoured of the memories of their past glories. When they woke up so late from their long lethargy, they were, like all late-comers, in a great haste to recover their place in the sun. They were then faced by the inexorable facts of actual weakness, underdevelopment and vast misery. The combination of resentment towards the West and the envious desire to appropriate and utilise its achievements and levers of power, plus the frustrations encountered in the attempt to skip centuries of social and economic development, led Arabs to put all the blame on imperialism—although in comparative terms the brunt of imperialism was felt much more heavily by other races.

World support for Zionist settlement, for which Arab consent was neither sought nor obtained, and then the establishment of Israel, assumed in the eyes of Arab nationalism the dimensions of a mortal injury, especially as it came from the hands of the Jews, whom they had been accustomed to despise as second-class citizens and a non-martial race of infidels.

The Palestine issue has become the symbol and focus of all Arab frustrations. Their sense of grievance blinds them to the historic rights, the background of tragedy behind the Jewish aspirations, the ardour and high idealism motivating them and the genuine interest of the civilised world in the restoration of Jewish statehood.

The student of Arab opinion and Arab thought is often horrified to watch the growth of the anti-Israel obsession to the point of it having become the cornerstone of a kind of systematic Manichean metaphysic, with the Jew as devil incarnate.

The paramount task at present is to put an end to the general atmosphere of 'kill him before he kills you.' The Arabs threaten to kill the Jews; the Jews then feel they must forestall the Arabs; the Arabs are convinced the Jews are out to kill them off, and so when an armed clash occurs they start running; the Arabs swear bloody vengeance; the Jews insist on maximum guarantees. Any historian knows what a corroding effect this sense of a state of mortal emergency has on peace, morality and freedom. The Arabs are now, understandably, in a state of shock. But one believes one perceives wiser and more prudent counsels stirring among some of them, although for the time being these are too inhibited to come out into the open.

Israel is still more deeply divided. There are those who anxiously 'await a telephone call from King Hussein,' hoping for an arrangement with him whereby Jordan would receive back most of the West Bank, except some strategic points and of course, excepting Jerusalem, plus access to and possibly control over the Muslim holy places. These hopes also assume that world-wide financial support, combined with a substantial Israeli contribution—by way of compensation—would not only make the resettlement of refugees possible, but also put Hussein back on his feet, and create a network of joint, international sponsored ventures in the form of vast works for desalination, irrigation, and so on, for the benefit of all concerned.

There are the others who, pointing to Arab intransigence, claim to see in the triumph of Israel arms the hand of God. Such a chance occurs only once in history, they say. The present generation of Israelis has no right to barter away the promised inheritance, which belongs to all generations. There can be no retreat from the strategic frontiers, particularly on the Jordan, the heights of Golan, and the Suez Canal. (Others would be content with the demilitarisation of Sinai.) They insist on the sacrosanct character of the geopolitical entity that is Palestine.

Romantics

While the mystics and romantics are obsessed with the danger from outside, the moderate realists fear the enormous difficulties inside, arising out of the presence of a large compact territorial Arab minority. They are also beset by grave moral scruples and are apprehensive of world public opinion.

To this the former, among them a surprising number of declared leftists, retort by condemning their adversaries as men of small Zionist faith, who also lack confidence in the ability of Israel to treat an Arab minority humanely and well and to solve all the social and economic problems involved.

In the hopeless view they take of the Arab readiness to recognise the existence of Israel, the hawks of Israel are most likely to add fuel to the hawks in the Arab world. This paradoxical 'alliance' can be countered, and the vicious circle broken, only by an 'alliance' of the moderate realists on both sides. And I can only hope that my friend Hourani and men like him will heed this appeal to their moral obligation towards their own people and mankind in general.

The Origins of the Middle East Crisis[1]

By Hal Draper[*]

We have just seen War No. 3 in the tragedy known as the Israel-Arab conflict; and we find ourselves in the position of being unable to cheer for either side in this clash of chauvinisms. At this time I am going to devote myself mainly to the myths and illusions about the Israeli side of the story, for the simple reason that it is these myths and illusions that you mainly read and hear about.

It is not possible to understand what has happened merely by looking at what happened in the last couple of weeks. Behind War No. 3 is a closely connected chain of events and issues going far back. The main link in this chain is the story of a *nation that has been destroyed*.

That sounds like an echo of what we hear all around, viz. the threat of the Arab states to destroy the state of Israel

[1] This article is a somewhat condensed and edited version of a talk given in Berkeley shortly after the outbreak of the Third Arab-Israeli War, dealing with the historical background of the conflict but not with the current situation, which was discussed separately. Fully detailed documentation for the material contained here may be found in a book which has just been published, *Zionism, Israel and the Arabs: The Historical Background of the Middle East Tragedy* (Berkeley, 1967), edited by myself, comprising articles from the Independent Socialist press. Ed.

[*] Hal Draper is an editor of *New Politics* and author of "Berkeley: The New Student Revolt." His article appeared in *New Politics*, Winter, 1967 and is reprinted by permission of the author. An article in a similar vein by the late Isaac Deutscher ("On the Israel–Arab War") was published in the *New Left Review*, (London), July–August, 1967. It was answered in detail by Simha Flapan in *Temps Modernes*, (Paris), November, 1967.

—the threat which is the hallmark of Arab chauvinism. But while this is a threat, there *was* a nation that was destroyed in Palestine—already. It is this destroyed nation whose fate has been the crux of the Middle East tragedy, for its fate has been used and is being used as a football by each side.

When I was born, there was an Arab nation in Palestine, in whose midst Jews had lived for 2000 years in relative peace. Where is this nation now, and what has been done to it? The answer is at the heart of the program which we face now.

Today the leaders of the Arab states are saying, "We aim to destroy the nation which inhabits Palestine," and they are rightly denounced for this. But toward the end of the 19th century, a movement arose which did in fact set itself the aim of destroying the nation which inhabited Palestine then; and moreover it did so. That movement was the Zionist movement.

Everyone talks nowadays about "*the* Jews" and "*the* Arabs," with doubtful justice. There are Jews and Jews, as there are Arabs and Arabs; and right now I am talking not about "the Jews," but about the Zionist movement. Israel today is run by the old men of the world Zionist movement, and it is still the Zionist ideology which rules Israeli policy. The European survivors of Hitler's death camps are not the Jews who run Israel; their terrible fate has been a tool used by the men who run Israel, so that the crimes of the Nazis have been used to deflect the attention of world public opinion from the crimes committed in Palestine.

For present purposes, there are three things to understand about this Zionist ideology, which still rules the rulers of Israel. To present the first, I quote a typical example of anti-Semitic literature:

> The converted Jew remains a Jew, no matter how much he objects to it . . . Jews and Jewesses endeavor in vain to obliterate their descent through conversion or intermarriage with the Indo-Germanic and Mongolian races, for the Jewish type is indestructible. . . . Jewish noses cannot be reformed, and the black wavy hair of the Jews will not change through conversion into blond, nor can its curves be straightened out by constant combing.

There is more of the same where this comes from. Obviously from the Nazi commentary on the Nuremberg Laws, or from Streicher's *Stürmer,* or perhaps from Gerald L. K. Smith? Not at all: it is from a classic of Zionism, Moses Hess' *Rom und Jerusalem.* It is easily possible to quote pages and pages more of this same mystical blood-tribalism from the best Zionist sources, all sounding as if it came from the arsenal of the anti-Semites.

For Zionism is, first of all, a doctrine about a tribal blood-mystique which makes all Jews a single nation no matter where they live or how. It asserts that Jews are inevitably *aliens* everywhere, just as the anti-Semites say they are; and that anti-Semitism is correct in feeling this. This is the first element in Zionism.

Secondly: it follows that the Jews must reconstitute their "nation" in a state territory; but not just *any* state territory. In fact there is a point of view called "territorialism," as distinct from Zionism, which looked for the establishment of a Jewish nation in a land other than Palestine. But Zionism demands that the Jewish "nation" take over Palestine—only Palestine; and by Palestine it means the ancient Jewish state and its boundaries, *Eretz Isroel,* no less. This is what the tribal mystique demands.

Thirdly: the Zionist ideology dictates that this Jewish state must be set up not only by Jews who want to live in such a state. One of the tasks of the Zionist movement is to move *all* Jews, from all countries of the world, into Palestine, now Israel. In Zionist slang, this is called the "Ingathering of the Exiles;" for it is an article of basic faith that all Jews living outside this territory are living literally in exile, and always will merely be exiles, nothing else. It was not very many years ago that a writer in *Davar,* the organ of the Israeli ruling party, made the suggestion that a good way of uprooting all those American Jews who declined to go to Israel was to send a gang of anti-Semitic agitators there to make the ground hot under their feet so that they would move. This, of course, is not usually the course recommended on paper, as against persuasion. But how persuasion graduates into denunciation and arm-twisting was seen in the early fifties when David Ben-Gurion, on a visit to the U.S., denounced the Zionist Organization of America as traitors to Zionism because its leaders were not working actively to get the entire Jewish population of the U.S. to move to Israel. It must be understood (though American Zionists systematically obfuscate it to the best of their ability) that the Israeli leaders and world Zionist leaders sincerely believe in their mission to "ingather" *all* the Jews of the world to the state of Israel, and that they have devoted their lives to this mission.

The Zionists have always been fond of saying that they are tired of the Jews being a "peculiar people," that they have been "peculiar" long enough. They want (they say) the Jews to be a people like any other, and to have a state just like any other state. In Israel, I would tell you, they have succeeded notably in *this* aim: Israel more and more has become a state like any other state. In this stridently militarist Zionist state, the current of Jewish humanism which was one of the glories of the Jewish people from Maimonides to Spinoza and after, is today represented only by a minority—a minority whose voices are rarely heard abroad, and hardly at all in the U.S.; but it is this minority which represents the only Israel with whom one can identify.

Soon after the creation of Israel the press was full of enthusiastic reports by American Jewish tourists who went to Israel and came back to relate the wonders that they saw there (and there are many to see). One that I remember most vividly was a tourist who was quoted as follows in the course of his burbling: "Why, you walk around Tel Aviv, and you know what? Even the *policemen* are Jewish!" That's true, naturally. The cops are Jewish in Israel—and they are still cops. The militarists in Israel are Jewish—and they are militarists. And the people who destroyed the Arab Palestinian nation which I mentioned were, alas, also Jewish—though I do not believe that they will go down in the annals of history alongside Maimonides and Spinoza.

The destruction of that Palestinian nation went through four periods. The first period goes from the beginning of the Zionist movement up to World War I. This was a period of slow immigration of Jews into Palestine and of gradual land-buying. By the time it ended Jews constituted something under 10 percent of the population. Despite Zionism's profession that this was the thin edge of the wedge in its long-term aim to establish a Jewish state in the land inhabited by Arabs, it was not taken seriously enough to occasion much resistance until the second period, inaugurated by the 1917 Balfour Declaration.

It was in this period that British imperialism, taking over the area, started its decades-long policy of playing Zionists against Arabs in order to maintain its imperialist control. The Zionist leadership willingly and knowingly collaborated with the British. They knew that, at this stage, it was not they who could control the Arab people living in the land; only British imperialism could do it for them. To be sure, they were not *puppets* of the British: they were junior partners, in an enterprise in which each partner considered that it was using the other for its own ends.

This was also the period of the beginning of Arab nationalism, of an Arab national-liberation movement. This movement had every right to fight for liberation from Britain (or in other parts of the Middle East, from France). To supporters of Arab freedom, the Zionist movement could have appeared only as what it actually was: a partner of the European imperialists. It makes no difference whatsoever that the Zionists played this baneful role not out of love for Britain but in pursuit of their own expansion. The fact is that Britain used the Zionist tool to increase the number of Jewish settlers so as to play them off against the indigenous Arab population. Thus it was inevitable that Jewish immigration should appear to the Arabs as a tool of imperialist domination, for it was so.

It was therefore during the 1920s that, for pretty much the first time in Palestine, there began sporadic Arab attacks against Jewish settlers. On the one side, these were the first stirrings of an Arab national liberation movement, directed not only against the British but also against the allies of the British who were at hand, viz. Zionist infiltrators into the country. On the other hand—and here you get the typically tragic element in this story which goes through it from beginning to end—these stirrings took on strong overtones of the backward social and religious aims of the Arab movement; for progressive social elements were weak, working-class formations were incipient. But this hardly can change the fact that there was a legitimate nationalist movement under way.

The third period—which was to prove decisive to the outcome—came with the onset of the Nazis' anti-Jewish drive, first in Germany itself, and then in the course of World War II in the rest of Nazi-occupied Europe, up to the mass extermination campaign and its death camps. It should be added that, in the period immediately following the war, there was also the onset of Soviet anti-Semitism on a big scale, thereby boosting the impact of what had happened during the war.

This is the period that everyone knows about; some think it is all one has to know. But there is more to this than meets the myopic eye.

To be sure, for the Jewish remnant Europe represented

burning ground: they had to get out—somehow, somewhere, anywhere. This plight of the Jewish refugees—one of the most terrible in the history of man's bestiality to man—was what dramatically captured the sympathy of everyone decent in the world; it is this that is tied up in the public mind with the exodus to Palestine. This is entirely true as far as it goes; but one has to know something else too. *This terrible plight and this great world sympathy were not enough to open the gates of a single Western country to those Jewish refugees!*

During those years we Independent Socialists called for opening the doors of the United States to the Jewish victims of Hitlerism, those who were left. I can tell you that in this great "liberal" country, crawling with liberals, there was hardly an echo of such a notion, of opening the doors of *this* country to the poor Jews for whom everyone's heart bled—in print.

One reason for this is clear and can be easily documented. Morris Ernst, the famous civil liberties lawyer who was involved at the time, has told the story, among others: about how the leaders of the Zionist movement exerted all the influence they could muster to make sure that the U.S. did *not* open up immigration to these Jews—for the simple reason that they wanted to herd these same Jews to Palestine. This is what their Zionist ideology demanded. White Christian America was only too glad to go along with this "solution"! Who wanted a few hundred thousand miserable Jewish refugees coming into the country? Not our liberal Americans, who were so heart-stricken by Nazi brutality. Not the British, who took in an inconsequential token number. Nor anyone else. These Jewish victims were people on the planet without a visa. Liberals in this country, as elsewhere, had a convenient way of salving their tender consciences; all they had to do was parrot the line which the Zionists industriously provided them: "They want to go only to Palestine . . ."

Now there is no point in anyone's arguing to what extent this was really true or not, or of how many it was true, because no one ever gave them the chance to decide whether they wanted to go to Palestine or to some other country that was open to them. The doors were shut against them, with the help of the whole Zionist apparatus and of other "influential" Jews who were no more enthusiastic about "flooding" the country with poor Jews than their WASP neighbors. First it was made damned sure that Palestine was the only possible haven, and then they might possibly be asked where they wanted to go, as if they had a free choice! In my eyes, this is one of the basest crimes committed by the Zionist leadership.

In this way the Jewish survivors of the Hitlerite death camps were herded toward Palestine, to keep the U.S. and other countries from being contaminated by their presence (for some) or to make sure that they were properly "ingathered" (for others). Of course, Palestine was not really open either, being still under the control of the British, but here at least the Zionist movement was willing to go all-out to crash the gates, with heavy financing from many an American Jew who himself had no sympathy for Zionism but could be convinced that Palestine was certainly a more suitable haven than New York.

This turn brought the Zionist movement into conflict with the same British imperialism whose junior partner it had been. The partners' paths now diverged. The Jewish refugees —fleeing from a horror behind them, and rejected on all sides—became the human material the Zionists needed to carry out the goal they had set a half century before: to dispossess the Arab nation of Palestine and install a Jewish state in its stead—and to do this with the sympathy of a good deal of the world.

The Palestinian Arabs, as well as their Arab neighbors, had a very simple comment to make on this situation: "Hitler's extermination program was a great crime, but why does that mean that *we* have to give up our land to the Jews? It is the world's problem, not just ours." I should like to see someone refute this.

We must note that by this time the Zionist movement had finally come out openly with its proclaimed intention of taking Palestine away as a Jewish state. This had been done in 1942, in the so-called "Biltmore Program." (Up to then, the Zionists had used doubletalk about a "Jewish homeland" to confuse the picture.) Now that the cards were on the table, there were even some Zionists—or at least people who considered themselves to be Zionists—who were outraged. It was around this time that the Ichud was founded in Palestine by Rabbi Judah Magnes. The idea of a bi-national state in Palestine was counterposed to the official Zionist program: instead of a "Jewish state" it meant a state in which both Jews and Arabs could live peacefully and tranquilly together; but it was rejected. Instead, the Zionists said, "We are going to take the whole country"; and they did.

Here I need only sketch how this happened. After a series of doubledealing maneuvers by the great powers (particularly the U.S., Britain and Russia) which it would take too long to go into, by 1947 the United Nations decided on a partition plan. There were to be two separate states in Palestine, a Jewish state and an Arab Palestinian state. By this time, there was indeed a Jewish majority in the territory assigned to the Jewish state—something like a 60% majority—and therefore one could feel that this majority had the right to invoke the right to self-determination. I might as well mention that, at that time (1948), I did myself believe and write that the Palestinian Jews had the *right* to make this mistaken choice (for, of course, a right exists only if it includes the right to make a mistake). I mention this only to make clear that I believed and wrote at that time that the attack on the new state of Israel by the Arab states was an aggression and a violation of the right to self-determination.

But at that moment Israel was still new-born, and there were different ways in which it could defend itself—in a progressive and democratic way, and in a racist and expansionist way. The answer to *that* historical question was not long in coming: it was given right away by the same Zionist leaders who were also the rulers of the new state power. From its first hour the Zionist power took the road of a reactionary and racist purge of the Arabs as such. At this point I am not talking about the foreign Arab states, but of the Arabs of Israel themselves, the great mass of whom never took up arms against Israel or aided the aggressors.

A new act in the Middle East tragedy begins here; although it is a crime smaller in magnitude than Hitler's against the Jews, it is still one of the most shameful in recent history. The Zionist rulers utilized the attack by the *foreign* Arab states to run the *Palestinian* Arabs off their land, by means of a series of laws and measures which were taken not only in 1948-49 but which went right on into the 1950s. The forty percent of the population which was Arab in the partitioned territory was reduced to about 10 percent in the new state of Israel. Immense proportions of Arab-owned land were simply robbed from them, by "legal" means. By 1954 over one-third of the Jewish population then in Israel was settled on land that had been stolen from the Palestinian Arabs. And the Arab state of Palestine which had been created by the partition never came into existence; by the end of the war, five sections of it had been grabbed by Israel and were never given up, and the West Jordan area was incorporated into the state of Jordan.

Thus the Arab nation of Palestine was destroyed, except as a discriminated-against remnant in Israel, and even the truncated Arab state of Palestine set up by partition was destroyed. I am entirely willing to denounce anyone who wants to destroy any existing state, including Israel; but some thought should be given to this recent history by those who are willing to denounce *only* the threat to destroy Israel.

The great land robbery of the Israeli Arabs was the despoiling of a whole people. It was carried out in various ways, but generally speaking the pattern was this: any Arab who had left his village during the war for any reason whatsoever was declared an "absentee" and his land was taken away by Zionist agencies. The Zionist myth has it that all these Palestinian Arabs left at the behest of the foreign Arab invaders and in cahoots with them. This is a big lie. There was a war on, and even if they *fled from* the Arab invaders and in fear of them, and even if they fled only to a neighboring village, they became "absentees." They also fled from the British; they not only fled from the invading Arabs but also fled from the Zionist troops—the Haganah and the Irgun. This was especially true after the massacre at Deir Yassin.

Deir Yassin was the name of an Arab village in Palestine, whose people were outstandingly *hostile* to the Arab invaders. In 1948 a battalion of the Irgun (the right-wing Zionist force) attacked the village. There were no armed men in the village, and no arms. Purely for terroristic purposes, the Irgun sacked the village and massacred 250 men, women and children. One hundred and fifty bodies were thrown down a well; 90 were left scattered around. This massacre was deliberately directed by the Irgun against a village known to be *friendly* to the Jews, as an example. Although the dirty job was done by the Irgun, the official-Zionist Haganah knew of the planned attack; immediately afterward the Irgun, instead of being pilloried in horror by the Zionist movement, was welcomed by the Haganah into a new pact of collaboration. (The Irgun's leader, Beigin, by the way, was taken into the Israeli cabinet along with General Dayan just before the outbreak of the recent Third War.)

Of course, the Irgun was able to show the way to the Haganah because it was semi-fascist; but the Haganah leaders learned fast. Before the First War had ended the Haganah too was attacking and ousting unarmed and non-belligerent

Arab villagers, although naturally not as brutally as the Irgun (since they were democrats and "socialists"). Especially after the Deir Yassin massacre, it was only necessary that any troops show up, and the Arab peasants got out of the way, as anyone else would do. They thus became "absentees," and their land was taken away by a series of laws over the next several years. *All* of the Zionist parties, from "left" to right, sanctioned this robbery. There was even a legal category known as "present absentees," who were very much present as Arab citizens of Israel but who were legally accounted to be "absentees" because they had been absent from their village on a certain date—and therefore could be legally robbed of their land. The largest portion of this stolen land went to the kibbutzim—not only the kibbutzim run by the Mapai (right-wing social democrats) but even more went to the kibbutzim of the Mapam (who claimed to be left socialists), whose leaders regularly made clear that their hearts bled for the plight of the Israeli Arabs. However, their hearts also bled for their land, even more.

Along the border areas, Palestinian Arabs were pushed over the line into the Gaza Strip, or into Jordan, and then they were shot on sight as "infiltrators" if they tried to come back. It was in ways like this—which I sketch here only briefly —that Israel's rulers created the massive Arab refugee problem. Literally they surrounded the country with a circle of hatred—*hatred which they themselves had caused*—the hatred of the despoiled Palestinian Arabs looking over from the other side of the border and seeing their own lands being tilled by strangers whom the Zionists had brought from thousands of miles away to take their place.

This robbery is not transmuted into justice just because some of these strangers were Jewish refugees from Europe against whom another crime had been committed by someone else. The Zionist agencies welcomed these despairing refugees to their new life by putting them on the marches of the hate-encircled state so that they would have to defend themselves, their lives, and their stolen gifts, from the previous Arab owners. (Thus the "exiles" were not only "ingathered" but also very useful.)

Meanwhile in Israel, the 10 percent of the Palestinian Arabs left—who had not only not taken up arms but had not fled— were placed under military control like an occupied enemy people, and discriminated against in many ways. It is not without reason that they have been called the "niggers of Israel";

but as a matter of fact the American Negroes would not have taken lying down what the Israeli Arabs had to endure for two decades.

On the borders—for example, in the Gaza Strip—the dispossessed and robbed Arabs lived a wretched existence under the control of Egypt, but the Egyptians only used them for their own purposes as pawns, while keeping their help to a minimum. They were not admitted into Egypt proper. They were forced to fester there so that their misery and hatred might make them a bone in the throat of the Israelis; at the same time Israel was as little interested as Nasser in arriving at a deal for the settlement of the Arab refugee problem.

Every now and then some of the refugees would "infiltrate" —that is, slip across into Israel to visit his own land or till his own soil or try to take back his own belongings—and would be shot to death by those same Jewish policemen and guards who so delighted the heart of the Jewish tourist mentioned earlier. As a result the Israelis complained bitterly about the "infiltrators" who were so evil as to do this. The terrible situation escalated. Infiltrators began to commit acts of sabotage on the property that had been stolen from them, or struck out more blindly at the robbers. The Israelis began to resort to organized military reprisals to terrorize them into acquiescence. In 1953 there was a massacre organized by Israeli armed forces in the Arab village of Kibya. In 1955— a year that more or less marked a turning-point for the worse —there was a big attack by an organized Israeli military force on Gaza; more and more Israeli leaders oriented toward "preventive" war, since military force was their only answer to the problem created by their own crimes. This was the traditional and classic answer of the militarist and expansionist mentality; it is the same answer as was recommended by General MacArthur on how to treat Koreans and Chinese and other such "gooks"—you show them who's master—that's what they can understand, etc. The answer of the Israeli militarists was, similarly: kill and terrorize the "gooks" and "teach them a lesson" so that they won't do it again.

There were negotiations over the plight of the Arab refugees but neither side was interested in a real settlement—not the Israeli side and not the Egyptian and Arab side. For Nasser, the Arab refugees leading their wretched existence were useful tools to harass the Israelis. As for Israel, at the same time that they argued that they could not restore the land to the Arabs they had robbed, they were industriously bringing in whole Jewish populations, from Yemen and Morocco, for example (not to speak of the whole Jewish population of the U.S. which Ben-Gurion was so vainly anxious to move to Israel). There was plenty of room in Israel for such hundreds of thousands of Jews, but in the negotiations over the Arab refugee problem there was not a *dunam* of land that could be spared. The decisive thing to remember is that, from the Zionist viewpoint, for every single despoiled Arab who would be readmitted to Israel there was a Jew who could therefore not be "ingathered."

The problem was not *how* Israel and the Arab states could have made peace; the problem was that neither side wanted to make peace, except of course on capitulatory terms. They did not then, and they do not now.

For Nasser, the Israel issue was a pawn in the inter-Arab struggle for power. It was also a useful distraction from the internal failures of his bureaucratic-military regime, which lacked any progressive domestic program. In both Egypt and Jordan, the pressure of the refugees within the country was relieved only by pointing them outward, against Israel. As for Israel, it must be remembered that Zionism still did not rule the "Land of Israel" as the Zionist program demanded; the "Land of Israel" still included territories outside of the state of Israel. Israeli expansionism was implicit in this, and also in the fact that, if room was going to be made for the millions of "exiles" who were to be ingathered, more land was needed. In 1955 Israeli leaders (some eagerly convinced of the necessity of "preventive" war, some dragging their feet) were looking for some pretext to launch a war against Egypt and the Arab alliance. As it happened, British and French imperialism brought them to launch that aggression themselves. In 1956, openly and in the sight of the whole world, side by side with the two leading European imperialisms (of which it was once again a junior partner), Israel invaded Egypt as its partners struck at the Suez Canal.

The point is not that Nasser is or was a dove of peace, himself, as has been made clear. One of the reasons why Nasser was not in a position to give warlike substance to his blowhard threats was that he was too preoccupied with internal difficulties and too weak. But if Nasser was no dove, it is still true that Israel exposed itself to the whole world as an open aggressor in alliance with European imperialism. Every dirty expansionist plan it had been accused of turned out to be true.

Even after the British and French enterprise failed, Israel fought to retain the land it had grabbed in Egypt and gave it up only after immense international pressure.

This pattern must be remembered in the light also of the way in which the recent Third War was initiated: i.e. with Nasser taking the situation to the brink, talking loudly about destroying Israel, while the Israelis went straight to the business at hand by precipitating the shooting war.

There is one other story to be told for this period—the story of a pogrom. This pogrom was directed against an Arab village in Israel named Kfar Kassem. On the day that Israel attacked Egypt in 1956, the Israeli government declared a new curfew for its Arab citizens (who, remember, were under military control anyway, even without a war). The new decree advanced the curfew from 11 p.m. to 5 p.m. Israeli officers showed up in Kfar Kassem, as well as other places, to make known the change on that day. They were told that the men had already gone out to the fields; the officers' reply was, roughly speaking, "Don't bother us with details." In the evening, when the men of the village returned from working in the fields after the new curfew hour, they were shot down in cold blood by the Israeli soldiers—for violating a curfew that had never been told them. The government admitted that 46 men were thus killed; the number wounded was not made public. The government admission applied only to Kfar Kassem but it was reliably reported that the same thing that day at other Arab villages. Even this much was admitted by the government only after a week had passed and the reports could no longer be hushed up. All of Israel was appalled. Some underlings were made the scapegoats.

It was clear, then, that the Zionist program of making Israel a "state like any other state" had come true: it had its own Jewish policemen, it had its own soldiers, it had its own militarists, and now it had its own pogroms.

In 1967 the road that started in Deir Yassin and goes through Kfar Kassem has now reached the bank of the Jordan, where Arab refugees are once again being pushed out and around by the Israelis, as they have been for the last 20 years. It would be useful to go through the whole chapter subsequent to 1956, leading up to the Third War, but, aside from time considerations, we would only find that it is more of the same thing: the tragedy of one reactionary chauvinism versus another reactionary chauvinism.

There is an image that haunts me, about this whole tragic

embroilment in the Middle East. Buck deer in the mating season will fight each other, and now and again it has happened that they will entangle their antlers and be unable to disengage. Unable to break loose, unable to win, locked in a static hopeless combat until they die and rot and their bleached bones are found by some hunter in the forest, their skeletons are grisly evidence of a tragedy which destroyed them both, ensnarled.

It may be that, in the Middle East entanglement, the Arabs, or some of the Arabs, can survive this conflict. But it is doubtful whether, in the long run, the Jews of Israel can. What the Zionists have made out of Israel is a new ghetto—a state ghetto with state boundaries. That's not a new life for the Jews; that is more of the old life of which the Jews have had more than their share. This generation of Zionist hawks ruling Israel is a curse. No matter how many more great military victories they win, the sea of Arab peoples ringing them cannot be eliminated from the picture, and hatred grows. It may be another decade or two before the Arab states become modernized enough to wage war effectively; and then it will take more than euphoria over military heroes to point a way for Israel.

There are some in Israel who know and say what has been said here—more who know and fewer who say—and it is to be hoped that the next generation will be more willing to listen to their kind, to the kind of Jews who represent what is best in the history of Jewish humanism and social idealism rather than those who worship the Moloch of a "state like any other state."

Perfidy and Aggression

By N. T. Fedorenko*

The attention of the whole world has been focussed in these past days on the Middle East, where Israel has committed open and perfidious aggression against the Arab states.

The United Nations Organization, whose mission it is to maintain international peace and security, naturally could not

* N. T. Fedorenko, Soviet Permanent Delegate to the U.N., played a leading part in the United Nations' discussions before, during and after the crisis of June, 1967. His article appeared in the Soviet weekly *New Times*, June 28, 1967.

pass by the Israeli aggression. First the Security Council was urgently called into session, to discuss, in particular, the Soviet demand for cessation of hostilities by Israel and withdrawal of Israeli troops from U.A.R., Jordanian and Syrian territory occupied as a result of the aggression. Then, on the initiative of the Soviet Union, a special emergency session of the General Assembly was convened on June 17.

The Security Council debates showed up the broad imperialist conspiracy against the Arab states and peoples of the Middle East. It was proved that the Israeli aggression was not an accidental thing, not the result of any mistake or misunderstanding. No, it was a carefully plotted imperialist provocation, the timing of which was planned on all sides. This aggression was to secure political changes in the Middle East in the interest of imperialism, notably American imperialism, to alter the "balance of strength" in the area. Its purpose was to undermine the Arab national-liberation movement, to weaken the progressive regimes in the U.A.R., Syria and other Arab countries. Israel acted as the instrument of more powerful imperialist states, and above all the U.S.

The Israeli army was built up and trained with the help of the imperialist Western Powers. Tel Aviv was given every protection and encouragement, particularly in Washington, to prepare it for aggression against the Arab states.

The peoples of the U.A.R. and other Arab countries have scored historic victories in these past years in their struggle to attain national independence and freedom. Important social restructuring and reform in the interests of the working masses has been carried out in these countries. The imperialists could not stomach the fact that in this struggle the Arab peoples lean on the friendship and support of the Soviet Union and other socialist states.

Writing in *U.S. News and World Report*, General Max Johnson, formerly planning officer for the U.S. Joint Chiefs of Staff, openly voiced the sentiment of the American military chiefs. "The growing hostility of Middle Eastern nations towards the United States and friendliness towards the Soviet Union," he wrote, "has been a strategic loss of great proportions." And he linked the events in Vietnam with the position in the Middle East, pointing out that this area was a "strategic crossroads" between Europe, Asia and Africa.

And indeed, remote though Southeast Asia and the Gulf of Tonkin are geographically from the Middle East and the Eastern Mediterranean, few will question that the American aggression in Vietnam was bound to have the most pernicious effect on the general political situation in the world; and it was by no means the last factor in Israel's aggression against the Arab states.

The colonialists also refused to accept that Arab riches should belong to the Arabs themselves and that it is the Arab countries' lawful right to determine their own path of development. The imperialist forces got busy and the Israeli aggression was unleashed just when more and more of the Arab countries had begun taking measures to consolidate national independence.

The Israeli aggression is pointed against the national freedom and state independence of the millions of Arabs—from Kuwait, Damascus and Baghdad to Cairo, Algiers and Casablanca. There is not a shadow of doubt that behind Tel Aviv stand the imperialist forces which want to hamstring the free national development of the Arab states. It is these forces that lavishly supplied Tel Aviv with the needful means and gave it economic, moral and political assistance and support.

It should be added that behind the Israeli extremists it is easy to discover not only the Pentagon generals but the incorrigible militarists in West Germany. That Bonn has directly abetted the Israeli extremists is not to be concealed by any smokescreens of "neutrality." Bonn not only engaged in incitement, it not only sacrificed diplomatic relations with a number of Arab states for the sake of close partnership with Israel; it also supplied arms and equipment for the Israeli army. At the height of the Middle East crisis, West Germany demonstratively dispatched a large consignment of gas-masks to Israel. Thus there grew up on the soil of fevered militarism, on the common basis of adventurism, of hatred for all things progressive, of hostility to the Arab peoples' struggle to consolidate independence and achieve social progress, an alliance of Tel Aviv extremist circles not only with Washington but with Bonn.

On the eve of the Israeli attack an atmosphere of hysteria was artificially created in the country and tension whipped up to prepare the ground for aggression. The Arab states were showered with accusations. The events that followed showed that the U.A.R., Syria and the other Arab states had no aggressive intentions, that they had not been preparing to strike, and that it was Israel that had been girding feverishly for its brigand attack on the Arab countries. It was not the peoples, not the Arab countries that had an interest in kindling military conflict, but the forces of imperialism, the oil monopolies, of whom Israel is the confederate.

It is not surprising that when the question of Israel's aggression against the Arab states came before the Security Council, the aggressor had open defenders and abettors there, who sought to obstruct the work of the Council and enable Israel to ignore the Council's decisions, gain time for more conquests, and carry out its criminal plans.

That is why the Security Council had to hold a practically continuous series of emergency meetings and pass three separate resolutions on what was in effect one and the same question, reiterating its demand that Israel cease hostilities forthwith.

Thanks to the support given them by the United States—a permanent member of the Security Council—and by certain other members of the Council, who prevented the passage of a decision condemning the aggressor and demanding the immediate withdrawal of his troops to the positions held before the hostilities, the Tel Aviv rulers were able insolently to ignore the Security Council decisions and continue and extend their aggression, overrunning more and more Arab territory.

Even after the Security Council had ordered an immediate ceasefire and termination of hostilities, Israel treacherously—contrary to two Security Council resolutions (of June 6 and 7)—invaded the Syrian Arab Republic, occupied part of its territory, and bombed Cairo and the Damascus area.

The Tel Aviv rulers deliberately deceived the Security Council, assuring it that Israel was complying with its decisions while in reality they continued the aggression. It came to light during the debates that the bombing attacks on Cairo and Damascus and the invasion of Syria had taken place at the very time when Israel's representative in the Security Council had been making his hypocritical speeches and misleading Council members so as to distract attention from the criminal acts of the Israeli military. The Israeli authorities also did everything they could to prevent the U.N. observers on the spot from discharging their functions and keeping the Security Council informed of what was happening.

This perfidy of Tel Aviv was indignantly condemned by the socialist and Afro-Asian members of the Security Council. The Soviet delegation called the Council's attention to the dangerous war psychosis that has come to reign in the Israeli capital. Threats and ultimatums of a rare insolence and cyni-

cism have been issuing from there. Plans of expansion, plans
of seizing new territories, plans of recarving the map of the
Middle East have been intensively prepared.

The overweening aggressors have taken over the notorious
nazi theories of geopolitics, of Lebensraum, of establishing a
"new order" and "vital frontiers" in the Middle East. The
peoples are familiar with these ultimatums, these insensate
theories, this talk of a "new order" and of recarving the political map. It was the nazi conquistadors that set out to recarve
the map of Europe and the world, and attempted by armed
force to impose what they called a "new order," until the
fascist beast's spine was broken by the combined efforts of
the Soviet Union and other peoples. How monstrous that
these devices of the nazi brigands, condemned by the International Military Tribunal in 1946, have now been revived by
a government claiming to represent a people which suffered
so bitterly at the nazi butchers' hands!

Incoming reports show that the Arab population of Gaza,
Jerusalem and other areas is being forcibly driven out. In the
territories seized by Israeli troops occupation authorities are
being set up, military governors of towns and regions are being appointed. Judging by all the indications, the system is
being employed which the nazi invaders used in the countries
they occupied in World War II.

Israel's Prime Minister Eshkol declared on June 12: "Have
no illusions, Israel will not agree to revert to the situation
which existed until a week ago. . . . We are entitled to determine what are the true and vital interests of our country
and how they shall be secured. The position that existed until
now shall never again return." General Moshe Dayan has proclaimed the same ambitions, declaring the other day that "if
they [the Arab countries] don't want to talk to us, to sit down
with us, then we shall stay where we are." "I don't think," he
went on, "that we should in any way give back the Gaza strip
to Egypt or the western part of Jordan to King Hussein."

Do these statements not show up the aggressor's true face
and his expansionist plans, carefully laid long beforehand and
executed when he thought the moment opportune?

Nor are the Israeli aggressors original in their methods of
carrying out their expansionist policies. Like the nazis, they
try to deceive the peoples by shifting the blame to the victim
of aggression. They also emulate their American masters, who
are waging barbarous war on the Vietnamese people and trying to dictate terms from positions of strength.

The facts go to show that, in the Middle East and in Southeast Asia and in Latin America alike, the same criminal hand is at work and the same imperialist methods are being employed. Like the soil of Vietnam, Arab soil has been drenched with napalm, and on it, too, infamous crimes against civilian populations have been and are still being perpetrated. It is all part of a single imperialist plot against freedom-loving peoples defending their sovereignty and freedom against colonial oppressors, upholding the great cause of national liberation.

In the Security Council the representative of Jordan, in a wrathful indictment of Tel Aviv, pointed to the similarity of Israel's policy and methods to the policy and methods of the nazis. "Both," he said, "have the concept of expansion, both have the concept of race, both have the concept of force, of acquiring lands by invasion and the use of force, and both have fifth columns."

Already in the first hours of Israel's aggression against the Arab states the Soviet Union branded the Israeli invaders and firmly demanded condemnation of their perfidious and criminal acts, immediate cessation of hostilities and the withdrawal of Israeli troops behind the armistice lines.

In a resolution tabled on June 8, the Soviet Union called on the Security Council to emphatically condemn Israel's aggressive acts and its violation of the Security Council resolutions, the U.N. Charter and the principles of the United Nations, and to demand that Israel immediately cease hostilities against neighbouring Arab states and withdraw all its troops from their territory to behind the armistice lines.

However, the United States, Britain and some other Western Powers, set their face against condemnation of the aggressor and the demand for the immediate withdrawal of his troops from the occupied territories. The Security Council proved unable to pass the decision that the emergency dictated. Yet under the U.N. Charter, as the organ primarily responsible for the maintenance of international peace and security, it should have done so.

Some Western representatives even tried to make out that the question of the withdrawal of Israel's troops from the occupied territories should be linked with some sort of other conditions, with a general settlement in the Middle East, and so on and so forth. The Soviet delegation firmly rejected all such attempts.

The Washington diplomats hastened to introduce their own resolution, which, so far from condemning Israel's aggression and demanding the withdrawal of its troops, actually attempted to put the Arab states at a disadvantage vis-à-vis the aggressor and hedge about the withdrawal of Israeli troops with various demands which in the final count would limit the Arab states' sovereign rights. Essentially, the American resolution only encouraged the Israeli extremists' expansionist ambitions. Accordingly, the Arab countries and the Soviet Union decidedly rejected it.

The Soviet delegation asked the U.S. and other Western delegations outright: Did they agree to the immediate and unconditional withdrawal of Israel's troops from the territories it had seized to behind the armistice lines? Were they willing to recognize that continued occupation of Arab territory by the Israeli armed forces was unlawful, criminal and contrary to the U.N. Charter and the elementary principles of modern international law? But the Security Council never did get a clear answer to these questions.

The representatives of India and Mali emphasized in their Security Council speeches the need to order withdrawal of both sides' armed forces behind the armistice lines and only then discuss other problems, relating to so-called deeper causes of the tension in the Middle East. The stand taken in the Council by India, in particular, was based on the well-known principle of international law that an aggressor must not be allowed to profit by his aggression.

Because of the Western Powers' attitude, however, the Security Council at the initial stage was only able to order the cessation of hostilities. But that was only a preliminary measure, essential to protect the victims of aggression from Israel's brigand forces. It was altogether insufficient. For it was the Security Council's duty under the U.N. Charter to put an end to the aggression and restore the lawful rights of the attacked Arab states—the U.A.R., Syria and Jordan.

The Soviet Union accordingly continued to insist that the Security Council should vote on the Soviet resolution. Yet even in the concluding phase of the Council's work the attitude of the Western members, notably the U.S. and Britain, who openly support Israel's aggressive policy, made it impossible for the Council to pass the necessary decision.

The Soviet resolution's demand for the immediate withdrawal of Israeli troops from the occupied Arab territories received the votes of the socialist (U.S.S.R. and Bulgaria) and Afro-Asian (India, Mali, Ethiopia and Nigeria) member countries of the Council. The Western states, while not venturing to vote openly against this lawful and just demand, resorted to the "hidden veto" by abstaining. Thus, the Soviet resolution did not go through.

Heavy responsibility for this rests on the states which failed in their duty as members of the Security Council. The result was to produce a situation that called for emergency action by the United Nations and all freedom-loving countries to stop the continuing aggression in the Middle East.

It was clear that further discussion of the matter in the Security Council could not at present yield the proper results. It thus became necessary to seek other ways of exerting a sobering influence on the aggressor.

In the circumstances the Soviet government felt that the U.N. General Assembly should discuss the situation, in accordance with Article 11 of the U.N. Charter, and take decisions designed to liquidate the consequences of the aggression and effect the immediate withdrawal of Israeli troops behind the armistice lines.

The Soviet government asked for a special emergency session of the U.N. General Assembly to be convened immediately for this purpose. A majority of U.N. member states responded at once with support for the Soviet government's proposal. It is significant, however, that the United States and Israel opposed this Soviet initiative.

The special emergency session of the General Assembly opened in New York on June 17. In view of the great importance of the question before it, the Soviet delegation is led by Premier Kosygin. Many other leading statesmen of U.N. member nations are also attending. The session has only begun. But one can already say that except for a narrow group of accomplices of the aggressor, the members of the U.N. uphold the rights of the Arab peoples.

Even now the Israeli aggressors remain on the soil they have seized from neighbouring Arab peoples. What are they counting on? Is Tel Aviv perhaps waiting for a special invitation? Does it think that the peoples of the world, the United Nations Organization, will accept its seizure and occupation of foreign territory? Does it imagine that the Arab countries, the Soviet Union, the socialist states and other freedom-loving peoples will allow it to profit by its insolent and perfidious aggression, to dictate terms from positions of strength, the positions of an invader seeking to wrest away by force lands that belong to Arab countries?

Anyone who imagines any such thing is profoundly mistaken. The Tel Aviv government should have no illusions: Israel will have to pay in full for its brigand actions. And the United Nations Organization must pass its authoritative judgment, must do its duty under the Charter.

New York
June 17

Holy War

By I. F. Stone*

Stripped of propaganda and sentiment, the Palestine problem is, simply, the struggle of two different peoples for the same strip of land. For the Jews, the establishment of Israel was a Return, with all the mystical significance the capital R implies. For the Arabs it was another invasion. This has led to three wars between them in twenty years. Each has been a victory for the Jews. With each victory the size of Israel has grown. So has the number of Arab homeless.

Now to find a solution which will satisfy both peoples is like trying to square a circle. In the language of mathematics, the aspirations of the Jews and the Arabs are incommensurable. Their conflicting ambitions cannot be fitted into the confines of any ethical system which transcends the tribalistic. This is what frustrates the benevolent outsider, anxious to satisfy both peoples. For two years Jean-Paul Sartre has been trying to draw Israelis and Arabs into a confrontation in a special number of his review, *Les Temps Modernes*. The third war between them broke out while it was on the press.

This long-awaited special issue on *Le conflit israélo-arabe* is the first confrontation in print of Arab and Israeli intellectuals. But it turns out to be 991 pages not so much of dialogue as of dual monologue. The two sets of contributors sit not just in separate rooms, like employers and strikers in a bitter labor dispute, but in separate universes where the simplest fact often turns out to have diametrically opposite meanings. Physics has begun to uncover a new conundrum in the worlds of matter and anti-matter, occupying the same space and time but locked off from each other by their obverse natures, for-

---

* I. F. Stone, a Washington correspondent for twenty-five years, is publisher and editor of *I. F. Stone's Weekly*. This essay first appeared in the *New York Review of Books* August 3, 1967, and is reprinted by permission of the author.

ever twin yet forever sundered. The Israeli-Arab quarrel is the closest analogue in the realm of international politics.

The conditions exacted for the joint appearance of Israelis and Arabs in the same issue of *Les Temps Modernes* excluded not only collaboration but normal editorial mediation or midwifery. Claude Lanzmann, who edited this special issue, explains in his Introduction that the choice of authors and of subjects had to be left "in full sovereignty" (*en toute souveraineté*) to each of the two parties. The Arabs threatened to withdraw if an article was included by A. Razak Abdel-Kader, an Algerian who is an advocate of Israeli-Arab reconciliation. When the Israelis objected that *Les Temps Modernes* at least allow Abdel-Kader to express himself as an individual, the Arabs insisted on an absolute veto: there would be no issue if Abdel-Kader were in it.

In his Preface Jean-Paul Sartre lays bare the conflicting emotions which led him to embark on so difficult a task as to attempt the role—in some degree—of peacemaker between Arab and Israeli. They awaken the memories of his finest hours. One was that of the Resistance. "For all those who went through this experience," M. Sartre writes, "it is unbearable to imagine that another Jewish community, wherever it may be, whatever it may be, should endure this Calvary anew and furnish martyrs to a new massacre." The other was Sartre's aid to the Arabs in their struggle for Algerian independence. These memories bind him to both peoples, and give him the respect of both, as the welcome he received in both Egypt and Israel last year attests. His aim in presenting their views is, he says wistfully, merely to *inform*. His hope is that information in itself will prove pacifying "because it tends more or less slowly to replace passion by knowledge." But the roots of this struggle lie deeper than reason. It is not at all certain that information will replace passion with knowledge.

The experiences from which M. Sartre draws his emotional ties are irrelevant to this new struggle. Both sides draw from them conclusions which must horrify the man of rationalist tradition and universalist ideals. The bulk of the Jews and the Israelis draw from the Hitler period the conviction that, in this world, when threatened one must be prepared to kill or be killed. The Arabs draw from the Algerian conflict the conviction that, even in dealing with so rational and civilized a people as the French, liberation was made possible only by resorting to the gun and the knife. Both Israeli and Arabs in other words feel that only force can assure justice. In this they agree, and this sets them on a collision course. For the Jews believe justice requires the recognition of Israel as a fact; for the Arabs, to recognize the fact is to acquiesce in the wrong done them by the conquest of Palestine. If God as some now say is dead, He no doubt died of trying to find an equitable solution to the Arab-Jewish problem.

The argument between them begins with the Bible. "I give this country to your posterity," God said to Abraham (Gen. XV:18) "from the river of Egypt up to the great river, Euphrates." Among the Jews, whether religious or secular mystics, this is the origin of their right to the Promised Land. The opening article in the Arab section of *Les Temps Modernes* retorts that the "posterity" referred to in Genesis includes the descendants of Ishmael since he was the son of Abraham by his concubine Ketirah, and the ancestor of all the Arabs, Christian or Muslim.

All this may seem anachronistic nonsense, but this is an anachronistic quarrel. The Bible is still the best guide to it. Nowhere else can one find a parallel for its ethnocentric fury. Nowhere that I know of is there a word of pity in the Bible for the Canaanites whom the Hebrews slaughtered in taking possession. Of all the nonsense which marks the Jewish-Arab quarrel none is more nonsensical than the talk from both sides about the Holy Land as a symbol of peace. No bit of territory on earth has been soaked in the blood of more battles. Nowhere has religion been so zestful an excuse for fratricidal strife. The Hebrew *shalom* and the Arabic *salaam* are equally shams, relics of a common past as Bedouins. To this day inter-tribal war is the favorite sport of the Bedouins; to announce "peace" in the very first word is a necessity if any chance encounter is not to precipitate bloodshed.

In biblical perspective the Jews have been going in and out of Palestine for 3,000 years. They came down from the Euphrates under Abraham; returned from Egypt under Moses and Joshua; came back again from the Babylonian captivity and were dispersed again after Jerusalem fell to the Romans in 70 A.D. This is the third return. The Arabs feel they have a superior claim because they stayed put. This appearance side by side in *Les Temps Modernes* provides less than the full and undiluted flavor of an ancient sibling rivalry. Both sides have put their better foot forward. The Arab section includes no sample of the bloodcurdling broadcasts in which the Arab radios indulge; the Israeli, no contribution from the right-wing Zionists who dream of a greater Israel from the Nile to the Euphrates (as promised in Genesis) with complete indifference to the fate of the Arab inhabitants. On neither side is there a frank exposition of the *Realpolitik* which led Arab nationalists like Nasser to see war on Israel as the one way to achieve Arab unity, and leads Jewish nationalists like Ben Gurion and Dayan to see Arab disunity and backwardness as essential elements for Israeli security and growth. No voice on the Arab side preaches a Holy War in which all Israel would be massacred, while no voice on the Israeli side expresses the cheerfully cynical view one may hear in private that Israel has no realistic alternative but to hand the Arabs a bloody nose every five or ten years until they accept the loss of Palestine as irreversible.

The picture, however, is not wholly symmetrical. There is first of all the asymmetry of the victorious and the defeated. The victor is ready to talk with the defeated if the latter will acquiesce in defeat. The defeated, naturally, is less inclined to this kind of objectivity. The editor, Claude Lanzmann, speaks of an "asymmetry between the two collections of articles which derives at one and the same time from a radical difference in their way of looking at the conflict and from the difference in the nature of the political regimes in the countries involved." Even if not expressly authorized by their governments or organizations to participate, M. Lanzmann explains, all the Arabs except the North Africans wrote only after consultation and defend a common position while the Israelis "as is normal in a Western style democracy" speak either for themselves or for one of their numerous parties. But this diversity may be exaggerated. On the fundamental issue which divides the two sides, no Arab contributor is prepared to advocate recognition of the state of Israel, while only one Israeli contributor is prepared to advocate its transformation into something other than a basically Jewish state.

The depth of this nationalistic difference may be measured by what happened to Israel's Communist party. Elsewhere national centrifugal tendencies have made their appearance in the once monolithic world of communism. In Israel the same nationalist tendencies split the Communist party into two, one Jewish the other Arab. The days when Arab Communists faithfully followed Moscow's line straight into the jails of Egypt, Iraq, Syria, and Jordan by supporting the 1947 partition plan have long passed away. Today Arab and Jewish

Communists no longer find common ground.[1] It would be hard to find an Arab who would agree with Moshe Sneh, head of the Jewish Communist party (Maki) in Israel, when he told *L'Express* (June 19-25), "our war is just and legitimate. What united the 13 Arab States against us, irrespective of their regime, was not anti-imperialism but pan-Arabism and anti-Jewish chauvinism." He added boldly that Moscow in supporting the Arabs had "turned its back on the politics of the international left and on the spirit of Tashkent." But even Sneh's bitter rival, Meir Vilner, the Jewish leader of, and one of the few Jews left in, the Arab Communist party (Rakka) expresses himself in *Les Temps Modernes* in terms with which no Arab contributor to it agrees. M. Vilner is for the return of all the refugees who wish to, for full equality to Arabs in Israel and for a neutralist policy, but he defends the existence of Israel as a legitimate fact and denies that "one can in any way compare the people (of Israel) to Algerian colons or the Crusaders." The comparisons rejected by the leader of the Arab Communist party in Israel are the favorite comparisons of the Arabs outside Israel. The diversity of viewpoint on the Israeli side thus ends with the basic agreement on its right to exist, and to exist as a Jewish state. This is precisely where the Arab disagreement begins.

The gulf between Arab and Jewish views becomes even clearer when one reads two supplementary pieces contributed by two French Jews, Maxime Rodinson, a distinguished sociologist and Orientalist, and Robert Misrahi, a well-known writer of the Left. The former takes the Arab and the latter the Zionist side. But while M. Misrahi's article appears with the Israelis, M. Rodinson's contribution—by far the most brilliant in the whole volume—appears alone. He refused, for reasons of principle, to appear in the Arab ensemble. It is not hard to see why. For while M. Rodinson gives strong support to every basic Arab historical contention, he is too much the humanist (and in the last analysis no doubt the Jew) to welcome an apocalyptic solution at the expense of Israel's existence. There is still a gulf between M. Rodinson's pro-Arab position and the most moderate view any Arab statesman has yet dared express, that of Tunisia's President Bourguiba. Bourguiba's famous speech in Jericho, March 3, 1965, is re-

[1] The relative strength of the two since the split may be seen from the fact that the Jewish branch was able to elect only one deputy while the Arab branch, which draws the largest vote among the Arab minority, elected three, two Arabs and one Jew.

printed in an appendix by *Les Temps Modernes,* along with an interview he gave *le Nouvel Observateur* (April 15) a month later. But Bourguiba's speech, though it created a sensation by its relative moderation, merely suggested that the Arabs proceed to regain Palestine as they did Tunisia by a series of more or less peaceful compromises. When *le Nouvel Observateur* asked him whether this did not imply the progressive disappearance of the State of Israel, he would not go beyond the cryptic reply, "That is not certain."

The Arab section of the symposium is nevertheless far from being uniform. A Moroccan, Abdallah Laroui, a professor of literature in Rabat, not only ends by saying that the possibilities of peaceful settlement must be kept open because a war would settle nothing, but even goes so far as to express the hope that the time may come when a settlement is possible without making a new exile, i.e., of the Israelis, pay for the end of another exile, i.e. of the Arabs from Palestine. He even suggests that under certain conditions, a Jewish community "with or without political authority"—a most daring remark—may prove compatible with Arab progress and development.

When we examine these conditions, we come to the heart of the fears expressed by the Arabs in this symposium. The Palestinian Arabs, from the first beginnings of Zionism, foresaw the danger of being swamped and dislodged by Jewish immigration. Neighboring Arab States feared that this immigration would stimulate a continuous territorial expansion at their expense and create a Jewish state powerful enough to dominate the area. The relative size and population of Israel when compared to its Arab neighbors are deceptive and may make these fears seem foolish, but historically the Middle East has often been conquered and dominated by relatively small bands of determined intruders. Even now, as the recent fighting showed, tiny Israel could without difficulty have occupied Damascus, Amman, and Cairo, and—were it not for the big powers and the UN—dictated terms to its Arab neighbors.

It was the attempt of the British to allay Arab apprehension by setting limits on Jewish immigration that precipitated the struggle between the British and the Jews. The 1917 Balfour Declaration, when it promised a "Jewish National Home" in Palestine, also said—in a passage Zionists have always preferred to forget—"that nothing shall be done which may prejudice the civil and religious rights of the existing non-Jewish communities in Palestine." British White Papers in 1922, in 1930, and again in 1939 tried to fulfill this companion pledge by steps which would have kept the Jews a permanent minority. It is this persistent and—as events have shown—justifiable Arab fear which is reflected in M. Laroui's article. In calling the Palestine problem "A Problem of the Occident" his basic point is that if the Occident wipes out anti-Semitism, or keeps it within harmless proportions, making refuge in Israel unnecessary for the bulk of Jewry, and Israel divorces its politics from the Zionist dream of gathering in all the Jews from Exile, this will end the danger of an inexorable expansion in search of *"lebensraum"* at the expense of the Palestinian Arabs, and finally make peace possible between the two peoples. Since immigration into Israel has dwindled in recent years, this Arab fear seems at the moment less a matter of reality than of Zionist theory and of a past experience which leads them to take it seriously.

The suggestion that Israel abandon its supra-nationalist dream finds its only echo on the other side of this collection of essays in Israel's No. 1 maverick and champion of Arab rights, Uri Avnery. Avnery was born in Germany in 1923 and went to Palestine at the age of ten, the year Hitler took power. He began his political career on the far nationalist right, as a member of the Irgun terrorist group in the struggle against the British, but has since swung over to the far left of Israeli opinion, to the point where he is considered anti-nationalist. In the wake of the first Suez war, he supported the Egyptian demand for evacuation of the Canal Zone and in 1959 he formed an Israeli committee to aid the Algerian rebels. At one time he organized a movement which asserted that the Israelis were no longer Jews but "Canaanites" and therefore one with the Arabs, forcibly converted remnants of the same indigenous stock. When this far-out conception attracted few Jews and even fewer Canaanites, he formed a "Semitic Action" movement which has now become "the Movement of New Forces." This polled 1.2 percent of the vote in the 1965 elections and by virtue of proportional representation put Avnery into Parliament. Avnery has been more successful as a publisher. He has made his weekly *Haolam Hazeh* ("This World") the largest in Israel by combining non-conformist politics with what the rather puritanical Israelis call pornography, though that weekly's girlie pictures would seem as old-fashioned as the *Police Gazette* in America.

Avnery writes in *Les Temps Modernes* that he would turn Israel into a secular, pluralist, and multi-national state. He would abolish the Law of Return which gives every Jew the right to enter Israel and automatically become a citizen. Avnery says this pan-Judaism of Zionism feeds the anti-Zionism of pan-Arabism by keeping alive "the myth of an Israel submerged by millions of immigrants who, finding no place to settle, would oblige the government to expand the country by force of arms."

Yet Avnery, who asks Israel to give up its Zionist essence, turns out to be a Jewish nationalist, too. After sketching out a plan for an Arab Palestinian state west of the Jordan, Avnery writes, "The Arabic reader will justly ask at this point, 'And the return of Israel to the limits of the UN Plan of 1947?'" Since Israel in the 1947-48 fighting seized about 23 percent more territory than was allotted to it in the 1947 partition plan, this implies a modification of frontiers in favor of the Arab state which was supposed to be linked with it in an economically united Palestine. But to this natural Arab question Avnery replies,[2] "Frankly we see no possibility of this kind. The Arab armies are already 15 kilometers from Israel's most populous city (Tel Aviv) and at Nathanya are even closer to the sea." The Arabs may feel that Avnery is as unwilling to give up the fruits of conquest as any non-"Canaanite." Avnery is as reluctant as any conventional Zionist to see his fellow Canaanite too close to Tel Aviv.

It is easy to understand why neither side trusts the other. In any case M. Sartre's symposium is a confrontation largely of moderates and Leftists, and on neither side do these elements command majority support. Another complexity is that while in settled societies the Left tends to be less nationalistic than the Right, in colonial societies the revolutionary left is often more nationalistic than the native conservative and propertied classes.

The overwhelming majority opinion on both sides, even as expressed in a symposium as skewed leftward as this one, shows little tendency to compromise. The Arabs argue that Israel is a colonialist implantation in the Middle East, supported from the beginning by imperialist powers; that it is an enemy of Arab union and progress; that the sufferings of the Jews

[2] Avnery was writing, of course, before the new outbreak of warfare had again changed these borders to Israel's advantage.

in the West were the consequence of an anti-Semitism the
Arabs have never shared; and that there is no reason why the
Arabs of Palestine should be displaced from their homes in
recompense for wrongs committed by Hitler Germany. M.
Laroui alone is sympathetic enough to say that if the Jewish
National Home had been established in Uganda, the Arabs
who felt compassion for the sufferings of the Jews of Europe
would have shown themselves as uncomprehending of the
rights of the natives as the West has been in Palestine. At
the other end of the Arab spectrum a fellow Moroccan, a
journalist, Tahar Benziane, ends up in classic anti-Semitism,
blaming the Jews themselves, their separatism and their sense
of superiority, for the prejudice against them. Benziane sees
the only solution not just in the liquidation of Israel but in
the disappearance of world Jewry through assimilation. His
would indeed be a Final Solution. This bitter and hateful
opinion, widespread in the Arab world, explains why Nazism
found so ready an echo before the war in the Middle East and
Nazi criminals so welcome a refuge in Egypt. It also disposes
of the semantic nonsense that Arabs being Semite cannot be
anti-Semitic!

The Zionist argument is that the Jewish immigration was a
return to the Jewish homeland. Robert Misrahi even goes so
far as to argue that the Jews had an older claim to Palestine
than the Arabs since the Jews had lived there in the ancient
kingdom of the Hebrews long before the Hegira of Mohammed! Misrahi argues the familiar Zionist thesis that their
struggle against Britain proves them to be anti-imperialist,
that their colonies are socialist, that their enemies are the
feudal elements in the Arab world, and that the Arab refugees
are the moral responsibility of the Arab leaders since it was
on their urging that the Arabs ran away.

There is a good deal of simplistic sophistry in the Zionist
case. The whole earth would have to be reshuffled if claims
2,000 years old to *irredenta* were suddenly to be allowed.
Zionism from its begining tried to gain its aims by offering
to serve as outpost in the Arab world for one of the great
empires. Herzl sought to win first the Sultan and then the
Kaiser by such arguments. Considerations of imperial strategy
finally won the Balfour Declaration from Britain. The fact
that the Jewish community in Palestine afterward fought the
British is no more evidence of its not being a colonial implantation than similar wars of British colonists against the mother
country, from the American Revolution to Rhodesia. In the

case of Palestine, as of other such struggles, the Mother Country was assailed because it showed more concern for the native majority than was palatable to the colonist minority. The argument that the refugees ran away "voluntarily" or because their leaders urged them to do so until after the fighting was over not only rests on a myth but is irrelevant. Have refugees no right to return? Have German Jews no right to recover their properties because they too fled?

The myth that the Arab refugees fled because the Arab radios urged them to do so was analyzed by Erskine B. Childers in the London *Spectator* May 12, 1961. An examination of British and US radio monitoring records turned up no such appeals; on the contrary there were appeals and "even orders to the civilians of Palestine, *to stay put.*" The most balanced and humane discussion of the question may be found in Christopher Sykes's book *Crossroads to Israel: 1917-48* (at pages 350-57). "It can be said with a high degree of certainty," Mr. Sykes wrote, "that most of the time in the first half of 1948 the mass exodus was the natural, thoughtless, pitiful movement of ignorant people who had been badly led and who in the day of trial found themselves forsaken by their leaders. . . . But if the exodus was by and large an accident of war in the first stage, in the later stages it was consciously and mercilessly helped on by Jewish threats and aggression toward Arab populations . . . It is to be noted, however, that where the Arabs had leaders who refused to be stampeded into panic flight, the people came to no harm." Jewish terrorism, not only by the Irgun, in such savage massacres as Deir Yassin, but in milder form by the Haganah, itself "encouraged" Arabs to leave areas the Jews wished to take over for strategic or demographic reasons. They tried to make as much of Israel as free of Arabs as possible.

The effort to equate the expulsion of the Arabs from Palestine with the new Jewish immigration out of the Arab countries is not so simple nor so equitable as it is made to appear in Zionist propaganda. The Palestinian Arabs feel about this "swap" as German Jews would if denied restitution on the grounds that they had been "swapped" for German refugees from the Sudetenland. In a sanely conceived settlement, some allowance should equitably be made for Jewish properties left behind in Arab countries. What is objectionable in the simplified version of this question is the idea that Palestinian Arabs whom Israel didn't want should have no objection to being "exchanged" for Arabic Jews it did want. One up-rooting cannot morally be equated with the other.

A certain moral imbecility marks all ethnocentric move-ments. The Others are always either less than human, and thus their interests may be ignored, or more than human, and therefore so dangerous that it is right to destroy them. The latter is the underlying pan-Arab attitude toward the Jews; the former is Zionism's basic attitude toward the Arabs. M. Avnery notes that Herzl in his book *The Jewish State,* which launched the modern Zionist movement, dealt with working hours, housing for workers, and even the national flag but had not one word to say about the Arabs! For the Zionists the Arab was the Invisible Man. Psychologically he was not there. Achad Ha-Am, the Russian Jew who became a great Hebrew philosopher, tried to draw attention as early as 1891 to the fact that Palestine was not an empty territory and that this posed problems. But as little attention was paid to him as was later accorded his successors in "spiritual Zionism," men like Buber and Judas Magnes who tried to preach *Ichud,* "unity," i.e. with the Arabs. Of all the formulas with which Zionism comforted itself none was more false and more enduring than Israel Zangwill's phrase about "a land without people for a people without a land." Buber related that Max Nordau, hearing for the first time that there was an Arab population in Palestine, ran to Herzl crying, "I didn't know that—but then we are committing an injustice." R. J. Zwi Werblowsky, Dean of the faculty of letters at the Hebrew University, in the first article of this anthology's Israeli section, writes with admirable objectivity, "There can be no doubt that if Nordau's reaction had been more general, it would seriously have paralyzed the *élan* of the Zionist movement." It took refuge, he writes, in "a moral myopia."

This moral myopia makes it possible for Zionists to dwell on the 1900 years of Exile in which the Jews have longed for Palestine but dismiss as nugatory the nineteen years in which Arab refugees have also longed for it. "Homelessness" is the major theme of Zionism but this pathetic passion is denied to Arab refugees. Even Meir Yaari, the head of Mapam, the leader of the "Marxist" Zionists of Hashomer Hatzair, who long preached bi-nationalism, says Israel can only accept a minority of the Arab refugees because the essential reason for the creation of Israel was to "welcome the mass of immigrant Jews returning to their historic father-land!" If there is not room enough for both, the Jews must have precedence. This is what leads Gabran Majdalany, a Baath Socialist, to write that Israel is "a racist state founded from its start on discrimination between Jew and non-Jew." He compares the Zionists to the Muslim Brotherhood who "dream of a Muslim Israel in which the non-Muslims will be the gentiles, second-class citizens sometimes tolerated but more often repressed." It is painful to hear his bitter reproach—

> Some people admit the inevitably racist character of Israel but justify it by the continual persecutions to which the Jews have been subjected during the history of Europe and by the massacres of the Second World War. We consider that, far from serving as justification, these facts constitute an aggravating circumstance; for those who have known the effects of racism and of discrimination in their own flesh and human dignity, are less excusably racist than those who can only imagine the negative effects of prejudice.

When Israel's Defense Minister, Moshe Dayan, was on *Face the Nation* June 11, after Israel's latest victories, this colloquy occurred.

> SYDNEY GRUSON: (*The New York Times*): Is there any possible way that Israel could absorb the huge number of Arabs whose territory it has gained control of now?
> GEN. DAYAN: Economically we can; but I think that is not in accord with our aims in the future. It would turn Israel into either a binational or poly-Arab-Jewish state instead of the Jewish state, and we want to have a Jewish state. We can absorb them, but then it won't be the same country.
> MR. GRUSON: And it is necessary in your opinion to maintain this as a Jewish state and purely a Jewish state?
> GEN. DAYAN: Absolutely—absolutely. We want a Jewish state like the French have a French state.

This must deeply disturb the thoughtful Jewish reader. Ferdinand and Isabella in expelling the Jews and Moors from Spain were in the same way saying they wanted a Spain as "Spanish," (i.e. Christian) as France was French. It is not hard to recall more recent parallels.

It is a pity the editors of *Les Temps Modernes* didn't widen their symposium to include a Jewish as distinct from an Israeli point of view. For Israel is creating a kind of moral schizophrenia in world Jewry. In the outside world the welfare of Jewry depends on the maintenance of secular, non-racial, pluralistic societies. In Israel, Jewry finds itself defending a society in which mixed marriages cannot be legalized, in which non-Jews have a lesser status than Jews, and in which the ideal is racial and exclusionist. Jews must fight elsewhere for their very security and existence—against principles and practices they find themselves defending in Israel. Those from the outside world, even in their moments of greatest enthusiasm amid Israel's accomplishments, feel twinges of claustrophobia, not just geographical but spiritual. Those caught up in Prophetic fervor soon begin to feel that the light they hoped to see out of Zion is only that of another narrow nationalism.

Such moments lead to a reexamination of Zionist ideology. That longing for Zion on which it is predicated may be exaggerated. Its reality is indisputable but its strength can easily be overestimated. Not until after World War II was it ever strong enough to attract more than a trickle of Jews to the Holy Land. By the tragic dialectic of history, Israel would not have been born without Hitler. It took the murder of six million in his human ovens to awaken sufficient nationalist zeal in Jewry and sufficient humanitarian compassion in the West to bring a Jewish state to birth in Palestine. Even then humanitarian compassion was not strong enough to open the gates of the West to Jewish immigration in contrition. The capitalist West and the Communist East preferred to displace Arabs than to welcome the Jewish "displaced persons" in Europe's postwar refugee camps.

It must also be recognized, despite Zionist ideology that the periods of greatest Jewish creative accomplishment have been associated with pluralistic civilizations in their time of expansion and tolerance: in the Hellenistic period, in the Arab civilization of North Africa and Spain, and in Western Europe and America. Universal values can only be the fruit of a universal vision; the greatness of the Prophets lay in their overcoming of ethnocentricity. A Lilliputian nationalism cannot distill truths for all mankind. Here lies the roots of a growing divergence between Jew and Israeli; the former with a sense of mission as a Witness in the human wilderness, the latter concerned only with his own tribe's welfare.

But Jewry can no more turn its back on Israel than Israel on Jewry. The ideal solution would allow the Jews to make their contributions as citizens in the diverse societies and nations which are their homes while Israel finds acceptance as a Jewish State in a renascent Arab civilization. This would end Arab fears of a huge inflow to Israel. The Jews have as much reason to be apprehensive about that prospect as the Arabs.

It can only come as the result of a sharp recrudescence in persecution elsewhere in the world. Zionism grows on Jewish catastrophe. Even now it casts longing eyes on Russian Jewry. But would it not be better, more humanizing, and more just, were the Soviet Union to wipe out anti-Semitism and to accord its Jews the same rights of cultural autonomy and expression it gives all its other nationalities? The Russian Jews have fought for Russia, bled for the Revolution, made no small contribution to Russian literature and thought; why should they be cast out? This would be a spiritual catastrophe for Russia as well as Jewry even though it would supply another flow of desperate refugees to an Israel already short of Jews if it is to expand as the Zionist militants hope to expand it.

Israel has deprived anti-Semitism of its mystique. For the visitor to Israel, anti-Semitism no longer seems a mysterious anomaly but only another variant of minority-majority friction. *Es is schwer zu sein a Yid* ("It's hard to be a Jew") was the title of Sholom Aleichem's most famous story. Now we see that it's hard to be a goy in Tel Aviv, especially an Arab goy. Mohammad Watad, a Muslim Israeli, one of the five Arabic contributors to the Israeli side of this symposium, begins his essay with words which startlingly resemble the hostile dialogue Jews encounter elsewhere. "I am often asked," he writes, "about my 'double' life which is at one and the same time that of an Arab and that of an Israeli citizen." Another Arab contributor from Israel, Ibrahim Shabath, a Christian who teaches Hebrew in Arabic schools and is editor-in-chief of *Al Mirsad,* the Mapam paper in Arabic, deplores the fact that nineteen years after the creation of Israel "the Arabs are still considered strangers by the Jews." He relates a recent conversation with Ben Gurion. "You must know," Ben Gurion told him, "that Israel is the country of the Jews and only of the Jews. Every Arab who lives here has the same rights as any minority citizen in any country of the world, but he must admit the fact that he lives in a Jewish country." The implications must chill Jews in the outside world.

The Arab citizen of Israel, Shabath complains, "is the victim today of the same prejudices and the same generalizations as the Jewish people elsewhere." The bitterest account of what they undergo may be found in an anonymous report sent to the United Nations in 1964 by a group of Arabs who tried unsuccessfully to found an independent socialist Arab movement and publication. Military authorities despite a Supreme Court order refused to permit this, and the courts declined to overrule the military. Their petition is reprinted in the Israeli section of this symposium. Though the military rule complained of was abolished last year, and police regulations substituted, it is too soon—especially because of the new outbreak of warfare—to determine what the effect will be on Arab civil liberties. Israelis admit with pleasure that neither in the Christian villages of Central Galilee nor in the Muslim villages of the so-called "Triangle" was there the slightest evidence of any Fifth Column activity. Those Israelis who have fought for an end of all discrimination against the Arabs argue that they have demonstrated their loyalty and deserve fully to be trusted.

It is to Israel's credit that the Arab minority is given place in its section to voice these complaints while no similar place is opened for ethnic minority opinion in the Arabic section. Indeed except for Lebanon and to some degree Tunisia there is no place in the Arab world where the dissident of any kind enjoys freedom of the press. There is no frank discussion of this in the Arab section. One of the most vigorous and acute expositions of the Arab point of view, for example, is an article by an Egyptian writer, Lotfallah Soliman, who has played a distinguished role in bringing modern ideas to the young intellectuals of his country since World War II. His autobiographical sketch says cryptically if discreetly "He lives presently in Paris." I stumbled on a more candid explanation. In preparing for this review, I read an earlier article in *Les Temps Modernes* (Aug.-Sept. 1960) by Adel Montasser on *La répression anti-démocratique en Egypte*. Appended to it was a list of intellectuals imprisoned by Nasser. Among them was Lotfallah Soliman. Obviously it's hard to be a free Egyptian intellectual in Nasser's Egypt. Many of those then imprisoned have since been freed, but it is significant that a writer as trenchant and devoted as Soliman has to work in exile.

It is true that the full roster of Arab minority complaints in Israel had to be presented anonymously for fear of the the authorities. But in the Arab section of this book no place was allowed even anonymously for the Jewish and the various Christian minorities to voice their compaints. As a result the Arab contributors were able to write as if their countries, unlike Europe, were models of tolerance. They hark back to the great days of Arabic Spain where (except for certain interludes not mentioned) Christian and Jew enjoyed full equality, religious, cultural, and political, with the Muslim: Spain did not become synonymous with intolerance, Inquisition, and obscurantism until the Christian Reconquest. But today no Arab country except, precariously, Lebanon, dimly resembles Moorish Spain. As a result the Jews from the Arabic countries tend to hate the Arab far more than Jews from Europe who have never lived under his rule, which often recalls medieval Christiandom. A glimpse of these realities may be found in the most moving article in this whole symposium. This is by Attalah Mansour, a young Christian Arabic Israeli novelist of peasant origin who has published two novels, one in Arabic and the other in Hebrew, and worked as a journalist on Avnery's paper *Haolam Hazeh* and on the staff of *Haaretz*, Israel's best and most objective daily paper. M. Mansour knows doubly what it is to be a "Jew." He is as an Arab a "Jew" to the Israelis and as a Christian a "Jew" to the Muslims. He tells a touching story of an accidental encounter in (of all places) the Paris Metro with a young man who turned out like him to be Greek-rite Christian though from Egypt. They exchanged stories of their troubles, like two Jews in the Diaspora. "We in Egypt," the younger stranger told him, "have the same feelings as you. There is no law discriminating between us and the Muslims. But the governmental administration, at least on the everyday level, prefers Mahmoud to Boulos and Achmed to Samaan"—i.e. the man with the Muslim name to the man with the Christian. "Omar Sherif the well known movie actor," the Egyptian Christian added, "is Christian in origin. But he had to change his Christian name for a Muslim to please the public." In Israel, similarly, Ibrahim often becomes Abraham to pass as a Jew and to avoid widespread housing discrimination.

If in this account I have given more space to the Arab than the Israeli side it is because as a Jew, closely bound emotionally with the birth of Israel,[3] I feel honor bound to report the

---

[3] I first arrived in Palestine on Balfour Day Nov. 2, 1945, the day the Haganah blew up bridges and watch towers to begin its struggle against the British and immigration restrictions. The following spring I was the first newspaperman to travel with illegal Jewish immigrants from the Polish-Czech

Arab side, especially since the US press is so overwhelmingly pro-Zionist. For me, the Arab-Jewish struggle is a tragedy. The essence of tragedy is a struggle of right against right. Its catharsis is the cleansing pity of seeing how good men do evil despite themselves out of unavoidable circumstance and irresistible compulsion. When evil men do evil, their deeds belong to the realm of pathology. But when good men do evil, we confront the essence of human tragedy. In a tragic struggle, the victors become the guilty and must make amends to the defeated. For me the Arab problem is also the No. 1 Jewish problem. How we act toward the Arabs will determine what kind of people we become: either oppressors and racists in our turn like those from whom we have suffered, or a nobler race able to transcend the tribal xenophobias that afflict mankind.[4]

Israel's swift and extraordinary victories have suddenly transmuted this ideal from the realm of impractical sentiment to urgent necessity. The new frontiers of military conquest have gathered in most of the Arab refugees. Zionism's dream, the "ingathering of the exiles," has been achieved, though in an ironic form; it is the Arab exiles who are back. They cannot be gotten rid of as easily as in 1948. Something in the order of 100,000 have again been "encouraged" to leave, but the impact on public opinion abroad and in Israel has forced the State to declare that it will allow them to return. While the UN proves impotent to settle the conflict and the Arab powers are unwilling to negotiate from a situation of weakness, Israel can to some degree determine its future by the way in which it treats its new Arab subjects or citizens. The wrangles of the powers will go on for months but these people must be fed, clothed, and housed. How they are treated

---

border through the British blockade. In 1947 I celebrated Passover in the British detention camps in Cyprus and in 1948 I covered the Arab-Jewish war. See my *Underground to Palestine* (1946) and *This Is Israel* (1948). I was back in 1949, 1950, 1951, 1956, and 1964.

[4] In September, Black Star will publish a vigorous little book *The Aryanization of the Jewish State* by Michael Selzer, a young Pakistani Jew who lived in Israel. It may help Jewry and Israel to understand that the way to a fraternal life with the Arabs inside and outside Israel must begin with the eradication of the prejudices that greet the Oriental and Arabic-speaking Jews in Israel who now make up over half the population of the country. The bias against the Arab extends to a bias against the Jews from the Arab countries. In this, as in so many other respects, Israel presents in miniature all the problems of the outside world. Were the rest of the planet to disappear, Israel could regenerate from itself—as from a new Ark—all the bigotries, follies, and feuds of a vanished mankind (as well as some of its most splendid accomplishments).

will change the world's picture of Israel and of Jewry, soften
or intensify Arab anger, build a bridge to peace or make new
war certain. To establish an Arab state on the West Bank
and to link it with Israel, perhaps also with Jordan, in a
Confederation would turn these Arab neighbors, if fraternally
treated, from enemies into a buffer, and give Israel the protection of strategic frontiers. But it would be better to give
the West Bank back to Jordan than to try to create a puppet
state—a kind of Arab Bantustan—consigning the Arabs to
second-class status under Israel's control. This would only
foster Arab resentment. To avoid giving the Arabs first-class
citizenship by putting them in the reservation of a second-class
state is too transparently clever.

What is required in the treatment of the Arab refugees
Israel has gathered in is the conquest both of Jewish exclusiv-
ism and the resentful hostility of the Arabs. Even the malarial
marshes of the Emek and the sandy wastes of the Negev could
not have looked more bleakly forbidding to earlier generations
of Zionist pioneers than these steep and arid mountains of
prejudice. But I for one have a glimmer of hope. Every year
I have gone to Palestine and later Israel I have found situations which seemed impossible. Yet Zionist zeal and intelligence overcame them. Perhaps this extraordinarily dynamic,
progressive, and devoted community can even if need be
transcend its essential self.

I was encouraged to find in this volume that the most objective view of the Arab question on the Israeli side was written by
Yehudah Harkabi, a Haifa-born professional soldier, a briga-
dier general, but a general who holds a diploma in philosophy
and Arabic studies from the Hebrew University and from
Harvard. He has written a book on *Nuclear War and Nuclear
Peace*. His article "Hawks or Doves" is extraordinary in its
ability to rise above prejudice and sentiment. He does not
shut his eyes at all to the Arab case. He feels peace can come
only if we have the strength to confront its full human reality.
"Marx affirms," he concludes, "that knowledge of the truth
frees man from the determinism of history." It is only,
General Harkabi says, when Israel is prepared "to accept the
truth in its entirety that it will find the new strength necessary
to maintain and consolidate its existence." The path to safety
and the path to greatness lies in reconciliation. The other
route, now that the West Bank and Gaza are under Israeli
jurisdiction, leads to two new perils. The Arab populations

now in the conquered territories make guerrilla war possible within Israel's own boundaries. And externally, if enmity deepens and tension rises between Israel and the Arab states, both sides will t / one means or another obtain nuclear weapons for the next round.

This will change the whole situation. No longer will Israeli and Arab be able to play the game of war in anachronistic fashion as an extension of politics by other means. Neither will they be able to depend on a mutual balance of terror like the great powers with their "second strike" capacity. In this pygmy struggle the first strike will determine the outcome and leave nothing behind. Nor will the great Powers be able to stand aside and let their satellites play out their little war, as in 1948, 1956, and 1967. I have not dwelt here on the responsibility of the great Powers, because if they did not exist the essential differences in the Arab-Israeli quarrel would still remain, and because both sides use the great Power question as an excuse to ignore their own responsibilities. The problem for the new generation of Arabs is the social reconstruction of their decayed societies; the problem will not go away if Israel disappears. Indeed their task is made more difficult by the failure to recognize Israel since that means a continued emphasis on militarization, diversion of resources, and domination by military men. For Israel, the problem is reconciliation with the Arabs; the problem will not go away even if Moscow and Washington lie down together like the lion and the lamb or blow each other to bits. But the great Powers for their part cannot continue the cynical game of arming both sides in a struggle for influence when the nuclear stage is reached. It is significant that the one place where the Israeli and Arab contributors to this symposium tend to common conclusions is in the essays discussing the common nuclear danger. To denuclearize the Middle East, to defuse it, will require some kind of neutralization. Otherwise the Arab-Israeli conflict may some day set off a wider Final Solution. That irascible Old Testament God of Vengeance is fully capable, if provoked, of turning the whole planet into a crematorium.

I. F. Stone Reconsiders Zionism

By Marie Syrkin*

In a lengthy review of *"Le conflit israelo-arabe,"* the special
issue of Jean-Paul Sartre's *Les Temps Modernes* devoted to
the Arab-Israel conflict, I. F. Stone re-examines the Zionist
case, (the *New York Review of Books,* August 3, 1967). Mr.
Stone explains that "as a Jew, closely bound emotionally with
the birth of Israel" he felt "honor bound to report the Arab
side, especially since the U.S. press is so overwhelmingly pro-
Zionist." Whatever the reasons for his posture, his conclusions
and arguments must stand on their own. It is unfortunate that
his declared stance as the man of "rationalist and universalist
ideals" offers a protective shade to the weighted scale in which
he judges Arab and Jewish claims. Familiar misstatements
dismissed as the usual anti-Israel line when coming from Arab
propagandists, the American Council for Judaism or Mr.
Fedorenko, are admittedly more distressing when repeated
by a respected writer of intellectual independence. Mr. Stone
concludes: "If God as some now say is dead, He no doubt
died of trying to find an equitable solution to the Arab-Jewish
problem." I am more inclined to attribute the demise to
despair at the wilful casuistry of some of the high-minded
disputants.

In reviewing the Arab and Israeli contributions to *Les
Temps Modernes,* Mr. Stone complains that both sides "have
put their better foot forward." The Arabs fail to include their
"blood-curdling broadcasts" demanding the extermination of
Israel; the Israeli section offers no contribution from "right-
wing Zionists" with expansionist dreams, also "no voice
on the Arab side preaches a Holy War in which all Israel
would be massacred, while no voice on the Israeli side expresses the cheerful cynical view one may hear in private that
Israel has no realistic alternative but to hand the Arabs a
bloody nose every five or ten years until they accept the loss
of Palestine as irreversible."

This plea for honesty disguises a dishonest equation. The
cries for the extermination of Israel, as every reader of the daily

* Marie Syrkin, formerly a Professor of English Literature, is now a mem-
ber of the Jewish Agency Executive in New York. Her answer to I. F.
Stone was published in *Midstream*, October, 1967. © The Theodor Herzl
Foundation, Inc.

press knows, emanate, beginning with Nasser, from the Presidents, Prime Ministers and Foreign Ministers of the Arab states; the expansionist visions of "the right-wing Zionists" are limited to a small group of extremists who at no time since the creation of Israel have controlled its government or have made its policy. On what basis does Mr. Stone equate the openly declared official policy of all the Arab states with the views of minority groups in Israel whose programs have been consistently repudiated by the Israeli people and government? And by what yardstick are the Arab will for a "Holy War in which all Israel would be massacred" and the Israeli will to oppose this ambition given a common measure? Mr. Stone describes the Israeli determination as "cheerfully cynical." Neither the adverb nor the adjective seems appropriate. I, too, have heard in many not so private conversations in Israel the view that as long as Arabs were bent on the destruction of the country, Israelis would be obliged to demonstrate, at whatever sacrifice, that it cannot be done; but to detect cheer or cynicism in this resolution is, to say the least, far-fetched.

The burden of Mr. Stone's analysis is the dispossessed Arab, and no matter where his argument strays he returns to this central question. Of the Arab refugees, Mr. Stone writes: "The argument that the refugees ran away 'voluntarily' or because their leaders urged them to do so until after the fighting was over not only rests on a myth but is irrelevant. Have refugees no right to return? Have German Jews no right to recover their properties because they too fled?" And he continues: "Jewish terrorism, not only by the Irgun, in such savage massacres as Deir Yassin, but in milder form by the Haganah itself, 'encouraged' Arabs to leave areas the Jews wished to take over."

First as to the "myth." It is hard to understand why Mr. Stone finds it necessary to quote a notoriously pro-Arab advocate like Erskine Childers or any other commentator to make his point. Mr. Stone was in Israel in 1948 and gave an enthusiastic account of the Israel struggle. In *This Is Israel*, published in 1948, Mr. Stone wrote: "Ill-armed, outnumbered, however desperate their circumstances, the Jews stood fast. The Arabs very early began to run away. First the wealthiest families went; it was estimated that 20,000 of them left the country in the first two months of internal hostilities. By the end of January, the exodus was already so alarming that the Palestine Arab Higher Committee in alarm asked neighboring Arab countries to refuse visas to these refugees and to seal the borders against them. *While the Arab guerrillas were moving in, the Arab civilian population was moving out."* (Emphasis added—M.S.)

Mr. Stone goes on to describe the "phenomenon" of the "sudden flight" of Arabs from Tiberias and Haifa. Not one word in Mr. Stone's first-hand, on-the-spot report suggests the "milder" terrorism of the Haganah which he now discovered in retrospect. On the contrary, his own account fully supports the "myth." Admittedly, Mr. Stone is entitled to change his mind about the rights of the Zionist case in the course of twenty years—there have been changes of heart in regard to Israel from Soviet Russia to De Gaulle—but he should not revise history. Either what he himself saw in 1948 or what he reads now about 1948 is accurate. Which is the myth and who is being mythopoic?

I can bear witness to the correctness of Mr. Stone's 1948 reporting. In June 1948, when I arrived in Israel the overwhelming sentiment of the Israelis was still bewilderment at the "phenomenon" of the mass flight of the Arabs. As I pieced together the diverse explanations, a fairly consistent picture emerged. The first waves of departure—in January by the well-to-do Arabs, in March by thousands of Arab villagers from the Sharon coastal plain after the picking of the citrus crop—were clearly in response to the directives of their leaders in anticipation of Arab bombardment. The Jewish farmers were so troubled by what the departure boded that they begged the Arabs to stay. This phase of the exodus was obviously disciplined and well-organized.

The process gathered momentum as the fighting increased and the Jews, instead of being driven into the sea, were proving victorious. When the Arabs of Tiberias suddenly fled in long convoys (the British provided transport) the astonished Jewish Community Council of Tiberias issued the following statement: "We did not dispossess them; they themselves chose this course. But the day will come when the Arabs will return to their homes and property in this town. In the meantime let no citizen touch their property." Such was the initial reaction in April, 1948.

The circumstances surrounding the flight of 70,000 Arabs from Haifa after the Haganah victory on April 22 has fortunately been fully reported by the British authorities who are surely free of the suspicion of pro-Jewish bias. On April

26 the Haifa British Chief of Police, A. J. Bridmead, reported: "The situation in Haifa remains unchanged. Every effort is being made by the Jews to persuade the Arab populace to stay and carry on with their normal lives, to get their shops and businesses open and to be assured that their lives and interests will be safe." In a supplementary report issued the same day, Bridmead repeated: "An appeal has been made to the Arabs by the Jews to reopen their shops and businesses in order to relieve the difficulties of feeding the Arab population. Evacuation was still going on yesterday and several trips were made by Z craft to Acre. Roads too were crowded. *Arab leaders* (my emphasis) reiterated their determination to evacuate the entire Arab population, and they have been given the loan of 10 three-ton military trucks as from this morning to assist the evacuation." On April 28 Bridmead was again reporting: "The Jews are still making every effort to persuade the Arab population to remain and settle back into their normal lives in the town."

A British eye-witness account published in the London *Economist* (October 2, 1948) offers an explanation for the stampede: "So far as I know, most of the British civilian residents whose advice was asked by Arab friends told the latter that they would be wise to stay. Various factors influenced their decision to seek safety in flight. There is but little doubt that by far the most potent of these factors was the announcement made over the air by the Arab Higher Executive urging all Arabs in Haifa to quit. The reason given was that upon the final withdrawal of the British the combined armies of the Arab States would invade Palestine and drive the Jews into the sea."

All this is familiar, readily available information and I am bringing Mr. Stone no news. I am concerned with his readers. It is obvious from the dates that the Arab exodus began months before "such savage massacres as Deir Yassin," which took place on April 9. (Note Mr. Stone's plural though the outrage perpetrated by the Irgun was a unique occurrence deplored and repudiated by the Jewish community of Palestine.) It is also obvious from Bridmead's report that "Arab leaders" with whom he was negotiating insisted on the evacuation of Haifa. None of this precludes the irrational panic and mass psychosis to which the Arabs fell prey; the exodus assumed proportions not anticipated by its instigators. However, the Jews can hardly be held responsible for the too complete success of the Arab scheme to clear the decks for an Arab invasion. The Arabs of Nazareth, who did not join the exodus, and other villages in Galilee that followed the example of Nazareth, were well able to withstand the Haganah "encouragement" that Mr. Stone suspects. The most straightforward explanation of Arab flight is still that provided by the Jordanian daily, *A—Difaa,* which voiced the sentiments of the refugees themselves: "The Arab governments told us, 'Get out so that we can get in.' So we got out, but they did not get in." (September 6, 1954.)

The Arabs fled; they were not driven out. Equally true is that the Jews of Palestine, at first baffled and alarmed by something they could not understand, subsequently shed no tears for defectors who had cast their lot with the Arab invaders. The Arab onslaught transformed the situation physically and psychologically.

So much for the "myth." How about Mr. Stone's argument that it is in any case "irrelevant"? When Mr. Stone asks, "Have German Jews no right to recover their properties because they too fled?" his implied comparison of the Palestinian Arabs with the Nazi victims and consequently of the Israelis and the Nazis is disquietingly reminiscent of the crudest Arab propaganda and of the diatribes of the representatives of the Soviet Union at the General Assembly. It is shocking to hear this line from Mr. Stone. What choice except the gas chamber remained for German Jews who did not manage to escape? Mr. Stone can hardly pretend that the Arabs ran from systematic extermination. This "too" thrown in so casually to associate the fate of German Jewry with that of the Palestinian Arabs in the reader's mind is a sample of Mr. Stone's fair play. If Mr. Stone is convinced of the unqualified right of all refugees to return, why does he not raise his voice for the return of millions of German refugees to East Prussia, Pomerania and Silesia? In the context of war and its aftermaths, such a demand would be as absurd as in the case of the Arab refugees. However, reparation for abandoned Arab property is another matter and subject to negotiation as the Israeli government has repeatedly stated.

The Arab states have made no secret of the objective of an Arab "return"—the liquidation of Israel. Nasser put it simply and candidly: "If the Arabs return to Israel, Israel will cease to exist." (*Zürcher Woche,* September 1, 1961.) The numerous official Arab pronouncements on "the refugees' right to annihilate Israel" are not the statements of extremist groups but official Arab policy enunciated by Arab statesmen. Consequently when Mr. Stone asks, "Have refugees no right to return?" and conjures up the image of despoiled and persecuted German Jews, he should consider Shukairy's Palestine Liberation Organization, an army of 300,000 refugees concentrated in the Gaza strip. That a would-be invading army fails of its purpose does not make it innocent or innocuous.

A good example of the complexities of the situation is provided by the new refugee problems resulting from the Israeli victory of June, 1967. Some 150,000 Arabs fled from the West Bank of Jordan to the East Bank. They fled for a variety of reasons chief among them the conviction that Israeli soldiers would massacre them; they had been promised that the victorious Arabs would slaughter every Israeli "man, woman and child." Hussein's broadcast to his people gave full instructions as to how to treat a conquered enemy: "Kill the Jews wherever you find them. Kill them with your hands, with your nails and teeth." It is hardly surprising that Arabs so commanded expected no better from the soldiers of Israel. As in 1948, Arab atrocity propaganda back-fired. But unlike 1948 the Israelis were neither bewildered nor alarmed. If Arabs preferred the East Bank of the Jordan to life on the West Bank under Israeli occupation, Israelis could readily make peace with this predilection. They remembered how savagely Jordan had shelled Jerusalem despite all urging by Israel that Hussein not join the Arab attack. They knew that had Israel been defeated there would have been no Jewish equivalent of the East Bank and no Jewish refugees. Nevertheless, after the cessation of hostilities, Israel agreed to repatriate all *bona fide* residents of the West Bank who had fled. Yet after this decision, in the course of the negotiations, the Jordanian Finance Minister, Abdul Wahab Majali, publicly urged the refugees to return "to help your brothers continue their political action and remain a thorn in the flesh of the aggressor until the crisis had been solved." It is hardly surprising that after this pronouncement some members of the Israeli Cabinet, meeting on August 13, several days after the Jordanian Finance Minister's counsel, raised the question of the advisability of the return of these "thorns." Though the Cabinet re-affirmed its previous decision despite this blatant provocation, no government can be expected to welcome a returning Fifth Column, even the Israeli.

No doubt just as Mr. Stone, despite his own testimony of 1948, now finds it possible to write of "the expulsion of the Arabs from Palestine" so the contemporary reports of correspondents who watched the trek of Arabs across the Allenby Bridge from the West Bank to the East Bank will weigh little with the scribes of the future or, for that matter, of the present. Already the whole anti-Semitic, anti-Israel cabal from fascist to Communist, from Black Power to White Power, is in full swing, as Soviet cartoons à la Streicher and accounts of Israeli "massacres" of Arabs in the publications of S.N.C.C. and of the white supremacist National States Rights party indicate. The notion that T.V., radio and instant reporting have made the distortion of events taking place under our eyes more troublesome than in the past appears to be increasingly naive. The Arab who on the Israeli side of the Allenby Bridge testifies in the presence of the Red Cross and neutral observers that he is leaving voluntarily, and signs a document to that effect, may tell an opposite tale to the Jordanians on the other side of the bridge. That the Jordanian government urges refugees to return and even ventures to recommend insurrection merely confirms the statement of the UNRWA chief representative in West Jordan who stated on July 4 that not one of the 20 refugee camps in West Jordan was affected by the hostilities during the war, nor one resident killed. (Reported by Martha Gellhorn in *The Guardian*.)

In a sense Mr. Stone is right when he declares that the discussion as to whether Arab refugees fled voluntarily or were driven out is "irrelevant." It is irrelevant because his objection to the resettlement of Arab refugees or to any reasonable accommodation with reality is based on his rejection of the right of Israel to exist as a Jewish State. He believes that General Dayan's statement, "We want a Jewish state like the French have a French state" must "deeply disturb the thoughtful Jewish reader." He is equally shocked by a reported conversation with Ben Gurion in which the latter said: "You must know that Israel is the country of the Jews and only of the Jews. Every Arab who lives here has the same rights as any minority citizen in any country of the world, but he must admit the fact that he lives in a Jewish country." Mr. Stone observes, "The implications must chill Jews in the outside world."

Presumably he accepts the existence of France, or Soviet Russia, or China, or the United States without frost-bite.

While we judge the democratic character of these states by the rights enjoyed by their ethnic or religious minorities, each of these states has a dominant majority culture. Why is a Jewish state, while giving full political rights to all its citizens and prepared to respect their cultural and religious differences, more disturbing than any other democratic national state? Israeli Arabs speak Arabic and are Moslems or Christians; the Jewish majority speaks Hebrew and is Jewish, and the Arabs would be the first to protest linguistic or religious "integration." Their minority rights are precious just as are the rights of minorities in the United States or, hopefully, in Soviet Russia. But Mr. Stone, thoroughly congealed, is only able to compare a Jewish state with Spain of the Inquisition and, in an indecent innuendo, with "more recent parallels."

If Mr. Stone were advocating the abolition of all national states and raising the vision of the Federation of the World and the Parliament of Man his ideological horror of a "Jewish country" would be comprehensible. But he is not unfurling a belated internationalist banner under whose folds the tribes will merge. On the contrary, he is sympathetic to national claims, and particularly sensitive to the claims of Arab nationalism. It is only Jewish nationalism that by definition becomes "narrow," "tribal," "exclusive," or "racist." For Israel to call itself a Jewish State is "supra-nationalist," unlike the other countries of the earth whose national character leaves thoughtful Jews and non-Jews unchilled. In the vocabulary of Jewish leftists as of Jewish bourgeois assimilationists (*vide* the Council of Judaism's espousal of Mr. Stone), Jewish nationalism is always "chauvinism"; it is never "emergent," "renascent," "progressive," "revolutionary." No matter how many national "liberation movements" may burgeon with radical and liberal approval in Asia or Africa, Jewish nationalism is a suspect growth to be eradicated as energetically by the hammer and sickle as by the fascist axe. A totalitarian Egypt, where former Nazi henchmen not only receive refuge but are influential in the government, is acclaimed in preference to socially advanced Israel. The Left has long abandoned its old-fashioned Utopian enchantment with internationalism and has developed a sturdy regard for the national identity of all the tribes of the globe—yellow, black, red—with the one exception already noted. I am certain that the same Russian Communists who proscribe the study of Hebrew in the Soviet Union as reactionary will, without batting an eyelash, endorse

S.N.C.C.'s suggestion that Swahili be taught in American public schools.

Mr. Stone finds nothing reprehensible in love of country if Arabs do the loving. Writing in *Ramparts* (July, 1967) he writes: "The refugees lost their farms, their villages, their offices, their cities, their country." In the mounting crescendo of this listing, the climactic "their country" is worth noting. And in the *New York Review of Books* he comments on the longing of the Arab refugees for Palestine. " 'Homelessness' is the major theme of Zionism but this pathetic passion is denied to Arab refugees." The homelessness in question here is, of course, national homelessness.

Mr. Stone stresses not only the Arab refugee who—whatever the explanation—left his home and his home town but the Palestinian who lost his country. And he charges the Zionists with a "moral imbecility" which enabled them to ignore the existence of a native Palestinian population when they began the return to the ancient homeland. Through the Jewish return to Palestine a Palestinian people was ruthlessly dispossessed. Here Mr. Stone echoes the theme song of Arab belligerence.

Though it seems late in the day to re-argue the ABC's of the Zionist case, the current barrage from both the extreme Right and Left makes a few reminders mandatory, particularly as many well-intentioned people are troubled by such charges. Did Jewish aggressors set up their homeland in total disregard of a native people with prior claims?

Now for the ABC's: To make his point Mr. Stone comes up with all kinds of nuggets from his mining of *Les Temps Modernes*. Herzl never mentioned the Arabs in *The Jewish State* (1896); Nordau wept when he learned of the existence of Arabs. Mr. Stone fails to mention the fact that by the time Herzl wrote *Old-New Land,* he was well aware of the Arabs and dreamed of happy co-existence. But whatever were the deficiencies of early Zionist fantasies, the Balfour Declaration issued in 1917 took full cognizance of the 600,000 local Arabs. The underlying assumption of the Declaration was that while over 97% of the huge territories liberated by the Allies from the Turks would be devoted to the setting up of independent Arab states, the "small notch" of Palestine would be reserved for the creation of a Jewish state. This "small notch" (Lord Balfour's term) was in 1922 further reduced by two-thirds through the amputation of the East Bank of Palestine for the establishment of Transjordan, later Jordan.

By the time the Mandate was in effect, five independent Arab states were established on the territory freed from Turkish rule. Saudi Arabia, Iraq, Syria, Lebanon and Transjordan were allotted an area covering, 1,200,000 square miles. The ten thousand square miles left to Western Palestine constituted less than 1% of the total area and was less than a third of the area originally promised by the Balfour Declaration. The Partition Resolution of 1947, accepted by the Jews and fought by the Arabs, further lopped away at the continually diminishing "notch." A glance at the map of the region shows the ratio between the huge Arab lands and the tiny state of Israel.

But the Arabs and their supporters reject this comparison as irrelevant. That the Arabs received much and the Jews little has nothing to do with the case. Arab nationalism cannot be sated by less than 100% gratification; 90% plus won't do. What about the Palestinian Arabs? Why should they surrender their Palestinian identity to become Syrians or Jordanians as the Jews irrationally suggest? True, all Arabs are brothers when the Pan-Arab dream beckons but it is criminal imperialist aggression to suggest that the Arabs, particularly the Palestinians, relinquish one jot of their national claim because of Jewish need, Hitler's victims and the rest. Such is the Arab argument.

If a genuine Palestinian nationalism had been violated then it would be Quixotic folly to ask the Arabs of Palestine to abandon their rights in favor of the unfortunate Jews. But did such a violation take place? At the end of World War I the inhabitants of the land treasured for centuries by Jews as Zion did not view themselves as a distinct Palestinian nation. *Palestine did not exist as a political or national entity as far as the Arabs were concerned.* For them it was merely a geographical locality, the south of Syria. Whereas no one doubts the fierce authenticity of Arab nationalism, *Palestinian* Arab nationalism is an artificial creation with no roots before the British Mandate. As recently as May 31, 1956, Ahmed Shukairy, the extremist chief of the Palestine Liberation Organization, declared before the Security Council: "It is common knowledge that Palestine is nothing but southern Syria."

Nor were the Zionist pioneers who came to an abandoned wasteland forty or fifty years ago afflicted by "moral imbecility." They may have been simple-minded in believing that the swamps they drained, the stony soil they irrigated—incidentally, swamps and deserts *purchased* at fancy prices by the Jewish National Fund—would make them welcome neighbors, but there was nothing wrong with their ethics. They were socialist idealists who believed that to reclaim a marsh through their own toil and devotion and to establish agricultural settlements on soil on which no one had been able to live for generations was a gain for all and a loss to none. They took literally the business about to each according to his need from each according to his capacity. The result of their personal sacrifices was the green country-side which now enables Arabs to point to the flourishing land of which they were "despoiled."

Simple-minded though the pioneers may have been in believing that their physical reclamation of desolate wastes would win them affection or gratitude, they were right in their estimate of the economic and demographic results of their labor. Far from dispossessing Arabs Zionist colonization resulted in their numerical increase.

According to the 1922 census taken by the British Government only 186,000 Arabs lived in the area which later became Israel. The increase in the Arab population of Palestine took place not only because of a very high rate of natural increase due to improved health conditions and standards of living but also because Palestine became a country of Arab *immigration* from adjacent Arab countries. Arabs were attracted, mainly from Syria and Egypt, to the Jewish areas of Mandated Palestine by the swift industrial and agricultural growth which the Jews had started and were constantly enlarging and diversifying. This is confirmed by the testimony in an UNRWA bulletin of 1962:

> A considerable movement of people is known to have occurred, particularly during the Second World War years when new opportunities of employment opened up in the towns and on military works in Palestine. These wartime prospects and, generally, the higher rate of industrialization in Palestine than in neighboring countries attracted many immigrants from those countries, and many of them entered Palestine without their presence being officially recorded.
> (UNRWA Reviews, Information Paper No. 6, Beirut, September, 1962.)

In the whole of Palestine the Arab population doubled between 1920 and 1940, growing from 600,000 to well over a million. In Jordan, closed to Jewish immigration, the population remained static. Paradoxically, in the period between the issuance of the Balfour Declaration and the establishment of Israel, Palestine changed from a country of Arab emigration to one of Arab immigration—a phenomenon observable in none of the adjacent Arab countries.

Perhaps the most telling demonstration of what had actually taken place has ironically been provided by Israel's June victory. When publicity focused on the Arab refugees, the overwhelming bulk were discovered dwelling on the West Bank, the part of Palestine annexed in 1948 by Jordan, and in Gaza, the Palestinian city, occupied by Egypt. The refugees, maintained by UNRWA in camps whose standard of living was higher than that of many an Arab village, had never left Palestine.

Will Mr. Stone, who deplores "Lilliputian nationalism," make a holy cause of a fixation on a particular village or street? No matter how dear a home or a home town to the residents, people are shifted despite their wishes for so trivial a cause as the construction of a new dam or highway. Israel, a country of immigrants gathered from remote corners of the world, understandably perceives no gross injustice in the resettlement of Arabs on territory formerly Palestine—or on adjacent territory—a resettlement requiring no adjustment in landscape, language, climate, religion or social mores. The opposition of the Arab states to any of the numerous proposals for the productive resettlement of the Palestinian Arabs is predicated on the simple proposition that Israel must be destroyed. Economically, territorially, above all, humanly, the deliberately created Arab refugee problem lends itself to just solution once the Arab premise of the liquidation of Israel swiftly through a hostile influx or slowly through an uncontrolled demographic change is abandoned. The pseudo-humanitarian premise that Arab nationalism in full panoply down to its most tenuous ramifications merits tender regard, whatever the cost to the one small Jewish state, only bolsters Arab appetite and intransigeance.

In addition to dwelling on the "expulsion" of the Arabs, Mr. Stone finds much wrong with Israel. He complains that Israel is creating a kind of "moral schizophrenia in world Jewry." Outside Israel, Jewish welfare depends on the existence of "secular, non-racial, pluralistic societies"; yet Jews defend a society in Israel in which "the ideal is racial and exclusionist." Israel is a theocratic state, with second-class Arab citizens and with ingrained prejudice against oriental Jews. Mr. Stone makes these charges categorically without offering a shred of evidence of their truth. Blanket denunciations, if false, can only be answered with a blanket denial. The one specific point Mr. Stone makes ("In Israel Jewry finds itself defending a society in which mixed marriages cannot be legalized") is patently untrue. Both in Israel and outside of Israel the requirements of rigid orthodoxy instead of being defended, are constantly under attack. If Mr. Stone read the Hebrew press he would appreciate the vigor of its self-criticism in this and other respects. Israel has many imperfections but to pretend that any of its inadequacies are its "ideal" rather than the result of human failure or of the economic and political pressures to which the small beleaguered land has been subject since its establishment is again to judge Israel by an invidious criterion applied to no other people. No country in the world has so bold a social vision or has tried so bravely to integrate the excluded of the earth who came to it—were they survivors of the gas chambers or despoiled Oriental Jews. Born in great travail to find an answer for Jewish need and to achieve Jewish national independence, it is not called upon to answer non-existent needs or desires which have ample scope for their satisfaction elsewhere.

Mr. Stone perceives a growing divergence between Jew and Israeli: "the former with a sense of mission as a Witness in the human wilderness, the latter concerned only with his own tribe's welfare." The reverse, of course, is true. It is the Israelis whose concerns are global, whose emissaries penetrated Hitler's Europe, who brought Eichmann to justice, whose instructors teach new and advanced social techniques to emergent countries in Africa, whose kibbutzim serve as laboratories to Africans and Indians and Burmese and Europeans, whose social dynamism and accomplishments inspire all poor and undeveloped countries. The world sympathy for Israel last June was not a tribute to tribal egoism but to courage and vision on an unprecedented scale.

Mr. Stone makes another nasty charge. Since Zionism "grows on Jewish catastrophe," it now "casts longing eyes on Russian Jewry." Mr. Stone wants to know if it would not be better if the Soviet Union wiped out anti-Semitism and gave equal rights to its Jewish citizens. Better than what? Better than another large-scale Jewish catastrophe which Israel apparently desires? This is a disgraceful accusation. Israel is in the foreground of Jewish agitation for unrestricted cultural rights for Russian Jews. Among the rights sought is the right of emigration for those Russian Jews who have families in Israel or elsewhere. Were there to be free emigration from Russia, Israel would be delighted if Russian Jews came. But that is a very different matter from desiring another "catastrophe" which would supply "another flow of desperate refugees to an Israel already short of Jews if it is to expand as the Zionist militants hope to expand it." Here we get a double dig; not only is Israel lusting for Jewish tragedy but it is expansionist. Let me tell Mr. Stone a secret: not only Zionist "militants" want Jewish immigration; all Israel does. The call for *"Aliyah"* (Immigration) has gone out not to "expand" but further to develop the country. Ben-Gurion's great dream is to "expand" into the Negev, the desert that constitutes two-thirds of Israel. This creative vision—to regenerate sand and stone as the Emek was reclaimed—is Israel's "hope." Mr. Stone who so eloquently expounds universal values and universal visions should be warier of lending his authority to vicious anti-Israel smears.

Finally Mr. Stone suggests: "The ideal solution would allow the Jews to make their contributions as citizens in the diverse societies and nations which are their homes while Israel finds acceptance as a Jewish State in a renascent Arab civilization. This would end Arab fears of a huge inflow to Israel." At first reading, most Zionists would enthusiastically embrace such a solution; that's what they have been wanting all along—a renascent Jewish state to be accepted by a renascent Arab civilization. Stone might be quoting Herzl. But a second reading is less reassuring. To calm Arab fears of a "huge inflow," Jewish immigration to Israel would presumably be restricted (though Mr. Stone appreciates that the prospect of an inundation is slight). If, despite his cautious phrasing, I read Mr. Stone correctly, the one group that the "exclusionist" Jewish state could rightly exclude would be Jews. Such is the *reductio ad absurdum* of Mr. Stone's universalism.

Given a will to peace on the part of the Arabs all the problems of the Arab-Israeli conflict can be settled reasonably and to the advantage of Jew and Arab. This includes the definition of boundaries and the integration of refugees into a productive life, but the elementary recognition of Israel's right to exist is the precondition of any settlement. And the emergence of Israel as a Jewish country with the same rights for self-defense and normal development as other democratic countries should scar no psyche able to envision "renascent" civilizations all over the globe.

A word of warning should be added. The Zionist visionaries who came with the Bible and socialist tracts to build a "just society" in the desert have lost many illusions. They have learned the stern lessons of recent history. I have watched this transformation. In 1936, on my first visit to Palestine I attended a seder in Ein Harod, a kibbutz in the Emek. In addition to the traditional questions—why is this night different?—the children asked *Kashes* of their own. One of the questions was, "Why do the Arabs live on the hills and we in the valley?". The answer, understandable only to those aware of the exposed position of the kibbutzim was, "Because we want peace and friendship."

The children who heard this answer grew up to fight for hills in three wars since 1948. Last July, three weeks after the end of the 1967 battles, I was in Galilee in a kibbutz shelled for months from the Syrian ridges. I saw the destroyed cottages and the underground shelters where the children routinely slept. The next morning I visited the Golan heights, the fortified Syrian hills bristling with Russian armor from which Syrian soldiers equally routinely attacked the kibbutz. The ridge was scaled by Israeli soldiers on the last day of the fighting and the bunkers dismantled in one of the toughest fights of the war. Perhaps the most illuminating circumstance of this battle was that the kibbutzim, not the Israeli military, insisted on the capture of the ridge: "Our children must sleep in bed not in shelters." Anyone standing among the masses of Russian armor on the ridge and seeing the guns pointed at the settlements would probably find it difficult to continue prating about Israeli expansionism. Until the Arabs make peace, Israel needs viable borders; as long as Israel is under attack by Arabs who outnumber her twenty to one, it will perforce be militant. If instead of indulging in strictly one-sided pieties, the self-declared humanists and universalists would unequivocally grant the rights of the farmer in valley rather than of the gunner on the hill, peace might come sooner. Otherwise the enemies of Israel may be caught in the vise of a self-fulfilling prophecy to the detriment of all.

UN Resolution 242:
A Common Denominator

By Gideon Rafael*

A variety of attributions and interpretations have been bestowed upon Resolution 242, depending upon the party which invoked its blessings. Some see in it a magic formula to dispel the Israel-Arab conflict; others regard it as a means of perpetuating it. But the real significance of that Resolution is that it has been accepted as a common denominator by the warring camps despite their differing views. In fact, Resolution 242 was never contemplated to be an act of revelation. It was the outcome of six months' of passionate on-stage United Nations debates and arduous backstage diplomatic wrangling.

When, at five o'clock in the afternoon of 22 November 1967, Ambassador Mamadou Boubacar Kante, representative of the Republic of Mali, pounded his Presidential gavel to announce that all the fifteen members of the Security Council had voted in favour of the British draft resolution—from now on to figure as Resolution 242—its adoption was not greeted with hymns of Hallelujah but rather with a sigh of relief that the United Nations had at long last acquitted itself of a tedious task. What the Security Council had achieved was to formulate a set of guide-lines for the establishment of a just and lasting peace between the Arab States and Israel, to be translated into treaty terms through agreement by the States themselves. What it had not accomplished was to reconcile the parties to the conflict.

Before the meeting rose for adjournment Mahmoud Riad, then Foreign Minister of Egypt, asked for the floor and enunciated the three articles of Egypt's political faith:

a) Israel is the aggressor and responsible for the war;

b) As the first step towards peace Israel must withdraw all its forces from all the territories occupied since 5 June;

c) The United Nations must recognise and respect the inalienable rights of the Palestine people.

Israel aggression, total withdrawal and the restoration of the rights of the Palestinian people have remained until this

* Israel Permanent Representative to the United Nations in 1967. Former Director-General of the Israeli Ministry for Foreign Affairs; at present Israeli ambassador in London. This article was originally published in *New Middle East* (June, 1973).

day the three pillars of Egypt's proclaimed policy. It may have changed occasionally its diplomatic tactics, but so far it has not deviated from its strategic objective.

At that same meeting, Foreign Minister Abba Eban summarised Israel's basic position, which has remained the cornerstone of its policy:

> 'We shall respect and fully maintain the situation embodied in the cease-fire agreement until it is succeeded by peace treaties between Israel and the Arab States ending the state of war, establishing agreed, recognised and secure territorial boundaries, guaranteeing free navigation for all shipping, including that of Israel, in all the waterways leading to and from the Red Sea, committing all signatories to the permanent and mutual recognition and respect of the sovereignty, security and national identity of all Middle Eastern States and ensuring a stable and mutually guaranteed security. Such a peace settlement, directly negotiated and contractually confirmed, would create conditions in which refugee problems could be justly and effectively solved through international and regional cooperation. . . .'

The Lessons of 1956 and the Objectives of 1962

To assess the essence and significance, the purpose and value of Resolution 242, one has to retrace the course of the political struggle which was waged in the United Nations during six tense months. It opened at the end of May 1967 when Egypt's preparations for offensive military action became manifest by the expulsion of the United Nations Emergency Force, the massive concentration of its forces in Sinai and the re-imposition of the blockade in the Straits of Tiran.

At the end of May, Foreign Minister Eban visited Paris, London and Washington in order to acquaint the heads of Governments with the full weight of the impending peril. Israel's Permanent Representative to the United Nations not only scornfully repudiated the slander and abuse with which the Arab and Soviet delegates were inundating the Security Council, but called upon that highest organ of the United Nations to stand up and to be counted in the face of a grave and imminent threat to international peace and security. Israel's envoys in the capitals of the world toiled to enlist understanding and support for it in its hour of destiny. Yet the Powers shirked their undertakings and the United Nations drowned in a flood of words with not a single drop of action in them.

In the wake of the armies clashing on the battlefield the diplomats took up the cudgels in the United Nations arena.

When the curtain rose at the Security Council in the early hours of Monday, 5 June, the Israel representative defined the main political objectives he was determined to pursue with the lessons of the 1956–57 political struggle well in mind:

To permit the momentum gained by Israel's Army in cutting through the formidable Egyptian build-up, to take its full course;

To prevent the adoption of any resolution calling for the withdrawal of forces prior to the establishment of peace, meaning that the Israel forces would remain on the cease-fire lines until replaced by agreed boundaries of peace;

To oppose any resurrection of the collapsed armistice régime and insist on the erection of a new structure of complete and lasting peace;

To cooperate closely with the United States to avoid the reactivation of that fatal Soviet-American vise whose closing jaws cracked in 1956 the position of America's friends and enabled its opponents to regroup and to recuperate their strength.

The Arab States on the other hand, staunchly supported by their Soviet allies, were guided by three diametrically opposite objectives:

The immediate unconditional and total withdrawal of Israel's forces from all the territories evacuated by the retreating Arab armies; in other words to return to the old armistice lines as the first step for the continued onslaught against Israel's very existence;

Condemnation of Israel as aggressor;

Full compensation to the Arab States for all war damages.

As soon as it became evident to the Soviet Government that contrary to the claims of Arab propaganda, the Israeli forces were advancing on that 5 June towards the Suez Canal, and not Egypt's armies towards Tel Aviv, the Soviet representatives hastened to secure United States support for a resolution that would call for a ceasefire and the immediate withdrawal of all forces to their previous positions. Encouraged by their experience of 1956 they believed that this exercise could be successfully repeated in 1967. The Arab Governments hoped that joint American-Soviet action would extricate them from the political and territorial consequences of their military debacle, that an American-Soviet salvage tug would tow their stranded ship back to the breached breakwaters of the old armistice lines.

But the United States had also learned from its 1956–57 experience. It had recognised that its policy then had helped the design of the Soviet Union to deepen its penetration into the Mediterranean area, to consolidate its position in the Middle East, had humiliated and estranged America's allies, and resurrected Nassar, the West's implacable adversary. Thus in 1967, American policy did not hasten to restore a dilapidated armistice régime which had broken down under the constant batterings of Arab assault and subversion, but insisted on a complete termination of the state of war and its replacement by a just and lasting peace.

From the very outset of the deliberations in the Security Council, and throughout their multiple stages, Israel's UN delegation maintained close contacts with the United States mission, in order to protect its political front line exposed to a constant assault by a formidable array of political forces commanding in the United Nations vast reserves of voting power. This cooperation was imperative to ensure the attainment of Israel's main objective: the transformation of the hostile Arab-Israel confrontation into a state of peaceful coexistence.

Arab Objectives

The debate in the Security Council ended with a resounding set-back for the Soviet and Arab delegations on every one of their claims. None of their proposals contained in a variety of draft resolutions calling for the withdrawal of the Israel forces, for its condemnation and for payment for war damages was adopted. In the United Nations forum the Arab Governments manifested an unusual measure of tenacity matched by an equal standard of obduracy. Undaunted by defeat in the Security Council, they carried their fight into the General Assembly. There they command the support of the entire Communist bloc from Cuba in the West to Mongolia in the East, of a dozen or so Muslim states and of a number of developing countries that traditionally side with them.

Upon the initiative of the Soviet Union, an Emergency Session of the General Assembly convened on 19 June. Moscow decided to send to New York its national diplomatic team captained by Prime Minister Kosygin, coached by veteran 'pro' Gromyko and composed of top flight diplomats, seasoned propagandists and master tacticians. Most of the Soviet bloc countries followed suit and despatched delegations also

led by their Prime Ministers. Against this redoubtable striking
force Israel put into the field a small but closely knit delegation of a handful of experienced career diplomats, led by
Foreign Minister Abba Eban and assisted by a group of parliamentary advisers.

In the General Assembly the Arab-Soviet coalition renewed
its offensive which had been repelled in the Security Council,
determined to attain its three objectives: condemnation, compensation and evacuation. When they failed to muster the
necessary votes for their extremist proposals, they sent their
strategic reserves into the field: Yugoslavia together with a
number of States traditionally aligned with the Arab countries, introduced a new draft resolution which though watered-
down in its style and wording pursued in its meaning the same
principal aim: unconditional Israel withdrawal without an
equivalent Arab advance towards peace.

Another move was initiated by a group of Latin American
states which linked the withdrawal clause to a change in Arab-
Israel relations. Their central plea was that the termination of
the state of war was a prior condition to withdrawal.

By mid-July the debates of the Emergency Session and the
behind-the-scenes diplomatic haggling had reached a deadlock.
Two opposing concepts were in conflict with no chance of
compromise in sight. Neither side could whip up the necessary voting majority. The Arab-Soviet bloc insisted on the
restoration of the pre-June situation. On the other side, a
powerful group of delegations, led by the United States, and
composed mainly of pro-Western States and a number of
developing countries, refuted the false allegations of Israel's
responsibility for the outbreak of the war and urged a new
constructive approach which would bring the Israel-Arab conflict to an end. This group drafted its proposals with caution
and restraint. It did not explicitly call for the establishment of
peace. It confined itself to the demand that the state of war
be terminated once and for all. On the question of the withdrawal of forces the resolution which was prepared by a number of Latin American states, did not differ substantially from
Arab-Soviet formulations except that it linked it to the termination of belligerency.

The Gromyko-Goldberg Connection

When it became clear to the Soviet delegation that its massive diplomatic and propaganda offensive designed to extricate

the Arab States from their self-inflicted predicament had bogged down, and that the Emergency Session was about to disperse without any results, the Soviet Ambassador in Washington, Anatoly Dobrynin, contacted Secretary of State Dean Rusk, to break the deadlock. He suggested a new formula which abandoned the demands for condemnation of Israel and payment of compensation to the Arab States. He concentrated on one principal objective: the immediate withdrawal by Israel from all the territories in exchange for a vague and noncommittal undertaking by the Arab States to relinquish their hostility. Rusk, well versed in the art of diplomacy in general and Soviet negotiating practices in particular, replied: 'What you are suggesting, Mr Ambassador, is to trade a horse for a rabbit.' 'What do you mean by that, Mr Secretary?' asked Dobrynin. Rusk explained: 'The horse is the withdrawal of the Israel forces and the rabbit is the trifle that you are offering in exchange.' But American diplomacy is also guided by the rule, which is always good diplomacy: never slam the door in the face of your interlocutor. Never cut off a probing exercise until you know exactly what the other side really is aiming at. Dean Rusk, therefore, agreed that Ambassador Goldberg, the United States representative to the United Nations, should be available for further contacts with Soviet representatives.

Ambassador Dobrynin hurried to New York. Intensive talks between him and Ambassador Goldberg began on 18 July. Their objective was to find a mutually acceptable formula. Their main difference centred around the 'horse-rabbit' equation. The principal issue remained the American position that withdrawal must be accompanied by a definite termination of the state of war. The Soviet representatives argued deviously that they too favoured this objective but that their Arab friends refused to accept a draft which would explicitly stipulate the cessation of belligerence. In an attempt to overcome this 'semantic allergy', Ambassador Goldberg suggested the following wording:

> 'The Arab States must recognise Israel's right to maintain its own national State and to live in peace and security, and, furthermore, the Arab States must give up all demands and actions that contradict this.'

But even this meek and involved formula did not satisfy Dobrynin. He objected to any wording which would require the Arab States to give unequivocal recognition of Israel's right to national independence. He answered with a counter-formulation:

'All States in the Middle East have a right to independence.'

The Israel delegation viewed with growing concern the gradual erosion of the American position. Foreign Minister Eban assisted by Israel's Permanent Representative to the United Nations and the Ambassador in Washington intervened strongly with the representatives of the United States to arrest this ominous drift. The American desire, however, to reach with the Soviet Union a parliamentary understanding in the United Nations was in this case a stronger motivating force for the State Department than to take a firm stand on a position designed to promote lasting peace between Israel and the Arab States.

To bolster its negotiating strength, the Soviet Government circulated through 'reliable channels' repeated hints that it would not remain indifferent to the continued occupation of Arab territories and would take appropriate steps if the political efforts were to fail. The United States, deeply and painfully involved in Vietnam, pursued at the time a cautious course in other international crises. It preferred a dubious diplomatic compromise to avoid further foreign complications. Moreover, some of the American policy experts believed that an accommodation with the Soviet Union would curb its ambitions to expand its influence in the Mediterranean.

These considerations seemed to have guided the State Department in directing Ambassador Goldberg to work for an American-Soviet compromise formula. When the talks with Ambassador Dobrynin failed to produce results, Foreign Minister Gromyko personally took over. He invited Ambassador Goldberg for a cup of Russian tea to gain American sympathy. Eventually both sides agreed on a compromise draft which was far closer to the Soviet position than to the policy enunciated by President Johnson in his speech of 19 June. Both parties to the bargain were fully aware that their real differences had simply been papered over. In parting, Gromyko suggested to Goldberg, true to classical Soviet diplomacy: 'Let's agree on the wording and differ on its interpretation.'

The Israel delegation learnt the full measure of the United States retreat only on the morrow of the Soviet-United States transaction when it was shown the text of the agreed draft resolution which read:

> The General Assembly....
> '1. Declares that peace and final solutions of this problem can be achieved within the framework of the Charter of the United Nations.
> '2. Affirms the principles under the Charter of:
> 'A. Withdrawal without delay by the parties to the conflict of their forces from territories occupied by them, in keeping with the inadmissibility of conquest of territory by war.
> 'B. Acknowledgment without delay by all member-States of the United Nations in the area; that each enjoys the right to maintain an independent national State of its own and to live in peace and security; and renunciation of all claims and acts inconsistent therewith.
> '3. Requests the Security Council to continue examining the situation in the Middle East with a sense of urgency, working directly with the parties and utilising a United Nations presence to achieve an appropriate and just solution of all aspects of the problem, in particular bringing to an end the long-deferred problem of the refugees and guaranteeing freedom of transit through international waterways.'

The reversal of the United States position was perhaps the most hazardous of all the many ups and downs which had occurred since the beginning of the United Nations deliberations in the Security Council on 5 June. The United States, in its attempt to close the gap between the differing American and Soviet positions on the question of withdrawal, retreated itself from its proclaimed policies. It was on the point of creating a situation as dangerous to Israel's future as it was detrimental to the prospects of peace in the Middle East. It abandoned in the American-Soviet draft not only the call for a lasting peace but even the demand for the termination of the state of war, while supporting a precipitate withdrawal by Israel. In effect, the United States had come very close to buying Dobrynin's rabbit, after all.

Everything was ready, then, for a grand finale of the Emergency Session. The Soviets undertook to secure the assent of the Arab delegations to the terms of the draft. But, Mr Gromyko was in for a major surprise, when he learnt the result of their consultations. They rejected the draft resolution. The Algerians and Syrians led the opposition and Egypt felt obliged to follow suit. Its negative stand doomed the Soviet-American initiative and relieved Israel from Big Power diplomatic encirclement.

Emergency Session Recessed

When this last effort to pass a resolution had failed, it was decided to wind up the Emergency Session without further delay. At the end of two months of this parliamentary tug-of-war, the situation presented itself as follows. The determined and unrelenting efforts made by the Soviet and Arab Governments since the military debacle in June, to mobilise international support for the immediate and unconditional withdrawal of the Israel forces, had failed. The United Nations organs declined to hold Israel responsible for the outbreak of the hostilities. All claims for the payment of war damages to the Arab States had been dismissed and dropped even by their sponsors. The Soviet-American accord had floundered on the rocks of Arab obstinacy. This was the optimum Israel could expect to achieve in the United Nations. The composition of the General Assembly, where the pro-Arab voting bloc can defeat any resolution not to its liking, makes it virtually impossible for Israel to marshal sufficient support for any of its objectives and in particular not for its central aim: the establishment of peace by negotiation.

Behind the scenes, however, diplomatic activity did not cease. Lord Caradon, Great Britain's permanent representative, led the group of activists. Early in October, he presented to the Israel delegation a draft resolution, a kind of see-saw puzzle, which he had pieced together from bits of the defunct Gromyko-Goldberg formula, seasoning it with ingredients from a previous Latin-American draft, and adding to it a new idea of appointing a special United Nations representative to act as mediator. Yet Lord Caradon's new model was a nonstarter. It did not commend itself to the Israel and other like-minded delegations. Israel agreed to consider a draft which would limit itself to the appointment of a special representative confined to the task of assisting the parties to enter into peace negotiations.

The diplomatic probings proceeded in an unhurried and relaxed atmosphere, until the calm was broken on 21 October by the stirring news that the Israel destroyer *Eilat* had been sunk by Soviet-made Egyptian missiles. In the wake of the shelling by Israel artillery of the refineries at Port Suez, on 24 October, the Security Council was called into urgent session. The international community was seized with anxiety that the cease-fire was about to collapse. The two incidents raised the Middle Eastern temperatures to a degree which the Big Powers considered perilously inflammable. The representative of the Soviet Union attacked Israel in his usual manner while completely disregarding the Egyptian aggression committed against the Israel naval vessel. To heighten the dramatic effect of their performance, the Soviets again circulated rumours of a possibility of their military intervention in case Israeli forces intended to operate on the Egyptian side of the Canal. The United States Government counselled caution and restraint, but in the Security Council it did not yield to Soviet fulminations. Thanks to the strenuous efforts of Ambassador Arthur Goldberg, a balanced resolution was adopted, calling upon both parties to cease all hostile acts and to observe scrupulously the cease-fire.

The military incidents on the Egyptian front expedited from now on the diplomatic activity. The pace of consultations was accelerated. The Soviet Union sent to New York its First Deputy Foreign Minister, Kusnetsov, a competent and skilled negotiator and a diplomat highly respected by his Western colleagues. His opening gambit was a conversation with Secretary Dean Rusk in Washington, where again he warned of the dangers of a Middle Eastern conflagration to which the Soviet Union could not remain indifferent. He indicated that the Arab Governments were now ready to accept the Gromyko-Goldberg formula which they had rejected only a few weeks ago. The permanent members of the Security Council—the Big Powers—incapable of reaching an agreement among themselves, encouraged the other ten members of the Council to try expeditiously their hand in drafting a resolution. But the ten equally could not reach agreement. Denmark and Canada stuck to their position that the central aim of any resolution should be the establishment of secure and recognised boundaries within the framework of a lasting and just peace. Opposing them was a group comprising India, Mali and Nigeria that tried to blend the Latin American principles of the termination of the state of war and the inadmissibility of acquisition of territory by war with the Arab demand of the unconditional withdrawal of the Israel forces from all the occupied territories. On 3 November, the ten non-permanent members of the Security Council informed their permanent colleagues of their failure to reach agreement.

Egypt; Surprise Move

The United States delegation, undeterred by the failure of other members of the Security Council to reach agreement, pursued its independent efforts to enlist support for a resolution of its own drafting. On 7 November while the American diplomatic activity was in full swing, the Egyptian delegation made a surprise move. It called for an urgent meeting of the Security Council. In his explanatory memorandum, the Representative of Egypt claimed that the meeting was necessary, 'because of the explosive situation in the Middle East resulting from Israel's refusal to withdraw its forces'. Yet he did not explain where it had been decided that Israel must withdraw, nor did he point to any resolution in this regard on which he could base his contention, because nothing of the kind had ever been ruled by any United Nations body.

Concurrently with the Egyptian sortie, India presented its own draft resolution. The United States countered by introducing their own proposal. In precipitating the convening of the Council. Egypt apparently was under the impression that it could muster a majority in favour of the Indian draft resolution. By taking this unexpected step it did not only surprise the United States representatives, but also antagonised them. For, in these critical weeks, while the delegates of the ten non-permanent members were consulting together, the United States representatives were engaged in secret and searching talks of clarification with the Egyptian Foreign Minister, Mahmoud Riad, and with King Husain, who was in New York at the time. They had obtained the consent of the King to the principles and formulations of the American draft which they presented to the Council on 7 November. Moreover, King Husain affirmed that his position had been endorsed by Nasser when they coordinated their moves at the United Nations at a meeting in Cairo on 17 September. The American representatives, in their conversations with Foreign Minister Riad, did not reach complete Egyptian consent to all the proposed wording but they were led to believe that Egypt had an interest in continuing the dialogue and was anxious to reach an agreement with them on a draft resolution. However the United States delegation realised later that while they were holding talks with Foreign Minister Riad, he was at the same time, urging the Indian delegation to proceed with the preparation of their own draft and to introduce it forthwith. Their proposal ran counter in its principal provisions to the United States position. The United States representatives did not conceal from Foreign Minister Riad their dismay at his double-dealing.

When the Council met on 9 November, it had before it two rival draft resolutions—the American and the Indian. The sponsors launched brisk campaigns to mobilise the required majority. India's prospects seemed to be far brighter than America's. At that time, the United States was not yet prepared to employ the ultimate United Nations diplomatic weapon, the veto, as a means of blocking undesirable draft resolutions. It relied on its power of persuasion in discussions with the delegates at the United Nations and with the Governments in the capitals. It was clear to all delegations, the Soviet Union and Egypt included, that any resolution unacceptable to the United States and rejected by Israel, would even if pushed through, carry no real political weight and have no influence on the situation in the Middle East.

The British Draft Resolution

In the face of this dilemma, Lord Caradon decided that the time was ripe to expedite his own efforts. He exerted considerable diplomatic skill and zeal to bridge the gap between the two draft resolutions. He now produced a proposal based in its essentials on the objectives of the American draft, adding to it formulations from earlier texts and some adaptations from the Indian draft.

Intrinsically, the new design 'made in Britain' was not much different from the American draft. It contained, however, two important modifications. Lord Caradon inserted into the preambular part a provision concerning the 'inadmissibility of the acquisition of territory by war'; and added to the one and only operative paragraph of the draft resolution which defined the terms of reference of the Special United Nations Representative, two essential provisions: agreement and acceptability. The Special Representative was to promote *agreement* between the parties concerned: and the peace settlement must be *acceptable* to them.

The preamble was altered in order to obtain Latin American support. While all this complicated backstage diplomacy was proceeding, Argentina and Brazil championed a draft of their own making which also was intended to be a compromise between the Indian and American proposals. It was based on the concepts of the proposal which the Latin American group had submitted unsuccessfully to the Emergency Session. The United States did not spare any effort to persuade the Governments of Argentina and Brazil to abandon their separate initiative which jeopardised Lord Caradon's endeavours to work out a unanimously acceptable compromise. He himself apparently felt that the only way to make Argentina and Brazil yield was to compensate them by incorporating into his own draft their peculiar doctrine of the inadmissibility of the acquisition of territory. But to lessen its significance and to indicate that this was not an operational provision but an abstract principle, he put it into the preamble and, for good measure, balanced it by adding another provision: 'The need to work for a just and lasting peace in which every State in the area can live in security.'

The change in the operational paragraph emphasising the need for agreement between the parties and the acceptability of a negotiated peace agreement was the result of arduous and sometimes tense discussions between Lord Caradon and the representatives of Israel who insisted, and won their point, that the resolution must reflect five guiding principles:

a) The central objective is the establishment of a just and lasting peace between Israel and the Arab States.

b) The withdrawal of Israel forces from the cease-fire lines would take place only after secure and recognised boundaries had been agreed upon within the terms of a peace treaty.

c) Peace must be the outcome of an agreement between the parties, achieved through free negotiations and not by outside imposition. Refuting the views of the French Representative expressed in one of his statements that it was unrealistic to expect negotiations without prior withdrawal, Mr. Eban answered. 'I invite the Council to understand that it is unrealistic to believe that withdrawal is possible without negotiation'.

d) Guaranteed freedom of navigation through all the international waterways in the area without limitations or reservations.

e) The United Nations Special Representative would be authorised to render good offices to the parties and not to act as a mediator presenting them with proposals of his own.

One difference between the American and British drafts was a curious omission in the British text of a provision contained in the United States draft, namely, to halt the arms race in the Middle East. The reason for its elimination is not clear. The first impression was that it was excluded out of consideration for the Soviet large-scale supplies of military equipment to the Arab countries, to replenish their arsenals depleted by combat losses. However, a Soviet draft resolution presented at the final stage of the Security Council debates included a similar call to halt the arms race couched in almost identical terms used in the United States text.

At the meeting of the Security Council on 15 November Ambassador Goldberg made a lucid and forceful presentation of his Government's policy in regard to the main issues to be embodied in the resolution:

'To seek withdrawal without secure and recognised boundaries, for example, would be just as fruitless as to seek secure and recognised boundaries without withdrawal. Historically there have never been secure and recognised boundaries in the area. Neither the Armistice lines of 1949 nor the cease-fire lines of 1967 have answered that description. Now such boundaries have yet to be agreed upon. An agreement on that point is an essential to a just and lasting peace, just as withdrawal is. Such boundaries cannot be determined by force. They cannot be imposed from the outside. For history shows that imposed boundaries are not secure and secure boundaries must be mutually worked out and recognised as part of the peace-making process.'

The next day Lord Caradon submitted formally the British draft resolution. The Arab representatives were still holding out on two points. They objected to 'recognised boundaries', since they were prepared to recognise only the 1949 Armistice lines. They insisted that the wording on evacuation of forces should state explicitly: 'Withdrawal of the Israel forces from *all* the territories occupied in the recent conflict.' The behind-the-scenes diplomatic activities reached a new high pitch. Lord Caradon tried without avail to obtain Israel's consent to dispense with the term 'recognised boundaries' and content itself with 'secure boundaries'. He also urged it to accept the insertion of a single little word, the definite article 'the' before the word 'territories', so that the text would read: 'withdrawal of Israeli forces from *the* territories'. He appeared to be disappointed when he encountered a resolute rejection of these changes which would have altered the very significance of the resolution in two of its most essential points. He tried to enlist the influence of the United States delegation to make Israel yield. However, it declined and made it clear that the United States would withdraw its support from the British draft, if it were to be changed by the omission or addition of even one single word.

The Withdrawal Formula Death at Summit Talks

When the Security Council met again on 17 November, the Soviet Representative, Deputy Foreign Minister Kusnetsov, took everybody by surprise with a brief and carefully worded statement. To gain his main objective, namely, a change in the withdrawal paragraph, he stressed that the Soviet Union supported the inalienable right of every State in the Middle East, including Israel, to national and independent existence. At the same time he urged that the resolution should express in unequivocal terms that Israel must withdraw its forces from all the occupied territories. When he eventually realised that the Western delegations were determined to resist even the slightest change in the British draft, he arranged for the Bulgarian representative to ask for an adjournment of the meeting until 20 November.

A well-tested feature of Soviet diplomacy is to wear their opponents down by prolonging the negotiating process until every political, tactical, psychological and propaganda device has been brought into full play. There was good reason for believing that in the end the Soviet Union would not veto the British draft resolution. A high-ranking and authoritative source close to the Soviet delegation expressed his opinion that, in the final analysis, the Soviets would vote for the British draft as it stood. All the same, Soviet diplomacy customarily does not yield until it has exhausted all its means. Even when it was evident that Egypt and Jordan were prepared as a result of an agreement reached in mid-November between King Husain and President Nasser, to accept the British draft without any changes, the Soviet delegation continued its parliamentary war of attrition in an endeavour to erode the text.

The evening before the meeting at which the decisive vote was to be taken, Kusnetsov sprang a new surprise. He informed the American delegation that he had been instructed by Moscow to present a new draft resolution—this time in the name of the Soviet Union alone. At the meeting of the Council, on 20 November, he tabled his proposal. Its main provisions reflected the defunct Gromyko-Goldberg formula, embellished by meaningless additions concerning the termination of the state of war and the need to restore peace and the establishment of normal conditions in the Middle East. It was obvious that this was a still-born initiative; but the adoption of the draft was not the purpose of the Soviet exercise. It was merely designed to serve as a delaying device. Once again Bulgaria's representative, the Soviet delegation's man Friday, asked for another adjournment of two days.

During that interval the Soviet Government made a concerted effort to press the United States to accept the wording. 'Withdrawal of Israel forces from *all the* territories'. They were so determined to achieve their purpose that they decided to carry their fight for the definite article to the highest level in Washington. During these two days Prime Minister Kosygin exchanged messages with President Johnson pleading for the acceptance of the Soviet change in return for their vote in favour of the amended British text. When President Johnson sternly declined Kosygin proposed a compromise: Instead of 'withdrawal from *all the* territories', he was ready to content himself with the wording 'from *the* territories occupied'. The summit correspondence ended, when the United States informed the Soviet Union in final and unmistakable terms that it would not agree to change even of an iota in the British draft. It is established Soviet negotiating practice to yield once they become convinced that they are up against a stone wall which can be neither breached nor by-passed.

When the Security Council met for its crucial session on 22 November after hectic last minute negotiations, the Soviet delegate raised his hand in unison with his American colleague and all the other delegates in favour of the unaltered original British draft. The resolution was passed unanimously and became Security Council Resolution 242. All the members had voted for the same text, but not all of them were prepared to recite it with the same incantation. Foreign Minister Eban in summarising the Israel position declared that only the original British text was the authorised version and the Government of Israel would refer to it alone in determining its position towards the resolution.

With American backing, the British delegate who had sponsored and presented the draft opposed last-minute attempts to confuse and distort the meaning of the resolution. Lord Caradon stated that the resolution:

'Opens the way to agreement and to action. It is the result of close and prolonged consultations with both sides and with all members of this Council. The draft resolution is a balanced whole. To add to it or to detract from it would destroy the balance and also destroy the wide measure of agreement we have reached together. It must be considered as a whole and as it stands. We have reached the stage when we want the resolution, the whole resolution and nothing but the resolution. The draft resolution does not belong to one side or the other or to any one delegation, it belongs to us all and that is the only resolution that will bind us and we regard its wording as clear.'

The Balance Sheet

The adoption of the resolution brought to an end the political struggle which began in May 1967, with the aim to prevent the outbreak of war. Because of its ineffectuality and lethargy to face the aggressive designs of the Arab States, the United Nations failed in this task. The contest ended in November, after Israel's successful resistance to the military threat, with a United Nations decision calling for the establishment of a lasting peace between the Arab States and Israel, the first call since 1953 by a United Nations organ categorically stating that nothing but the conclusion of a negotiated peace could solve the Israel-Arab conflict.

During the long months of the debates in the United Nations, Israel's opponents were compelled to abandon one demand after another, whereas Israel gained support for its positions. The Security Council did not call for immediate, unconditional and total withdrawal of the Israel forces; it called, instead for qualified withdrawal to secure and recognised boundaries; it rejected all attempts to saddle Israel with the responsibility for the outbreak of the hostilities; it insisted on the termination of the state of war imposed by the Arab States and the cessation of all hostile acts such as blockade and boycott conducted by them against Israel for more than 20 years; it did not adopt a formula concerning itself with the 'rights of the Palestinian people', but recommended a just settlement of the refugee problem; it did not advocate the imposition of a settlement, but favoured a negotiated peace agreement. Though it mentioned an abstract principle of inadmissibility of non-acquisition of territory by war, it also spelt out the fundamental principle of the Charter of the inadmissibility of war itself. It stressed the main Charter clause which outlawed the use of force or even the threat to resort to force—a situation to which Israel had been exposed from the very first day of its independent statehood. On these basic principles Resolution 242 is founded. Its purpose and significance is its insistence that the parties should withdraw from hostility and belligerency and advance towards a system of peaceful and good neighbourly relations.

For over five years now, Resolution 242 has served a variety of purposes: many a Government, hesitant to take an independent stand on the Israel-Arab conflict has found it a useful noncommittal political hide-out. Arab Governments have used it as a barrier behind which they entrenched themselves in their refusal to negotiate a peace treaty with Israel. But it also had served as an agreed basis for Israel and the Arab States to enter into the Jarring talks, until the UN Representative brought them to a standstill by departing from his terms of reference. And perhaps one day it will serve again as a platform for true negotiations, when the Arab states have reached the conclusion that it is more beneficial to live in peace with Israel than to fight it.

Over the years various Arab States have claimed that peace depends on the implementation of that Resolution—to be effected without negotiations or agreement between the parties. Only those who believe that it is possible for the three pillars of unwisdom of the resolution adopted in Khartoum in summer 1967: 'No recognition of Israel, no negotiations, no peace'—to co-exist with the positive provisions of Resolution 242: The establishment of peace by agreement, the recognition of each State's right to independence and the establishment of a system of relations guaranteeing to all States of the region to dwell in peace and security—can maintain the fictitious view that Resolution 242 is a self-implementing proposition. To this day, the most agile performers of diplomatic acrobatics have failed to reconcile the abysmal contradiction of Resolution 242's positive principles with the continued adherence to the sterile negations of the Khartoum position. . . .

Since its adoption, Resolution 242 has remained the principle work-horse of the diplomatic ploughmen. Its wording, principles and provisions are sign-posts pointing the way to the negotiating table. It is not a detailed blue-print for peace, but rather an outline to guide the peace-makers. The sooner the parties to the conflict meet around the drawing board to draft the terms of peace, the earlier they will be able to move into a new, safe and comfortable dwelling of peaceful relations.

PART V

From War to War

The documents and articles contained in the present section refer to developments since the Six Day War in 1967, with the exception of the National Covenant of the Palestine Liberation Organization. This manifesto, drawn up in May 1964, superseded the earlier Draft Constitution. The Palestine Liberation Organization is the biggest of the Palestinian refugee organizations; its manifesto has been modified since in various points. The Al Fatah "Seven Points" and the interview with the leader of the organization, Yaser Arafat, both published in 1969, offer more recent interpretations of the aims of this movement. The Arab National Movement (the predecessor of the Popular Front) was founded in the Lebanon in 1948. It did not join Al Fatah which in its view was not radical enough and it has since split into two factions led by Dr. George Habbash and Naif Hawatme respectively. The Platform of the Popular Front for the Liberation of Palestine' was formulated by the latter, the extreme left-wing faction of the movement. General Harkavi, the author of several studies on Arab-Israeli problems, now teaches at the Hebrew University, Jerusalem. The essay on Fatah Doctrine is taken from a more detailed study: "Fedayeen Action and Arab Strategy" published by the Institute of Strategic Studies in London in December 1968.

Nasser's speech at the Arab Socialist Union Congress in March 1969 and the Syrian Ba'th Party Resolution of April 1969 reflect the stand taken by the Egyptian and Syrian governments in the dispute since the armistice of June 1967. The excerpts from articles by Hassanain Haykal, the leading Egyptian journalist, define in more detail the objectives of the war of attrition against Israel as seen from Cairo. Ahmad Baha Ed-Dine is another prominent Egyptian journalist, editor of the weekly Mussawar; the ideas expressed in his article were later discussed at greater length in a book by the same author which attracted much attention in Arab circles. "Two Years Later" written by Foreign Minister Abba Eban and General Dayan's speech present Israeli points of view on both the short-term issues involved in the Arab-Israeli dispute and the long-term perspectives. Yehoshua Arieli is professor of history at the Hebrew University, Jerusalem; his speech reflecting the opinions of the anti-annexationist movement in Israel was made at an international symposium in Tel Aviv in March 1969 sponsored by the monthly New Outlook. "Sartre looks at the Middle East again" is based on an interview with Arturo Schwartz, editor of the Quaderni del Medio Oriente. Sartre had visited the Middle East shortly before the Six Day War. Prof. Bernard Lewis argues in his essay originally written for Foreign Affairs, that the two main problems of the area—the East-West rivalry and the Arab-Israeli conflict—while likely to persist are not necessarily connected. Prof. Uri Ra'anan of the Fletcher School of Law and Diplomacy discusses in his contribution first published in Midstream in May 1969 Soviet interest in the Middle East and the possibilities of U.S.-Soviet agreement.

Security Council Resolution on the Middle East, November 22, 1967

THE SECURITY COUNCIL,

Expressing its continuing concern with the grave situation in the Middle East,

Emphasizing the inadmissibility of the acquisition of territory by war and the need to work for a just and lasting peace in which every state in the area can live in security.

Emphasizing further that all member states in their acceptance of the Charter of the United Nations have undertaken a commitment to act in accordance with Article 2 of the Charter,

1. *Affirms* that the fulfillment of Charter principles requires the establishment of a just and lasting peace in the Middle East which should include the application of both the following principles:

(i) Withdrawal of Israeli armed forces from territories of recent conflict;

(ii) Termination of all claims or states of belligerency and respect for and acknowledgment of the sovereignty, territorial integrity and political independence of every state in the area and their right to live in peace within secure and recognized boundaries free from threats or acts of force;

2. *Affirms further* the necessity

(a) For guaranteeing freedom of navigation through international waterways in the area;

(b) For achieving a just settlement of the refugee problem;

(c) For guaranteeing the territorial inviolability and political independence of every state in the area, through measures including the establishment of demilitarized zones;

3. *Requests* the Secretary General to designate a special representative to proceed to the Middle East to establish and maintain contacts with the states concerned in order to promote agreement and assist efforts to achieve a peaceful and accepted settlement in accordance with the provisions and principles in this resolution.

4. *Requests* the Secretary General to report to the Security Council on the progress of the efforts of the special representative as soon as possible.

The Palestinian National Charter:
Resolutions of the Palestine National Council

Charter*

1. Palestine is the homeland of the Arab Palestinian people; it is an indivisible part of the Arab homeland, and the Palestinian people are an integral part of the Arab nation.

2. Palestine, with the boundaries it had during the British Mandate, is an indivisible territorial unit.

3. The Palestinian Arab people possess the legal right to their homeland and have the right to determine their destiny after achieving the liberation of their country in accordance with their wishes and entirely of their own accord and will.

4. The Palestinian identity is a genuine, essential, and inherent characteristic; it is transmitted from parents to children. The Zionist occupation and the dispersal of the Palestinian Arab people, through the disasters which befell them, do not make them lose their Palestinian identity and their membership in the Palestinian community, nor do they negate them.

5. The Palestinians are those Arab nationals who, until 1947, normally resided in Palestine regardless of whether they were evicted from it or have stayed there. Anyone born, after that date, of a Palestinian father—whether inside Palestine or outside it—is also a Palestinian.

6. The Jews who had normally resided in Palestine until the beginning of the Zionist invasion will be considered Palestinians.

* Decisions of the National Congress of the Palestine Liberation Organization held in Cairo July 1–17, 1968.

7. That there is a Palestinian community and that it has material, spiritual, and historical connection with Palestine are indisputable facts. It is a national duty to bring up individual Palestinians in an Arab revolutionary manner. All means of information and education must be adopted in order to acquaint the Palestinian with his country in the most profound manner, both spiritual and material, that is possible. He must be prepared for the armed struggle and ready to sacrifice his wealth and his life in order to win back his homeland and bring about its liberation.

8. The phase in their history, through which the Palestinian people are now living, is that of national struggle for the liberation of Palestine. Thus the conflicts among the Palestinian national forces are secondary, and should be ended for the sake of the basic conflict that exists between the forces of Zionism and of imperialism on the one hand, and the Palestinian Arab people on the other. On this basis the Palestinian masses, regardless of whether they are residing in the national homeland or in diaspora, constitute—both their organizations and the individuals—one national front working for the retrieval of Palestine and its liberation through armed struggle.

9. Armed struggle is the only way to liberate Palestine. Thus it is the overall strategy, not merely a tactical phase. The Palestinian Arab people assert their absolute determination and firm resolution to continue their armed struggle and to work for an armed popular revolution for the liberation of their country and their return to it. They also assert their right to normal life in Palestine and to exercise their right to self-determination and sovereignty over it.

10. Commando action constitutes the nucleus of the Palestinian popular liberation war. This requires its escalation, comprehensiveness, and the mobilization of all the Palestinian popular and educational efforts and their organization and involvement in the armed Palestinian revolution. It also requires the achieving of unity for the national struggle among the different groupings of the Palestinian people, and between the Palestinian people and the Arab masses, so as to secure the continuation of the revolution, its escalation, and victory.

11. The Palestinians will have three mottoes: national unity, national mobilization, and liberation.

12. The Palestinian people believe in Arab unity. In order to contribute their share toward the attainment of that objective, however, they must, at the present stage of their struggle,

safeguard their Palestinian identity and develop their consciousness of that identity, and oppose any plan that may dissolve or impair it.

13. Arab unity and the liberation of Palestine are two complementary objectives, the attainment of either of which facilitates the attainment of the other. Thus, Arab unity leads to the liberation of Palestine, the liberation of Palestine leads to Arab unity; and work toward the realization of one objective proceeds side by side with work toward the realization of the other.

14. The destiny of the Arab nation, and indeed Arab existence itself, depend upon the destiny of the Palestine cause. From this interdependence spring the Arab nation's pursuit of, and striving for, the liberation of Palestine. The people of Palestine play the role of the vanguard in the realization of this sacred national goal.

15. The liberation of Palestine, from an Arab viewpoint, is a national duty and it attempts to repel the Zionist and imperialist aggression against the Arab homeland, and aims at the elimination of Zionism in Palestine. Absolute responsibility for this falls upon the Arab nation—peoples and governments —with the Arab people of Palestine in the vanguard. Accordingly, the Arab nation must mobilize all its military, human, moral, and spiritual capabilities to participate actively with the Palestinian people in the liberation of Palestine. It must, particularly in the phase of the armed Palestinian revolution, offer and furnish the Palestinian people with all possible help, and material and human support, and make available to them the means and opportunities that will enable them to continue to carry out their leading role in the armed revolution, until they liberate their homeland.

16. The liberation of Palestine, from a spiritual point of view, will provide the Holy Land with an atmosphere of safety and tranquility, which in turn will safeguard the country's religious sanctuaries and guarantee freedom of worship and of visit to all, without discrimination of race, color, language, or religion. Accordingly, the people of Palestine look to all spiritual forces in the world for support.

17. The liberation of Palestine, from a human point of view, will restore to the Palestinian individual his dignity, pride, and freedom. Accordingly the Palestinian Arab people look forward to the support of all those who believe in the dignity of man and his freedom in the world.

18. The liberation of Palestine, from an international point of view, is a defensive action necessitated by the demands of self-defense. Accordingly, the Palestine people, desirous as they are of the friendship of all people, look to freedom-loving, and peace-loving states for support in order to restore their legitimate rights in Palestine, to re-establish peace and security in the country, and to enable its people to exercise national sovereignty and freedom.

19. The partition of Palestine in 1947 and the establishment of the state of Israel are entirely illegal, regardless of the passage of time, because they were contrary to the will of the Palestinian people and to their natural right in their homeland, and inconsistent with the principles embodied in the Charter of the United Nations, particularly the right to self-determination.

20. The Balfour Declaration, the Mandate for Palestine, and everything that has been based upon them, are deemed null and void. Claims of historical or religious ties of Jews with Palestine are incompatible with the facts of history and the true conception of what constitutes statehood. Judaism, being a religion, is not an independent nationality. Nor do Jews constitute a single nation with an identity of its own; they are citizens of the states to which they belong.

21. The Arab Palestinian people, expressing themselves by the armed Palestinian revolution, reject all solutions which are substitutes for the total liberation of Palestine and reject all proposals aiming at the liquidation of the Palestinian problem, or its internationalization.

22. Zionism is a political movement organically associated with international imperialism and antagonistic to all action for liberation and to progressive movements in the world. It is racist and fanatic in its nature, aggressive, expansionist, and colonial in its aims, and fascist in its methods. Israel is the instrument of the Zionist movement, and a geographical base for world imperialism placed strategically in the midst of the Arab homeland to combat the hopes of the Arab nation for liberation, unity, and progress. Israel is a constant source of threat vis-à-vis peace in the Middle East and the whole world. Since the liberation of Palestine will destroy the Zionist and imperialist presence and will contribute to the establishment of peace in the Middle East, the Palestinian people look for the support of all the progressive and peaceful forces and urge them all, irrespective of their affiliations and beliefs, to offer

the Palestinian people all aid and support in their just struggle for the liberation of their homeland.

23. The demands of security and peace, as well as the demands of right and justice, require all states to consider Zionism an illegitimate movement, to outlaw its existence, and to ban its operations, in order that friendly relations among peoples may be preserved, and the loyalty of citizens to their respective homelands safeguarded.

24. The Palestinian people believe in the principles of justice, freedom, sovereignty, self-determination, human dignity, and in the right of all peoples to exercise them.

25. For the realization of the goals of this Charter and its principles, the Palestine Liberation Organization will perform its role in the liberation of Palestine in accordance with the Constitution of this Organization.

26. The Palestine Liberation Organization, representative of the Palestinian revolutionary forces, is responsible for the Palestinian Arab people's movement in its struggle—to retrieve its homeland, liberate and return to it and exercise the right to self-determination in it—in all military, political, and financial fields and also for whatever may be required by the Palestine case on the inter-Arab and international levels.

27. The Palestine Liberation Organization shall cooperate with all Arab states, each according to its potentialities; and will adopt a neutral policy among them in the light of the requirements of the war of liberation; and on this basis it shall not interfere in the internal affairs of any Arab state.

28. The Palestinian Arab people assert the genuineness and independence of their national revolution and reject all forms of intervention, trusteeship, and subordination.

29. The Palestinian people possess the fundamental and genuine legal right to liberate and retrieve their homeland. The Palestinian people determine their attitude toward all states and forces on the basis of the stands they adopt *vis-à-vis* the Palestinian case and the extent of the support they offer to the Palestinian revolution to fulfill the aims of the Palestinian people.

30. Fighters and carriers of arms in the war of liberation are the nucleus of the popular army which will be the protective force for the gains of the Palestinian Arab people.

31. The Organization shall have a flag, an oath of allegiance, and an anthem. All this shall be decided upon in accordance with a special regulation.

32. Regulations, which shall be known as the Constitution of the Palestine Liberation Organization, shall be annexed to this Charter. It shall lay down the manner in which the Organization, and its organs and institutions, shall be constituted; the respective competence of each; and the requirements of its obligations under the Charter.

33. This Charter shall not be amended save by [vote of] a majority of two-thirds of the total membership of the National Congress of the Palestine Liberation Organization [taken] at a special session convened for that purpose.

Resolutions*

1. The PLO reaffirms its previous attitude concerning Security Council Resolution 242 which obliterates the patriotic and national rights of our people and treats our national cause as a refugee problem. It therefore refuses categorically any negotiations on the basis of this Resolution at any level of inter-Arab or international negotiation including the Geneva Conference.

2. The PLO will struggle by all possible means and foremost by means of armed struggle for the liberation of the Palestinian lands and the setting up of a patriotic, independent, fighting peoples' regime in every part of the Palestine territory which will be liberated. It affirms that this will only be accomplished through major changes in the balance of forces to the advantage of our people and their struggle.

3. The PLO will struggle against any proposal to set up a Palestine entity at the price of recognition, peace and secure boundaries, giving up the historic right and depriving our people of its right to return and to self-determination on its national soil.

4. The PLO will consider any step toward liberation which is accomplished as a stage in the pursuit of its strategy for the establishment of a democratic Palestinian state, as laid down in the decisions of previous National Council meetings.

5. The PLO will struggle together with patriotic Jordanian forces for the creation of a Jordanian-Palestinian patriotic front, the object of which will be the establishment of a patriotic, democratic regime in Jordan which will make common cause with the Palestinian entity which will arise as a result of struggle and conflict.

* Cairo (June, 1974).

6. The PLO will struggle for the establishment of a fighting union between the Palestinian and Arab peoples and between all Arab liberation forces agreed on this program.

7. The Palestine national authority will strive to call on the Arab states in confrontation [with Israel] to complete the liberation of the whole of the soil of Palestine as a step on the way to comprehensive Arab unity.

8. The PLO will strive to strengthen its solidarity with the socialist countries and world forces of liberation and progress to thwart all Zionist, reactionary, and imperialist designs.

9. In the light of this program, the PLO will strive to strengthen patriotic unity and raise it to the level at which it will be able to fulfill its patriotic and national tasks and duties.

10. In the light of this program, the revolutionary command will prepare tactics which will serve and make possible the realization of these objectives.

Al Fatah

The Seven Points,
passed by the Central Committee of Al Fatah *January, 1969*

1. *Al Fatah*, the Palestine National Liberation Movement, is the expression of the Palestinian people and of its will to free its land from Zionist colonisation in order to recover its national identity.

2. *Al Fatah*, the Palestine National Liberation Movement, is not struggling against the Jews as an ethnic and religious community. It is struggling against Israel as the expression of colonisation based on a theocratic, racist and expansionist system and of Zionism and colonialism.

3. *Al Fatah*, the Palestine National Liberation Movement, rejects any solution that does not take account of the existence of the Palestinian people and its right to dispose of itself.

4. *Al Fatah*, the Palestine National Liberation Movement, categorically rejects the Security Council Resolution of 22 November 1967 and the Jarring Mission to which it gave rise.

This resolution ignores the national rights of the Palestinian people—failing to mention its existence. Any solution claiming to be peaceful which ignores this basic factor, will thereby be doomed to failure.

In any event, the acceptance of the resolution of 22 November 1967, or any pseudo-political solution, by whatsoever party, is in no way binding upon the Palestinian people, which is determined to pursue mercilessly its struggle against foreign occupation and Zionist colonisation.

5. *Al Fatah,* the Palestine National Liberation Movement, solemnly proclaims that the final objective of its struggle is the restoration of the independent, democratic State of Palestine, all of whose citizens will enjoy equal rights irrespective of their religion.

6. Since Palestine forms part of the Arab fatherland, *Al Fatah,* the Palestine National Liberation Movement, will work for the State of Palestine to contribute actively towards the establishment of a progressive and united Arab society.

7. The struggle of the Palestinian People, like that of the Vietnamese people and other peoples of Asia, Africa and Latin America, is part of the historic process of the liberation of the oppressed peoples from colonialism and imperialism.

An Interview with "Abu Ammar" (Yaser Arafat)

Q.—Al Fatah has offered an alternative to the Jews in Palestine—that is the creation of a progressive, democratic State for all. How do you reconcile this with the slogan "Long live Palestine Arab and Free?"

Abu Ammar.—A democratic, progressive State in Palestine is not in contradiction to that State being Arab. The social, geographical and historical factors play a major role in determining the nature and identity of any State. Anyone who has tried to look at the Palestinian problem in its historic perspective would realise that the Zionist State has failed to make itself acceptable because it is an artificially created alien state in the midst of an Arab world.

Palestine has acquired its identity through the historical development of the area. It is impossible for any Palestinian State to isolate itself from its geographical surroundings. It has been proved historically that any State, created on the land of Palestine which had been alien to the area, was unable to survive.

* Text of an interview with the leader of *Al Fatah*, published in *Free Palestine*, August, 1969.

It is claimed that the main reason for the establishment of the State of Israel was to find a solution to the Jewish problem, but the experience of the past twenty years has proved that the absorbing capacity of the State has been insufficient to solve the problem of the 16 million Jews in the world.

The Zionist Movement has, as a result, to face one of two alternatives: either to carry on an expansionist policy which will enable it to absorb all the Jews of the world or to admit the failure of its experience and try and find a solution for those Jews who have been uprooted from their countries of origin to be settled on the land of Palestine.

We have offered our solution: that is the creation of a democratic Palestinian State for all those who wish to live in peace on the land of peace. Such a State can only acquire stability and viability by forming a part of the surrounding area, which is the Arab area. Otherwise this State with its Jewish, Christian and Moslem citizens would be another alien and temporary phenomena in the area, which will arouse the antagonism of its neighbours, exactly as did the first Jewish State and the Crusaders' State. Neither of these States lasted for more than 70 years.

The word Arab implies a common culture, a common language and a common background. The majority of the inhabitants of any future State of Palestine will be Arab, if we consider that there are at present 2,500,000 Palestinian Arabs of the Moslem and Christian faiths and another 1,250,000 Arabs of the Jewish faith who live in what is now the State of Israel.

Q.—The immediate objective of your Movement is the liberation of your occupied homeland. What are your long-term objectives after achieving liberation? How do you envisage the future State of Palestine?

Abu Ammar.—As you have rightly mentioned, the immediate objective of Al Fatah is the total liberation of Palestine from Zionism and the destruction of any racial or sectarian notion which might exist among the Arabs.

Accordingly, we believe the only way to realise our objective is by overcoming our differences and achieving national unity. Our struggle in its present stage is a struggle for survival and for recovering our national identity. We aim ultimately at the establishment of an independent, progressive, democratic State in Palestine, which will guarantee equal rights to all its citizens, regardless of race or religion.

We wish to liberate the Jews from Zionism, and to make them realise that the purpose behind the creation of the State of Israel, namely to provide a haven for the persecuted Jews, has instead thrown them into a ghetto of their own making.

We wish to help build a progressive society based on liberty and equality for all. We also aim at participating actively in any struggle led by any Arab nation to achieve freedom and independence and to help build the united progressive Arab society of the future.

We support the struggle of all oppressed peoples in the world and we believe in the right for self-determination to all nations. We do not know for how long our struggle will go on until the liberation of our homeland is achieved. It might be a few years, or perhaps tens of years. It will be up to the generation that will finally liberate Palestine to decide upon the structure of their State.

Q.—The Palestine National Liberation Movement has certainly been able to achieve a break-through in what used to be a Zionist domain: the Western Leftist movements. Al Fatah has become to many synonymous with freedom fighting and an expression of struggle against oppression everywhere. Yet the new Zionist propaganda tactic is to smear it, by accusing it of accepting help from what is termed by them as "reactionary sources". What have you to say to this?

Abu Ammar.—Our Revolution accepts help, whether technological, material or military, from all sources. We seek the support of all those who wish to see Palestine liberated from Zionism, provided it is unconditional. We address ourselves equally to those who wish to offer help because they wish to see the Holy places liberated or to those revolutionaries in Africa, Asia and Latin America who consider our struggle as part of the struggle against oppression everywhere.

We have formed very strong ties with the liberation movements all over the world—in Cuba, in China, in Algeria and in Vietnam. We must not forget that in a war of liberation we should make use of every available source and means that will help us reach our ultimate goal—that is the liberation of our homeland.

I would also like to point out that other nations who have entered a war of liberation have adopted the same methods: for example in Vietnam the National Liberation Front includes 23 different organisations ranging from the Catholics and Buddhists to the Communists.

Can anyone accuse the Vietnamese Revolution of being a reactionary force? Add to this that the Palestinian Revolution in undertaking to lead the struggle against the Zionists, and to prevent any further aggression against the rest of the Arab world is entitled to use all the resources available in the Arab area.

Q.—Plans for a "peaceful settlement" of what is termed as an "Arab-Israeli" conflict seem to be speeding up, with the Four Power talks going ahead. Both the United States and the Soviet Union are eager to impose such a solution. How will Al Fatah react or rather act?

Abu Ammar.—The United Nations Security Council and the Big Powers have chosen to call their solutions "peaceful", whereas, in fact they are political solutions which are in no way related to peace as they all aim at safeguarding the state of Israel and ignoring the Palestinian Revolution. As such we declare that we will not under any circumstances accept any so-called peaceful solution which is being concocted by either the "Big" States or the "Small" States. We regard any such settlement as a document of self-humiliation which our people are forcibly asked to accept.

I believe that if our generation is unable to liberate its homeland, it should not commit the crime of accepting a fait accompli, which will prevent the future generations from carrying on the struggle for liberation.

What seems strange is that the call for a peaceful settlement started to be heard only when the Zionist enemy began to feel the blows dealt him by our Revolution.

I would like to mention here that immediately following the June War 1967, when President Johnson was asked about the problem in the Middle East, he replied, "is there a problem?" This goes to prove that a problem exists only when Israel considers it as existing. We, the Palestinian people, refuse to capitulate or to give legality to usurpation. As long as Israel is an invading, racialist, fascist State, it will be rejected. Let no one think that any resolution taken outside the will of the Palestinians will ever acquire viability or legality.

We have waited twenty years for world conscience to awaken, but it was at the cost of more dispersion. And here I would like to state that in this we do not only have the support of the Palestinian masses, but also of the whole Arab masses. We must also not forget that our Movement started before the 5th of June 1967, with the purpose of liberating

Palestine and we will not throw our arms until victory, no matter who stands in our way.

Q.—Your Movement has on more than one occasion declared that it will not interfere in the affairs of other Arab countries. Don't you think that owing to recent developments in certain neighbouring Arab countries, this policy should be revised, especially as these developments aim at threatening the Palestinian Revolution?

Abu Ammar.—We will not interfere in the internal affairs of any Arab country that will not in its turn put obstacles in the way of our Revolution or threaten its continuation.

Q.—During her last visit to Britain, Golda Meir denied the existence of a Palestinian people or a Palestinian resistance movement. What is your answer?

Abu Ammar.—Her predecessor, Levi Eshkol, also denied our existence for a very long time. Yet before his death, in an interview with the American magazine *Newsweek,* he had to admit that we do exist. In 1967 Moshe Dayan claimed that the Palestinian resistance was like an egg in his hand, which he could crush any time. Yet in 1969 he was quoted as advising the Israelis to "deepen their graves". Our answer therefore to Golda Meir and to anyone who doubts our existence can be found in our actions inside the occupied territories, whether in Haifa or Jerusalem or Tel Aviv or Eilat or elsewhere. Besides, you are now living amongst us and you can judge whether a Palestinian Resistance Movement exists or not.

Q.—Besides the military field, what are Al Fatah's achievements, for example, in other fields such as the emancipation of women, the education of children, social services and so on?

Abu Ammar.—As a progressive revolution, we consider that all members of our society, whether men or women, should enjoy equal rights. We therefore encourage the total emancipation of all our women and we endeavour to give them every opportunity to participate actively in our struggle. The Palestinian woman has since the days of the Mandate fought side by side with our men. In the occupied territories at present, it is our valiant sisters who are leading the civilian resistance against the occupying forces.

We do not place any obstacles or restrictions in the face of any woman who wishes to join in our Movement. In fact, we are encouraging them to join both our military and political ranks.

As for the education of children, we have established schools for both girls and boys; we have the "Cubs" training centers, we have organizations for caring for the families of our martyrs. We have founded our own hospitals and clinics which provide free medical treatment to the displaced persons in their camps. In fact, we know that our struggle is a long-term one and we are preparing ourselves accordingly.

Q.—How many times did you personally cross the Jordan since 1967?

Abu Ammar.—I do not answer personal questions, but I have entered the occupied territories every time that my military command has asked me to do so.

Q.—Do you consider your struggle as part of the struggle against imperialism and colonialism everywhere and why?

Abu Ammar.—Our struggle is part and parcel of every struggle against imperialism, injustice and oppression in the world. It is part of the world revolution which aims at establishing social justice and liberating mankind. Outside the Palestinian and Arab masses our greatest support comes from all freedom-loving people who have realised the true nature of Zionism and its association with imperialism and neo-colonialism. Israel's natural allies are sufficient proof of this. We only have to look at the support it receives from the United States, at its close links with the racist Republics of South Africa and Rhodesia.

As for its ties with the puppet regime of South Vietnam, let us only remember that its defence minister Moshe Dayan found it necessary and useful to spend a few months there learning their methods. The 1956 aggression against Egypt is another very clear example of the reasons for the creation of a Zionist state in the area. To sum up, we consider Israel as playing the new role of the East India Company in the Middle East.

Q.—Do you accept non-Palestinians in your fighting forces?

Abu Ammar.—We have at present both Arab and non-Arab freedom fighters in our ranks.

Q.—Why do you think Al Fatah has had such an appeal on both the national and international levels?

Abu Ammar.—Al Fatah has revolutionised the approach to the Palestinian problem. It has been the active force behind the resurgence of the Palestinian entity, which has established itself as the major element in the conflict. It is a true expression of the new Arab determination to resist invasion and oppression. Above all, it is part of the world movements for liberation and as such must attract freedom-loving people everywhere. Al Fatah was the first movement which translated the Palestinian aspirations into actions and which by its nature represents the true Palestinian determination.

Platform of the Popular Front for the Liberation of Palestine

1. Conventional War is the War of the Bourgeoisie. Revolutionary War is People's War

The Arab bourgeoisie has developed armies which are not prepared to sacrifice their own interests or to risk their privileges. Arab militarism has become an apparatus for oppressing revolutionary socialist movements within the Arab states, while at the same time it claims to be staunchly anti-imperialist. Under the guise of the national question, the bourgeoisie has used its armies to strengthen its bureaucratic power over the masses, and to prevent the workers and peasants from acquiring political power. So far it has demanded the help of the workers and peasants without organising them or without developing a proletarian ideology. The national bourgeoisie usually comes to power through military coups and without any activity on the part of the masses, as soon as it has captured power it reinforces its bureaucratic position. Through widespread application of terror it is able to talk about revolution while at the same time it suppresses all the revolutionary movements and arrests everyone who tries to advocate revolutionary action.

The Arab bourgeoisie has used the question of Palestine to divert the Arab masses from realising their own interests and their own domestic problems. The bourgeoisie always concentrated hopes on a victory outside the state's boundaries, in Palestine, and in this way they were able to preserve their class interests and their bureaucratic positions.

The war of June 1967 disproved the bourgeois theory of conventional war. The best strategy for Israel is to strike rapidly. The enemy is not able to mobilise its armies for a long period of time because this would intensify its economic crisis. It gets complete support from US imperialism and for these reasons it needs quick wars. Therefore for our poor people the best strategy in the long run is a people's war. Our people must overcome their weaknesses and exploit the weaknesses of the enemy by mobilising the Palestinian and Arab peoples. The weakening of imperialism and Zionism in the Arab world demands revolutionary war as the means to confront them.

2. Guerrilla Struggle as a Form of Pressure for the "Peaceful Solution"

The Palestinian struggle is a part of the whole Arab liberation movement and of the world liberation movement. The Arab bourgeoisie and world imperialism are trying to impose a peaceful solution on this Palestinian problem but this suggestion merely promotes the interests of imperialism and of Zionism, doubt in the efficacy of people's war as a means of liberation and the preservation of the relations of the Arab bourgeoisie with the imperialist world market.

The Arab bourgeoisie is afraid of being isolated from this market and of losing its role as a mediator of world capitalism. That is why the Arab oil-producing countries broke off the boycott against the west (instituted during the June war) and for this reason McNamara, as head of the World Bank, was ready to offer credits to them.

When the Arab bourgeoisie strive for a peaceful solution, they are in fact striving for the profit which they can get from their role as mediator between the imperialist market and the internal market. The Arab bourgeoisie are not yet opposed to the activity of the guerrillas, and sometimes they even help them; but this is because the presence of the guerrillas is a means of pressure for a peaceful solution. As long as the guerrillas don't have a clear class affiliation and a clear political stand they are unable to resist the implication of such a peaceful solution; but the conflict between the guerrillas and those who strive for a peaceful solution is unavoidable. Therefore the guerrillas must take steps to transform their actions into a people's war with clear goals.

3. No Revolutionary War Without a Revolutionary Theory

The basic weakness of the guerrilla movement is the absence of a revolutionary ideology, which could illuminate the horizons of the Palestinian fighters and would incarnate the stages of a militant political programme. Without a revolutionary ideology the national struggle will remain imprisoned within its immediate practical and material needs. The Arab bourgeoisie is quite prepared for a limited satisfaction of the needs of the national struggle, as long as it respects the limits that the bourgeoisie sets. A clear illustration of this is the material help that Saudi Arabia offers *Al Fatah* while *Al Fatah* declares that she will not interfere in the internal affairs of any Arab countries.

Since most of the guerrilla movements have no ideological weapons, the Arab bourgeoisie can decide their fate. Therefore, the struggle of the Palestinian people must be supported by the workers and peasants, who will fight against any form of domination by imperialism, Zionism or the Arab bourgeoisie.

4. The War of Liberation is a Class War Guided by a Revolutionary Ideology

We must not be satisfied with ignoring the problems of our struggle, saying that our struggle is a national one and not a class struggle. The national struggle reflects the class struggle. The national struggle is a struggle for land and those who struggle for it are the peasants who were driven away from their land. The bourgeoisie is always ready to lead such a movement, hoping to gain control of the internal market. If the bourgeoisie succeeds in bringing the national movement under its control, which strengthens its position, it can lead the movement under the guise of a peaceful solution into compromises with imperialism and Zionism.

Therefore, the fact that the liberation struggle is mainly a class struggle emphasises the necessity for the workers and peasants to play a leading role in the national liberation movement. If the small bourgeoisie take the leading role, the national revolution will fall as a victim of the class interests of this leadership. It is a great mistake to start by saying that the Zionist challenge demands national unity for this shows that one does not understand the real class structure of Zionism.

The struggle against Israel is first of all a class struggle. Therefore the oppressed class is the only class which is able to face a confrontation with Zionism.

5. The Main Field of Our Revolutionary Struggle is Palestine

The decisive battle must be in Palestine. The armed people's struggle in Palestine can help itself with the simplest weapons in order to ruin the economies and the war machinery of their Zionist enemy. The moving of the people's struggle into Palestine depends upon agitating and organising the masses, more than depending upon border actions in the Jordan valley, although these actions are of importance for the struggle in Palestine.

When guerrilla organisations began their actions in the occupied areas, they were faced with a brutal military repression by the armed forces of Zionism. Because these organisations had no revolutionary ideology and so no programme, they gave in to demands of self-preservation and retreated into eastern Jordan. All their activity turned into border actions. This presence of the guerrilla organisations in Jordan enables the Jordanian bourgeoisie and their secret agents to crush these organisations when they are no longer useful as pressure for a peaceful solution.

6. Revolution in Both Regions of Jordan

We must not neglect the struggle in east Jordan for this land is connected with Palestine more than with the other Arab countries. The problem of the revolution in Palestine is dialectically connected with the problem of the revolution in Jordan. A chain of plots between the Jordanian monarchy, imperialism and Zionism have proved this connection.

The struggle in east Jordan must take the correct path, that of class struggle. The Palestinian struggle must not be used as a means of propping up the Jordanian monarchy, under the mask of national unity, and the main problem in Jordan is the creation of a Marxist-Leninist party with a clear action programme according to which it can organise the masses and enable them to carry out the national and class struggle. The harmony of the struggle in the two regions must be realised through co-ordinating organs whose tasks will be to guarantee reserves inside Palestine and to mobilise the peasants and soldiers in the border-territories.

This is the only way in which Amman can become an Arab

Hanoi: —a base for the revolutionaries fighting inside Palestine.

Al Fatah's Doctrine

by Y. Harkabi*

Fatah's Major Conceptions

Fatah's prescription for facing the challenge inherent in [its] dilemma was Revolutionary War waged on guerilla warfare lines. Its merit is that it does not require such long and tedious preparations as a conventional war, for it can be launched with small forces. Revolutions, *Fatah* reasons, once set in motion, generate their own forces and acquire momentum. 'The armed struggle is the basic factor for expanding the revolution and its continuation; in short, causing a revolution in the life of this society. Such historic changes are usually achieved by wars, calamities and uncontrollable economic fluctuations. The nearest means of producing such a convulsion and a great historic change in the course of the national development of the Arab nation is by creating an appropriate environment for a decisive fateful battle between the Arabs and the Zionist enemy.'

Arab politicians usually subordinated the Palestinian issue to their interests and policy, and manipulated it accordingly. *Fatah* signifies an attempt to reverse this trend and subordinate all other Arab problems to the goal of liberating Palestine. Before, the Palestinians orbited round the Arab state; now, *Fatah* tries to stage a Copernican revolution, and reverse the relationship.

The Objective of War

Fatah sets out the objective of the war against Israel in bold type: 'The liberation action is not only the wiping out of an Imperialist base but, what is more important, the extinction of a society [*Inqirad mujtama*]. Therefore armed violence will necessarily assume diverse forms in addition to the liquidation of the armed forces of the Zionist occupying state,

* Reprinted by special permission from *Adelphi Papers* No. 53 (December, 1968), "Fedayeen Action and Arab Strategy." Institute of Strategic Studies, London.

namely, it should turn to the destruction of the factors sustaining the Zionist society in all their forms: industrial, agricultural, and financial. The armed violence necessarily should also aim at the destruction of the various military, political, economic, financial and intellectual institutions of the Zionist occupation state, to prevent any possibility of a re-emergence of a new Zionist society. Military defeat is not the sole goal in the Palestinian Liberation War, but it is the blotting out of the Zionist character of the occupied land, be it human or social.' Or: 'The Jewish state is an aberrant mistaken phenomenon in our nation's history and therefore there is no alternative but to wipe out the existential trace [*Alathar al-wujudi*] of this artificial phenomenon.'

Lt.-Col. Sha'ir, an officer in the command of the PLO Army, also expresses the objective in unmistakable terms: 'The chief objective and the fundamental effort for the Popular War concerning the liberation of Palestine is the reoccupation of the usurped land regardless of the method, be it smashing or annihilation [*Ibada*], because the enemy when he usurped Palestine did not think of the fate of our people, of things holy to it and its lawful rights, in the lands of his forefathers.'

Arab declarations of objectives frequently used extreme expressions like 'throwing the Jews into the sea' which implied genocide. *Fatah* endeavours in its publications to avoid such notorious expressions, stressing that the purpose is limited to the destruction of the state, not of its people. The formula most frequently used in its writings is 'liquidation, or the uprooting of the Zionist existence or entity.' However, when the implications of this objective come to be spelled out, it is realised that Zionism is not only a political regime or a superstructure of sorts, but is embodied in a *society*. Therefore, this *society* has to be liquidated, which underlines that achieving it will require a great deal of killing. The Arabs' objective of destroying the state of Israel (what may be called a 'politicide') drives them to genocide. Since the existence of Israel is founded on the existence of a concentration of Jews so their dispersion should precede the demise of the state. Thus, despite *Fatah's* efforts, it comes back to the Arab objective in its extremist version.

Fatah stresses that Jews will be allowed to live in a democratic Arab Palestine after Israel's extinction. In order for the country to become Arab again, the sheer numerical predominance of Jews over Palestinian Arabs requires part of the Jewish population to disappear. How?

Fatah's recognition of the right of a Jewish minority to exist is nothing new. It recalls the fundamental Islamic position, which grants the Jews security on the condition of their subordination as a tolerated minority.

The Arab position is enmeshed in this complexity arising from the impossibility of destroying Israel as a state without destroying a considerable part of her inhabitants. To escape from this dilemma the Arab objective is sometimes expressed in another formula showing perhaps improved articulation without changing the issue: 'the de-Zionization of Israel.' Since the basic meaning of Zionism was the achievement of Jewish statehood, de-Zionizing Israel has only one implication, that Israel will cease being a Jewish state; not Israel but Palestine. Israel and Zionism are organically connected. De-Zionizing Israel is only a contradiction in terms.

Fatah senses the difficulties in the Arab position: 'Examining the Palestinian issue from all its aspects, we realize the necessity to satisfy many parties by our solution. For instance, if we consider world public opinion has some weight and influence, we must put out a solution which will satisfy public opinion or be acceptable to it, even be it with difficulty. Of course, when we speak about the need for satisfying world opinion, we do not mean in the kind of solution to the Palestine issue, but in its method. Public opinion has no right to dispute the imperative necessity of its solution [i.e. by destruction of the state], but its right to know the method, so that public opinion will not castigate us with Fascism, anti-Semitism or other inhuman epithets.'

What is more important for the present discussions is the influence of the objective on the nature of the war by which *Fatah* hopes to achieve its aim. Such a war is different from one directed towards a change of the political regime, or towards harassment of the representatives of a remote country until the government prefers to relinquish its rule in that area. In order to achieve the purpose of liquidating a society or wiping out its 'existential trace,' war must be of great extent and intensity and become really total.

The question that is crucial to any evaluation of *Fatah's* position is the degree to which guerrilla warfare can suit such an objective. This will be taken up at the conclusion of this paper.

Palestinian Activism

Fatah exhorted the Palestinians to become the driving force in the conflict, not by agitation in the Arab countries as they had previously, not by pushing the Arab states to action, but by starting actual fighting themselves. *Fedayeen* action should be developed into a fully fledged War of National Liberation. Only by what *Fatah* terms an 'armed struggle' can the Palestinians solve their problems and regain Palestine.

Fatah stressed its disbelief in the possibility of a political solution. Arab politics are treated, especially before the six-day war, with marked disapproval. Politics are sickening when juxtaposed with the sublimity of the 'armed struggle.' The Palestinians will be able to concentrate on their conflict only if they extricate themselves from inter-Arab rivalries and exercise neutrality. If they take sides in any Arab issue, they will antagonize the opponents of the side they support, who will then try to make things difficult for them. The Palestinian problem should be put above Arab politics. Only by freeing themselves from Arab rivalries will the Palestinians be able to acquire liberty of action in their affairs.

There are inconsistencies in the writings and pronouncements of *Fatah* on how far the Palestinians are capable of accomplishing by themselves the liberation of Palestine. On the one hand, there are announcements that the forces of the Palestinian masses are irresistible and can achieve this goal. On the other hand, there is recognition that the last stroke will have to be dealt by the concerted forces of the Arab armies.

The war *Fatah* aspires to wage is called, in its parlance, the 'Palestinian Revolution,' to signify as well the transformation it will cause in the Palestinians themselves who from passive onlookers will become dynamic fighters.

This trend towards Palestinian activism and the Palestinization of the conflict has to be seen against its historical background. Its psychological aspects should also be tackled, otherwise the human dimension of such developments will evade us. However, in offering psychological explanations, it should always be borne in mind how tentative they are so long as they are based on intuition, and how corrupting they may be by inspiring in the writer, and even the reader, a false sense of clairvoyance.

The mid-1960s saw the re-emergence of the Palestinians as

contestants in the Arab-Israel conflict, after about seventeen years in which the confrontation was mainly at states level. The entry of the Arab armies into the war in 1948 transformed the conflict from a civil one between Jews and Arabs in Palestine, or an intra-state war, to an inter-state war. The activities surrounding the setting up of the Palestine Liberation Organization and the *Fedayeen* organizations signify in some respects an attempt to revert to the previous state of affairs. This development of the Palestinians' reassertion embodied elements of both protest and reproach towards the Arab states for their failure to fulfil their obligation towards the Palestinians. *Fatah,* by emphasizing that the 'Palestinian people is the only true available stock [*Rasid*] for the war of return,' insinuates that the others are not so trustworthy.

On the other hand, the Arab states handing over to the Palestinians the leading role in the conflict implied an abdication of sorts by the Arab states and an avowal of their failure. It is not mere coincidence that the Summit Meetings which established the PLO were convened as a result of, presumably, the most dismal of Arab failures between 1948 and the six-day war. All the Arab leaders had committed themselves to preventing Israel from completing her project of pumping water from Lake Tiberias (what Arabs called 'the diversion of the Jordan'). When the time came, they realized their helplessness.

The relationship between the Palestinians and the Arabs has always been ambivalent, each accused the other of being responsible for their inadequacies in the conflict. The Arab states blamed the Palestinians for selling land to the Jews, for their feeble resistance during the Mandate, and for their acting as agents for Israel Intelligence. Their existence epitomized the calamities that befell the Arab world as a result of the Arab–Israel conflict, and the Palestinians were blamed for them.

The Palestinians blamed the Arab states for their half-hearted activities in the conflict, their irresolution, internal bickerings, the restrictions they imposed on the Palestinians, and their manipulation of the conflict to their narrow interests.

Despite that element of protest against the Arab states embodied in the Palestinians' organizations, they could be created only with the help of some Arab official quarters. The PLO did not come into being only by Palestinian spontaneity. It was established from above by the Summit Meetings and derived its authority and part of its finances from them. The *Fatah* acted under the aegis of the Syrian radical Baath. Thus protest and dependence intermingled.

Palestinian activism came in the early 1960s to be cherished widely in Palestinian circles. Palestinian initiative seemed vital after the Arab states' failure. Mr. Nashashibi ends his book as follows: 'Oh Palestinians, if you do not restore the land, you will not return to it, and it will not return to you.'

An important factor in the Palestinian move for the 're-Palestinization' of the conflict was the influence of the Algerian War. It was a source of both pride and inspiration. If the Algerians prevailed over a great power such as France, so it was argued, there was hope in defeating small Israel.

Hence the effort to draw analogies between Algeria and Palestine and the effort to describe Israel as only another colonialist case, whose fate is doomed as part of the general historical trend of the liquidation of colonies.

Palestinian ideologists argued that previous presentation of the conflict as an inter-state one was erroneous. It was an Imperialist ruse aimed at excluding the Palestinians from their natural role, thus 'liquidating' the conflict. This argument was, too, an apologia for the Arabs themselves as they too described the conflict as international. They were only deluded and their failing was only naïvety. Both Israel and the Imperialists conspired to blur the 'liberation' aspect of the conflict.

Naming the conflict a 'War of National Liberation' after it had already reached a mature age, and the identification of 'War of National Liberation' with guerrilla warfare, produced among Palestinians an inclination to project it backwards and describe the conflict as if the Palestinians had waged continuous popular guerrilla warfare against the Jews. The history of the events in Palestine from World War I is being rewritten to appear as a continuous popular resistance and heroic uprisings. The blame for failure is focused on the leadership. Naji Alush in his book *Arab Resistance in Palestine 1917–1948* gives a Marxist explanation for this failing. Because of its class interests the Palestinian leadership tied its destiny to colonialism, and betrayed the national cause.

Palestinian radio programmes abound with plays and descriptions of brave resistance against the Jews in Palestine. Small ambushes or attacks on Jewish settlers are elevated into heroic acts of guerrilla warfare. Thus, heroism anticipated in the future is reinforced by inspiration drawn from the past, and if the real past cannot be a source of such inspiration, some retouching is done. Such an account may have another merit: it implies that the Palestinians are not only imitators of Mao and Che, but preceded them.

The allure of activism is presumably very powerful for the Palestinians. The Palestinians suffered not only from the agony of defeat, deprivation, refugee status, living in camps, but from contempt by the other Arabs. Losing their land and property was a blow to their dignity, as traditionally the criterion for position and prestige in Arab society is ownership of real estate. Activism and 'revolutionarism' are means of gaining self-respect, especially for the younger generation. This generation is ambivalent towards their parents—they reproach them for their weaknesses and failings, calling them 'the generation of defeat,' or 'the defeated generation' (*Jil al-Hazima, Al-Jil al-Munhar*). Whereas the young generation dubbed itself (already before the six-day war) the 'generation of resistance' or 'the generation of revenge' (*Jil al-Muqawama, Jil-al-Naqma*). On the other hand, in order to bolster themselves up as Palestinians, they have to praise the Palestinian record and stress the continuity of the struggle.

Activism has the psychological function of atoning for past failings and inadequacies. It symbolizes the Palestinians' regeneration, and a reaction against fatalism, proverbial in Arab society, about which the young generation feels uneasy. Activism is a manly quality, hailed in a masculine society, and a reaction against emotionalism treated derogatorily in Arab political literature, including *Fatah's*. 'Revolutionarism' (*Thauria*) exerts a strong influence in most of the Arab world signifying a radical change, spectacular and forceful, a protest against the past, and a guarantee of success for the future. The adjective 'revolutionary' is attached to all kinds of nouns in Arab political literature as a word of approbation and optimism.

Fatah described what this Palestinian revolution will accomplish: 'The staging of the revolutionary movement is a conscious transcendence of the circumstances of the Arab Palestinian people, of the traditional leadership, of the stagnated situations, of the opportunism and the self-seeking political arrangements, or those directed from beyond the Palestinian pale, it is a rejection of this fragmented reality. The Palestinian revolutionary movement on this level is a social revolution and a mutation in the social relationship of the Palestinian Arab people.'

Adulation of Violence

It is not by sheer accident that the third *Fatah* pamphlet entitled *The Revolution and Violence, the Road to Victory* is a selective précis of Frantz Fanon's book *The Wretched of the Earth*. Fanon's influence is manifested in other *Fatah* writings, especially on the psychological impact of Israel on the Arabs and on the transformations that their armed struggle will produce in the Palestinians. 'Violence,' 'Violent Struggle' and 'Vengeance' are expressions of great frequency in *Fatah* literature. The reader of these texts is introduced to a world of simmering frustrated hatred and a drive for unquenchable vengeance.

Violence is described as imperative in wiping out colonialism, for between the colonialist and the colonized there is such a contradiction that no coexistence is possible. One of the two has to be liquidated. (Descriptions of the Arab–Israel conflict as both a zero-sum game and a deadly quarrel are frequent in Arab publications.) Such a conflict is 'a war of annihilation of one of the rivals, either wiping out the national entity, or wiping out colonialism. . . . The colonized will be liberated from violence by violence.' The 'Palestinian Revolution' is such a cataclysmic event that it can only be achieved by violence.

Violence liberates people from their shortcomings and anxieties. It inculcates in them both courage and fearlessness concerning death. Violence has a therapeutic effect, purifying society of its diseases. 'Violence will purify the individuals from venom, it will redeem the colonized from inferiority complex, it will return courage to the countryman.' In a memorandum to Arab journalists, *Fatah* stated: 'Blazing our armed revolution inside the occupied territory [i.e. Israel, it was written before the six-day war] is a healing medicine for all our people's diseases.'

The praising of violence as purgative, may imply also an element of self-indictment for flaws which will now be rectified, and a desire to exorcize the record of failings. The praising of violence may have as well the function of giving cathartic satisfaction as a substitute for operational action.

Violence, *Fatah* asserts, will have a unifying influence on people, forging one nation from them. It will draw the individuals from the pettiness of their ego, and imbue them with the effusiveness of collective endeavour, as bloodshed will produce a common experience binding them together. Thus, 'the territoriality, [i.e. the fragmentation into different Arab states] which was imposed by Imperialism and Arab leaderships and which was sustained by traditional circumstances in the societies, will end.'

The struggle, besides its political goals, will have as a by-product an important impact on those who participate in it. It is 'a creative struggling' (*Nidalia khallaqa*). Violence, Revolutionarism, Activism, 'the battle of vengeance,' 'armed struggle,' all coalesce in an apocalyptic vision of heroic and just aggression, meting out revenge on Israel.

Engineering a Revolution

Fatah ideologists have been inclined to deal with general ideas of guerrilla warfare, rather than specifying in detail how their objectives will be accomplished through it. Like the other exponents of guerrilla warfare *Fatah* deals with the more practical problems, by means of tracing the phases by which the war or the revolution will evolve. It is called 'revolution' in which warfare proper is only a part of a larger complex of activities, mobilizing the support and the participation in the struggle of the masses, and their own transformation through it.

The Pamphlet entitled *How Will the Armed Popular Revolution Explode?* dwells on the mechanism and process of this 'revolution.' It explains that a revolution originates when the oppressed people become aware of the evils of the present reality, and as a result of the growth of an urge to avenge themselves upon it. Needless to say, the reality here is Israel. Though the feelings of revolt against the oppressive reality are spontaneous, they have to be assisted and to be organized. The revolution has to be orchestrated by stages, by its leaders, the 'Revolutionary Vanguard.'

In *Fatah's* descriptions of the stages and their names there are some inconsistencies. They may originate either from different authorship, reflecting diverse influences, or be caused by simple imprecision and vagueness. This vagueness is even more accentuated by the lack of differentiation between the organizational and the operational aspects of the stages, and the relationship between the two.

The parts of *Fatah's* writings which deal with the phases of war make uneasy reading. *Fatah's* terminology and formulation may seem both esoteric and highfalutin'. However, what may be more wearisome for the reader who is not versed in such parlance is the generality and abstraction of the discussion. It contains a mixture of a terminology influenced by Marxist literature, attempting to interpret developments in a rational way, with mythical overtones expressed in figures of speech like the 'ignition' or 'detonation' or a revolution, and leaves the reader wondering how it is to be done.

The organizational stages symbolize the expansion of the circles of those involved in the revolution or war. Stage one is the *Formation of the Revolutionary Vanguard*. This is achieved by 'the movement of revolutionary gathering of the revengeful conscious wills.' 'The individual of the Revolutionary Vanguard is distinguished by his revolutionary intuition.' His task is 'to discover the vital tide in his society, for its own sake and for its usefulness for action and movement, and then to realize what obstacles hamper his movement in accordance with history's logic.' Thus, 'the Revolutionary Vanguard signifies the type of human who interacts positively with the reality [of his predicament], and so elevates himself by his consciousness until he releases himself from reality's grip, in order to pursue the superseding of this reality by another, which differs basically in its values and traits. To take a concrete example, the reality of Arab Palestinian people is fragmented, disfigured and corrupted, and shows signs of stagnation. However, despite this stagnation and immobility, the historical direction imposes the existence of a current of vitality among the Palestinian people, so long as the Palestinian man treasures vengeance on this reality. As this wish for vengeance grows, the current of vitality congeals in the form of a Revolutionary Vanguard.'

The second stage is the *Formation of the Revolutionary Organization*. In it the Revolutionary Vanguard achieves a psychological mobilization of the Palestinian masses by stimulating their urge for revenge, until 'the constructive revolutionary anxiety embraces all the Palestinian Arabs.' It is thus called the stage of *Revolutionary Embracing* (*Al-Shumul al-Thauri*). Indoctrination of the masses will not precede the staging of the armed struggle but will be achieved by it. 'Mistaken are those who advocate the need for rousing a national consciousness before the armed struggle assumes a concrete form. . . . Ineluctably the armed struggle and mass consciousness will go side by side, because the armed struggle will make the masses feel their active personality and restore their self-confidence.' The Vanguard will galvanize the masses by means of its example and sacrifice in guerrilla activities.

Fatah's publications state that irresistible might is stored in the Arab masses. They are 'latent volcanoes,' they are the main 'instrument' of the struggle. This explosive capacity has to be activated and this task is allotted to the Vanguard.

The revolution's success is dependent on co-operation between the Vanguard and the masses. 'The Revolution in its composition has a leadership and a basis, necessitates the accomplishment of a conscious interaction between the basis, which is the masses, and the leadership, in order to ensure the revolution's success and continuation.'

The third stage is the *Formation of the Supporting Arab Front.* Popular support for the 'Palestinian Revolution' is to be secured in all Arab countries in order to safeguard rear bases in Arab countries for the war, and as a means of putting pressure on the Arab governments not to slacken or deviate from aiding the Palestinian Revolution by pursuit of their local interests. The Supporting Arab Front is thus expressed on two levels, the popular and the governmental. The popular support is used as an instrument of pressure against the Arab governments.

In the same publications the overall development of the revolution is divided into two major stages: one, *Organization and Mobilization,* called elsewhere the *Phases of Revolutionary Maturing,* comprises the organizational stages already enumerated. The second stage is called that of the *Revolutionary Explosion (Marhal atal-Tafjir al-Thauri).* The stage of the Revolutionary Explosion is described in colourful language: 'The hating revengeful masses plunge into the road of revolution in a pressing and vehement fashion as pouring forces that burn everything that stands in their way.' In this stage 'tempests of revenge' will be let loose. However, the Vanguard should ensure mass discipline to prevent violence going berserk. 'The Revolution's Will should obey its regulating brain.'

While the first stage is preparatory, the second is the main interesting stage. Unfortunately, *Fatah's* description of it is rather rudimentary. Even the question of the timing of its beginning is not clear. *Fatah* specified: 'Our operations in the occupied territory can never reach the stage of the aspired revolution unless all Palestinian groups are polarized around the revolution.' *Fatah* does have an ambition to become the central leader of all the Palestinians, proving that the other movements, which have not matured round what has been described as a Revolutionary Vanguard like itself, are artificial and 'counterfeited.' Thus the stage of revolution will arrive only when *Fatah* has mobilized *all* the Palestinians.

Nevertheless, *Fatah's* small action at the beginning of January 1965 is frequently hailed as the 'detonation of the revolution,' implying that the revolution started then. By the same token, at the beginning of 1968, *Fatah's* official journal celebrated the fourth anniversary 'of our Palestinian people's revolution in the occupied territory.' Perhaps this ambiguity as to the timing of the revolutionary stage stems from *Fatah's* emphasis of the need to precipitate action. Once action is launched the development proceeds spontaneously.

Influences

The theories of guerrilla warfare have been developed in the twentieth century several times over. They have been popularized and romanticized to the extent of becoming almost part of this generation's culture. No wonder that *Fatah* repeats ideas expounded elsewhere. It would be excessive to expect its approach to be completely original, nor does it pretend to be all original. Actually, the temptation to pose as original is less than the confidence Fatah can draw from the success of these theories in China, Algeria, Cuba or Vietnam. These successes are presented as precedents guaranteeing *Fatah's* success as well. The feeling of kinship of sorts in a family of successful revolutionaries and guerrilla fighters inspires optimism and pride. Thus, *Fatah* makes no bones about its indebtedness to the exponents of guerrilla warfare. Its spokesmen are fond of explaining that, although they have learnt from others, they rely only on their own specific experience. No doubt the singularity of the Palestinian case limits the possibility of benefiting from lessons from elsewhere.

The main guerrilla treatises of Mao Tse-tung, Giap, Che Guevara and Régis Debray, have been translated into Arabic in several editions, and serialized in the press. In its main series of 'Revolutionary Lessons and Trials,' *Fatah* published pamphlets bearing the titles *The Chinese Experience, The Vietnamese Experience,* and *The Cuban Experience.*

In their books on guerrilla warfare, General Talas and Colonel Sha'ir too give long and detailed accounts of the doctrines of guerrilla warfare as developed by its major exponents.

Though Algeria, as an Arab case, should have served as the main source of inspiration, it seems that the greatest influence was exerted by Cuba. (Algeria has not codified her guerrilla experience in the same way as the other guerrilla practitioners. At least such a publication, if it does exist, has not come to the general notice. Perhaps the reason is that Boumedienne was more of a commander of the regular forces outside Algeria in Tunisia than a guerrilla leader.)

The reasons for *Fatah's* seeing Cuba as the main source of inspiration seem obvious: Mao has stressed that guerrilla warfare can succeed only in a large country like China where the guerrillas can establish a base out of the reach of enemy forces. Mao has specified that guerrilla warfare cannot succeed in a country the size of Belgium. Mao's words thus disprove *Fatah,* whereas Cuba is a success story of guerrilla warfare in a small country.

Che Guevara radiates optimism. He lightheartedly urged taking the plunge before conditions matured, while Mao is both more cautious and sombre. The first sentence of the *Fatah* pamphlet on Cuba reads: 'The Cuban experience has proved the error of those who see a need for waiting until the maturing of the objective and the subjective circumstances for the revolution, instead of the continuous effort to accelerate the formation of these circumstances.'

In China and Vietnam the bearers of the revolution were the Communist Party. *Fatah* disapproves of the need to set out as a party. In Cuba it all started from the wanderings of the first twelve people in the Sierra Maestra. Thus the Cuban model suits *Fatah* better, precisely because it was not a popular movement.

General Talas, who dedicated his book to Guevara, and praises him to the skies as the 'guide of War of National Liberation,' explains in the introduction that his main contribution was the idea of the 'revolutionary focus,' the nucleus of the revolt which, though numerically small, can start the movement off and win.

Representatives of *Fatah* and the other organizations established relations with China, Vietnam and Cuba, and were given help and advice. Some of *Fatah's* leaders were sent to Algeria and China for training.

During the years 1963 to 1967 there was a spate of articles in the Arab press on the different aspects of Arab strategy against Israel. A wide range of problems was discussed, such as the kind of war the Arabs should wage, how it should be initiated, analyses of strategic strengths and weaknesses of the two sides, the impact of nuclear weapons—should Israel acquire them, problems arising from Western intervention, the influence of Egyptian missiles, the timing of war, the possibilities of a preventive war by Israel, and the whole field of guerrilla warfare.

To the strategic analyst part of this material may seem amateur—an exercise in imitation of the style of strategic discussions in the West. However, these publications are interesting, as they throw light on the mood and thinking of some important Arab circles. It would be tedious to try fully to report on the views expressed. My purpose is to isolate some of the strands of thought on guerrilla warfare, and Arab strategy in general, not in a micro-historic way—tracing chronologically the details of the debate in Arab countries, identifying the people who took part in it, and the circles they represented—but rather in a conceptual way, reconstructing the possible different positions on the problem of the Arab programme of action against Israel.

Fedayeen not the Solution

The basic suitability of guerrilla warfare as advocated by *Fatah* was questioned. Naji Alush writing his book in 1963–64 directed his criticism against articles published in 1962 in *Our Palestine*, the journal in which *Fatah* made its ideological debut. Alush asked, 'Why should we suppose that the Israeli Army will stand with its hands tied in the face of *Fedayeen's* attacks? The Israeli Army will destroy Arab villages and cities, and even may take a decisive step, and, for example, occupy the whole West Bank. . . .

'The Journal considered that in the present circumstances the Arab armies are incapable of wiping out Israel, whereas it sees that the Palestinian entity is capable of accomplishing

this miracle. How will it be? With the help of the Arab states
and the non-Arab states?

'Naturally we see the Revolutionary Road, which *Our Palestine* has chosen, as an unwarranted one, because it is built
on improvisation, excitement and spontaneity. It will restore
the issue to 1947 [i.e. to another defeat]. . . .

'Smashing Israel cannot be done by *Fedayeen's* attacks
because of the completeness of her preparations and arms.'

The relevance of the Algerian case to the Palestinian condition came under criticism from several quarters. Naji Alush
admonished, 'The legend of the liberation of Algeria may push
the liberation of Palestine into an abyss. The heroic triumph
of the Algerian revolt made some Palestinians and some progressive Arabs fancy that following the same road will bring
the same result.'

Alush spelled out the differences between Algeria and Palestine, invoking the authority of an analysis by Professor Walid
Al-Khalidi:

1. *The Combat Area.* Algeria was a colony with a small
French minority and ten million Algerians. Palestine is divided
into three: a small Arab minority in Israel concentrated in a
few zones, and limited in its possibilities of action; the West
Bank has become a Jordanian colony occupied by the 'Forces
of the Desert and mercenaries,' where the Palestinians are
prohibited from organizing themselves; the Gaza Strip is administered as occupied territory by an Arab government, with-
holding from its inhabitants self-government which might have
transformed them into a nucleus from which serious action
for the liberation of Palestine could have been developed. The
Palestinians in Gaza and the West Bank have first to overcome Arab government domination, before they can organize
themselves for war.

2. *The Nature of the Battle.* In Algeria it was a battle for
independence . . . which is not the case in Palestine. There
is a battle for the uprooting of a state recognized by the
United Nations, supported by world public opinion and the
principal capitalist states. . . . Britain and the United States
were ready to accept the independence of Algeria, but they
are not ready to accept the liquidation of the Zionists' state.
The Algerian struggle for independence could be compared to
the Palestinians' struggle before 1948 . . . after 1948 the nature of the situation changed in Palestine.

3. Algerians could have bases in Tunisia and Morocco.

However, no Arab government will tolerate the organization of the Palestinians on its territory, unless they constitute a part of its forces and are subservient to its policy.

4. *The Problem of Power.* The Algerian people could paralyse, by employing guerrilla warfare, a large French army, owing to the vastness of Algeria which is 852,600 square miles, in which there were many mountains, thick bushes and roadless regions, which rendered movement of the army difficult and made way for successful guerrilla warfare. As regards Palestine, most of the occupied territory is a plain, settled with fortified settlements, connected by an extensive network of roads, which facilitates army movements and renders the task of *Fedayeen* difficult.

5. When the revolution erupted in Algeria, its active organizations were in Algeria. As regards the Palestinians, the organization of a revolution must grow outside of the occupied territory. . . . Since the revolutionary organizations are outside the boundaries of the Zionists' state, any action by them necessitates an armed invasion against which the usurping state will launch a military operation directed against the Arab neighbouring countries.

6. In Algeria, the fighters were men attached to their people who left the towns and their sham for the bosom of the masses. The propagandists of revolution in Palestine are chatterboxes of the bourgeoisie who prefer coffee houses in Beirut, Damascus, or Gaza to the sands of the occupied territory and the mountains of what was left in Palestine west of the Jordan. They organize themselves in Gaza, Lebanon, and Kuwait issuing thousands of proclamations without remembering once where the battlefield is, or discovering its boundaries and purpose.

7. Arab states' aid to Algeria was very small, yet, despite its smallness, Algeria achieved victory because her conditions made that meagre aid sufficient. However, in the battle for Palestine, the aid will not be adequate even if it is large. This is because the aim is to uproot the usurping state and not to spread fear and ruin inside its borders. The Palestinian people, divided and oppressed, cannot mobilize the necessary power to squash the Zionists' state which is defended by 300,000 well-trained and well-armed soldiers.

8. The Algerian campaign took a territorial shape [i.e. pertaining to one Arab people or state] . . . the struggle stopped at the traditional borders of Algeria, and it recognized the

borders drawn by colonialism. This nature of territoriality made the Palestinians demand a territorial struggle [i.e. by the 'Palestinian entity' as distinct from the rest of the Arabs], but that is impossible in Palestine. Algeria could be liberated without a clash with Tunisia or Morocco and their reactionary governments, while the revolutionary operation for the liberation of Palestine must collide with the Government of Jordan.'

No doubt this is sound criticism. It spares the need for a military evaluation of guerrilla prospects in the area, which, coming from an Israeli, might be suspected as partisan.

"The Struggle Continues"

President Nasser's Speech at the opening of the second session of the Arab Socialist Union National Congress at Cairo University, March 27, 1969.

In the name of God the All-Merciful, we open the Arab Socialist Union National Congress.

Brothers, before beginning with the proceedings of the session I ask you to observe one minute's silence in memory of General Abd al-Mun'im Riyad—the brave soldier who offered his life on the battlefield and who gave a high example of Egyptian military honour, and in memory of all our heroic martyrs on the Egyptian front, and the martyrs of the Palestine resistance and the martyrs of the Palestine masses confidently and faithfully struggling on their soil.

Compatriots, members of the ASU National Congress, your Congress is now holding its second session in accordance with the 30th March statement—that the elected ASU National Congress should exist until the effects of the aggression were overcome and should hold a plenary session every three months to follow up and guide the stages of the struggle and adopt whatever it deemed appropriate in this respect.

Although the agenda of this session includes many questions, the foremost question under the 30th March statement —and the primary question of concern to the masses—is one before any other: this is the question of the comprehensive struggle of our people and nation to restore and establish their rights and to liberate and honour the land. There is no other issue before this question, under the 30th March statement and by virtue of our masses' concern. There is no other issue above this question by virtue of the current phase of the foremost issue of comprehensive Arab struggle, which is the centre of attention and the sphere of every sacrifice and hope we offer or expect.

This session of the National Congress begins when our struggle is in a very important and at the same time very dangerous phase. This phase is reflected in particular in both the military and political sides of the Middle East crisis.

On the military side, the phase is apparent in the continued escalation of military operations along the Egyptian front, the escalation of the Palestine resistance organisations, and the escalation of the Palestine people's steadfastness, which is openly and fully challenging the Israeli occupation. At the same time, the enemy's wrath has escalated. We see the effects of this in the repeated raids on Jordanian towns and cities on the pretext of deterring the Palestine resistance.

Brothers, this means that with this escalation we are entering a stage which is inevitable, with the continuation of Israeli aggression on one side, and on the other with our increased capacity for steadfastness and daily support for our comprehensive force in defending our sacred rights. We are now entering a stage in which we should expect strikes by the enemy and in which we should return the enemy's strikes more heavily. We will discuss this in detail later.

On the political side, the phase is apparent in the collaboration of international political activity surrounding the Middle East crisis, which is crystallising in the forthcoming meeting of the four big-power permanent member States of the Security Council, which issued the 22nd November 1967 resolution on the Middle East crisis. The meeting, coming about eighteen months after adoption of the resolution, is to discuss that resolution and what has been done to implement it, in the midst of pressures affirming to every fair observer and every individual sincerely concerned about peace that the Middle East crisis cannot possibly wait any longer.

It is a miracle that the crisis has lasted so long without exploding—an explosion which would have far-reaching and unlimited effects. This means that politically and militarily we are entering a very critical and sensitive stage. Representatives of the four big powers will meet in New York. These powers will study and debate various possibilities. The importance of the subject is that the attitude of these four powers will be a new measurement that will help us clearly and beyond doubt to determine the attitudes of enemies and friends. Perhaps I should sincerely say that the attitudes of the various States in this connection will determine for each the extent of their relations with our Arab nation for years to come, whatever the consequences.

In this connection, and without awaiting other details on the political side, which I will deal with later, I wish to explain to you that the destiny of the Middle East will be determined in the Middle East itself and that nobody can dictate to the Arab nation what this nation regards as against justice or its lawful, historical rights. Peace cannot be imposed, but peace can come by itself if justice forms the basis. We should always remember that the balance of power may change but the foundations of justice are always firmly rooted and perpetual.

Brother compatriots, members of the Congress, the current session of your Congress begins with a new military and political phase—a phase in which events are moving faster and taking a serious turn. Therefore we must be extremely alert, cautious and fully prepared. . . .

Brothers, we will now take a look at some of our fronts near the enemy lines.

First, the Egyptian front. When we refer to the Egyptian front, we begin with the issue of the reconstruction of the armed forces. We all know the situation of our armed forces after the aggression and the cease-fire decision. The reconstruction of our armed forces was a difficult operation. It was not at all an easy operation. First of all we were in need of arms, then we needed reorganisation, then we needed hard training. All this requires the exertion of great efforts and means that our officers and soldiers must accustom themselves to leading a hard—a very hard—life. Naturally, the formation, organisation, and training of our armed forces is not enough. We must also train the brains that command these forces and units. This too has not been an easy task. The formation, training and command of all levels of our leadership has not been easy. When we speak about the reconstruction of the armed forces, we mean that we are reconstructing an army in whose arming, organisation, training and command we have confidence. The armed forces command is the brain that directs the battle and fighting. We also refer to the standard and efficiency of the men in our armed forces.

All these operations were delicate operations that require

planning. What was wanted was fighting spirit, a spirit of sacrifice, and the restoration of confidence in our armed forces after the defamatory campaign to which our armed forces had been exposed in the world.

In reality we lost the battle in 1967 without coming face-to-face with the enemy. We lost the war without entering into it. We lost the battle without fighting. Despite this, our armed forces were exposed to many defamatory campaigns. The only confrontation in 1967 took place on 5th June. On that day, our armed forces fought well. However, in view of what happened to our air force on 5th June, instructions to withdraw were issued on 6th June. So, since we did not have the opportunity to enter the war we cannot say that we lost. We did not have the opportunity to confront the enemy. What happened was that an attempt was made to defame our armed forces so that the people would lose their confidence in the armed forces and so that the armed forces would lose confidence in themselves.

Therefore, after the organisation and arming of our armed forces and after the creation of a command, we had to examine the standard of our men and the spirit of confidence which was restored. We had to see that the fighting spirit was spread among all members of our armed forces. We had to feel the spirit of sacrifice return among the members of our armed forces and to see that cohesion was present between officers and men. We had to see that everyone was sacrificing his time and that we worked day and night.

Brothers, I saw all this during my visits to the armed forces. The people gave a good example of their feelings when they attended the funeral of the martyr Abd al-Mun'im Riyad. Abd al-Mun'im Riyad worked till midnight every day. All members of the armed forces knew this. He used to pay constant visits to army units. He had constant discussions with everyone. The members of our armed forces were used to sudden visits by Abd al-Mun'im Riyad at any post.

During my recent visits to the armed forces at the time of the feast [Id al-Adha], a soldier spoke to me about a certain issue. When the soldier approached me I thought that he was going to complain to me or that he was going to refer to a private issue. However, he did not speak to me about a private issue. He spoke about an issue concerning the use of the arms in his unit. In fact, when he said what he wanted, I asked him: Do you not want anything? He said: No, I do not want

anything. I asked him: Have you no complaints? He said: No,
I have no complaints. I asked him: From what college did
you graduate? He said: I graduated from the Faculty of Arts
of Cairo University. We discussed the subject he brought up.
Abd al-Mun'im Riyad also spoke to him on the same subject.
At the end of our visit that night we went to rest. After
dinner I noticed that Abd al-Mun'im Riyad had asked for the
soldier who spoke to us earlier. Riyad sat down with him and
asked him about the details of the subject for which he had
had no time during the visit. He sat with him and talked
about all issues.

This is the spirit of our men in the armed forces. This is
the spirit of the Chief of Staff of our armed forces and the
spirit of a soldier of the Egyptian armed forces which are now
in position on the battlefield.

Brothers, the efforts to train our armed forces are great. We
know that the enemy had been preparing for this battle since
1956. This fact appeared in books written by the enemy. They
said they were mobilising themselves until they saw that we
were about to become stronger than they. They launched their
aggression against us at that time so that they could prevent
us from becoming their superiors.

We have learned many lessons from what happened in
1967. We are now working hard day and night to make good
our losses. With regard to training, training means one is
deprived of leave for a long period, for there is training day
and night. We feel that the officers and men of the armed
forces are doing difficult work and are assuming heavy responsibilities. They work for long periods without leave, but every
one of them knows that we want to make good our losses in
the shortest period possible. We also want to use the weapons
we have received with full competence. This is as far as training is concerned.

As far as science and technology is concerned, we are en-
deavouring to catch up with what we have missed in all types.
We are developing and expanding our war industry. When I
speak in this way some people may think that I am divulging
secrets. Well, I am not divulging secrets. How can we enter
the war if we are not trained and if we do not have a command, arms and armed forces in which we have complete
confidence?

With regard to arms, the subject of the supply of arms

demands our careful consideration. By such consideration we learn a few lessons, and also we can be more sure of the correctness of the course we have maintained. Several points have to be considered in this matter.

(i) The Soviet Union is supplying us with the weapons we need. Immediately after the setback and the aggression the Soviet Union began supplying us with arms, with aircraft. We were able in a short period to obtain enough arms to help us meet any Israeli aggression. Had it not been for these arms we could not have succeeded in attaining a position from which we could answer or repel the enemy.

(ii) The United States and its allies are supplying arms to our enemy. There is a distinction between the US supply of arms to Israel and the Soviet supply of arms to us. After the June 1967 aggression Israel had more arms than it needed, while we hardly had enough. Moreover, we needed the arms to defend our homelands and to liberate our occupied territories. The supply of arms to Israel—which was the aggressor —could only mean that Israel was being encouraged to continue the aggression and to insist on achieving gains from this aggression.

(iii) The Soviet Union is supplying us with the arms we need without exerting pressure on our current financial resources, which are bearing the heavy burden of the war. It is enough to tell you that we have not yet paid a single penny for all the arms we have received so far from the Soviet Union. The first consignment of arms we received from the Soviet Union was free. After that, all other arms consignments were paid for with long-term loans.

I want you to know that the United States gives arms to Israel practically free of charge. The US Export-Import Bank offers Israel long-term loans with which it purchases arms for nominal sums, while generous American donations to Israel take care of these loans when the time for payment comes.

(iv) When arms are obtained from States and not by smuggling, the matter is no longer a commercial deal but is firmly linked with the countries exporting the arms. A country cannot possibly give arms to a country contrary to its own policy. This means quite frankly that the imperialist powers cannot give arms to countries which openly oppose and challenge imperialism, even if these countries are ready to pay for the arms in hard currency. They cannot get the arms until they succumb to imperialism, or if there is hope of making them succumb to imperialism. We tried this with Britain in 1953 and with the United States in 1954. I want to say quite clearly that supposing we did have the foreign hard currency to purchase the arms, if we could manage that—and I say that we could manage—if we had the currency and went to Washington or London to purchase the arms, we would not get anything. Proof of this is clearly before our eyes.

(v) From the point of view of our national independence, in particular from the point of view of our main and basic existence, our supply of arms from the Soviet Union is a firm guarantee and the only door open to us. This makes us always feel most grateful for the Soviet Union's attitude to us, to our questions of destiny and to our legitimate struggle for our cause.

We have obtained arms from the Soviet Union since 1955. From 1955 to this date, the Soviet Union has neither dictated any political restriction nor made a single condition. It has not made any request which could affect our national prestige. Relations are based mainly on the belief in the popular liberation movement, hostility to imperialism, and resistance to imperialist influence and plans.

After obtaining arms, we must grasp arms. The armed forces are now day and night doing so, grasping and training so that the arms may have full weight on the battlefield. After obtaining the arms, we asked the Soviet Union to provide us with Soviet military technicians—who are at present with our armed forces in their various units and corps. We asked the Soviet Union for technicians and have insisted on our request. Why? To compensate for shortcomings. These shortcomings appeared in various fields in June 1967—in the use of arms, in the command and in various aspects. We also asked the Russians to assist us in training, in grasping arms, and in modernising the various commands—from the supreme to the subordinate commands. I insisted on requesting Soviet experts for deployment with the armed forces because of my conviction that to confront the Israeli enemy we needed the full assistance of Soviet arms and also of those who could instruct us on the use of the arms and who could help us in command training.

In fact, we have benefited a great deal in the recent months from the Soviet experts and advisers who are with our units. They have left their families behind and are earnestly working with us day and night so that we may benefit from their experience and so that our armed forces may attain full proficiency to enable them to stage the battle to liberate the land. . . .

Brother citizens, members of the National Congress. Before leaving the subject of the Egyptian front to view the remaining Arab fronts surrounding the enemy, we must stop carefully to consider the excellent activities that the Arab Sinai Organisation has begun to carry out. The activities of this organisation, which was founded by the young people of Sinai and by other groups of young people from the whole of the homeland who have voluntarily joined its ranks—who defied danger and found their way to this dear part of our nation—began to be felt a few months ago.

During the past few weeks the organisation began to expand its activities in extremely dangerous circumstances, and to fight the enemy in unsuitable natural conditions. Despite all this, the young people of this organisation carried out their great and extremely dangerous tasks in solemn silence. Their attacks were direct. They came face-to-face with the enemy's military forces concentrated in the desert. Our young people formed fighting patrols and clashed with the enemy. They raided enemy headquarters and laid mines. Not a single day passed without the sound of the explosion of these mines reaching the enemy's ears. These explosions inflicted personal and material losses on the enemy.

Regardless of the enemy's repeated threats of revenge against the activities of this organisation, no one is now able to prevent these national young people from carrying out their role in the battle. The Arab fida'iyin action is linked with the Israeli occupation of Arab soil. Therefore, as long as this occupation continues, the people's resistance against it cannot be stopped. This resistance is manifested in all possible ways, both in a negative way and in a popular or military way. This resistance will continue until the end of the occupation.

Brothers, we shall now move on to consider the other fronts of Arab military action. The matters I shall discuss are not secret, because some of Israel's leaders have discussed them and the facts may have also been published by newspapers in Israel or in some Arab newspapers.

The second point I want to discuss is the eastern command. Actually, ever since June 1967 we have been thinking of co-ordinating the joint Arab fronts. Meetings and other long secret meetings actually took place, until it was eventually possible to establish the eastern front and form a command for this eastern front. This command is actually of great importance. Therefore it is necessary that there should be an eastern front and a western front. It is also necessary that there should be complete co-ordination between the eastern and western fronts. The enemy is aware of this importance and of what can possibly result from the formation of strong eastern and western fronts.

The importance of the eastern front was stressed in one of the books of the Strategic Studies Institute. The book points out that Israel's principal target these days is to break up this eastern front. I can say that the establishment of the eastern front has succeeded to a great extent. What has been achieved?

The eastern front has been formed, composed of Syria, Iraq and Jordan. A command for this eastern command has been formed and complete co-ordination has been achieved between the forces of Syria, Iraq and Jordan. What I am now saying is not a secret, because the Israeli Defence Minister discussed it in the Israeli newspapers. Contacts are now taking place between the eastern front and Kuwait and Saudi Arabia.

After this short discussion of the eastern front, I will now speak about the resistance forces. We have spoken about the resistance forces before and revealed our view on them. We have also spoken of our policy. Our policy towards the resistance forces is summed up in consolidation of the resistance forces by every material and military means. We have also said that it is the right of the Palestine people to resist occupation, to fight and to demand their full rights.

We will now speak about the Palestine popular resistance. As we speak about the Palestine popular resistance, which has broken out everywhere in the territory the enemy occupied after June 1967, we must mention the resistance being carried out in valiant Gaza—the Palestine Arab people in valiant Gaza, these people who refuse to surrender. We are aware of the difficult circumstances the people of Gaza are facing in economic and other ways. Despite these circumstances, however, Gaza refuses in every way—through its young men, its sons, its daughters, its men and its old people—refuses to surrender or to keep silent.

We must also mention the Palestine popular resistance in the West Bank. We must mention the Palestine popular resistance in Jerusalem and the reaction by Israel, seeking to turn Jerusalem into a Jewish city. I tell our brothers, the people of Jerusalem, that we, the people of the UAR, give our pledge that we shall in no circumstances accept the fait accompli Israel seeks to impose in Jerusalem. Arab Jerusalem is a part of the Arab nation and no one can abandon Arab Jerusalem. . . .

Brother citizens, I am aware that there is a big question in your mind and in the mind of our people and nation. The question is: When will the battle be? I should like to tell you —out of a sense of responsibility—that I cannot answer this question. I can only say that everything physically possible is being mobilised for the day of the battle. In fact, superhuman efforts are being made for the battle. This is being done with the work, knowledge, faith and resolve of our men in all fields of national struggle, both at the front and on the home front immediately behind it.

Therefore I hope that you will see eye to eye with me that we should not accelerate the battle to make it take place before its due time, not even by one day. However, I promise you in the meantime that we shall not delay the battle, not even by one day, from the date it is due.

Brother citizens, members of the National Congress, before leaving military matters to discuss political matters, I must remind you that the War Minister will be here with you tomorrow at a closed session to give you further details which you would like to know and on which you may ask for explanations. The same thing will apply to the Foreign Minister, who will also attend the closed session with you tomorrow. He will talk to you about things that you would like to know within his field.

For this reason, I shall make my talk about political matters as brief as possible so as not to place obstacles before the contacts among the four big Powers which will begin in the next few days. However, it might be appropriate to review certain general topics so that we may not expect more than the circumstances allow.

1. No one can ask us to do more than we committed ourselves to do when we accepted the 22nd November 1967 Security Council resolution. Despite our absolute belief in a principle which we have declared and which we shall untiringly repeat—that what has been taken by force can be regained only by force—we have presented everything possible,

within the principles in which we believe, to the UN Middle
East envoy Gunnar Jarring, who is to supervise the implementation of the Security Council resolution.

2. We have realised from the beginning that any hope in
Ambassador Jarring's mission is difficult to realise because
Israel rejects the Security Council resolution. It rejects the
resolution because it provides for two things of great importance. These are: (i) the need for withdrawal from Arab
territories occupied after 5th June, and (ii) that no territory
can be annexed by aggression. Israel wants to expand and is
seeking land. We have brought to the attention of the world
statements by Israeli leaders and officials sufficient to condemn
them and to expose their intentions and plans.

3. Towards the end of last year the problem was again
taken to the Security Council in an indirect manner. It was
evident then that Ambassador Jarring was unable to proceed
with his mission and that the authority issuing the resolution
should express another view on it before it was too late.

4. Since that time three new attempts have emerged. The
first was a timetable presented by the Soviet Union for the
implementation of the resolution. The second was a set of
ideas contributing to the implementation of the resolution.
These ideas have been presented by France for discussion at
a four-power meeting, proposed by her, to include the four
big powers which are permanent Security Council members,
in their capacity as the effective force in the Council. Finally,
a few days ago, there was the US working document.

5. I do not want to express an opinion after which it might
be said that we are making difficulties before the meeting of
the big four powers. However, I cannot conceal from you that
the USA bears a great responsibility for the dangerous road
on which the Middle East crisis is proceeding. From the beginning of the crisis, the US attitude has been identical to that
of Israel all along the line and without reservations, despite
its alleged friendships with the Arab world—which are a subject of great doubt—and despite its enormous interests in the
Arab world—about which there is no doubt. Following the
recent US Presidential elections, which brought in a new government, we tried—and I add further that we are still trying
—but I am bound in honesty to say immediately that so far
I do not see any indications of a change in the US attitude,
which supports Israel all the way.

Brothers, after perusing the recent US working document, I can assert that the US attitude is one of complete support for the Israeli point of view. I have only one answer to this US support for Israel—the constant support before and after June 1967—I have only one answer. It is that we Arabs will in no circumstances surrender or accept any pressure.

Brothers, the Israeli newspapers reported that the USA had accepted Israel's point of view, during Eban's visit, on the subject of negotiations between the Arabs and Israel and on the subject of refugees. The Israeli newspapers said that the USA had adopted Israel's point of view on these subjects.

Brothers, the serious situation that may arise if the big four countries, in their capacity as the principal powers in the Security Council, are unable to find a means of implementing the Council's resolution—this situation we and everybody are aware of.

Brother compatriots, members of the National Congress, whatever the case may be, before and after all this, one fact above all remains. Our Arab nation will always have the last word concerning the most important issues of its struggle. Our nation will not give up any of its principles, rights or territory. It will work, struggle, resist and fight so that its destiny will always be guarded by its will. God is its supporter. Peace be with you.

Syrian Ba'th Party Congress Resolutions

Text of statement by Ba'th Regional Command on the Party's Extraordinary Fourth Regional Congress, April, 1969.

Brother citizens, the Extraordinary Fourth Regional Congress was convened at a time when the Arab nation stands, with all its present and future aspirations and hopes, at a cross roads. It will either assert itself, its freedom and its rights in life and determine its future, or slip again into a lost road to live deprived and powerless. This national situation imposed itself on the conference throughout. In a responsible spirit the past stage, including both its achievements and its gaps, was reviewed. In the light of this, the Congress was able to arrive at a unified view of the future, avoiding the gaps and enabling the achievements to take effect. It was also able to surmount the crisis and begin a new stage which it is hoped will be filled with action and achievement.

The recent crisis tackled by the Congress is not the first of its type in the history of the Party. Throughout its march, the Party, like any other revolutionary party, has faced bitter strife from within and acute domestic struggles, but has always emerged strong and more capable of confronting future events however hard these may be. Nevertheless, in view of the present circumstances of the Arab homeland, the recent crisis was the most dangerous and sensitive crisis for the future of the current stage of our people. The Syrian Region, in the light of its doctrinal line which it raised through the Party's leadership, has become one of the main guarantees for continuing the line opposing colonialism, imperialism and Zionism in a constructive way. Prompted by our national and domestic responsibility, it behooves us to defend the Party leading the revolution in this Region.

There were various past and recent causes for the difficult, hard conditions which the Arab homeland has experienced since the setback, and the Party's own conditions have played a major role in these causes. In the light of the situation imposed by the setback, liberation has become the noblest and principal aim of this stage, and the armed struggle has become the axis of the Party's policy in all fields. It was natural that views should differ on the means and methods to guarantee the best possible situation for confronting the occupation and aggression in our land. This has led to attitudes which differ in certain aspects from the attitudes of the political Command.

Those resolutions adopted by Congresses convened after 23rd February [1966] on building up the Party and developing sound Party relations have not been fully implemented. Furthermore, there has been a co-ordination between the implementation of the Congresses' resolutions on domestic policy and the realisation of the slogan "Every citizen has his role in the battle" on the one hand, and major advances in building the material base of the revolution on the other. There has also been no coordination between the will of the revolution to build the ideological army and the provision of the means and the adoption of the practical steps necessary to achieve this.

In addition to a number of other factors, these circumstances have led to the appearance of the signs of a crisis which continued to develop to the point when some measures were adopted that led to a collision course. The crisis thus extended beyond the Party framework to become a .domestic and national crisis which affected both the Arab masses and leaders. Action to end this crisis in a manner ensuring Party unity and the preservation of the revolution became a general domestic and national demand.

The Party's bases, represented by the Regional Congress members, called for an extraordinary Congress in accordance with the Party's statutes. The Command agreed to call the Congress for an extraordinary session which was attended by the representatives of the various popular organisations and some Party organisations abroad. The meetings continued from 20th March to 31st March 1969. The reports submitted to the Congress regarding the crisis and its causes, as well as ways of tackling it, were discussed. The congress discussions were comprehensive, objective, and within the framework of the domestic and national responsibility demanded by the present fateful stage.

Brother citizens, on the basis of the fateful circumstances facing the Arab nation, which dictate that the main aim of the Arab people in this stage should be the liberation of the land from the colonialist Zionist occupation and working for the unification of all the human, military, political and economic efforts and resources and placing them in the service of the armed struggle to achieve the aim of liberation; and out of the Party's obligation to face its historic responsibilities towards the Arab revolution; the Congress has adopted the following resolutions and recommendations: . . .

In connection with the battle. Everything we say, build and plan is in accordance with the logic of the current fateful battle in all its dimensions and requirements. This Region has had a clear policy towards the battle based on principle. The policy was drawn up by the former Party Congresses on the basis of the slogan "Everything for the battle." In addition to affirming the resolutions of the former Congresses in this connection, the Congress has decided: (a) To complete popular mobilisation in keeping with the new stage. (b) To stress the achievement of effective co-ordination between the Arab fronts.

In the field of Arab policy. The Party has always believed that Arab unity and the battle in which the Arab nation is now engaged are two faces of the same fact, namely the Arab nation's awareness of its nationhood. Both are a living and practical expression of this awareness. Any step on the path to comprehensive unity gives support to the battle and is a step towards victory. Any victory we win in the battle will undoubtedly strengthen the Arab people's self-confidence and self-knowledge, and their ability to apply this knowledge in establishing unity.

In view of the fateful circumstances of the Arab homeland and the hostile plot against the Arab land and national existence, and on the strength of its absolute faith in the sound character of the Arab nation, the Congress has recommended the following: (a) That all initiatives be taken to achieve any possible step towards unity with the progressive Arab States, to work in all circumstances to create an atmosphere for unity, and to produce with these States a unified policy for the present stage. (b) To continue the work to bring all Arab resources into the battle and to achieve a unified Arab military stand and provide the necessary atmosphere for this stand.

In the field of foreign policy. The Congress views with satisfaction the fact that this Region has done everything necessary to strengthen relations with our friends, especially the Soviet Union and the States of the socialist camp, and to develop these relations to serve the battle of freedom and existence in which the Arab nation is engaged. Also, the Congress expresses satisfaction that this Region has responded to France's ban on arms for Israel, and that the Region is willing to develop friendly relations with France and do everything necessary to encourage the just French policy concerning the aggression. The Congress is gratified at this Region's firm stand towards all those States whose attitudes have proved them to be enemies of the Arab people and this people's legitimate aspirations to a free dignified life. These States include particularly the USA, Britain and Western Germany.

The Congress has also viewed with satisfaction the great efforts by this Region in political struggle on the international level, including influencing world opinion—a political struggle which supports the armed struggle. The Congress has decided to continue to work for implementation of the Party Congresses' resolutions on foreign affairs, stressing especially the Party's strategy of faith in armed struggle, rejection of so-called peaceful solutions, and the determination of our attitude towards other States in the light of their policies on the Palestine issue.

In the Party field. (a) All measures adopted because of the crisis shall be abolished and the Command shall restore the situation to normality immediately. (b) The Regional Congress denounces the exchanges of uncorroborated accusations which accompanied the crisis and enhanced it, and asks the Command to pay special attention to dealing with such a phenomenon, which threatens proper moral practices within the Party. (c) The Party bases called for a Regional Congress and the Command's response to this call has strengthened the Party's organisational principles and confirmed that the solution to any crisis within the Party can only be achieved through its institutions.

Brother citizens, the concern for the forward march of the Party and the revolution shown by friends throughout the world, many Arab brothers and honourable progressive and mass organisations in this country, and the responsible, mature attitude shown by all citizens throughout the crisis, have greatly impressed the Party's bases and Congress members. The Party Command praises these friendly and fraternal attitudes and renews its pledge to perform all its commitments of struggle in domestic, Arab and international policies. The Command underlines the importance of complete expression, in both policies and actions, of the Arab people's historic determination to retrieve the usurped land and restore the disgraced dignity.

Long live the struggle of the Arab people against imperialism and Zionism! Long live the struggle of the Palestinian Arab people for the liberation of their usurped land! Glory and immortality to the martyrs of the resistance and fida'iyin movements throughout the battlefields!

(Signed) The Regional Command of the Ba'th Party.

The Strategy of the War of Attrition

By Hassanain Haykal*

The coming stage of the struggle will be full of great and precious sacrifices. No matter how saddening or painful this

* Excerpts from articles published in *Al Ahram*, March 27, April 11, April 25, 1969.

may be, it is a destiny from which there can be no escape in view of several considerations arising from the battle fronts in the Arab-Israeli conflict:

1. ... In the Israeli view, supported so far by Britain and the USA the present cease-fire lines provide an opportunity for forcing the Arab nation to submit completely to a plan for domination of which Israel is only the spearhead. This view assumes that, placed as they are along the cease-fire lines, the Arabs are in no position to reject anything.

In the Arab view, supported by the USSR and understood by France, the present cease-fire lines are new burdens in an old crisis, a new more serious complication in an already dangerous situation, and such a complication twice compounded would be the last foundation on which any long or short-term solution can be based.

2. Israel believes that the present cease-fire lines will enable it to exert a dual-purpose pressure on Egypt, Syria and Jordan to secure the following:

(a) Recognition of the 1948 armistice lines as the international boundaries of Israel; (b) annexation of new areas, on the West Bank, the Golan Heights, and perhaps in the Egyptian Sinai desert as well where claims might exist but have not been made public yet.

In the face of this dual-purpose pressure, however, none of the three Arab States directly concerned can either: (a) make any bargains over its national territory under any pressure; ... once a State concedes part of its territory, it collapses and loses any justification for its continued existence; or (b) decide on anything inside the Palestinian territory, because the Palestinian people now speak for themselves and nobody has the right to speak on their behalf, particularly in matters affecting their land. ...

3. There is a time bomb in the shape of the cease-fire lines. This is a dangerous situation for which the influence of the USA and of pro-Israeli world opinion are to blame more than anybody else. ... It was inevitable that the cease-fire lines turned into a time bomb, for the Arab States which accepted the cease-fire did so because they had no alternative and because they wanted to wait for the results of the efforts that might be made by the forces concerned with the peace of the area and the world. But the state of no alternative is liable to change and waiting has a limit.

The enemy has poured fuel on the fire. When the enemy

felt the Arab impatience growing at the cease-fire lines, he tried to prolong the situation by the only means he has: violence. . . .

It is only natural for us to become impatient at the cease-fire lines. Likewise, the enemy's violence will increase, for this is his nature. Accordingly, we must expect that the enemy will increase his violence, extending it to the entire cease-fire lines and beyond them to any spot he can.

All this means that a different stage of confrontation will develop and will be full of great and precious sacrifices, as I have already said. We shall lose heroes. . . . We shall lose installations built with much sweat. . . .

I was one of those who after the battles of 1967 wrote frankly that one of the advantages achieved by the enemy was his occupation of Sinai which had brought the Canal area within range of his guns. No matter how hard or painful this may be, the area installations must be considered exposed to danger. Undoubtedly, it is one of our prime duties to defend every wall against the enemy guns as long as this is possible. But the vulnerability of the areas to the enemy guns must not for one single moment prevent us from acting. Otherwise, the enemy would be successful in using the hostage as he had calculated from the start. In fact, this area has been in danger since the day it came within range of the enemy guns in June 1967. Whatever solution is achieved for the Middle East crisis —even if it is a peaceful or diplomatic solution—the enemy will most likely vent his wrath by pouring fire into this area before withdrawing from it.

The phase which prevailed for almost a year after the June battles could be described as the phase of calm along the cease-fire lines. It was a phase in which calm was the rule and impatience was the exception, expressing signs of the Arab rejection that has been suppressed by the state of waiting without alternative.

But for some months, the features of a new phase have been developing and have not taken clear shape. It is the phase of impatience along the cease-fire lines. It is a phase in which impatience is the rule and calm is the exception. This phase will grow every day because the enemy has only violence, and human experience has shown that violence does not extinguish fires but fans them, turning impatience into indignation, indigation into wrath, and wrath into an explosion. The enemy's losses during the growing phase of impatience will be great no matter how hard he tries to conceal or deny them. We shall benefit from this phase no matter how many heroes we lose in the battlefield, no matter how valuable the installations exposed to enemy fire on and away from the battlefield. I will only speak of some of the benefits and completely ignore the rest.

1. The enemy has exploited the shock the Arabs suffered following their defeat in the battles of June 1967 and the period of calm that followed, to unburden himself of the commitments of general mobilisation which he could not endure for long because of his limited manpower resources. . . .

2. When the Arab resistance operations rose in intensity inside the occupied territory, the enemy employed a brigade of paratroopers to help the Nahal, police and intelligence forces. He also employed a squadron of helicopters, learning from the US experiences in Vietnam. Thus the enemy's burden was increased.

3. When the civil disobedience waves began against the enemy authority and later turned into bloody clashes in Gaza, Nablus, Hebron and Jerusalem, the enemy rushed to set up an electronic defence line to prevent the resistance men from entering the occupied territory. Thus, he was able to divert some of his forces to deal with the Palestinian cities which rose with pride and dignity against the enemy's authority and presence. The line, however, failed to achieve the desired aim and the enemy had to deploy part of his force in the occupied area surrounding Jerusalem.

4. When the artillery exchanges along the Suez Canal increased and Egyptian armed resistance patrols entered Sinai, as the Israeli delegate to the Security Council said, and fought battles near the Mitlah pass, the enemy immediately thought of setting up a defence line of steel installations along the East bank of the Canal. This led to more clashes and the Egyptian artillery fire was so strong that it destroyed a large part of these installations and prevented the setting up of others. Israel then rushed to declare partial mobilisation to reinforce its troops in Sinai. Thus, the size of the Israeli forces almost doubled, from one and a half divisions to almost three divisions.

5. With the continuation of the artillery operations along the Egyptian front and the pouring of troops into Sinai, Israel

resorted to another method for dealing with the resistance organisations. It is called "active pursuit" by aircraft. . . .

6. The use of Israeli aircraft in such battles is likely to have several effects: (a) the aircraft will be in constant need of maintenance due to extensive use. (b) The aircraft will be continuously exposed to being shot down . . . (c) The Arab fighters will become accustomed to living under the threat of air strikes and to fighting this threat. This in itself will help to dispel the state of unjustified panic that had developed after the six-day battles. Furthermore, aircraft may be effective in strategic operations but in tactical operations, without the conditions of a comprehensive war, the effect will be limited, particularly on fighters who are helped by the nature of the ground on which they are fighting and by their training to protect themselves against air attacks.

7. When Israel increased its troop concentrations in Sinai, the Arab Sinai organisation began to play its most serious part, for this increase has provided it with more targets for more effective blows. . . .

The new phase along the battle fronts has meant the following to us: (1) Loss of more heroes; (2) further exposure of our installations to danger; (3) the cease-fire line is proving to the world everyday that it is a time bomb; (4) the growing belief of our masses in their right to self-defence and their power to practise it, despite the shackles imposed by the stage of waiting without alternative; and (5) preparation of our fighters for the battle so that they will not be taken by surprise as in June 1967.

To the enemy, the new phase has meant: (1) Increase in the occupation costs; (2) loss of more blood; (3) exhaustion of more equipment; and (4) increase of economic burdens because of the confrontation.

The difference between us and the enemy is that whatever losses we suffer will not be high compared with our losses in June 1967, while anything the enemy loses will be great after its cheaply won victory in 1967. . . .

The Israeli enemy does not appear to be at his best these days. Usually our enemy is orderly and organised, but these days he appears confused and contradictory. There is a great deal of evidence of this. . . . Perhaps the most striking evidence of apparent confusion and contradiction can be summed up as follows:

1. So far the enemy has not taken an appropriate decision on the defence of his positions in Sinai. Will he adopt a static or mobile defence? Both methods have advantages and contain dangers. Static defence from reinforced positions would save him men and would not require him to increase his concentrations in the open desert. It would at the same time rob him of his best advantage: the capability of rapid movement. . . .

2. When the recent fierce artillery battles began, the Israeli Defence Minister Gen. Moshe Dayan described them "as a kind of fireworks—neither harmful nor beneficial." Nevertheless, a few days later the Israeli Army began constructing what they later called the Bar Lev Line, after the Israeli Army Chief of Staff. It seems Bar Lev was once one of the leading proponents of the static defence method. The Bar Lev Line is composed of more than 100 reinforced concrete positions. . . . When the Egyptian artillery destroyed more than half of these fortified positions, the enemy rapidly increased his concentrations in the desert.

3. When the Egyptian forces advanced one step in their strategy of positive defence and launched combat patrol operations across the Canal to attack the Israeli positions and engage in face-to-face combat with the men and officers in those positions, the enemy's behaviour was a vivid example of his state of confusion and contradiction. The first operation was carried out last Sunday night. The enemy kept it secret despite his losses. He did not expect Egypt to say anything about it because any such statement would be tantamount to an admission of violating the cease-fire line by crossing the Suez Canal. When the Egyptian military spokesman mentioned the operation in his daily statement about incidents on the fighting front, the enemy appeared surprised. The enemy restrained himself, and eighteen hours after the operation and three hours after the statement by the Egyptian military spokesman, he hastened to issue an admission of the operation. He tried however to minimise its significance. . . .

When Monday night's operation followed, Israel was the first to issue a statement on it. Again Israel's statement was an attempt to minimise the significance of the operation. This attempt was reinforced by the statement of the UN Israeli Delegate that instructions had been issued to him to lodge a complaint against Jordan to the President of the Security Council on operations of the "saboteurs"—meaning the Palestine resistance organisations—but that Israel did not intend to lodge any complaint about operations by the Egyptian combat patrols, because those operations were so insignificant as to deserve no attention.

Nevertheless, at dawn on Tuesday the Israeli Air Force retaliated against an Egyptian radar unit which is on Jordanian territory in accordance with the requirements of the direct military co-ordination between the two countries and within the framework of the activities of the Eastern Command. . . . Even the Israeli retaliatory operation was not as well planned as usual. The Israeli raid on the Egyptian radar position near the town of Mazar in the Karak district did not take the Egyptian anti-aircraft artillery responsible for protecting the position by surprise, even though the attack took place at dawn. Radar equipment worth not more than 10,000 dollars was destroyed, but Israel lost a Vautour and a Mirage worth not less than 10,000,000 dollars. . . .

My purpose in this article is not merely to cite the evidence of the enemy's current state of confusion and contradiction. This is only an introduction to my purpose. But there is one question that must be answered in connection with this introduction before arriving at my main purpose. The question is: What is the explanation of this current state of the enemy?

The only explanation is that on most of the Arab fronts the enemy is facing something for which he is not prepared. . . .

On the Egyptian front, to be specific, the Israeli enemy imagined that any bullet fired on the Egyptian front would be "a political bullet" intended either to bring pressure to bear on the great Powers to convince them that the Middle East situation was about to explode, or to influence the Arab masses and convince them of the earnest intention to fight. Conceived in this frame of mind, Israel's assessments overlook the most important factor in the Arab stand on all the fighting fronts: the incentive of liberation. The enemy forgets that the picture changed fundamentally after 1967. Before then, the enemy claimed the Arabs were working to bring about his defeat. . . . Since 1967, the enemy no longer accuses the Arabs of working to defeat him, although in fact their sole aim in life is now to bring about his defeat by any means. The enemy acquits the Arabs now not because he feels reassured about their intentions, but because he feels reassured about their present capabilities. Yet, the enemy forgets the incentive of liberation, which was not as strong before 1967. . . . In view of this powerful incentive, the enemy should not make his calculations according to the traditional criteria, but on the basis of different factors that will definitely prove their effectiveness. . . . After the introduction and the related question, the purpose of this article is to draw attention to a number of vital points at the present stage of the Arab-Israeli struggle.

1. The Israeli enemy will soon wake up from the confusion and contradiction that now afflict him. This is because he has many means, above all his military strength, which will enable him to recover his balance quickly. Military force will be the first means the enemy will use intensively to rid himself of the state of confusion and contradiction now afflicting him. This means that the enemy will strike violent blows so as at least to regain the initiative and, if he can, to reduce the pent-up power of the Arab incentive of liberation which has gathered force since the setback. . . .

The Israelis planned their war with us in a modern, logical way which involved no miracles or near-miracles. But when they arrived to fight us, we were not really there. This was due to many factors—previously discussed by me—which imposed defeat without a fight on the Arab force. Acute anxiety prevailed in Israel before the decision was taken to enter the war on 5th June 1967. Israel's Grand Old Man Ben Gurion was against the risk. The former Premier Levi Eshkol was hesitant. Israel entered a war which the Arabs entered not with their strength but with their shortcomings. In fairness, and according to all sources of reference, it must be said that the units that had the opportunity to fight acquitted themselves well. The reasons for the Arab shortcomings were at a higher level than the sacrifices of those who fought. It will suffice to say that four-fifths of the Egyptian force in Sinai did not have an opportunity to engage the enemy. . . .

The first thing, then, the enemy will use to recover his balance and rid himself of the state of confusion and contradiction that now afflicts him is his military strength. He will strike with it because it is the only weapon he has, and because the legend of its victory is the most precious thing he possesses. All this means that the enemy will strike and strike violently. He cannot recover his balance and regain the initiative unless he drives the Arabs back, at least psychologically, to their position at the end of the battles of June 1967.

2. No one should exaggerate in presenting the evidence of Israel's confusion and contradiction. This is not yet the end, nor even the beginning of the end. What is now taking place on the Arab fronts is closer to being the beginning of the beginning. The next part of the road will be rough beyond imagination. I can even say that the famous saying that we will wrest our territory from the enemy's occupation inch by inch is not a mere slogan but it is most probably what will actually happen, because we will fight on every inch of this land.

We must face the rough road with steady hearts and not be swayed by joy one day because the enemy lost two or three aircraft, or because dozens of his soldiers fell to our guns, or because our fighting patrols hit his positions. We must, in return, expect unlimited losses in men and equipment on our side. If one day we give ourselves to tumultuous rejoicing, we may find ourselves in the grip of gloomy grief the next day. We must not let the days pass in this way—one very cold and another very hot. . . .

What I said about the need to put the brakes on feelings now may appear to be a call for people to become computers, devoid of sentiment. This is impossible, because it is inhuman. This is not exactly what I am asking. I am trying to avoid further human misfortune. . . . It is usual for many to resort to hope to bridge the wide gap between reality and their desires. The danger is that such hopes may become day-dreams. Day-dreams may exceed capability and disable it. This will double the strength of any enemy strikes. . . .

Someone might contradict by asking: Why do I say this when we are moving along a road which we must follow to the end? The answer is: This is what should really be said at this time and in these circumstances. It is the nature of war to strike, to be prepared to be struck by the enemy without letting this be a surprise, and to be prepared at all times to give death to the enemy, and to take death from him. Such is the nature of war. . . .

To my mind there is one chief method which cannot be ignored or avoided in tipping the balance of fear and assurance in the Arab-Israeli conflict in favour of the Arabs. This course, which meets all the requirements and necessities and is in harmony with logic and nature—this main course to tip the balance in our favour, or merely precisely to adjust it, is: to inflict a clear defeat on the Israeli Army in battle, in one military battle.

I should like to be more specific because there is no room under present conditions for irresponsible talk. I would make the following points: (1) I am not speaking about the enemy's defeat in the war, but his defeat in a battle. There is still a long way to go before the enemy can be defeated in the war. The possibilities for this are still not within sight. But the enemy's defeat in one battle presupposes capabilities which could be available at an early stage in the long period before the end of the war. (2) I am not speaking of a battle on the scale of that of 5th June 1967—a 5th June in reverse, with the Arabs taking the initiative and Israel taken by surprise. Most likely 5th June will not be repeated either in form or in effect. In the coming battle neither we nor the enemy will be taken by surprise. . . . I am speaking about a limited battle which would result in a clear victory for the Arabs and a clear defeat for Israel—naturally within the limits of that battle. (3) The requirements and necessities I am speaking about, and which will impose the military battle, do not include any marked consideration for the so-called revenge for injured Arab dignity. . . .

To these three reservations regarding the battle, which I consider necessary and vital, I should like to add more, in the hope that they will give a clearer picture of what I am saying. (1) The current artillery exchanges along the Egyptian front are not the battle I am thinking of—the battle that I feel the requirements and necessities are imposing. What I am envisaging is far greater and broader. The artillery exchanges are important, indeed very important, but they are not the battle which can achieve the aim of inflicting a clear defeat on the Israeli Army. (2) Neither are the activities of the resistance organisations at their present level the battle I am thinking of or the battle imposed by the requirements and possibilities. . . . (3) In simple and general terms the battle I am speaking about . . . is one in which the Arab forces might, for example, destroy two or three Israeli Army divisions, annihilate between 10,000 and 20,000 Israeli soldiers, and force the Israeli Army to retreat from the positions it occupies to other positions, even if only a few kilometres back.

I am speaking, then, about a battle and not the war; about a battle that is limited as battles naturally are; about a real battle, however, resulting in a clear defeat for the Israeli Army. Such a limited battle would have unlimited effects on the war. . . .

1. It would destroy a myth which Israel is trying to implant in the minds—the myth that the Israeli Army is invincible. Myths have great psychological effect. . . .

2. The Israeli Army is the backbone of Israeli society. We can say that the greatest achievement placed on record by the Arab resistance against Zionism—an achievement resulting from the simple act of refusal—has been to dispel the Zionist dreams. Because of the Arab refusal, Israel has become a military stronghold and Israeli society has become the society of a besieged stronghold—a military garrison society. . . .

3. Such a battle would reveal to the Israeli citizens a truth which would destroy the effects of the battles of June 1967. In the aftermath of these battles, Israeli society began to believe in the Israeli Army's ability to protect it. Once this belief is destroyed or shaken, once Israeli society begins to doubt its Army's ability to protect it, a series of reactions may set in with unpredictable consequences.

4. Furthermore, such a battle would shake the influence of the ruling military establishment. The establishment has the whip hand in directing and implementing Israeli policy on the excuse of acting as Israel's sole protector and guardian of Zionist plans.

5. Such a battle would destroy the philosophy of Israeli strategy, which affirms the possibility of "imposing peace" on the Arabs. Imposing peace is in fact, a false expression which actually means "waging war."

6. Such a battle and its consequences would cause the USA to change its policy towards the Middle East crisis in particular, and towards the Middle East after the crisis in general.

There are two clear features of US policy. One which concerns the Middle East crisis, is that the USA is not in a hurry to help in finding a solution to the crisis. No matter how serious or complicated the situation may become, the USA will continue to move slowly as long as Israel is militarily in a stronger position. This situation would surely change once the Israel position of strength was shaken.

The other phenomenon concerns the Middle East after its present crisis. It is that the USA sees in Israel an instrument for attaining its aims in the area. No matter how far the Arabs go in their revolt against the US influence and how much they

defy this influence, the US aims are guaranteed as long as
Israel remains capable of intimidating the Arabs. If Israel's
ability to intimidate becomes doubtful, US policy will have
to seek another course. Israel has proved to the USA that for
the time being it is more useful to it than the Arabs. Although
all the US interests in the Middle East lie with the Arabs, the
USA continues to support Israel. The strange contradiction
in the Middle East at present is that the USA is protecting
its interests in the Arab world by supporting Israel. Israel is
thus the gun pointed at the Arabs, the gun which the USA is
brandishing to attain its aims and protect its interests. . . .

After all this, the question remains: is such a battle
possible?

The answer is: I do not claim military experience, yet I
say that there is no doubt or suspicion as to the possibilities
of such a battle which could inflict defeat on the Israeli Army.
My belief is based on the following considerations:

1. The only myths in the Israeli system are those fabricated by bold and daring propaganda or by great imagination.
Israeli society is not a straw as some believe, nor a rock as
others imagine. . . . Israeli society cannot live independently.
It is a society which cannot produce any genuine economic
or political force. What matters most is the intrinsic force and
not the apparent force, which is deceptive in most cases.
Myths that are based on apparent force are bound to be dispelled by experience, especially if met by a capable force.

2. Israel has lost its once-in-a-lifetime opportunity. After
5th June 1967 its myth acquired all the elements it needed.
Yet Israel could not attain its goal of turning the end of the
battle into the end of the war. Arab steadfastness proved that
the battle has ended but the war will continue. Thus Israel
has lost its opportunity.

3. In any future battle, the Israeli Army would fight under
conditions different from those in all previous battles. The
Israeli Army would not be able to advance easily from its
present positions along the Jordan river, the Suez Canal and
the Golan Heights without finding itself passing through
densely populated Arab areas, with the danger that these
would absorb all its striking forces, exhaust it and make it
easy to pounce on the Israeli Army's scattered remains one
by one. With the exception of the Air Force effort, the Israeli
Army would have to fight a sustained battle or a defensive

battle, whereas it is accustomed to fighting offensive battles with its characteristic tactics of indirect approach and fast outflanking movements. The Israeli lines of communication between the bases and the fronts have become long and arduous, especially in times of operations. As a result of the long lines of communication it would be impossible for the Israeli Army to move quickly on the Arab fronts as it did in the past when it was able to strike on one front and then switch its forces by its short lines of communication to strike at another Arab front. . . .

4. In any future battle the Israeli Army would face Arab armies with different standards of fire power and its use, different command structures benefiting from past experience, and a higher morale, as the Arab forces would be aware of fighting for the heart of their homeland and not only for its borders.

At the beginning of my article I said that a battle ending in a clear defeat for the Israeli Army should be the chief method of tipping the balance of fear and assurance. . . . I did not say it is the only method because there are other secondary methods. . . . I will give the following examples in this respect.

1. Our acceptance of the Security Council resolution on the Middle East—the resolution which international society has endorsed—is a valuable step, particularly since Israel has rejected the resolution and thereby defied the whole of international society. Despite Israel's daily proclaimed disrespect for the international organisation, the question is not so simple. I mean that the Israeli citizens' awareness of being at odds with the entire world will undoubtedly influence their mood, and so affect the balance of fear and assurance in the Arab-Israeli conflict.

2. The Soviet Union's support for the Arabs and its continued help to them in rebuilding their military forces after the tragedy of June 1967 will undoubtedly affect the feelings of the Israeli people in the balance of fear and assurance.

3. France's stand cannot fail to affect the balance of fear and assurance for the Israeli inhabitants who realise that the greater part of their military power in 1967 came from France and that—from 1954 to 1964 at least—France was an ally of Israel joined by special ties.

4. The current four-power talks in New York arouse

Israel's suspicions, to say the least, because they indicate clearly that the Middle East crisis cannot for long remain confined to the Middle East and that it might lead to a nuclear confrontation between the great Powers. The talks may produce a solution to the problem which—to put it at its lowest—will fail to give Israel everything it feels to be within its reach. Irrespective of their results and what the Arabs think of these results, the talks will play their part in affecting the balance of fear and assurance in the Israeli people's feelings.

I expect Israel will take this article and submit a copy of it to the Security Council, as it has done in the past, saying: Look, they admit that the battle is the only course and that the political attempts are only secondary courses paving the way for the chief method. Taking all the Israeli attempts into consideration, and we must admit its tireless activities, I should like to say: Our aim is to eliminate the aggression. How we wish that all the secondary methods might lead to the attaining of that aim! Facts and evidence keep reminding us that what has to be done must be done.

Returning to Palestine

By Ahmed Baha Ed-Dine

The withdrawal of the forces of aggression behind the frontiers of June 5, 1967 is undoubtedly the logical slogan, conforming with the phase through which we are passing at this time. It denotes the scope of the "first indispensable step" which has to be taken before we can even contemplate going on to the next stages. *Nevertheless, it would be an error to imagine that "the elimination of the consequences of aggression" implies the restoration of the exact same situation in the Arab world as existed prior to the aggression.*

Many situations will change and many ideas and methods will be modified.

We should also now be thinking of what ought to change— in particular with regard to the Palestinian problem itself.

The most elementary lesson we can draw from the defeat is to ask ourselves the following question: Have the ways we have been following up to now in order to try to solve the

Palestinian problem been adequate or should we be thinking of other means and new methods ... with a view to fully restoring the rights of the Arabs?

The conditions which existed in the Arab world from 1948 to 1967 fossilized the Arab position towards the Palestinian problem. For close to twenty years, the Arabs have obtained no other result than a verbal "rejection" of the state of affairs created in 1948. Now that this "frozen" situation has been thawed by Israeli aggression, we find ourselves facing a new situation that can be molded anew.

At this time, news is reaching us concerning the heroic Palestinian resistance put up in the occupied territory—a resistance which is the only serious step imaginable prior to realizing and consolidating our aims. Consequently we must draw the most important lesson of our defeat from that reality.

Before we envisage the possibility of different circumstances, of leaving the defense trenches in order to tackle the Palestine problem anew, we must admit that the simplest and most important "line of defense" against Israel would be, in the first place, for *Palestine to become a reality*.

The Zionist invasion of 1948 succeeded in tearing away one part of Palestine while we Arabs, instead of preserving what was left to us of that country, and seeing to it that it was made monolithic, firm and able to demand its rights, set about dismembering that part of the territory of Palestine which we controlled.

The Zionist invasion of 1948 set out to gather together Jewish immigrants and refugees from all over the world and to transform them into active citizens—farmers, artisans and fighters; while the Arabs, reconciled themselves to the Palestinian citizens of being transformed into emigrants and refugees.

In the course of the years, the idea of creating a Palestinian entity and a Palestinian organization took form and began to develop. It is thus that the Palestinian (Liberation) Organization came into being, although it lacked one of the most important conditions enabling it to speak on behalf of the people and the homeland; namely, the territory. Yet, this territory, though reduced, did exist. The Palestinian "struggle" was consequently directed from Cairo, Beirut and every other Arab country—but not Palestine.

This state of affairs gave the world the feeling that Palestine no longer existed; that there was no real Palestinian people laying claim to its own territory; that it was merely a case of the neighboring Arab states putting up a resistance to another state named Israel.

Somewhat similar situations—but with innumerable variants and nuances—have been imposed on some other countries by international and colonialist circumstances. In this way Korea was divided into two sides, each side claiming to represent the country's only authentic state; but neither did away with itself because the colonialists were occupying the other state. In Vietnam, foreign forces imposed divisions upon the country, recognizing the victory of the national revolution in North Vietnam and preserving a colonialist base in the South. But the amputated nation which did not succeed in having its own right triumph fully—instead of knuckling under, mustered its strength and turned itself into a base for the liberation of its usurped, colonized nation.

What should we do, as a result?

Restore the Name of Palestine

It is clear that the indispensable point of departure, which must be examined and organized immediately, is the re-establishment of a state called Palestine. This state would include Jordan—consisting of the West and the East Bank of the Jordan—and the Gaza sector. In other words, it would comprise the remaining parts of Palestine, to which would be added the area which was Transjordan and which has become integrated with Palestine in the course of the years. It might be argued that this proposal would change nothing and simply suggest a change of name. Our reply to this is that any political initiative may confine itself to titles and be void of substance, but may equally, by persevering action, bring about a radical change and assume a new substance.

Only the restoration of the name, "Palestine," could have a major psychological—and subsequently political—influence on the world, and affect the future of this problem. The authentic name of the country would be reborn; the Palestinian state, of which one part was usurped, would rise up solidly along the front line against the usurper and claim its legitimate rights.

The re-establishment of the name of Palestine on Palestinian soil should be accompanied by the return of the Palestinian people to the soil of Palestine.

What actually has happened during the past nineteen years to the Palestinian people, with the exception of those who stayed in their own homes on the West Bank of the Jordan?

The Palestinian faced the following dilemma: either to become a powerless refugee living in tents, or to become an ex-Palestinian emigrant in some other part of the world— Canada, Latin America or one of the Arab countries from Algeria to the West to Kuwait in the East.

Who emigrated? The most capable, competent and gifted of Palestine's sons. Those who had succeeded in their careers as businessmen, engineers, doctors, economists and journalists. The elite among these competent and intelligent people had no other path open before them than emigration, than working outside Palestine and choosing some other nationality than the Palestinian. Only those who had left families in their country of origin kept up any ties with Palestine, while the others detached themselves from it completely. Thus, at the very same time that Israel was knocking at every door to attract Jews from Yemen, from Europe and the Maghreb in order to transform them into citizens and thereby enhance the density of her own population and her demographic and social solidity, the Arabs, for their part, were allowing the Palestinian entity, as a demographic reality and as a civilization, to disintegrate, to disperse, and gradually to lose its most precious asset: its human resources.

Build a New Life

The restoration of the name of the Palestinian state would of course be of no value as long as it was not accompanied by real action aimed at turning the tide of emigration and dispersion into one of return and regrouping. Before talking of "returning" to occupied Palestinian territory, we must achieve the return to the territory where Palestinians are still living. The Arab bulwark deployed to face Israel cannot be composed of a desert zone of refugee camps and of a society becoming more depleted from day to day. On the contrary, it should be supported by a society that is economically, socially, politically and therefore militarily, powerful.

A different kind of life must be launched in Palestine—a

life that could absorb the capacities of its people, that would not encourage them to emigrate but instead would attract former emigrants to return to their country. Though it is true that such a new life is an expression of the duty of patriotism and the wish to solve the Palestine problem, it is no less true that Palestine must make it possible for all to work there, to live, to advance and to develop in that country.

Our call for a return to Palestine is not a marginal or secondary problem. Despite the current international and political interest surrounding the Palestinian problem it is indispensible that a Palestine exist. Palestine, which is the principal party to this problem must affirm its presence, demonstrate that it exists, and prove that its existence is real and meaningful. It must express its claims and exert continuing pressure. It was precisely the feeling of the importance of this factor that undoubtedly prompted the Summit Conferences to create a Palestinian entity represented by the Palestine Liberation Organization. What was it, however, that caused that organization to fail and what was its weak point? The factor which proved fatal to the organization was the lack of a territory, and of a people attached to that territory. Its existence was more fragile than that of the Jewish Agency before the creation of the State of Israel. In fact, the Jewish Agency and even the Zionist Movement itself only owe their effectiveness to the fact that they were attached to a territory, to their concentration on Palestinian territory, through the agricultural settlements, the towns and the population centers which they controlled.

The call for a return is not a subsidiary problem. The human factor is the decisive one in this national struggle, the bitter struggle which sets noble national destinies against those of an invading people that is seeking to create a new nationalism. In the final instance, it is the human factor which will prove decisive, and above all, it will be the Palestinian human factor, aided and supported by the Arab human factor as its strategic extension. The Palestinian human factor does not depend only on quantity but also on quality; as much in the sphere of education as of skills, productivity and the country's economic, political, social and military institutions.

It is of little importance, after all, what the regime of the country will be: whether it will be a monarchy or something else. The homeland is greater than the regime in power. People may disagree regarding the regime, with all that this implies, but there can be no disagreement concerning the national homeland itself. No one makes it a pre-condition that the regime of his country be according to his own tastes before thinking of living, working and fighting there. The Palestinian's feelings concerning the return to the country and the Palestinian cause, his struggle and activities, should be no less strong than that of the Jew who emigrates from the other end of the earth to a country he has never seen, which he does not know and whose language he does not even speak. Undoubtedly, the Palestinian attachment is no less powerful than that attraction.

Let the Palestinian of today—of Lebanese, Kuwaiti or Argentinian nationality be able to benefit solely from his Palestinian nationality. The Palestinians must be in Palestine if Palestine is to belong to the Palestinians.

Those who are ready to sacrifice their lives today fighting in the occupied territories under extremely difficult conditions show that they are tackling the problem in a sound manner and that their way is perfectly feasible.

Should the Refugees Live in Tents?

The proposal, however, raises a delicate and sensitive point —of the Palestinian refugees. And here I refer to those living in the camps situated around Israel's frontiers in Gaza, Syria, Lebanon and Jordan. Since 1948, that is, for the past 20 years, approximately one million Palestinians have been living in tents in the refugee camps supported by international welfare organizations. Their circumstances are such that they cannot lead any sort of civilized lives; they are not cultivating the land, they are not working and they are not learning properly.

They are living in tents because they constitute the main contingent of those who were literally driven off their land and out of their dwellings. Their kind of life symbolizes to them the determination of the Palestinian people to reoccupy their homes, or at least to apply the resolutions successively adopted by the United Nations in their favor. No one wants to eliminate the refugee problem either by abandoning their right to return or by diverting them from claiming that right. The following question arises, however: should this large mass of Palestinian people, after 20 years of living in tents, continue to live in these same tents for a further period, whose duration no one knows?

I believe that to be impossible, unjust to the refugees and without any purpose.

In this comprehensive proposal I have put forward for the renaissance of "the Palestinian state," I don't have any precise answers to this question. But, nevertheless, I can define the objective and refer it to the writers, the experts, the thinkers and the politicians to discuss the ways it could be fulfilled.

The aim is a double one:

1. to reform the life of that dispersed mass of human beings on the land of Palestine which we control. These people should, upon Palestinian soil, transform themselves into a powerful, enlightened, advanced and productive society, that will promote its agriculture and arm itself. A kind of "powerful climate" along the front line with Israel could be created. Finally, this human mass will no longer find itself behind barriers of infirmity, illiteracy, incapacity and stunted development;

2. to prevent any action liable to put an end to their right to return or in any way to undermine their cause.

I do not believe that this is impossible to achieve.

It is exceedingly important not to liquidate their problem since it is the spearhead of the entire Palestinian affair as a whole. But it is equally important for the refugees to become an efficient and influential force so that they may become a Palestinian Arab power. Let us recall once more that the Jews also constructed camps for the refugees they took in, but in these camps they worked, they trained for jobs, they lived and produced.

This is the proposal I am putting forward.

I will allow myself to return to one point. The problem of settling the land, of forming an attachment to it and of turning it into a powerful base, may appear to be of secondary importance, not pointing to a clear and rapid solution. But then, there are no easy, decisive, and rapid solutions for any of the world's really great problems. Nevertheless, in the course of time a new influential and unalterable situation can be created through initiatives, decisions and actions.

Israel is keenly aware of this problem; that is why she has always based her actions accordingly. Therefore, right after seizing any parcel of land she sets out to establish a settlement there. That is—a populated, productive fighting unit organically attached to the soil; in other words, it sets out rapidly to create a new demographic, geographic and political reality.

This is how the Israelis have been acting for almost a century, ever since the first Jewish immigrants began to arrive in Palestine. And that is how they acted only a few days ago when they began to set up new settlements near Jerusalem.

A Soldier Reflects on Peace Hopes

By Moshe Dayan*

At this course, people learn how to make war. But on this occasion, if I may, I should like to discuss the other side of the picture—the question of peace between us and the Arabs, or, more precisely, the problematics of peace. In a brief address, obviously, it is impossible to treat the subject exhaustively, and I, at all events, am not capable of doing so. I shall therefore merely try to cast some light on the subject.

I have chosen Dr. Arthur Ruppin as one personality who casts light on the subject. He came to Israel for the first time in 1907, was expelled "forever" by the Turkish Governor Jemal Pasha, and came back to the country after the English conquest, this time really forever.

Two unique elements are involved, if we wish to present the problem through the eyes of Dr. Ruppin. The first is the period in which he lived. From 1920 to 1942, Dr. Ruppin was one of the architects of the Zionist venture, the "father of Zionist settlement." This was the inter-war era, a concentrated period of 20 successive years, whose distance from us lends itself to evaluation and review. At the same time, the period is not quite so distant that its links with the present day are severed. From this standpoint of distance on the one hand, and links on the other, it might perhaps be proper to pinpoint 1936 as the focal year of the period. This was the year of the riots, which raged 30 years before the Six Day War.

Not only was the period unique, but perhaps the man

---

* Text of an address by General M. Dayan to a graduating class at the Israel Army Staff and Command College (*Jerusalem Post*, September 27, 1968).

himself more so. Not the man as a typical representative of the period, but Dr. Ruppin with his special qualities, which permitted him to see things with greater clarity, depth and honesty than many other men of his day.

Dr. Ruppin was a humanist by nature, a man of conscience, and when he encountered the "Arab question," he wanted to be persuaded that Zionism could be fulfilled without detriment to the Arabs of Palestine. In his education and schooling alike, he was a scientist, and he studied things not only through their concrete expression, but also through the forecast of their future development and transformation. Above all, Ruppin was a man of action: "For the Jews of Europe," he wrote in his diary, "Zionism is a religion, but for me, it means action." And in the "Arab question," he did not look for appropriate formulas but for practical solutions. Moreover, since his life was utterly dedicated to Jewish settlement in Israel, he inevitably saw the "Arab question" as it was reflected through settlement. The ground he had his feet on was Zionist fulfillment, and he was only prepared to turn his gaze towards what was capable of achievement, without quitting this basic posture.

I cannot conclude my remarks about Ruppin the man, without including a paragraph from Berl Katznelson's eulogy of him:

> From generation to generation we see the 36 righteous men, whom we depict in the form of drawers of water, foresters or peasants. It would never occur to us to seek one of these 36 righteous men on some congress platform, in an office, in a university chair, or among public figures. I would not have used this figure of speech, had I considered it an exaggeration. Ruppin embodied unique characteristics which we associate solely with the 36 righteous men. He was modest without being self-effacing. He was not infected by the taint of power. Even the great publicity which he enjoyed from time to time in the course of his functions left him unspoiled.

I do not think it would be too outrageous of me to assume that most of the people here have not read the three volumes of Dr. Arthur Ruppin's autobiography. I shall therefore permit myself, in the following, to quote relevant extracts from this diary of his.

Ruppin was put in charge of Zionist settlement in Israel in 1920, after the First World War. He obviously anticipated that with the collapse of the Ottoman Empire, the wave of national liberation would also reach the Arab countries, and the Palestine Arabs as well. In the first days of his work he may perhaps have not realized the implicatiòns of this development for Zionism. But in 1923, three years after taking over his functions, not only did the "Arab question" reveal itself to him, but he also discovered that his predecessors had overlooked it.

At this period, in 1923, Ruppin underwent the first phase in his approach to the "Arab question." He not only recognized the existence of the problem but even diagnosed a solution, namely the merging and integration of the Jews among the peoples of the Middle East. Although he was already nearing his fifties, his criticism of others, and his confidence in himself, are steeped in the spirit of youth. In 1923 he wrote in his diary:

> Herzl's conception was naive, and can be explained by the fact that he failed utterly to understand the conditions among the peoples of the Orient, and create, along with our brethren of the same race—the Arabs (and the Armenians)—a new Near East cultural community. More than ever before, it appears to me, Zionism can only find its justification in the racial association of the Jews with the peoples of the Near East. I am currently gathering material for a book about the Jews, whose basic premise will be the racial issue. I propose to include pictures of the ancient Oriental peoples, and of the modern populations, and to portray types which were to be found in the past, as well as in the present, among the group of nations of Syria and Asia Minor. I intend to show that those very same types are still to be found among present-day Jewry.

Ruppin understood that this approach implied a fundamental change in the Zionist concept, but he was not deterred by this fact. "Zionism will last" he wrote, "only if it is given a radically different scientific basis." The need to set Zionist fulfillment on a scientific foundation, the aspiration to find in Zionism some justification vis-à-vis the Palestine Arabs, and the need to lay down realistic answers based on a knowledge of local conditions—these principles are an integral part of Ruppin's nature. He clung to them later too, even when he discovered that the question was more complicated than it appeared at first, and required other solutions.

Ruppin did not hold on for very long to this idea of integration among the Arab peoples. As soon as he got to know realities better, he sensed that the common racial origins of

Israelis and Arabs, and the resemblance between the Jewish nose and the Armenian nose, did not constitute an adequate basis on which to construct a "new Near East cultural community." In 1925, Ruppin arrived at the second phase of the "Arab question"—the bi-national phase.

During his bi-national state phase, which coincided with his adherence to the Brit Shalom Movement, which he founded in 1926 and left after differences with his fellow-members in 1929, Ruppin believed that Eretz Israel ought to be a common state for two nations. The Jews and the Arabs, in other words, should continue their existence as different and separate peoples, and not merge into a "new cultural community"—but at the same time they should maintain one single state, a bi-national state.

At this point, two things should be stressed. First, as Ruppin grew more and more immersed in his Zionist work and increased in stature, his awareness of the need to ensure the further independent continuation of the profound. He believed that this could be attained, if the aims of Zionism were realized. "World history knows no laws, not even the laws of reasonableness. There is therefore no sense in predicting the future. This is also the answer to those who claim to 'prove' that Zionism has no future." (1932) The second thing is that he saw the essence of Zionism as persistent and expanding immigration and settlement. He regarded these as "essential conditions," and did not diverge from them even when he feared there might be a contradiction between Zionism and the "Arab question."

As early as 1928, in fact, inner doubts of this sort troubled him. "In that conversation it became clear how difficult it is to realize Zionism and still bring it continually into line with the demands of general ethics. I was well and truly depressed. Will Zionism indeed deteriorate into a pointless chauvinism? Is there in fact no way of assigning, in Israel, a sphere of activity to a growing number of Jews, without oppressing the Arabs? I see a special difficulty in the restricted land area. Surely the day is not far off, when no more unoccupied land will be available and the settlement of a Jew will automatically lead to the dispossession of an Arab *fellah?* What will happen then?"

The idea of the bi-national state was supposed to reply to three problems. The first problem was that of nationality.

Each people would preserve its own nationality. The second problem was to prevent the Jews dominating the Arabs, and vice-versa. "Under the aegis of the League of Nations, Eretz Israel must become a state in which Jews and Arabs live side by side, as two nations with equal rights. Neither shall be dominant, and neither shall be enslaved." On the third problem, that of Jewish immigration and the dispossession of the Arabs, Ruppin wrote: "Just as it is the right of the Arabs to remain in the country, so is it the right of the Jews to immigrate thereto." (1929)

This phase, like its predecessor, was a revolutionary one. Here again, as before, Ruppin believed that points of difference could be ironed out objectively speaking but in order to achieve this, other mistakes must not be repeated. "We want to extricate ourselves from the error which was prevalent in Europe for 100 years, and which caused the World War— namely that only one nation can rule in one state."

As regards the abstract formulation, the bi-national state may have provided the answer for Ruppin to the question of how Arabs and Jews would live in common. But as he came to know realities better, he discovered more and more difficulties, and Ruppin, with his intellectual integrity, did not allow generalizations to obscure factual truth. "I am therefore convinced that a number of serious conflicts of interest exist between the Jews and the Arabs. For the time being I do not see how these conflicts can be resolved in such a way as to allow the Jews the possibility of free immigration, and free cultural and economic development—things which are essential conditions for Zionism and in such a way that the interests of the Arabs should not be impaired, on the other hand." (1928)

Ruppin knew, moreover, that the idea of the bi-national state was merely an ideological point of departure, an indication of framework within whose bounds he hoped it would be possible to solve the problem. "In the course of debates within the Brit Shalom Movement, we formulated the concept that the solution must necessarily lie within a bi-national state . . . even the bi-national state, obviously, gave a general reply to the problem, and it was my intention to make use of the Brit Shalom further, as a means of clarifying decisive questions, which would emerge from this general answer." (1936)

And the questions, in fact, still remain: "The 'conflicts of interest' were of a substantive nature." There was the question of land. "On every site where we purchase land and where we settle people, the present cultivators will inevitably be dispossessed." Thus he wrote about immigration: "Since our immigrants, for the vast majority, are people without means, the possibility should not be ruled out that these immigrants would take away the livelihood of the Arabs." Then there was the different standard of living and other factors.

But the main difficulty stemmed from the fact that the Arabs simply did not want the Jews to come to Eretz Israel. Every solution—including the establishing of a bi-national state—faced the alternative of either making allowances for the views and desires of the Arabs, and putting an end to Zionism, or carrying on with immigration, land purchase and settlement, while denying the right of the Arabs of Palestine to determine the future of the country. Any solution, or arrangement, which would be contingent on the agreement of the Arabs, or on the introduction of a democratic constitution whereby decisions on questions at issue would be taken by a majority (an Arab majority naturally)—this implied the cessation of immigration, and of Jewish economic development.

Ruppin understood this, and in his letter to Hans John (May 30, 1928) he wrote: "During our last conversation, you pointed out quite rightly that all the Arabs of Eretz Israel oppose the Zionist Movement, and until we are capable of suggesting a satisfactory solution to the conflict of interests they will carry on being our antagonists. If, under these circumstances, a constitution worthy of the name were granted, it would stand to reason that the Arabs would make use of all the rights assured them by the constitution, to prevent, as a majority, all economic progress on the part of the Jewish minority. The meaning of this would be, quite simply, the end of the Zionist movement."

The crux of the problem, therefore, lies in the impossibility of arriving at agreement and cooperation with the Arabs. But, at this stage, Ruppin still believed that it was possible to find the "redeeming formula," which would serve as a bridge for understanding between Arabs and Jews. And so he founded the Brit Shalom Movement.

As time went on, the "Arab question" did not become any less grave, but in fact worsened. In 1936, Ruppin needed to find a solution for it, no less than he did in 1923, and in fact more. He saw this as a vital necessity, not just to resolve the conflict with the Arabs, but also in order to put relations with himself and with his conscience into proper order. But was there a way of squaring the circle? Did the magic formula exist, to reach agreement with the Arabs, "without thereby ceding the fundamentals of Zionism?"

I was at odds with the other members of the Brit Shalom, in my appraisal of the prospects of reaching an agreement with the Arabs. In this respect, the Brit Members displayed great optimism. They thought that economic advantages, and certain political guarantees, would in themselves be calculated to persuade the Arabs to accept the Jewish national home. There was nothing new in this concept. It was, in fact, just a continuation of the false approach towards the Arabs, which had prevailed in the Zionist movement from its beginning. Nobody ever imagined, beforehand, that those very same Arabs who during the days of Turkish oppression were prepared with equanimity to accept year by year a few hundred meek Jews who lived on *halluka* charity, would struggle by force against tens or hundreds of thousands of strong, straight-backed Zionists at a time when the country was under a free British administration. The 'peaceful infiltration,' which they hoped for so much, proved in reality to be a deceptive illusion. If we could learn any lesson from the history of the world in recent decades, this lesson would be that the political posture of nations is not dependent on considerations of good sense, but on instincts. All the economic advantages, and all the logical considerations, will not move the Arabs to give up the control of Eretz Israel in favour of the Jews, after they consider it was handed to them, or to share this control with the Jews, as long as the Arabs constitute the decisive majority in Eretz Israel. I gave expression to these ideas in a letter to Dr. Jacobson, December 3, 1931, when I wrote: What we can get today from the Arabs—we don't need. What we need—we can't get.

The year 1936 brought Ruppin to the third phase of his approach to the "Arab question." He ceased believing in the possibility of persuading the Arabs to agree to cooperate. No "legal formula," no "political guarantees," no "economic advantages," and no "negotiations" would bring the Arabs to consent to the Jews' return to Zion. This was undoubtedly due not only to the cumulative failures of attempts at dialogues with the Arab leaders, but also to the fact that the Arabs' anti-Zionist political stand grew a great deal more outspoken, and found expression in bloody outbreaks of violence, especially during the 1936 riots.

What next? What are the conclusions? After 16 years of

trial and inner doubts, Ruppin demolished his own entire
ideological structure. He had long since abandoned the Brit
Shalom Movement. He was perhaps disappointed, he was
certainly wiser, but he did not despair, on any account:

> Nowadays, I personally am in a mood of calm and dispassion. I
> have formulated the following theory for myself: It is only natural
> and inevitable, that Arab opposition to Jewish immigration should
> find an outlet from time to time in outbreaks of this sort. It is
> our destiny to be in a state of continual warfare with the Arabs,
> and there is no other alternative but that lives should be lost. This
> situation may well be undesirable, but such is the reality. If we
> want to continue our work in Eretz Israel, against the desires of
> the Arabs—then we shall be compelled to take such loss of life
> into consideration!

As regards his own conscience, and as regards his self-re-
counting, Ruppin was calm and dispassionate. He had formulated a theory for himself, and it satisfied him. But what of the
practical aspect? "And what ought to be done in order to reduce
or remove tensions between the two peoples, since after all, this
tension cannot continue interminably? To my mind, no negotiations with the Arabs today can help us move forward, since the
Arabs still hope to be able to get rid of us, over our heads . . .
not negotiations, but the development of Eretz Israel, as we increase our ratio of the population, and strengthen our economic
power, can lead to a lessening of tension. When the time comes,
and the Arabs realize that it is not a question of negotiations, in
which they are asked to grant us something which we do not
yet have, but of conceding the existence of a reality, then the
weight of facts will lead to a lessening of tension."

To create the facts: immigration, settlement, economic development and so forth. In these activities, Ruppin sees not only
the fulfillment of Jewish longings. Once translated into facts,
they will also convince the Arabs to stop fighting against us.
"We must increase our strength and our numbers, until we
reach parity with the Arabs. The life or death of the Zionist
movement will depend on this. . . . Perhaps a bitter truth, but
it is the truth with a capital T." (1936) "The weight of facts—
the increase of our strength and numbers will lead to a lessening
of tension with the Arabs. When will we reach that stage? Within five to ten years." (1936) In this time-table, things like the
policy of Hitler, the World War and the end of the Mandate,
were not taken into account.

Ruppin's heart-searching over the path to agreement with the Arabs had thus come full circle. The fulfillment of Zionism embodied the solution to the "Arab question." Does this mean that Ruppin realized he was wrong, while his colleagues in the leadership, whom he called "naive" and "ignorant of the Arab problem," were correct? Not at all. The prevalent point of view held that the "Arab question" should be left alone, and it would find its own solution thanks to the prosperity, the development, the progress and the culture which the Jews would bring to the Arabs of the country. Ruppin, on the other hand, stopped dealing with the "Arab question," because he realized that the Arabs would not agree to Zionism, *in spite* of all these things.

In the years that followed, developments were determined as a result of factors unconnected with the pattern of relationships between the "Arab question" and Zionist fulfillment. Nevertheless, I should like to quote Ruppin's point of view on two more issues: the Peel Commission's partition proposal, and the White Paper. They are of interest for the subject of this lecture—if not directly, then indirectly.

Apart from Ruppin, the British Empire too was in a quandary in those years, over the question of Arabs and Jews in Eretz Israel. The solution it proposed (the Peel Commission, 1939) was partition—not integration, not a bi-national state, and not cooperation. This means the establishment of separate states for Jews and Arabs. The Jewish State was assigned an area of some 5,000 sq.km. To give some idea of the proportion, the State of Israel, today, has an area of 20,250 sq.km., in other words four times as large, while the area within the present cease-fire lines is 88,000 sq.km., 18 times larger than the area of the "Jewish State" in the Peel Commission's proposals.

On August 1, 1937, Ruppin wrote:

> After studying the partition proposal, I have come to the conclusion that we shall not be able to absorb the 300,000 Arabs in it. Since it will be impossible to get them to leave of their own accord, it is essential that the Jewish State should have other boundaries, inside of which not 300,000 but at the most 100,000 Arabs, would remain. I have put my "personal" plan for the new Jewish State in writing. According to this plan, the area will be reduced from 5m to 1.5m. dunams.

It should be recalled that in those days there were 363,000 Jews in Eretz Israel, and the 100,000 Arabs whom Ruppin was ready to absorb in the Jewish State would have been equivalent to 750,000 Arabs, absorbed by the Jewish State we have today.

During the Zionist Congress in Zurich, Ruppin brought to the Zionist Executive his proposal to give up two-thirds of the area proposed by the Royal Commission, and to establish a midget Jewish State on an area of 1.5 million dunams. After the Executive meeting he wrote in his diary: "I explained my ideas to him [Weizmann]. I did not feel they made a great impression . . ." (1937) We may disagree with Ruppin's conclusion, but we cannot accuse him of not having learnt the bitter lesson of life side-by-side with the Arabs.

And finally—the White Paper:

> The White Paper was eventually published yesterday. It contains no surprise. . . . I do not know why, but this document irritates me far less than it irritates all the other Jews. Is it because I have grown old, and my senses are dulled? Or perhaps it is because I no longer believe in policies on paper? This White Paper is a direct function of a specific political setup (a united Arab front, England's fear of the Arabs) and it will be just as short-lived as this political setup. (1939)

Chief of staff, officers and guests: I trust you will forgive me for having spoken at length. In other circumstances, I would have been able to end at this point. But in the present forum and in these days, in surveying the development of Ruppin's ideas on the Arab question, I do not want to avoid making a number of concrete observations.

Firstly about what Ruppin called "political setup." When he said that the White Paper was the product of a political setup, and that this would leave nothing of the White Paper when it vanished, he was perfectly correct. Ruppin understood this, not because old age had dulled his senses, but because he had amassed wisdom during his years of work. His view of the White Paper was the result of his understanding, and not of dull senses.

Between then and now, the political setup has in fact changed entirely. A Jewish State has been established, with close to three million inhabitants. We have been victorious in three wars. We have an army whose strength should not be underestimated, and a people standing behind it, investing huge sums of money to aid our economy. Second, the dimensions have changed. When Ruppin thought in terms of Arabs, he meant the Palestine Arabs. When we talk about Arabs nowadays, we mean the Arab states. Not only that, but these states are also supported by the world's second greatest power—the Soviet Union.

Dimensions have changed in the "demographic question" in terms of the size of our own population as well as that of the Palestine Arabs. Geographically, too, there have been changes in the areas settled by us, as well as the areas occupied by our forces today.

Third, the facts are no longer the same. Ruppin was wrong to hope that by creating facts, tensions between us and the Arabs would be lessened. What greater "creation of facts" could there be than the establishment of the State, the concentration of 2.5m. Jews there, and the victories in three wars? But despite this, do the Arabs today agree to sign a peace agreement with us? The facts have been created, but the tension is no less than it was before.

Here I shall permit myself to add one observation. We see the facts which we ourselves create, but everybody who believes that facts are decisive in this issue, must remember that the Arabs, too, could well point to facts—their large and steadily increasing numbers, their influence in the world, the oil resources at their disposal, and so forth. In other words, everybody who adheres to the formula whereby the facts we create will bring the other side to accept us, can just as well point to significant facts on the Arab side the moment he steps into the Arabs' shoes.

At any rate, if we return to Ruppin's forecasts, the facts he hoped for, as regards the increase in strength and numbers, did come to pass. But I fear that they have not yet convinced the Arabs to accept us, or our political existence, to regard us as an acceptable neighbour state with equal rights. Perhaps Ruppin's error on this point stemmed from the fact that he thought in rational categories, whereas Arab opposition stems from emotions.

Fourth, there is his letter to Jacobson of April 12, 1931—about the prospects of an agreement with the Arabs, in which he said: "What we can get today from the Arabs, we don't need. What we need—we can't get." This definition sounds to me very up-to-date, when I sometimes read that today the Arabs are offering us the 1947 partition plans.

And finally, today too, unfortunately, a year after the war, and despite the fact that we are standing on the Suez Canal and on the River Jordan, in Gaza and in Nablus; despite all our efforts—including a willingness for far-reaching concessions—

to bring the Arabs to the peace table—the things which Ruppin said 32 years ago still seem sound. It was during the 1936 riots that he wrote:

> The Arabs do not agree to our venture. If we want to continue our work in Eretz Israel against their desires, there is no alternative but that lives should be lost. It is our destiny to be in a state of continual warfare with the Arabs. This situation may well be undesirable, but such is the reality.

Annexation and Democracy

By Yehoshua Arieli*

My subject today is democracy and the problem of the occupied territories. I will commence by saying that more than one year and a half has elapsed since the war; the peace that was expected at the close of the war hasn't come and the prospects of obtaining it seem to be decreasing. This change in the prospects of peace and of the perspective in general has also led to changes in attitudes towards the occupied territories. It actually seemed at one time that the policies conducted particularly in Samaria and Judea held hopes of creating some kind of normalization. Today, things look different, but then it appeared as if the policy of open bridges would help maintain the status quo without harming too much the national sentiments of the population of these territories.

The same thing happened as far as Sinai is concerned. It can be said that the Sinai Peninsula has become a permanent element in not only military, but also, to some extent, economic planning. As far as the Sinai Peninsula is concerned, here too there seems to be a growing impression that occupation will be maintained for a long time. The formula which the National Unity Government adopted a year and half ago of holding on to the territories until a negotiated peace has been achieved, has for all practical purposes turned into an excuse not to state the terms and aims of the peace and at the same time not to define clearly the aims and methods in the occupied territories, in the fear that any definition concerning either peace or the territories would lead to breaking up the coalition and the beginning of a domestic struggle that all sides, of course, want to avoid.

* Reprinted by special permission from *New Outlook*, July, 1969.

It is therefore not surprising that in this present, what seems to be interim and undefined period, there is a growing tendency, of indeterminate strength, to believe that it is to Israel's advantage to hold on as long as possible, or forever, to the status quo. This view has been explicitly formulated by the group that has made it its ideology: the Movement for a Greater Israel. I am convinced that if the views of this group, or of those knowingly or not close to it, were adopted as policy by the Government, they would have led us to the edge of the abyss and threatened the very existence of the State of Israel. They would destroy our democracy, damage our souls and create a fanatic and retrogressive society in Israel, culturally and morally. Indeed, you have to be either a demagogue or very naive to say that the path to peace is a short one and that we are sure to find it. There is, however, a tremendous difference between policies that are imposed upon us by the force of reality and those we choose for ourselves as desirable. The partisans of annexation and of including the territories within the State of Israel as an aim and goal of policy, bar the way to any other solution and are prepared to endanger both peace and security for an aim which may have various justifications, into which I won't go here.

The question that arises is, therefore, what would happen— and I shall speak only of the domestic aspects—if we really carried out the policy of permanently including the territories formally, or even informally, within the borders of the State of Israel.

I see the danger in three fields: in that of the political regime, of society, and of personal and collective attitudes. The famous Spanish-American philosopher, George Santayana, once said that anyone who isn't prepared to learn from history will have to repeat it. Those who love their country and are concerned over its fate must look at the problems not from the aspect of the present situation or of our desires, but historically, and ask, what will happen, how will our society develop in the supposed new situation of annexing the territories. Implementing a program of that kind would lead to immediate changes in two fields: in our international status and in the composition of the society that for practical purposes would be under the jurisdiction of the State of Israel; in other words, the national composition of our population. As I have already pointed out, the State of Israel has so far defined its position in keeping with international practice, that is that a settlement reached with the signing of a peace treaty would include the return of the occupied territories to a full or at least great extent.

However, if, in one way or another, we were to begin actually to annex the territories and to ignore the fact that we were only in an interim situation, our international situation would change radically. It could be assumed—and today after the illusions that certain circles cultivated concerning America have proven false —it is even clearer that theoretical or practical policies of annexation would have left us in a situation of international isolation, and facing not only a U.N. condemnation but the danger of perhaps being expelled from the U.N. or of the application of sanctions. If we assume that for domestic reasons the United States would not have wanted to participate, these sanctions would be made the responsibility of other countries who were ready to apply them, and we would thereby become a country under siege.

The Siege Situation

I do not want to prophecy whether the State of Israel would be ready to enter into that situation or could hold out in such a situation. For the sake of argument I will assume that we could hold out in a situation of siege and total isolation, the way Rhodesia is actually doing. In many ways, though, of course, the situation isn't the same. Our geopolitical environment is unlike that of Rhodesia. We don't have the tremendous support of a great and rich country like South Africa, nor do the new nations of Africa resemble the Arab world. But let us assume for a moment that we could succeed in holding out in such a situation. There is no doubt that for a state under siege the permanent condition of life is one of war as a natural state of affairs, of being permanently preoccupied with fighting for its very existence. Both society and government would have to reorganize themselves on the basis of a permanent state of emergency. All the economic and human resources would be permanently mobilized to maintain the state's existence and security; the planning and control of manpower resources and economic factors would be concentrated in the hands of an emergency authority. In such conditions no country can allow itself the luxury of party politics or of using the country's resources for the wasteful ways of a working democracy. Actually a kind of unity would have to be established that would not permit any deviations or outlays that were not related to the emergency situation. In this situation, the State cannot be dependent upon a public opinion which may not always support it and will have to guide public opinion and impose on it those views that fit in with what the government thinks necessary for the emergency.

In such a situation the society would also adopt the hierarchical structure of the army command in which the borders between civil and military fields would tend to disappear and in which a new ruling bureaucratic, technological, military and managerial elite would be formed, no longer dependent upon institutions and processes based on the democratic procedure of elections, representation and public control. A state of emergency demands internal cohesion and cannot afford freedom of expression. Censorship and public indoctrination would become necessary to maintain the state of emergency.

We can also assume that the Arab population of the territories would intensify its resistance and terror if this situation became a permanent one for it. The authorities would therefore have to apply increasingly harsh measures of repression, leading to a further vicious circle of terror and repression. Concomitantly with the society's adaption to the state of emergency politically and socially, a process of psychological adaptation would also have to take place. It is impossible to maintain a situation of war under conditions of emergency and fear for an extended time, without the individual's developing defense mechanisms making it possible to withstand the tension of continuing danger and strain.

This last need creates a tendency to reject any criticism coming from the outside and to develop a fanatic nationalism and selfrighteousness refusing to consider any alternatives or to listen to the voice of doubt. A value system will come into being centered completely around the values and norms of national cohesion and national identification. There would also come into being a strange combination of narrow-minded tribalism and fanatic, historic nationalism. That is the kind of combination that exists today in South Africa and which, to some extent, has always been present in situations like those described above.

Ultimately we would be driven into a situation that the American sociologist, Harold Lasswell, has called the "garrison state." This is not a new phenomenon; it has appeared in history at various times and in similar situations. The Spartan community was like that, as were the states established by the feudal warrior-classes in the Middle Ages, the Turkish Mongols at certain times, Sweden at the beginning of the 18th and France in the 19th centuries. As for the 20th century, I shall only recall Japan and South Africa, and, to a certain degree, Soviet Russia.

I have just spoken of the problems implied by international isolation which could be a result of adopting decisions in keeping with the views of our maximalist movement. However, even if we assume, for the sake of argument, that we won't have to face that kind of situation, that we won't be isolated, that we will find persons or groups or countries to help us out of the siege, the question still remains: What will our situation be like politically and socially from the standpoint of the relations between the Arab minority and ourselves if we absorb the large Arab minority of the occupied territories into our midst.

Arabs in a Jewish State

There is no doubt that if we add the Arabs of the West Bank and Gaza to our present Arab citizens, we are talking about one and a quarter million inhabitants today. If we assume that the Arab natural increase and our natural increase plus immigration remain more or less stable, it is not hard to see that within a short time the Arab minority will grow to about 40 per cent. How will a state with a 40 per cent Arab minority be able to maintain and develop its institutions and unique democratic character?

Among the members of the Greater Israel Movement, and its knowing and unknowing supporters, there are some who argue that it would be possible to grant immediate civil rights to the large minority on condition that the State forego its national and Zionist character. I have no debate with these people since it is clear that giving up the State's mission puts the situation of the Arabs in a new light, though I doubt whether the Arab side, for its part, would be prepared to give up its own national character. My argument, however, is with those circles who, in the name of Jewish history, of the historic rights of the Jewish people, of Israel's security as a Jewish State, want to annex this minority and thereby, with their own hands, destroy the character of our society as both a Jewish society and a democratic one.

We, therefore, have to ask what would happen if, as we would be obliged to do, we granted equal civil rights to this large Arab minority. From this standpoint, the State of Israel is undoubtedly not like other countries. There are countries, especially in the West, and my example is the United States, where both nationality and citizenship are defined in general and universal terms. That is—both citizens and the state are defined in inclusive terms permitting any person to become a citizen and identify himself with the state. The definition of citizens may either be historical or universal as in the United States and to some lesser extent in the enlightened democracies of Europe.

The situation in Israel is different. Without going into evaluations or into details, Israel is the national state *par excellence*. It is the classic antithesis to American democracy from the viewpoint of national character. The State of Israel's uniqueness lies first and foremost in the simple fact that it was formed and exists in order to solve the problem of the Jewish people as a whole, which is dispersed the world over and which can return to its land if it wants. What is more, this state's function is not limited, as in most of the countries existing today, to those problems deriving from the existing population within its borders. The state's functions are transcendental—that is, go beyond the borders of the State and beyond the given present to the future and to the people as a whole, in order to solve its problem.

It is clear now that for this kind of state and nationalism the possibilities of non-Jewish identification are limited. Even when the non-Jew has full rights, can identify with the society as one maintaining law and security, supplying services and the possibilities of livelihood and personal development, he can only if he is a Zionist at heart identify himself with the transcendental aims of the state. This is true too for the Arab community living in the country who are citizens of Israel and whom we considered full citizens. Though this minority never fled or was caused to flee from the country, has lived and chosen to live with us from the very beginning, has developed with the State of Israel itself, improved its situation and found many common points of contact with the state, there is still no doubt that this minority has been torn in its hearts and in its loyalties.

However, there is a considerable difference between the situation of the Arab citizens of Israel and the large minority we are adding to them, on whom we are imposing citizenship against its will, which has been educated in blind hatred for 20 years, has gone through the suffering of the refugee camps and therefore justly or unjustly looked upon this country as an expropriator. In practice, we can assume that this minority would never be ready to accept citizenship, and if it accepted it with its 40 per cent minority, would form an irredentist movement destroying the democratic structure of the country and compelling us against our will to move from a situation of equality and equal citizenship to increasing repression and all that involved.

Dangers of Discrimination

I therefore, don't assume that that would be the path we would take. It is much more reasonable to assume that those supporting this aim are actually talking of what they call encouraging emigration of a transition period without civil rights. It is clear that as long as this encouragement of emigration is left to natural trends, it will not succeed. The Arabs have learnt the lesson that it doesn't pay to leave this country if there is no need. This encouragement would, therefore, have to adopt other methods, which would only intensify the hatred of the refugees and worsen their situation immeasurably, or compel us to go over to a situation of open discrimination.

It is clear that a situation of complete discrimination would bring us back to the same situation that I spoke of when I spoke of the results of international isolation. It would put us into a situation where the state would have to deny to one part of its population its essential rights. It would have to differentiate between the one community and the other, and here I would like to quote Abraham Lincoln, changing only one word, that: a democratic government cannot remain for a long time half democratic and half oppressive. It must change and become either the one or the other. I have no doubt what would happen to us. We would have to adapt ourselves to a state that was unwillingly turning into a police state, to a government whose need to maintain a special class with the responsibility for repression would affect its own mentality. We would have lost our souls for some additional territory.

I have drawn for you here the two results that seem to me to be inevitable if we make the inclusion of the Arab community and the annexation of territory an end in itself rather than a temporary problem which we have to solve. Finally I would like to point out that in these circles—which to my sorrow include persons who grew up in the labor movement and were educated to socialism—we find developing a kind of nationalist and mythological mentality which prepare them psychologically and intellectually for a situation in which one part of the State would become a ruling people and the other part a people without rights and without self-determination.

I don't say that these attitudes are held today by a large part of the Jewish community. On the contrary, I am sure that their part is small, though it is very influential and vocal especially in the mass media. But I would like to warn ourselves not to allow ourselves to drift against our will and by endless improvisations, into a position and situation that will force us into roles and activities we would abhor and avoid by all means if we had a choice.

PART VI

The Yom Kippur War
and After

The documents included in this section refer to the situation in the Middle East created as the result of the "fourth round." Particularly illuminating are the speeches by Egyptian President Anwar Sadat, which deal with the prehistory of this war and Egypt's relations with the Soviet Union and the United States, and provide the official Egyptian version of the last phase of the war after Israeli troops crossed the Suez Canal. After the end of the war a commission was appointed by the Israeli parliament, the Knesset, to investigate why Israel was taken by surprise on October 6, 1973, and also the setbacks suffered during the first days of the war. This commission, headed by Justice S. Agranat, prepared a detailed report—of which, however, only a small part has been published. Yasir Arafat's speech at the U.N. General Assembly on November 13, 1974, restates the case of the Palestine Liberation Organization, while Dr. Habbash's interview reflects the more radical position taken by his organization, the Popular Front for the Liberation of Palestine. In his speech Arafat stated that "we include in our perspective all Jews now living in Palestine who choose to live with us there in peace and without discrimination." The slogan of a democratic Palestine cannot, however, be easily coordinated with the demand to preserve the Arab character of Palestine. General Harkabi's essay analyzes this contradiction on the basis of discussions between leading members of the Palestinian resistance.

Speech (October 15, 1973)

By Hafiz al-Asad*

Brother compatriots, brother military men, sons of our Arab people, with great pride in you and your great steadfastness I address you today from the bastion of steadfastness, the immortal Damascus whose great steadfastness against the enemy's barbarous raids has become the symbol of the steadfastness of our entire Arab homeland and a cause for pride of all our Arab nation. This city will remain as towering as [Mount] Qasyun in the protection of its sons who are meeting the challenges with strong resolve and who are facing difficulties, no matter how big, with more resolve and iron will and increased determination to achieve victory.

The steadfastness of Damascus stems from the steadfastness of its sister towns of this struggling country; from the steadfastness of Homs, Latakia, Tartus and Baniyas, and also from the steadfastness of Cairo and every capital, town and village in the Arab homeland. This is because, basically, this steadfastness is the practical expression of the will of our people and their determination to live the life of dignity to which they aspire and to make bright the future that they wish for themselves and for all the peoples of the world.

Ten days ago I addressed you on the day which marked the end of a stage during which the enemy had wanted his repeated aggressions to consolidate occupation and expansion and pave the way for imposing his will on our nation. Today I address you as the battle takes its real shape as a full war of liberation. Its first achievement has been the liberation of the Arab will from the elements of pressure. God willing, it will

* President and Supreme Commander of the Armed Forces, Syria. Radio and television broadcast (Damascus).

end with the liberation of the land which its sons have long desired.

In those 10 glorious days of ferocious battles waged by our armed forces with all their arms and with extreme manhood, bravery and unshakable faith in victory—in those days of magnificent, heroic steadfastness of our people we corrected many erroneous ideas which had almost become established abroad about our nation. We have restored self-confidence to the Arab individual after dressing his wounded dignity and proving to the enemy and all the world that our people are not an easy prey that the enemy thought it could easily swallow. We have proved that certain death awaits anyone who tries to humiliate our people or debase an inch of our land.

You have revived the traditions of our glorious nation, of the fathers and the forefathers. You have pleased God, the homeland and the sense of moral goodness. With chaste blood you have charted on the map of Arab struggle a road which will never change after today. It is a road to victory.

You have been supporting the cause of your nation and therefore your nation rose to support your steadfastness. You have been with the cause of freedom and therefore the free men in the world rushed to express their support for your giant stand. They have expressed it in various ways.

You have won the respect, appreciation and admiration of everyone. The reason for all this was our steadfastness, both by civilians and military, in our readiness to meet hardship with selflessness and in our insistence on proceeding steadily towards the goal, regardless of how costly the sacrifice or however long the road.

During these critical days I was, through my senses and feelings, with every individual. I was with the soldier, the NCO and officer while smashing the enemy tanks with his tank, shelling the concentrations of aggressors with his gun and directing precise fire at the enemy planes which fell in wreckage on the ground; I was with the pilot while defending the homeland's sky with his plane, chasing the enemy planes and smashing the legend of the invincible Israeli air force; I was with the sailor while protecting our coasts with his naval unit and gun and writing new chapters of Arab glory on the seas; I was with every citizen of our noble people; with the worker in his factory while operating the machine with one hand and carrying arms with the other; with the peasant while tilling the land and carrying his rifle; with the employee in his office while doing his duty towards his compatriots in the best manner and with a sense of responsibility; with the man responsible for security and civil defence while carrying out his duties with loyalty and devotion; with the doctor and the nurse as they stood in complete readiness and preparedness to fulfill humane and national duties; with the merchant in his shop as he met the needs of citizens with high patriotic spirit; with the housewives as they cared for the families and children; and with the army of loyal and sincere citizens in their various jobs as they managed the homeland's daily life.

Brothers, you may have questions on your mind which you would probably expect me to answer. Or perhaps you wish me to talk about national and international activities related to the battle, whether these were of a positive or negative nature. But you realize that war has its conditions and requirements which make it incumbent upon us to avoid discussing any matter that would not benefit the war effort.

Nevertheless, in this regard I am anxious to point out that our steadfastness in the war of liberation has begun to give the slogan, "pan-Arabism of the battle", a practical and real meaning. In this regard I would like to express, on your behalf, the greatest appreciation for the role of the sisterly Iraqi forces whose men fought heroically against the enemy and whose blood was mixed with that of their brothers in the Syrian forces. Their participation in the battle has been a true expression of the pan-Arabism of the battle. Greetings to the Iraqi Army and to our people in sisterly Iraq.

The day will come when the Saudi forces and the Jordanian forces will also take part in the battle and play their role in the national battle. Also, the two sisterly states Algeria and Libya, from the first moment [of the battle] took the initiative to give practical backing and actual support with various forms. The United Arab Amirates and the state of Qatar also extended a helping hand.

The support that was given to the northern front was matched by support to the western front where the valiant Egyptian forces are fighting major battles against the enemy after they humiliated him and defeated him. This defeat made the enemy resort to contradictions and exposed him to the entire world. This happened when the Egyptians crossed the Suez Canal, destroyed the enemy fortified positions and continued their advance into Sinai steadily and with strength.

If this indicates anything, it indicates Arab unity. It also indicates that our nation is alive. Our unity and vitality appear most gloriously during crises and hardships. We should not forget that our steadfastness is the fundamental and basic factor in every stand. On this rock all the enemy's attempts will be crushed. Continuous steadfastness increases the rally of the Arab nation around us and their support for us will double.

Our heroes have transformed Israel's aggression, since 6th October, to a retreat of the enemy forces. As I told you on that day, our forces rushed to repulse the aggression, forcing the occupation forces to withdraw before them. They continued their advance and expelled the enemy forces from Mount Hermon, Qunaytirah, Jibbin, Khushniyah, Jukhadar, Awl Al, Tall al-Faras and Rafid and other villages and positions in the Golan. They inflicted on the enemy losses which deeply shook the Zionist entity. At that time, while the enemy was hiding his losses and defeats from the people of Israel and from the outside world—a method which he is still following—we in turn kept quiet about the victories of our forces and postponed announcing them.

While the enemy's reports and statements exposed themselves day after day and uncovered more contradictions, we preferred to wait before announcing what we had achieved and until the repelling of the enemy forces is final and the liberation of the land is complete.

We could have announced the liberation of the greater part of the Golan on the fourth day of the battle. The faith of our armed forces in God—praise be to Him—as well as our armed forces' confidence in our people, their proper use of the good weapons in their possession, and their faith in the cause they are fighting for have all reflected on the course of fighting through the victories that our forces have achieved and are still achieving in every field and on every level. The heroic acts of our army have compelled the enemy to admit that the battle is tough and that the fighting is intense.

On our part, we have not anticipated an easy victory or that the enemy would accept his expulsion from our land without ferocious resistance. We know the enemy's expansionist ambitions and know that there are forces encouraging these ambitions and supporting the attempts to achieve these ambitions. In the aftermath of his losses and defeats in the first days of fighting, the enemy hastened to enlist the help of these forces, asking them for assistance and large numbers of foreigners to offset his losses in men in the various corps, particularly the air force as well as new weapons to offset his losses in weapons. With the quick supplies he received and which were added to the calculated reserve forces, the enemy heavily concentrated on one sector of our front and began to exert pressure with the larger part of his forces, tanks and planes and was able to achieve a limited penetration of our lines. Nevertheless, our forces initiated a quick reply and waged, from new positions, fierce fighting in which every member of our forces fought most valiantly and repulsed the enemy counter-offensive and inflicted heavy losses on his tanks and planes and forced him to retreat.

Our forces continue to pursue the enemy and strike at him and will continue to strike at enemy forces until we regain our positions in our occupied land and continue then until we liberate the whole land.

We know that our enemy has a source to supply him and offset his losses in men and weapons. However, we are confident of the resources of our people and nation and the sources of our support. I say to those who are supporting the falsehood and aggression of Israel that they should consider and think of the consequences that their hostile aggressive attitudes will have on their many interests in the Arab homeland. By gaining the animosity of the masses of our nation, they are arousing the anger of these masses. And when peoples become angry, no force can stand in their way.

Brother compatriots, brother soldiers, freedom and dignity have a price and the price is no doubt costly. However, we are ready to pay this price in order to preserve honour, to defend freedom, to liberate the land and to regain the rights so that we can give the coming Arab generations their right to an affluent life and a shining, smiling future in which they can enjoy freedom, security, reassurance and peace.

We are knocking at the door of freedom with our hands and with all our strength, realizing that the enemies of peoples do not voluntarily recognize the freedom of these peoples. We are determined that the liberation of the land and the achievement of victory in this war be the great goal from which we shall not budge, God willing. For the sake of the great goal, every sacrifice and effort will be cheap. As long as our goal is great and as long as we believe in this goal, our effort and struggle will be commensurate with our goal. As long as we believe in the goal, all enemy efforts and psychological warfare tactics will be defeated and fail and will definitely not affect the morale of our people and their ability to hold out and resist.

We are a people who, in the hour of decisiveness, are capable of creating miracles. The hour of decisiveness has come. Let us adapt ourselves to continue the war of liberation to its victorious end. Let us continue the war of liberation with a deep breath, believing in God, confident in ourselves and of our ability to make victory with our own hands.

Finally, on your behalf, I convey a greeting—coming from a heart full of love and appreciation—to all the men of our armed forces. I hail their courage, valour, high efficiency, firm faith in the cause of their homeland and their certain capability to wrest the right. Greetings from the heart to every Arab soldier who is helping to make victory in the battle of liberation certain. Greetings to every one of you. Let us all reiterate at all times: either martyrdom or victory.

Message to Hawari Boumedien (October 9, 1973)

By Leonid I. Brezhnev*

President Hawari Boumedien [of Algeria] late last night received the USSR Ambassador, who handed him an important message from the CPSU Central Committee General Secretary on the Middle East situation. The message said:

The responsibility for the new military flare-up in the Middle East lies wholly and completely with the Tel Aviv leaders. While enjoying the support and protection of imperialist circles, Israel continues its aggression started in 1967 against the Arab countries, and foils every effort to establish a just peace in the Middle East and deliberately carries out provocations, including armed provocations, against Syria, Egypt and Lebanon, thus aggravating to the extreme the situation in this region.

I believe, dear comrade President, you agree that [in] the struggle at present being waged against Israeli aggression, for the liberation of Arab territories occupied in 1967 and the safeguarding of the legitimate rights of the Arab people of Palestine, Arab fraternal solidarity must, more than ever be-

* As broadcast at Algiers.

fore, play a decisive role. Syria and Egypt must not be alone in their struggle against a treacherous enemy. There is an urgent need for the widest aid and support of the progressive regimes in these countries who, like Algeria, are the hope for progress and freedom in the Arab world.

The Central Committee of the CPSU and the Soviet Government are firmly convinced that the Algerian leaders, who are widely experienced in the anti-imperialist struggle, understand full well all the peculiarities of the present situation and that, guided by the ideals of fraternal solidarity, will use every means and take every step required to give their support to Syria and Egypt in the tough struggle imposed by the Israeli aggressor.

Dear comrade President, your high personal prestige in the Third World countries which in particular contributed to the great success of the fourth non-aligned conference, clearly gives you the indisputable means to act with the Arab states with a view to bringing about a united stand in the face of the common danger.

As for the Soviet Union, it gives to the friendly Arab states multilateral aid and support in their just struggle against the imperialist Israeli aggression.

Speech (October 16, 1973)

By Anwar Sadat*

In the name of God, brothers and sisters, I would have liked to have come to you before today and meet you and the masses of our people and nation, but I was preoccupied with what you know about and in the way you want. I am confident that you will understand and excuse me.

However, I felt your presence and that of our people and nation with me in every opinion. I felt your presence and that of our people and nation with me in every decision. You were all with me in the matter that I have shouldered as an expression of the will of the nation and of the destiny of a people.

Then I found it suitable to come to you today to speak to you and to the masses of our people and the peoples of our nation as well as to a world that is interested in what is hap-

* Address to the People's Assembly (Cairo).

pening in our land because it is closely related to humanity's gravest issues, the issue of war and peace. This is because we do not consider our patriotic and national struggle as a local or regional phenomenon, since the area in which we live has its strategic and cultural role at the heart of the world and the centre of its movement. And since the events are important and the developments were successive and the decisions were decisions of destiny, I would like to begin straight away with what I would like to talk to you about. I shall concentrate on two points: war and peace.

First, war. I do not think you expect me to stand before you so that we can together boast about what we have achieved in 11 days of the most important and gravest—in fact the greatest and most glorious—days in our history.

Perhaps the day may come when we shall sit together, not to boast, but to remember and to study and also to teach our children and grandchildren generation after generation the story and hardships of struggle, the bitterness and sufferings of defeat and the sweetness and hopes of victory. Yes, the day will come when we shall sit and relate what everyone of us has done in his own position and how everyone of us shouldered his trust and carried out his role. We shall tell how the heroes of this people and this nation came out in pitch black days to carry the lighted torches to lighten the path so that their nation can cross the bridge between despair and hope. The time will come for all that.

I think you will agree with me that we have problems and tasks to which we must devote all our time and efforts. If I may pause a little—although I know that you are craving to hear more—then I say the following:

(1) Regarding myself I have tried to fulfil my pledges to God and to you exactly three years ago today. I pledged to God and to you that the question of liberating the patriotic and national soil was the first responsibility I assumed in loyalty to our people and to everyone. I pledged to God and to you that I would spare no efforts or sacrifices, regardless of their costs to me, for the sake of enabling the nation to reach a situation where it can raise its will to the level of its aspirations. For I have always believed and still do that a wish not backed by will is like daydreaming. My love for and loyalty to this homeland refused to fall prey to the mirage or fog of daydreaming. . . .

I say without pretence that history will record for this nation that its setback was not a downfall but a passing stumble, and that its movement was not an outburst but a lofty rise. Our people have exerted unlimited efforts, made unlimited sacrifices and shown unlimited maturity. More important than all that—the efforts, sacrifices and maturity—the people have maintained unlimited faith. This was the dividing line between the setback and failure.

I have felt that from the first day I assumed responsibility and willingly accepted the burdens God placed on my shoulders, I knew that the people's faith was the foundation. If the foundation were sound, then we could regain everything that we lost and once again return to the place we retreated from. Despite many manifestations, some of which were natural and others fabricated owing to the psychological warfare waged against us, the question facing me and others every succeeding day was: is the foundation sound? I was confident that no psychological warfare, no matter how fierce, could affect the firmness of this foundation. So long as the foundation was all right, then everything else should be all right. The rest was nothing but a storm in a teacup, as they say.

I (? admit) we faced many real problems, problems in the services, supply, and production and also in political work. I knew the truth, but I was not in a position to explain it. I knew that we had to make life bearable for the people and at the same time take precautions for what was expected. I was certain that the day would come when the truth would be known to others as it was clear to me. When the truth is known, the people will know and appreciate it. I thank God.

(3) There were clear indications that the entire Arab nation was in a state of rupture. I thought this was natural because of social and cultural reasons that were aggravated by the bitterness of the setback. Some asked me and asked themselves as well: Will the nation be able to face its terrible trial while in this state of rupture? I used to say: In addition to its natural causes, this rupture reflects the contrast between reality and hope. There is no advantage in this. I even believed that there would be no cure or rest from what the nation's conscience was suffering from, except when the nation would face the moment of challenge. At certain times I was not prepared to enter into futile discussions: Should we deal with the rupture before facing the challenge, or accept the challenge despite the presence of indications of rupture? My opin-

ion has been that nations can discover themselves or their mettle only through engaging in struggle. The greater the challenge is, the greater will be the awakening of the nation and its discovery of its capabilities.

I do not deny the existence of social and cultural differences, for this is the course of history. But at the same time I realize that great nations, when faced with great challenges, are capable of clearly determining the priorities for themselves in a way that leaves no room for doubt. I have believed in the soundness and firmness of the call of Arab nationalism. I have been aware of the various interactions which motivate the progress of the one nation. But I have also been confident that unity of action would impose itself on all the powers, quarters and currents because they would all realize that the present condition is not one for competition between various interpretations, but one of struggle involving the life or death of an entire nation, thank God.

(4) I have been aware of the quality of our armed force. When I spoke about them I was not predicting the future or speculating. I have come up from the ranks of these armed forces and personally lived according to their traditions. I had the honour of serving in their ranks and under their banners. The record of these forces is bright, but our enemies —old and new imperialism and world Zionism—concentrated against this record in a terrible manner because they wanted to make the nation doubt its shield and its sword. I had no doubt whatsoever that these armed forces were the victim but never the cause of the 1967 setback.

In 1967 these forces would have been able to fight with the same valour and courage with which they are fighting today had their military command not lost its nerve after the strike against which Abd an-Nasir [Nasser] had warned, or had the command not issued an order at that time for a general retreat from Sinai without Abd an-Nasir's knowledge as well. These forces were not given the chance to fight in defence of the nation, its honour and its soil. They were not defeated by the enemy but were exhausted by the conditions, which did not give them a chance to fight. I participated with Jamal Abd an-Nasir in the rebuilding of the armed forces. Then destiny decreed that I should bear the responsibility of completing the rebuilding operation as well as of being their supreme commander.

The Egyptian armed forces have achieved a miracle by any

military standard. They have fully devoted themselves to their duty. They have efficiently absorbed all the weapons and methods of training of the modern age, as well as its sciences.

When I gave them the order to reply to the enemy's provocation and to check his deceit, they proved themselves. After the orders were given them, these forces took the initiative, surprised the enemy and threw him off balance with their quick movement. I shall not be exaggerating to say that military history will make a long pause to study and examine the operation carried out on 6th October 1973 when the Egyptian armed forces were able to storm the difficult barrier of the Suez Canal which was armed with the fortified Bar Lev Line to establish bridgeheads on the east bank of the Canal after they had, as I said, thrown the enemy off balance in six hours.

The risk was great and the sacrifices were big. However, the results achieved in the first six hours of the battle in our war were huge. The arrogant enemy lost its equilibrium at this moment. The wounded nation restored its honour.

The Middle East political map has changed. While we say so out of pride, as some of the pride is faith, we are duty bound to record here, on behalf of the people and this nation, our absolute confidence in our armed forces; our confidence in their command, which drew up the plan; our confidence in the officers and men who have implemented the plan with fire and blood. We record our confidence in the armed forces' faith and knowledge, our confidence in the armed forces' arms and in their capability of absorbing the arms, I say in brief that this homeland can be assured and feel secure, after fear, that it now has a shield and a sword.

From here I want to draw your attention with me to the northern front, where the great Syrian army is fighting one of the most glorious battles of the Arab nation under the loyal and resolute command of brother President Hafiz al-Asad.

I want to tell our brothers on the northern front: You made a promise and you were faithful to the promise. You made a friendship and you have turned out to be the most honest friends. You have fought and you have proved to be the most courageous fighters. You have fought like men and stood fast like heroes. We could not have found more reassuring and praiseworthy men in this comradeship in which we had to fight together against a common enemy, the enemy of the whole Arab nation.

We have been the vanguards of the battle. Together we have borne its brunt and paid most dearly with our blood and resources. We shall continue the fighting and defy danger. We shall continue, backed by our brothers who have sincerely and faithfully joined the battle, to pay the price in sweat and blood until we reach an objective acceptable to us and to our nation in this serious stage of its continuous struggle.

That was about war—and now that about peace. When we speak about peace we must remember and not forget—just as others also must not pretend to forget—the real reasons for our war. You will allow me specifically and categorically to put some of these reasons to you.

(1) We have fought for the sake of peace, the only peace that really deserves to be called peace—peace based on justice. Our enemy sometimes speaks about peace. But there is a vast difference between the peace of aggression and the peace of justice. David Ben Gurion was the one who formulated for Israel the theory of imposing peace. Peace cannot be imposed. The talk about imposing peace means a threat to wage war or actually waging it.

The great mistake our enemy has made is that he thought the force of terror could guarantee security. But the futility of this theory has been proved in practice on the battlefield. It has been proved that if this theory did work at one time, due to the weakness of the opposite side, it does not work if these people rally their forces every day. I do not know what David Ben Gurion would think if he were in command in Israel today. Would he have been able to understand the nature of history or would he be like the Israeli command today —in opposition to history?

Peace cannot be imposed. The peace of a fait accompli cannot exist and cannot last. There can only be peace through justice alone. Peace cannot be established through terror however oppressive and whatever illusions the arrogance of power or the stupidity of power might give. Our enemy has persisted in this arrogance and stupidity not only over the past six years, but throughout the past 25 years—that is, since the Zionist state usurped Palestine.

We might ask the Israeli leaders today: Where has the theory of Israeli security gone? They have tried to establish this theory once by violence and once by force in 25 years. It has been broken and destroyed. Our military power today challenges their military power. They are now in a long pro-

tracted war. They are facing a war of attrition which we can
tolerate more and better than they can. Their hinterland is
exposed if they think they can frighten us by threatening the
Arab hinterland. I add, so they may hear in Israel: We are
not advocators of annihilation, as they claim.

Our Zafir-type trans-Sinai Egyptian Arab rockets are now
in their bases ready to be launched at the first signal to the
deepest depth in Israel.

We could have given the signal and the order from the very
first moment of the battle, particularly as the Israelis' haughti-
ness and vicious pride gave them the illusion that they could
bear greater consequences than they really could sustain. But
we are aware of the responsibility of using certain types of
arms, and we ourselves restrain ourselves from using them. The
Israelis should remember what I once said and still say: an eye
for an eye, a tooth for a tooth and death for death.

(2) We do not fight to attack the territory of others, but
we fought and will continue to fight for two objectives: (a) to
restore our territory which was occupied in 1967; and (b) to
find ways and means to restore and obtain respect for the
legitimate rights of the people of Palestine.

These are our objectives in accepting the risks of the fighting. We have accepted them in reply to unbearable provocations. We were not the first to begin these, but we acted in
self-defence to defend our land and our right to freedom and
life.

Our war was not for aggression, but against aggression.
In our war we did not depart from the values and laws of
international society as stipulated in the UN Charter, which
the free nations have written with their blood after their victory over Fascism and Nazism.

We may say that our war is a continuation of humanity's
war against Fascism and Nazism; for, by its racist claims and
its reasoning of expansion through brute force, Zionism is
nothing but a feeble replica of Fascism and Nazism which is
contemptible rather than frightening and calls for disdain
more than for hatred.

In our war we have behaved in accordance with the provisions and spirit of the UN Charter, and not vice versa. In
addition, we have behaved out of respect for the UN resolutions, both those of the General Assembly and of the Security
Council.

Brothers and sisters, the entire world has supported our

rights and praised our courage in defending these rights. The world has realized that we were not the first to attack, but that we immediately responded to the duty of self-defence. We are not against but are for the values and laws of the international community. We are not warmongers but seekers of peace. The world has realized all this, and in the light of it sympathizes with our cause.

Today, the world sympathizes with us more out of its respect for our determination to defend this cause. We were sure of world sympathy, and now we are proud of its respect for us. I tell you in all sincerity and honesty that I prefer world respect, even without sympathy, to world sympathy that is without respect. I thank God.

Brothers and sisters, a single state has differed from the whole world—not just from us, but from the whole world, as I said. This state is the United States. The United States claims it was shocked because we tried to repulse the aggression. We do not understand how or why the United States was shocked. This state, it said, was not only shocked but has recovered from the shock without coming to its senses.

It is regrettable and sad that this should be the attitude of one of the two superpowers in this age. We were expecting; or perhaps wishing, despite all the indications and experiences, that the United States would recover from the surprise and come to its senses. But this did not happen. We have seen the United States recovering from the surprise and turning towards manoeuvres. Its first objective is to stop the fighting and bring a return to the lines that existed before 6th October. We could have been angered by this inverse logic, but we were not. This is because, on the one hand, we are confident of ourselves, and, on the other, we really do want to contribute to world peace.

The world is entering an era of detente between the two superpowers. Now we oppose the policy of detente. We had one reservation about this policy and this reservation still exists. If we want the world, after a world war has become impossible, to enter an era of peace, then peace is not an abstract or absolute meaning. Peace has one single meaning: that all the peoples of the world should feel that it is peace for them and not peace imposed on them.

I would like to say before you and to all the world that we want the policy of detente to succeed and to be consolidated.

We are prepared to contribute to the success of this consolidation. But we rightly believe that this cannot happen while aggression is being committed against an entire Arab nation, which lies strategically in the heart of the world and possesses its most important economic resources. Any disregard of this logical fact is not only disregard but also an insult, which we do not accept, either for ourselves or for the world, which is aware of the importance and value of this area in which we live. Therefore, the world must realize now that this area can give and can withhold.

Brothers and sisters, the United States, after a manoeuvre we refused even to discuss—especially after we had forged the path of right with the force of arms—has resorted to a policy that neither we nor our Arab nation can keep silent about. It has established a quick bridge to transport military aid to Israel. The United States was not content with the fact that it was its arms that enabled Israel to obstruct all attempts for a peaceful solution of the Middle East question. It has now involved itself in something with more serious and more dangerous consequences.

While we are fighting aggression and are trying to remove its nightmare from over our occupied territories, the United States rushes to the aid of the aggressor to compensate him for his losses and to supply him with what he did not have before.

The United States has established a sea and air bridge along which new tanks, new aircraft, new guns, new rockets and new electronics [equipment] pour into Israel. We tell them: This will not frighten us. But before matters reach the point of no return, you and we must understand: What is this leading to, and for how long? Where [are you going] to, when we and not Israel shape the map of the Middle East? Where to, when your entire interests are with us and not with Israel? Where to and for how long?

Brothers and sisters, I have thought of sending President Richard Nixon a letter in which I would clearly define our position. But I hesitated lest this might be misinterpreted. For this reason, I have decided instead to address an open message to him from here. This is a message dictated not by fear but by confidence. It is a message that emanates not from weakness but from a genuine desire to protect peace and bolster detente. I wish to tell him clearly that our aim in the war is well known and there is no need for us to explain it again. If you want to know our terms for peace, then here is our peace plan:

(1) We have fought and will fight to liberate our territories which the Israeli occupation seized in 1967 and to find a means to retrieve and secure respect for the legitimate rights of the Palestinian people. In this respect, we uphold our commitment to the UN resolutions, [those of] the General Assembly and the Security Council.

(2) We are prepared to accept a cease-fire on the basis of the immediate withdrawal of the Israeli forces from all the occupied territories, under international supervision, to the pre-5th June 1967 lines.

(3) We are prepared, as soon as the withdrawal from all these territories has been completed, to attend an international peace conference at the United Nations, which I will try my best to persuade my comrades, the Arab leaders directly responsible for running our conflict with the enemy [to accept]. I will also do my best to convince the Palestine people's representatives about this so that they may participate with us and with the assembled states in laying down rules and regulations for a peace in the area based on the respect of the legitimate rights of all the peoples of the area.

(4) We are ready at this hour—indeed at this very moment —to begin clearing the Suez Canal and to open it for world navigation so that it may resume its role in serving world prosperity and welfare. I have actually issued an order to the head of the Suez Canal Authority to begin this operation on the day following the liberation of the eastern bank of the Canal. Preliminary preparations for this operation have already begun.

(5) In all this, we are not prepared to accept any ambiguous promises or loose words which can be given all sorts of interpretations and only waste time in useless things and put our cause back to the state of inaction, which we no longer accept whatever reasons the others may have or whatever sacrifices we have to make. What we want now is clarity: clarity of aims and clarity of means.

Brothers and sisters, we have said our word. I pray to God Almighty that all will understand it within its true framework and will see it squarely and will assess matters rightly. The present hours demand the courage and the minds of men.

For our part, we are facing these hours with the humility of those who are true to God, to themselves, to their nation and to mankind. The biggest battles ever fought with conventional weapons, even in the wars between the giants, are taking place during these hours. Destinies are being shaped and relations are being determined during these hours. The relations that are being determined will impose themselves on the future and are asserting themselves even now.

During these hours heroes are marching forward. During these hours martyrs are falling or, rather, rising up. Conflicting feelings are felt during these hours, hours during which the feelings of happiness are mixed with other deep feelings. This is because we wanted and still want right and not war. But we wanted and still want right even if war was imposed on us. When the elation of victory filled all hearts, I—between myself and my God—was aware of all the sufferings we are undergoing for the sake of victory. I have been following the news of our victory with humility because I know the truth. The dear Almighty has taught us: You have been destined to fight although it is hateful to you [Koranic verse].

Brothers and sisters, these are the moments in which we know ourselves and know our friends and our foes. We have known ourselves; we have known our friends. They have been the most sincere and loyal friends that we could ask for. We have always known our enemy. We do not wish to increase the number of our enemies. On the contrary, we have given one message after another, one notification after another and one warning after another so as to give everyone an opportunity to make revisions [of their attitudes], hoping they would retreat. However, we are, God willing, capable, after saying the word and giving notification and warning, of dealing one blow after another. We shall know when, where and how to do so if they want to escalate what they are doing now.

The entire Arab nation, on whose behalf I take the liberty to speak, has not forgotten the positions taken up during these hours. The Arab nation will not forget the friends of these hours who stand with it. It will not forget the enemies of these hours who stand with its enemy.

God, be our support and guide. God, bless our people and our nation. God, you have promised and your promise is truth. If you support God He will support you and guide your steps. Peace be upon you.

Press Conference (October 31, 1973)

By Anwar Sadat*

. . . The second reason for accepting the cease-fire, in addition to the two superpowers' guarantees of this cease-fire and the immediate implementation of the resolution, is that frankly I do not fight against America. I fought Israel for 11 days. As the Israeli Defence Minister said yesterday, his ammunition would have run out in three days. This was also my assessment. But I am not prepared to fight America.

There was reaction to the cease-fire in this country, in the Arab nation and within our armed forces. But these are the reasons just as I am giving them. It is for these two reasons that I accepted the cease-fire.

In the military situation, there was this question of the wedge in the Deversoir area. In those 11 days everything was taking place in the east, then the new weapons arrived.

This operation reminds me of a similar one which took place about the end of the second world war. The attack was called the two-lands attack. The Allies had closed in on Germany. Then one day the weather forecast said the weather would not be good for flying. The Germans launched a suicidal operation and drove a huge wedge between the allied forces. It was a huge, suicidal operation. Acting on that famous Goebbels formula, the Germans wove a big story. Actually, Germany's fate was decided before that attack. Germany was finished, but it still carried out that desperate attack.

This was what happened. The Deversoir operation was exactly the same operation. It was a desperate operation. They came to the west bank for the purpose of causing confusion in the German fashion, as I told you. We noticed that Israel had adopted the Nazi mentality in all its actions, even in regard to the Bar Lev line they had set up to face us and the other lines behind it. It was exactly like the so-called Atlantic Wall. The Bar Lev line was the first wall followed by three

* Excerpt from a press conference at Cairo.

other lines behind it. It was exactly like the situation in Normandy. They borrowed German methods and Goebbels's propaganda methods as well.

They created the Deversoir gap. It was a suicidal operation like that of the two-lands attack. It was, in fact, a small affair. We do not deny that there were errors on our part. The main purpose and aim of all this was for it to be a psychological and political operation rather than a military operation so that they could weave the big story that they have been weaving in the past five or six days. They created a major uproar in Europe saying that they were about 50 kilometres or miles from Cairo, that they were on the west side and so forth. It was a huge psychological warfare operation to draw the attention of the whole world to the Israeli military.

The Israeli militarists themselves know better than anyone else that the wedge existing today, the pocket existing today on the west bank, is no more than a pocket. As a result the Israeli militarists exploited the cease-fire. They violated the cease-fire after we had accepted it and advanced so that they could say: We are about 50 miles from Cairo. We are on the west bank and are occupying so many square miles. We have seized a town, etc., etc., so we can make up for the Egyptian crossing and the storming of the Bar Lev line.

Our Egyptian young soldiers in the east, whether in the Second or Third Armies, are standing firm. The Israeli operation was no more than a psychological warfare operation. They tried to create a military victory out of it. It was a desperate operation, the aims of the operation are no more than psychological and political ones.

Now they say that they have cut off the Third Army's lines of communication and that they have encircled the Third Army. Just for your information, the Third Army is not only on the east [bank]. The Third Army holds a sector in the east and a larger sector in the west. They know what part of the Third Army is facing them in the west. The positions are intermingled. In the east there is the Third Army. So they came behind in the west. Behind them directly is the rest of the Third Army, or the major part of it. The positions are intermingled, but they wanted to claim: We have taken the west bank and encircled the Third Army.

The story of the Third Army has been exploited in the Goebbels manner. As I have told you, the Third Army has occupied positions and stands as firm as a rock on the east bank, that is, a part of the Third Army. The major part is in the west behind the Israelis. They know this, but they carried out the operation after the cease-fire and put me in a dilemma. Because, with the major part of the Third Army behind them in the west, I could storm my way through and finish off all these people between the east and the west, between the two flanks of the army, but we had committed ourselves to the cease-fire and were embarking on a new affair.

If peace is what is required, then we want peace. I am putting pressure on and restraining my military personnel with great difficulty, because they want to settle this matter and this entire problem. Settling it is easy and the Israelis know this. They know that settling it is easy. I reveal what the Israelis said. This is exposed and verbatim so that I will tell them, and they hear me now [as heard]. They told each other that their position, verbatim, is fragile. They hear me now.

My military personnel are asking me [to continue to fight] but I say let us not break the cease-fire. Let us not have more war. We want to proceed towards solving [the issue]. This is the reason for Isma'il Fahmi's visit to Washington. Presidents Brezhnev and Nixon are aware of all the details of this, minute by minute.

This is the military situation. There is one more point about the military situation. They went to Suez. The Goebbels of Tel Aviv announced that they had occupied Suez. They also took a picture of Mrs. Meir near one of the oil tanks in Suez. For three days they tried to occupy Suez but could not.

The UNEF commander entered Suez. He announced that there was nobody at all in Suez, that it has not been occupied, and that Suez is Egyptian. They wanted to occupy one of the canal towns, particularly Suez because the Canal is named after it. [They tried] for three days. Suez town's resistance and the number of tanks it destroyed merits great praise. The resistance prevented the Israelis from occupying an inch of Suez town.

The Israelis stayed out near Zaytiyah. They brought Mrs. Meir and took her picture near one of the Zaytiyah oil tanks. This was a psychological operation aimed at shaking us. This would enable them to claim that Suez is finished and that they are marching towards Cairo. This is Goebbels's method of propaganda. This is psychological warfare. No, we will not be affected. Our nerves are very strong.

Speech (April 3, 1974)

By Anwar Sadat*

I want to digress here a while to talk about the war decision. You recall that in 1971, I announced that this year must be the year of decision. You also recall that during the same year, 1971, only a few months had passed since I assumed my office. I made an initiative on 4th February 1971 after the termination of the second cease-fire, which was due to be ended on 5th February 1971, for the sake of peace.

The US Secretary of State, Mr. Rogers, came in May 1971. You will also recall that he announced he had nothing to request from Egypt—nothing. After the announcement of the initiative in February, he announced in May that he had nothing to request from Egypt and that Egypt had fully done its part. At that time, we also answered Jarring's memorandum of 8th February 1971.

We waited. May and June passed. On 6th July 1971, I received notification from the US Secretary of State that the United States would intervene to achieve a peaceful solution in accordance with the initiative I had submitted. They asked some questions, including a question about the Egyptian-Soviet treaty which was concluded at that time, May 1971.

After the US Secretary of State had visited here, President Podgornyy came. We concluded the treaty in late May. They [the Americans] put questions, and I answered them. My answer has always been that all our decisions express our free will. Since 23rd July 1952, our will has been free to take whatever decision we see fit to take.

July passed without anything happening. August and September passed. On 11th October 1971 I went to the USSR. I had a long session with the three Soviet leaders. As I have told you before, and as you heard at the [ASU] Central Committee, we reached agreement. We removed the clouds that existed in our relations with the USSR. We agreed in October 1971 on specific deals, and the arms were to arrive before the end of 1971. They asked about the year of decision, why I held to this and why I insisted that the situation be reactivated militarily—because there was no other way.

* Students' conference (Alexandria). Excerpts.

I explained the matter to them very clearly and frankly and in a friendly manner. As I have said, we agreed on arms deals, and the arms were to arrive before the end of 1971.

Relations between ourselves and the United States at that time were not progressing well. On the contrary, their promises in May and July and their failure to fulfil all these promises prompted me to reveal the true American attitude to the people. I attacked them most violently.

This is because the attitude of the US Secretary of State at that time was indeed regrettable. He had reason to feel ashamed and I did shame him before our people, the Arab nation and the whole world.

In 1971, when the first shipments began to arrive, we were supposed to be able to make a decision on the battle on 8th December. I was in the Soviet Union in October. October passed and so did November. And then December came, but there was absolutely no information about the arrival of any shipments or anything. On 8th December the battle between India and Pakistan began. As we all know, the Soviet Union had commitments towards India. We entered December and then more than half of December had gone by—nothing had arrived. The understanding was that these shipments would arrive in October, November and December so that before the end of 1971 we could make a decision and begin operations.

At that time I notified the Soviet Union. About the middle of December I told them that there were only 15 days left before the end of the year and we did not yet even have the dates for the arrival of shipments or vessels. We had no information about them and they had not appeared. I had fixed the year as the year of decision, and therefore I asked if I could visit them in order to avert this situation and that we might solve it together. They fixed a date for my visit—not in January 1972 but in February 1972. This was so that the whole of December and January might have passed, and so would February. As a matter of fact, I almost rejected this date. However, I always place the sublime interest of the cause and the country above personal considerations.

As you have seen, in the past three years, I have experienced and suffered a great deal. I learned [something about the background] afterwards. I went [to the Soviet Union] in February and, as I understood it, their purpose in delaying the date was to let me calm down or cool off a little. This was because I had fixed 1971 as the year of decision and they did not approve of it. Actually they did not approve of any action other than political or diplomatic action.

I went in February, and two months after February in the same year—that is in April. This time they had asked that I visit them and insisted on it because Nixon was going to visit them in May. The first summit conference in Moscow was in May 1972. I visited the Soviet Union again late in April. It was the fourth time. The first was in March 1971. The second was in October 1971. The third in February 1972, and the fourth in April 1972.

The core of the discussion between us was—and I always said it—that the issue would not be activated or solved without military action. The Soviet Union's view was against military action. The discussions used to finish up with the view that even in order to reach a peaceful solution, Israel must be made to feel that we are in a position to talk about a peaceful solution from a position of strength, not weakness. This was the result that we used to end up with, and they used to promise to supply us with arms, etc. etc.

I am not saying this to belittle the arms that we have received. I am continuing the explanation. The April 1972 meeting was held, as I told you, and we agreed at that meeting that after the summit meeting between President Nixon and Secretary Brezhnev in May, [the process of] consolidating Egypt's capability would begin quickly because we agreed that there would be nothing new in the US position in 1972 since it was an election year in the United States. We also agreed that after the elections, that is immediately after November, we had to be prepared. They agreed to this.

I returned from this visit, and in May the summit conference was held in Moscow. I waited for a notification, and after 14 days, I received a notification, including an analysis by the Soviet Union similar to what we had predicted, that is, that there was nothing new in the US position because the US position viewed Egypt and the Arabs as a motionless corpse and they only respect force. So if Egypt and the Arabs were a motionless corpse, why should they [the Americans] act or change their position? The Soviet analysis was the same as our predictions before the April visit, and it came after 14 days. I replied and said: All right, now that the analysis is the same as the one we agreed upon, the questions, as agreed upon with you, are the following:

There were seven clauses—this, that and the other thing.
Therefore, as we agreed, these clauses were to have reached
me by November. We would then be standing on solid ground
after the US elections in November. If they spoke about a
peaceful solution, we would be standing on solid ground and
in a position to speak and say yes or no—we reject or we
agree. Why should a solution be proposed to us when we are
weak? The solution proposed would exactly reflect the extent
of our strength.

My reply was sent to them and I said simply that my reply
was on its way. A whole month passed during which I received no answer. We calculated in days the period between
the Moscow visit, that is the meeting, and November so as
not to lose a single day for the seven clauses that I had requested and that we had agreed upon. A whole month passed.
The first 15 days passed before I received the analysis and
one month before I received an answer. I was surprised by
the answer I received. There was absolutely no mention of
anything about the battle except in the last three lines of the
answer.

Before that, there was the statement about the Moscow
summit meeting between the two giants. The statement included the phrase military relaxation—military relaxation
while Israel had complete superiority and we were short of
several things. However, we were asked to embark on military relaxation. What did this mean? It meant that if such
military relaxation took place in the area at a time when
Israel was superior and we were at the level of our position
at that time, the question would not be solved. It would be
a case of the stronger side dictating conditions to us. We
would either accept or reject. Whether we accepted or not,
they would say: We are staying where we are and that is all.

When I received the answer a month later and it included
absolutely no mention of what we had agreed upon in April,
I made my decisions regarding the Soviet experts, a decision
that you learned about in the summer. As I said afterwards,
the real aim of these decisions was also strategic; analysts
should have been more aware than they were—because anyone who had studied my decisions even a little would have
understood that I intended to enter a battle when I ousted
the Soviet experts. The Soviet experts were not fighters. They
would not enter the battle with me. In fact, they were banned
from going near the Canal. All of them were here in the in-

terior as experts on arms and other types of training. Some were manning SAM-3 missiles after the Abu Za'bal raid.

Our sons were already trained and ready to take over everything. In fact, when the Soviet experts left, our sons took over the SAM-3 emplacements in a matter of seconds. There was no vacuum at all that would have left a gap in our air defences. This never happened because our sons took over immediately.

Actually, my purpose, as I have said, was a pause with the friend on the one hand and, on the other, to tell everyone that I was entering the battle—a 100 per cent Egyptian battle. No one at all can claim that anyone has fought it for me. I do not even have experts for weapons training. That was among the reasons for my decision at that time.

The situation continued. Our brothers in the Soviet Union took a long time despite the fact that I sent the Prime Minister, who was Dr. Aziz Sidqi at that time. I sent him because before we proclaimed the decision [on the Soviet experts] we had to agree on a joint declaration in order to cover anything that the West might exploit. They refused and we declared it unilaterally. The issue was settled and the decision was implemented.

Relations remained frozen between us and the Soviet Union all during the summer. The decisions were taken in July. Relations remained frozen all during the summer until October came, when our brother, President Hafiz al-Asad, went to Moscow and intervened in the matter. Dr. Aziz Sidqi left on 16th October and then returned. It was clearly apparent that relations had begun to move again. However, this was on the surface only. In fact and in essence, relations did not move at all.

It was necessary for the Soviet Union to take time to find out that I did not carry out the operation in agreement with the United States behind their backs. I allowed them to take enough time to find out that the matter was not a dagger in their back in agreement with the United States or others. Not at all. It was a national decision. It was a pause to tell them this procedure was unacceptable—a procedure which amounts to a kind of "wait a little, cool off a little, you cannot move until we want you to move". We do not accept this. We do not accept this procedure. It is not according to our will, which has been free since 23rd July 1952. No one at all can direct us or impose any trusteeship on us.

In December 1972 three months were left before the expiration of an agreement between us and them over facilities in the Mediterranean. We gave them facilities in the Mediterranean, not bases. We do not give bases to anyone. Since 23rd July no one has had bases here with us. We are non-aligned. However, we have extended facilities to them. The agreement was to end in March 1973. Five years would have passed of the agreement, for it was concluded in 1968. The agreement stipulates that three months before its expiry the two sides will agree either to terminate or renew it. At that time, relations were disrupted—exactly as I have told you, and everything was at a standstill.

I asked Field Marshal Isma'il to call the Russian General at the Embassy here and tell him that we had decided for our part, to extend the facilities for another period. This happened three months before the expiration of the agreement.

Nevertheless, I still say that the USSR stood by us in the dark moments of 1967. We are a grateful people. We do not forget past favours.

The Field Marshal called the General and told him about this. The facilities have remained ever since. Early in 1973, Field Marshal Isma'il and Hafiz Isma'il left for the USSR. The two of them concluded a deal. After February 1973 our relations began to be, or to become, normal. Some of [the arms included in] this deal began reaching us after Field Marshal Isma'il's return from the USSR.

As I have told you and as you have already heard from me, the decision on the battle was made last April, April 1973. As I have told you, some of the deal began reaching us after the Field Marshal's return in February. We were happy that our relations would return to normal. But the USSR persisted in the view that a military battle must be ruled out and that the question must await a peaceful solution.

The month of June came and with it the second summit conference between President Nixon and Brezhnev. The first meeting was held in Moscow in May 1972. As I have told you, that meeting resulted in military relaxation. This meant that everything must stop and that Israel would remain superior and that we would remain in our position. It was clear from the statement issued in June 1973 that the two super powers had taken another leap forward. They agreed that nothing should happen anywhere in the world. They agreed to abide by this. The only [trouble] spot left in the world was the Middle East. The Vietnam issue was decided. Nothing would happen there. So the Middle East was the only spot left. Nothing should happen here and everyone should await a peaceful solution. On reading the statement, we found that our issue had been put into cold storage pending a peaceful solution.

Security Council Resolution 338
(October 22, 1973)

THE SECURITY COUNCIL

1. Calls upon all parties to the present fighting to cease all firing and terminate all military activity immediately, no later than 12 hours after the moment of the adoption of this decision, in the positions they now occupy;

2. Calls upon the parties concerned to start immediately after the cease-fire the implementation of Security Council Resolution 242, (1967) in all of its parts;

3. Decides that immediately and concurrently with the cease-fire, negotiations start between the parties concerned under appropriate auspices aimed at establishing a just and durable peace in the Middle East.

Statement in the Knesset
(October 23, 1973)

By Golda Meir

Members of the Knesset:

On 22 October the Government of Israel unanimously decided to respond to the approach of the U.S. Government and President Nixon and announce its readiness to agree to a cease-fire according to the resolution of the Security Council following the joint American-Soviet proposal.

According to this proposal, the military forces will remain in the positions they hold at the time when the cease-fire goes into effect.

The implementation of the cease-fire is conditional on reciprocity. Our decision has been brought to the notice of the Foreign Affairs and Security committee, and now to the notice of the Knesset.

As regards the second paragraph of the Security Council resolution, the Government decided to instruct Israel's representative at the United Nations to include in his address to the Security Council a passage clarifying that our agreement to this paragraph is given in the sense in which it was defined by Israel when it decided in August 1970 to respond positively to the United States Government's initiative for a cease-fire, as stated in the United Nations on 4 August, 1970, and by the Prime Minister in the Knesset on the same day. This was also made clear to the U.S. Government. Israel's acceptance of a cease-fire with Egypt is conditional upon Egypt's agreement, but is not conditional upon Syria's agreement to a cease-fire, and vice-versa.

The Government also decided to clarify with the U.S. Government a series of paragraphs intimately connected with the content of the Security Council resolution and the procedure required by it. It is our intention to clarify and ensure, inter alia, that:

> The cease-fire shall be binding upon all the regular forces stationed in the territory of a State accepting the cease-fire including the forces of foreign States, such as the armies of Iraq and Jordan in Syria and also forces sent by other Arab States which took part in the hostilities.
>
> The cease-fire shall also be binding upon irregular forces acting against Israel from the area of the States accepting the cease-fire.
>
> The cease-fire shall assure the prevention of a blockade or interference with free navigation, including oil tankers in the Bab-el-Mandeb straits on their way to Eilat.
>
> It shall ensure that the interpretation of the term referring to 'negotiations between the parties' is direct negotiations—and, naturally, it must be assured that the procedures, the drawing up of maps and the subject of cease-fire supervision shall be determined by agreement.

A subject of great importance, one dear to our hearts, is the release of prisoners. The Government of Israel has decided to demand an immediate exchange of prisoners. We have discussed this with the Government of the United States, which was one of the initiators of the cease-fire.

I spoke about this with the Secretary of State, Dr. Kissinger. We will insist on an immediate exchange of prisoners. When Dr. Kissinger's plane arrived at Andrews Air Base, the State Department spokesman, Mr. McCloskey, made the following statement to newsmen:

"We believe one of the early priorities should be a release of prisoners on both sides, and we and the Soviet Union have pledged our efforts to obtain assurances that this will be done as a priority matter."

I stress again that this subject is one of the principal tests of the cease-fire, and that there will be no relaxation of our demand that the obligations undertaken by the initiators of the cease-fire be indeed carried out.

I will say several things about our military situation on the Syrian and Egyptian fronts before the cease-fire:

On the Syrian Front

The lines we are holding today on the Syrian front are better than those we held on the 6th of October.

Not only do we now hold all the territory which was under our control before, but our situation has been considerably improved by the holding of positions on the Hermon ridge and also on the front line in the east, which has shifted the previous cease-fire line to a better line supported by a strong flank in the north, on the Hermon ridge.

On the Egyptian Front

The Egyptians did indeed gain a military achievement in crossing the Canal, but in a daring counter-offensive by the Israel Defense Forces, our forces succeeded in regaining control of part of the Eastern Canal line, and to gain control of a large area west of the Canal, an area which opens before us both defensive and offensive possibilities:

(a) This deployment deprives the Egyptian army of its capacity to constitute an offensive threat in the direction of Sinai and Israel, and also prevents them from being able to attack essential installations or areas in our territory.

(b) The forces of the I.D.F. west of the Suez Canal constitute a strong military base for the development of operations initiated by us if required.

In connection with the cease-fire issue, the U.S. Secretary of State, Dr. Henry Kissinger, and his aides called here on their way from Moscow to Washington. The visit was an appropriate opportunity for a thoroughgoing discussion of questions arising from the cease-fire, as well as for an exchange of views, in a friendly spirit, on what was about to happen and what was called for as a result of Israel's response to the U.S. Government's request for agreement to a cease-fire. During this visit, we continued and strengthened the contacts which preceded the Security Council resolution.

In all our contacts with the United States, I learnt that not only does the U.S. have no plan for the borders and other components of peace, but that it is its view that those who offer their 'good services' should see to it that the parties themselves—and they alone—should make proposals, plans, for the future.

Furthermore, I must emphasize that, in accordance with authoritative information to hand, the Moscow talks contained nothing more than is contained in the Security Council resolution. I have to inform you that the Syrian Government has so far not responded to the cease-fire resolution. The fighting on that front continues, and the I.D.F. will operate there in accordance with its plans.

As for the Egyptian front—firing against our forces has not yet ceased, and the I.D.F. is obliged to operate as required as long as the firing continues.

At this stage, I will state only that we are examining the conduct of the Egyptians with close military and political attention. Should Egypt persist in belligerent activity, we shall deem ourselves free to take any action and move called for by the situation.

I shall not go into elaborate evaluations of the political activity which preceded the cease-fire. In any event, it was not we who made approaches concerning a cease-fire. As far as the situation on the fronts was concerned, there was no reason for such an approach on our part. It was not we who initiated the timing and clauses of the Security Council's resolution. On the fronts, our forces were not in an inferior battle position. As aforesaid, we deemed it right to respond to the call of the United States and its President, since:

(a) The State of Israel, by its nature, has no wish for war, does not desire loss of life. All Governments of Israel have been convinced that war would not promote peace.

(b) The cease-fire proposal has come when our position is firm on both fronts, when the achievements we hold are of great value and justify agreement to a cease-fire, despite the enemy's achievement east of the Suez Canal.

(c) We responded to the call by the United States and its President out of appreciation and esteem for its positive policy in the Middle East at this time.

Great importance attaches to our response insofar as concerns the continued strengthening of Israel, with particular reference to the continued military and political aid in the war that has been forced upon us . . .

The Egyptian rulers' attitude to war and to loss of life is different from ours. On record is the statement by the Egyptian President concerning his readiness to sacrifice millions of his people. On 16 October, after the I.D.F. had succeeded in establishing a bridgehead west of the Canal, the Egyptian President delivered a boastful address, mocked at a cease-fire and said inter alia:

> "We are prepared to agree to a cease-fire on the basis of withdrawal of the Israeli forces from all the occupied territories forthwith—under international supervision—to the pre 5 June 1967 lines."

Only a few days passed and Egypt agreed to a cease-fire. Not one of the conditions raised by Sadat in his speech was included in the Security Council resolution.

Paragraph 3 of the Security Council resolution says:

> "The Security Council decides that immediately and concurrently with the cease-fire, negotiations start between the parties concerned under appropriate auspices aimed at establishing a just and durable peace in the Middle East."

According to the agreed version of representatives of the U.S.A., the meaning of negotiations between the parties is direct negotiations between Israel and her neighbors on the subject of a just and enduring peace. No such explicit statement was included in Resolution 242 of the Security Council. Moreover, the present resolution also specifies the timing of the beginning of these negotiations—immediately and concurrently with the cease-fire. And there is no need to stress that we attribute great importance to paragraph 3 of the Security Council resolution, if our neighbors will indeed carry it out . . .

On various occasions the Government of Israel has officially defined its attitude towards Security Council Resolution 242. These statements were made from international platforms and at diplomatic meetings, and we have brought them to the knowledge of the Knesset, its Defense and Foreign Affairs Committee and the public at large.

At this time I shall refer to one statement made on 4 August, 1970, to the U.S. Government, to the United Nations and to the Knesset. This statement too, is connected with a cease-fire, and I shall not tire the Knesset by quoting it in full. However, I consider it necessary to quote from my statement in the Knesset on 5 August. This statement was made on the eve of possible talks with the Arab States, and it is still completely valid.

> "Israel has publicly declared that, by virtue of her right to secure borders, defensible borders, she will not return to the frontiers of 4 June 1967, which make the country a temptation to aggression and which, on various fronts, give decisive advantages to an aggressor. Our position was and still remains that, in the absence of peace, we will continue to maintain the situation as determined at the cease-fire. The cease-fire lines can be replaced only by secure, recognized and agreed boundaries demarcated in a peace treaty.
>
> "In accepting the American Government's peace initiative, Israel was not asked to, and did not, undertake any territorial commitments. On the contrary, the Government of Israel received support for its position that not a single Israeli soldier will be withdrawn from the cease-fire lines until a binding contractual peace agreement is reached."

This terrible war that was forced upon us reinforces our awareness of the vital need for defensible borders, for which we shall struggle with all our vigor.

It is worth noting that, since the outbreak of the war on Yom Kippur, the terrorists have also resumed activities from Lebanese territory. Up to this morning, during this period of 17 days, 116 acts of aggression have been perpetrated, 44 civilian settlements on the northern border have been attacked and shelled, and some 20 civilians and 6 soldiers were killed or wounded in these actions. Our people living in the border settlements may be confident that Israel's Defense Forces are fully alert to this situation. Despite the defensive dispositions operative on this front, it has been proved once again that defensive action alone is not sufficient to put an end to acts of terror.

The war in which we are engaged began with a concerted attack on two fronts. The aggressive initiative afforded our enemies preliminary achievements—but, thanks to the spirit and strength of Israel's Defense Army, which is backed by the entire nation, this attack was broken. The aggressors were thrown back. Considerable portions of their forces were destroyed, and the I.D.F. broke through and crossed the cease-fire lines. From holding battles our forces went over to the offensive and gained brilliant achievements.

On both fronts our forces are now holding strong positions beyond the cease-fire lines, unbroken in spirit. The people is united in support of our army.

Israel wants a cease-fire. Israel will observe the cease-fire on a reciprocal basis, and only on that basis. With all her heart Israel wants peace negotiation to start immediately and concurrently with the cease-fire. Israel is capable of evincing the inner strength necessary for the promotion of an honorable peace within secure borders.

We shall be happy if such readiness is also shown by the people and Government of Egypt. However, if the rulers of Egypt propose to renew the war, they shall find Israel prepared, armed and steadfast in spirit ...

The Agranat Commission Report

On the Public Atmosphere

This report, which is the third—and last—report of the Commission, deals with the subject of the Israel Defence Forces' preparation for the Yom Kippur War in general and with the subject of the operations it conducted in order to contain the enemy. These are the last remaining subjects which the Commission was empowered to investigate, by its terms of reference. With the submission of this report, we reconfirm our conclusions in the first partial report of April 1, 1974, which dealt with the subject of information and its evaluation and the IDF's preparedness in the days before the war, and our reasons for these conclusions, contained in the second partial report of July 10, 1974, which may now be regarded as final conclusions. Accordingly, all three reports must be deemed to be "the Commission's report," within the meaning of section 19(a) of the Inquiry Commissions Law, 1968.[1]

Before discussing the contents of this report we wish to

[1] One matter, which was garbled in the first partial report must be rectified: Where it is stated that the Prime Minister decided in favour of "total mobilization of the reserves," the words in quotation marks should be replaced by the following: "mobilization as recommended by the Chief of Staff and later approved by the Cabinet."

say a few words about the public atmosphere in which most of our report was prepared. Even before the appointment of this Commission there was a deeply-rooted feeling amongst many citizens that grave blunders had been committed by both the military and civilian authorities. This feeling undoubtedly contributed to the tension even before the Commission began its work and led to the expectation that the Commission would complete its work and publish a report exposing the blunders and errors and naming those responsible therefore with the utmost expedition.

However, the immense scope and breadth of the inquiry made it impossible for the Commission to meet these expectations. This was not appreciated by all sections of the public, particularly since the Commission's work was conducted in camera and in the strictest secrecy. The members of the Commission could well appreciate this and were not unduly hampered by the atmosphere of tension referred to above, while remaining alive to the necessity of taking considerable care to refrain from allowing themselves to be influenced by any preconceived opinions.

However, when the first partial report of the Commission was published in April 1974, on the assumption that the public was entitled to know as soon as possible what conclusion had been reached by the members of the Commission with respect to those subjects whose investigation they had completed, there were certain members of the public, including public figures and journalists, who did not agree with these conclusions and recommendations and who did not confine their criticism to the merits of these conclusions—fair and substantive criticism being of course both permissible and desirable in a democratic regime—but resorted to allegations of "favouritism" and "discrimination" on the part of members of the Commission.

It should be noted that just as the law makes it a criminal offence to defame a judge within the framework of his judicial duties, so does it prohibit the publication of insulting and defamatory matter against members of inquiry commissions. But even apart from these provisions it is obvious that there is nothing more likely to poison the atmosphere than allegations of this nature against judges or members of inquiry commissions.

Furthermore, section 41(a) of the Judges Law prohibits the publication of anything likely to influence the course of a court action and this applies equally to the proceedings of inquiry commissions. The purpose of this provision is to prevent the conclusions of a court (or inquiry commission) or tribunal from being influenced by anything save the evidence before it and at the same time to prevent creating, by means of "trial by the press" any preconceived ideas in the minds of the public as to what conclusions and decisions a tribunal should draw.

During the course of our inquiry, however, articles and comments on the subject matter pending before us appeared which were in blatant contravention of these provisions with respect to sub justice. Furthermore, some of the matter published was as irresponsible as to constitute an infringement of the vital demands of security, besides being inaccurate and false. This manifestation provided not only a general cause for alarm but it hindered the Commission from proceeding quietly with its work, particularly since the Commission was unable to reveal the real truth to the public.

This tense—and even ugly—atmosphere made our mission, which was sufficiently difficult as it was, almost impossible, and this raises the question of the future of inquiry commissions, in general, within the framework of the present law. If despite the fact that we were exposed to the barbs of insulting and non-substantive criticism, without being able to react to and refute it publicly we should still have decided to continue with our mission, this was only because we regarded its completion as of the greatest importance and likely to contribute towards enabling the Government to face the test confronting it: that of strengthening and improving the organism on which the safety of the State depends—the IDF.

We wish to make a further general remark at this stage: we do not see any cause for apologising for the fact that it took us 14 months of almost continuous sessions to complete our inquiry, in the light of the number of involved and complicated subjects included in our terms of reference and of the fact that we studied each of them thoroughly and in the greatest detail.

Blocking Actions

In connection with this subject it is important to note the following:

The wealth of documentation, together with the detailed testimony of most ranking officers, permitted us to examine the blocking actions in detail.

The documentation includes discussions and decisions at the government general staff and area command level; orders and reports made at the various military levels; conversations between senior officers before and during the battles; battle-field developments from the point of view of the divisions, brigades and battalions, etc.

We strove mainly to elicit from the mass of material the decisive questions, to pinpoint basic faults and to point to the lessons to be learned from them in order that these might be implemented in the future.

We did not find it to be our task to analyse the political-strategic decisions, the goals of the war or the principles of one war plan or another. These were for us background for examination of the conduct of the battles (in order to examine, for example, if this conduct involved substantial deviations from the principles fixed for the execution of counter-attacks or if some of the steps taken to stop the enemy went counter to IDF battle doctrine).

As for the conduct of battle commanders, evaluation in certain instances involved purely professional judgements and we have recommended that these be investigated by the IDF.

We have decided to concentrate our investigation of the blocking actions in the events of October 8 on the southern front and the events of October 6–7 (till the afternoon) on the northern front. The reasons, in brief, follow:

We had two alternatives—either to examine in a general way all the battles involved in the blocking stage or to analyse in depth the battle that was decisive. We chose the second. Our job was not to write the history of the blocking actions—that would have involved years of work—but to pinpoint the main defects uncovered in this stage.

Many of the defects in this stage derive from the element of surprise. A distinction must be made between the southern and the northern fronts. In the south, the surprise was complete both in time and method of attack so that no effective steps were taken beforehand. In the north, on the other hand, the surprise mainly involved the objectives of the enemy and his method, not so much the attack itself. We chose to examine the battle of October 8 in the south because these were to be the first time that the IDF took the initiative.

What caused this battle to go wrong, among other things, was the deviation from the objectives defined by the Chief of

Staff as well as lack of control on the part of the command and its inability to correctly read the progress of the battle. Furthermore, some of the steps taken that day by various command echelons stemmed consciously or unconsciously from opinions formed by commanders a long time before the Yom Kippur War and not from an analysis of the current situation. It is not our purpose to contradict or endorse these assumptions but only to examine to what extent it was appropriate to apply them given the circumstances.

From this, it is clear that a detailed study should be of the lessons and implications of this battle. It had a far-reaching effect on the entire strategy adopted thereafter by the IDF in the war and it also had potential or actual political implications.

In the South

The exhaustive consideration, running to 746 pages, which we have devoted to these battles, is divided into four parts: the build-up of the forces, the plan, the fighting (the political level, the General Staff and the Command), and the divisions in the battle.

In summing up the results of the battles of October 8, we note the following:

Although the battles failed inasmuch as they did not attain the objectives set by the Southern Command, they were of great significance in the progress of the war. They contained the enemy's bridgeheads, preventing him from completely achieving the first stage of his plan. Although one reserve division was unsuccessful in its attempt to wipe out the bridgeheads, its hard fight contributed to the containment of the enemy's advance and prepared the ground for counterattack. Although another reserve division did not fight for most of that same day due to reasons beyond its control and although it sustained heavy losses on the evening of October 8 and the morning of October 9, these battles opened the way for further moves.

On Tuesday afternoon, October 9, the division deployed for a westward advance. The attempt did not succeed. But when the battle ended towards evening, a battalion reached the vicinity of the canal and thereby exposed the weak spot in the Egyptian alignment through which the IDF would subsequently cross the canal.

Finally, it must again be stressed that on the battlefields where these fights were waged, there were unsurpassed manifestations of sacrifice and bravery on the part of officers and men alike.

At the conclusion of discussions of the October 8 battles, the Commission adds some reservations and remarks about the evidence submitted on this subject.

In the North

These battles were analyzed in a special section covering 311 pages. At the outbreak of the war, and in its early stages, certain basic facts characterized the situation of the Northern Command.

The Command was aware that hostilities might break out and took appropriate measures. Reinforcements were sent in and although the number of units was fewer than considered necessary for the defence of the Golan Heights in the event of an overall war, the imbalance was not intolerable. Units on the Golan were on a relatively high state of alert, although they too were taken aback by the scope and timing of enemy operations when war broke out.

The regulars who fought on the Golan in the initial stages distinguished themselves generally by their stubborn fight and their perseverance, like the reserves who joined them later. Supreme courage was manifest at all levels. At the front itself, units led by junior officers showed great resource. Their sometimes independent and even lone operations influenced the tide of battle in certain cases.

After the Syrian attack had been stemmed, the Northern Command switched from a situation in which the enemy had penetrated to the vicinity of the River Jordan and endangered Eastern Galilee, over to a counter-offensive which left the troops close to the enemy capital and in control of the Hermon crest.

The interim reports issued last year covered the intelligence aspect in the days before the fighting began. The probe of the intelligence aspect after the fighting began, covered the quality and organization of intelligence work, which preceded and accompanied the October 8 offensive on the southern front, as well as the intelligence reaching the units which took part in the fighting itself.

Some of the lessons emerging from what the Intelligence Corps did on the eve of the war and how it functioned hold true for the course of the fighting as well. In the initial stages, field intelligence as such scarcely existed. The Intelligence Corps, moreover was shackled by preconceived patterns of thought.

On the Southern Front, faulty intelligence had a considerable influence on the battles to stem the Egyptian advance.

Officers' Control

The degree of control of the situation, exercised by officers at various levels and their control of the units at their command, constituted a central problem in the battles to stem the Egyptian advance, and to a lesser degree the Syrian advance.

When the war broke out, this problem largely stemmed from the difficulties of applying the theory of control and reporting, in the sudden sharp transition, with only the slightest warning, from a state of lull, to a state of overall war.

Difficulties of control continued to exist after the initial stages as well. Accordingly, the probe also covered the various elements involved in control by officers, in time of war, as applied during the battles to stem the enemy advance. This showed up a series of faulty procedures and erroneous concepts.

Future of the Defence Forces

This, as our previous reports, is of a sharply critical nature. Clearly this is the result of the investigative function we were called upon to carry out. At the same time it is important to emphasize that our eyes were upon the future of the Israel Defence Forces and of the State—so that that which should be corrected will in fact be so.

The true test of any army is not only in its being able to win when it has the initiative, but precisely when it starts from difficult circumstances and goes ahead to victory. However, having been witnesses to the brilliance with which the army of the people stood up to its difficult test, it is essential to ensure that it will not have to meet a similar test in the future and it was this that we bore in mind in drawing up the three reports. It is to be hoped that the lessons to which we have pointed will be assimilated and that our recommendations will be implemented.

And finally, on the long road of this investigation, we could live—insofar as this is possible through hearing of testimony—the experiences of our soldiers, their sacrifice and their heroism. And this only strengthened our recognition that the task entrusted to us was not only a heavy public responsibility but a great privilege.

Discipline Indivisible

The Commission paid special attention to the question of discipline in the army, which it considered of great importance. For this reason it weighed publishing this section of the report in full, but finally decided that security considerations would not permit it.

The subject of discipline has been on the army's agenda all along, the Commission noted. How strict discipline should be, the unfavourable influence at times of civilian society, the kind of means to be used to impose discipline—these and other questions have always been discussed by the General Staff.

Army discipline expresses itself in the fact that the individual soldier accepts the authority of his superiors, which is itself based upon army regulations for the purpose of carrying out a military task, whether routine or operational.

This discipline can be administrative, that is, concerned with the daily behaviour of the soldier, or technical, concerned with care of equipment, or operational, concerned with soldier's behaviour in carrying out his duty in an operation against the enemy.

Army drill aims to make it "second nature" for the soldier to carry out his special duties in battle despite the external and subjective pressures upon him.

Discipline, command and obedience characterize the military profession. Without discipline an army is transformed into an armed mass unable to perform correctly. Administrative shortcomings can exist in any army, but without good discipline they cannot be corrected.

The more complex the means of warfare, the larger the size of the forces, the longer the chain of command, and the greater the deployment and dispersal of forces and the speed of battle, the greater becomes the need for discipline and proper administration.

Discipline is indivisible. For example, a soldier who becomes accustomed in time of peace not to observe the minor rules, such as in matters of personal appearance, without being alerted to this failure by his superior officer, will in the end be negligent in carrying out operational orders.

Moreover, the soldier cannot be expected to carry out his orders scrupulously, if he sees that his commanding officer does not demand the same of himself.

A soldier who is not scrupulous in matters of personal cleanliness will in the end also not be scrupulous about the cleanliness and fitness of his personal weaponry. A soldier who becomes used to violating traffic laws in peace-time, and sees his commanding officer doing the same, won't observe the rules of moving traffic in war and will thus impede the flow of forces to the front.

The conclusion is that good habits of discipline in small matters as in large add up to fatefully affect the preservation of life and equipment.

Captivity

While the Commission was collecting general testimony, it heard about various situations in which soldiers were taken prisoner. This material was referred to the Chief of Staff, for his study, so that he could take the appropriate decisions.

Training

The Commission considered it important to conduct an additional study of the Army's preparedness and deployment before the war, and its manner of fighting during the battles to stem the enemy advance, from the standpoint of officers' and soldiers' training before the war. The aim of this additional study was to point up what was wrong institutionally in the system of training, its aims and its content. Lessons could thus be drawn, and improvements made.

The Commission therefore asked R/A Haim Laskov (Res.), a former head of IDF training, to prepare a special chapter as a supplement to this report. Submitted as R/A Laskov's separate opinion, it nevertheless largely fits in with the rest of this report. It expands on the training aspect, where it concerns battle intelligence regimen and discipline, emergency depot units, and the battles of October 8.

Sharon Supported

We wish to dwell on a particular question on the subject of discipline, which gave rise to public debate in the wake of a press interview ("Ma'ariv" of January 25, 1974) granted by Major-General (Res.) Ariel Sharon, and from which it would appear that in his opinion, there are certain circumstances in which a commander may refrain from carrying out an operational order addressed to him.

When General Sharon appeared before us as a witness we examined him on this question, in order to set the record straight. General Sharon testified to having been disturbed by a question of conscience in the wake of something which happened on one of the final days of the Yom Kippur War. On that day, he had been ordered to lead the division under his command to attack a certain target. He had believed that implementation of the order would result in many casualties and that if the commander who had issued the order had been fully aware of the situation on the battlefield—knowledge which he lacked in General Sharon's opinion—he would not have issued the order. He, General Sharon, therefore opposed the order for hours, but finally, the order not having been rescinded, he obeyed it and carried out the attack. Discovering no achievements thereafter to induce him to change the opinion he held before the operation, he cites this instance as an example of an order which it would have been justified not to carry out, answering for it thereafter. In his testimony, he stressed that such cases are very rare.

We believe that Major-General Sharon's outlook, as he described it to us is consistent with military discipline. At a time of battle—and we are not of course dealing here with an order which has to be carried out forthwith—very rare instances may occur in which the commander who receives an order is convinced that if his commander was fully aware of the facts in the field he would not insist on its being carried out. Thus he who receives the order is caught on the horns of a dilemma, between his obligation to carry out any order, unless it is clearly illegal, and his conviction that on the basis of the facts of the situation, such an order is out of the question.

When a commander finds himself in such a situation, and he has exhausted all the accepted means, insofar as these are at his disposal in the circumstances, to have the order changed: informing the commander who gave the order of the facts of the situation, and trying to persuade him to change the order, appealing against the order to a higher echelon—and all to no avail, the commander is then obliged by military law to carry out the order to the best of his ability, and afterwards demand the establishment of a committee of inquiry to investigate the circumstances under which the order was given and carried out.

If he does not carry out the order, his superior officer may remove him from his command forthwith, and he is then liable for court-martial for deliberate refusal to obey an order, and all that remains is for him to inform the court-martial of his grounds for not carrying out the order, as an extenuating circumstance.

Final Remarks

It is generally accepted by the IDF that there were serious disciplinary faults. A minority of the commanders believed these did not adversely affect the IDF's fighting conduct during the Yom Kippur War. Our opinion on the basis of the evidence before us is different. We explained above that there is a strong link between the level of everyday discipline in the army and the quality of performance during the supreme test of war. The readiness to sacrifice and the ability to improvise as they were revealed during the Yom Kippur War—and these are not substitutes for discipline—to a large extent extricated the army from its straits. But who knows what hitches might have been prevented had a greater degree of discipline been added to the readiness to fight.

One cannot promote trust in the IDF, insofar as it has been impaired, by banal declarations and demands for an attitude of cilivian trust in respect to the army. Our public is linked by a thousand threads to the army, and reserve soldiers know very well what is going on within it. If the soldier and the junior officer work in a climate in which there is proper discipline, fulfilment of standing army orders and proper administration based on fixed rules, there is a corresponding increase in mutual trust within the ranks, in willingness to join the permanent army and in devotion of soldiers at all levels. And there will disappear of its own accord the regrettable occurrence of reserve soldiers speaking badly of the army, and the army will gain the full public trust it enjoyed in the past.

There can be no postponing the effort to remedy things that are wrong; this must be integrated with the difficult task of broadening the forces and physically strengthening them, because between these two there is a strong reciprocal link. The IDF and Israel's people are indeed one. Thus it is precisely for the IDF, and primarily for its senior command, to pave the way for the elimination of faults which began to penetrate into its ranks from the civilian sector—and thus to make a decisive contribution to the improvement of society generally. The IDF is capable of meeting this difficult task for which it was given instruments and sanctions that are not at the disposal of civilian society.

Interview (August 3, 1974)

By George Habbash*

Q. What is your analysis of the Palestinian and Arab political situations after the October War?

A. Almost nine months have elapsed since the cease-fire; during this time, some Arab and some international powers have worked from the principle of political struggle based on Security Council Resolutions 242 and 338 to insure the Israeli withdrawal from the Arab territories, on the one hand, and to achieve what was called giving the Palestinian people their full right to self-determination.

What are the results of this policy? Part of the Arab land was regained—on the Syrian and Egyptian fronts—but in lieu of what? What exactly is the price?

On the imperialistic level: the prominent achievement of American imperialism as a result of this policy is the return of American influence to the area, and the continuous expansion of this influence politically, economically and morally. This truth reaffirms the enemy's nature and its aggres-

* General Secretary of the Popular Front for the Liberation of Palestine. Excerpts from *Al-Hadaf* (Beirut).

sive identity, in spite of all attempts by the subservient systems and reactionary forces to decorate imperialism's ugly face. The results of the return of imperialism's influence to the area affected the close relations between the USSR and the Arab people. These are the most important concrete truths that surfaced during the recent nine months.

On the Arab level: in return for the disengagement steps on the Egyptian and Syrian fronts, those systems sacrified their power of military confrontation which enables them to continue the struggle and secures for them the complete extraction of their rights. Additionally, there was the step of lifting the oil embargo from the imperialistic countries which supported Zionism in its war against the Arab people.

Here, it must be indicated that the proposed plans of "settlement" might be affected by the internal developments in America (for example, the Watergate scandal) or any developments that may occur in the world. But what must be clear is that America will remain eager and will push in the direction of settlement as long as this "settlement" guarantees the return of its interests and their continuity for the longest possible interval. Therefore, efforts will continue in the direction of more steps towards "settlement." Based on this obvious principle, in return for every piece of land recovered by the Arab side, the Arabs are required to pay the price to the imperialistic powers and Israel—part of this price paid to imperialism and part to Israel.

Q. What is the position of the Front toward the official visit of the PLO delegation, headed by Yasser Arafat, to the USSR in August of this year?

A. The Front decided not to join the delegation. This position is not against the USSR despite our disagreements on many issues. Rather, we consider the USSR a power that is supporting our people's struggle. We also consider the Soviets friends of the Arab and Palestinian struggle. It is a mistaken position to put the Soviets and the Americans in one basket for only their general convergence of opinion concerning Resolution 242 and their agreement on the general lines of a political settlement. We consider the USSR a friend of the Palestinian struggle. We are convinced that the continuity of the Palestinian political and military struggle and our success in guaranteeing this continuity, eventually to the level that will mobilize the Arab masses according to a well-rooted revolutionary political line, will definitely lead to a reconsideration by the USSR of the nature of the existing struggle in the area, and the truths about the presence of the Zionist state which means no more than the existence of a racist, fascist and aggressive state. No peace will materialize as long as the Zionist state exists. This is the only conclusion that can be drawn by our masses based on this fact. The day will come when the Communist and leftist powers will uncover the true core and substance of the Zionist system.

We should not misinterpret international contradictions. The Front's decision not to participate in the PLO's delegation to Moscow does not express a position estranged from the Soviets, for whom we possess every appreciation, but it is a position against the PLO's leadership who wished the delegation travelling to Moscow to be "homogeneous." In our opinion, homogeneity means the common representation of a political line, which is the line leading towards political settlement. But we must keep in mind that within the Palestinian circle there exist two completely contradictory political lines, one on either end. One line wants the PLO to be a part of the political settlement and the other line considers this a dangerous national divergence, and considers the present mission of the struggle to keep the PLO outside the boundaries of the settlement. Based on this came our demand that the delegation be composed of all the member organizations of the Executive Council so that the delegation fairly represents the coexisting and contradictory political lines within the Liberation Organization.

There is another reason for our nonparticipation in the organization's delegation to Moscow: the delegation which was appointed to travel left without the Executive Council of the organization discussing the specific missions to be deliberated with our Soviet comrades, and without specifying a position on all the subjects proposed. The unilateral decision-making of the PLO must not continue. Our position is an expression of our rejection of the sense of unilateral decision-making that is predominant in the leadership of the PLO.

Q. What practical steps will the "rejection front" take at the Palestinian and Arab levels?

A. In fact what is called the rejection forces is nothing but an expression of Palestinian and Arab forces that emerged from an analysis, summarized as follows: the Palestinian revolution is strained and ends when it becomes a part of the political settlement presently proposed, and the continuity of the revolution is only ensured by resisting and fighting the proposed political settlement plans. These forces now work as though they are one front. But such a front did not arise until now. It is the duty of these forces to organize one front that has its own political programme, a list of specified organizational interrelationships and consolidated struggle programmes. Presently it is the duty of this front to work within the framework of the Liberation Organization to prevent its complete deviation, so that the Liberation Organization does not become part of the settlement.

But, in the event that the PLO goes to Geneva, the rejection front becomes the sole representative of the continuity of the revolution.

The subject that should be given chief priority is the necessity for the transformation of these Palestinian and Arab forces from the state of reflexive cooperation to the state of a clear frontal format according to a precise political programme.

Q. What is the PFLP's understanding of the relationship between the resistance and the Arab masses for the near future?

A. We believe that the Palestinian resistance will not be able to get out of the dilemma it is living in if it remains dependent on the masses of the Palestinian people, even if the revolutionary Palestinian party existed and the united Palestinian front existed. Even though important, it is not sufficient to defeat the plans of imperialism since the subject is really the balance of power. Because of this, the only true way out from the resistance's dilemma is for the Palestinian revolution to become an integral part of the Arab revolution, fused with it in all sections of the Arab nation. It is the Palestinian, Jordanian, Syrian, Egyptian, Iraqi and Lebanese masses who are able to guarantee the victory of our Palestinian people's struggle. When the Palestinian military struggle movement becomes able to move from a geographical and human depth that is not confined by the boundaries of the land of Palestine or the west and east banks, but extends to include all the lands surrounding Palestine, then the military struggle feature will rely upon such a human and geographical depth. At that time, it will be an impossibility for the oppressing forces to hit the Palestinian revolution.

Q. What is the explanation of the Front's acceptance of the ten points during the recent Palestinian National Council?

A. It is important for me to clarify what I heard and what reverberated during and after the convention—that I had personally, and in my own hand-writing, initiated these ten points. All what was said are lies and it is sad that attempts to slander our position as a popular front in front of the Palestinian masses occurred, whether premeditatedly or not. I put together some points as a basis for a political programme that might be agreed upon by the National Council during its twelfth convention. These points cumulatively put the resistance movement outside the framework of the settlement by opposing it in a way that cannot be disputed. Among those points is the definitive rejection of Resolution 242 and the Geneva Conference. The points which I wrote in the name of the Popular Front are in line with the political line represented by the Popular Front. But the ten points which the Palestinian National Council adopted are a compromise position attempting to prevent the explosion within the Palestinian circle. There have been several attempts aimed at concealing the contradictions within the Palestinian circle. But I take this opportunity to declare at the top of my voice that two contradictory political lines exist within the PLO, and the necessity of maintaining the struggle against any attempt to cover or weaken this contradiction is imperative.

One political line says that the only way open for the resistance movement is to enter into the framework of the political solution and to struggle within this framework to achieve whatever is possible. On the other hand, there is another line that believes in the continuity of the revolution and in staying away from political settlements in spite of the imperialistic powers' proposed dissolution attempts and plots.

There can be no real and strong national unity, in the long run, based upon the ten points . . . National unity cannot exist except upon a unified political stand: the Liberation Organization must reject in a clear and firm way, free from ambiguity or misunderstanding, all the forms of the proposed settlements.

In this respect, I announce in the name of the PFLP that it is important for us to remain within the PLO inasmuch as the Liberation Organization remains outside the framework of the Geneva Conference. Participation in the Geneva Conference means to us a dangerous national deviation which we will fight with all our power, based on the strength of the masses. When the Organization is in Geneva, the subject becomes black and white . . .

The attempts to dissolve the contradictions in the Palestinian circle must not continue. It is incorrect to state that disagreements do not exist. We must not bury our heads in the sand. There is a line that is devoted to the subservient Arab bourgeois system's policy of trying to dampen and cover the Palestinian and Arab proletariat's line in its struggle against the subservient bourgeois policy, on the Arab and Palestinian levels . . .

Q. What are the PFLP's expectations on the Lebanese front for the next phase?

A. Of course, it is necessary to expect attacks on the resistance and especially in Lebanon. This is a scientific deduction. Why? Because the proposed settlement aims at containing the Palestinian resistance. This is a fact. And it is natural for the resistance movement to hesitate in front of the humiliating format that American imperialism will propose to contain the revolution. At the same time, there will be a plan drawn to direct political and military attacks on the Palestinian resistance movement so that the resistance is compelled at the end to enter into the framework of the settlement from a position of weakness, permitting the plan to achieve its aims. This point must be engrained in our minds because the resistance in Lebanon still constitutes a revolutionary feature. The Palestinian gun is still held up in this area. Through the ability of the resistance movement to express its political line to the Palestinian and Arab masses through its overt existence in this and other circles, it is natural for the enemy to work against the existence of this revolutionary feature until he reaches the position that enables him to contain the resistance movement within a format that does not conflict with the basic benefits of his imperialistic appendages and his long-range benefits . . .

What do I mean exactly?

Any Israeli imperialistic reactionary plan against the resistance as a whole will face opposition from all the resistance movement. We will find ourselves in front of the picture of May again. In other words, all the resistance movement will have a united stand. Will the enemy be able to come and isolate and attack the Popular Front in Shatila? No. Because that will result in a confrontation with all the Palestinian guns, whether carried by a Popular Front or Fateh member. All will face this attempt. By this we see the difficulty of directing a military blow to the resistance movement. But what may happen is that some Palestinian forces, for some excuse or another, based upon the claim of enforcing discipline in the camps, will hit another Palestinian group with the blessing of the reactionary forces. Here occurs intact the painful blow to the resistance movement as a whole.

The area in this case will be full of action. Thus, we must keep our eyes open in order to prevent the enemy from achieving its objectives. Of course, the principal dependence or main line in facing any plots of any kind aiming to hit the Palestinian resistance in any form is that of complete fusion between the resistance and the Lebanese mass movement. It is only this format of fusion that can crush all the plots.

Address to the UN General Assembly (November 13, 1974)

By Yasir Arafat*

Mr. President, I thank you for having invited the Palestine Liberation Organization to participate in this plenary session of the United Nations General Assembly. I am grateful to all those representatives of States of the United Nations who contributed to the decision to introduce the question of Palestine as a separate item of the agenda of this Assembly. That decision made possible the Assembly's resolution inviting us to address it on the question of Palestine.

The roots of the Palestinian question reach back into the closing years of the 19th century, in other words, to that period which we call the era of colonialism and settlement as we know it today. This is precisely the period during which Zionism as a scheme was born; its aim was the conquest of Palestine by European immigrants, just as settlers colonized, and indeed raided, most of Africa. This is the period during which, pouring forth out of the west, colonialism spread into the further reaches of Africa, Asia, and Latin America, building colonies everywhere, cruelly exploiting, oppressing, plundering the people of those three continents. This period persists into the present. Marked evidence of its totally repre-

* Excerpts (29th Session).

hensible presence can be readily perceived in the racism practised both in South Africa and in Palestine.

Just as colonialism and its demagogues dignified their conquests, their plunder and limitless attacks upon the natives of Africa with appeals to a "civilizing and modernizing" mission, so too did waves of Zionist immigrants disguise their purposes as they conquered Palestine. Just as colonialism as a system and colonialists as its instrument used religion, color, race and language to justify the African's exploitation and his cruel subjugation by terror and discrimination, so too were these methods employed as Palestine was usurped and its people hounded from their national homeland.

Just as colonialism heedlessly used the wretched, the poor, the exploited as mere inert matter with which to build and to carry out settler colonialism, so too were destitute, oppressed European Jews employed on behalf of world imperialism and of the Zionist leadership. European Jews were transformed into the instruments of aggression; they became the elements of settler colonialism intimately allied to racial discrimination.

Zionist theology was utilized against our Palestinian people: the purpose was not only the establishment of Western-style settler colonialism but also the severing of Jews from their various homelands and subsequently their estrangement from their nations. Zionism is an ideology that is imperialist, colonialist, racist; it is profoundly reactionary and discriminatory; it is united with anti-Semitism in its retrograde tenets and is, when all is said and done, another side of the same base coin. For when what is proposed is that adherents of the Jewish faith, regardless of their national residence, should neither owe allegiance to their national residence nor live on equal footing with its other, non-Jewish citizens—when that is proposed we hear anti-Semitism being proposed. When it is proposed that the only solution for the Jewish problem is that Jews must alienate themselves from communities or nations of which they have been a historical part, when it is proposed that Jews solve the Jewish problem by immigrating to and forcibly settling the land of another people—when this occurs exactly the same position is being advocated as the one urged by anti-Semites against Jews.

Thus, for instance, we can understand the close connection between Rhodes, who promoted settler colonialism in southeast Africa, and Herzl, who had settler colonialist designs upon Palestine. Having received a certificate of good settler colonialist conduct from Rhodes, Herzl then turned around and presented this certificate to the British Government, hoping thus to secure a formal resolution supporting Zionist policy. In exchange, the Zionists promised Britain an imperialist base on Palestine soil so that imperial interests could be safeguarded at one of their chief strategic points.

The Jewish invasion of Palestine began in 1881. Before the first large wave of immigrants started arriving, Palestine had a population of half a million; most of the population was either Moslem or Christian, and only 20,000 were Jewish. Every segment of the population enjoyed the religious tolerance characteristic of our civilization.

Palestine was then a verdant land, inhabited mainly by an Arab people in the course of building its life and dynamically enriching its indigenous culture.

Between 1882 and 1917 the Zionist Movement settled approximately 50,000 European Jews in our homeland. To do that it resorted to trickery and deceit in order to implant them in our midst. Its success in getting Britain to issue the Balfour Declaration once again demonstrated the alliance between Zionism and imperialism. Furthermore, by promising to the Zionist movement what was not hers to give, Britain showed how oppressive the rule of imperialism was. As it was constituted then, the League of Nations abandoned our Arab people, and Wilson's pledges and promises came to nought. In the guise of a mandate, British imperialism was cruelly and directly imposed upon us. The mandate document issued by the League of Nations was to enable the Zionist invaders to consolidate their gains in our homeland.

In the wake of the Balfour Declaration and over a period of 30 years, the Zionist movement succeeded, in collaboration with its imperialist ally, in settling more European Jews on the land, thus usurping the properties of Palestine Arabs.

By 1947 the number of Jews had reached 600,000: they owned about 6 percent of Palestinian arable land. The figure should be compared with the population of Palestine which at that time was 1,250,000.

As a result of the collusion between the mandatory Power and the Zionist movement and with the support of some countries, this General Assembly early in its history approved a recommendation to partition our Palestinian homeland. This took place in an atmosphere poisoned with questionable actions and strong pressure. The General Assembly partitioned what it had no right to divide—an indivisible homeland. When we rejected that decision, our position corresponded to that of the natural mother who refused to permit King Solomon to cut her son in two when the unnatural mother claimed the child for herself and agreed to his dismemberment. Furthermore, even though the partition resolution granted the colonialist settlers 54 percent of the land of Palestine, their dissatisfaction with the decision prompted them to wage a war of terror against the civilian Arab population. They occupied 81 percent of the total area of Palestine, uprooting a million Arabs. Thus, they occupied 524 Arab towns and villages, of which they destroyed 385, completely obliterating them in the process. Having done so, they built their own settlements and colonies on the ruins of our farms and our groves. The roots of the Palestine question lie here. Its causes do not stem from any conflict between two religions or two nationalisms. Neither is it a border conflict between neighboring states. It is the cause of a people deprived of its homeland, dispersed and uprooted, and living mostly in exile and in refugee camps.

With support from imperialist and colonialist Powers, it managed to get itself accepted as a United Nations Member. It further succeeded in getting the Palestine Question deleted from the agenda of the United Nations and in deceiving world public opinion by presenting our cause as a problem of refugees in need either of charity from do-gooders, or settlement in a land not theirs.

Not satisfied with all this, the racist entity, founded on the imperialist-colonialist concept, turned itself into a base of imperialism and into an arsenal of weapons. This enabled it to assume its role of subjugating the Arab people and of committing aggression against them, in order to satisfy its ambitions for further expansion on Palestinian and other Arab lands. In addition to the many instances of aggression committed by this entity against the Arab States, it has launched two large-scale wars, in 1956 and 1967, thus endangering world peace and security.

As a result of Zionist aggression in June 1967, the enemy occupied Egyptian Sinai as far as the Suez Canal. The enemy occupied Syria's Golan Heights, in addition to all Palestinian land west of the Jordan. All these developments have led to the creation in our area of what has come to be known as the "Middle East problem." The situation has been rendered more serious by the enemy's persistence in maintaining its unlawful occupation and in further consolidating it, thus establishing a beachhead for world imperialism's thrust against our Arab nation. All Security Council decisions and appeals to world public opinion for withdrawal from the lands occupied in June 1967 have been ignored. Despite all the peaceful efforts on the international level, the enemy has not been deterred from its expansionist policy. The only alternative open before our Arab nations, chiefly Egypt and Syria, was to expend exhaustive efforts in preparing forcefully to resist that barbarous armed invasion—and this in order to liberate Arab lands and to restore the rights of the Palestinian people, after all other peaceful means had failed.

Under these circumstances, the fourth war broke out in October 1973, bringing home to the Zionist enemy the bankruptcy of its policy of occupation, expansion and its reliance on the concept of military might. Despite all this, the leaders of the Zionist entity are far from having learned any lesson from their experience. They are making preparations for the fifth war, resorting once more to the language of military superiority, aggression, terrorism, subjugation and, finally, always to war in their dealings with the Arabs.

It pains our people greatly to witness the propagation of the myth that its homeland was a desert until it was made to bloom by the toil of foreign settlers, that it was a land without a people, and that the colonialist entity caused no harm to any human being. No: such lies must be exposed from this rostrum, for the world must know that Palestine was the cradle of the most ancient cultures and civilizations. Its Arab people were engaged in farming and building, spreading culture throughout the land for thousands of years, setting an example in the practice of freedom of worship, acting as faithful guardians of the holy places of all religions. As a son of Jerusalem, I treasure for myself and my people beautiful memories and vivid images of the religious brotherhood that was the hallmark of our Holy City before it succumbed to catastrophe. Our people continued to pursue this enlightened policy until the establishment of the State of Israel and their dispersion. This did not deter our people from pursuing their humanitarian role on Palestinian soil. Nor will they permit their land to become a launching pad for aggression or a racist camp predicated on the destruction of civilization, cultures, progress and peace. Our people cannot but maintain the heritage of their ancestors in resisting the invaders, in assuming the privileged task of defending their native land, their Arab nationhood, their culture and civilization, and in safeguarding the cradle of monotheistic religion.

By contrast, we need only mention briefly some Israeli stands: its support of the Secret Organization in Algeria, its bolstering of the settler-colonialists in Africa—whether in the Congo, Angola, Mozambique, Zimbabwe, Azania or South Africa—and its backing of South Vietnam against the Vietnamese revolution. In addition, one can mention Israel's continuing support of imperialists and racists everywhere, its obstructionist stand in the Committee of Twenty-Four, its refusal to cast its vote in support of independence for the African States, and its opposition to the demands of many Asian, African and Latin American nations, and several other States in the Conferences on raw materials, population, the Law of the Sea, and food. All these facts offer further proof of the character of the enemy which has usurped our land. They justify the honorable struggle which we are waging against it. As we defend a vision of the future, our enemy upholds the myths of the past.

The enemy we face has a long record of hostility even towards the Jews themselves, for there is within the Zionist entity a built-in racism against Oriental Jews. While we were vociferously condemning the massacres of Jews under Nazi rule, Zionist leadership appeared more interested at that time in exploiting them as best it could in order to realize its goal of immigration into Palestine.

If the immigration of Jews to Palestine had had as its objective the goal of enabling them to live side by side with us, enjoying the same rights and assuming the same duties, we would have opened our doors to them, as far as our homeland's capacity for absorption permitted. Such was the case with the thousands of Armenians and Circassians who still live among us in equality as brethren and citizens. But that the goal of this immigration should be to usurp our homeland, disperse our people, and turn us into second-class citizens—this is what no one can conceivably demand that we acquiesce in or submit to. Therefore, since its inception, our revolution has not been motivated by racial or religious factors. Its target has never been the Jew, as a person, but racist Zionism and undisguised aggression. In this sense, ours is also a revolution for the Jew, as a human being, as well. We are struggling so that Jews, Christians and Moslems may live in equality enjoying the same rights and assuming the same duties, free from racial or religious discrimination.

We do distinguish between Judaism and Zionism. While we maintain our opposition to the colonialist Zionist movement, we respect the Jewish faith. Today, almost one century after the rise of the Zionist movement, we wish to warn of its increasing danger to the Jews of the world, to our Arab people and to world peace and security. For Zionism encourages the Jew to emigrate out of his homeland and grants him an artificially-created nationality. The Zionists proceed with their terrorist activities even though these have proved ineffective. The phenomenon of constant emigration from Israel, which is bound to grow as the bastions of colonialism and racism in the world fall, is an example of the inevitability of the failure of such activities.

We urge the people and governments of the world to stand firm against Zionist attempts at encouraging world Jewry to emigrate from their countries and to usurp our land. We urge them as well firmly to oppose any discrimination against any human being, as to religion, race, or color.

Why should our Arab Palestinian people pay the price of such discrimination in the world? Why should our people be responsible for the problems of Jewish immigration, if such problems exist in the minds of some people? Why do not the supporters of these problems open their own countries, which can absorb and help these immigrants?

Those who call us terrorists wish to prevent world public opinion from discovering the truth about us and from seeing the justice on our faces. They seek to hide the terrorism and tyranny of their acts, and our own posture of self-defense.

The difference between the revolutionary and the terrorist lies in the reason for which each fights. For whoever stands by a just cause and fights for the freedom and liberation of his land from the invaders, the settlers and the colonialists, cannot possibly be called terrorist; otherwise the American people in their struggle for liberation from the British colonialists would have been terrorists, the European resistance against the Nazis would be terrorism, the struggle of the Asian, African and Latin American peoples would also be terrorism, and many of you who are in this Assembly Hall were considered terrorists. This is actually a just and proper struggle consecrated by the United Nations Charter and by the Universal Declaration of Human Rights. As to those who fight against the just causes, those who wage war to occupy, colonize and oppress other people—those are the terrorists, those are the people whose actions should be condemned, who should be called war criminals: for the justice of the cause determines the right to struggle.

Zionist terrorism which was waged against the Palestinian people to evict it from its country and usurp its land is registered in our official documents. Thousands of our people were assassinated in their villages and towns, tens of thousands of others were forced at gun-point to leave their homes and the lands of their fathers. Time and time again our children, women and aged were evicted and had to wander in the deserts and climb mountains without any food or water. No one who in 1948 witnessed the catastrophe that befell the inhabitants of hundreds of villages and towns—in Jaffa, Lydda, Ramle and Galilee—no one who has been a witness to that catastrophe will ever forget the experience, even though the mass blackout has succeeded in hiding these horrors as it had hidden the traces of 385 Palestinian villages and towns destroyed at the time and erased from the map. The destruction of 19,000 houses during the past seven years, which is equivalent to the complete destruction of 200 more Palestinian villages, and the great number of maimed as a result of the treatment they were subjected to in Israeli prisons, cannot be hidden by any blackout.

Their terrorism fed on hatred and this hatred was even directed against the olive tree in my country, which has been a proud symbol and which reminded them of the indigenous inhabitants of the land, a living reminder that the land is Palestinian. Thus they sought to destroy it. How can one describe the statement by Golda Meir which expressed her disquiet about "the Palestinian children born every day"? They see in the Palestinian child, in the Palestinian tree, an enemy that should be exterminated. For tens of years Zionists have been harassing our people's cultural, political, social and artistic leaders, terrorizing them and assassinating them. They have stolen our cultural heritage, our popular folklore and have claimed it as theirs. Their terrorism even reached our sacred places in our beloved and peaceful Jerusalem. They have endeavoured to de-Arabize it and make it lose its Moslem and Christian character by evicting its inhabitants and annexing it.

I must mention the fire of the Aksa Mosque and the disfiguration of many of the monuments, which are both historic and religious in character. Jerusalem, with its religious history and its spiritual values, bears witness to the future. It is proof of our eternal presence, of our civilization, of our human values. It is therefore not surprising that under its skies the three religions were born and that under that sky these three religions shine in order to enlighten mankind so that it might express the tribulations and hopes of humanity, and that it might mark out the road of the future with its hopes.

The small number of Palestinian Arabs who were not uprooted by the Zionists in 1948 are at present refugees in their own homeland. Israeli law treats them as second-class citizens —and even as third-class citizens since Oriental Jews are second-class citizens and they have been subject to all forms of racial discrimination and terrorism after confiscation of their land and property. The have been victims to bloody massacres such as that of Kfar Kassim; they have been expelled from their villages and denied the right to return, as in the case of the inhabitants of Ikrit and Kfar-Birim. For 26 years, our population has been living under martial law and has been denied the freedom of movement without prior permission from the Israeli military governor—this at a time when an Israeli law was promulgated granting citizenship to any Jew anywhere who wanted to emigrate to our homeland. Moreover, another Israeli law stipulated that Palestinians who were not present in their villages or towns at the time of the occupation were not entitled to Israeli citizenship.

The record of Israeli rulers is replete with acts of terror perpetrated on those of our people who remained under occupation in Sinai and the Golan Heights. The criminal bombardment of the Bahr-al-Bakar School and the Abou Zaabal factory are but two such unforgettable acts of terrorism. The total destruction of the Syrian city of Kuneitra is yet another tangible instance of systematic terrorism. If a record of Zionist terrorism in South Lebanon were to be compiled, the enormity of its acts would shock even the most hardened: piracy, bombardments, scorched earth, destruction of hundreds of homes, eviction of civilians and the kidnapping of Lebanese citizens. This clearly constitutes a violation of Lebanese sovereignty and is in preparation for the diversion of the Litani River waters.

Need one remind this Assembly of the numerous resolutions adopted by it condemning Israeli aggressions committed against Arab countries, Israeli violations of human rights and the articles of the Geneva Conventions, as well as the resolutions pertaining to the annexation of the city of Jerusalem and its restoration to its former status?

The only description for these acts is that they are acts of barbarism and terrorism. And yet, the Zionist racists and colonialists have the temerity to describe the just struggle of our people as terror. Could there be a more flagrant distortion of truth than this? We ask those who usurped our land, who are committing murderous acts of terrorism against our people and are practising racial discrimination more extensively than the racists of South Africa, we ask them to keep in mind the United Nations General Assembly resolution that called for the one-year suspension of the membership of the Government of South Africa from the United Nations. Such is the inevitable fate of every racist country that adopts the law of the jungle, usurps the homeland of others and persists in oppression.

For the past 30 years, our people have had to struggle against British occupation and Zionist invasion, both of which had one intention, namely the usurpation of our land. Six major revolts and tens of popular uprisings were staged to foil these attempts, so that our homeland might remain ours. Over 30,000 martyrs, the equivalent in comparative terms of 6 million Americans, died in the process.

When the majority of the Palestinian people was uprooted from its homeland in 1948, the Palestinian struggle for self-determination continued under the most difficult conditions. We tried every possible means to continue our political struggle to attain our national rights, but to no avail. Meanwhile, we had to struggle for sheer existence. Even in exile we educated our children. This was all a part of trying to survive.

The Palestinian people produced thousands of physicians, lawyers, teachers and scientists who actively participated in the development of the Arab countries bordering on their usurped homeland. They utilized their income to assist the young and aged amongst their people who remained in the refugee camps. They educated their younger sisters and brothers, supported their parents and cared for their children. All along the Palestinian dreamed of return. Neither the Palestinian's allegiance to Palestine nor his determination to return waned; nothing could persuade him to relinquish his Palestinian identity or to forsake his homeland. The passage of time did not make him forget, as some hoped he would. When our people lost faith in the international community which persisted in ignoring its rights and when it became obvious that the Palestinians would not recuperate one inch of Palestine through exclusively political means, our people had no choice but to resort to armed struggle. Into that struggle it poured its material and human resources. We bravely faced the most vicious acts of Israeli terrorism which were aimed at diverting our struggle and arresting it.

In the past 10 years of our struggle, thousands of martyrs and twice as many wounded, maimed and imprisoned were offered in sacrifice, all in an effort to resist the imminent threat of liquidation, to regain our right to self-determination and our undisputed right to return to our homeland. With the utmost dignity and the most admirable revolutionary spirit, our Palestinian people has not lost its spirit in Israeli prisons and concentration camps or when faced with all forms of harassment and intimidation. It struggles for sheer existence and it continues to strive to preserve the Arab character of its land. Thus it resists oppression, tyranny and terrorism in their ugliest forms.

It is through our popular armed struggle that our political leadership and our national institutions finally crystalized and a national liberation movement, comprising all the Palestinian factions, organizations, and capabilities, materialized in the Palestine Liberation Organization.

Through our militant Palestine national liberation movement, our people's struggle matured and grew enough to accommodate political and social struggle in addition to armed struggle. The Palestine Liberation Organization was a major factor in creating a new Palestinian individual, qualified to shape the future of our Palestine, not merely content with mobilizing the Palestinians for the challenges of the present.

The Palestine Liberation Organization can be proud of having a large number of cultural and educational activities, even while engaged in armed struggle, and at a time when it faced the increasingly vicious blows of Zionist terrorism. We established institutes for scientific research, agricultural development and social welfare, as well as centers for the revival of our cultural heritage and the preservation of our folklore. Many Palestinian poets, artists and writers have enriched Arab culture in particular, and world culture generally. Their profoundly humane works have won the admiration of all those familiar with them. In contrast to that, our enemy has been systematically destroying our culture and disseminating racist, imperialist ideologies; in short, everything that impedes progress, justice, democracy and peace.

The Palestine Liberation Organization has earned its legitimacy because of the sacrifice inherent in its pioneering role, and also because of its dedicated leadership of the struggle. It has also been granted this legitimacy by the Palestinian masses, which in harmony with it have chosen it to lead the struggle according to its directives. The Palestine Liberation Organization has also gained its legitimacy by representing every faction, union or group as well as every Palestinian talent, either in the National Council or in people's institutions. This legitimacy was further strengthened by the support of the entire Arab nation, and it was consecrated during the last Arab Summit Conference which reiterated the right of the Palestine Liberation Organization, in its capacity as the sole representative of the Palestinian people, to establish an independent national State on all liberated Palestinian territory.

Moreover, the Palestine Liberation Organization's legitimacy was intensified as a result of fraternal support given by other liberation movements and by friendly, like-minded nations that stood by our side, encouraging and aiding us in our struggle to secure our national rights.

Here I must also warmly convey the gratitude of our revolutionary fighters and that of our people to the nonaligned countries, the socialist countries, the Islamic countries, the African countries and friendly European countries, as well as all our other friends in Asia, Africa and Latin America.

The Palestine Liberation Organization represents the Palestinian people, legitimately and uniquely. Because of this, the Palestine Liberation Organization expresses the wishes and hopes of its people. Because of this, too, it brings these very wishes and hopes before you, urging you not to shirk a momentous historic responsibility towards our just cause.

For many years now, our people has been exposed to the ravages of war, destruction and dispersion. It has paid in the blood of its sons that which cannot ever be compensated. It has borne the burdens of occupation, dispersion, eviction and terror more uninterruptedly than any other people. And yet all this has made our people neither vindictive nor vengeful.

Nor has it caused us to resort to the racism of our enemies. Nor have we lost the true method by which friend and foe are distinguished.

For we deplore all those crimes committed against the Jews, we also deplore all the real discrimination suffered by them because of their faith.

I am a rebel and freedom is my cause. I know well that many of you present here today once stood in exactly the same resistance position as I now occupy and from which I must fight. You once had to convert dreams into reality by your struggle. Therefore you must now share my dream. I think this is exactly why I can ask you now to help, as together we bring out our dream into a bright reality, our common dream for a peaceful future in Palestine's sacred land.

As he stood in an Israeli military court, the Jewish revolutionary, Ahud Adif, said: "I am no terrorist; I believe that a democratic State should exist on this land." Adif now languishes in a Zionist prison among his co-believers. To him and his colleagues I send my heartfelt good wishes.

And before those same courts there stands today a brave prince of the church. Bishop Capucci. Lifting his fingers to form the same victory sign used by our freedom-fighters, he said: "What I have done, I have done that all men may live on this land of peace in peace." This princely priest will doubtless share Adif's grim fate. To him we send our salutations and greetings.

Why therefore should I not dream and hope? For is not revolution the making real of dreams and hopes? So let us work together that my dream may be fulfilled, that I may return with my people out of exile, there in Palestine to live with this Jewish freedom-fighter and his partners, with this Arab priest and his brothers, in one democratic State where Christian, Jew and Moslem live in justice, equality, fraternity and progress.

Is this not a noble dream worthy of my struggle alongside all lovers of freedom everywhere? For the most admirable dimension of this dream is that it is Palestinian, a dream from out of the land of peace, the land of martyrdom and heroism, and the land of history, too.

Let us remember that the Jews of Europe and the United States have been known to lead the struggles for secularism and the separation of Church and State. They have also been known to fight against discrimination on religious grounds.

How can they continue to support the most fanatic, discriminatory and closed of nations in its policy?

In my formal capacity as Chairman of the Palestine Liberation Organization and leader of the Palestinian revolution I proclaim before you that when we speak of our common hopes for the Palestine of tomorrow we include in our perspective all Jews now living in Palestine who choose to live with us there in peace and without discrimination.

In my formal capacity as Chairman of the Palestine Liberation Organization and leader of the Palestinian revolution I call upon Jews to turn away one by one from the illusory promises made to them by Zionist ideology and Israeli leadership. They are offering Jews perpetual bloodshed, endless war and continuous thraldom.

We invite them to emerge from their moral isolation into a more open realm of free choice, far from their present leadership's efforts to implant in them a Masada complex.

We offer them the most generous solution, that we might live together in a framework of just peace in our democratic Palestine.

In my formal capacity as Chairman of the Palestine Liberation Organization, I announce here that we do not wish one drop of either Arab or Jewish blood to be shed; neither do we delight in the continuation of killing, which would end once a just peace, based on our people's rights, hopes and aspirations had been finally established.

In my formal capacity as Chairman of the Palestine Liberation Organization and leader of the Palestinian revolution I appeal to you to accompany our people in its struggle to attain its right to self-determination. This right is consecrated in the United Nations Charter and has been repeatedly confirmed in resolutions adopted by this august body since the drafting of the Charter. I appeal to you, further; to aid our people's return to its homeland from an involuntary exile imposed upon it by force of arms, by tyranny, by oppression, so that we may regain our property, our land, and thereafter live in our national homeland, free and sovereign, enjoying all the privileges of nationhood. Only then can Palestinian creativity be concentrated on the service of humanity. Only then will our Jerusalem resume its historic role as a peaceful shrine for all religions.

I appeal to you to enable our people to establish national independent sovereignty over its own land.

Today I have come bearing an olive branch and a freedom-fighter's gun. Do not let the olive branch fall from my hand. I repeat: do not let the olive branch fall from my hand.

War flares up in Palestine, and yet it is in Palestine that peace will be born.

Rabat Conference Resolution
(October 29, 1974)

The Rabat summit issued a five-point resolution on the questions of Palestinian representation and the future of the West Bank. Voicing unanimous support for the PLO, the summit:

Affirms the right of the Arab Palestinian people to the return of its homeland and its right to self-determination.

Affirms the right of the Palestinian people to set up an independent national authority under the leadership of the Palestine Liberation Organization, in its capacity as the sole legitimate representative of the Palestinian people, on any liberated Palestinian land. The Arab countries are resolved to support such an authority once it is established.

Declares its support for the Palestine Liberation Organization in exercising its national and international responsibilities within the framework of Arab commitments.

Calls upon Jordan, Egypt, Syria and the PLO to outline a joint formula for the coordination of their relations in the light of the above decisions, and for their implementation.

Notes the undertaking by all Arab countries to consolidate the national Palestinian unity, and avoid intervention in the Palestinian action.

Arabs and Jews

By Edward W. Said*

During 1970 and 1971 a reasonably articulate Arab in the United States would frequently be asked to participate in pub-

* Edward W. Said is Professor of English and Comparative Literature at Columbia University. This is the revised text of a talk delivered at the Annual Convention of the Association of Arab-American University Graduates, held in Washington, D.C., October 19–21, 1973, during the fourth Arab-Israeli war. The text of the lecture is reprinted with kind permission from *Palestine Studies* (Winter, 1974).

lic discussions on the Middle East question. On one occasion
I was preceded to the lectern by an Israeli speaker who, I
thought then, had the lack of irony to say that it was the
Arabs that had always seen themselves as the chosen people.
Obviously this heedless remark was a later embarrassment to
him as a Jew, and it was easy to mock him with his own
observation. This incident isn't perhaps of tremendous value
now, except that it did come back during the anxious and
confusing days of the fourth Arab-Israeli war. You began to
realize that what as an intellectual of secular persuasion you
have always believed, that there is really no such thing as a
divinely chosen race, has a disquieting additional meaning.
No, the Jews are not a chosen people, but Jews and Arabs
together, one as oppressor and the other as oppressed, have
chosen each other for a struggle whose roots seem to go deeper
with each year, and whose future seems less thinkable and
resolvable each year. Neither people can develop without the
other there, harassing, taunting, fighting; no Arab today has
an identity that can be unconscious of the Jew, that can rule
out the Jew as a psychic factor in the Arab identity; conversely,
I think, no Jew can ignore the Arab in general, nor can he im-
merse himself in his ancient tradition and so lose the Palestinian
Arab in particular and what Zionism has done to him. The more
intense these modern struggles for identity become, the more
attention is paid by the Arab or the Jew to his chosen opponent,
or partner. Each is the other.

I can recall that as a child before 1948 in Palestine and
Egypt the foreigners with which I was surrounded here and
there stood out with a hard and almost cold difference from
me. The Englishman or the Frenchman or the Greek had
recognizable patterns of speech and even dress, gestures
unique to each, and so on. Yet the Jew, whether he was
Egyptian, Palestinian, Italian or British, seemed to seep
through those harder identities and be mixed up with mine.
Usually of course, nothing was said, but there was a felt
correspondence between us nevertheless. Maybe this experience was not common to many Arabs: I don't really know.
Now, however, there is a corporate Arab-Jewish identity, so
overlaid with events, with insults, wars, humiliations and fear,
all those seeming inevitabilities; but there are only the rarest
occasions for judging how in victimizing each other—most
often at the instigation of imperialist powers—we have shared
little except conflict and a gradually diminished human reality.

Every Arab has his own national identity to protect his spirit from the fraying ordeals of Arabism-Israelism, that ugly padlock of one-against-one tension. For the Egyptian there is an unbroken national Egyptian history that has endured for eighty centuries; this is a sovereign life whose richness astounded even Herodotus. For the Palestinian perforce his national identity is an embattled resistance to dispossession and extinction; yet for most of the world he has seemed like cigarette ash, moved from corner to corner, threatened always with irreversible dispersion. How many partisans of Jewish immigration to Israel recognize that every penny spent for that purpose also buys a Palestinian more time as an exile from his country?

However, all Arabs have suffered both in the Middle East and in the West. The Arab is seen as the disruptor of Israel's existence, or, in a larger view, as a surmountable obstacle to Israel's creation in 1948. This has been part of the Zionist attitude toward the Arab, especially in the years before 1948 when Israel was being promulgated ideologically. Palestine was imagined as an empty desert waiting to burst into bloom, its inhabitants minimized as inconsequential nomads possessing no stable claim to the land and therefore no cultural permanence. At worst, the Arab today is conceived of as a bloody-minded shadow that dogs the Jew and that interrupts the smoothly flowing "democracy" of Israeli life. In that shadow—because Arab and Jew are Semites—can be placed whatever latent mistrust the Westerner still feels towards the Jew. The Jew of pre-Nazi Europe has split in two: a Jewish hero, constructed out of a revived cult of the adventurer-pioneer, and the Arab his creeping, mysteriously fearsome shadow. Thus isolated from his past the Arab has seemed condemned to being local colour or to chastisement at the hands of Israeli soldiers and tourists, kept in his place by American Phantom jets, American cluster bombs and napalm, and UJA money.

If I may digress here for a little it is to point out that the Arabs and Islam have always been a singuar problem for the largely Christian West. As an instance there is the attitude of the West to Islam during the Middle Ages, the great age of Islamic civilization, roughly from the ninth through the eleventh centuries. This attitude is the subject of a book, *Western Views of Islam During the Middle Ages,* by the Chichele Professor of Modern History at Oxford, R. W.

Southern. To the Western thinkers who tried to understand Islam and the Arab achievement a great problem constantly supervened: how to explain a religion, a society, a civilization which in many ways parallelled that of the Christian West, yet which was, on the one hand, immeasurably more mature, powerful, and civilized, and on the other hand, a civilization which was immeasurably different and non-Christian. "In understanding Islam," Southern says,

> the West could get no help from antiquity, and no comfort from the present. For an age avowedly dependent on the past for its materials, this was a serious matter. Intellectually the nearest parallel to the position of Islam was the position of the Jews. They shared many of the same tenets and brought forward many of the same objections to Christianity. But Christian thinkers had at their disposal an embarrassing wealth of material for answering the Jewish case; and the economic and social inferiority of the Jews encouraged the view that their case could be treated with disdain. Nothing is easier than to brush aside the arguments of the socially unsuccessful, and we can see this verified in the melancholy history of the Jewish controversy in the Middle Ages.... But Islam stubbornly resisted this treatment. It was immensely successful. Every period of incipient breakdown was succeeded by a period of astonishing and menacing growth. Islam resisted both conquest and conversion, and it refused to wither away. (pp. 4–5)

Even during the comparatively remote period of which Southern speaks we have the Western habit of associating the unfamiliar with the inferior—how ironically prophetic of the Arab-Israeli conflict of today as it is also of the implicit attitude of identifying Jew with Arab.

I point this out with the intention only of showing that the relation between Islam and Arabs on the one hand, and the West on the other has a long and unhappy history. Not infrequently, as Southern says, Judaism and Islam were considered together as more or less interchangeable problems. In referring to all this I do not by any means wish to characterize the present political relationship between Arabs, Jews and the West as something reducible to a doctrinal problem in the Middle Ages. I wish only to show that the impoverishment of the Arab and of Islam, as well as Judaism, at the hands of the Christian West has behind it a long and complex background of unsatisfactory dealings. In part it is this background that illuminates the commonly accepted view of the Arab that is found in the West today, where—as I said a while ago—the Israeli appears as the Champion of Western-ism and modernity and democracy, whereas it is the Arab who is subservient, obscure and strangely to be feared.

Although in many ways, the war from the Arab viewpoint went better than one had expected—and this sense of restored self-esteem is something it would be hypocritical ever for an Arab to deny—there are strong reasons for thinking of this war in particular as having been a very dangerous business indeed. I am not thinking exclusively, or even principally, about dangers of its escalating into World War Three, or of the increased risk of superpower confrontation. It is entirely to have been expected that the US would request funds for aid to Israel and for Cambodia simultaneously, and for President Nixon to use the war to divert attention from his shady misadventures. The risks taken by superpowers, the mindlessness and the lack of respect for human issues, are risks of course, but they seem less immediate to me at this point than other ones. For so unusual and eccentric a conflict as the one between the Arabs and Israel breeds unusual and eccentric consequences. In the past and even now one such consequence has been the total absence of engagement; each side denied the other, each in his own way. Since 1967 this has been far less true of the Arabs than it has of the Israelis; I think that one can say this as an Arab quite honestly without fear of being accused of nationalist pride. From the governments to the people there seemed a growing willingness, perhaps because there was no real option, to deal with the unpleasant fact of Israel's presence. It is probably this willingness that accounts for the far more popular and determined sort of struggle that Arabs are presently waging on the field today. At last the Arabs have discovered that Israel, and Israel's strength, are *real*, which means that Israel can be fought and fought bravely if necessary. There is no mythology here.

For the Israeli since 1967 there seemed to have emerged two kinds of Arabs: one, the intransigent rebellious type of fellow, the so-called terrorist, the wicked enemy of Israel, and two, the good Arab, the reasonable man, with whom it was always pleasant to flirt, to exchange left-wing ideas, dovish sentiment, and so on. Yet in neither case was there a determination to open up the questions about which the conflict, from the Arab side at least, turned; there was no willingness, for example, seriously to discuss the rights of the Palestinians, except after all the pieties about Jewish statehood had been pronounced, all the necessities of maintaining the Law of

Return and other undiscussable privileges of that sort. All talk of the right of Palestinians was thereafter invalidated, and such talk seemed only to be a way of standing with Israel's strength and, at the same time, maintaining a good conscience.

If this seems a harsh statement, and if it discounts too much the often-courageous stand of Israelis who were critical of their government's policy of the illegal occupation of Arab territories, the denial of the Palestinian's existence, and so on, nevertheless I believe it is right to say that such positions in Israel were always hampered by something called "realism." Realism dictated that any talk of seriously modifying the immigration laws and the completely Jewish institutions of the state was tantamount to being a fool or a knave or a traitor or all three. Realism, one was very often told by realists, was taking the country's mood into consideration, the fervent nationalism, the unchangeable characteristics of the state of Israel as it was presently constituted, and even Jewish racism. Those were realities with which one was not supposed to argue since they had the force of reality, of history, and—even though it wasn't always mentioned—the force of military power. Realism therefore was the uncrossable line, rather like that formidable Bar-Lev line, which assured one that here at last was something absolutely secure and powerful, and it—far more than Arab good intentions or promises or whatever—guaranteed reality. So one could discuss Palestinian rights rather as one could discuss the question of the annexation of the Sinai, as a choice one might or might not make, depending on the attractiveness of the argument put forward on its behalf, and above all, on its realism.

Many former doves in Israel and perhaps in America have now seen that they were wrong and "unrealistic." That is, they feel that if what they had argued for had become state policy, then Israel—so they say—would now be fighting Arabs in the streets of Tel Aviv. As an instance there is a letter to the *New York Times* of October 17, 1973 by a whole team of high-flying (former) doves, including Shlomo Avineri, Jacob Talmon, and Gershom Sholem. Here are some typical excerpts:

> We, the undersigned, have always used our right as free men to express our views on our country's policies, both external and internal; and some of us have disagreed with some of these policies

in the past. The real issue today, as it was in 1967, is the determination by Egypt and Syria to destroy Israel....

The Egyptian and Syrian attack against us on the Day of Atonement has led us to the painful conclusion that the policy of the present governments of the Arab states is to go to any length to destroy Israel....

The Arab doctrine of prior agreement by Israel to withdraw from territory is illogical and unacceptable. Everyone of us is wholly convinced that our very existence today is due to the fact that this doctrine was rejected by us. The way in which the Egyptian and Syrian attack was prepared and launched must convince the world that this rejection was thoroughly justified...

This is a very strange realism indeed. For the state policy was precisely *not* to yield an inch, not to engage the Arabs in any serious way except as bodies to be raped and spaces to be entered violently at will, and it was that same realistic policy that led to the latest war. For instead of seeing that the realism of the situation since 1967 is that one cannot by sheer sightless force impose one's will on anyone, no matter how badly beaten, the neo-realists see instead that realism calls for more, not less, stubbornness and realism of the old variety. As if all the bombing done by the Nazis in World War Two, and all the US bombing in Vietnam had anything for their effect but a strengthening of the people's will to resist. As if the Bar-Lev line was anything more than an invitation to Egypt to cross it and attempt rightfully to retake her occupied territory. *This* realism is something missing from the conflict even now. And it is this missing realism, this missing chapter in the history of Israel's existence among the Arabs, that is very dangerous.

All of us in the United States have witnessed the sometimes appalling spectacle and sound of media coverage of the latest conflict. Most of the time it seems as if we are watching either a football game, with favourites and villains, hometeams and visitors, or as if we are watching a horse opera, with marshals, Indians and bad guys. Language is out of all touch with reality. Arabs, always mobs of them, faceless, voiceless, dark, and frightening, are always *claiming* to have done something. Israelis, who look like Bohemians of some sort, *are* doing things; the interviews are uniformly of some clever glib fellow like General Herzog, or a friendly infantryman from the Bronx. Bombing, napalming, strafing of Arabs is perfectly all right, for isn't it with Arabs that American bombs were designed to deal, using clean hands, as with a sub-

human other? How hard it is to watch the silent faces of
Arab suffering on the anonymous ruthless face of American
TV! When the Israelis cross the Golan Heights they are going
"into Syria," as if the Golan were somewhere else. But one is
constantly struck by one theme: the hardship endured by the
Israelis, and always their hope and optimism. This isn't a
war, it's a pastime: at least that's the impression one gets, as
if fighting Arabs was like ridding the backyard of a few
miscellaneous pests. On one occasion during the war's second
week, an irrepressible CBS reporter steps up to an obviously
dead-tired Israeli soldier (an American) and asks him,
whether after eleven days in the field it's worth it. "Yes"
comes back the answer, "if it's the last time anything is
worth it." Earlier in the war the answer wasn't quite so weary;
usually one heard things like, it'll be over in a couple of days,
we'll break their bones, then we'll be home for the weekend.
Now, a more resigned note creeps in: for the last time, anything is worth the effort. There are several interpretations
possible for this change in tone. But mainly, I think, one gets
the feeling that the realism of the present situation is that
once we beat the Arabs this time, they will never never dare
come near us again.

Let me give one more example of this realism, or rather,
this extraordinary absence of realism. One of the classical
texts on Zionism is Arthur Hertzberg's anthology called *The
Zionist Idea, A Historical Analysis and Reader* (Meridian
Books, New York, 1960). The book is a six-hundred page
compilation of excerpts from the principal figures in the history of Zionism, from Alkalai and Kalischer to Ben Gurion,
Silver and Weizmann. The readings cover a span of about a
hundred years, precisely those years during which Zionism
went from a theory to a movement. An astounding fact is
that in this six-hundred page book there are scarcely a dozen
pages that refer to Arabs, that so much as mention them as
in some way constituting, for a part of the hundred years in
question, half and more than half of the question of Palestine.
This is no hastily thrown together book of readings. It is
intended as a reliable and scholarly guide to the most representative as well as the best of Zionist thought. And this book,
as with the major thrust of Zionism, has absolutely nothing to
say about the Arabs whose presence in Palestine must have
reminded the Zionist from time to time of another people on
the land, and there for a long time. Aside from Magnes,

Jabotinsky, and Buber, Arabs are less even than an incidental difficulty to the Jewish question, which, in every other case, is remarkable for the sustained and the often profound attention it receives from the thinkers, ideologists and theorists that Hertzberg anthologizes.

This is "realism." For behind this sort of thought and practice is an even more intensified disengagement from reality. Can anyone seriously believe that another defeat will make all the Arabs stop bothering Israel and go away? Yes, people seriously believe that, even a whole nation believes that. As if the effort were no greater and no more difficult than ridding a small area of a nest of unwanted rodents. Has it occurred to no one to say to those people: if you beat the Arabs this time, the next time will be a shorter interval away than you expect? That continued tyranny does not break the will or the back of a people, and that popular resistance grows, rather than lessens, with every blow? Even American intellectuals who had the freedom to make these truths apparent never, or very rarely, did—once again, because in the interests of realism it was better to repeat the tired truths of Israeli official realism.

But to be honest amongst ourselves as well, we must say what about this war has been a threat to us. Not that we might lose because we have learned how to deal with defeat. But that, in parallel with the Israelis, we will start to believe that our Middle East can be restored to us either by war or by negotiation as a pristine, unspotted land, free of its past enemies, ours for the taking. That is out of the question. There is no future that is entirely free of the past, and there is certainly no future without an adequate understanding of the present. For the Arab today there must be an understanding that years and years of war with the Israelis, possibly with the great powers as well, will not bring a utopia in the end. Certain processes, which inhere in the struggle, must be acknowledged. First of all, there can be no struggle on the popular or on the individual level without drastic changes. This is a truism. Among these changes the giving up of certain ideas, at very great cost, is one of the most difficult to endure. We must give up, once and for all, the idea that we shall have a Middle East that is as if Zionism had never happened. The Israeli Jew is there in the Middle East, and we cannot, I might even say that we must not, pretend that he will not be there tomorrow, after the struggle is over. This is something very obviously to be faced directly and immediately by the Palestinian who has always fought for his right to be there. It is not for me to say what the right of the Israeli Jew is or should be, but *that* he is, that he exists with an obviously special attachment to the land is something we must face. We must face it directly, and not through the distorting glasses of an imperialist project which, alas, is the only way we have had to face it; quite justly we have rejected it on the grounds that such a vision scants us completely. But how then do we face it? We cannot avoid the continued presence between us and the Israelis of distrust, war, and even the deepest hate. Those cannot be wished away simply, but they can be isolated and seen as secondary attributes of the struggle, the result of circumstances in which Palestinian Arabs and diaspora Jews were victims of powers and historical circumstances that made either violence or the total absence of any sort of meaningful engagement the only two alternatives.

This latest war was a result of such conditions and circumstances. It has made violence on the field of battle the only acceptable language to both sides and the only language understood by the world at large; this idea is not mine alone, for I find it in the editorial declaration, put more approvingly than I would, made on the front page of *al-Nahar* (Beirut), October 8. The violence of war, however, brings very limited results, despite the heady feeling that combatants get as they fight. I myself despise the violence of war. It would seem that one of the perceptions Israelis now have about violence in the past should be that violence of that kind obstructs vision and impedes understanding. These limitations of war apply no less to the Arabs. War leaves the major tasks still very much to be undertaken. But for the past several years, particularly here and generally among diaspora Jews and expatriate Palestinians and Arabs, there have been taking place other sorts of violence which are more productive and perhaps even creative. I am not speaking here of hijacking, kidnapping, robbery, or other forms of free enterprise of that kind, for those, I think, lead politically and morally to nothing. The violence I have in mind is the activity that takes place when, for instance, a Jew or an Israeli is forced psychologically and morally to confront the fact of the Palestinian's presence before him, his presence as a human and political and national and moral entity with which he, as a Jew and as an Israeli, must deal, and to which he must answer. War today has made such a confrontation possible of course, as never before since 1948, but I believe that we cannot stop there: just as we must not forget that during those black years since 1967 it was mainly the Palestinians who kept our spirits alive. There has to be acknowledgement of the human and the political reality which includes both Arabs and Israelis for the reason alone that their day-to-day reality includes the other as foe and as presence. This is the kind of realism that I would oppose to the Israeli pseudo-realism of which I spoke a moment ago. It is a realism that takes in as much as possible of what has happened, of what has been felt and experienced, on both sides. It will take in the dense human reality which has hitherto been denied by one side to the other, and it encompasses not only the discovery of this reality but also the political and emotional pressures—of memory, of war, of threats, of humiliation, of fear above all—whose impressions on all our spirits are very deep. In the United States such confrontations, such interhuman violence of a constructive type have taken place, and I would urge no Arab to shrink from it. Without the Israeli and the Jew most of our twentieth century Arab history is not fully intelligible. Israel has made us more clear to ourselves, in ways we have not liked, in ways that we have justly resisted—but the fact of Israel's role is to be acknowledged nevertheless. If Israel cannot rise to such challenges, if it is doomed to the moral and political dullness that every day violated the Judaic prophetic traditions, *there is no reason at all* why we should so fail! We must not fail.

Thus a major and dangerous consequence of this war is that these reckonings of Arabs with Israelis and Jews might not take place. One reason, as I have said, is the hindering violence of war itself, which gives a combatant the sense that all is solved, or solvable, by war. A second is the setting of this war, which is not simply in the Middle East, but obviously in the media, on the world stage, amidst great power rivalry, and all up and down the great, even unlimited dimensions of history. In other words this war is dangerous not because it might spread to include more participants, but because it will spread to include more elements and perspectives that also obscure the vision, impede understanding, and finally blunt one's humanity. I mean, quite frankly, that this war takes on the symmetry of a blood feud, one side retaliating for the evils of the other, while the roots of the struggle get forgotten

and become unknown to those who struggle the hardest. An
Arab becomes only a reaction to an Israeli, and an Israeli
only a killer of Arabs. As Yeats put it speaking of such a
situation: "The best lack all conviction, while the worst/ Are
full of passionate intensity." Such a war can appeal, and indeed often does appeal, to the worst in one—I've already
spoken of the base feelings of latent anti-Semitism that
emerge as the world watches us, the sense that in watching
Jews and Arabs killing each other one is watching a fun
gladiatorial contest, that there is "our" side and "their" side,
and so on. We must not forget that loss of life, and terrible
expenditure of blood and treasure on both sides, has taken
place; and, however much it concerns an idea in conflict with
another, it is over a land whose place is both central and
absolute for the Arab and the Jew. One of Mahmoud Dar-
wish's short poems can be read as a reminder to both sides
that the land is in some measure theirs together: the excerpt I
shall read comes from a collection entitled "Diary of a Palestinian Wound," and it is dedicated to Fadwa Toukan.

> This is the land that sucks in the flesh of martyrs;
> Summer's returns are wheat and flowers.
> Worship the land!
> In its bowels we are salt and water:
> But on its breast we are a wound, warring.

The perspective of the poem is a long one and a cyclical
one almost; I take it as an invitation to see the struggle in
Palestine as a joint one, a struggle that devastates and which,
from this long perspective, also enriches the land's moral and
human worth to its people. For those of us who, for one
reason or another, have lived at some geographical distance
from the struggle there is no need, however, to consider ourselves outside the struggle, or apart from it in any serious way.
For those of us who believe very strongly that there can be
no long-term solution of the problem of Palestine without the
reckonings of which I have been speaking, then our perspective must include ourselves as participants in the struggle, in
its devastating and enriching aspects, in certain very specific
ways. In the first place, I believe that each of us must feel
called to contribute to the discussion on the crucial issues
facing the Arabs at large. By this I mean that we avoid the
following of party lines, or more important, of vague general ideas—like Arab unity, or peace with justice—and turn
instead to a committed investigation of, and involvement in

precisely the kind of Arab world in which we would like to live. This is especially true, it would seem, of Palestinians who have not often realized, I think, that the Palestine for which they have struggled and continue to struggle is yet to be made, is still in the making. For most people Palestine is but a word or an idea; it must descend from that ideal world and enter the world of actuality without much more delay. And only the potential citizens of Palestine can initiate and sustain such a process, give it precise shape and determine its content.

In the second place I would say that we must work at establishing a workable system of relationships that will enable us to connect profitably our past with our present and our future. My feeling is that too many of us have felt that our past is too distant, our present too unpalatable and our future too hazy; we have felt that our traditions are cumbersome and worn out, daily life too trivial, and our potential much beyond our capacities for realization. Perhaps the problem is that we rely too heavily upon the perceptual modes we have learned, under stress, from the West. Who is it today who can seriously say that he is not thoroughly tired of the sterile debates on such subjects as the conservative and the orthodox movement in Islam, or the Westernizers and the reactionaries, or British interests versus Russian interests, and on and on? The answer is not simply to speak happily of Arab development and Arab oil, but to put ourselves politically and spiritually in the closest touch with our resources, which may be orthodox or modern or neither, but which cannot be something toward which we are sullenly hostile. Of such resources I would say the principal ones are neither oil nor money but rather our staggeringly complex cultural system, which accommodates an infinite series of particular experiences, experiences sectarian, topographical, political, religious, historical, and sociological, with a general Arab-Islamic worldview; and, a second principal resource, the almost unparalleled access we have as a modern people to the traditions of a rich past. There can be no people whose modern birth took place in so short a time and with such remarkable natural and material wealth, and at the same time incorporated within its modern life so much of its stable traditionalism. These two resources alone require human, social and political exploitation of a sort that will occupy many future generations.

In the last place, and at the risk of sounding perhaps a

little conservative, I would say that a wide perspective must necessarily take into account the present state of affairs, not as something to be lamented or joked about, but something about which to be concerned. There are institutions, from governments to school systems to legal processes, in the Arab world and amongst Arab communities here whose functioning at present may be unsatisfactory but whose necessity, even as a minimum, is very serious. I think also, for example, about those Palestinian Arab institutions now functioning in the occupied territories such as Bir Zeit College. Such things cannot be abandoned while we research the theory of revolutionary practice in the New Jerusalem. There are realities of power and government with which we, as the most revolutionary group perhaps, cannot afford to misunderstand or be ignorant of. I think that we face a real test of our vision as we set about dealing with these presences, not as something to be put aside until the correct plan or the most perfect solution happens upon us, but more or less as a call upon our inventiveness and generosity and our intelligence. Each one of us I suppose has a hold on him of some urgency in the contemporary Arab world or in contemporary Arab life; it is that hold with which one must begin, not with a vague theoretical desire to reform the world, nor, as I have been saying about the Israeli, with a very definite wish to exclude all but the small part of reality which obsesses one. From that beginning on our involvement gets more specific and more strong, and this takes place in ways that I haven't the opportunity now to describe. But what I have tried to describe is the fairly complex and rich process which connects Arabs with each other and with Jews in what is now a terrible and costly struggle but which, one can hope, will turn out to have been a step made during the long revolution.

The Meaning of "A Democratic Palestinian State"*

By Y. Harkabi

1. The Internal Debate

The crux of the Arab conflict with Israel has been the problem of safeguarding the country's Arab character. Arab de-

* Excerpts from an article originally published in 1970, with a postscript of 1974. From Y. Harkabi: *Palestinians and Israel*, Jerusalem, 1974.

mands during the Mandate for the prohibition of the sale of land to Jews and curtailment of Jewish immigration served the same purpose: that of keeping the ownership of land and Palestine's ethnic character inviolate. The difficulties confronting the Arabs in their attempt to halt Judaization were aggravated with the end of the Mandate and the foundation of the State of Israel: from then on it was a question of turning back the wheel of history and erasing the Jewish state.

The problem of eliminating the Jewish state is heightened by the presence of a considerable Jewish population. For a Jewish state depends upon the existence of Jewish citizens, and therefore elimination of the state requires in principle a "reduction" in their number. Hence the frequency and dominance of the motif of killing the Jews and throwing them into the sea in Arab pronouncements. Their position, insofar as it was *politicidal* (i.e., calling for annihilation of a state), was bound to have *genocidal* implications, even had the Arabs not been bent upon revenge.

When, after the Six-Day War, the Arabs realized that their wild statements had harmed their international reputation, they moderated their shrill demands for the annihilation of Israel. Arab propagandists denied that they had ever advocated the slaughter of the Jewish population, asserting that, at most, "Jewish provocations" had aroused their anger and wild statements which, they alleged, were not meant to be taken literally. Ahmed Shukeiry insisted that he never advocated throwing the Jews into the sea, that the whole thing was merely a Zionist libel. What he meant, he explained, was that the Jews would return to their countries of origin by way of the sea: "They came by the sea and will return by the sea" (*Palestine Documents for 1967*, p. 1084).

After the Six-Day War, Arab spokesmen put forward the concept of "a Democratic Palestinian State in which Arabs and Jews will live in peace." This slogan was well received and regarded by the world at large as evidence of a new Arab moderation. Many people overlooked the ambiguity of the pronouncement and disregarded the fact that it did not contradict basic Arab contentions: for the wording might well imply the reduction of Jews to an insignificant minority, which would then be permitted to live in peace. Once this line was adopted, its meaning was keenly debated among the Palestinian Arabs.

An indication of the slogan's true significance, as understood by the Palestinian organizations, is found in a circular to its members sent by the Popular Democratic Front for the Liberation of Palestine, reporting on the deliberations of the sixth session of the Palestinian National Assembly. This fedayeen organization, headed by Na'if Hawatmeh, broke away from George Habash's Popular Front for the Liberation of Palestine in February 1969. A delegation of the Popular Democratic Front proposed to the Assembly that the slogan "Democratic State" should be given "a progressive content." The Assembly rejected their proposal suggesting that the main purpose of the "Democratic State" concept was to improve the Arab image. Moreover, the inclusion of this slogan in the national program would, it was stressed, impair the Arab character of Palestine. Nevertheless, since it had been well received abroad, the Assembly considered it worth retaining.

The relevant passage in the Popular Democratic Front's report entitled "Internal Circular concerning Debates and Results of the Sixth National Assembly" reads:

> The slogan "The Democratic Palestinian State" has been raised for some time within the Palestinian context. Fatah was the first to adopt it. Since it was raised, this slogan has met with remarkable world response. Our delegation presented the Congress [i.e., the Assembly] with a resolution designed to elucidate its meaning from a progressive aspect, opposing in principle the slogan of throwing the Jews into the sea, which has in the past seriously harmed the Arab position.
>
> When the subject was first debated, it was thought that there was general agreement on it. But as the debate developed, considerable opposition showed itself. In the course of the discussion the following views came to light.
>
> 1. One which maintains that the slogan of "The Democratic Palestinian State" is a tactical one which we propagate because it has been well received internationally.
>
> 2. Another suggests that we consider this slogan to be strategic rather than tactical, but that it should be retained even though it is not a basic principle. This position, but for a mere play of words, corresponds to the previous one.
>
> 3. The third view was more straightforward in rejecting the slogan and its progressive content as proposed by our delegation. The position of this faction was based on the assertion that the slogan contradicts the Arab character of Palestine and the principle of self-determination enshrined in the National Covenant of the [Palestine] Liberation Organization, and that it also advocates a peaceful settlement with the Jews of Palestine....

In this way the "democratic solution" is presented as a compromise between two chauvinistic alternatives—a Jewish state, and driving the Jews into the sea—as if these were comparable propositions. By this supposedly fair solution, the Arabs renounce the extermination of Jews, and the Jews renounce their state. Although the Palestinian state will become a popular democracy, its Arab character will be preserved by being part of a larger "democratic" Arab federation. The final paragraph is meant to repudiate objections that a democratic Palestine would remain, owing to its mixed population, an anomaly among the Arab states and difficult to digest within the framework of Arab unity.

The Democratic Front's pronouncement may be mistakenly interpreted as favoring a binational state: "The Palestinian state will eliminate racial discrimination and national persecution and will be based on a democratic solution to the conflict brought about by the coexistence (*ta'āyush*) of the two peoples, Arabs and Jews" (*The Present Situation* . . ., p. 136). The recognition of "a Jewish people" is a significant innovation. Hitherto Arabs have mostly held that Jews constitute only a religion and do not therefore deserve a national state. However, this admission of a Jewish nationhood is qualified, for Jews as a people are not entitled to a state of their own but must settle for incorporation in a state of Palestinian nationality. Their nationhood, therefore, has only cultural and not national-political dimensions. Thus, Hawatmeh tells Lutfi al-Khuli, editor of *at-Tali'a:*

> We urged initiation of a dialogue with the Israeli socialist organization Matzpen, which advocates an Arab-Jewish binational state. But we have not been able to convince Matzpen to adopt a thoroughly progressive, democratic position on the Palestine question which would mean liquidation (*tasfiaya*) of the Zionist entity and establishment of a democratic Palestinian state opposed to all kinds of class and national suppression (*at-Tali'a*, November, 1969, p. 106).

The proposal for a binational state, as advocated by Matzpen, is not sufficiently progressive for Hawatmeh. In his view, Jewish nationhood implies only cultural autonomy for a religious community. But this is no innovation; Mr. Shukeiry was prepared to grant the same.

2. Bafflements and Contradictions

In Arab journalism, particularly in periodicals, interesting articles and symposia are often published concerning social prob-

lems, self-criticism and the Arab-Israel conflict. Israeli newspaper reporting usually skips over these articles because it is
by its nature more concerned with political events, more with
Arabs' actions and less with their ideas. Such journalistic
portrayal of the Arab world becomes pallid because of the
absence of the human-ideological dimension of events. Human
beings not only operate, they also think about their actions.
Furthermore, our concern for the opponent's reflections tends
to humanize him by viewing him along with all his human
problems. The Six-Day War and its aftermath raised questions for the Arabs and stimulated them to reassess their
procedure in the conflict. They began to grapple with the
question of their *objective* in the conflict. This wrestling is
primarily concerned now with the slogan "Democratic Palestinian State."

In the weekly supplement of the Beirut newspaper *al-Anwar*
(March 8, 1970), a long symposium was published concerning the meaning of the slogan "The Democratic State," in
which the views of most of the prominent fedayeen organizations were represented. A translation of extracts (italicized
text) from this symposium is here presented, along with comments by the author and a summary concerning its significance.

Representative of the Democratic Front: ... The adoption of
a particular slogan, in our estimation, does not stem from a
subjective position or a subjective desire but from a study and
analysis of the evolution of the objective situation, the objective possibilities present in society and within history—moving
forces, as well as the nature of the potential evolution of
these forces in the future. ...

Coexistence (ta'āyush) *with this entity* (*Israel*) *is impossible, not because of a national aim or national aspiration of
the Arabs, but because the presence of this entity will determine this region's development in connection with world
imperialism, which follows from the objective link between it
and Zionism. Thus, eradicating imperialist influence in the
Middle East means eradicating the Israeli entity. This is something indispensable, not only from the aspect of the Palestinian people's right of self-determination, and in its homeland, but also from the aspect of protecting the Arab national
liberation movement, and this objective also can only be
achieved by means of armed struggle. ...*

The representative of the Arab Liberation Front (a fedayeen organization under Iraqi influence): *There is no special [separate] solution for the Palestine issue. The solution must be within the framework of the Arab revolution, because the Palestine issue is not merely the paramount Arab issue but the substance and basic motivation of the Arab struggle. If the Arab nation suffers from backwardness, exploitation and disunity, these afflictions are much more severe in Palestine. That is, the Arab cause in the present historical stage is epitomized in the Palestine issue. . . .*

The liberation of Palestine will be the way for the Arabs to realize unity, not to set up regional State No. 15, which will only deepen disunity. The unified State will be the alternative to the Zionist entity, and it will be of necessity democratic, as long as we understand beforehand the dialectical connection between unity and Socialism. In the united Arab State all the minorities—denominational and others—will have equal rights . . .

The intention is not to set up a Palestinian State as an independent unit, but to incorporate it within a unified Arab State which will be democratic because it is progressive, and which will grant the Israeli Jews minority rights.

Shafiq al-Hut (a leader of the PLO and head of its Beirut office): *. . . The Palestinian problem is that of a Zionist-colonialist invasion at the expense of a land and a people known for thirteen centuries as the Palestinian Arab people. . . .*

I side with Farid al-Khatib in holding that there is no benefit in expatiating upon the slogan "Democratic Palestinian State." I hope the fedayeen organizations will not do so, although I would encourage discussion of it by those who are not in responsible positions. Whatever discussion of it there is on the part of the fighting groups may cause a sense of helplessness, despair or weakness. . . .

As far as it concerns the human situation of the Jews, which Farid al-Khatib mentioned, we should expose the Zionist movement and say to the Jew: The Zionist movement which brought you to Palestine did not supply a solution to your problem as a Jew; therefore you must return whence you came to seek another way of striving for a solution for what

*is called "the problem of the persecuted Jew in the world."
As Marx has said, he (the Jew) has no alternative but to be
assimilated into his society. . . .*

*Even if we wished, by force of circumstances, a Democratic
Palestinian State "period," this would mean its being non-
Arab. Let us face matters honestly. When we speak simply
of a Democratic Palestinian State, this means we discard its
Arab identity. I say that on this subject we cannot negotiate,
even if we possess the political power to authorize this kind
of decision, because we thereby disregard an historical truth,
namely, that this land and those who dwell upon it belong to
a certain environment and a certain region, to which we are
linked as one nation, one heritage and one hope—Unity,
Freedom and Socialism. . . .*

The implication that the Israeli Jews would be allowed to
stay in the Democratic State raises difficulties concerning its
Arab character.

*If the slogan of the Democratic State was intended only
to counter the claim that we wish to throw the Jews into the
sea, this is indeed an apt slogan and an effective political and
propaganda blow. But if we wish to regard it as the ultimate
strategy of the Palestinian and Arab liberation movement,
then I believe it requires a long pause for reflection, for it
bears upon our history, just as our present and certainly our
future.*

Representative of as-Sa'iqa (a Syrian fedayeen organization): *I was among those who thought five years ago that
we must slaughter the Jews. But now I cannot imagine that,
if we win one night, it will be possible for us to slaughter
them, or even one tenth of them. I cannot conceive of it,
neither as a man, nor as an Arab.*

*If so, what do we wish to do with these Jews? This is a
problem for which I do not claim to have a ready answer.
It is a problem which every Arab and Palestinian citizen has
an obligation to express his opinion about, because it is yet
early for a final, ripe formulation to offer the world and those
living in Palestine.*

*Thus, I think that among many Jews, those living in Pales-
tine, especially the Arab Jews, there is a great desire to return
to their countries of origin, since the Zionist efforts to trans-*

form them into a homogeneous, cohesive nation have failed. There is a well-known human feeling—yearning for one's homeland, one's birthplace. There are a number of known facts concerning the Jews living in Palestine today which clearly point to this feeling among them. They desire to return to their countries of origin, especially Jews from the Arab region. . . .

Moderator: *. . . Can we consider the Kurdish problem and the manner of its solution as similar to the Jewish problem and its solution under the heading of the slogan of one Democratic State? . . .*

Representative of the Liberation Front: *Our view of the subject of Kurdish national rights follows from objective and historical considerations which substantially contradict the nature and objectives of the Zionist movement. The Kurds comprise a nationality having a distinct, well-known historical, geographical and human dimension. . . .*

Farid al-Khatib: *As far as the Arab character of the Democratic State is concerned, the Jews in Palestine have the right to express their view concerning the Arab character of the Democratic State in a democratic manner. And although it is possible to say that the Democratic State is Arab, and to say furthermore that it is a union, it is advisable to hold back additional information until the appropriate stages in the evolution of the resistance are reached. When the Zionist movement came to Palestine, it first sought a refuge, afterward a homeland, and then a State; and now it is striving to build an empire within and outside Palestine.*

Zionism also disclosed its objectives in stages.

There is nothing to be gained by summoning the Jews in the Zionist State to join the national liberation movement, as Shafiq al-Hut proposed, when he advocated convening the unified State at once. This will not convince the Jews of the world and world public opinion.

As far as it concerns the number of Palestinians, all those who emigrated to Latin America in the nineteenth century, and those who live in the desert, in exile, under conquest, or in prison, all are citizens in the State. For example: the number of Bethlehemite residents living in South America exceeds the number of those Bethlehemites living in occupied

Palestine, and the combined total [of all Palestinians] is not less than that of the Jews now living in the Zionist State. . . .

The Palestinians are more numerous than the Israeli Jews and will determine the character of the State.

Shafiq al-Hut: *First, how can Farid (al-Khatib) think that the Jews and Zionists who came to set up an empire in our country have the privilege to express their democratic right in the Palestinian State? Second, how can he claim that it is difficult to convince Jewish citizens to join the liberation movement?*

Farid al-Khatib: *I think that most of the Jews living in Palestine are groups of people who were deceived by the Zionist movement and the world imperialist movement. And the Jew, as a man, has the right to express his opinion in a democratic manner regarding his future life after the collapse of the Zionist State, which is opposed to the Democratic State insofar as it discriminates between the Eastern Jew and the Western Jew and the Circassian Jew.*

The second point: The greatest ambition of the revolution is to draw the Jews of the Zionist State into the ranks of the resistance movement. . . . But what I wanted to say is that it is difficult to persuade the Jews to join the resistance movement because its immediate objective is to dissolve the Zionist contradiction within the Zionist State. . . .

Representative of the Democratic Front: *It seems to me that many of the disagreements that exist concerning this idea can be traced to some manner of misunderstanding or lack of communication. . . . This State is not bi-national in the sense that there would be two national States joined together in one form or another. This solution must be rejected, not only because it is inconsistent with our own desire, but also because it is not a true democratic solution. It is rather a solution that will represent the continuation of the national conflict which exists between the Jews and Arabs, not a solution of this conflict. It is impossible to speak of a democratic solution if it is powerless to eliminate the conflict between the different denominations and peoples within the Democratic State. When we speak of democracy it must be clear that we do not mean liberal democracy in the manner of "one man, one vote."*

OLD ILLUSIONS AND NEW AWARENESS

If the number of Jews living in Israel is not reduced, then, on a national level their quantitative and qualitative weight will dilute the Arab character of the liberated state, and on a personal level there will not be sufficient room for these Jews as well as for the Palestinians who supposedly *all* desire to return. In order to evade these difficulties, the spokesmen in the symposium try to breathe life into old ideas: that the Jews brought to the country were misguided by Zionist deceit (Zionism therefore not being a vital need), and that they remain by coercion (criticism by Israelis of themselves and their state, in a manner unknown in Arab countries, is interpreted as a sign of hatred for the state and a desire to emigrate). On these grounds it is believed that the Jews would rejoice at the opportunity to leave. An interesting element of self-deception is added, that the Jews from Arab countries wish to return to their countries of origin. One may suspect that this illusion contains the psychological dimension of *amour-propre* and self-adulation: the Arabs are so good and were so kind to the Jews that it is inconceivable for the Jews not to desire ardently to return to live under their protection. However, along with these notions, there are signs of recognition that this is a false hope, and that the Jews have nowhere to return to, especially those born in the country, who will soon become the majority of the Jewish community. An attempt to grapple with these contradictory notions is most evident in the words of the as-Sa'iqa representative, who maintains at one and the same time that most Israeli Jews have nowhere to go, and yet that many will emigrate.

The spokesmen also try to evade this problem by claiming that the Israeli Jews are not a people. Their attachment to the country is therefore weak, and the hope that they will emigrate is reinforced. Moreover, in the clash between the Jewish group, whose cohesion is supposedly religious and not national, and the group whose cohesion is national, the latter will prevail, thereby determining the character of the country. Therefore, even if a considerable Jewish community remains there will be no such thing as a partnership between two homogeneous groups, creating a bi-national state. The Democratic Front, which stresses the Palestinianism of the Democratic State more than its Arab character, also regards membership in an Arab unity as inherent in the very idea of the

Democratic State, while the Iraqi organization rejects the notion of the Palestinian State and regards it at best as a district within a unified state. (For this organization, the struggle in Palestine has the value of a catalyst for the rest of the changes in Arab countries, or a spark that will ignite a revolution that will spread to all of them.) Along with these hopes of reducing the number of Jews in the Democratic State there is the notion of tipping the population scales in the Arabs' favor by considering all Palestine Arabs, wherever they may live, as prospective citizens of the state according to an Arab Law of Return of sorts.

All the participants in the symposium agree that the Jews do not presently constitute a people. However, the recognition gnaws at some of them that nationalism is not something static but an evolution, and as time goes on, the Jews in Israel will become consolidated into a people and a nation. Hence the conclusion that this process must be forestalled by the founding of a Palestinian State. The temporal factor thus works against the idea that the Israelis are not a people, and against the possibility of founding a Palestinian State. It is no accident that Shafiq al-Hut vigorously maintains the essential and permanent nature of the Jewish status as nonpeople and non-nation. According to the view presented by Arabs, only a people has the right of political self-determination and deserves a state of its own. If the Jews are indeed becoming a people, this means that they are in the process of acquiring these rights.

AN ARAB PANDORA'S BOX

For most of the participants, the slogan "Democratic State" is merely tactical, the aim being to give the outside world a positive impression and to enchant the Israelis who, as the speaker who describes Fatah's views says, will only eventually discover its full meaning. For the Democratic Front this is presumably not merely a slogan, but a *principle* they sincerely hold as an implication of the progressivism they profess. However, even they wrestle with the slogan; they safeguard themselves by various qualifications or *hedges:* the state will be a member within an Arab federation, and the democracy will not be formal, nor expressed in a numerical representation, but a "true" democracy of "the contents"—that is, its policy will represent progressiveness as expressed by "the Palestinian revolution." The final qualification is their insistence upon the precondition for establishing the Democratic State, that Israel be destroyed.

For those who regard the slogan "Democratic State" as merely a tactic, the problem arises that it is impossible to lead the public only by tactical slogans; one must present the objectives of a national vision. While the slogan "Democratic State" may be helpful externally, it is quite destructive internally, impairs the state's Arabism and undermines confidence in the feasibility of "returning" to the country, if it would not be evacuated. Shafiq al-Hut states bluntly that acceptance of this slogan means abandoning the idea of Arabism. From the Arab viewpoint another two-fold question arises: 1) if the Jews are a people, it is doubtful whether they will consent to live in a non-Jewish state, and hence the expressed hope that they will emigrate; 2) since the Palestinians are a people, they will certainly be opposed to returning to a state which is not Arab.

It appears that the Palestinians and Arabs are beginning to sense the difficulty of their ideological position. In the past they could be content with the formulations "restoration of rights" and "restoration of the homeland," which were restricted to the meaning of the objective as bearing upon what would be given to the Arabs, and the implication concerning what would be taken away from the Jews was overlooked. Arab spokesmen in foreign countries are still striving to focus on the need to rectify the injustice inflicted on the Palestinians, while evading the implication of this rectification for the Jews. The necessity of defining the position in all its aspects and the debate concerning the Democratic Palestinian State undermine the Arab position. The slogan of a "Democratic State" seemed to be an escape from a genocidal position, but it was revealed as the first step of retreat, and the source of problems and bewilderment. I think it is no exaggeration to say that this slogan opened a Pandora's box for the Arab position in the conflict. Hence the deep apprehensions of all the participants in the discussion concerning this slogan, and the dramatic agreement of everyone at the end of it that the slogan "Democratic State" is premature, even though this contradicted the previous insistence by some on the need for a clear definition of the objective.

It appears that those who formulated the Palestinian Covenant of 1968 sensed the difficulties inherent in the Arab posi-

tion and wished to anticipate them by nailing down the qualification that only a small Jewish minority (the descendants of
those who came to the country before 1917) would be given
citizenship in "the liberated state," thus assuring the Arab
character of the country. If this stipulation manifests radicali-
zation of the position, the reason was probably the apprehension that otherwise the ground would begin sliding beneath
the Arab position.

The slogan of the "Democratic State" was offered as an
escape from the odium that Article 6 of the 1968 Covenant
brought upon the PLO stand, and as if the former superseded
the latter, even without the formal act of amending the
Covenant. It seems that the difficulties in which the idea of
the Democratic State is enmeshed and the internal controversies it aroused, as expressed in this symposium, explain
why Article 6 has not been amended, despite the fact that it
damaged the Palestinian cause.

3. Postscript

The slogan of the "Democratic State" was hailed by Arab
spokesmen as an all-important innovation demonstrating the
liberal humanitarian nature of the Palestine movement. Yasser
Arafat, to strengthen this impression, even said that its president can be Jewish. However, scrutiny shows that it is
neither so liberal nor new.

The objective of setting up a Democratic Palestine was
enshrined in the resolutions of the Eighth Palestinian National
Assembly (March 1–5, 1971). The resolution was carefully
formulated and it does not say, as Palestinian spokesmen
purport to interpret the slogan, that *all* Israelis will be allowed
to stay, but that the state will be based on equality of rights
for all its citizens: "The future state in Palestine . . . will be
Democratic, in which all will enjoy the same rights and obligations." This is quite compatible with the quantitative limitation included in the infamous Article 6 of the 1968 Covenant.

It is not new. All along the Palestinians have repeatedly
declared that their state will be democratic. That is part of
the spirit of the age, when even autocratic regimes call themselves democratic. For instance, the Congress, which set up
the "All-Palestine Government" in Gaza and which unanimously elected the former Mufti of Jerusalem, Hajj Amin al-
Husaini, as its president, proclaimed on October 1, 1948 "the

establishment of a free and democratic sovereign state. In it the citizens will enjoy their liberties and their rights. . . ."

Even if the slogan of the "Democratic State" were free of inconsistency and insincerity it is not acceptable to the Israelis. The Israelis have no less a right to national self-determination than the Palestinian Arabs. They do not want to become Palestinians of Jewish faith; they intend to remain Israelis.

The difficulties for the Arabs inherent in the slogan of the "Democratic State" caused a decline in its discussion at subsequent Palestinian Congresses. This does not mean that it was discarded, as the alternative is to fall back on the brutality of the former, blatant, politicidal-genocidal position.

No Need To Worry Now

Perhaps the most common attitude is to concentrate at this stage on the demand for "self-determination for the Palestinians in their homeland" and leave the rest. This demand is an objective that can be easily justified. Defining the final objective now, it is argued, is a waste of time, and only a source of bafflement. Political objectives should be set in a time sequence. The problem of reconciling the existence of a large Jewish community with the conversion of the country into a Palestinian state is one for the distant future and should not bother the Arabs and Palestinians now. Now they should exert all their efforts in the struggle against Israel and in attaining of their national and social objectives. The achievement of these and the return of the Palestinians will produce new conditions which may solve the entire problem.

This approach was already alluded to in the Symposium. It has been expressed with greater clarity by Alias Murqus in his book criticizing the platform of the Lebanese Communist Party (LCP) at its Second Congress in the summer of 1968. Murqus commends the LCP stand in defining that the "final solution to the Palestinian problem should be based on positions of principle, stemming from the inalienable right of the Palestinian Arabs in their land and homeland and hence their right to return there and achieve their self-determination . . . as the existence of the Jews in Palestine cannot impair the Palestinian natural and historical right in their homeland." He stresses that "the final solution to the Palestinian problem is Palestine as an Arab homeland," and as regards the future it calls for "the complete eradication of the State of Israel." He goes on:

> How shall we reconcile the existence of two million Jews and two million Palestinian Arabs? This is not our task or yours now. Let us define our objective in principle and nothing more. Let us define the present way to the goal: The fighting and the falling of hundreds of thousands from the Arabs and the Jews (from the Arab more than from the Jews). With the victory of the Algerian revolution the majority of the French, young and old, went, returned to France. With Arab victory in the Near East (the battle will be longer, fiercer and with heavier casualties), it is possible that the Jews in great numbers will return whence they came—Baghdad, Allepo, Yemen, Morroco, Tunisia, Algeria, Egypt, Poland and other places, to France, or they will settle in Canada, the USA and Australia. This problem should not worry us, as its solution is by the struggle (*Marxism, Leninism and the World and Arab Development in the Platform of the Lebanese Communist Party*, (Arabic) Dar al-Haqiqa, Beirut, 1970, pp. 362–363).

Peace with Egypt?

By Walter Laqueur*

Any discussion of the current prospects for peace between Israel and the Arab countries has to begin by rehearsing the history of the Middle East between the Six-Day War of June 1967 and the Yom Kippur War of October 1973. Efforts to reach a peace settlement in those seven years were protracted, highly complicated, and ultimately futile. All the many plans that were proposed—the Rogers plan, the Jarring plan, and the nameless others—seem now of merely academic interest (although it is entirely possible that one or another of them will be disinterred for future use). The story of these negotiations is a melancholy one, not least for the question it raises of possible opportunities missed by the various parties to the conflict, especially Israel. Not that Israel ignored any genuine peace overture from the Arabs; there was none. But it is another matter whether an interim accommodation might not have been reached with Egypt alone, based on a demilitarization of the Sinai, and whether such an arrange-

* Reprinted with kind permission from *Commentary* (March, 1974).

ment would not have lessened the likelihood of a new round of fighting.

After the Arab attack of October 1973 it was noted in Israel that the strategic depth offered by the Sinai was in fact a lifesaver; had the attack been launched from the pre-June 1967 lines it would have threatened Israel's very existence. This is very true. But the argument assumes that the 1967 borders were the only feasible alternative to the Bar Lev line, when in fact a demilitarized Sinai might have functioned as a more effective warning zone than did the Suez Canal. Nor can it be taken for granted that the attack itself was inevitable, since Egypt faced a great many problems at home and abroad, and had some sort of interim agreement been reached on the Sinai, the Egyptians might not have felt such an overriding urgency to recover all the lost territories.

Similarly, a settlement might have been made with Jordan; although not with Syria. Yet Syria in isolation could not have caused a great deal of damage. The same goes for Al-Fatah and its rival groups, who would anyway have kept up their sporadic attacks from across the border and the hijacking of airplanes. In the course of time, however, the Palestinians might have come to see that they could no longer rely on the Arab governments in their struggle and they too might have come to accept the existence of the state of Israel.

This particular line of thinking was dismissed in the late 60's as a dangerous delusion by those who claimed to know Arab political psychology. Yet it later appeared that the terrorist organizations were actually afraid of a more flexible Israeli policy, lest it put them out of business. "Thank God for Dayan," wrote Yasir Arafat in retrospect:

> After the 1967 defeat, Arab opinion, broken and dispirited, was ready to conclude peace at any price. If Israel, after its lightning victory, had proclaimed that it had no expansionist aims and withdrawn its troops from the conquered territories, while continuing to occupy certain strategic points necessary to its security, the affair would have been easily settled. . . .[1]

Arafat exaggerates: the affair would not have been easily settled. Still, there was a chance that de-escalation might have worked, and the truth is that those opportunities which did exist were not explored.

[1] Quoted in John K. Cooley, *Green March, Black September* (New York, 1973), p. 99.

The reasons for this were manifold. Deep down the Israelis have always inclined toward a "worst-case" analysis of their situation, arising perhaps from a determination (which is hardly difficult to understand in the light of recent history) not to take any risks with Jewish lives. Arab leaders had threatened Israel with extinction for many years prior to 1967, and these threats could not easily be dismissed as idle. When in the wake of the 1967 war the Arabs officially opted at the Khartoum conference for a policy of immobility ("No peace, no recognition, no negotiation") it was only natural for Israel to react accordingly. Any other course would have been interpreted as evidence of weakness, and it was well known that Arabs respected strength alone. From a military point of view the 1967 armistice lines seemed ideal. Before the war, Jordanian territory extended to within 30 km. of Tel Aviv, Egyptian territory to within 80; now the Egyptians were many hundreds of kilometers away, and the Jordanians were beyond the Jordan River. Israeli planes could reach Cairo in a few minutes' time. A good case could be, and was, made for not withdrawing from these lines—quite apart from the biblical prophecies and other divine injunctions invoked by the few Israeli annexationists.

No one in Israel expected all the territories taken in the Six-Day War to be retained, at least at first. Immediately after the war Moshe Dayan came out against an Israeli presence at the Suez Canal, Abba Eban warned against an "intoxication with victory," David Ben-Gurion on more than one occasion reiterated that a strong army, although vital, was no substitute for a political solution which in his view should include a return of the West Bank under agreed terms and a satisfactory settlement of the Sinai issue. Differences of opinion within the ranks of the Israeli government itself manifested themselves in such proposals as the Allon plan, recognizing the Palestinian Arabs' right to self-determination. But as time went on, Dayan, Golda Meir, Israel Galili, and other Israeli leaders became increasingly pessimistic about the prospects of a peace settlement. As long as the Arabs were unwilling to talk, Israel had to stand fast. A growing reluctance was felt even to discuss the possible terms of a settlement. The general attitude became that the Arab-Israeli confrontation, like every other conflict in history, had to run its full course. At some date in the future, when the Arabs were psychologically ready to accept the existence of Israel, it would be possible to find mutually acceptable solutions to all the outstanding questions—but for the time being Israel had to stand firm.

This policy had much to recommend it, but it also had several major flaws. It ignored the fact that the Arab-Israeli conflict was not purely regional in character, and that with regard to the two superpowers involved, an asymmetry existed between American support for Israel and Soviet support for the Arabs: America had to consider its other interests in the Middle East whereas the Soviet Union could give all-out assistance to its clients. It underrated the effective force of the Arab armies built up by the Russians since 1967. It overrated détente. And, above all, it did not take into consideration the growing importance of the oil weapon as a means of isolating Israel on the international scene: as far as Western Europe and Japan were concerned, Israel was expendable but Arab oil was not. The international constellation, in brief, was changing, and not in Israel's favor. A major power might have stood by and watched these changes with some degree of equanimity; a small country did so at its peril.

With the end of the 1973 war came a new willingness in Israel to rethink the Arab-Israeli dispute, and to consider new ways of settling it. A spate of articles and speeches, symptomatic of the confusion caused by war, suggested all kinds of panaceas: a National Security Council, a mutual-defense pact with the U.S., a "charismatic minister of information." Only after an interval of several weeks were serious attempts undertaken to analyze the lessons of the October war in broader perspective and greater depth. This soul-searching coincided with the electoral campaign in which the parties had to clarify their policies for the future. The right-wing Herut claimed in its election propaganda that the people of Israel had won a magnificent victory on the battlefield and should not have to pay for the defeat of the Western world on the oilfields of Arabia; but Herut also denied that it was a "war party" and asserted that it was much better equipped than the Labor coalition to lead Israel toward peace. The Liberals, Herut's partners in the Likud coalition, advocated a more moderate line, suggesting Israeli concessions in return for peace; the debate among Liberals was whether these concessions should be spelled out or not.

As for the Labor alignment, it had to accommodate conflicting trends in its declared policy. The preamble of the 14-point program accepted last November stated that "Our platform must reflect the lessons of the Yom Kippur War." But what were these lessons, apart from the need (on which everyone agreed) to maintain the strength of the defense forces? The platform insisted on defensible borders based on a territorial compromise. There would be no return to the June 1967 boundaries; a peace agreement with Jordan would be based on the existence of two independent states—Israel, with Jerusalem as its capital, and an Arab state to the east; efforts would be made to continue settling Israelis in the occupied areas "in keeping with cabinet decisions giving priority to national security considerations." The last point was a concession to the "hawks" in the Labor alignment, but as a whole the Labor platform constituted a decisive victory for the doves and a retreat from the maximalist demands voiced before the war.

By sheer coincidence, the Labor platform was published on the same day the demands of the Arabs were made known at the Algiers meeting of Arab heads of state. These stated that the struggle against the Zionist "invasion" was a long-term historic responsibility which would call for many more trials and sacrifices. A cease-fire was not peace, which would come only when a number of conditions had been met, two among them paramount and unequivocal: first, the evacuation by Israel of all occupied Arab territories and above all Jerusalem; second, the re-establishment of full national rights for the Palestinian people. Yet inasmuch as no objections were voiced to negotiations with Israel, something which the Khartoum conference in 1967 had expressly rejected, it appeared to many observers that the "moderate" line of President Sadat had won out in Algiers. The final communiqué stated that the meeting had been a great success, but since Iraq and Libya boycotted the conference, and Syria subsequently decided not to participate in the Geneva conference at all, Arab unity could by no means be said to be complete. As the weeks passed the Algiers resolution was shrilly rejected by Arab extremists. A broadcast emanating from Baghdad on December 21, 1973 (the day the Geneva talks opened) announced: "The masses will not be bound by the regimes of treason and defeatism at the Geneva conference." Radio Tripoli asked: "Has our Arab nation become so servile in the eyes of those leaders [i.e., Sadat] that they belittle its dignity and injure its pride without fearing its wrath?"

Israel's "khaki elections" took place on the last day of the old year. If public-opinion polls published last September are to be trusted, the results would have been similar even if the war had not taken place. The Labor alignment, deeply split and under fire from within not only because of the military handling of the war but for the lack of flexibility shown by Mrs. Meir's inner circle in recent years, lost ground. Were it not for the obvious necessity to preserve the unity of the alignment in view of the international situation, it is quite possible that both Mrs. Meir and General Dayan might have had to resign under pressure from large sections of their party. But Likud had no cause to be overjoyed by the results of the elections either; if the party of Menahem Begin could not overtake its rivals in such nearly ideal conditions, it never would—unless, of course, the Labor alignment should disintegrate entirely.

The campaign was confused because the Israeli voter was not given a clear choice. As one Israeli commentator wrote, "Those who want to purchase Dayan must buy Allon. Those who want the Liberals must buy Begin." In the absence of a clear choice, the outcome of the elections was bound to be inconclusive: no clear mandate emerged for any one course of action. Menahem Begin may have been relieved not to receive more votes than he did; victory would have almost certainly compelled him to make concessions in Geneva contrary to what he promised during the campaign. Yet the absence of consensus—more accurately, the sharp polarization of public opinion—will make the task of the Israeli negotiators beyond the first stage of the talks very difficult. The effect of the vote, the London *Economist* wrote, was to block any government from making the vital decisions that the Geneva talks demand. Since such a state of affairs cannot continue for very long, the deadlock will probably be broken either by new fighting or by a new election, or perhaps both.

II

Throughout history there has been one kind of war notoriously difficult to conclude: the war of faith, the holy war, the crusade. In these conflicts it is not the leader or the government of the other side that is the enemy, but every individual in the enemy camp.

To what extent do the Arabs regard their conflict with

Israel as a religious war, or a war of national liberation, to use the modern parlance? The recent Algiers summit conference proclaimed that the war aim of the Arab states was the restoration of the national rights of the Palestinian Arabs, that the Palestine Liberation Organization was the only legal representative of the Palestinians, and that its interpretation of the "national rights" was binding. The PLO interpretation was in turn laid down in the Palestinian National Covenant of July 1968, which says that the establishment of Israel is "null and void." The Algiers resolution, in other words, as much as stated that the purpose of any peace conference would be to discuss the liquidation of Israel.

In the eyes of some, this means that it is pointless for Israel to attend the Geneva conference. Fortunately, however, even in the war aims of religious or quasi-religious movements a discrepancy often exists between the desirable and the possible. In theory Catholics and Protestants should not coexist to this day, nor should Muslims and Christians, or Communists and non-Communists. All such movements have come at one stage or another to the realization that with an enemy who cannot be defeated, temporary compromises have to be made. The old enmity, the *odium theologicum*, is itself subject to gradual erosion as such compromises become permanent; the formulas of hatred may linger on but they no longer carry the same conviction.

At the Geneva peace conference Israel will establish in due course whether, at this stage in the conflict, a readiness to compromise has been reached by the Arab states. With regard to Egypt in particular a peace conference may have been long overdue. So far as the psychological readiness of other Arabs to accept the existence of Israel is concerned, the conference may turn out to be premature. Geneva may be just the beginning of a long process, perhaps the first in a series of conferences that will be interrupted by crises, pressure, threats, breakdown, new fighting, new negotiations.

The Geneva peace conference opened on December 21 in an atmosphere of cautious optimism. President Nixon had said soon after the alert in October that the prospects for peace had never before been so good. Dr. Kissinger, in his opening speech at the conference, spoke of a "historic chance for peace"; there were promising noises from Jerusalem, Moscow, and even Cairo. All this optimism was based, no doubt, on the undisputed fact that immediately after a war

the prospects almost always seem brightest and formerly unacceptable conditions suddenly seem acceptable after all.

It was not by chance that the conference concentrated in
its first phase on Israel and Egypt; and certainly the issue of
troop disengagement, an issue speedily settled in the agreement signed on January 17, was not the only motivating factor. The Israel-Egypt "problem" does not at first glance seem
insurmountable. If Egyptian sovereignty over Sinai were
recognized and Egypt were to accept an effective system of
demilitarization, there would then remain only the matter of
a token Israeli demilitarized zone and the question of the
Gaza Strip and Sharm el-Sheikh. Neither side is particularly
eager to accept responsibility for Gaza (though neither will
admit it) and the importance of Sharm el-Sheikh to Israel
has been somewhat exaggerated (the recent Egyptian blockade at Bab el-Mandeb almost nullified the strategic usefulness
of an Israeli presence at Sharm el-Sheikh). Assuming that
Israel were to withdraw gradually from Sinai and the Egyptians were to accept the principle of demilitarization, a settlement between the two countries could be envisaged—following hard bargaining, of course.

Israel, however, would hardly agree to withdraw in return
for a mere armistice, and it is here that the real difficulties
may set in. Egypt has assured its Arab allies that it will under
no circustances make peace with Israel unless Israel withdraws from all occupied Arab territories and unless the national rights of the Palestinians are restored. The official interpretation of this formula, as I have noted, means the
liquidation of the state of Israel. There are, however, several
other interpretations possible and there are, in addition, legitimate grounds for doubting the strength of Egypt's commitment to the cause of its allies.

For twenty-five years Egypt has borne the brunt of the
struggle against Israel, yet pan-Arab feeling is less deeply
rooted in Cairo than elsewhere in the Arab world. Even the
late Gamal Abdel Nasser, the champion of pan-Arabism,
recognized toward the end of his life that he had taken upon
himself an impossible and thankless task. In the struggle
against Israel Egypt has received a great deal of verbal aid
and unsolicited advice, but when the hour of truth comes,
as it did in October 1973, little more than token support is
ever forthcoming from its Arab friends. Syria and Iraq harbor
strong feelings of resentment toward Egypt; leadership in the

Arab world, they maintain, should rightfully be theirs. Colonel Qaddafi of Libya has on many occasions decried Egypt's "decadence" and "corruption," and there is not much love lost between Egypt and Algeria either. The Egyptians for their part regard Syria and Iraq as semi-barbaric lands and they have contempt for the Palestinians.

All in all, there is a strong inclination inside Egypt today to put Egyptian interests first, pan-Arab interests second. The Six-Day War came as a great shock to Egypt, and there was universal agreement that the shame of 1967 had to be expiated on the field of battle and Sinai regained. But with these aims achieved, Egypt may no longer feel an overriding obligation to champion the further struggle against Israel. To be sure, one can find hundreds of articles and dozens of books published in Egypt all proclaiming the inadmissibility of a Jewish state in the Middle East. But these declarations should not necessarily be taken at face value. If Israel could be made to disappear overnight, no Egyptian leader would object, but the prospect of many more years of hard fighting and severe damage to the country has little appeal. The Egyptian army was eager to fight for Ismailia; it is not so eager to fight (much less to die) for Nablus and Tulkarm. When addressing their more radical Arab brethren, Egyptians will stress that the final goal is the total liberation of the whole of Palestine, but this, they are apt to add quickly, will happen only in a generation or two or perhaps three. In the meantime much water will have flowed down the Nile and the Jordan.

It should have been Israeli policy after 1967—and especially after Nasser's death in 1970—to concentrate on a separate deal with Egypt, and this should be its foremost objective now. I do not wish to discount the difficulty of accomplishing this objective. Egypt is desperately poor, and financially dependent on Saudi Arabia and the Persian Gulf states. These countries for a variety of reasons, have a vested interest in the prolongation of the struggle against Israel, which for them is tantamount to an insurance policy against the radical forces in the Arab world that threaten their own existence. Sadat's position is stronger now than before the war, but this is not saying much. Nor would an Egyptian-Israeli deal mark the end of the Arab-Israeli conflict, and in the event of a new flare-up the danger would always exist that Egypt might be drawn into the campaign. Finally, an opening to Egypt on Israel's part would involve a basic psychological reorientation: since 1948 Egypt has been *the* enemy for Israel. Nevertheless, despite all these considerations, the fact remains that the interests of the two countries are not necessarily incompatible, and normal, if not friendly, relations between them should not be ruled out as a future possibility. There will be many realignments in the Arab world in the years to come and, unlikely as this may appear now, it is by no means unthinkable that one day Israel will break out of its present isolation and align itself with one or more of the Arab countries against one or more of the others.

For if a settlement with Egypt entails grave risks, the two other alternatives are even more dangerous. One is not to give up anything, the other to tackle the problem at its core and strive for a settlement which would satisfy the Palestinian Arabs. As for the first, if one assumes (as some do) that any Israeli withdrawal is bound to be just the first step in the gradual dismemberment of the country as a whole by its Arab neighbors, it would of course be preferable in every respect to make a stand now, rather than later when the boundaries will be harder to defend. Israel is already isolated, according to this view, and there is no further point in trying to appease world opinion by capitulation. The U.S. in the last resort can be counted on to remain steadfast, for its prestige is deeply involved and Israel is by now a cornerstone of its foreign policy. This line of thought, if put into action, would almost certainly bring about a new war in the Middle East, perhaps within a few months, for Sadat is under considerable domestic pressure to show results or to renew the fighting. But the prospect does not deter the advocates of such a policy. A new war, they argue, might be a protracted and hard struggle, but in the end Israel would win and this time the victory would be decisive.

A more sophisticated version of the hard-line argument maintains that since the deck has been stacked in advance, it would be fatal for Israel to act "reasonably" and "responsibly" in the present situation, as it is being urged to do on all sides. A superpower like the Soviet Union can swallow whole countries and go uncriticized, while Israel is denied the right to defensible borders and is expected to conform to the wishes of the great powers. Since the game is fixed, why not behave "irrationally" —like the Arab oil producers, say, or the Arab terrorists? There would be much general indignation, the Russians would issue threats, a few more countries would break off relations, pressure would be exerted by Washington, but nothing much worse would be likely to happen. The coming years will in any case see far-reaching changes in world politics—perhaps the total collapse of Europe, or, less likely, the reassertion of Europe's power. War might break out between the Soviet Union and China. International relations are increasingly being dictated by the law of the jungle, and unless Israel adapts itself to these conditions, the argument concludes, its chances of survival will be slim. Israel should be tough, unpredictable, and to a certain degree irresponsible.

This reasoning cannot be dismissed out of hand (for the simple fact that anything is possible in politics) but the chances of such a policy in the real world cannot be rated high. It underestimates the extent of Israel's military and economic dependence on the United States, and exaggerates American readiness to help Israel in the future. But even more decisively, it is not a policy that the government of a democratic country can easily pursue.

Then there is the alternative of an accommodation with the Palestinians—in every way the ideal solution. If Palestinians and Israelis could reach agreement on the basis of the establishment of a Palestinian state on the West Bank, Israeli willingness to take back some refugees, and the resettlement elsewhere of those for whom a home could not be found, an end would be put to the conflict once and for all. For the fate of the Palestinian Arabs is the heart of the matter; without a solution of this issue, the wider conflict will not be solved.

Unfortunately, however, the Palestinian issue is also the least tractable by far of all the issues of contention between Israel and the Arab world. A Palestinian Arab state would not be economically viable, and would be heavily dependent on the other Arab countries and the Soviet Union. Moreover, the policy of such a state would most likely be dictated not by the forces of peace but by the radical elements, which would consider the West Bank merely a base for the continuation of the armed struggle against Israel. Nor does the domestication of the terrorists seem a likely prospect for the near future. The main Palestinian organizations, Fatah and PLO, deny the Israelis' right to national self-determination, and their aim is the destruction of the "Zionist state." When they speak of the "democratic secular Palestinian state" that will replace Israel, they mean an Arab state in which Jews would have the right to be buried in their own cemeteries.

Thus, whatever the Geneva conference may achieve, it will almost certainly not bring an overall peace to the area. But if the chances for overall peace are remote, there does exist now (as after 1967) an opportunity for defusing the conflict, for rendering unlikely the renewal of fighting on a large scale. This can be done principally by Israel's meeting the basic demands of the Egyptians—gradual withdrawal of Israeli foreigners from large parts of the Sinai and the recognition in principle of Egyptian sovereignty there, in exchange for demilitarization. Unless this demand is met, a new outbreak of hostilities seems likely, with the almost certain outcome a peace settlement dictated by the superpowers and even more detrimental to Israel's interests.

III

The prospect of an imposed settlement by the superpowers to the detriment of Israel raises the specter of the infamous Munich conference of 1938. And, in fact, Czechoslovakia in the late 1930's has been invoked rather frequently in the last few months as offering an instructive analogy to the situation in which Israel now finds itself. A small democratic country in the center of Europe, Czechoslovakia was dismembered in two stages following a decision dictated by the powers. "Munich" and "appeasement" have become part of our political vocabulary, shorthand words connoting a sellout à la 1938. There are those who see such a sellout—of Israel—shaping up in today's Middle East.

Drawing historical parallels is always dangerous and sometimes downright misleading, but there is no denying that a comparison with Czechoslovakia is of some help in understanding the present situation. Though democratic in character, Czechoslovakia contained a substantial minority—3,500,000 Germans —which, from the very beginning, did not want to be part of the Czechoslovak state formed after World War I, gravitating rather toward Germany; the stronger Germany became, the stronger the pull toward Berlin. Hitler demanded the "return" of the Sudeten regions, where the German minority was concentrated; the Czechs maintained that these regions were economically and militarily vital to Czechoslovakia.

All through 1938, while the Nazis were stepping up the pressure on Prague, a great deal of sharp criticism was being voiced in the West about the state of affairs inside Czechoslovakia. The British and French press published scathing condemnations of the Czechs for their treatment of the German minority.

The Czech state, it was claimed, was an artificial creation, founded a mere twenty years before in what was now seen to have been a regrettable error. The idea that France should "commit suicide," or that a "single Frenchman should die for this misbegotten state" was grotesque. Not surprisingly, the Jews too were brought in; Léon Daudet, son of a famous father, wrote in 1938 in *L'Action Française:* "Peasant or worker, the average Frenchman is expected to commit suicide at the merest nod of a Jew who detests him, in some obscure and faraway village of which he hasn't the vaguest idea." Later that same year, Neville Chamberlain echoed these sentiments in similar terms: the Paris treaty-makers had committed an error, he declared, and the treaty should have been revised long ago; it was unthinkable to Chamberlain that Britons should go to war for a faraway land about which they knew nothing.

The anti-Czech comment of 1938, which bears an uncanny resemblance to remarks in the Western press, particularly the British and French, during the recent Middle East crisis and after, was by no means limited to the Right or to proponents of *Realpolitik.* The Left too castigated Czechoslovakia for not being a genuinely neutral country like Switzerland; France and Britain after all could not play the role of international policeman forever. Czech policy was called a danger to world peace; although the term "détente" had not yet been invented, the phrase used at the time was just as expressive: "*Conciliation entre les états democratiques.*" The only alternative to such concilation was the unleashing of war. What the world needed was disarmament, and in the long run Czechoslovakia too was assured it would find security in a disarmed world.[2]

The status of Czechoslovakia was supposed to be settled by the agreements reached in Munich. The Sudeten regions were returned to Germany in exchange for an international guarantee of the new boundaries of Czechoslovakia against unprovoked aggression. Yet when, six months later, German troops invaded what remained of Czechoslovakia after Munich, no one came to the rescue.

Munich provides some highly instructive lessons about the psychology of appeasement and the value of international guarantees, and as such it is useful as a warning in the present negotiations. But there is a danger in pushing the analogy too far.

[2] Michael Harrington in a recent article has offered the current version of this argument. See his "Israel, the War, and American Politics," *Midstream,* December 1973.

Not every peace treaty in world history has been violated, after all, nor every international guarantee ignored. The lessons of Munich, that is to say, are of limited value as a guide for the future and cannot in my view be used as an alibi by those who oppose any concessions whatsoever on Israel's part.

The international constellation and the balance of power in the Middle East do not resemble Europe in 1938. Czechoslovakia faced a relentless enemy who could not possibly be deflected from his course. Israel, on the other hand, confronts a coalition of states that have neither the cohesion nor the power of Nazi Germany. That this coalition should have come into being at all was unusual—to a certain extent it may have come into being as a result of Israeli diplomatic inflexibility—and it will last only by a miracle. Hitler was reasonably certain that Czechoslovakia, facing the overwhelming power of the Reich, would not fight. And as for the Czechs, surrender meant the loss of independence, in itself a national disaster but not the end of the Czech people. For many centuries the Czechs had survived under foreign rule, and the conviction was strong that sooner or later Hitler's policy would lead to a war in which the Germans would be defeated, and then an independent Czechoslovakia would rise again—as indeed it did seven years later. No such hope exists for Israel, and this in itself precludes an Israeli surrender. But Israel is not only more resolute than Czechoslovakia, it is also infinitely stronger. Even Hitler would not have attacked Czechoslovakia if, for argument's sake, it had meant risking the destruction of Berlin, Munich, and other German centers.

For Israel, the years to come, fraught as they will be with danger, will require not only constant military preparedness, a high degree of flexibility, and economic sacrifice, but also, very likely, political concessions. Nevertheless, and despite the efficaciousness of the oil weapon in Arab hands, the outlook is not all that unpromising. As long as the "Zionist menace" overshadowed all other factors in the Arab political consciousness, a certain degree of unity prevailed in the Arab world. But as the "enemy" assumes a lower profile, all the suppressed dissensions among Arab nations and Arab ideologies are bound to reassert themselves. The fact that some Arab countries will earn fabulous riches during the years to come while others will not is going to exacerbate existing divisions; sooner or later, there will be a free-for-all for the spoils. The oil-producing countries are already becoming increasingly unpopular all over the world because of their extortionist policies, and they are going to have to defend themselves and their riches against more immediate dangers than Israel. Assuming that the global balance of power does not radically change in the next decade, that America does not become substantially weaker, and that some sort of détente continues to hold between the two super-powers, the risk will be reduced of an all-out Arab attack.

But in the final analysis, Israel's fate will depend on its own policies and on its own inner character. It certainly cannot afford the luxury of an internal factional war such as once before in history caused the destruction of a Jewish commonwealth. Israel in the days to come will need unity, strong nerves, and a readiness to compromise combined with a firm resolve to repel any new threat to its existence.

The Arab-Israeli Conflict

By Elie Kedourie*

At its beginnings just over half a century ago, what is now known as the Arab–Israeli conflict was relatively simple and limited, but since then—and this is perhaps its most important and ominous characteristic—it has become progressively more complicated and envenomed.

The Zionists in whose favour the Balfour declaration was issued in November 1917 had been neither numerically important nor politically significant before the world war in the territory which shortly afterwards came to be officially called Palestine. They were known to the original inhabitants as immigrant foreigners upon whom the Ottoman authorities—whether at the time of Abd al-Hamid or later—did not look with much favour and whose ingress they tried to restrict as much as possible; and known also for their agricultural settlements which were occasionally involved in friction and dispute with their rural and nomadic neighbours.

The Balfour declaration, therefore, could not but come as a shock to a population which, being overwhelmingly Muslim, was already disoriented by the collapse of a Muslim authority which had lasted for four centuries, and its replacement by Christian European conquerors. And these conquerors were

* From *Arab Political Memoirs and Other Studies* (London: Frank Cass, 1974).

proposing to bestow privileges, the extent of which was uncertain, on this handful of foreigners, privileges which in the end might even lead Jews to exercise power over the Muslims who had hitherto believed in their divinely ordained right to rule over Christians and Jews. This feeling of Muslim superiority which a century of reverses at the hands of Europe had shaken but also exacerbated, goes far to make intelligible the uncompromising opposition which from the very beginning the Palestinians offered to Zionism. Also the very vagueness of the Balfour declaration, while arousing the worst fears of the Palestinians, encouraged them to hope that unyielding and strenuous opposition might lead to the declaration being interpreted restrictively, or even actually disowned.

But, when all is said and done, the conflict between the Zionists and their opponents all through the 1920s and the first half of the '30s, remained confined to Palestine. Opposition to Zionism erupted in riots and violence in 1920, 1921 and 1929. The first two incidents may be seen as unsuccessful attempts by the Palestinians to overawe and intimidate a new government and compel it to bow to their wishes. Whilst the third—and most serious—outbreak, that of 1929, coming as it did after a period of actual Jewish emigration from Palestine, may be interpreted as a bid by the mufti of Jerusalem at once to demonstrate his supremacy in Palestinian Arab politics, and to hurry the Jews on their way out. But such incidents, serious as they were, involved only the Mandatory, the Zionists and the Arabs of Palestine, and hardly involved other governments or groups. Indeed, it may be argued that the mufti may have been right in 1929 when he reckoned that Zionism was a declining force.

The advent of Hitler in 1933 introduced an entirely new and unforeseen element in the Palestinian problem. It increased, beyond any previous expectation, the demand for immigration into Palestine; imbued the Zionist leaders with a new sense of urgency and imposed new pressures on them; and by upsetting the European balance, indirectly weakened the British position in the Mediterranean and encouraged those who wanted to challenge it. Nazism, in short, seriously complicated the Palestine problem, made it perhaps well-nigh intractable. The British, we may note in passing, have been repeatedly blamed for encouraging Zionist settlement in a country occupied by a large group of people naturally unwilling to be swamped and dominated by another, aggressive and enterprising, group. This, however, is to condemn *ex post facto*, for no one in 1917 could have reasonably foretold the rise and triumph of Nazism which, by confronting European Jewry with sudden ruin and destruction, overturned the assumptions and expectations on which the Balfour declaration policy implicitly rested.

The next complication which befell Palestine dates from 1938–9. In 1936 strikes organized by the Arab higher committee degenerated into serious disorders. This compelled the British government to look anew at the problem. A Royal Commission was appointed which recommended in 1937 partition of the country into Arab and Jewish areas as the measure most likely to issue in appeasement and to produce a settlement. The government first accepted this line of policy, but soon afterwards it began to have second thoughts. It appointed in 1938 a technical commission ostensibly to examine further the detailed scheme of partition proposed by the Royal Commission, the chairman of this commission, however, being given secretly to understand that partition was no longer the policy which the government favoured. A new departure was clearly being envisaged.

The new policy was unveiled at the end of 1938, when the government announced the convening of a conference on Palestine, to which were to be invited not only the Jewish Agency and representatives of the Palestinian Arabs, but also, on the one hand, representatives of Arab states—even of a state as far away as Yemen—and on the other, of world Jewry, the latter being, in point of political importance or sovereign attributes, by no means the equal or the equivalent of the Arab states. This was a fateful and perhaps fatal move, the consequences of which even now are far from being exhausted. For this move recognized and sanctioned the intervention of a number of sovereign states in the affairs of a territory under British control. For the administration of Palestine, Great Britain was indeed responsible to the League of Nations, but it had certainly hitherto not acknowledged responsibility to a collection of states who shared more or less vaguely the epithet 'Arab'. Indeed, up to the middle of 1937, we find the British government firmly resisting Egyptian and Iraqi attempts to intervene officially in Palestinian affairs.

Whatever the various reasons and justifications for this new policy, it was one which appreciably limited British freedom of action, since the right to intervene, once conceded to outsiders, would be difficult if not impossible again to withdraw. This was to burden future British policy, as well as Palestine and the

Palestinians with—to use a legal metaphor—a heavy servitude. There is no evidence that the British government was disquietened by this prospect. When an annex to the Charter of the Arab League in 1945 officially stated that the signatories had a collective right of intervention, the British government never protested at a claim now all the more enhanced for being enshrined in a formal instrument.

This development exacerbated the conflict in Palestine by introducing a large number of sovereign states, each with their particular, and conflicting, interests into what had been a relatively limited dispute between two groups in a mandated territory. The consequence of such a step appeared clearly in the Palestine war of 1948–9. After the U.N. vote, in November 1947, to partition Palestine—the very solution proposed by the Royal Commission ten years before—and the British decision to lay down the mandate which followed, King Abdullah decided that here at last was an opportunity to enhance a position which he had ever regarded as beneath his abilities and deserts. First he hoped that, supported by Iraq, he would compel the Zionists to accept his overlordship without a fight. When this failed, he embarked on war. Up to the end of April 1948, Egypt was not contemplating military intervention, but she could not allow the Hashemites to aggrandize themselves by annexing Palestine. At the last minute, therefore, an Egyptian army, by all accounts unprepared for battle, was ordered to march into Palestine. Syria, fearful of Abdullah's ambitions, likewise intervened. The conflict between Palestinians and Zionists thus became embroiled with the discordant ambitions of Egypt and Syria, Jordan and Iraq, all the more intransigent for being proclaimed in the ideological vocabulary of pan-Arabism, rather than expressed in the more modest language of interests.

The next complication in the Palestine problem first appeared in 1955–6, and became manifest in all its danger during the Six-Day war and since. The conflict, which initially was local to Palestine, and then was transformed into a regional conflict, now became inextricably involved in the rivalries of the great powers. This happened because the Soviet Union began to exert the power and influence which Tsarist Russia used traditionally to have in the region and which, so to speak, unnaturally disappeared between 1917 and 1955. In the Suez affair, the Israeli government deliberately took advantage of the British and French quarrel with Egypt in order to defeat and neutralize the most important of its enemies. An American-Soviet 'collusion'—

an appropriate term to use in this context—prevented it from gaining its object. This American-Soviet collusion ruined British and French power and influence in the Mediterranean and the middle east, thus destroying the possibility of the rivalry between the two super-powers being effectively mediated or moderated by the action of other powers as used to happen in the classical eastern question before 1914. As became clear during and after the Six-Day war, the U.S.A. and the Soviet Union now stand face to face in the middle east, and their conflict is linked precisely with the Arab-Israeli conflict. This is an inherently unstable and dangerous position, made even more dangerous by the fact that neither super-power is fully in control of the actions of its clients, and is thus liable to get drawn into quarrels neither sought nor foreseen.

These then are the parties involved in this conflict: the Zionists, who have succeeded in creating and maintaining the State of Israel; the native Palestinians; the Arab States; and the U.S.A. and the U.S.S.R. Each of these parties will influence, more or less as the case may be, the further course of the conflict and any possible settlement. There is a great deal of variety in the aims and purposes of these parties, as well as in the price which they are prepared to pay for attaining them. But for all of them the conflict may be said to be primarily political (and therefore, at times, military). Political in the sense that two groups (the Israelis and the Palestinians) dispute sovereign control over a territory; political also in the sense that this original dispute has become for other local states a means for attaining regional primacy or increasing their territory; political lastly in the sense that each of the super-powers sees in this dispute a way of increasing its power and influence in the Mediterranean and middle east, and of diminishing that of its rival.

But the political conflict between Israel and its neighbours is further complicated by what might be called a cultural conflict, or perhaps misunderstanding. A clue to its nature may be gathered from the frequency with which the dispute between Israel and her neighbours is described as a conflict between 'Jews' and 'Arabs'. Are these two groups actually in conflict? Jews as a group certainly have an identity supplied by a religion which has kept them together. So far as 'culture' goes—if by culture we mean broadly a way of life—the Jews have experienced huge variations of culture throughout their history. Some of them, in particular, have shared, or still share, the culture of those called 'Arabs'. To the extent that there is cultural conflict, it must be between the 'Arabs' and those Jews who have not shared in their outlook, values and way of life.

But who are the 'Arabs'? Some sixty years ago, the term 'Arab' generally meant Bedouin. Since then this term has undergone a great change. It has ceased primarily to designate a group of nomads; it has rather become an ideological term indicating an aspiration to create a new political order, in which all 'Arabs' would be members of an autonomous, sovereign entity. In this new usage, who the 'Arabs' are has changed from time to time, and even now the notion is not yet quite stable. But one thing at least can be affirmed, namely, that they are, in an overwhelming majority, Muslim, that they are, and have been part of the Muslim world and of an Islamic culture. Islam has generally looked upon Jews as a subject community docile and unwarlike, to be treated with contemptuous tolerance, and whom it is quite unthinkable to consider as political equals. This surely accounts for a great deal of intransigence with which the Palestinians and the Arab states have refused sometimes in clear disregard of their interests to negotiate directly or to sit at the same table with Zionists or Israelis. But the Jews with whom they had to deal in Palestine were, in fact, the antithesis of the Jews to whom the Muslims were accustomed. They were politically activist, aggressive and by no means deferential towards Muslims.

On the contrary, the Jews who invented Zionism and worked for the establishment of the State of Israel, coming from eastern Europe, and imbued with European notions and prejudices, were wholly pre-occupied with European issues and European problems. They knew little about the indigenous inhabitants of Palestine, and looked down upon them as backward, primitive and incompetent. The history of the Palestine problem from the Balfour declaration to the Six-Day war must have served to confirm them in this view. The political conflict over Palestine has thus been further complicated by mutual incomprehension, to which have contributed, on the one hand, the European prejudices of the Zionists, and, on the other, the Muslim prejudices of the Arabs. Misunderstanding, it has been said, makes the world go round. Mutual contempt is another story.

To review this conflict and its progressive exacerbation is thus to admit the unlikelihood of a speedy settlement. What must increase pessimism is that a state of war between Israel and its neighbours has now lasted for almost a quarter of a century and that, as we may suspect, it has become for various governments a cosy habit and a convenient state of affairs. It is said, no doubt with a great deal of truth, that a state of war enables the Israeli government to transform a heterogeneous collection of immigrants into a homogeneous nation-state, and to mobilize the sympathies and resources of world Jewry. It is probably just as true that military régimes, such as those of Egypt, of Syria and of Iraq, apprehend in a state of peace a serious threat to their stability, or even to their very existence.

But let us review in turn the various parties to the conflict, their ability to make peace, and the inducements and pressures which may incline them thereto. On the Arab side, it seems to be the case that ability to influence the course of the quarrel is almost in inverse proportion to a party's vital interest in it. This is, and has been, most true of the Palestinians. For some twenty years, from the British occupation until the end of 1938, the Palestinian leaders attempted by continuous pressure and protest, as well as by occasional violence, to resist the establishment and extension of the National Home to which the mandatory was committed. This campaign almost from the beginning went hand in hand with the campaign of Hajj Amin al-Husayni, whom Sir Herbert Samuel had tacitly allowed to become mufti of Jerusalem in 1921, to establish his dominance over the Palestinians. In declaring his uncompromising hostility to Zionism the mufti indeed faithfully expressed the sentiments of those whom he claimed to lead; but it remains true that he was leader not because he was elected or appointed by the Palestinians, but only owing to the initial support of the mandatory, to his subsequent use of the *Waqf* resources which the government allowed him to control without any supervision, and in the later stages to a campaign of murder and terrorism. He was thus practically free to pursue whatever policy he liked, and in the end was tempted by armed rebellion, intrigues with Italy and Germany, and with elements in Syria and Iraq who wanted to use the Palestine issue as a weapon in their own struggle for power. His policies failed, and he may fairly be said to have served his people ill.

The period 1937–9 may be considered a watershed in the sombre, disaster-strewn history of the Palestinians. It was then that the mufti fled to the Lebanon, an action which, in retrospect, marks the failure of his policies. Self-appointed and self-seeking as he was, yet his policies, however unwise or undesirable, in their fashion were primarily concerned with the interests of the Palestinians. When the Arab states were invited at the end of 1938 to intervene in the Palestine problem, Palestinian interests necessarily became a pawn or a weapon in the hands of these states in their pursuit of power and primacy. Between 1939 and the Six-Day war the Palestinians had no say or no control over their affairs. Such leadership as Hajj Amin and his lieutenants had provided was dispersed and destroyed, and the Arab states and the Arab League undertook to defend the Palestinians' interests. During this period, successive catastrophes befell the Palestinians which they have been utterly powerless to avert.

Since the Six-Day war the Palestinians have once again come to the fore. Once again leaders claim to speak in their name and to defend their particular interests. The character and the tactics of these leaders bear a disturbing resemblance to those of the 1930s: In so far as they are not promoted or supported for its purposes by one or other of the Arab states, they too are self-appointed. Undoubtedly in their utter hostility to Israel, they speak for all the Palestinians, but these have no say whatever over policies or tactics, which are decided by small groups in secret. Again like Hajj Amin, the new leaders have a partiality for guerrilla warfare. This partiality has indeed been reinforced by the great popularity which the doctrine of Mao, Guevara and the Vietcong have found in Asia and Africa. Quite recently, Yassir Arafat, the leader of the Palestine Liberation Organization, declared in an interview (*Le Monde*, 12 November 1970): 'I will tell you why the Americans, in spite of their undoubted power, do not have, and will never have the upper hand over the Vietcong: a guerrilla movement which has popular support is invincible. No electronic machine is able to measure the will of our people to conquer their right to life and freedom. Their ability to resist is practically infinite'.

The words were uttered after three years of fruitless guerrilla action against Israel—fruitless itself, and fruitless in that guerrilla warfare has not been changed (as the theory requires) into a 'people's war'. These words also followed the clash with King Husayn's army which has decisively shown that, in middle eastern conditions at any rate, a resolute government disposing of planes, tanks and artillery, is more than a match for guerrillas who wish to take it over. Even if Husayn were killed or deposed, it is by no means clear that the guerrillas would be able to take over Jordan. If this is so, then the future for Palestinian resistance is not bright. At best, the guerrillas may become a kind of IMRO (Internal Macedonian Revolutionary Organization), able to use spasmodic terror, but quite unable to effect a substantial change. There is another reason for pessimism: if as has been here argued, it was a misfortune for the Palestinian cause to be, so to speak, pan-Arabized, then the guerrilla organizations in relying, as they must, on this or that Arab state, are doing nothing to save the Palestinians from the ruinous attentions of their protectors.

The guerrillas then are unlikely to achieve military victory over Israel, or to force it to give in to their demands. The clash with the Jordanians indicates that they are also unlikely to be able to force an Arab state to wage war on their behalf. It follows that they are not in a position, should they want it, on their own to negotiate or conclude a compromise peace with Israel. A peace of this kind which did not suit Jordan or Syria or Egypt can easily be upset by them. Jordan which, after the Palestinians, is the party most vitally interested in the conflict, is in scarcely a better position.

To Abdullah's ambitions, as has been seen, must be attributed in large part the outbreak of war in 1948. But bold and ambitious as he was, yet he was not a man to persist in a manifestly unprofitable enterprise. Having emerged from the war of 1948 as the only beneficiary on the Arab side, he was quite willing to attempt a settlement with his fellow-beneficiary Israel. But Jordan was no longer the pastoral emirate over which he had ruled for a quarter of a century. It now included a large and turbulent population of Palestinians, many of them refugees: it was he who had made this bed and he must now lie on it. He had to reckon with these Palestinians in his attempts at a settlement, and with the trouble which a defeated and embittered Egypt would make for him among the Palestinians. His room for manoeuvre became very exiguous, and the final reckoning came when they assassinated him in that Jerusalem which he had wanted so much to possess. His grandson was at no time in a better position to negotiate. Much as he wanted a settlement, particularly after the Six-Day war, he too has never been in a position to conclude it on his own. A satisfactory peace for him must include the return of the west bank, if not of east Jerusalem. A Jordan permanently confined within the frontiers of the old emirate would destroy his prestige and put his throne at risk. But even if he could make a satisfactory deal with the Israelis, he would not be in a position to go through with it in the face of opposition from other members of the Arab League, and particularly Egypt.

Let us consider the character of this opposition, leaving aside Egypt for the moment. The opposition is likely to come from countries like Syria, Iraq, Libya or Algeria—none of them as intimately touched by the conflict as Jordan, the two latter being indeed very far from the scene. This opposition would be expressed in activist and doctrinaire terms, in the style customary to a party like the Ba'th in Syria or Iraq, or the FLN in Algeria. A passage in a recent article by the Algerian minister of information and culture, Ahmed Taleb-Ibrahimi, provides an excellent specimen of this style and outlook. He wrote (*Le Monde*, 12 September 1970):

> No smoke-screen and no inspired article will make us forget the decisive importance of the potential power of the Arab masses who are already impressing on those who were meditating a treacherous blow, that the Palestinian cause cannot be betrayed with impunity.
>
> Today's struggle [referring to Husayn's recent attack on the guerrillas] must not be taken for a classic battle, as was the case in the Spanish civil war, where some parties try out their weapons. It is not a matter of tanks or rockets. The resistance must be organized and must spread to all the Arab countries. For those who think to justify their defeatism (which, of course they call realism) by declaring that the struggle in the East takes place under peculiar conditions, is different from the struggle of the Vietminh or of the FLN, examples are not lacking which prove that resistance can develop in mountains as well as in cities, in the steppes as well as in deserts of sand or ice. The problem is not one of terrain, but of will: what in the end is victorious is not war material, however perfected, but rather the man who operates the weapon, and the faith which moves the man.
>
> To take another point, how can Algeria advise the Palestinian resistance to accept that which it had refused to accept for itself twelve years ago? A cease-fire in present-day conditions reminds us too much of that '*paix des braves*' by means of which it was hoped to undermine the morale of the Algerians.

Rhetoric of this style invites, and sometimes compels, political activity of a similar style. But even if it did not, even if those who use it have no intention of themselves being carried away by it, they may yet consider that their interest requires the encouragement of intransigence. Algeria is a rival of Egypt in north Africa, and one way by which to assert her claim is to adopt an uncompromising stand over Palestine. Again, Syria and Iraq, both governed by Ba'hist officers consumed with mutual dislike, confronting each other in a gladiatorial posture, and in any case looking on King Husayn as fair game for revolutionaries, would also have good reason to encourage, singly or in unison, an uncompromising stand.

But by themselves, neither Iraq nor Syria nor Algeria are decisive, just as the Palestinian guerrillas and Jordan can effect nothing on their own. For all these parties are dwarfed and overshadowed by Egypt which, it is no exaggeration to say, holds, among Israel's enemies, the key to a settlement. Egypt's involvement in the Palestine conflict was a deliberate step by Faruq to secure primacy in the middle east. The adventure, in a sense, cost him his throne. But his ambition was taken over by those who overthrew him, and from beginning to end Nasser sought, by means of a victory over Israel, to crush his opponents in the Arab world and establish Egypt as *the* middle-eastern great power. Egypt's resources and military capacity did not prove equal to such an aim, the pursuit of which has brought so far nothing but loss and catastrophe. But Nasser's régime and his prestige had become intimately bound up with this policy. As is known, so long as he was unwilling to consider a settlement which might advertise and consecrate the failure of this policy, no other Arab state or group would have dared even enter into negotiations. This was because Nasser's prestige and Egypt's power were too great to be challenged by the other Arab states. Whether Nasser himself would have been prepared to abandon the policy he took over from Faruq, and to work for a purely Egyptian-Israeli settlement will never now be known.

His successors do not enjoy his prestige either inside or outside Egypt, and this may in fact be one potent reason why they dare not abandon a policy associated with one who, because of his death in office, has so to speak become the tutelary deity of the régime. What is clear at any rate is that they persist in using the rhetoric of pan-Arabism and in proclaiming themselves the champions of all the Arabs against Israel. Thus, in a declaration in the National Assembly, Anwar al-Sadat said that the struggle was for them 'the priority of all priorities'. By struggle he meant 'the total liberation of all occupied Arab territories, with no exception whatever. To give up anything whatever means giving up everything'. Again: 'To give up the total liberation of these territories is tantamount to submitting to the Israeli imperialist aggressor and those who give him support. No one in the Arab world will agree to the liberation of one portion of the territory, and the abandonment of another. Let the world understand that we are against all half-solutions, all bargaining and all auctions.' The U.A.R. he stated, 'is unshakeably convinced that the Arab nation is one, that its progress is one and that its aspirations are the same for all the Arabs.' (*Le Monde*, 21 November 1970). This is the language of Nasserism. But Sadat has also introduced a new, Islamic, accent which must greatly appeal to, and move, his audience. In an eloquent address delivered in April 1972 on the anniversary of the Prophet's birthday he compared the struggle on which his people were engaged to the trials which faced Muhammad at the beginning of his apostolate. We are fated, he said, to fight the battle to liberate our land and, with our land, Jerusalem, the first *qibla* and third *haram*. 'We will, with God's help' he affirmed, 'take it back from those of whom our Book says that lowliness and submissiveness is their lot.' Sadat also declared that he refused to negotiate directly with people whom the Prophet had found, in his dealings with them, to be vile, treacherous and faithless. (Text of Sadat's address reproduced in an appendix in Fu'ad Matar, *Russya al-nasiriyya wa Misr al-misriyya* (Nasserite Russia and Egyptian Egypt), Beirut, 1972, pp. 202–5). Whether these words represent an extension of Nasserism, or are used to cover a retreat from it, time will tell.

Egypt has never been powerful enough to win, or even to maintain its position—witness the occupation of Sinai and the closure of the canal, but has been powerful enough to prevent a settlement. Israel, contrariwise, has been powerful enough to win many campaigns and improve its positions, but not powerful enough to impose a settlement. Hence the deadlock, and the mutual and cumulative mistrust. But as between Israel and its neighbours the position is asymmetrical in one respect which is crucial. The Israelis are convinced that the conflict is for them a life-and-death issue, that a defeat or a retreat for them will end not merely in a humiliating peace but in the destruction of their state. Hence another element of intransigence. But what kind of a settlement, one may ask, does Israel envisage? The answer is by no means clear, and this very lack of clarity is in itself yet one more obstacle to a settlement. Israel's objective has always been twofold: recognition and secure frontiers. The Six-Day war put it at least in the short term in a better bargaining position, but did not bring the attainment of these aims nearer. It may have even perhaps made this more difficult, since the conquest of so much territory in 1967 has tempted some Israeli politicians to believe that they could attain both recognition and a larger Israeli territory, or else that Israel, secure behind the shield of its new conquests, need not sacrifice anything for recognition by its neighbours. Since Israel's is a parliamentary régime in which government has been carried on from the start by means of coalitions, it has always been easier to register disagreement over policies, than to resolve on a particular policy. Moreover, disagreement about policy is accompanied by confusion about the character of the conflict in which Israel is engaged.

The conflict at the outset was one with the indigenous population of Palestine. During the 1920s and '30s the belief widely prevailed among Zionist leaders that this local conflict could somehow be dissolved if the Palestinians could be submerged in a wider Arab entity. The Zionists, in other words, were themselves pan-Arabs. Events have shown this line of reasoning to be quite fallacious, but many Israeli leaders still hanker after it. They now do so in the belief that to admit the existence of Palestinians as Palestinians is somehow to throw doubt on the legitimacy of Israel and its right to the territory it occupies. Hence the curious immobility of Israeli policy after 1967. Internal deadlock—political and intellectual—in Israel reinforces the external deadlock.

But Israel and its enemies, checkmated by one another, find themselves further constrained by their dependence on the super-powers who, of course, are primarily concerned with the safeguard and advancement of their own interests, and for whom the middle east is merely one element in a world-wide rivalry and the Arab–Israeli conflict by no means the most important issue in the middle east. It was to outflank and neutralize the American and, generally, the western positions in the middle east that the U.S.S.R. began an active policy in Egypt in 1955. In the decade which followed the Soviet stake in the middle east and in the Mediterranean increased enormously. Its naval contingent in the Mediterranean, its liberal supply of arms to Egypt, Syria, Iraq and other Arab states, its financing of the high dam: all these meant that Soviet prestige became bound up with the survival and success of those Arab states which had become its clients. It is the logic of this situation, rather than deliberate choice, which has made the U.S.A. the patron and protector of Israel. For it has been a constant theme of Soviet propaganda that just as the Soviets were committed to the protection of the Arab states, so the United States was committed to the protection of Israel. The Six-Day war and the events which followed somehow seemed to give body and reality to this propaganda. By espousing so unconditionally the cause of the defeated Arab states, the U.S.S.R. forced the U.S.A. to link its prestige to the survival of Israel and to its protection against defeat. Such a position is necessarily irksome to the U.S.A. which, by reason of its interests elsewhere in the middle east, cannot afford to seem unconditionally to support Israel. Hence the continuous ambiguity and tension in the relations between these two states. One reason, presumably, for American initiatives to break the deadlock between Israel and its neighbours is eagerness to escape from the position into which the Soviets have cornered them.

The American position, seemingly weak, is not, however, without its strength. Its protégé, Israel, has a stranglehold over the Suez Canal, to open which is a more pressing Soviet than American interest. Israel, again, is militarily superior to its neighbours and does not need the kind of direct support which the U.S.S.R. has had to give Egypt. Lastly, so long as the protégés of the Soviets are involved with Israel, they cannot busy themselves very much with subverting states such as Saudi Arabia or the Lebanon to protect which is an American interest. Whether the U.S.A. considers these as strong cards, and whether it would consider them nonetheless worth sacrificing for the sake of a local settlement with the Soviets, we do not yet know. If the former is the case then the deadlock is likely to last for some time, if the latter then a new situation will emerge about which it is fruitless to speculate. For in such a situation what will be important will be not the exact territorial character of an Arab-Israeli settlement, but rather the stance in which the super-powers and their protégés will find themselves for prosecuting their ambitions in an area which seems doomed to turbulence and disorder for a long time to come.

The Egyptian-Israeli Accord on Sinai
(September 1, 1975)

The Government of the Arab Republic of Egypt and the Government of Israel have agreed that:

ARTICLE I

The conflict between them and in the Middle East shall not be resolved by military force but by peaceful means.

The agreement concluded by the parties Jan. 18, 1974, within the framework of the Geneva peace conference constituted a first step towards a just and durable peace according to the provisions of Security Council Resolution 338 of Oct. 22, 1973; and they are determined to reach a final and just peace settlement by means of negotiations called for by Security Council Resolution 338, this agreement being a significant step towards that end.

Article II

The parties hereby undertake not to resort to the threat or use of force or military blockade against each other.

Article III

(1) The parties shall continue scrupulously to observe the cease-fire on land, sea and air and to refrain from all military or paramilitary actions against each other.

(2) The parties also confirm that the obligations contained in the annex and, when concluded, the protocol shall be an integral part of this agreement.

Article IV

A. The military forces of the parties shall be deployed in accordance with the following principles:

(1) All Israeli forces shall be deployed east of the lines designated as lines J and M on the attached map.

(2) All Egyptian forces shall be deployed west of the line designated as line E on the attached map.

(3) The area between the lines designated on the attached map as lines E and F and the area between the lines designated on the attached map as lines J and K shall be limited in armament and forces.

(4) The limitations on armament and forces in the areas described by paragraph (3) above shall be agreed as described in the attached annex.

(5) The zone between the lines designated on the attached map as lines E and J will be a buffer zone. On this zone the United Nations Emergency Force will continue to perform its

functions as under the Egyptian-Israeli agreement of Jan. 18, 1974.

(6) In the area south from line E and west from line M, as defined in the attached map, there will be no military forces, as specified in the attached annex.

B. The details concerning the new lines, the redeployment of the forces and its timing, the limitation of armaments and forces, aerial reconnaissance, the operation of the early warning and surveillance installations and the use of the roads, the U.N. functions and other arrangements will all be in accordance with the provisions of the annex and map which are an integral part of this agreement and of the protocol which is to result from negotiations pursuant to the annex and which, when concluded, shall become an integral part of this agreement.

ARTICLE V

The United Nations Emergency Force is essential and shall continue its functions, and its mandate shall be extended annually.

ARTICLE VI

The parties hereby establish a joint commission for the duration of this agreement. It will function under the aegis of the chief coordinator of the United Nations peace-keeping missions in the Middle East in order to consider any problem arising from this agreement and to assist the United Nations Emergency Force in the execution of its mandate. The joint commission shall function in accordance with procedures established in the protocol.

ARTICLE VII

Nonmilitary cargoes destined for or coming from Israel shall be permitted through the Suez Canal.

ARTICLE VIII

(1) This agreement is regarded by the parties as a significant step toward a just and lasting peace. It is not a final peace agreement.

(2) The parties shall continue their efforts to negotiate a final peace agreement within the framework of the Geneva peace conference in accordance with Security Council Resolution 338.

ARTICLE IX

This agreement shall enter into force upon signature of the protocol and remain in force until superseded by a new agreement.

The U.S. Proposal for Early-Warning System in Sinai

In connection with the early-warning system referred to in Article IV of the agreement between Egypt and Israel concluded on this date and as an integral part of that agreement (hereafter referred to as the basic agreement), the United States proposes the following:

[1]

The early-warning system to be established in accordance with Article IV in the area shown on the attached map will be entrusted to the United States. It shall have the following elements:

A. There shall be two surveillance stations to provide strategic early warning, one operated by Egyptian and one operated by Israeli personnel. Their locations are shown on the map attached to the basic agreement. Each station shall be manned by not more than 250 technical and administrative personnel. They shall perform the functions of visual and electronic surveillance only within their stations.

B. In support of these stations, to provide tactical early warning and to verify access to them, three watch stations shall be established by the United States in the Mitla and Gidi Passes as will be shown on the agreed map.

These stations shall be operated by United States civilian personnel. In support of these stations, there shall be established three unmanned electronic-sensor fields at both ends of each pass and in the general vicinity of each station and the roads leading to and from those stations.

[2]

The United States civilian personnel shall perform the following duties in connection with the operation and maintenance of these stations:

A. At the two surveillance stations described in paragraph 1A, above, United States personnel will verify the nature of the operations of the stations and all movement into and out of each station and will immediately report any detected divergency from its authorized role of visual and electronic surveillance to the parties to the basic agreement and the UNEF.

B. At each watch station described in paragraph 1B above, the United States personnel will immediately report to the parties to the basic agreement and to UNEF any movement of armed forces, other than the UNEF, into either pass and any observed preparations for such movement.

C. The total number of United States civilian personnel assigned to functions under these proposals shall not exceed 200. Only civilian personnel shall be assigned to functions under these proposals.

[3]

No arms shall be maintained at the stations and other facilities covered by these proposals, except for small arms required for their protection.

[4]

The United States personnel serving the early-warning system shall be allowed to move freely within the area of the system.

[5]

The United States and its personnel shall be entitled to have such support facilities as are reasonably necessary to perform their functions.

[6]

The United States personnel shall be immune from local criminal, civil, tax and customs jurisdiction and may be accorded any other specific privileges and immunities provided for in the UNEF agreement of Feb. 13, 1957.

[7]

The United States affirms that it will continue to perform the functions described above for the duration of the basic agreement.

[8]

Notwithstanding any other provision of these proposals, the United States may withdraw its personnel only if it concludes that their safety is jeopardized or that continuation of their role is no longer necessary. In the latter case the parties to the basic agreement will be informed in advance in order to give them the opportunity to make alternative arrangements. If both parties to the basic agreement request the United States to conclude its role under this proposal, the United States will consider such requests conclusive.

[9]

Technical problems including the location of the watch stations will be worked out through consultation with the United States.

Annex to the Sinai Agreement

Within five days after the signature of the Egypt-Israel agreement, representatives of the two parties shall meet in the military working group of the Middle East peace conference at Geneva to begin preparation of a detailed protocol for the implementation of the agreement. In order to facilitate preparation of the protocol and implementation of the agreement, and to assist in maintaining the scrupulous observance of the cease-fire and other elements of the agreement, the two parties have agreed on the following principles, which are an integral part of the agreement, as guidelines for the working group.

1. DEFINITIONS OF LINES AND AREAS

The deployment lines, areas of limited forces and armaments, buffer zones, the area south from line E and west from line M, other designated areas, road sections for common use and other features referred to in Article IV of the agreement shall be as indicated on the attached map (1:100,000—U.S. edition).

2. BUFFER ZONES

(a) Access to the buffer zones shall be controlled by the UNEF, according to procedures to be worked out by the working group and UNEF.

(b) Aircraft of either party will be permitted to fly freely up to the forward line of that party. Reconnaissance aircraft of either party may fly up to the middle line of the buffer zone between E and J on an agreed schedule.

(c) In the buffer zone, between line E and J, there will be established under Article IV of the agreement an early-warning system entrusted to United States civilian personnel as detailed in a separate proposal, which is a part of this agreement.

(d) Authorized personnel shall have access to the buffer zone for transit to and from the early-warning system; the manner in which this is carried out shall be worked out by the working group and UNEF.

3. Area South of Line E and West of Line M

(a) In this area, the United Nations Emergency Force will assure that there are no military or paramilitary forces of any kind, military fortifications and military installations; it will establish checkpoints and have the freedom of movement necessary to perform this function.

(b) Egyptian civilians and third-country civilian oil-field personnel shall have the right to enter, exit from, work and live in the above-indicated area, except for buffer zones 2A, 2B and the U.N. posts. Egyptian civilian police shall be allowed in the area to perform normal civil police functions among the civilian population in such numbers and with such weapons and equipment as shall be provided for in the protocol.

(c) Entry to and exit from the area, by land, by air or by sea, shall be only through UNEF checkpoints. UNEF shall also establish checkpoints along the road, the dividing line and at other points, with the precise locations and number to be included in the protocol.

(d) Access to the airspace and the coastal area shall be limited to unarmed Egyptian civilian vessels and unarmed civilian helicopters and transport planes involved in the civilian activities of the area, as agreed by the working group.

(e) Israel undertakes to leave intact all currently existing civilian installations and infrastructures.

(f) Procedures for use of the common sections of the coastal road along the Gulf of Suez shall be determined by the working group and detailed in the protocol.

4. AERIAL SURVEILLANCE

There shall be a continuation of aerial reconnaissance missions by the U.S. over the areas covered by the agreement following the same procedures already in practice. The missions will ordinarily be carried out at a frequency of one mission every seven to 10 days, with either party or UNEF empowered to request an earlier mission. The U.S. will make the mission results available expeditiously to Israel, Egypt and the chief coordinator of the U.N. peace-keeping mission in the Middle East.

5. LIMITATION OF FORCES AND ARMAMENTS

(a) Within the areas of limited forces and armaments the major limitations shall be as follows:

(1) Eight (8) standard infantry battalions.

(2) Seventy-five (75) tanks.

(3) Sixty (60) artillery pieces, including heavy mortars (i.e., with caliber larger than 120 mm.), whose range shall not exceed 12 km.

(4) The total number of personnel shall not exceed eight thousand (8,000).

(5) Both parties agree not to station or locate in the area weapons which can reach the line of the other side.

(6) Both parties agree that in the areas between lines J and K, and between line A (of the disengagement agreement of Jan. 18, 1974) and line E, they will construct no new fortifications or installations for forces of a size greater than that agreed herein.

(b) The major limitations beyond the areas of limited forces and armament will be:

(1) Neither side will station nor locate any weapon in areas from which they can reach the other line.

(2) The parties will not place anti-aircraft missiles within an area of 10 kilometers east of line K and west of line F, respectively.

(c) The U.N. Force will conduct inspections in order to insure the maintenance of the agreed limitations within these areas.

6. PROCESS OF IMPLEMENTATION

The detailed implementation and timing of the redeployment of forces, turnover of oil fields and other arrangements called for

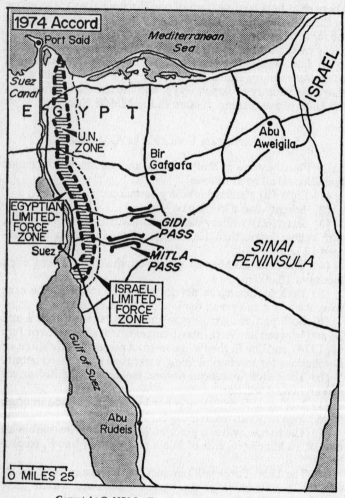

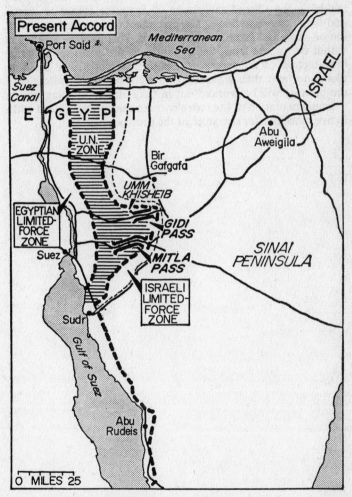

Present Accord

Mediterranean Sea

Port Said

ISRAEL

Suez Canal

E G Y P T

U.N. ZONE

Abu Aweigila

Bir Gafgafa

UMM KHISHEIB

EGYPTIAN LIMITED-FORCE ZONE

GIDI PASS

Suez

MITLA PASS

SINAI PENINSULA

ISRAELI LIMITED-FORCE ZONE

Sudr

Gulf of Suez

Abu Rudeis

0 MILES 25

Copyright © 1975 by The New York Times Company.
Reprinted by permission.

by the agreement, annex and protocol shall be determined by the working group, which will agree on the stages of this process, including the phased movement of Egyptian troops to line E and Israeli troops to line J. The first phase will be the transfer of the oil fields and installations to Egypt. This process will begin within two weeks from the signature of the protocol with the introduction of the necessary technicians, and it will be completed no later than eight weeks after it begins. The details of the phasing will be worked out in the military working group.

Implementation of the redeployment shall be completed within five months after signature of the protocol.

PART VII

Camp David
and War in Lebanon

The years following the 1973 war were filled with dramatic events. President Anwar Sadat's visit to Jerusalem began a round of new peace plans and culminated in the Camp David accords, an Egypt-Israel peace treaty, and proposals for West Bank autonomy. Other Arab states and the Palestinians rejected this framework. The Israeli governments of Prime Minister Menachem Begin and his successor, Yitzhak Shamir, continued settlement activities on the West Bank. Saudi Crown Prince Fahd suggested a new Arab position, hinting at acceptance of Israel, but this was watered down by the 1982 Arab summit. The Israeli invasion of Lebanon set off a new chain of events. Secretary of State George Shultz indicated heightened U.S. concern over the issues involved, a massacre of Palestinians by Lebanese Christians provoked further feelings of urgency, and the Reagan Plan proposed a future peace arrangement involving Arab recognition of Israel and a Jordan–West Bank federation. This, too, was rejected by Israel, the PLO, and Jordan and was followed by an internal revolt, led by Said Musa under Syrian sponsorship, in the largest PLO group, Al Fatah.

Harold H. Saunders: U.S. Foreign Policy and Peace in the Middle East (November 12, 1975)*

Mr. Chairman, a just and durable peace in the Middle East is a central objective of the United States. Both President Ford and Secretary Kissinger have stated firmly on numerous occasions that the United States is determined to make every feasible effort to maintain the momentum of practical progress toward a peaceful settlement of the Arab-Israeli conflict.

We have also repeatedly stated that the legitimate interests of the Palestinian Arabs must be taken into account in the negotiation of an Arab-Israeli peace. In many ways, the Palestinian dimension of the Arab-Israeli conflict is the heart of that conflict. Final resolution of the problems arising from the partition of Palestine, the establishment of the State of Israel, and Arab opposition to those events will not be possible until agreement is reached defining a just and permanent status for the Arab peoples who consider themselves Palestinians. . . . The U.S. has provided some $620 million in assistance—about sixty-two percent of the total international support ($1 billion) for the Palestinian refugees over the past quarter of a century.

Today, however, we recognize that, in addition to meeting the human needs and responding to legitimate personal claims of the refugees, there is another interest that must be taken into account. It is a fact that many of the three million or so people who call themselves Palestinians today increasingly regard themselves as having their own identity as a people and desire a voice in determining their political status. As with any

* Prepared statement of Harold H. Saunders, Deputy Assistant Secretary for Near Eastern and South Asian affairs, before the House Foreign Affairs Subcommittee on the Middle East.

people in this situation, there are differences among themselves, but the Palestinians collectively are a political factor which must be dealt with if there is to be a peace between Israel and its neighbors.

The statement is often made in the Arab world that there will not be peace until the "rights of the Palestinians" are fulfilled, but there is no agreed definition of what is meant and a variety of viewpoints have been expressed on what the legitimate objectives of the Palestinians are:

Some Palestinian elements hold to the objective of a binational secular state in the area of the former mandate of Palestine. Realization of this objective would mean the end of the present state of Israel, a member of the United Nations, and its submergence in some larger entity. Some would be willing to accept merely as a first step toward this goal the establishment of a Palestinian state comprising the West Bank of the Jordan River and Gaza.

Other elements of Palestinian opinion appear willing to accept an independent Palestinian state comprising the West Bank and Gaza, based on acceptance of Israel's right to exist as an independent state within roughly its pre-1967 borders.

Some Palestinians and other Arabs envisage as a possible solution a unification of the West Bank and Gaza with Jordan. A variation of this which has been suggested would be the reconstitution of the country as a federated state, with the West Bank becoming an autonomous Palestinian province.

Still others, including many Israelis, feel that with the West Bank returned to Jordan, and with the resulting existence of two communities—Palestinian and Jordanian—within Jordan, opportunities would be created thereby for the Palestinians to find self-expression.

In the case of a solution which would rejoin the West Bank to Jordan or a solution involving a West Bank/Gaza state, there would still arise the property claims of those Palestinians who before 1948 resided in areas that became the State of Israel. These claims have been acknowledged as a serious problem by the international community ever since the adoption by the United Nations of Resolution 194 on this subject in 1948, a resolution which the United Nations has repeatedly reaffirmed and which the United States has supported. A solution will be further complicated by the property claims against Arab states of the many Jews from those states who moved to Israel in its early years after achieving statehood.

In addition to property claims, some believe they should have the option of returning to their original homes under any settlement.

Other Arab leaders, while pressing the importance of Palestinian involvement in a settlement, have taken the position that the definition of Palestinian interests is something for the Palestinian people themselves to sort out, and the view has been expressed by responsible Arab leaders that realization of Palestinian rights need not be inconsistent with the existence of Israel.

No one, therefore, seems in a position today to say exactly what Palestinian objectives are. . . . What is needed as a first step is a diplomatic process which will help bring forth a reasonable definition of Palestinian interests—a position from which negotiations on a solution of the Palestinian aspects of the problem might begin. The issue is not whether Palestinian interests should be expressed in a final settlement, but how. There will be no peace unless an answer is found.

Another requirement is the development of a framework for negotiations—a statement of the objectives and the terms of reference. The framework for the negotiations that have taken place thus far and the agreements they have produced involving Israel, Syria, and Egypt, has been provided by United Nations Security Council Resolutions 242 and 338. In accepting that framework, all of the parties to the negotiation have accepted that the objective of the negotiations is peace between them based on mutual recognition, territorial integrity, political independence, the right to live in peace within secure and recognized borders, and the resolution of the specific issues which comprise the Arab-Israeli conflict.

The major problem that must be resolved in establishing a framework for bringing issues of concern to the Palestinians into negotiation, therefore, is to find a common basis for the negotiation that Palestinians and Israelis can both accept. This could be achieved by common acceptance of the above-mentioned Security Council resolutions, although they do not deal with the political aspect of the Palestinian problem.

A particularly difficult aspect of the problem is the question of who negotiates for the Palestinians. It has been our belief that Jordan would be a logical negotiator for the Palestinian-related issues. The Rabat Summit, however, recognized the Palestinian Liberation Organization as the "sole legitimate representative of the Palestinian people." . . .

However, the PLO does not accept the United Nations Security Council resolutions, does not recognize the existence of Israel, and has not stated its readiness to negotiate peace with Israel; Israel does not recognize the PLO or the idea of a separate Palestinian entity. Thus we do not at this point have the framework for a negotiation involving the PLO. We cannot envision or urge a negotiation between two parties as long as one professes to hold the objective of eliminating the other —rather than the objective of negotiating peace with it.

There is one other aspect to this problem. Elements of the PLO have used terrorism to gain attention for their cause. Some Americans as well as many Israelis and others have been killed by Palestinian terrorists. The international community cannot condone such practices, and it seems to us that there must be some assurance if Palestinians are drawn into the negotiating process that these practices will be curbed.

This is the problem which we now face. If the progress toward peace which has now begun is to continue, a solution to this question must be found. We have not devised an American solution, nor would it be appropriate for us to do so. This is the responsibility of the parties and the purpose of the negotiating process. But we have not closed our minds to any reasonable solution which can contribute to progress toward our overriding objective in the Middle East—an Arab-Israeli peace. The step-by-step approach to negotiations which we have pursued has been based partly on the understanding that issues in the Arab-Israeli conflict take time to mature. It is obvious that thinking on the Palestinian aspects of the problem must evolve on all sides. As it does, what is not possible today may become possible.

Our consultations on how to move the peace negotiations forward will recognize the need to deal with this subject. As Secretary Kissinger has said, "We are prepared to work with all the parties toward a solution of all the issues yet remaining —including the issue of the future of the Palestinians." We will do so because the issues of concern to the Palestinians are important in themselves and because the Arab governments participating in the negotiations have made clear that progress in the overall negotiations will depend in part on progress on issues of concern to the Palestinians. We are prepared to consider any reasonable proposal from any quarter, and we will expect other parties to the negotiation to be equally open-minded.

Brookings Institution Panel:
Towards Peace in the Middle East
(December 1975)*

The study group reached five main conclusions.

1. *U.S. interests.* The United States has a strong moral, political, and economic interest in a stable peace in the Middle East. It is concerned for the security, independence, and well-being of Israel and the Arab states of the area and for the friendship of both. Renewed hostilities would have far-reaching and perilous consequences which would threaten those interests.

2. *Urgency.* Whatever the merits of the interim agreement on Sinai, it still leaves the basic elements of the Arab-Israeli dispute substantially untouched. Unless these elements are soon addressed, rising tensions in the area will generate increased risk of violence. We believe that the best way to address these issues is by the pursuit of a comprehensive settlement.

3. *Process.* We believe that the time has come to begin the process of negotiating such a settlement among the parties, either at a general conference or at more informal multilateral meetings. While no useful interim step toward settlement should be overlooked or ignored, none seems promising at the present time and most have inherent disadvantages.

4. *Settlement.* A fair and enduring settlement should contain at least these elements as an integrated package:

(a) *Security.* All parties to the settlement commit themselves to respect the sovereignty and territorial integrity of the others and to refrain from the threat or use of force against them.

(b) *Stages.* Withdrawal to agreed boundaries and the establishment of peaceful relations carried out in stages over a period of years, each stage being undertaken only when the agreed provisions of the previous stage have been faithfully implemented.

(c) *Peaceful relations.* The Arab parties undertake not only to end such hostile actions against Israel as armed incursions, blockades, boycotts, and propaganda attacks, but also to give

---

* This is a summary from the Brookings Report, drafted by a panel of diplomats and academicians, including future U.S. National Security Adviser Zbigniew Brzezinski.

evidence of progress toward the development of normal international and regional political and economic relations.

(d) *Boundaries.* Israel undertakes to withdraw by agreed stages to the June 5, 1967, lines with only such modifications as are mutually accepted. Boundaries will probably need to be safeguarded by demilitarized zones supervised by UN forces.

(e) *Palestine.* There should be provision for Palestinian self-determination, subject to Palestinian acceptance of the sovereignty and integrity of Israel within agreed boundaries. This might take the form either of an independent Palestine state accepting the obligations and commitments of the peace agreements or of a Palestine entity voluntarily federated with Jordan but exercising extensive political autonomy.

(f) *Jerusalem.* The report suggests no specific solution for the particularly difficult problem of Jerusalem but recommends that, whatever the solution may be, it meet as a minimum the following criteria:

—there should be unimpeded access to all of the holy places and each should be under the custodianship of its own faith;

—there should be no barriers dividing the city which would prevent free circulation throughout it; and

—each national group within the city should, if it so desires, have substantial political autonomy within the area where it predominates.

(g) *Guarantees.* It would be desirable that the UN Security Council endorse the peace agreements and take whatever other actions to support them the agreements provide. In addition, there may well be need for unilateral or multilateral guarantees to some or all of the parties, substantial economic aid, and military assistance pending the adoption of agreed arms control measures.

5. *U.S. role.* The governments directly concerned bear the responsibility of negotiation and agreement, but they are unlikely to be able to reach agreement alone. Initiative, impetus, and inducement may well have to come from outside. The United States, because it enjoys a measure of confidence of parties on both sides and has the means to assist them economically and militarily, remains the great power best fitted to work actively with them in bringing about a settlement. Over and above helping to provide a framework for negotiation and submitting concrete proposals from time to time, the United States must be prepared to take other constructive steps, such as offering aid and providing guarantees where desired and needed. In all of this, the United States should work with the

USSR to the degree that Soviet willingness to play a constructive role will permit.

Platform of the Likud Coalition
(March 1977)*

The Right of the Jewish People to
the Land of Israel (Eretz Israel)

a. The right of the Jewish people to the land of Israel is eternal and indisputable and is linked with the right to security and peace; therefore, Judaea and Samaria will not be handed to any foreign administration; between the sea and Jordan there will only be Israeli sovereignty.

b. A plan which relinquishes parts of western Eretz Israel, undermines our right to the country, unavoidably leads to the establishment of a "Palestinian State," jeopardizes the security of the Jewish population, endangers the existence of the State of Israel, and frustrates any prospect of peace.

Genuine Peace—Our Central Objective

a. The Likud government will place its aspirations for peace at the top of its priorities and will spare no effort to promote peace. The Likud will act as a genuine partner at peace treaty negotiations with our neighbors, as is customary among the nations. The Likud government will attend the Geneva Conference. . . .

d. The Likud government's peace initiative will be positive. Directly or through a friendly state, Israel will invite her neighbors to hold direct negotiations, in order to sign peace agreements without pre-conditions on either side and without any solution formula invented by outsiders ("invented outside").

At the negotiations each party will be free to make any proposals it deems fit.

Settlement

Settlement, both urban and rural, in all parts of the Land of Israel is the focal point of the Zionist effort to redeem the

* Excerpts from Prime Minister Begin's election platform.

country, to maintain vital security areas and serves as a reservoir of strength and inspiration for the renewal of the pioneering spirit. The Likud government will call the younger generation in Israel and the dispersions to settle and help every group and individual in the task of inhabiting and cultivating the wasteland, while taking care not to dispossess anyone.

Arab Terror Organizations

The PLO is no national liberation organization but an organization of assassins, which the Arab countries use as a political and military tool, while also serving the interests of Soviet imperialism, to stir up the area. Its aim is to liquidate the State of Israel, set up an Arab country instead and make the Land of Israel part of the Arab world. The Likud government will strive to eliminate these murderous organizations in order to prevent them from carrying out their bloody deeds.

President Anwar Sadat:
Peace with Justice (November 20, 1977)*

. . . I come to you today on solid ground to shape a new life and to establish peace. We all love this land, the land of God, we all, Moslems, Christians and Jews, all worship God.

Under God, God's teachings and commandments are: love, sincerity, security and peace.

I do not blame all those who received my decision when I announced it to the entire world before the Egyptian People's Assembly . . . with surprise and even with amazement. . . .

Many months in which peace could have been brought about have been wasted over differences and fruitless discussions on the procedure of convening the Geneva conference. All have shared suspicion and absolute lack of confidence.

But to be absolutely frank with you, I took this decision after long thought, knowing that it constitutes a great risk, for God Almighty has made it my fate to assume responsibility on behalf of the Egyptian people, to share in the responsibility of the Arab nation, the main duty of which, dictated by responsibility, is to exploit all and every means in a bid to save

* Excerpts from speech delivered by the Egyptian President before the Israeli Parliament.

my Egyptian Arab people and the pan-Arab nation from the horrors of new suffering and destructive wars, the dimensions of which are foreseen only by God Himself. . . .

Those who like us are shouldering the same responsibilities entrusted to us are the first who should have the courage to make determining decisions that are consonant with the magnitude of the circumstances. We must all rise above all forms of obsolete theories of superiority, and the most important thing is never to forget that infallibility is the prerogative of God alone.

If I said that I wanted to avert from all the Arab people the horrors of shocking and destructive wars I must sincerely declare before you that I have the same feelings and bear the same responsibility toward all and every man on earth, and certainly toward the Israeli people.

Any life that is lost in war is a human life, be it that of an Arab or an Israeli. A wife who becomes a widow is a human being entitled to a happy family life, whether she be an Arab or an Israeli.

Innocent children who are deprived of the care and compassion of their parents are ours. They are ours, be they living on Arab or Israeli land.

They command our full responsibility to afford them a comfortable life today and tomorrow.

For the sake of them all, for the sake of the lives of all our sons and brothers, for the sake of affording our communities the opportunity to work for the progress and happiness of man, feeling secure and with the right to a dignified life, for the generations to come, for a smile on the face of every child born in our land—for all that I have taken my decision to come to you, despite all the hazards, to deliver my address.

I have shouldered the prerequisites of the historic responsibility and therefore I declared on Feb. 4, 1971, that I was willing to sign a peace agreement with Israel. This was the first declaration made by a responsible Arab official since the outbreak of the Arab-Israeli conflict. Motivated by all these factors dictated by the responsibilities of leadership on Oct. 16, 1973, before the Egyptian People's Assembly, I called for an international conference to establish permanent peace based on justice. I was not heard.

I was in the position of man pleading for peace or asking for a cease-fire, motivated by the duties of history and leadership, I signed the first disengagement agreement, followed by the second disengagement agreement in Sinai.

Then we proceeded, trying both open and closed doors in a bid to find a certain road leading to a durable and just peace. . . .

How can we achieve permanent peace based on justice? Well, I have come to you carrying my clear and frank answer to this big question, so that the people in Israel as well as the entire world may hear it. All those devoted prayers ring in my ears, pleading to God Almighty that this historic meeting may eventually lead to the result aspired to by millions.

Before I proclaim my answer, I wish to assure you that in my clear and frank answer I am availing myself of a number of facts which no one can deny.

The first fact is that no one can build his happiness at the expense of the misery of others.

The second fact: never have I spoken, nor will I ever speak, with two tongues; never have I adopted, nor will I ever adopt, two policies. I never deal with anyone except in one tongue, one policy and with one face.

The third fact: direct confrontation is the nearest and most successful method to reach a clear objective.

The fourth fact: the call for permanent and just peace based on respect for United Nations resolutions has now become the call of the entire world. It has become the expression of the will of the international community, whether in official capitals where policies are made and decisions taken, or at the level of world public opinion, which influences policymaking and decision-taking.

The fifth fact, and this is probably the clearest and most prominent, is that the Arab nation, in its drive for permanent peace based on justice, does not proceed from a position of weakness. On the contrary, it has the power and stability for a sincere will for peace.

The Arab declared intention stems from an awareness prompted by a heritage of civilization, that to avoid an inevitable disaster that will befall us, you and the whole world, there is no alternative to the establishment of permanent peace based on justice, peace that is not swayed by suspicion or jeopardized by ill intentions.

In the light of these facts which I meant to place before you the way I see them, I would also wish to warn you, in all sincerity I warn you, against some thoughts that could cross your minds. . . .

First, I have not come here for a separate agreement between Egypt and Israel. This is not part of the policy of Egypt. The problem is not that of Egypt and Israel.

An interim peace between Egypt and Israel, or between any Arab confrontation state and Israel, will not bring permanent peace based on justice in the entire region.

Rather, even if peace between all the confrontation states and Israel were achieved in the absence of a just solution of the Palestinian problem, never will there be that durable and just peace upon which the entire world insists.

Second, I have not come to you to seek a partial peace, namely to terminate the state of belligerency at this stage and put off the entire problem to a subsequent stage. This is not the radical solution that would steer us to permanent peace.

Equally, I have not come to you for a third disengagement agreement in Sinai or in Golan or the West Bank.

For this would mean that we are merely delaying the ignition of the fuse. It would also mean that we are lacking the courage to face peace, that we are too weak to shoulder the burdens and responsibilities of a durable peace based upon justice.

I have come to you so that together we should build a durable peace based on justice to avoid the shedding of one single drop of blood by both sides. It is for this reason that I have proclaimed my readiness to go to the farthest corner of the earth.

Here I would go back to the big question:

How can we achieve a durable peace based on justice? In my opinion, and I declare it to the whole world, from this forum, the answer is neither difficult nor is it impossible despite long years of feuds, blood, faction, strife, hatreds and deep-rooted animosity.

The answer is not difficult, nor is it impossible, if we sincerely and faithfully follow a straight line.

You want to live with us, part of the world.

In all sincerity I tell you we welcome you among us with full security and safety. This in itself is a tremendous turning point, one of the landmarks of a decisive historical change. We used to reject you. We had our reasons and our fears, yes.

We refused to meet with you, anywhere, yes.

We were together in international conferences and organizations and our representatives did not, and still do not, exchange greetings with you. Yes. This has happened and is still happening.

It is also true that we used to set as a precondition for any negotiations with you a mediator who would meet separately with each party.

Yes. Through this procedure, the talks of the first and second disengagement agreements took place.

Our delegates met in the first Geneva conference without exchanging direct word, yes, this has happened.

Yet today I tell you, and I declare it to the whole world, that we accept to live with you in permanent peace based on justice. We do not want to encircle you or be encircled ourselves by destructive missiles ready for launching, nor by the shells of grudges and hatreds.

I have announced on more than one occasion that Israel has become a fait accompli, recognized by the world, and that the two superpowers have undertaken the responsibility for its security and the defense of its existence. As we really and truly seek peace we really and truly welcome you to live among us in peace and security.

There was a huge wall between us which you tried to build up over a quarter of a century, but it was destroyed in 1973. It was the wall of an implacable and escalating psychological warfare.

It was a wall of the fear of the force that could sweep the entire Arab nation. It was a wall of propaganda that we were a nation reduced to immobility. Some of you had gone as far as to say that even for 50 years to come, the Arabs would not regain their strength. It was a wall that always threatened with a long arm that could reach and strike anywhere. It was a wall that warned us of extermination and annihilation if we tried to use our legitimate rights to liberate the occupied territories.

Together we have to admit that that wall fell and collapsed in 1973. Yet, there remains another wall. This wall constitutes a psychological barrier between us, a barrier of suspicion, a barrier of rejection; a barrier of fear, of deception, a barrier of hallucination without any action, deed or decision.

A barrier of distorted and eroded interpretation of every event and statement. It is this psychological barrier which I described in official statements as constituting 70 percent of the whole problem.

Today, through my visit to you, I ask you why don't we stretch out our hands with faith and sincerity so that together we might destroy this barrier? Why shouldn't our and your will meet with faith and sincerity so that together we might remove all suspicion of fear, betrayal and bad intentions? . . .

Ladies and gentlemen, to tell you the truth, peace cannot be worth its name unless it is based on justice and not on the occupation of the land of others. It would not be right for you to demand for yourselves what you deny to others. With all frankness and in the spirit that has prompted me to come to you today, I tell you you have to give up once and for all the dreams of conquest and give up the belief that force is the best method for dealing with the Arabs.

You should clearly understand the lesson of confrontation between you and us. Expansion does not pay. To speak frankly, our land does not yield itself to bargaining, it is not even open to argument. To us, the nation's soil is equal to the holy valley where God Almighty spoke to Moses. Peace be upon him.

We cannot accept any attempt to take away or accept to seek one inch of it nor can we accept the principle of debating or bargaining over it.

I sincerely tell you also that before us today lies the appropriate chance for peace. If we are really serious in our endeavor for peace, it is a chance that that may never come again. It is a chance that if lost or wasted, the resulting slaughter would bear the curse of humanity and of history.

What is peace for Israel? It means that Israel lives in the region with her Arab neighbors in security and safety. Is that logical? I say yes. It means that Israel lives within its borders, secure against any aggression. Is that logical? And I say yes. It means that Israel obtains all kinds of guarantees that will ensure these two factors. To this demand, I say yes.

Beyond that we declare that we accept all the international guarantees you envisage and accept. We declare that we accept all the guarantees you want from the two superpowers or from either of them or from the Big Five or from some of them. Once again, I declare clearly and unequivocally that we agree to any guarantees you accept, because in return we shall receive the same guarantees.

In short then, when we ask what is peace for Israel, the answer would be that Israel lives within her borders, among her Arab neighbors in safety and security, within the framework of all the guarantees she accepts and which are offered to her.

But, how can this be achieved? How can we reach this conclusion which would lead us to permanent peace based on justice? There are facts that should be faced with courage and clarity. There are Arab territories which Israel has occupied and still occupies by force. We insist on complete withdrawal from these territories, including Arab Jerusalem.

I have come to Jerusalem, the city of peace, which will always remain as a living embodiment of coexistence among believers of the three religions. It is inadmissible that anyone should conceive the special status of the city of Jerusalem within the framework of annexation or expansionism. It should be a free and open city for all believers.

Above all, this city should not be severed from those who have made it their abode for centuries. Instead of reviving the precedent of the Crusades, we should revive the spirit of Omar Emil Khtab and Saladin, namely the spirit of tolerance and respect for right.

The holy shrines of Islam and Christianity are not only places of worship but a living testimony of our interrupted presence here. Politically, spiritually and intellectually, here let us make no mistake about the importance and reverence we Christians and Moslems attach to Jerusalem.

Let me tell you without the slightest hesitation that I have not come to you under this roof to make a request that your troops evacuate the occupied territories. Complete withdrawal from the Arab territories occupied after 1967 is a logical and undisputed fact. Nobody should plead for that. Any talk about permanent peace based on justice and any move to ensure our coexistence in peace and security in this part of the world would become meaningless while you occupy Arab territories by force of arms.

For there is no peace that could be built on the occupation of the land of others, otherwise it would not be a serious peace. Yet this is a foregone conclusion which is not open to the passion of debate if intentions are sincere or if endeavors to establish a just and durable peace for our and for generations to come are genuine.

As for the Palestine cause—nobody could deny that it is the crux of the entire problem. Nobody in the world could accept today slogans propagated here in Israel, ignoring the existence of a Palestinian people and questioning even their whereabouts. Because the Palestine people and their legitimate rights are no longer denied today by anybody; that is nobody who has the ability of judgment, can deny or ignore it.

It is an acknowledged fact, perceived by the world community, both in the East and in the West, with support and recognition in international documents and official statements. It is of no use to anybody to turn deaf ears to its resounding voice, which is being heard day and night, or to overlook its historical reality.

Even the United States of America, your first ally, which is absolutely committed to safeguard Israel's security and existence and which offered and still offers Israel every moral, material and military support—I say, even the United States has opted to face up to reality and admit that the Palestinian people are entitled to legitimate rights and that the Palestine problem is the cause and essence of the conflict and that so long as it continues to be unresolved, the conflict will continue to aggravate, reaching new dimension.

In all sincerity I tell you that there can be no peace without the Palestinians. It is a grave error of unpredictable consequences to overlook or brush aside this cause.

I shall not indulge in past events such as the Balfour Declaration 60 years ago. You are well acquainted with the relevant text. If you have found the moral and legal justification to set up a national home on a land that did not all belong to you, it is incumbent upon you to show understanding of the insistence of the people of Palestine for establishment once again of a state on their land. When some extremists ask the Palestinians to give up this sublime objective, this in fact means asking them to renounce their identity and every hope for the future.

I hail the Israeli voices that called for the recognition of the Palestinian people's right to achieve and safeguard peace.

Here I tell you, ladies and gentlemen, that it is no use to refrain from recognizing the Palestinian people and their right to statehood as their right of return. We, the Arabs, have faced this experience before, with you. And with the reality of the Israeli existence, the struggle which took us from war to war, from victims to more victims, until you and we have today reached the edge of a horrible abyss and a terrifying disaster unless, together, we seize this opportunity today of a durable peace based on justice.

You have to face reality bravely, as I have done. There can never be any solution to a problem by evading it or turning a deaf ear to it. Peace cannot last if attempts are made to impose fantasy concepts on which the world has turned its back and announced its unanimous call for the respect of rights and facts.

There is no need to enter a vicious circle as to Palestinian rights. It is useless to create obstacles, otherwise the march of peace will be impeded or peace will be blown up. As I have told you, there is no happiness [based on] the detriment of others.

Direct confrontation and straightforwardness are the short-cuts and the most successful way to reach a clear objective. Direct confrontation concerning the Palestinian problem and tackling it in one single language with a view to achieving a durable and just peace lie in the establishment of that peace. With all the guarantees you demand, there should be no fear of a newly born state that needs the assistance of all countries of the world.

When the bells of peace ring there will be no hands to beat the drums of war. Even if they existed, they would be stilled.

Conceive with me a peace agreement in Geneva that we would herald to a world thirsting for peace. A peace agreement based on the following points:

Ending the occupation of the Arab territories occupied in 1967.

Achievement of the fundamental rights of the Palestinian people and their right to self-determination, including their right to establish their own state.

The right of all states in the area to live in peace within their boundaries, their secure boundaries, which will be secured and guaranteed through procedures to be agreed upon, which will provide appropriate security to international boundaries in addition to appropriate international guarantees.

Commitment of all states in the region to administer the relations among them in accordance with the objectives and principles of the United Nations Charter. Particularly the principles concerning the nonuse of force and a solution of differences among them by peaceful means.

Ending the state of belligerence in the region.

Ladies and gentlemen, peace is not a mere endorsement of written lines. Rather it is a rewriting of history. Peace is not a game of calling for peace to defend certain whims or hide certain admissions. Peace in its essence is a dire struggle against all and every ambition and whim.

Perhaps the example taken and experienced, taken from ancient and modern history, teaches that missiles, warships and nuclear weapons cannot establish security. Instead they destroy what peace and security build.

For the sake of our peoples and for the sake of the civiliza-tion made by man, we have to defend man everywhere against rule by the force of arms so that we may endow the rule of humanity with all the power of the values and principles that further the sublime position of mankind.

Allow me to address my call from this rostrum to the people of Israel. I pledge myself with true and sincere words to every man, woman and child in Israel. I tell them, from the Egyptian people who bless this sacred mission of peace, I convey to you the message of peace of the Egyptian people, who do not harbor fanaticism and whose sons, Moslems, Christians and Jews, live together in a state of cordiality, love and tolerance.

This is Egypt, whose people have entrusted me with their sacred message. A message of security, safety and peace to every man, woman and child in Israel. I say, encourage your leadership to struggle for peace. Let all endeavors be channeled toward building a huge stronghold for peace instead of building destructive rockets.

Introduce to the entire world the image of the new man in this area so that he might set an example to the man of our age, the man of peace everywhere. Ring the bells for your sons. Tell them that those wars were the last of wars and the end of sorrows. Tell them that we are entering upon a new beginning, a new life, a life of love, prosperity, freedom and peace.

You, sorrowing mother, you, widowed wife, you, the son who lost a brother or a father, all the victims of wars, fill the air and space with recitals of peace, fill bosoms and hearts with the aspirations of peace. Make a reality that blossoms and lives. Make hope a code of conduct and endeavor. . . .

PLO: Six-Point Program (December 4, 1977)*

In the wake of Sadat's treasonous visit to the Zionist entity, all factions of the Palestinian Resistance Movement have decided to make a practical answer to this step. On this basis, they met and issued the following document:

We, all factions of the PLO, announce the following:

FIRST: We call for the formation of a "Steadfastness and Confrontation Front" composed of Libya, Algeria, Iraq, Democratic Yemen, Syria and the PLO, to oppose all capitulation-

* Signed by leaders of the PLO's constituent organizations in Tripoli, Libya.

ist solutions planned by imperialism, Zionism and their Arab tools.

SECOND: We fully condemn any Arab party in the Tripoli Summit which rejects the formation of this Front, and we announce this.

THIRD: We reaffirm our rejection of Security Council resolutions 242 and 338.

FOURTH: We reaffirm our rejection of all international conferences based on these two resolutions, including the Geneva Conference.

FIFTH: To strive for the realization of the Palestinian people's rights to return and self-determination within the context of an independent Palestinian national state on any part of Palestinian land, without reconciliation, recognition or negotiations, as an interim aim of the Palestinian Revolution.

SIXTH: To apply the measures related to the political boycott of the Sadat regime.

In the name of all the factions, we ratify this unificatory document.

Arab League Summit Conference Declaration (December 5, 1977)*

With a sense of complete pan-Arab responsibility, the conference discussed the dimensions of the current phase through which the Arab cause in general and the Palestinian question in particular are passing and the American-Zionist plans aimed at imposing capitulatory settlements on the Arab nation, prejudicing the established national rights of the Palestinian people, liquidating the national Arab accomplishments and striking at the Arab liberation movement as a prelude to subduing the Arab area and controlling its destiny and tying it to the bandwagon of world imperialism.

The conference also discussed the visit made by President Sadat to the Zionist entity as being a link in the framework of the implementation of the hostile schemes. . . .

Those attending the conference studied the current situation with all of its dimensions and concluded that the objectives of the plot are as follows:

---

* Excerpts. The Arab League Summit Conference was held in Tripoli, Libya, December 2–5, 1977.

To undermine the possibility of the establishment of a just and honorable peace which would safeguard the national rights of the Arab nation and guarantee for it the liberation of its occupied territories, the foremost of which is Jerusalem, and for the Palestinian people their established national rights.

. . . To enable the forces hostile to the Arab nation, headed by the United States, to realize gains that will upset the international balance in favor of the Zionist-imperialist forces and Zionism and undermine the national independence of the Afro-Asian and Latin American countries.

To establish an alliance between the Zionist enemy and the current Egyptian regime aimed at liquidating the Arab issue and the issue of Palestine, split the Arab nation and forfeit its national interests.

Out of its belief in the nature of the Zionist and imperialist challenges aimed at weakening the Arab will for liberation and harming the firm national rights of the Palestinian people which have been confirmed by international legitimacy—the foremost of which is their right to return and decide their own destiny and build their independent state on the soil of their homeland under the leadership of the PLO, which is the sole legitimate representative of the Palestinian people—and proceeding from the reality of pan-Arab and historic responsibility, the summit conference decided the following:

1. To condemn President al-Sadat's visit to the Zionist entity since it constitutes a great betrayal of the sacrifices and struggle of our Arab people in Egypt and their armed forces and of the struggle, sacrifices and principles of the Arab nation. While appreciating the role of the great Egyptian people in the national struggle of the Arab nation, the conference stresses that Egypt is not the beginning or the end and that if the Arab nation is great with Egypt, the latter's greatness is only possible within the Arab nation, without which it can only diminish in importance.

2. To work for the frustration of the results of President al-Sadat's visit to the Zionist entity and his talks with the leaders of the Zionist enemy and the subsequent measures including the proposed Cairo meeting. The conference warns that anyone who tries to pursue a similar line or to have any dealings with the said results shall be held responsible for his deed nationally and on the pan-Arab level.

3. To freeze political and diplomatic relations with the Egyptian Government, to suspend dealings with it on the Arab and international levels and to apply the regulations, provisions

and decisions of the Arab Boycott against Egyptian individuals, companies and firms which deal with the Zionist enemy.

4. To decide not to take part in Arab League meetings which are held in Egypt and to undertake contacts with the Arab League member states to study the question of its headquarters and organs and the membership of the Egyptian regime.

5. The conference salutes the Palestinian Arab people, who are standing fast in the occupied homeland, including all of their national and other popular organizations which are struggling against the occupation and which reject the visit of al-Sadat to occupied Palestine. The conference also warns against any attempt to prejudice the legitimacy of the PLO representation of the Palestinian people.

6. The conference takes satisfaction in recording the preliminary positions taken by the Arab states which have denounced the visit and rejected its consequences. Out of its responsibility and in compliance with its commitment and collective resolutions, the conference calls on these states to adopt practical measures to face the serious character of this capitulatory policy, including the suspension of political and military support. The conference also condemns the disgraceful stands adopted by those who praise this visit or support it and warn them of the consequences of their despondent and defeatist policies.

7. The conference appeals to the Arab nation on the official and popular levels to provide economic, financial, political and military aid and support to the Syrian region, now that it has become the principal confrontation state and the base of steadfastness for dealing with the Zionist enemy and also to the Palestinian people represented by the PLO.

8. The conference greets our Arab people in sisterly Egypt and particularly their national and progressive forces, which have rejected the capitulatory policy being pursued by the Egyptian regime as being a betrayal of the sacrifices of the people and their martyrs and an insult to the dignity of their armed forces.

9. In asserting the importance of the relationship of struggle and nationalism between Syria and the Palestinians, the Syrian Arab Republic and the PLO announce the formation of a unified front to face the Zionist enemy and combat the imperialist plot with all its parties and to thwart all attempts at capitulation. The Democratic and Popular Republic of Algeria, the Socialist People's Libyan Arab Jamahiriyah and the PDRY [People's Democratic Republic of Yemen—South Yemen] have

decided to join this front, making it the nucleus of a pan-Arab front for steadfastness and combat which will be open to other Arab countries to join.

10. Members of the pan-Arab front consider any aggression against any one member as an aggression against all members.

The conference pledges to the Arab nation that it will continue the march of struggle, steadfastness, combat and adherence to the objectives of the Arab struggle. The conference also expresses its deep faith and absolute confidence that the Arab nation, which has staged revolutions, overcome difficulties and defeated plots during its long history of struggle— a struggle which abounds with heroism—is today capable of replying with force to those who have harmed its dignity, squandered its rights, split its solidarity and departed from the principles of its struggle. It is confident of its own capabilities in liberation, progress and victory, thanks to God.

The conference records with satisfaction the national Palestinian unity within the framework of the PLO.

Prime Minister Menachem Begin: Autonomy Plan for the Occupied Territories (December 28, 1977)*

. . . With the establishment of peace we shall propose the introduction of an administrative autonomy for the Arab residents of Judea, Samaria and the Gaza Strip on the basis of the following principles:

The administration of the military rule in Judea, Samaria and the Gaza Strip will be abolished. In Judea, Samaria and the Gaza Strip an administrative autonomy of, by and for the Arab residents will be established. The residents of Judea, Samaria and the Gaza Strip will elect an administrative council which will be composed of 11 members. The administrative council will act according to the principles postulated in this document. Every resident 18 years old or older, regardless of his citizenship or the lack of it, will be entitled to vote for the administrative council. Every resident who is 25 years old or older the day the list of candidates for the administrative council is presented will be entitled to be elected to the ad-

* Excerpts from the Prime Minister's speech to the Israeli Parliament.

ministrative council. The administrative council will be elected in general, direct, personal, equal and secret elections. . . .

The administrative council will establish the following departments: department of education; department of transportation; department of construction and housing; department of industry, commerce and tourism; department of agriculture; department of health; department of labor and social betterment; department for the rehabilitation of refugees; department of legal administration and supervision of the local police force. The administrative council will issue regulations pertaining to the activities of those departments.

Security and public order in the areas of Judea, Samaria and Gaza will be entrusted to the Israeli authorities. . . .

Residents of Judea, Samaria and Gaza, regardless of their citizenship or lack of it, will have the free option to receive either Israeli or Jordanian citizenship. . . . A committee of representatives of Israel, Jordan and the administrative council will be established to examine the law in Judea, Samaria and the Gaza district and to determine which laws will remain valid, which will be abolished and what the authority of the administrative council will be to issue regulations. The decisions of this committee will be adopted unanimously.

Israeli residents will be entitled to purchase land and settle in the areas of Judea, Samaria and Gaza. Arab residents of Judea, Samaria and the Gaza district who become, in accordance with the free option granted them, Israeli citizens will be entitled to purchase land and settle in Israel. A committee of representatives of Israel, Jordan and of the administrative council will be established to determine immigration rules for the areas of Judea, Samaria and Gaza. The committee will postulate those rules which will permit Palestinian refugees outside Judea, Samaria and Gaza immigration in a reasonable volume into these areas. The decision of the committee will be adopted unanimously.

Israeli residents and the residents of Judea, Samaria and the Gaza district will be assured free movement and free economic activity in Israel, in Judea, in Samaria and in the Gaza district.

The administrative council will name one of its members to represent it before the Government of Israel for the purpose of discussing common issues, and one of its members will represent it before the Government of Jordan for the discussion of common issues.

Israel insists on its rights and demand for its sovereignty

over Judea, Samaria and the Gaza Strip. Knowing that other demands exist, it proposes, for the sake of the agreement and of peace, to leave the question of sovereignty in those areas open.

Regarding the administration of the places holy to the three religions in Jerusalem, a special proposal will be prepared and presented, insuring free admission for all believers to the places sacred to them.

These principles will lend themselves to reexamination after a period of five years. . . .

We do not even dream of the possibility—if we are given the chance to withdraw our military forces from Judea, Samaria and Gaza—of abandoning those areas to the control of the murderous organization that is called the PLO. . . . This is history's meanest murder organization, except for the armed Nazi organizations. It also bragged two days ago about the murder of Hamdi al-Qadi, deputy director of the Education Bureau in Ramallah.

It is a frightening proposition that someone's solution to the problems in the Middle East might be a single bullet dispatched to the heart of Egyptian President as-Sadat as the PLO's predecessors did at Al-Aqsa Mosque to King Abdallah. One single bullet. No wonder that the Egyptian Government has declared that should such a single shot be fired, Egypt would retaliate with a million shots. We wish to say that under no condition will that organization be allowed to take control over Judea, Samaria and Gaza. If we withdraw our army, this is exactly what would happen. Hence, let it be known that whoever desires an agreement with us should please accept our announcement that the IDF will be deployed in Judea, Samaria and Gaza. And there will also be other security arrangements, so that we can give to all the residents, Jews and Arabs alike, in Eretz Yisrael a secure life—that is to say, security for all. . . .

. . . We have a right and a demand for sovereignty over these areas of Eretz Yisrael. This is our land and it belongs to the Jewish nation rightfully. We desire an agreement and peace. We know that there are at least two other demands for sovereignty over these areas. If there is a mutual desire to reach an agreement and to promote peace—what is the way?

Should these contradictory demands remain, and should there be no answer to the collision course between them, an agreement between the parties would be impossible. And for this reason, in order to facilitate an agreement and make peace, there is only òne possible way. One way and no other: to agree to decide that the question of sovereignty remain open and to deal with people, with nations. That is to say, administrative autonomy for the Arabs of Eretz Yisrael; and for the Jews of Eretz Yisrael—genuine security. This is the fairness that is inherent in the content of the proposal. And in that spirit the proposal was also accepted abroad. . . .

President Jimmy Carter:
Statement on Palestinian Rights (January 4, 1978)*

It is an honor and a pleasure for us to be in this great country, led by such a strong and courageous man.

Mr. President, your bold initiative in seeking peace has aroused the admiration of the entire world. One of my most valued possessions is the warm, personal relationship which binds me and President Sadat together and which exemplifies the friendship and the common purpose of the people of Egypt and the people of the United States of America.

The Egyptian-Israeli peace initiative must succeed, while still guarding the sacred and historic principles held by the nations who have suffered so much in this region. There is no good reason why accommodation cannot be reached.

In my own private discussions with both Arab and Israeli leaders, I have been deeply impressed by the unanimous desire for peace. My presence here today is a direct result of the courageous initiative which President Sadat undertook in his recent trip to Jerusalem.

The negotiating process will continue in the near future. We fully support this effort, and we intend to play an active role in the work of the Political Committee of Cairo, which will soon reconvene in Jerusalem.

We believe that there are certain principles, fundamentally, which must be observed before a just and a comprehensive peace can be achieved.

· First, true peace must be based on normal relations among the parties to the peace. Peace means more than just an end to belligerency.

· Second, there must be withdrawal by Israel from territories occupied in 1967 and agreement on secure and recognized borders for all parties in the context of normal and

* Delivered in Aswan, Egypt.

peaceful relations in accordance with U.N. Resolutions 242 and 338.

· Third, there must be a resolution of the Palestinian problem in all its aspects. The problem must recognize the legitimate rights of the Palestinian people and enable the Palestinians to participate in the determination of their own future.

Some flexibility is always needed to insure successful negotiations and the resolution of conflicting views. We know that the mark of greatness among leaders is to consider carefully the views of others and the greater benefits that can result among the people of all nations which can come from a successful search for peace.

Mr. President, our consultations this morning have reconfirmed our common commitment to the fundamentals which will, with God's help, make 1978 the year for permanent peace in the Middle East.

Camp David Frameworks for Peace
(September 17, 1978)*

Preamble

The search for peace in the Middle East must be guided by the following:

—The agreed basis for a peaceful settlement of the conflict between Israel and its neighbors is United Nations Security Council Resolution 242, in all its parts.

—After four wars during thirty years, despite intensive human efforts, the Middle East, which is the cradle of civilization and the birthplace of three great religions, does not yet enjoy the blessings of peace. The people of the Middle East yearn for peace so that the vast human and natural resources of the region can be turned to the pursuits of peace and so that this area can become a model for coexistence and cooperation among nations.

—The historic initiative of President Sadat in visiting Jerusalem and the reception accorded to him by the Parliament, government and people of Israel, and the reciprocal visit of Prime Minister Begin to Ismailia, the peace proposals

* Excerpts. This document was signed by Egyptian President Anwar Sadat and Israeli Prime Minister Menachem Begin and witnessed by President Jimmy Carter at Camp David, in Thurmont, Maryland.

made by both leaders, as well as the warm reception of these missions by the people of both countries, have created an unprecedented opportunity for peace which must not be lost if this generation and future generations are to be spared the tragedies of war.

—The provisions of the Charter of the United Nations and the other accepted norms of international law and legitimacy now provide accepted standards for the conduct of relations among the states.

—To achieve a relationship of peace, in the spirit of Article 2 of the United Nations Charter, future negotiations between Israel and any neighbor prepared to negotiate peace and security with it, are necessary for the purpose of carrying out all the provisions and principles of Resolutions 242 and 338.

—Peace requires respect for the sovereignty, territorial integrity and political independence of every state in the area and their right to live in peace within secure and recognized boundaries free from threats or acts of force. Progress toward that goal can accelerate movement toward a new era of reconciliation in the Middle East marked by cooperation in promoting economic development, in maintaining stability, and in assuring security.

—Security is enhanced by a relationship of peace and by cooperation between nations which enjoy normal relations. In addition, under the terms of peace treaties, the parties can, on the basis of reciprocity, agree to special security arrangements such as demilitarized zones, limited armaments areas, early warning stations, the presence of international forces, liaison, agreed measures for monitoring, and other arrangements that they agree are useful.

Framework

Taking these factors into account, the parties are determined to reach a just, comprehensive, and durable settlement of the Middle East conflict through the conclusion of peace treaties based on Security Council Resolutions 242 and 338 in all their parts. Their purpose is to achieve peace and good neighborly relations. They recognize that, for peace to endure, it must involve all those who have been most deeply affected by the conflict. They therefore agree that this framework as appropriate is intended by them to constitute a basis for peace not only between Egypt and Israel, but also between Israel and each of its other neighbors which is prepared to negotiate peace with Israel on this basis. With that objective in mind, they have agreed to proceed as follows:

A. West Bank and Gaza

1. Egypt, Israel, Jordan and the representatives of the Palestinian people should participate in negotiations on the resolution of the Palestinian problem in all its aspects. To achieve that objective, negotiations relating to the West Bank and Gaza should proceed in three stages:

(a) Egypt and Israel agree that, in order to ensure a peaceful and orderly transfer of authority, and taking into account the security concerns of all the parties, there should be transitional arrangements for the West Bank and Gaza for a period not exceeding five years. In order to provide full autonomy to the inhabitants, under these arrangements the Israeli military government and its civilian administration will be withdrawn as soon as a self-governing authority has been freely elected by the inhabitants of these areas to replace the existing military government. To negotiate the details of a transitional arrangement, the Government of Jordan will be invited to join the negotiations on the basis of this framework. These new arrangements should give due consideration both to the principle of self-government by the inhabitants of these territories and to the legitimate security concerns of the parties involved.

(b) Egypt, Israel, and Jordan will agree on the modalities for establishing the elected self-governing authority in the West Bank and Gaza. The delegations of Egypt and Jordan may include Palestinians from the West Bank and Gaza or other Palestinians as mutually agreed. The parties will negotiate an agreement which will define the powers and responsibilities of the self-governing authority to be exercised in the West Bank and Gaza. A withdrawal of Israeli armed forces will take place and there will be a redeployment of the remaining Israeli forces into specified security locations. The agreement will also include arrangements for assuring internal and external security and public order. A strong local police force will be established, which may include Jordanian citizens. In addition, Israeli and Jordanian forces will participate in joint patrols and in the manning of control posts to assure the security of the borders.

(c) When the self-governing authority (administrative council) in the West Bank and Gaza is established and inaugurated, the transitional period of five years will begin. As soon as possible, but not later than the third year after the beginning of the transitional period, negotiations will take place to determine the final status of the West Bank and Gaza and its relationship with its neighbors, and to conclude a peace treaty between Israel and Jordan by the end of the transitional period. These negotiations will be conducted among Egypt, Israel, Jordan, and the elected representatives of the inhabitants of the West Bank and Gaza. Two separate but related committees will be convened, one committee, consisting of representatives of the four parties which will negotiate and agree on the final status of the West Bank and Gaza, and its relationship with its neighbors, and the second committee, consisting of representatives of Israel and representatives of Jordan to be joined by the elected representatives of the inhabitants of the West Bank and Gaza, to negotiate the peace treaty between Israel and Jordan, taking into account the agreement reached on the final status of the West Bank and Gaza. The negotiations shall be based on all the provisions and principles of UN Security Council Resolution 242. The negotiations will resolve, among other matters, the location of the boundaries and the nature of the security arrangements. The solution from the negotiations must also recognize the legitimate rights of the Palestinian people and their just requirements. In this way, the Palestinians will participate in the determination of their own future through:

1) The negotiations among Egypt, Israel, Jordan and the representatives of the inhabitants of the West Bank and Gaza to agree on the final status of the West Bank and Gaza and other outstanding issues by the end of the transitional period.

2) Submitting their agreement to a vote by the elected representatives of the inhabitants of the West Bank and Gaza.

3) Providing for the elected representatives of the inhabitants of the West Bank and Gaza to decide how they shall govern themselves consistent with the provisions of their agreement.

4) Participating as stated above in the work of the committee negotiating the peace treaty between Israel and Jordan.

All necessary measures will be taken and provisions made to assure the security of Israel and its neighbors during the transitional period and beyond. To assist in providing such security, a strong local police force will be constituted by the self-governing authority. It will be composed of inhabitants of the West Bank and Gaza. The police will maintain continuing liaison on internal security matters with the designated Israeli, Jordanian, and Egyptian officers.

During the transitional period, representatives of Egypt, Israel, Jordan, and the self-governing authority will constitute a continuing committee to decide by agreement on the modalities of admission of persons displaced from the West Bank and Gaza in 1967, together with necessary measures to prevent disruption and disorder. Other matters of common concern may also be dealt with by this committee.

Egypt and Israel will work with each other and with other interested parties to establish agreed procedures for a prompt, just and permanent implementation of the resolution of the refugee problem.

B. Egypt-Israel

1. Egypt and Israel undertake not to resort to the threat or the use of force to settle disputes. Any disputes shall be settled by peaceful means in accordance with the provisions of Article 33 of the Charter of the United Nations.

2. In order to achieve peace between them, the parties agree to negotiate in good faith with a goal of concluding within three months from the signing of this Framework a peace treaty between them, while inviting the other parties to the conflict to proceed simultaneously to negotiate and conclude similar peace treaties with a view to achieving a comprehensive peace in the area. The Framework for the Conclusion of a Peace Treaty between Egypt and Israel will govern the peace negotiations between them. The parties will agree on the modalities and the timetable for the implementation of their obligations under the treaty.

C. Associated Principles

1. Egypt and Israel state that the principles and provisions described below should apply to peace treaties between Israel and each of its neighbors—Egypt, Jordan, Syria and Lebanon.

2. Signatories shall establish among themselves relationships normal to states at peace with one another. To this end, they should undertake to abide by all the provisions of the Charter of the United Nations. Steps to be taken in this respect include:

(a) full recognition;

(b) abolishing economic boycotts;

(c) guaranteeing that under their jurisdiction the citizens of the other parties shall enjoy the protection of the due process of the law.

3. Signatories should explore possibilities for economic development in the context of final peace treaties, with the objective of contributing to the atmosphere of peace, cooperation and friendship which is their common goal.

4. Claims Commissions may be established for the mutual settlement of all financial claims.

5. The United States shall be invited to participate in the talks on matters related to the modalities of the implementation of the agreements and working out the timetable for the carrying out of the obligations of the parties.

6. The United Nations Security Council shall be requested to endorse the peace treaties and ensure that their provisions shall not be violated. The permanent members of the Security Council shall be requested to underwrite the peace treaties and ensure respect for their provisions. They shall also be requested to conform their policies and actions with the undertakings contained in this Framework.

. . . The following matters are agreed between the parties:

(a) the full exercise of Egyptian sovereignty up to the internationally recognized border between Egypt and mandated Palestine;

(b) the withdrawal of Israeli armed forces from the Sinai;

(c) the use of airfields left by the Israelis near El Arish, Rafah, Ras en Naqb, and Sharm el Sheikh for civilian purposes only, including possible commercial use by all nations;

(d) the right of free passage by ships of Israel through the Gulf of Suez and the Suez Canal on the basis of the Constantinople Convention of 1888 applying to all nations; the Strait of Tiran and the Gulf of Aqaba are international waterways to be open to all nations for unimpeded and non-suspendable freedom of navigation and overflight;

(e) the construction of a highway between the Sinai and Jordan near Elat with guaranteed free and peaceful passage by Egypt and Jordan; and

(f) the stationing of military forces listed below.

Stationing of Forces

A. No more than one division (mechanized or infantry) of Egyptian armed forces will be stationed within an area lying approximately 50 kilometers (km) east of the Gulf of Suez and the Suez Canal.

B. Only United Nations forces and civil police equipped with light weapons to perform normal police functions will be stationed within an area lying west of the international border and the Gulf of Aqaba, varying in width from 20 km to 40 km.

C. In the area within 3 km east of the international border there will be Israeli limited military forces not to exceed four infantry battalions and United Nations observers.

D. Border patrol units, not to exceed three battalions, will supplement the civil police in maintaining order in the area not included above.

The exact demarcation of the above areas will be as decided during the peace negotiations.

Early warning stations may exist to ensure compliance with the terms of the agreement.

United Nations forces will be stationed: (a) in part of the area in the Sinai lying within about 20 km of the Mediterranean Sea and adjacent to the international border, and (b) in the Sharm el Sheikh area to ensure freedom of passage through the Strait of Tiran; and these forces will not be removed unless such removal is approved by the Security Council of the United Nations with a unanimous vote of the five permanent members.

After a peace treaty is signed, and after the interim withdrawal is complete, normal relations will be established between Egypt and Israel, including: full recognition, including diplomatic, economic and cultural relations; termination of economic boycotts and barriers to the free movement of goods and people; and mutual protection of citizens by the due process of law.

Egypt-Israel Peace Treaty (March 26, 1979)*

ARTICLE I

1. The state of war between the Parties will be terminated and peace will be established between them upon the exchange of instruments of ratification of this Treaty.

* Excerpts from peace treaty drawn up at Camp David meetings.

2. Israel will withdraw all its armed forces and civilians from the Sinai behind the international boundary between Egypt and mandated Palestine, as provided in the annexed protocol . . . and Egypt will resume the exercise of its full sovereignty over the Sinai. . . .

ARTICLE II

The permanent boundary between Egypt and Israel is the recognized international boundary between Egypt and the former mandated territory of Palestine . . . without prejudice to the issue of the status of the Gaza Strip. The Parties recognize this boundary as inviolable. Each will respect the territorial integrity of the other, including their territorial waters and airspace.

ARTICLE III

. . . Each Party undertakes to ensure that acts or threats of belligerency, hostility, or violence do not originate from and are not committed from within its territory, or by any forces subject to its control or by any other forces stationed on its territory, against the population, citizens or property of the other Party. Each Party also undertakes to refrain from organizing, instigating, inciting, assisting or participating in acts or threats of belligerency, hostility, subversion or violence against the other Party, anywhere, and undertakes to ensure that perpetrators of such acts are brought to justice.

The Parties agree that the normal relationship established between them will include full recognition, diplomatic, economic and cultural relations, termination of economic boycotts and discriminatory barriers to the free movement of people and goods, and will guarantee the mutual enjoyment by citizens of the due process of law.

Arab League Summit Communiqué (March 31, 1979) *

As the Government of the Arab Republic of Egypt has ignored the Arab summit conferences' resolutions, especially those of the sixth and seventh conferences held in Algiers and

* Excerpts. The communiqué was issued in Baghdad, Iraq.

Rabat; as it has at the same time ignored the ninth Arab summit conference resolutions—especially the call made by the Arab kings, presidents and princes to avoid signing the peace treaty with the Zionist enemy—and signed the peace treaty on 26 March 1979;

It has thus deviated from the Arab ranks and has chosen, in collusion with the United States, to stand by the side of the Zionist enemy in one trench; has behaved unilaterally in the Arab-Zionist struggle affairs; has violated the Arab nation's rights; has exposed the nation's destiny, its struggle and aims to dangers and challenges; has relinquished its pan-Arab duty of liberating the occupied Arab territories, particularly Jerusalem, and of restoring the Palestinian Arab people's inalienable national rights, including their right to repatriation, self-determination and establishment of the independent Palestinian state on their national soil.

. . . The Arab League Council, on the level of Arab foreign ministers, has decided the following:

1. A. To withdraw the ambassadors of the Arab states from Egypt immediately.

B. To recommend the severance of political and diplomatic relations with the Egyptian Government. The Arab governments will adopt the necessary measures to apply this recommendation within a maximum period of one month from the date of issuance of this decision, in accordance with the constitutional measures in force in each country.

2. To consider the suspension of the Egyptian Government's membership in the Arab League as operative from the date of the Egyptian Government's signing of the peace treaty with the Zionist enemy. This means depriving it of all rights resulting from this membership.

3. To make the city of Tunis, capital of the Tunisian Republic, the temporary headquarters of the Arab League. . . .

Foreign Minister Andrei Gromyko:
On the Camp David Agreement
(September 25, 1979) *

The Middle East problem, if divested of the immaterial, boils down to the following—either the consequences of the

* From a speech delivered to the UN General Assembly by the Soviet Foreign Minister.

aggression against the Arab states and peoples are eliminated or the invaders get a reward by appropriating lands that belong to others.

A just settlement and the establishment of durable peace in the Middle East require that Israel should end its occupation of all the Arab lands it seized in 1967, that the legitimate rights of the Arab people of Palestine including the right to create their own state be safeguarded and that the right of all states in the Middle East, including Israel, to independent existence under conditions of peace be effectively guaranteed.

The separate deal between Egypt and Israel resolves nothing. It is a means designed to lull the vigilance of peoples. It is a way of piling up on a still greater scale explosive material capable of producing a new conflagration in the Middle East. Moreover, added to the tense political atmosphere in this and the adjacent areas is the heavy smell of oil.

It is high time that all states represented in the United Nations realized how vast is the tragedy of the Arab peoples of Palestine. What is the worth of declarations in defence of humanism and human rights—whether for refugees or not—if before the eyes of the entire world the inalienable rights of an entire people driven from its land and deprived of a livelihood are grossly trampled upon?

The Soviet policy with respect to the Middle East problem is one of principle. We are in favour of a comprehensive and just settlement, of the establishment of durable peace in the Middle East, a region not far from our borders. The Soviet Union sides firmly with Arab peoples who resolutely reject deals at the expense of their legitimate interests.

Yasir Arafat: Interview on Camp David (November 19, 1979)*

First, we must consider the events in the occupied land, since it is one of the main fronts on which we are fighting the Camp David plot. At the same time, it is a front against which the tripartite alliance—Carter, Begin, al-Sadat— launched their counterattack in retaliation for the resolutions of the Front of Steadfastness and Confrontation and those of the Baghdad summit and the Arab foreign and economy

* Interview in the Algerian newspaper *Al-Sha'b*.

ministers' conference, which implemented all resolutions that were agreed upon.

This attack centered on our people in the occupied land by means of fascist, mean and oppressive measures in addition to the confiscation of land, building of settlements and terrorism such as deportation of the population, arrest and mass punishment against towns and villages as well as confiscation of springs. Our kinfolk's reply was magnificent and is now crowned by this splendid popular uprising against the Zionist authorities, protesting against the Zionist authorities' decision to deport one of our cadres and leaders in the occupied land: Bassam ash-Shak'ah, the Nablus mayor.

The other face of the battle is the mounting war of attrition against the Lebanese and Palestinian peoples. The most modern weapons, even the internationally banned ones, are being used in this war. This is resulting in the destruction of many Lebanese towns and villages and Palestinian camps and in the eviction of hundreds of thousands of Lebanese and Palestinian people. Actually, this terrorist and hellish plan is still continuing, and the Zionist enemy leaders continue to implement it. This, however, will neither intimidate us nor make us hesitate to reply to the enemy actions, both in the occupied land and in southern Lebanon, and with all forms of the military and political struggle. We have practiced this and we will never retreat. We have all the Arabs on our side. Our steadfastness has proved that the Arab nation does not lack will and steadfastness. . . .

President Hafiz al-Asad: Speech
(March 8, 1980) *

To us, to the whole world and as outlined in the UN resolutions, peace means Israel's complete withdrawal from the occupied Arab territories and the acknowledgement of the Palestinians' inalienable rights, including their right to determine their own destiny and set up their independent state. Peace under the Camp David accords means Israel's false withdrawal from Sinai—and it has not yet withdrawn—so that eventually it would be in a position to take all Egypt.

To us, peace means that Arab flags should fly over the

---

* Excerpts from a speech delivered in Damascus by the Syrian President.

liberated territories. Under the Camp David accords, peace means that the Israeli flag should be hoisted in an official ceremony in Cairo, while Israel is still occupying Egyptian, Syrian and Palestinian territory and is still adamantly denying Palestinian rights.

To us, peace means we should exercise our free will. Under the Camp David accords, peace means that the al-Sadat regime should keep Egypt's doors wide open to a Zionist economic, cultural and psychological invasion. It also means that Israel should continue to expand settlements.

To us, peace means a step further toward Arab unity. Under the Camp David accords, peace means Egypt should disengage from the Arab nation and move closer to usurper and aggressor Israel.

We do not make any distinction between one Arab territory and another, while the Camp David partners insist on making a distinction between Egyptian territory and other Arab territories.

The whole world calls for the establishment of a Palestinian state, while al-Sadat and his two allies talk about autonomy. The whole world knows, and the Israeli opposition leaders confirm, that the autonomy farce is a figment of Begin's imagination which he presented during his visit to Ismailia. On the other hand, al-Sadat presents autonomy as the distillation of his genius and most ideal solution.

Israel stresses daily that it will not withdraw from the West Bank and Gaza at any time in the future, and al-Sadat does not stop speaking about great hopes for the success of the autonomy farce. Despite their meager means, our heroic people in the occupied territory are resisting and waging a mighty struggle against the plot. But al-Sadat is using every material and psychological pressure on these people to force them to surrender to the plot.

The world condemns Israel's policy and aggression and supports the just Arab cause. But al-Sadat considers his close friend Begin as the messenger of peace, and his own Arab nation as the enemy of peace. Al-Sadat makes peace with the Israeli leaders and slanders the Arab nation, to which he has turned his back, forgetting that Egypt is part of this nation.

As for the third party, or the full partner as they like to call it, or the honest broker as it likes to call itself, it is determined not to annoy the Israeli leaders even in words. It is not prepared to draw a line between U.S. and Israeli interests in this region. To the United States, therefore, Israeli interests must come first, before anything else.

The Palestine question is the central issue of our struggle and the substance of our cause. We consider the PLO the sole legitimate representative of the Palestinian people. We will continue to support and strengthen the Palestinian revolution against all potential dangers. Syria and the Palestinian revolution are in one trench, something which must be understood by both friend and foe.

I frankly and truly say that the Soviet Union is the real friend of all peoples fighting for their freedom and independence. In my opinion, the imperialists have discovered from experience that they cannot weaken this friendship. But this does not mean that they will stop their attempts to destroy this friendship if they can. We know that we need the assistance of this big friend in our current battle. We must not miscalculate. This is a big battle. Israel is backed by the United States with large quantities of sophisticated weapons. Therefore, how can we possibly shut our eyes to a maneuver aimed at dragging us into a conflict with this big friend and closing the door through which we obtain assistance in the fiercest confrontation that we and all Arabs have in this age?

European Council: Venice Declaration
(June 13, 1980)*

The heads of state and government and the ministers of foreign affairs . . . agreed that growing tensions affecting this region constitute a serious danger and render a comprehensive solution to the Israeli-Arab conflict more necessary and pressing than ever.

. . . The time has come to promote the recognition and implementation of the two principles universally accepted by the international community: the right to existence and to security of all the states in the region, including Israel, and justice for all the peoples, which implies the recognition of the legitimate rights of the Palestinian people.

All of the countries in the area are entitled to live in peace within secure, recognized and guaranteed borders. The neces-

* Excerpts from a declaration by the European Council issued at the conclusion of a two-day conference in Venice.

sary guarantees for a peace settlement should be provided by the United Nations by a decision of the Security Council and, if necessary, on the basis of other mutually agreed procedures. The Nine declare that they are prepared to participate within the framework of a comprehensive settlement in a system of concrete and binding international guarantees, including guarantees on the ground.

A just solution must finally be found to the Palestinian problem, which is not simply one of refugees. The Palestinian people, which is conscious of existing as such, must be placed in a position, by an appropriate process defined within the framework of the comprehensive peace settlement, to exercise fully its right to self-determination.

. . . These principles apply to all the parties concerned, and thus the Palestinian people, and to the Palestine Liberation Organization, which will have to be associated with the negotiations.

. . . The Nine stress that they will not accept any unilateral initiative designed to change the status of Jerusalem and that any agreement on the city's status should guarantee freedom of access of everyone to the holy places.

The Nine stress the need for Israel to put an end to the territorial occupation which it has maintained since the conflict of 1967, as it has done for part of Sinai. They are deeply convinced that the Israeli settlements constitute a serious obstacle to the peace process in the Middle East. The Nine consider that these settlements, as well as modifications in population and property in the occupied Arab territories, are illegal under international law.

Concerned as they are to put an end to violence, the Nine consider that only the reunification of force or the threatened use of force by all the parties can create a climate of confidence in the area, and constitute a basic element for a comprehensive settlement of the conflict in the Middle East. . . .

Israel Government: Fundamental Policy Guidelines (August 5, 1981)*

The right of the Jewish people to the land of Israel is an eternal right that cannot be called into question, and which is intertwined with the right to security and peace.

* Excerpts from Begin Government's Second Coalition agreement.

The Government will continue to place its aspirations for peace at the head of its concerns, and no effort will be spared in order to further peace. The peace treaty between Israel and Egypt is a historic turning point in Israel's status in the Middle East.

The Government will continue to use all means to prevent war.

The Government will diligently observe the Camp David agreements.

The Government will work for the renewal of negotiations on the implementation of the agreement on full autonomy for the Arab residents of Judea, Samaria and the Gaza Strip.

The autonomy agreed upon at Camp David means neither sovereignty nor self-determination. The autonomy agreements set down at Camp David are guarantees that under no conditions will a Palestinian state emerge in the territory of western "Eretz Yisrael."

At the end of the transition period, set down in the Camp David agreements, Israel will raise its claim, and act to realize its right of sovereignty over Judea, Samaria and the Gaza Strip.

Settlement in the land of Israel is a right and an integral part of the nation's security. The Government will act to strengthen, expand and develop settlement. The Government will continue to honor the principle that Jewish settlement will not cause the eviction of any person from his land, his village or his city.

Equality of rights for all residents will continue to exist in the land of Israel, with no distinctions [on the basis] of religion, race, nationality, sex, or ethnic community.

Israel will not descend from the Golan Heights, nor will it remove any settlement established there. It is the Government that will decide on the appropriate timing for the imposition of Israeli law, jurisdiction and administration on the Golan Heights.

Prince Fahd ibn Abd al-Aziz: The Fahd Plan (August 7, 1981)*

. . . There are a number of principles which may be taken as guidelines toward a just settlement; they are principles which

---

* Excerpts from an interview in Jidda with Saudi Arabian Crown Prince Fahd, now King of Saudi Arabia.

the United Nations has taken and reiterated many times in the
last few years. They are:

First, that Israel should withdraw from all Arab territory
occupied in 1967, including Arab Jerusalem.

Second, that Israeli settlements built on Arab land after
1967 should be dismantled.

Third, a guarantee of freedom of worship for all religions
in the holy places.

Fourth, an affirmation of the right of the Palestinian people
to return to their homes and to compensate those who do not
wish to return.

Fifth, that the West Bank and the Gaza Strip should have a
transitional period, under the auspices of the United Nations,
for a period not exceeding several months.

Sixth, that an independent Palestinian state should be set up
with Jerusalem as its capital.

Seven, that all states in the region should be able to live in
peace.

Eight, that the United Nations or member states of the United
Nations should guarantee to execute these principles. . . .

I wish to reaffirm that the principles of a just comprehensive
solution have become familiar and do not require great effort:

1. An end to unlimited American support for Israel.

2. An end to Israeli arrogance, whose ugliest facet is embodied in Begin's government. This condition will be automatically fulfilled if the first condition is fulfilled.

3. A recognition that, as Yasir Arafat says, the Palestinian
figure is the basic figure in the Middle Eastern equation.

West Bank Palestinians: Reactions to Camp David
(August 30, 1981) *

The Palestinian masses in the occupied West Bank and Gaza
Strip continue to reject the declaration made by Sadat and
Begin . . . that they had agreed to resume talks concerning
so-called "autonomy" for the inhabitants of the West Bank
and the Gaza Strip. A large number of Palestinian figures and
personalities have commented . . . that the autonomy plan
does not concern them in any respect, and that they consider
the autonomy plan to be a conspiracy directed against the

* Excerpts from an article in the Algerian newspaper *Al-Sha'b*.

hopes and aspirations of the Palestinian people who are striving to attain their legitimate rights—which have been established by the international community, as represented by the UN....

Dr. Amin al-Khatib, head of the Federation of Charity Associations in Jerusalem, said: "I do not believe that any plan for a solution to the Palestine problem which does not include the establishment of an independent Palestinian state in the territory of Palestine will be successful, no matter how skillfully its sponsors choose names for it and think up methods of attempting to convince us to accept it. We are quite confident that a people such as the Palestinian people, who have gone through great hardships and have become seasoned concerning all different types of plans and half-solutions, will not be able to accept or be content with any solution other than a Palestinian state. . . .

"We have the following to say to Sadat: 'The Palestinian people, inside the occupied territories, do not wish to have you speak or negotiate in their behalf. Give both yourself and us some peace and do not bother us with this whirlpool which is called "autonomy." ' "

Zalikhah Shihabi, the head of the Jerusalem Women's Federation, said: "Everything concerning autonomy—whether it be the autonomy talks, resumption of such talks, their cessation, or the breaking off of such talks altogether—does not concern us. The reason for this is that we know that it is merely a waste of time, and the objective of those who are calling for autonomy is to decrease the resentment of world public opinion against them, to attempt to outflank and encircle the PLO, and to flee from the truth which is shining as brightly as the sun. This truth is that the PLO is the only body authorized to discuss all matters which concern the Palestine question. All of us here agree that there should be an independent Palestinian state. Anything other than that will only meet with rejection and indifference on the part of the Palestinian people."

Mustafa 'Abd al-Nabi al-Natshah, deputy mayor of Hebron: "Autonomy is a continuation of military occupation, only with a mask over it. Autonomy, which is tantamount to local rule, does not contain any of the elements of establishing an independent state. It is a deception utilized in order to impose permanent occupation and would confer permanent legitimacy upon the military occupation. This is something which we totally reject."

Ibrahim al-Tawil, mayor of al-Birah, said: "Our people have not rejected autonomy for no reason. The rejection is based on the convictions of Palestinians living both inside and outside the occupied territories. What is called 'autonomy' is nothing more than a creation of the occupation and a part of it. Agreeing to this autonomy means conferring legitimacy upon the occupation."

Mr. al-Tawil then asked: "What kind of autonomy is it that does not grant our Palestinian people their legitimate rights— people who, like any other people, are demanding to live in peace and tranquility?"

He added: "Autonomy, as the Israelis understand it, means withdrawing army patrols and leaving [military] camps and settlements all over the West Bank. Furthermore, Begin has threatened to open the doors of his jails if any of the autonomy officials think about establishing their own state. So what is this autonomy which is nothing more than another version of the occupation? What it is is the deception and misleading of world public opinion and the other people of the world."

Mr. al-Tawil asserted that there are no people—and that there never will be people—who will participate in carrying out this step. He said that if there were any such mercenaries, they would not represent anybody and would not number even 1 person out of 10,000. He said that all [Palestinian] citizens reject this plan.

Walid Khalidi: Regiopolitics: Toward a U.S. Policy on the Palestine Problem (Summer 1981)*

. . . The Arab world is a baffling political universe. . . . What distinguishes the Arab world from the global setting is the intensity of its transnational resonance and of its impact, both negative and positive, across the sovereign frontiers of individual Arab states. To be sure, what echoes within this area of resonance is often a protracted cacophony. Yet beneath the

* Excerpts from an article in *Foreign Affairs,* Summer 1981. Walid Khalidi is a professor of political studies at the American University of Beirut, Lebanon, a visiting professor of government at Harvard University, and a member of the Palestine National Council.

confused signals there is a logic of sorts. This is the continuing struggle between centripetal and centrifugal forces. The former are grounded in the ideologies of pan-Arabism and pan-Islamism and their non-doctrinaire versions, which take the form of sentiments, cultural solidarity, interpersonal contacts and enlightened self-interest. The latter stem from the more restrictive perspectives of individual states, ruling elites and leaders, and ethnic, sectarian and tribal subnational forces.

Within the Arab world six issues dynamically interact: (1) the Palestine problem; (2) the Arab-Israeli conflict; (3) domestic change and instability; (4) oil policies; (5) inter-Arab relations; and (6) relations with the outside world.

It would be ludicrous to maintain that the non-resolution of the Palestine problem and the resulting perpetuation of the Arab-Israeli conflict are responsible for all developments (or those adverse to the West) in all the other "fields" listed above. But it would be sloppy "Regiopolitics" to fail to assess their significance. . . .

Change and domestic instability in the Arab world preceded the emergence of the Palestine problem and will presumably be around after its resolution. But the rapidity and extent of change, and the intensity of the cultural backlash against it, are relatively recent phenomena in the Arab world. Since 1948 incumbent Arab regimes have been at the receiving end of monumental demands from internal opposition forces and regional rivals bent on delegitimizing them in the name of Palestine. In the new circumstances of rapid change and regional turbulence, the non-resolution of the Palestine problem could constitute the bushels of straw that could break the backs of some Arab regimes.

. . . Since the mid-1930s, when Palestinian guerrillas first attacked the Iraq Petroleum Company pipelines in Mandatory Palestine, the *threat* to interrupt oil supplies, *armed attack* on oil installations, *disruption* in the flow or transport of oil and the *imposition of embargoes* have been—with the singular exception of the recent Iraqi-Iranian conflict—exclusively connected in the Arab world with the non-resolution of the Palestine problem and the perpetuation of the Arab-Israeli conflict. . . .

. . . Many centrifugal forces in the Arab world operate independently of any ramifications of the Palestine problem. A list enumerating "purely" inter-Arab conflicts would be a long one. But from the U.S. point of view these conflicts do not adversely involve the U.S. image or interests quite in the same way, if at all, as do inter-Arab tensions related to the Arab-Israeli conflict.

Given the dynamics of the Arab area of resonance, the oil-rich Arab countries do not constitute a cohesive sub-system in any meaningful political sense within it. Both their affiliation with the West and their conservative regimes makes these states particularly vulnerable to the pressure of the Palestine problem both domestically and in their inter-Arab relations. This pressure has been a major cause of polarization among the Arab states as a whole. Its most destabilizing effect has been the outbidding tactics, both offensive and defensive, that the Arab states have used against each other in the name of Palestine.

The outbidding process has taken place not only between radical and conservative regimes but also between conservative regimes (e.g., Hashemite Iraq and Saudi Arabia in the 1950s) and between the radicals themselves. By and large the conservatives have been at the receiving end, but sometimes they have gone on the offensive against the radicals (e.g., Jordanian and Saudi Arabian castigation of Nasser for hiding behind the United Nations Emergency Force in 1966–67). In imposing the 1973 embargo the conservatives were demonstrating to Arab public opinion that they were second to none in their espousal of the cause of Palestine. The agony of Lebanon (reminiscent of Spain in the 1930s) is the most poignant example of the spillover effect of the non-resolution of the Palestine problem into inter-Arab relations.

A point can be made that, notwithstanding the foregoing, the Palestine problem has been the principal "unifying" factor in inter-Arab politics and that its resolution would give momentum to centrifugal forces. At worst the fervent proponents of Arab fragmentation might perhaps be persuaded to endorse a Palestinian settlement if only with their own objective in mind. . . .

. . . The Palestine problem and Arab-Israeli conflict have had the following broad effects on Arab relations with the West and the U.S.S.R. (1) They have resulted in the deepening and perpetuation of Arab political alienation from the West—an alienation which admittedly had historico-cultural roots older than the Palestine problem and was also a product of the Arab experience of European colonialism in general. Western, and particularly American, sponsorship of Israel and a perceived unwillingness to solve the Palestine problem largely counterbalanced the positive effects of decolonization on Arab-Western relations. With West European colonial disengagement completed, the onus of the non-resolution of the Palestine problem was shifted increasingly to the United States. (2) At the same time, the attractiveness of Soviet military and diplomatic help has increased in proportion to American backing of Israel. In fact, the Palestine problem provided the main Soviet entrée into the Arab world, affording Moscow the opportunity to champion the most popular Arab cause at the expense of the West. (3) While the fundamentally nationalist ideology of even the most radical Arab regimes has set limits on Soviet influence and while disillusionment with Soviet help has developed in many countries, the non-resolution of the Palestine problem has supplied the most powerful motivation (and rationalization) for continued reliance on the U.S.S.R. And while the Arab cultural backlash in its nationalist and religious manifestations has involved "repudiation" of both East and West, the emotional and intellectual balance of Arab public and elite opinion remains in favor of the U.S.S.R. (4) Western military support of Israel has led to Soviet military support of the Arabs. The vicious circle this established has reinforced the Arab emotional and intellectual tilt in favor of the Soviets, especially with the younger generations. . . .

No one knows what an Arab world bereft of the Palestine problem would look like, but there are excellent reasons for trying to find out. For Israel a settlement of the Palestine problem will mean the end of war. For the Palestinians a sovereign Palestinian state on the West Bank, in the Gaza Strip, and in East Jerusalem in coexistence with Israel—the terms on which the PLO would settle—means a haven from their diaspora and a repository for their vast potential for constructive achievement. The endorsement by Fatah, the mainstream PLO group, of a settlement along these lines will isolate and contain the Palestinian and Arab dissidents. Such a settlement would remove a primary source of instability throughout the Arab states' system. It could improve the prospects for functional inter-Arab regional cooperation. Agitation on behalf of Palestine would markedly decline. The interruption of oil supplies resulting from such agitation will lose its rationale, while that resulting from an Arab-Israeli war will be precluded. The continual Arab-American confrontation over Palestine in international forums will end. The incentive for Arab acquisition of nuclear weapons to match Israel's will become less cogent. Such Arab military dependence on outside powers as has been generated by the Arab-Israeli conflict will significantly diminish. Superpower collision in the Middle East will lose a hitherto ever-present catalyst.

The rationale for American coyness about moving forward on a settlement could be reduced to three arguments: (1) the PLO and the radical Arabs are unwilling to contemplate a reasonable and honorable settlement; (2) the same is true for the U.S.S.R.; (3) what might be described as the Cohabitation Argument—the removal of Egypt through Camp David from the Arab-Israeli military equation—makes it possible to live with the new status quo. . . . The PLO is excluded from peace negotiations on the ground that it is a terrorist organization. This is hypocritical and unadult. Like every liberation movement in history the PLO has used terrorist tactics. . . .

The PLO is likewise ruled out of court because of the provisions in its Covenant which deny the legitimacy of the state of Israel and call for the liberation of "the whole of Palestine." One way of looking at the Covenant is to view it as a gratuitous tract of hate against an altogether innocent party. Another is to see it in relation to the evolution of the Palestine problem and the tribulations of Palestinian disinheritance and statelessness. Nevertheless, whatever its background the Covenant is maximalist, unrealistic and no basis for a settlement.

The Palestine National Council (PNC), the highest PLO authority, has met 12 times since the adoption of the present Covenant in 1968. If the resolutions adopted by successive PNCs are read in sequence, a movement away from maximalism and in the direction of accommodation is unmistakable. This movement is noticeable on four levels: (1) from explicit emphasis on the objective of the liberation of the "whole" or the "entire" soil of Palestine to the discarding of these adjectives; (2) from explicit reliance on "armed struggle" as the only means for the achievement of liberation to increasing expressions of the need for political activity in addition to this "armed struggle," and of readiness to attend international peace conferences as well as to meet with "progressive" Jewish elements from both inside and outside Israel; (3) from repeated statements about the "secular democratic state" over the whole of Palestine as the ultimate objective to an increasing de-emphasis of this objective; and (4) from repeated and vehement rejection of a "political entity" or a "ministate" in the post-1967 Occupied Territories to an implied though conditional acceptance of such a state. It remains to make explicit what is implied in this movement. This is the task of quiet diplomacy.

The Arab countries that are pivotal for a solution of the Palestine problem are the radicals: Syria and Iraq. Neither Jordan nor Saudi Arabia could sponsor a solution unacceptable to both or either of these two. Damascus and Baghdad are the ideological capitals of pan-Arabism, and in fact much of the tension between them is over its leadership. . . .

If Syria, Iraq and the PLO have a veto among Arabs over a Palestinian settlement, the Saudi role is no less indispensable. The cornerstone of Saudi diplomacy in the post-Nasser era has been the effort to forge a moderate inter-Arab consensus on the Palestine problem, oil policies, regional disputes and international relations in general. Intrinsic to this Saudi diplomacy has been bridge-building with the radicals, Syria and Iraq, and Fatah. No other Arab capital is on speaking terms with as many Arab (and Muslim) capitals as Riyadh. This makes the Saudis the ideal interlocutor between the Arabs (and Muslims) and the West. The greater the prestige of Saudi Arabia in the Arab world, the greater the impact of its moderating influence. . . .

The assumption that the U.S.S.R. has no interest in a Palestine settlement may or may not be true. What is unquestionable is that the U.S.S.R. will wreck a solution composed and orchestrated exclusively by the United States. The thrust of the top Soviet leadership's advice to the PLO has been along the lines the PLO will now accept. The mercurial nature of Arab regimes with regard to Moscow may have generally sunk into Soviet political consciousness and the Soviets may by now be aware that all Arab regimes are fundamentally nationalist. Further, the Soviets may not relish being dragged to the brink of confrontation with the United States by a runaway ad hoc Arab military coalition—a likely eventuality should no solution of the Palestine problem materialize. They may not relish the prospect of an Arab client being humiliated in a future Arab-Israeli war, nor view with equanimity the Arab trend toward the acquisition of nuclear weapons. . . .

That the Camp David status quo is something the United States can live with is the most dangerous illusion. There is in fact no such status quo. Within the Camp David framework Israeli colonization policies in the Occupied Territories have been changing the situation on the ground so rapidly that before long the physical basis of a Palestinian settlement will have been removed for all time. No Arab regime (including Egypt) can be reconciled to the permanent loss of the Occupied Territories. Israeli retention of the West Bank, the Gaza Strip, and East Jerusalem *as well as* the Golan maximizes the probability of Arab reaction. The religious ferment in the region could reconfirm Jerusalem's credentials as a catalyst for crusades. Continued public silence by Washington on Israel's colonization policies is no asset to the United States in the worlds of Arabdom and Islam. It reinforces the already formidable Israeli constituency against the evacuation of the Occupied Territories. . . .

President Hosni Mubarak: Egypt and Israel (October 14, 1981)*

Egypt, the state and the people, is continuing along the road to a lasting and comprehensive peace based upon the framework that has been agreed upon at Camp David and that is based on the peace treaty between Egypt and Israel in letter and in spirit. Egypt, the state and the people, will spare no effort or time in continuing the autonomy talks until we put the Palestinian people along the beginning of the correct course for achieving their legitimate rights.

We, as the late leader repeatedly declared, do not speak on behalf of the Palestinian people. We do not claim that we are achieving the final solution of the question. The Palestinian people are the owners of the right and owners of the first and last responsibility for solving their problem. However, we are continuing in our role, dictated by our historical responsibility. We will make all efforts and pave the way for a transitional period during which the Palestinian people will determine their fate.

Egypt, the state and the people, is implementing the peace treaty. Egypt's position before the complete Israeli withdrawal in April 1982 is the same as Egypt's position after the complete withdrawal.

It pleases me to announce to you that we have received categorical assurances that the final Israeli withdrawal will take place on schedule, without delay and without slowing down. This coming 25th of April will, God willing, not pass without

* Excerpts from the Egyptian President's inaugural address.

Egypt's flag waving high over Rafah, Sharm ash-Shaykh and every foot of the sacred land of the Sinai. The martyr of justice will have thus given his country and nation the greatest fulfillment by liberating the territory, restoring dignity and opening the road to a great future. With this historic event, the glorious Egyptian people and their valiant armed forces will have completed their most tremendous achievement in their contemporary history, lighting an eternal flame on the sands of Sinai that time cannot extinguish. Brothers, the historic peace initiative undertaken by our departed leader was the initiative of 42 million Egyptians. In fact, today that initiative does not belong only to the Egyptian people but also to all the peoples of the world.

Since President Reagan assumed power, the United States has announced the continuation of the U.S. commitment as a full partner in all the peace steps that are now taking their normal course.

I take this opportunity to declare to all the peoples of the world that the Egyptian people, who have faith in the peace miracle achieved by the hero of peace, today believe even more strongly in the continuation of the peace process, today they are more determined to protect all the fruits of peace.

The result of the referendum on my assumption of the responsibility on Sadat's road is the best evidence of the will and decision of the Egyptian people. It is a will for peace and it is a decision for peace.

U.S.-Israel Memorandum of Understanding
(November 30, 1981) *

PREAMBLE

This Memorandum of Understanding reaffirms the common bonds of friendship between the United States and Israel and builds on the mutual security relationship that exists between the two nations. The Parties recognize the need to enhance strategic cooperation to deter all threats from the Soviet Union in the region. Noting the long-standing and fruitful cooperation for mutual security that has developed between the two countries, the Parties have decided to establish a framework

* Excerpts. Memorandum announced simultaneously in Washington and Jerusalem.

for continued consultation and cooperation to enhance their national security by deterring such threats in the whole region.

The Parties have reached the following agreements in order to achieve the above aims:

ARTICLE I

United States-Israeli strategic cooperation, as set forth in this Memorandum, is designed against the threat to peace and security of the region caused by the Soviet Union or Soviet-controlled forces from outside the region introduced into the region. It has the following broad purposes:

A. To enable the Parties to act cooperatively and in a timely manner to deal with the above mentioned threat;

B. To provide each other with military assistance for operations of their forces in the area that may be required to cope with this threat;

C. The strategic cooperation between the Parties is not directed at any State or group of States within the region. It is intended solely for defensive purposes against the above mentioned threat.

ARTICLE II

1. The fields in which strategic cooperation will be carried out to prevent the above mentioned threat from endangering the security of the region include:

A. Military cooperation between the Parties, as may be agreed by the Parties;

B. Joint military exercises, including naval and air exercises in the eastern Mediterranean Sea, as agreed upon by the Parties;

C. Cooperation for the establishment and maintenance of joint readiness activities, as agreed upon by the Parties;

D. Other areas within the basic scope and purpose of this agreement, as may be jointly agreed.

Israeli Law on the Golan Heights (December 14, 1981)*

1. The law, jurisdiction and administration of the State shall apply to the Golan Heights. . . .

* Source: Israel Press Office.

2. This law shall become valid on the day of its passage in the Knesset.

3. The Minister of the Interior shall be charged with the implementation of this law, and he is entitled, in consultation with the Minister of Justice, to enact regulations for its implementation and to formulate in regulations transitional provisions and provisions concerning the continued application of regulations, orders, administrative orders, rights and duties which were in force on the Golan Heights prior to the application of this law.

Defense Minister Ariel Sharon: Israel's Security (December 15, 1981)*

As I see them, our main security problems during the 1980's will stem from external threats to Israel, her integrity and her sovereign rights . . .

One—The Arab confrontation.

Second—The Soviet expansion which both builds on the Arab confrontation and at the same time provides it with its main political and military tools.

Later on, I will comment on the implications in terms of political and military requirements in order to cope with the threat and to ensure Israel's national security in the 1980's.

Starting with the Arab challenge, I must touch upon the three major factors which, in my mind, contribute the most to sustain Arab enmity and confrontation at a level that presents an actual danger to our security and which, I believe, will continue to sustain it in the foreseeable future—at a level which might confront us with a potential threat to the existence and integrity of Israel.

Those factors are:

A. First, the national ideology of radical Arab regimes (such as in Syria, Libya, Iraq and South Yemen) and their political and strategic ambitions which motivate them to invest, on a first-priority basis, in the creation of a political-military setting designed to serve a strategy of political and military stages for the liquidation of the State of Israel.

* Excerpts from a speech by Defense Minister Ariel Sharon at the Center for Strategic Studies, Tel Aviv University.

The main elements of this strategy of stages can be summed up as follows:

1) A combined effort of sustained political pressure and, when needed, limited military action aimed at the harassment and weakening of Israel.

2) The build-up of a military power, conventional and eventually nonconventional, to be used in appropriate conditions in the future, for a decisive onslaught against Israel.

3) The third element of the strategy is the political and military reliance on the Soviet Union, to ensure the Arab capability to initiate and carry out the confrontation.

4) The fourth element is to maximize the political strategic impact of the oil weapon.

5) And the fifth is the political and military backing to the PLO as an instrument to carry out terrorist activities. This constitutes a central element in the strategy of stages, so long as Israel's deterrent posture and other political considerations prevent the formation of an Arab coalition, ready to wage war.

That brings me to the second major factor, which is the PLO. On the challenge presented by the PLO, I will say only this: The PLO poses a political threat to the very existence of the State of Israel and remains one of the main obstacles to the resolution of the Palestinian problem on the basis of the Camp David accords.

It constitutes a framework for terrorist organizations operating against Israel, in its territory or in the world at large, with the following purposes:

—To undermine the domestic stability in Israel and its security.

—To generate international pressure on Israel.

—To drag the confrontation states to war against Israel.

—To deter Arab countries and moderate Palestinian elements from negotiations with Israel on the basis of Camp David.

The third factor is one of growing concern to us and to the Western world, and might well develop as the main challenge of the 1980's. It has to do with the Soviet strategy of expansion in the Middle East and Africa. The Soviet strategy is under no pressure of time, but its achievements since the middle of the 1950's are really impressive. . . . It is a strategy of expansion which, if not checked, could eventually enable the Soviet Union:

—To ensure a sea-control capability in the Mediterranean, the Indian Ocean, the Red Sea and the Persian Gulf.

—To establish the military infrastructure for direct or indirect operations.

—To expand and penetrate other key countries in the Middle East and the Persian Gulf, from the direction of Afghanistan, Iraq, South Yemen and Syria.

—To outflank NATO's eastern tier (Turkey) through Iran, Iraq, Syria and Lebanon.

—To outflank NATO's southern tier in the Mediterranean, through Libya, Syria and Algeria.

—To gain control over other key countries in Africa, from the direction of Libya, Algeria, South Yemen, Ethiopia, Mozambique, Angola and Congo-Brazzaville. . . .

Today, as in the past two decades, the Soviet strategy of expansion in the area continues to build on:

—Arab regimes which Soviet political and military support enables to survive, to carry out their own ambitions and to maintain military confrontations—including the confrontation with Israel.

—Radical elements and terrorist organizations, which Soviet political and military support enables to create upheavals threatening to shift the region towards Soviet political-strategic patronage.

The shadow of Soviet presence in the Middle East and Africa endangers the stability of the region and vital interests of the free world. I want to stress this point with all possible emphasis. The greatest danger to the free world in the 1980's would be to continue to indulge in the wishful thinking and the inaction which have characterized Western attitudes to Soviet gradual expansion during the last two decades. . . .

Obviously, in order to be able to protect our national security interests, we will have to ensure our ability to maintain a balance of forces and a qualitative and technological edge over any combination of Arab war coalition; in other words:

—To prevent war by maintaining a deterrent posture against the threats to the existence of Israel.

—Should deterrence break down and war erupt, to ensure a military capability to preserve the integrity of Israel's territory, in any war-opening situation including a sudden Arab attack, and to disrupt the war coalition by damaging the core of its offensive capability.

To achieve these goals, we will have to structure our military strength on new approaches, taking into account:

—The lack of territorial depth and therefore the necessity to establish a strong territorial defense system, based on populous and high quality settlement of key border areas in Judaea, Samaria, the Gaza district, the Golan Heights, the Galilee and the Negev.

—The need to provide maximum protection to human life.

—The need to develop and produce weapon systems and equipment which should enable us to maintain a permanent qualitative advantage over Arab confrontation states—including with regard to advanced and sophisticated equipment they might get from Eastern and Western sources.

As a rule, while striving to establish ties of strategic cooperation with the United States to enhance stability and security in the region as a whole, we will continue to ensure our own independent ability to cope with the Arab military threats to our existence and security.

In order to cope with the threat, Israel cannot build on a balance of power based on a simple quantitative ratio of military forces. We cannot hope to match Arab numbers. Therefore, Israel's defense policy will have to ensure our ability to maintain a military balance based, beyond the quantitative ratio, on a clear qualitative and technological superiority. Israel is confronted by the challenge of maintaining a balance in peace of countries which have practically no limitations in funds to finance their military effort and furthermore in the . . . military technology and sophisticated weaponry they receive from all three sources—the Soviet, the American and the West-European supply sources, which are all competing by the same means for influence and economic advantages. Among the three sources of supply the United States remains sensitive to the need of maintaining a balance in the Arab-Israeli confrontation. But there is no control on the influx of armament from Soviet and European sources. Therefore, Israel has to build on her independent capability to develop and produce systems which are vital to ensure our qualitative advantage and our security. This puts a tremendous burden on our defense budget and on Israel's national economy. . . . The second "safety valve" if I can use that concept, in our defense policy, is our resolve and our ability to prevent the disruption of the territorial military status in neighboring countries. That includes our resolve.

—One—To prevent the violation of security arrangements laid down in political agreements such as in the Sinai with Egypt, and the Golan with Syria. It must be crystal clear: We did sign the peace treaty with Egypt and we faithfully carry out its provisions of withdrawal to the international border, but we have no intention to accept any violation of the status and of the security arrangements in the Sinai as agreed between us.

—Two—We will prevent any violation of the status quo ante in south Lebanon.

—Three—We will prevent any change in the geographical-military status of the confrontation area which might present unacceptable threat such as the massive introduction of Iraqi forces into Jordan or southern Syria or Syrian forces into Jordan. Such an accumulation of forces in the confrontation area would endanger our very existence and is therefore unacceptable to Israel. . . .

The third element in our defense policy for the 1980's is our determination to prevent confrontation states or potentially confrontation states from gaining access to nuclear weapons. Israel cannot afford the introduction of the nuclear weapon. For us it is not a question of a balance of terror but a question of survival. We shall therefore have to prevent such a threat at its inception.

There are three major elements in our defense policy for the 1980's. We shall, of course, also maintain our freedom of action and our ability to act in order to overcome the terrorist threat. To sum up—in order to strengthen the foundation of its national security, in face of the direct Arab threat as well as in face of the challenge from outside the region, Israel will make special efforts:

—One—To ensure our qualitative advantage and maintain the required balance of forces.

—Two—To expand and consolidate our economic, industrial, scientific, demographic and physical infrastructure, so as to carry the burden of our national security.

—Three—To hold political negotiations from a position of security for the purpose of continuing the peace process between Israel and her neighbors.

—Four—To consolidate and nurture national unity in Israel, as well as the ties between Israel and the Jewish people in the Diaspora.

—Five—To enhance strategic cooperation with the United States and to develop security relationships with Middle-Eastern and African countries and with other countries in the world. In that respect, I want to stress that Israel is not a liability but an asset, as the United States has gradually come to realize. For the common defense of the Free World, beyond our military capabilities, Israel has to offer an example of true democracy and stability in the midst of regional uncertainties and upheavals, and moreover the capability to contribute to the well-being of developed and less-developed nations, in many important fields such as science, medicine, food production and sophisticated agricultural technology in general.

Yitzhak Shamir:
Israel's Role in a Changing Middle East
(Spring 1982)*

Traditionally, the twin goals of Israel's foreign policy have always been peace and security—two concepts that are closely interrelated: Where there is strength, there is peace—at least, shall we say, peace has a chance. Peace will be unattainable if Israel is weak or perceived to be so. This, indeed, is one of the most crucial lessons to be learned from the history of the Middle East since the end of the Second World War—in terms not only of the Arab-Israel conflict, but of the area as a whole.

The Middle East is a mosaic of peoples, religions, languages and cultures. Although the Muslim-Arab culture is predominant, it has not produced any homogeneity. A vast number of currents—religious and political—are vying with each other, cutting across political borders. The region is permanently in ferment, and frequently unrest flares up in violence, terror, insurrection, civil strife and open and sometimes prolonged warfare. . . .

The most remarkable feature, in our context, of these chronic manifestations of unrest and belligerence is the fact that the great majority of them have nothing to do with Israel or with the Arab-Israel conflict. There were some outsiders, 20 and 30 years ago, who sincerely, but out of ignorance, believed that a solution of the Arab-Israel conflict would lead to regional stability and open a new era of progress. Nothing could be further from the truth. There have, it is true, been four major wars between Israel and its Arab neighbors. However, a full count of the instances of trouble and strife, both domestic and international, in North Africa and Western Asia,

---

* Excerpts from an article in *Foreign Affairs,* Spring 1982. Yitzhak Shamir became Israel's Foreign Minister in March 1980 and its Prime Minister in October 1983.

would show that the overwhelming majority have no connection whatsoever with the Arab relationship to Israel. . . .

Reduced to its true proportions, the problem is clearly *not* the lack of a homeland for the Palestinian Arabs. That homeland is Trans-Jordan, or eastern Palestine. There are, however, 1.2 million Palestinian Arabs living in the territories which have been administered by Israel since 1967 in Judea, Samaria and Gaza. Their status and problems were discussed at great length at Camp David. The granting of sovereignty to those areas was ruled out by Israel. A second Palestinian Arab state to the west of the River Jordan is a prescription for anarchy, a threat to both Israel and Jordan, and a likely base for terrorist and Soviet penetration. Hence, it was finally resolved at Camp David to implement an Autonomy Plan for the inhabitants of those areas, on a five-year interim basis. The proposal was made by Israel and accepted by the other partners of the Camp David accords, Egypt and the United States. It is not intended as the ultimate solution of the problem represented by these areas and their inhabitants, but as an interim arrangement designed to achieve two objectives: (a) to allow the Arab inhabitants of these areas the fullest feasible freedom in running their own lives, and (b) to create optimal conditions of peaceful coexistence between Arab and Jew.

Israel has made it clear, at Camp David and since, that it has a claim to sovereignty over Judea, Samaria and Gaza. In order, however, to keep the door open to a solution that will be acceptable to the parties, as envisaged at Camp David, Israel has deliberately refrained from exercising its rights under this claim. The claim will undoubtedly be presented at the end of the five-year interim period, and, while it is realized that there will be a similar claim on the Arab side, by that time one would hope that the kind of atmosphere will have been created that will make it possible to reach an agreement involving a solution acceptable to both sides. It should be clearly understood, therefore, that just as Israel is refraining from pushing its own solution at this time, by the same token the Arab side must refrain from pushing now for measures or the adoption of principles (such as self-determination, an embryo parliament in the autonomous territories, and the like) that would clearly fall beyond the parameters of Camp David and that would tend to prejudge the ultimate outcome of the negotiations on the final status of these areas. Autonomy, in other words, must be allowed to perform the function it was intended to perform—namely, to serve as an interim arrangement, pending the ultimate solution that is to be addressed at a later stage.

Meanwhile, Israelis and Arabs are learning to coexist in Judea, Samaria and Gaza—ultimately the best way to reconciliation and peace. Israelis will continue to reside in those areas. As in the past, this will not be done, of course, at the expense of the Arab inhabitants and their property. But, as Judea and Samaria constitute the heartland of the Jewish people's birth and development as a nation, Israel will not be party to a design that would deny Jews residence in those areas.

No less important, the Israeli presence in these areas, both civilian and military, is vital to Israel's defense—as should be abundantly clear against the background of the recent history of the region and of Israel's patent inability to maintain a large standing army on its borders. The defunct pre-1967 armistice lines—which for nearly 20 years proved to be a prescription for chronic instability and warfare—have long since ceased to have any relevance in the context of the search for a viable Middle East peace. Certainly, Israel will not entertain any notion of a return to those lines or anything approximating them. On this point there is, in Israel, virtually universal agreement.

A final word on the Palestinian subject. There are some, no doubt well-intentioned but largely unaware of some very important facts, who have proposed that Israel negotiate with the PLO. They point to the absence of any organized voice, other than the PLO, representing "the Palestinians" and to the existence of ostensibly moderate elements in that organization that may be encouraged to seek a political solution that would include recognition of Israel.

The real problem is not whether to deal with the PLO or not, but whether it would serve any useful purpose whatsoever. Even if one were to overlook their bloodthirsty modus operandi, their subservience to Soviet aims and their key role in international terror, the PLO's very raison d'être is the denial of Israel's right to exist, thinly veiled behind the cover of an ostensibly legitimate call for Palestinian statehood. The very act of granting the PLO a status—any status—in the political negotiations would be self-defeating. It would elevate its standing from that of a terrorist organization to that of a recognized aspirant to a totally superfluous political entity. Hence, association of the PLO with any aspect whatsoever of the political process and the prospects of peace are mutually exclusive.

On its part, Israel will do everything it can to ensure that the peace treaty with Egypt will serve as a solid base from which to expand the peace process toward a wider circle of participants. This can be achieved only by means of an Israel-Egypt partnership that is encouraged by active U.S. participation. It has a chance of success, provided that no alternative proposals and plans other than the Camp David accords are introduced into the process. No one is so naïve as to believe that this is a goal which will be easily attained. But this combination of states, working together toward a worthy and vital objective, has already proved its capacity to overcome obstacles and make progress. Together, they are a formidable force for stability that cannot be bypassed by any factor in the Middle East. In order for this policy to bear fruit, much patience and persistent effort are required. . . .

The magnitude of Israel's sacrifice for the achievement of the peace treaty has not been given proper recognition by the international community. From 1968 onward, Israel invested $17 billion in the Sinai Peninsula—in airfields, military installations, development of oilfields, infrastructure, towns and farm villages. The cost of the military redeployment to the Negev is estimated at $4.4 billion. Beyond the financial burden, and the strategic significance of the withdrawal from Sinai, the uprooting of several thousand Israelis who built their homes in the townships and villages along the eastern edge of Sinai is a traumatic event that has made a deep imprint on the entire nation.

With the transfer of the Sinai Peninsula to Egyptian sovereignty and the normalization of relations with Egypt under the peace treaty, Israel has gone a long way toward implementing the provisions of the 1967 U.N. Security Council Resolution 242. The Sinai Peninsula, it should be remembered, covers more than 90 percent of the territory that came into Israel's possession in the Six-Day War. Thus Israel has demonstrated, through concrete action and considerable risk and sacrifice, that it seeks peace and coexistence with its neighbors. It is now up to its neighbors to come forth with a similar demonstration of peaceful intent and readiness. . . .

Thus, within the context of a powerful, basically unchanging ideological rejection of Israel, there are two conflicting currents coursing through the Arab world. One—which is, as of now, the prevailing current—rejects the Jewish State wholly and without reservation, in theory and in practice. The other —only just beginning to crack the surface of developments in the Middle East—accepts the fact of Israel's existence and is ready, in some sort of pragmatic fashion, to come to terms with that existence. Israel is learning to live with this reality, and to try to build on the hope that, in the course of time, this pragmatism can be developed into something more permanent and more meaningful.

A crucial role in determining the future direction of events in the region can be played by forces and influences outside the region.

The history of the involvement of foreign governments in Middle Eastern politics is not a happy one. Attracted by the strategic importance of the region and, more recently, by its immense natural resources and bank deposits, most governments have sought to apply a political gloss to their perceived economic interests by making political statements on the Arab-Israel issue in response to Arab pressures.

. . . Arab hopes of exercising the military option against Israel would not have been sustained as they are if not for the immense supplies of sophisticated offensive military supplies from Russia. The Soviet Government has steadily increased its political and military support of the PLO in spite of, or perhaps because of, this organization's central role in international terror and its declared aim of destroying Israel and its population. This totally one-sided stand by the Soviet Union is compounded by its policy of boycotting Israel, and of persisting in its non-relations with Israel since 1967.

Soviet actions demonstrate clearly that the Soviet Union is opposed to peace in the Middle East, is bent on expanding its presence and influence in the region at the expense of regional stability, and has no problem in the choice of means to achieve its objective. Public opinion is far from being a factor in Soviet decisionmaking. . . .

Peace is fundamental to Israel's way of life, and Israel's determination to achieve it is permanent. Security is a vital guarantee of the viability and maintenance of peace. Together these two objectives provided the conceptual framework that produced the Camp David accords, and the march along this road must continue unabated.

A program for continued action to secure regional stability and peace must originate from the countries and governments that will have to implement the peace and live by it. Israel believes that it should include the following elements:

1. Negotiations between Israel and each of its neighbors, aimed at agreement on a just and lasting peace, laid out in formal peace treaties, that would provide for the establishment of normal diplomatic, economic and good-neighborly relations.

2. Recognition of the sovereignty and political independence of all existing states in the region, and of their right to live in peace within secure and recognized boundaries, free from threats or acts of force, including terrorist activity of any kind.

3. Autonomy for the Arab inhabitants of Judea, Samaria and the Gaza district for a five-year interim period, as set forth in the Camp David accords, and deferment of the final determination of the status of these areas until the end of this transitional period.

4. Restoration of the full independence of Lebanon, through the withdrawal of Syrian and PLO forces from Lebanese territory.

5. Negotiations, among all the states of the Middle East, aimed at declaring the region a nuclear-weapons-free zone, for the security and well-being of all its inhabitants.

Boutros Boutros-Ghali: The Foreign Policy of Egypt in the Post-Sadat Era (Spring 1982)*

. . . Broadly speaking, Egyptian foreign policy in the last three decades has been directed toward two main challenges: how to contain Israeli ambitions and how to solve the Palestinian problem, the core of the Middle East crisis. This task, difficult in itself and rendered more complex by virtue of the multifaceted nature of the conflict, has been further complicated by the differences among Arabs, and the inability of some to adopt a rational attitude or to discard shortsighted policies toward the problem.

Thus, Egypt's efforts to resolve the contradictions between Palestinian national rights and Israeli national aims had to take place in the framework of an equation that would strike a balance between Egypt's conviction that Arab initiative is an important factor in any peace process and the necessity for her to exercise her traditional leadership in order to break the deadlock that has existed for well over 30 years. . . .

* Excerpts from an article in *Foreign Affairs,* Spring 1982. Boutros Boutros-Ghali is Minister of State for Foreign Affairs of the Arab Republic of Egypt.

President Sadat presented the elements of Egypt's peace plan before the Knesset, as follows:

—the termination of the Israeli occupation of all the Arab territories occupied since 1967, including East Jerusalem;

—the realization of the inalienable rights of the Palestinian people and their rights to self-determination including the right to establish their own state;

—the right of all states in the area to live in peace within secure boundaries, based on the recognition that the security of international borders can be established through agreed-upon arrangements and international guarantees;

—the commitment by all states in the region to conduct relations among themselves according to the purposes and principles of the U.N. Charter, in particular the peaceful settlements of disputes and the abstention from the threat or use of force; and

—the termination of the state of belligerency in the area.

Thus it was abundantly clear that Egypt viewed the Palestinian problem as being at the very heart of the Middle East conflict and that an unjust peace that would not guarantee the rights of the Palestinian people would have no future. Indeed, Egypt is seeking a comprehensive peace and not a separate or bilateral agreement with Israel. And during long hours of negotiations with the Israelis, Egyptians have sought to link the withdrawal of Israeli forces from Egyptian territory to the withdrawal of Israeli forces from Palestinian territory. Every effort was exerted by Egypt to associate the solution of the Egyptian question with that of the Palestinian question, in order to lay special emphasis on her comprehensive approach to the peace process. . . .

What Egypt has in mind is that the Palestinians and other Arab parties concerned join these negotiations. It is obvious, however, that only tangible and positive results would induce them to do so. Hence the emphasis laid by Egypt on the necessity for the Israelis to adopt a number of confidence-building measures, to discard the policies of economic sabotage, psychological warfare and cultural frustration being conducted against the Palestinians in the occupied lands. . . .

Occupation by Israel of the West Bank and Gaza will have to end, for three million Israelis cannot go on forever governing one-and-a-half million Palestinians and ignoring their national rights and aspirations.

Needless to say, Egypt feels as strongly about ending the occupation of the Golan Heights as she does about ending the occupation of Gaza and the West Bank, including East Jerusalem. Egypt rejects totally both the annexation of East Jerusalem and that of the Golan, as illegal, unacceptable and obnoxious measures that are not conducive to the atmosphere that is necessary to reach a peaceful comprehensive solution. Such unilateral measures contradict the letter and the spirit of the Camp David accords. Egypt in an official statement on December 15, 1981, strongly condemned the Israeli decision to extend Israeli law, jurisdiction and administration to the occupied Syrian territory of the Golan Heights and termed it an illegal measure and a violation of international law and the Charter of the United Nations. In U.N. Security Council Resolution 242, which is the basis of the Camp David accords, it is stipulated that the acquisition of territory by war is inadmissible and that it is essential to respect the sovereignty and territorial integrity of every state in the area, including Syria.

When Saudi Arabia took the bold step of putting forward what has become known as the "Fahd Peace Plan," Egypt could only welcome the fact that a major Arab state would opt for a constructive approach that could end the indecisiveness that has plagued the Arab scene. The Saudi proposals are a set of principles derived from Security Council Resolution 242 and other U.N. resolutions. But to translate these principles into practical realities, one would still need a framework and a negotiating process, which Camp David has provided. In other words, the Saudi proposals are not an alternative to Camp David, but they need a "Camp David" to be implemented satisfactorily.

Thus, Egypt does not consider that peace in the Middle East is her own exclusive concern. Any proposals are welcomed by Egypt provided that they build upon what has already been achieved through Camp David, take into account what has already been acquired through the present negotiations, and meet with the approval of all the parties concerned. Until such a formula is proposed and accepted by these parties, Egypt under President Mubarak is intent on pursuing the negotiations and efforts to reach a comprehensive, peaceful solution that would bring justice and security for all. Egypt is equally intent on continuing to play her historical role in the peace process and in the negotiations that may take place between the Arabs and Israel to achieve that goal.

The diplomatic relations established between Egypt and Israel will, needless to say, continue at the same level. As stipulated in the peace treaty, relations between the two countries are "normal" relations, the word normal meaning exactly what it says and not implying in any way a concept of special relations, alliance or strategic cooperation. This kind of cooperation might be envisaged the day a comprehensive and just peace is achieved, but nothing in the peace treaty commits Egypt to anything that goes further than normal relations between any two given countries.

The role of the United States in establishing a just, comprehensive peace cannot be overemphasized. The full partnership role played by the United States in the negotiations between Egypt and Israel has borne fruit in the form of the peace treaty. It is expected that the United States would continue to play the same positive role in order to achieve a just and lasting solution to the Palestinian problem, the crux of the Middle East problem.

Egypt's conviction is that American participation in the peace negotiations is an essential element. This participation has been instrumental in reaching the Camp David accords and the peace treaty. But there is an even more vital role for U.S. diplomacy to play in helping to define the terms of full Palestinian autonomy and to convince the Israelis that only a self-governing Palestinian body with wide-ranging jurisdiction in all fields would have a chance to be accepted by the Palestinians. The United States can also play a part in convincing the Palestinians and the Palestine Liberation Organization (PLO) that their legitimate rights can be obtained by negotiation and that they can find their place in the family of nations through a peaceful and legitimate process. But to be able to do that, the United States would have to start talking to the Palestinians, to the organization that is accepted by the majority of them as representative of their aspirations, to the organization that is recognized by the majority of nations—namely the PLO. Contacts have to be established between the U.S. government and the PLO and not only through impromptu meetings in the corridors of the United Nations or at diplomatic parties. This was the gist of the message carried by President Sadat on his last trip to Washington in August 1981. This remains a strong belief of Egyptian diplomacy. . . .

Certain Arab governments criticize the peace process but have been unable to unite not only behind an alternative process but even behind the goals to be attained by such a process. This failure on the part of the Arab governments emphasizes the importance of Egypt's leadership. In playing a leading role in the search for a peaceful and just solution to the Arab-Israeli conflict, Egypt maintains a balance between her own national interests and the wider interests of the Arab nations. . . .

Sooner or later, Egypt's actions will make the other Arab governments grasp that the withdrawal of Israeli forces and the return of Sinai to full Egyptian sovereignty constitute a valuable precedent, in accordance with the text of the Egyptian-Israeli Treaty of Peace, which states in its preamble that: "The (Camp David) Framework is intended to constitute a basis for peace not only between Egypt and Israel, but also between Israel and each of its Arab neighbors. . . ." The success of the Camp David accords is bound to have a "snowball" effect and give the peace process more strength, more dynamism and more credibility in Arab eyes. Sooner or later, Arab governments are bound to join the peace process and Egypt's efforts to induce them to do so will be successful.

This is because the present disagreement between Egypt and a number of Arab countries is not in any way the first inter-Arab dispute and will not be the last.

In spite of the severance of diplomatic relations between Cairo and those Arab capitals, transnational relations have continued and even increased: more than two million Egyptian workers, technicians and experts, teachers, doctors and judges are performing a well-appreciated mission in these Arab countries; private Arab investment continues to flow into Egypt; and Cairo remains the favorite destination of Arab tourists. Thousands of Arabs of every nationality are learning in schools and colleges in Egypt, and Arab military and police officers are still being trained in Egyptian academies.

Reconciliation at the official level between Egypt and the governments of the other Arab states is bound to come and President Mubarak has made it quite clear that Egypt does not object to such a reconciliation. Ever since his accession to the presidency, he has underlined the futility of press campaigns among Arabs that can only exacerbate the differences, and he has urged Egyptian journalists and editors to refrain from attacking or abusing Arab governments.

There is hardly any doubt, however, that a rapprochement between Cairo and the dissenting Arab capitals will have to take into account the reality of the relations existing between Egypt and Israel. Egypt would not be the only country able to maintain relations both with Israel and the Arab states. A number of countries in the area itself manage to do that quite successfully, namely Turkey, a Muslim country, and Cyprus which has diplomatic representatives from both Israel and the PLO. Besides, the European and the Latin American countries and the United States all have excellent relations with both the Arab states and Israel. So why should the same thing be impossible to realize in Egypt's case? Certainly the fact that Egypt is an Arab country might seem to complicate the issue, but should not the Arabs accept from a sister state what they readily accept from others? . . .

Secretary of State George P. Shultz: Congressional Testimony (July 12, 1982)*

In late 1974 I visited Beirut, at the time a beautiful and thriving city, even then marked by the presence of Palestinian refugees. But since then Lebanon has been racked by destruction, enduring the presence of armed and assertive PLO and other forces.

Coherent life and government are impossible under those conditions and inevitably Lebanon became a state in disrepair. The Lebanese deserve a chance to govern themselves, free from the presence of the armed forces of any other country or group. The authority of the Government of Lebanon must extend to all its territory.

The agony of Lebanon is on the minds and in the hearts of us all. But in a larger sense Lebanon is but the latest chapter in a history of accumulated grief stretching back through decades of conflict. We are talking here about a part of the globe that has had little genuine peace for generations. A region with thousands of victims—Arab, Israeli and other families torn apart as a consequence of war and terror. What is going on now in Lebanon must mark the end of this cycle of terror rather than simply the latest in a continuing series of senseless and violent acts.

We cannot accept the loss of life brought home to us every day even at this great distance on our television screens; but at the same time we can, as Americans, be proud that once again it is the United States, working most prominently through President Reagan's emissary, Ambassador Philip

* Excerpts from confirmation hearing for the Secretary of State–designate before the Senate Foreign Relations Committee.

Habib, that is attempting to still the guns, achieve an equitable outcome and alleviate the suffering.

Mr. Chairman, the crisis in Lebanon makes painfully and totally clear a central reality of the Middle East: The legitimate needs and problems of the Palestinian people must be addressed and resolved—urgently and in all their dimensions. Beyond the suffering of the Palestinian people lies a complex of political problems which must be addressed if the Middle East is to know peace. The Camp David framework calls as a first step for temporary arrangements which will provide full autonomy for the Palestinians of the West Bank and Gaza. That same framework then speaks eloquently and significantly of a solution that "must also recognize the legitimate rights of the Palestinian people."

The challenge of the negotiations in which the United States is, and during my tenure will remain, a full partner, is to transform that hope into reality. For these talks to succeed, representatives of the Palestinians themselves must participate in the negotiating process. The basis must also be found for other countries in the region, in addition to Israel and Egypt, to join in the peace process.

Our determined effort to stop the killing in Lebanon, resolve the conflict, and make the Government of Lebanon once again sovereign throughout its territory underscores the degree to which our nation has vital interests throughout the Arab world. Our friendly relations with the great majority of Arab states have served those interests and, I believe, assisted our efforts to deal with the current Lebanon crisis.

But beyond the issues of the moment, the importance to our own security of wide and ever-strengthening ties with the Arabs is manifest. It is from them that the West gets much of its oil; it is with them that we share an interest and must cooperate in resisting Soviet imperialism; it is with them, as well as Israel, that we will be able to bring peace to the Middle East.

Finally, and most important, Mr. Chairman, the Lebanese situation is intimately linked to the vital question of Israel's security. Israel, our closest friend in the Middle East, still harbors a deep feeling of insecurity. In a region where hostility is endemic, and where so much of it is directed against Israel, the rightness of her preoccupation with matters of security cannot be disputed. Nor should anyone dispute the depth and durability of America's commitment to the security of Israel or our readiness to assure that Israel has the necessary means to defend herself. I share in this deep and enduring commitment. And more, I recognize that democratic Israel shares with us a deep commitment to the security of the West.

Beyond that, however, we owe it to Israel, in the context of our special relationship, to work with her to bring about a comprehensive peace—acceptable to all the parties involved—which is the only sure guarantee of true and durable security.

Prime Minister Menachem Begin: The Wars of No Alternative and Operation Peace for Galilee (August 8, 1982)*

Let us turn from the international example to ourselves. Operation Peace for Galilee is not a military operation resulting from the lack of an alternative. The terrorists did not threaten the existence of the State of Israel; they "only" threatened the lives of Israel's citizens and members of the Jewish people. There are those who find fault with the second part of that sentence. If there was no danger to the existence of the state, why did you go to war?

I will explain why. We had three wars which we fought without an alternative. The first was the War of Independence, which began on November 30, 1947, and lasted until January 1949. . . . We carried on our lives then by a miracle, with a clear recognition of life's imperative: to win, to establish a state, a government, a parliament, a democracy, an army— a force to defend Israel and the entire Jewish people.

The second war of no alternative was the Yom Kippur War and the War of Attrition that preceded it. What was the situation on that Yom Kippur day [October 6, 1973]? We had 177 tanks deployed on the Golan Heights against 1,400 Soviet-Syrian tanks; and fewer than 500 of our soldiers manned positions along the Suez Canal against five divisions sent to the front by the Egyptians.

It is any wonder that the first days of that war were hard to bear? I remember Gen. Avraham Yaffe came to us, to the

* Excerpts from a speech delivered at the National Defence College in Israel.

Knesset Foreign Affairs and Defence Committee, and said: "Oy, it's so hard! Our boys, 18- and 19-year-olds, are falling like flies and are defending our nation with their very bodies."

In the Golan Heights there was a moment when the O/C Northern Command—today our chief of staff—heard his deputy say, "This is it." What that meant was: "We've lost: we have to come down off the Golan Heights." And the then O/C said, "Give me another five minutes."

Sometimes five minutes can decide a nation's fate. During those five minutes, several dozen tanks arrived, which changed the entire situation on the Golan Heights.

If this had not happened, if the Syrian enemy had come down from the heights to the valley, he would have reached Haifa—for there was not a single tank to obstruct his armoured column's route to Haifa. Yes, we would even have fought with knives—as one of our esteemed wives has said—with knives against tanks. Many more would have fallen, and in every settlement there would have been the kind of slaughter at which the Syrians are experts.

In the south, our boys in the outposts were taken prisoner, and we know what happened to them afterwards. Dozens of tanks were destroyed, because tanks were sent in piecemeal, since we could not organize them in a large formation. And dozens of planes were shot down by missiles which were not destroyed in time, so that we had to submit to their advances.

Woe to the ears that still ring with the words of one of the nation's heroes, the then defence minister, in whose veins flowed the blood of the Maccabees: "We are losing the Third Commonwealth."

Our total casualties in that war of no alternative were 2,297 killed, 6,067 wounded. Together with the War of Attrition—which was also a war of no alternative—2,659 killed, 7,251 wounded. The terrible total: almost 10,000 casualties.

Our other wars were not without an alternative. In November 1956 we had a choice. The reason for going to war then was the need to destroy the *fedayeen,* who did not represent a danger to the existence of the state.

However, the political leadership of the time thought it was necessary to do this. As one who served in the parliamentary opposition, I was summoned to David Ben-Gurion before the cabinet received information of the plan, and he found it necessary to give my colleagues and myself these details: We are going to meet the enemy before it absorbs the Soviet weapons which began to flow to it from Czechoslovakia in 1955.

In June 1967 we again had a choice. The Egyptian army concentrations in the Sinai approaches did not prove that Nasser was really about to attack us. We must be honest with ourselves. We decided to attack him.

This was a war of self-defence in the noblest sense of the term. The government of national unity then established decided unanimously: We will take the initiative and attack the enemy, drive him back, and thus assure the security of Israel and the future of the nation.

As for Operation Peace for Galilee, it does not really belong to the category of wars of no alternative. We could have gone on seeing our civilians injured in Metulla or Kiryat Shmona or Nahariya. We could have gone on counting those killed by explosive charges left in a Jerusalem supermarket, or a Petah Tikva bus stop.

All the orders to carry out these acts of murder and sabotage came from Beirut. Should we have reconciled ourselves to the ceaseless killing of civilians, even after the agreement ending hostilities reached last summer, which the terrorists interpreted as an agreement permitting them to strike at us from every side, besides Southern Lebanon? They tried to infiltrate gangs of murderers via Syria and Jordan, and by a miracle we captured them. We might also not have captured them. There was a gang of four terrorists which infiltrated from Jordan, whose members admitted they had been about to commandeer a bus (and we remember the bus on the coastal road).

And in the Diaspora? Even Philip Habib interpreted the agreement ending acts of hostility as giving them freedom to attack targets beyond Israel's borders. We have never accepted this interpretation. Shall we permit Jewish blood to be spilled in the Diaspora? Shall we permit bombs to be planted against Jews in Paris, Rome, Athens or London? Shall we permit our ambassadors to be attacked?

There are slanderers who say that a full year of quiet has passed between us and the terrorists. Nonsense. There was not even one month of quiet. The newspapers and communications media, including *The New York Times* and *The Washington Post,* did not publish even one line about our capturing the gang of murderers that crossed the Jordan in order to commandeer a bus and murder its passengers.

True, such actions were not a threat to the existence of the state. But they did threaten the lives of civilians whose number we cannot estimate, day after day, week after week, month after month.

During the past nine weeks, we have, in effect, destroyed the combat potential of 20,000 terrorists. We hold 9,000 in a prison camp. Between 2,000 and 3,000 were killed and between 7,000 and 9,000 have been captured and cut off in Beirut. They have decided to leave there only because they have no possibility of remaining there. The problem will be solved.

We have destroyed the best tanks and planes the Syrians had. We have destroyed 24 of their ground-to-air missile batteries. After everything that happened, Syria did not go to war against us, not in Lebanon and not in the Golan Heights.

For our part, we will not initiate any attack against any Arab country. We have proved that we do not want wars. We made many painful sacrifices for a peace treaty with Egypt. That treaty stood the test of the fighting in Lebanon; in other words, it *stood the test*.

The demilitarized zone of 150 kilometres in Sinai exists, and no Egyptian soldier has been placed there. From the experience of the 1930s, I have to say that if ever the other side violated the agreement about the demilitarized zone, Israel would be obliged to introduce, without delay, a force stronger than that violating the international commitment: not in order to wage war, but to achieve one of two results: restoration of the previous situation, i.e., resumed demilitarization, and the removal of both armies from the demilitarized zone; or attainment of strategic depth, in case the other side has taken the first step towards a war of aggression, as happened in Europe only three years after the abrogation of the demilitarized zone in the Rhineland.

Because the other Arab countries are completely incapable of attacking the State of Israel, there is reason to expect that we are facing a historic period of peace. It is obviously impossible to set a date.

It may well be that "The land shall be still for 40 years." Perhaps less: perhaps more. But from the facts before us, it is clear that, with the end of the fighting in Lebanon, we have ahead of us many years of establishing peace treaties and peaceful relations with the various Arab countries.

The conclusion—both on the basis of the relations between states and on the basis of our national experience—is that there is no divine mandate to go to war only if there is no alternative. There is no moral imperative that a nation must, or is entitled to, fight only when its back is to the sea, or to the abyss. Such a war may avert tragedy, if not a Holocaust, for any nation; but it causes it terrible loss of life.

Quite the opposite. A free, sovereign nation, which hates war and loves peace, and which is concerned about its security, must create the conditions under which war, if there is a need for it, *will not be* for lack of alternative. The conditions must be such—and their creation depends upon man's reason and his actions—that the price of victory will be few casualties, not many.

President Ronald Reagan: The Reagan Plan (September 1, 1982)*

My fellow Americans, today has been a day that should make us proud. It marked the end of the successful evacuation of the Palestine Liberation Organization (PLO) from Beirut, Lebanon. This peaceful step could never have been taken without the good offices of the United States and, especially, the truly heroic work of a great American diplomat, Ambassador Philip Habib [President's special emissary to the Middle East]. Thanks to his efforts, I am happy to announce that the U.S. Marine contingent helping to supervise the evacuation has accomplished its mission. Our young men should be out of Lebanon within 2 weeks. They, too, have served the cause of peace with distinction, and we can all be very proud of them.

But the situation in Lebanon is only part of the overall problem of conflict in the Middle East. So, over the past 2 weeks, while events in Beirut dominated the front page, America was engaged in a quiet, behind-the-scenes effort to lay the groundwork for a broader peace in the region. For once, there were no premature leaks as U.S. diplomatic missions traveled to Mid-East capitals, and I met here at home with a wide range of experts to map out an American peace initiative for the long-suffering peoples of the Middle East, Arab and Israeli alike.

* Speech to the nation by President Reagan from Burbank, California.

It seemed to me that, with the agreement in Lebanon, we had an opportunity for a more far-reaching peace effort in the region, and I was determined to seize that moment. In the words of the scripture, the time had come to "follow after the things which make for peace."

Tonight, I want to report to you on the steps we have taken and the prospects they can open up for a just and lasting peace in the Middle East. America has long been committed to bringing peace to this troubled region. For more than a generation, successive U.S. administrations have endeavored to develop a fair and workable process that could lead to a true and lasting Arab-Israeli peace. Our involvement in the search for Mid-East peace is not a matter of preference, it is a moral imperative. The strategic importance of the region to the United States is well known.

But our policy is motivated by more than strategic interests. We also have an irreversible commitment to the survival and territorial integrity of friendly states. Nor can we ignore the fact that the well-being of much of the world's economy is tied to stability in the strife-torn Middle East. Finally, our traditional humanitarian concerns dictate a continuing effort to peacefully resolve conflicts.

When our Administration assumed office in January 1981, I decided that the general framework for our Middle East policy should follow the broad guidelines laid down by my predecessors. There were two basic issues we had to address. First, there was the strategic threat to the region posed by the Soviet Union and its surrogates, best demonstrated by the brutal war in Afghanistan; and, second, the peace process between Israel and its Arab neighbors. With regard to the Soviet threat, we have strengthened our efforts to develop with our friends and allies a joint policy to deter the Soviets and their surrogates from further expansion in the region and, if necessary, to defend against it. With respect to the Arab-Israeli conflict, we have embraced the Camp David framework as the only way to proceed. We have also recognized, however, that solving the Arab-Israeli conflict, in and of itself, cannot assure peace throughout a region as vast and troubled as the Middle East.

Our first objective under the Camp David process was to insure the successful fulfillment of the Egyptian-Israeli Peace Treaty. This was achieved with the peaceful return of the Sinai to Egypt in April 1982. To accomplish this, we worked hard with our Egyptian and Israeli friends, and eventually with other friendly countries, to create the multinational force which now operates in the Sinai.

Throughout this period of difficult and time-consuming negotiations, we never lost sight of the next step of Camp David: autonomy talks to pave the way for permitting the Palestinian people to exercise their legitimate rights. However, owing to the tragic assassination of President Sadat and other crises in the area, it was not until January 1982 that we were able to make a major effort to renew these talks. Secretary of State Haig and Ambassador Fairbanks [Richard Fairbanks, Special Negotiator for the Middle East Peace Process] made three visits to Israel and Egypt early this year to pursue the autonomy talks. Considerable progress was made in developing the basic outline of an American approach which was to be presented to Egypt and Israel after April.

The successful completion of Israel's withdrawal from Sinai and the courage shown on this occasion by Prime Minister Begin and President Mubarak in living up to their agreements convinced me the time had come for a new American policy to try to bridge the remaining differences between Egypt and Israel on the autonomy process. So, in May, I called for specific measures and a timetable for consultations with the Governments of Egypt and Israel on the next steps in the peace process. However, before this effort could be launched, the conflict in Lebanon preempted our efforts. The autonomy talks were basically put on hold while we sought to untangle the parties in Lebanon and still the guns of war.

The Lebanon war, tragic as it was, has left us with a new opportunity for Middle East peace. We must seize it now and bring peace to this troubled area so vital to world stability while there is still time. It was with this strong conviction that over a month ago, before the present negotiations in Beirut had been completed, I directed Secretary of State Shultz to again review our policy and to consult a wide range of outstanding Americans on the best ways to strengthen chances for peace in the Middle East. We have consulted with many of the officials who were historically involved in the process, with Members of the Congress, and with individuals from the private sector; and I have held extensive consultations with my own advisers on the principles I will outline to you tonight.

The evacuation of the PLO from Beirut is now complete. And we can now help the Lebanese to rebuild their war-torn country. We owe it to ourselves, and to posterity, to move quickly to build upon this achievement. A stable and revived Lebanon is essential to all our hopes for peace in the region. The people of Lebanon deserve the best efforts of the international community to turn the nightmares of the past several years into a new dawn of hope.

But the opportunities for peace in the Middle East do not begin and end in Lebanon. As we help Lebanon rebuild, we must also move to resolve the root causes of conflict between Arabs and Israelis. The war in Lebanon has demonstrated many things, but two consequences are key to the peace process:

First, the military losses of the PLO have not diminished the yearning of the Palestinian people for a just solution of their claims; and

Second, while Israel's military successes in Lebanon have demonstrated that its armed forces are second to none in the region, they alone cannot bring just and lasting peace to Israel and her neighbors.

The question now is how to reconcile Israel's legitimate security concerns with the legitimate rights of the Palestinians. And that answer can only come at the negotiating table. Each party must recognize that the outcome must be acceptable to all and that true peace will require compromises by all.

So, tonight I am calling for a fresh start. This is the moment for all those directly concerned to get involved—or lend their support—to a workable basis for peace. The Camp David agreement remains the foundation of our policy. Its language provides all parties with the leeway they need for successful negotiations.

· I call on Israel to make clear that the security for which she yearns can only be achieved through genuine peace, a peace requiring magnanimity, vision, and courage.

· I call on the Palestinian people to recognize that their own political aspirations are inextricably bound to recognition of Israel's right to a secure future.

· And I call on the Arab states to accept the reality of Israel and the reality that peace and justice are to be gained only through hard, fair, direct negotiation.

In making these calls upon others, I recognize that the United States has a special responsibility. No other nation is in a position to deal with the key parties to the conflict on the basis of trust and reliability.

The time has come for a new realism on the part of all the

peoples of the Middle East. The State of Israel is an accomplished fact; it deserves unchallenged legitimacy within the community of nations. But Israel's legitimacy has thus far been recognized by too few countries and has been denied by every Arab state except Egypt. Israel exists; it has a right to exist in peace behind secure and defensible borders; and it has a right to demand of its neighbors that they recognize those facts.

I have personally followed and supported Israel's heroic struggle for survival ever since the founding of the State of Israel 34 years ago. In the pre-1967 borders, Israel was barely 10 miles wide at its narrowest point. The bulk of Israel's population lived within artillery range of hostile Arab armies. I am not about to ask Israel to live that way again.

The war in Lebanon has demonstrated another reality in the region. The departure of the Palestinians from Beirut dramatizes more than ever the homelessness of the Palestinian people. Palestinians feel strongly that their cause is more than a question of refugees. I agree. The Camp David agreement recognized that fact when it spoke of the legitimate rights of the Palestinian people and their just requirements. For peace to endure, it must involve all those who have been most deeply affected by the conflict. Only through broader participation in the peace process—most immediately by Jordan and by the Palestinians—will Israel be able to rest confident in the knowledge that its security and integrity will be respected by its neighbors. Only through the process of negotiation can all the nations of the Middle East achieve a secure peace.

These then are our general goals. What are the specific new American positions, and why are we taking them?

In the Camp David talks thus far, both Israel and Egypt have felt free to express openly their views as to what the outcome should be. Understandably, their views have differed on many points.

The United States has thus far sought to play the role of mediator; we have avoided public comment on the key issues. We have always recognized—and continue to recognize—that only the voluntary agreement of those parties most directly involved in the conflict can provide an enduring solution. But it has become evident to me that some clearer sense of America's position on the key issues is necessary to encourage wider support for the peace process.

First, as outlined in the Camp David accords, there must be a period of time during which the Palestinian inhabitants of the West Bank and Gaza will have full autonomy over their own affairs. Due consideration must be given to the principle of self-government by the inhabitants of the territories and to the legitimate security concerns of the parties involved.

The purpose of the 5-year period of transition, which would begin after free elections for a self-governing Palestinian authority, is to prove to the Palestinians that they can run their own affairs and that such Palestinian autonomy poses no threat to Israel's security.

The United States will not support the use of any additional land for the purpose of settlements during the transition period. Indeed, the immediate adoption of a settlement freeze by Israel, more than any other action, could create the confidence needed for wider participation in these talks. Further settlement activity is in no way necessary for the security of Israel and only diminishes the confidence of the Arabs that a final outcome can be freely and fairly negotiated.

I want to make the American position well understood: The purpose of this transition period is the peaceful and orderly transfer of authority from Israel to the Palestinian inhabitants of the West Bank and Gaza. At the same time, such a transfer must not interfere with Israel's security requirements.

Beyond the transition period, as we look to the future of the West Bank and Gaza, it is clear to me that peace cannot be achieved by the formation of an independent Palestinian state in those territories. Nor is it achievable on the basis of Israeli sovereignty or permanent control over the West Bank and Gaza.

So the United States will not support the establishment of an independent Palestinian state in the West Bank and Gaza, and we will not support annexation or permanent control by Israel.

There is, however, another way to peace. The final status of these lands must, of course, be reached through the give-and-take of negotiations. But it is the firm view of the United States that self-government by the Palestinians of the West Bank and Gaza in association with Jordan offers the best chance for a durable, just and lasting peace.

We base our approach squarely on the principle that the Arab-Israeli conflict should be resolved through negotiations involving an exchange of territory for peace. This exchange is enshrined in U.N. Security Council Resolution 242, which is, in turn, incorporated in all its parts in the Camp David agreements. U.N. Resolution 242 remains wholly valid as the foundation stone of America's Middle East peace effort.

It is the United States' position that—in return for peace—the withdrawal provision of Resolution 242 applies to all fronts, including the West Bank and Gaza.

When the border is negotiated between Jordan and Israel, our view on the extent to which Israel should be asked to give up territory will be heavily affected by the extent of true peace and normalization and the security arrangements offered in return.

Finally, we remain convinced that Jerusalem must remain undivided, but its final status should be decided through negotiations.

In the course of the negotiations to come, the United States will support positions that seem to us fair and reasonable compromises and likely to promote a sound agreement. We will also put forward our own detailed proposals when we believe they can be helpful. And, make no mistake, the United States will oppose any proposal—from any party and at any point in the negotiating process—that threatens the security of Israel. America's commitment to the security of Israel is ironclad. And, I might add, so is mine.

During the past few days, our ambassadors in Israel, Egypt, Jordan, and Saudi Arabia have presented to their host governments the proposals in full detail that I have outlined here today. Now I am convinced that these proposals can bring justice, bring security, and bring durability to an Arab-Israeli peace. The United States will stand by these principles with total dedication. They are fully consistent with Israel's security requirements and the aspirations of the Palestinians. We will work hard to broaden participation at the peace table as envisaged by the Camp David accords. And I fervently hope that the Palestinians and Jordan, with the support of their Arab colleagues, will accept this opportunity.

Tragic turmoil in the Middle East runs back to the dawn of history. In our modern day, conflict after conflict has taken its brutal toll there. In an age of nuclear challenge and economic interdependence, such conflicts are a threat to all the people of the world, not just the Middle East itself. It is time for us all—in the Middle East and around the world—to call a halt to conflict, hatred, and prejudice; it is time for us all to launch a common effort for reconstruction, peace, and progress.

It has often been said—and regrettably too often been true—that the story of the search for peace and justice in the Middle East is a tragedy of opportunities missed. In the aftermath of the settlement in Lebanon we now face an opportunity for a broader peace. This time we must not let it slip from our grasp. We must look beyond the difficulties and obstacles of the present and move with fairness and resolve toward a brighter future. We owe it to ourselves—and to posterity—to do no less. For if we miss this chance to make a fresh start, we may look back on this moment from some later vantage point and realize how much that failure cost us all.

These, then, are the principles upon which American policy toward the Arab-Israeli conflict will be based. I have made a personal commitment to see that they endure and, God willing, that they will come to be seen by all reasonable, compassionate people as fair, achievable, and in the interests of all who wish to see peace in the Middle East.

Tonight, on the eve of what can be a dawning of new hope for the people of the troubled Middle East—and for all the world's people who dream of a just and peaceful future—I ask you, my fellow Americans, for your support, and your prayers in this great undertaking.

Twelfth Arab Summit Conference: Final Statement (September 9, 1982) *

. . . In view of the grave conditions through which the Arab nation is passing and out of a sense of historical and pan-Arab responsibility, their majesties and excellencies and highnesses the kings, presidents and emirs of the Arab nation discussed the important issues submitted to their conference and adopted the following resolution in regard to them.

I. The Arab-Israeli Conflict

The conference greeted the steadfastness of the Palestine revolutionary forces, the Lebanese and Palestinian peoples and the Syrian Arab Armed Forces and declared its support for the Palestinian people in their struggle for the retrieval of their established national rights.

Out of the conference's belief in the ability of the Arab nation to achieve its legitimate objectives and eliminate the aggression, and out of the principles and basis laid down by

* The Twelfth Arab Summit Conference convened in Fez, Morocco, on November 25, 1981, was adjourned, and resumed again on September 6, 1982.

the Arab summit conferences, and out of the Arab countries' determination to continue to work by all means for the establishment of peace based on justice in the Middle East and using the plan of President Habib Bourguiba, which is based on international legitimacy, as the foundation for solving the Palestinian question and the plan of His Majesty King Fahd ibn 'Abd al-'Aziz which deals with peace in the Middle East, and in the light of the discussions and notes made by their majesties, excellencies and highnesses the kings, presidents and emirs, the conference has decided to adopt the following principles:

1. Israel's withdrawal from all Arab territories occupied in 1967, including Arab Jerusalem.

2. The removal of settlements set up by Israel in the Arab territories after 1967.

3. Guarantees of the freedom of worship and the performance of religious rites for all religions at the holy places.

4. Confirmation of the right of the Palestinian people to self-determination and to exercise their firm and inalienable national rights, under the leadership of the PLO, its sole legitimate representative, and compensation for those who do not wish to return.

5. The placing of the West Bank and Gaza Strip under UN supervision for a transitional period, not longer than several months.

6. The creation of an independent Palestinian state with Jerusalem as its capital.

7. Security Council guarantees for the implementation of those principles.

8. The drawing up by the Security Council of guarantees for peace for all the states of the region, including the independent Palestinian state.

9. Security Council guarantees for the implementation of these principles.

II. The Israeli Aggression Against Lebanon

The conference declares its strong condemnation of the Israeli aggression against the Palestinian people, and draws the attention of international public opinion to the gravity of this aggression and its consequences on stability and security in the region.

The conference has decided to back Lebanon in everything that will lead to the implementation of the Security Council resolutions, particularly Resolutions 508 and 509 calling for the withdrawal of Israel from Lebanese territory up to the recognized international borders.

The conference affirms the solidarity of the Arab states with Lebanon in its tragedy, and its readiness to render any assistance it demands to remedy and put an end to this tragedy. The conference has been notified of the decision of the Lebanese Government to end the task of the Arab Deterrent Forces in Lebanon provided that negotiations be conducted between the Lebanese and Syrian Governments to make the arrangements in the light of the Israeli withdrawal from Lebanon.

El-Hassan Bin Talal: Jordan's Quest for Peace (Fall 1982)*

. . . Because Jordan is a small country, we are often discounted as a major factor in what is clearly the greatest threat to international security. We do not have a large population like Egypt or Syria. We do not have a position of military superiority like Israel. We do not have oil like Saudi Arabia or Iraq. So, then, why is Jordan important? Do we assert its centrality because we are Jordanian?

No, Jordan's views are important. Apart from the Sinai, which is in the process of being returned to Egypt, most of the territory Israel occupied in 1967, and therefore which is referred to in U.N. Security Council Resolution 242, was Jordanian. East Jerusalem was Jordanian. There are more Palestinians in Jordan than in any other state, most of them refugees from the wars of 1948 and 1967. Jordan and Israel have outstanding territorial conflicts dating from 1948. Although it is our position and belief that the Palestine Liberation Organization is and can only be the sole representative of the Palestinian people, still it is incontestable that large numbers of Arabs in the West Bank continue to attend closely to Jordan's actions and policies.

It is clear today that the sine qua non of any general and effective settlement of the Arab-Israeli conflict must address and resolve the Palestinian issue. It is not our purpose here to posit the requirements for such a resolution; indeed, the re-

* Excerpts from an article in *Foreign Affairs,* Fall 1982. El-Hassan Bin Talal is the Crown Prince of Jordan.

quirements are part of the dispute. What is clear, however, is that all parties today recognize that, to use the words of former U.S. Assistant Secretary of State Harold Saunders, "The Palestinians collectively are a political factor which must be dealt with if there is to be a peace between Israel and its neighbors." Even a cursory review of Israeli statements demonstrates conclusively that there too is a recognition of the crucial nature of the Palestinian problem. Whether in terms of "autonomy" proposals or hints that the Palestinians already have their state in Jordan, it is evident that Israeli leaders, too, have come to accept, implicitly or explicitly, the unavoidable fact that no settlement is possible without dealing with the Palestinian problem.

We Jordanians must add that, practically speaking, a settlement must also take into account our perceptions. Small as Jordan is, our country is politically, socially, economically, militarily and historically inseparable from the Palestinian issue. Not that we can speak in place of the Palestinians; we cannot. As His Majesty King Hussein has said recently, "Palestinians alone have the right to determine their future. There are no other options acceptable to Jordan nor is there any substitute for the Palestine Liberation Organization, the sole legitimate representative of the people of Palestine. . . ." We cannot speak in place of the Palestinians. At the same time, however, as a leading Jordanian social scientist has written, "The Jordanians and Palestinians are now one people, and no political loyalty, however strong, will separate them permanently."

Consider for a moment the following:

—Half Jordan's population is Palestinian.

—The West Bank and East Jerusalem, both captured by Israel in 1967, were part of Jordan.

—If there is large-scale Palestinian migration as a result of any regional settlement, Jordan will necessarily be greatly affected.

—Virtually all Palestinians currently resident in Jordan are Jordanian nationals.

—Israel and Jordan have vital interests in development of regional water resources in the Jordan River. Israel has already illegally diverted much of the Jordan River, but the importance of cooperation in the future cannot be overestimated. In other areas such as tourism, there is also substantial need for cooperation.

—After any settlement as before it, Jordan will share a long border with Israel. For us, development is not just an abstract goal, but a pressing need. We do not wish to continue to divert so much of Jordan's small resource base to a costly armaments program to defend our overexposed position or in order to reduce the risks along this extended border.

—Pending the creation of a Palestinian state, it is still Jordan which pays the salaries and pensions of West Bank officials; it is Jordan that bears some development costs of the territory and whose approval is necessary for such projects; it is in the Jordanian parliament that the inhabitants of the West Bank are represented; it is Jordanian law that has effect in the West Bank. This is not to deny that Israel is also involved in these activities, for that is true, albeit a clear violation of international law. Rather, we intend only to show how concrete and contemporary are Jordan's interests. . . .

. . . Yet lately we in Jordan have begun to hear and read that "Jordan opposes an Arab-Israeli settlement." Let us be clear on this point: no one, no country, no people wants a settlement more than we do. Certainly, no one pays a heavier price for the continuation of the conflict than do we here in Jordan.

After the 1967 War, other Arab governments learned—and what a costly lesson—what we had known for almost two decades: Israel was to be an enduring reality of the Middle East, and the issue was not to undo the 1947 injustice to Palestinians and all Arabs but rather to constrain an Israel hungry for territorial expansion and powerful enough to obtain it.

Perhaps it is germane to say at this point that we Jordanians do not have a precise blueprint of a settlement in mind. Indeed, I believe I can speak for all the Arab countries, and probably for Israel too, in saying that the range of ideas or alternatives or minimums or maximums that is advanced in any of our countries is appallingly varied. For us Jordanians, there are a few clear-cut requirements. Certainly, the same can be said for Egyptians, Israelis, Iraqis, Palestinians, Saudis and Syrians. We have learned through successive tragedies to keep our requirements few, to question them, to be sure they are truly vital. This is true also of other Arab parties. Sadly, it is not true for Israel, whose list of requirements has grown with each passing year. . . .

In spite of Israel's intransigence, which is growing apace with her appetite, the Arab governments including Jordan still seek a settlement. We have to, for let us be candid: Israel has designs on the West Bank, East Jerusalem, the Golan Heights, and southern Lebanon—whose territories are these? Arab territories. We do not want to provide a pretext for further Israeli expansion. So, yes Jordan, and, yes, the other Arab states near Israel favor a settlement.

Yet it is true that we do not favor *any* settlement. Neither Jordan, nor Syria nor Lebanon nor Saudi Arabia nor Egypt nor Israel—none of the Middle East countries—is prepared to accept, or should be prepared to accept, "peace at any price." Again, let us all be honest. A "settlement" that did not resolve the Palestinian problem, or the question of the Golan, or Israel's or Jordan's or Lebanon's or Syria's rights to exist with reasonable security within a recognized territory—such an outcome would be no settlement at all, for natural forces would be at work to overturn it before it was signed. We understand Israel's needs, and believe Israel's truly vital requirements can be met, but we too have a few vital requirements. Each nation must enjoy some security as a result of a settlement, and none of us can have perfect security, for as has often been shown, one nation's perfect security is another's perfect insecurity.

It is true that agreement on what a settlement should look like is lacking both within and among Arab states, as it is lacking in fact within Israel and between Israel and other states. But a resolution to the conflict is much less likely to be found

—if Israel continues to expand what are clearly illegal settlements in the occupied territories;

—if Israel continues to decide unilaterally to annex Arab land;

—if private land is confiscated to be handed out to Israeli settlers;

—if peace agreements are made in the name of rather than with other parties;

—if Israel continues to play with internal vulnerabilities of Arab states, increasing instability and distrust;

—if Israel continues to play with internal vulnerabilities of seeing her role as a regional policeman.

Let there be no mistake. I am not holding the Arabs blameless for the depth and duration of the Arab-Israeli conflict. For too long Arab states thought the monumental injustice perpetrated against the Palestinian people in 1948 was the only reality. For too long many Arabs held that justice would be served in the end, that justice would triumph, and could see only a return to their lands by the refugees as just. After all, we knew the Palestinian Arabs, native to the land, as our Arab brothers. We did not know the Jews who had suddenly seized it. What was to happen to them? Arabs didn't care; they cared deeply, though, about the Palestinians. This was unrealistic. Today, we understand that the Palestinian problem must be dealt with *in the context* of the existence of Israel. Nevertheless, that problem *must* be resolved. We Arabs too have some requirements, but there is no question that we seek, favor, and deeply desire a resolution to this disastrous conflict.

It must be noted that the Israeli annexation of Arab Jerusalem and the Golan have both taken place in the aftermath of the Egyptian-Israeli peace treaty. Even Israelis never claimed historic rights to the Golan. Now that they have purported to annex the Golan Heights, can anyone doubt that the next step will be the West Bank? Never mind the concept of autonomy. Never mind the ideas of Palestinian self-rule. It is clear that Israel is intent upon adding this Arab territory to Greater Israel.

It was the inevitability of this result to the Camp David separate peace that led us to remain outside the discussions. We ask for a process of peace, not a process of annexation. Jordan and other Arab governments want a true peace, a peace of compromise, a peace that will allow Arab and Jew and Christian to live side by side in this region so important to all three faiths and the many peoples who embrace them. We seek a peace that will not force us to divert our meager resources to a constant cycle of arming to deter others and defend ourselves, a peace that will allow us to develop our land, our people, and our society both economically and spiritually, not bury the people in the land with continuing bitterness and hatred.

And what are the essentials of such a peace? Clearly, the modalities must be negotiated, but several prerequisites are manifestly central to bring about a peace that can endure. Happily, the prerequisites are few. Sadly, they are more elusive today than they were when President Sadat traveled to Jerusalem.

First, it is clear that the Palestinians must be allowed to freely exercise their national right of self-determination. The whole world, including the United States, and implicitly even Israel, has recognized that the Palestinian problem is at the core of the continuing Middle East tragedy. Put another way, there will never be a true peace in the region until this first requirement is met.

The second requirement is Israeli withdrawal from territories occupied in the 1967 War. Indeed, these two requirements may be viewed as related. We understand that timing can be important, that security measures (such as arms or forces limitations, observers, and the like) may be an integral part of any agreement. Issues such as security measures, juridical status, corridors of transit and communication, representation, foreign nationals, and so forth are important and are proper subjects of negotiation. Moreover, it is clear that in some cases security requirements may dictate minor modifications to specific lines previously disputed. Yet, such exchanges must result from negotiations aimed at *mutual* security and based on the two principles we have identified, not as a result of force or threat. . . .

The United States has important—some would say, vital—interests in the Middle East. It is also true that we have critical interests in the West, not least with the United States. Much in our tradition is shared, from our great monotheistic traditions to our prolonged and close association with Western Europe. We have resources of faith as well as of minerals; America has resources of science and technology as well as capital. The world is interdependent, and those Arabs who ignore or castigate our interdependence with the West, like their counterparts here, are out of step with more than their compatriots—they are out of step with reality itself.

Thus, when some Arabs say that American or Western interests are at risk in the continued failure to achieve a settlement, what they are really saying is that world interests, our interests as well as yours, are at stake. A future that condemns us to pervert the nature and value of our relationship into that of a gunrunner's, that forces America's friends to confront and even do violence to other friends, that perpetuates poverty and ignorance and narrowly limits the resources to overcome these common enemies—this is not a hopeful destiny, this is not a humane destiny, this is not an acceptable destiny. . . .

The Kahan Commission Report (February 7, 1983)*

Before we discuss the essence of the problem of the indirect responsibility of Israel, or of those who operated at its behest,

---

* Excerpts from the report of the Kahan Commission to investigate the massacre at the Sabra and Shatilla refugee camps, which was signed by Chairman Yitzhak Kahan and members Aharon Barak and Yona Efrat.

we perceive it to be necessary to deal with objections that have been voiced on various occasions, according to which if Israel's direct responsibility for the atrocities is negated—i.e., if it is determined that the blood of those killed was not shed by I.D.F. [Israel Defence Force] soldiers and forces, or that others operating at the behest of the state were not parties to the atrocities—then there is no place for further discussion of the problem of indirect responsibility. The argument is that no responsibility should be laid on Israel for deeds perpetrated outside of its borders by members of the Christian community against Palestinians in that same country, or against Muslims located within the area of the camps. A certain echo of this approach may be found in statements made in the Cabinet meeting of 9.19.82, and in statements released to the public by various sources.

We cannot accept this position. If it indeed becomes clear that those who decided on the entry of the Phalangists into the camps should have foreseen—from the information at their disposal and from things which were common knowledge —that there was danger of a massacre, and no steps were taken which might have prevented this danger or at least greatly reduced the possibility that deeds of this type might be done, then those who made the decisions and those who implemented them are indirectly responsible for what ultimately occurred, even if they did not intend this to happen and merely disregarded the anticipated danger. A similar indirect responsibility also falls on those who knew of the decision: it was their duty, by virtue of their position and their office, to warn of the danger, and they did not fulfill this duty. It is also not possible to absolve of such indirect responsibility those persons who, when they received the first reports of what was happening in the camps, did not rush to prevent the continuation of the Phalangists' actions and did not do everything within their power to stop them.

. . . We would like to note here that we will not enter at all into the question of indirect responsibility of other elements besides the State of Israel. One might argue that such indirect responsibility falls, inter alia, on the Lebanese Army, or on the Lebanese government to whose orders this army was subject, since despite Major General Drori's urgings in his talks with the heads of the Lebanese Army, they did not grant Israel's request to enter the camps before the Phalangists or instead of the Phalangists, until 9.19.82. It should also be noted that in meetings with U.S. representatives during the critical days, Israel's spokesmen repeatedly requested that the U.S. use its influence to get the Lebanese Army to fulfill the function of maintaining public peace and order in West Beirut, but it does not seem that these requests had any result. One might also make charges concerning the hasty evacuation of the multi-national force by the countries whose troops were in place until after the evacuation of the terrorists.

. . . As has already been said above, the decision to enter West Beirut was adopted in conversations held between the Prime Minister and the Defense Minister on the night between 14–15 September 1982. No charge may be made against this decision for having been adopted by these two alone without convening a Cabinet session. On that same night, an extraordinary emergency situation was created which justified immediate and concerted action to prevent a situation which appeared undesirable and even dangerous from Israel's perspective. There is great sense in the supposition that had I.D.F. troops not entered West Beirut, a situation of total chaos and battles between various combat forces would have developed, and the number of victims among the civilian population would have been far greater than it ultimately was. The Israeli military force was the only real force nearby which could take control over West Beirut so as to maintain the peace and prevent a resumption of hostile actions between various militias and communities. The Lebanese Army could have performed a function in the refugee camps, but it did not then have the power to enforce order in all of West Beirut. Under these circumstances it could be assumed that were I.D.F. forces not to enter West Beirut, various atrocities would be perpetrated there in the absence of any real authority; and it may be that world public opinion might then have placed responsibility on Israel for having refrained from action.

The demand made in Israel to have the Phalangists take part in the fighting was a general and understandable one; and political, and to some extent military, reasons existed for such participation. The general question of relations with the Phalangists and cooperation with them is a saliently political one, regarding which there may be legitimate differences of opinion and outlook. We do not find it justified to assert that the decision on this participation was unwarranted or that it should not have been made.

It is a different question whether the decision to have the Phalangists enter the camps was justified in the circumstances that were created.

In our view, everyone who had anything to do with events in Lebanon should have felt apprehension about a massacre in the camps, if armed Phalangist forces were to be moved into them without the I.D.F. exercising concrete and effective supervision and scrutiny of them. All those concerned were well aware that combat morality among the various combatant groups in Lebanon differs from the norm in the I.D.F., that the combatants in Lebanon belittle the value of human life far beyond what is necessary and accepted in wars between civilized peoples, and that various atrocities against the noncombatant population had been widespread in Lebanon since 1975. It was well known that the Phalangists harbor deep enmity for the Palestinians, viewing them as the source of all the troubles that afflicted Lebanon during the years of the civil war.

The decision on the entry of the Phalangists into the refugee camps was taken on Wednesday (9.15.82) in the morning. The Prime Minister was not then informed of the decision. The Prime Minister heard about the decision, together with all the other ministers, in the course of a report made by the Chief of Staff at the Cabinet session on Thursday (9.16.82) when the Phalangists were already in the camps. Thereafter, no report was made to the Prime Minister regarding the excesses of the Phalangists in the camps, and the Prime Minister learned about the events in the camps from a BBC broadcast on Saturday (9.18.82). With regard to the following recommendations concerning a group of men who hold senior positions in the Government and the Israel Defense Forces, we have taken into account [the fact] that each one of these men has to his credit [the performance of] many public or military services rendered with sacrifice and devotion on behalf of the State of Israel. If nevertheless we have reached the conclusion that it is incumbent upon us to recommend certain measures against some of these men, it is out of the recognition that the gravity of the matter and its implications for the underpinnings of public morality in the State of Israel call for such measures.

The Prime Minister, the Foreign Minister, and the Head of the Mossad

We have heretofore established the facts and conclusions with regard to the responsibility of the Prime Minister, the Foreign Minister, and the head of the Mossad. In view of what we have determined with regard to the extent of the responsibility of each of them, we are of the opinion that it is sufficient to determine responsibility and there is no need for any further recommendations.

The Minister of Defense, Mr. Ariel Sharon

We have found, as has been detailed in this report, that the Minister of Defense bears personal responsibility. In our opinion, it is fitting that the Minister of Defense draw the appropriate personal conclusions arising out of the defects revealed with regard to the manner in which he discharged the duties of his office—and if necessary, that the Prime Minister consider whether he should exercise his authority under Section 21-A(a) of the Basic Law of the Government, according to which "the Prime Minister may, after informing the Cabinet of his intention to do so, remove a minister from office."

The Chief of Staff, Lt.-Gen. Rafael Eitan

We have arrived at grave conclusions with regard to the acts and omissions of the Chief of Staff, Lt.-Gen. Rafael Eitan. The Chief of Staff is about to complete his term of service in April, 1983. Taking into account the fact that an extension of his term is not under consideration, there is no [practical] significance to a recommendation with regard to his continuing in office as Chief of Staff, and therefore we have resolved that it is sufficient to determine responsibility without making any further recommendation.

Closing Remarks

In the witnesses' testimony and in various documents, stress is laid on the difference between the usual battle ethics of the I.D.F. and the battle ethics of the bloody clashes and combat actions among the various ethnic groups, militias, and fighting forces in Lebanon. The difference is considerable. In the war the I.D.F. waged in Lebanon, many civilians were injured and much loss of life was caused, despite the effort the I.D.F. and its soldiers made not to harm civilians. On more than one occasion, this effort caused I.D.F. troops additional casualties. During the months of the war, I.D.F. soldiers witnessed many sights of killing, destruction, and ruin. From their reactions (about which we have heard) to acts of brutality against civilians, it would appear that despite the terrible sights and experiences of the war and despite the soldier's obligation to behave as a fighter with a certain degree of callousness, I.D.F. soldiers did not lose their sensitivity to atrocities that were perpetrated on noncombatants either out of cruelty or to give vent to vengeful feelings. It is regrettable that the reaction by I.D.F. soldiers to such deeds was not always forceful enough to bring a halt to the despicable acts. It seems to us that the I.D.F. should continue to foster the [consciousness of] basic moral obligations which must be kept even in war conditions, without prejudicing the I.D.F.'s combat ability. The circumstances of combat require the combatants to be tough—which means to give priority to sticking to the objective and being willing to make sacrifices—in order to attain the objectives assigned to them, even under the most difficult conditions. But the end never justifies the means, and basic ethical and human values must be maintained in the use of arms.

Among the responses to the commission from the public, there were those who expressed dissatisfaction with the holding of an inquiry on a subject not directly related to Israel's responsibility. The argument was advanced that in previous instances of massacre in Lebanon, when the lives of many more people were taken than those of the victims who fell in Sabra and Shatilla, world opinion was not shocked and no inquiry commissions were established. We cannot justify this approach to the issue of holding an inquiry, and not only for the formal reason that it was not we who decided to hold the inquiry, but rather the Israeli Government resolved thereon. The main purpose of the inquiry was to bring to light all the important facts relating to the perpetration of the atrocities; it therefore has importance from the perspective of Israel's moral fortitude and its functioning as a democratic state that scrupulously maintains the fundamental principles of the civilized world.

We do not deceive ourselves that the results of this inquiry will convince or satisfy those who have prejudices or selective consciences, but this inquiry was not intended for such people. We have striven and have spared no effort to arrive at the truth, and we hope that all persons of good will who will examine the issue without prejudice will be convinced that the inquiry was conducted without any bias.

Yasir Arafat: Speech to Palestine National Council (February 14, 1983)*

To those against whom war is made, permission is given to fight because they have been wronged; and truly God is most powerful for their aid. They are those who have been expelled from their homes in defiance of right, for no cause except that they say, our Lord is God.

. . . The struggle will continue until the aims of our Arab nation are achieved. It will continue so that its domain is protected. . . . This commitment is based on deep conviction and pan-Arab nobility and the revolutionary reunion which has driven and still drives our revolution in strength and gallantry to continue our militant road and our armed revolution until we achieve our firm national rights which are not open to disposal, including our right to return, self-determination, and the establishment of our independent Palestinian state on our national Palestinian soil and until our fluttering banners are raised over holy Jerusalem, capital of our independent Palestine, and over its minarets and over its churches and over its walls. . . .

. . . Our Palestine National Council is convened in these difficult and grave times through which our Arab nation is passing in the shadow of the fateful challenges to our civilization as an Arab nation, and not only as a Palestinian revolution and not as joint Lebanese-Palestinian forces, but as an Arab nation. It is a question of to be or not to be, in the shadow of the U.S. imperialist-Zionist onslaught whose nails and daggers pierce the body of our Arab nation. It tries to spread its domination over our entire Arab nation; it tries to control our resources and tries to annex us to its sphere of influence.

Here is the importance of the posture, the mighty posture displayed by the joint Lebanese-Palestinian forces, and the steadfastness which they continue to display in their confrontation of this all-embracing American onslaught. In the same vein is the unequalled steadfastness of our joint forces and our militant masses in face of the Israeli military operation, fully paid for by the United States, by the racist military clique in the Zionist invasion army, in order to commit these

---

* Excerpts from a speech in Algiers.

barbarous crimes against the Lebanese and Palestinian people. These crimes reached the summit of barbarism and savagery as is clear from the massacres and butchery in the Sabra and Shatila camps after the gallant fighters of the joint forces had destroyed the arrogance and pomposity of the enemy and turned him back.

Your fighters stood fast in Beirut. Your masses stood fast in Beirut. Your nation stood fast by you in Beirut in the face of untiring attempts by the United States to exhaust the entire Arab nation and kneel before the aggressors, the Zionist invaders and the U.S. imperialists. In 88 days the pride of our contemporary Arab history . . . stood fast in the face of technological supremacy and challenged the superior and sophisticated U.S. military machine. . . .

Brother President, friends, brothers, by standing fast in Beirut a new phase began in our Arab history. Israel's blitzkrieg wars and its imaginary blitzkrieg victories have ended forever in the face of your mujahidin brothers who have died as martyrs for the existence and dignity of our entire Arab nation. Yes, brother, this is a new phase of our history which we enter with strength and belief after the volcano which erupted in Beirut. It is a phase of Arab transformation with all its values and concepts and with all that surrounds it. Imperialist balances and everything based upon them will not live long after the eruption of this volcano in Beirut.

Beirut has exposed everything. It has exposed everything and nothing is left to our Arab nation except the deep roots produced by the free and noble people and the mujahidin.

. . . For 18 years we have been fighting for our homeland through our Palestinian revolution. Through this last stage of our people's long march, that hard and difficult march, we have learned from our own experiences and those of revolutionaries all over the world that national unity is the guarantee for victory and that the independence of national decision away from all pressures and negative influences is the basis for crystallizing the national personality of our Palestinian people. We have learned that armed struggle complements political struggle in all fields. Despite all obstacles and hurdles and mines—and they are many—we have been guided by these bases. . . .

The rallying of our Palestinian people, internally and externally, around their armed revolution is the protective shield on which the arrows of the aggressors and the plotters always fall. Whatever the disguises and however hard the parties to the plot hide or try to hide themselves, and whatever forms the plot takes, after the Beirut events, they cannot deceive our people and our masses. No force, however great and however much acclaimed, can transform the giant who stood fast in Beirut and Lebanon into a dwarf. . . . Our decision comes from our people and from the barrel of a gun. . . . These firm national objectives, which are not open to modification, are that our people shall live in their homeland, free and as masters.

I beg our Arab nation, and after the Arab summit in Fez approved the Arab peace plan and after the visit paid by the Arab seven-member committee to world capitals, I say to every Arab that peace is the peace of the strong. I say peace is the peace of the strong and there is no peace for the weak or for those who bend. Therefore, our Arab nation is called upon to mobilize all its energies and all its military and political and mass capabilities to confront the challenges of destiny imposed on us at this critical stage which our Arab nation is now experiencing. . . .

We do not fight for the sake of fighting and do not reject for the sake of rejection. We fight for the freedom of our homeland and people and for the sake of our dignity. We reject anything—far or near—that harms our firm national rights. On this basis, the PLO asks all countries in the world to stand beside it in the face of the Israeli aggression, stressing that there is no solution to the Middle East crisis, no peace, no stability, and no security in this region, without the firm national rights of the Palestinian people.

While clinging to the rifle and shouldering it in the face of aggression in order to defend our people and land and for the sake of our freedom, we are advocates of peace based on meeting our people's firm national rights, including the right to return, the right to self-determination, and the right to establish an independent Palestinian state on their natural soil with holy Jerusalem as the capital. Our choice to establish a confederation with our people in fraternal Jordan is a genuine expression of our conviction in comprehensive Arab unity. . . .

Our national unity is the basis of our action and movement, our independent national decision is our guide, which cannot be faulted in defining the target. It is inevitable that our National Council should lay down political programs which fulfill the requirements and reply to the challenges. Ultimately, it is inevitable that we should have absolute unity founded on a democratic and creative basis. Let thousands of flowers blossom but in the gardens of the revolution! . . .

The PLO, entering its new revolutionary stage with firm and strong steps, turns to all those who are free and honorable in the world to stand beside our people's just struggle. At the same time, when the revolution starts this new and regenerated uprising, it reaches out—as it has always done—to all the world's liberation movements. It clasps their hands and stands beside them with all our capabilities.

We turn, with greetings and appreciation, to our friends in the socialist bloc led by the friendly Soviet Union, to the nonaligned countries, to the Islamic countries, to the African countries, and to the friendly countries for their support and their stand beside the just and legitimate struggle of our people. We greet and stand beside the free and revolutionary people in South Africa and Namibia and warmly greet all the free and revolutionary people in America, Latin America, and Asia. We are with every struggler against imperialism, Zionism, and colonialism. We are with every struggler against oppression and racial discrimination and for a better life and future.

Palestine National Council: Political Statement (February 22, 1983)*

On the Palestinian Level:

1. Palestinian National Unity:

The battle of steadfastness of heroism in Lebanon and Beirut epitomizes Palestinian national unity in its best form. The PNC affirms continued adherence to independent Palestinian decisionmaking, its protection, and the resisting of all pressures from whatever source to detract from this independence.

Palestinian Armed Struggle:

The PNC affirms the need to develop and escalate the armed struggle against the Zionist enemy. It affirms the right

* Excerpts from the PNC Political Statement issued in Algiers at the concluding session.

of the Palestine revolution forces to carry out military action against the Zionist enemy from all Arab fronts. . . .

2. The Occupied Homeland:

The PNC salutes our steadfast masses in the occupied territory in the face of the occupation, colonization, and uprooting. It also salutes their comprehensive national unity and their complete rallying around the PLO, the sole legitimate representative of the Palestinian people, both internally and externally. The PNC condemns and denounces all the suspect Israeli and American attempts to strike at Palestinian national unanimity and calls on the masses of our people to resist them. . . .

The National Council salutes the steadfastness of its people living in the areas occupied in 1948 and is proud of their struggle, in the face of racist Zionism, to assert their national identity, it being an indivisible part of the Palestinian people. The council asserts the need to provide all the means of backing for them so as to consolidate their unity and that of their national forces.

Our Dispersed People:

The PNC asserts the need to mobilize the resources of our people wherever they reside outside our occupied land and to consolidate their rallying around the PLO as the sole legitimate representative of our people. It recommends to the Executive Committee to work to preserve the social and economic interests of Palestinians and to defend their gained rights and their basic liberties and security.

Contacts With Jewish Forces:

. . . The PNC calls on the Executive Committee to study movement within this framework in line with the interest of the cause of Palestine and the Palestinian national interest.

On the Arab Level:

Deepening cohesion between the Palestinian revolution and the Arab national liberation movement throughout the Arab homeland so as to effectively stand up to the imperialist and Zionist plots and liquidation plans, particularly the Camp

David accords and the Reagan plan, and also ending the Zionist occupation of the occupied Arab land, relations between the PLO and the Arab states shall be based on the following:

A. Commitment to the causes of the Arab struggle, first and foremost the cause of and struggle for Palestine.

B. Adherence to the rights of the Palestinian people, including their right to return, self-determination, and the establishment of their own independent state under the leadership of the PLO—rights that were confirmed by the resolutions of the Arab summit conferences.

C. Adherence to the question of sole representation and national unity and respect for national and independent Palestinian decisionmaking.

D. Rejection of all schemes aimed at harming the right of the PLO to be the sole representative of the Palestinian people through any formula such as assigning powers, acting on its behalf, or sharing its right to representation.

The Arab Peace Plan:

The PNC considers the Fez summit resolutions as the minimum for political moves by the Arab states, moves which must complement military action with all its requirements for adjusting the balance of forces in favor of the struggle and Palestinian and Arab rights. The council, in understanding these resolutions, affirms it is not in conflict with the commitment to the political program and the resolutions of the National Council.

Jordan:

Emphasizing the special and distinctive relations linking the Jordanian and Palestinian peoples and the need for action to develop them in harmony with the national interest of the two peoples and the Arab nation, and in order to realize the rights [as] the sole legitimate representative of the Palestinian people, both inside and outside the occupied land, the PNC deems that future relations with Jordan should be founded on the basis of a confederation between two independent states.

Lebanon:

1. Deepening relations with the Lebanese people and their National Forces and extending support and backing to them

in their valiant struggle to resist the Zionist occupation and its instruments.

2. At the forefront of the current missions of the Palestinian revolution will be participation with the Lebanese masses and their National and democratic forces in the fight against and the ending of Zionist occupation.

Relations With Syria:

Relations with sister Syria are based on the resolutions of successive PNC sessions which confirm the importance of the strategic relationship between the PLO and Syria in the service of the nationalist and pan-Arab interests of struggle and in order to confront the imperialist and the Zionist enemy, in light of the PLO's and Syria's constituting the vanguard in the face of the common danger.

The Steadfastness and Confrontation Front:

The PNC entrusts the PLO Executive Committee to have talks with the sides of the pan-Arab Steadfastness and Confrontation Front to discuss how it should be revived anew on sound, clear, and effective foundations, working from the premise that the front was not at the level of the tasks requested of it during the Zionist invasion of Lebanon.

Egypt:

The PNC confirms its rejection of the Camp David accords and the autonomy and civil administrations plans linked to them. The council calls on the Executive Committee to develop PLO relations with Egyptian nationalist, democratic, and popular forces struggling against moves to normalize relations with the Zionist enemy in all their forms.

Reagan's Plan:

Reagan's plan, in style and content, does not respect the established national rights of the Palestinian people since it denies the right of return and self-determination and the setting up of the independent Palestinian state and also the PLO—the sole legitimate representative of the Palestinian people—and since it contradicts international legality. Therefore, the PNC rejects the considering of this plan as a sound basis for the just and lasting solution of the cause of the Palestine and the Arab-Zionist conflict.

Barry Rubin: United It Stalls: The PLO
(March 21, 1983) *

Can the Palestine Liberation Organization develop a pragmatic diplomatic policy following its crushing military defeat in Lebanon? The sixteenth Palestine National Council meeting in Algiers last month disappointed those who had hoped so. Although the PLO may be adapting to the new situation, its pace is so slow and hesitant as to throw into doubt its ability or desire to negotiate before it is too late. With Israel daily tightening its hold on the West Bank, and Jordan considering initiatives in its own right, the Palestinian leadership seems again to have thrown away opportunities, and to be further than ever from its goals.

In recent years the PLO has gradually shifted away from its old, unattainable objective of destroying Israel and replacing it with an Arab state. The PLO now proposes a Palestinian state in the West Bank and Gaza, though it persists in refusing to recognize Israel. Last September President Reagan suggested a plan for a Jordanian-Palestinian federation with a large measure of Palestinian self-rule. Since then the Administration has hoped—and a large segment of the media has grasped at straws to imply—that the PLO might accept this proposal. The current government of Israel opposes all these ideas, but President Reagan hopes to induce Prime Minister Begin to change his policy.

The result of the convention of the PNC, the PLO's parliamentary body, was both a clear-cut political victory for Yasir Arafat and a reminder of just how narrow is his room for maneuvering. The Reagan plan was rejected, and resolutions discouraged a proposed negotiating tactic to circumvent PLO-Israel mutual nonrecognition—the creation of a joint Jordanian-Palestinian delegation in which West Bank inde-

* Barry Rubin is a senior fellow at the Georgetown University Center for Strategic and International Studies. The article was published in *The New Republic*, March 21, 1983, reprinted by permission of *The New Republic*, © 1983, The New Republic, Inc.

pendents would represent the Palestinians, but take orders from PLO headquarters.

Observers have often overestimated Arafat's courage or ability to change PLO policy, given the caution bred by his constant struggle to mollify PLO factions and Arab regimes that use money, competing militancy, and even assassination in attempts to control the organization. Arafat's own weapons include cagey ambiguity in political positions and consensus above all. These tools have served him well, but also block any moving away of the PLO from a maximalist and rejectionist stance.

There are thus two ironies in the PLO's politics. First, the very policies that preserve the organization also freeze it into self-defeating negativism. Second, Arafat's strong position as leader is best protected by minimum use of his potential leverage. With time no longer on its side and deprived of its base in Lebanon, the PLO may well find such flaws fatal.

PNC Chairman Khalid Fahum and Arafat themselves sketched out, in milder but equally determined language, the reasons why the Reagan plan was unacceptable to the PLO. They scorned it for disregarding refugees' "right to return" to what is now Israel, self-determination, establishment of an independent Palestinian state with East Jerusalem as its capital, and recognition of the PLO as its sole legitimate representative. These four points all concern major issues; the Reagan plan cannot be adjusted to meet them.

Thus the PNC political resolution rejected the U.S. proposal in fairly clear language: "Reagan's plan, in style and content, does not respect the established national rights of the Palestinian people. . . . Therefore, the PNC rejects the considering of this plan as a sound basis for the just and lasting solution of the cause of the Palestine and the Arab-Zionist conflict." Fatah leader Salah Khalif said in his speech—not quoted in the U.S. press—"I have not heard a single Palestinian say that he accepted Reagan's plan."

The PNC took a more favorable position on a confederation with Jordan, which Arafat even defended as an expression of Arab unity. But there was no question of accepting domination from Amman. The resolution called for "a confederation between two independent states." Our people shall live in their homeland, free and as masters," said Arafat. The PNC was suspicious about allowing the Jordanians or West Bank mayors to negotiate with the Americans or Israelis. The PNC final resolution called for: "Rejection of all schemes aimed at harming the right of the PLO to be the sole representative of the Palestinian people through any formula such as assigning powers, acting on its behalf, or sharing its right of representation."

If the PLO does change course, the Arab regimes will have a great deal to do with it. Despite Syria's negativism, the majority of involved Arab governments favor some accommodation with Israel for the first time in history. Egypt, Jordan, Saudi Arabia, and even Iraq take this "moderate" position. The Saudis, however, have been quite timid, even by their standards, in trying to influence the PLO. Their Fez summit resolution, endorsed by the PNC meeting, called for an independent Palestinian state in all the occupied territories with only the vaguest offer of recognition for Israel. So far they have not offered much encouragement to Reagan's efforts.

The PLO's anti-Americanism remains particularly strident. As PLO spokesmen repeatedly stress, the United States is Israel's main supplier of arms and aid, while U.S. guarantees to protect Palestinians in West Beirut proved worthless in the Sabra and Shatila massacres. Arafat's closing oration portrayed Lebanon as a PLO victory, and blamed setbacks on United States involvement. Washington received no thanks for saving the PLO leadership and troops in West Beirut from complete destruction. In Arafat's words, Ambassador Philip Habib and President Reagan decided "to destroy the foundation of the PLO." He even claimed, "The U.S. 6th fleet . . . was the one that carried out the Israeli military landings. . . ." But things in Lebanon were not really so bad: "They speak of this invincible [Israeli] army. But, brothers, by God I have not found it invincible. . . . I wish all my nation was with me to see the feebleness of this army."

Such rhetoric is aimed at building morale, but it also shapes thinking. PLO strategy is still tied to positions based on illusion or internal politics. Reporters and commentators like to suggest that the failure of the PLO or of Jordan to accept the Reagan plan results from a lack of U.S. credibility and an inability to bring rapid Israeli withdrawal from Lebanon or a settlement freeze on the West Bank. But aside from the misdeeds of the Begin government, the fact is that the PLO has principled differences with American objectives and the Jordanians are hard put to join in without an Arab mandate or PLO acquiescence. The PLO only offers Hussein the unattractive option of risking a great deal to establish a PLO-led state. Unless the Arab side can produce a better offer, Washington will have no incentive to put pressure on Israel, and the creeping annexation of the West Bank will continue. . . .

Jordan's Refusal to Join the Reagan Peace Initiative (April 10, 1983)*

Since the Israeli aggression of June 1967, and through our awareness of the dangers and repercussions of the occupation, Jordan has accepted the political option as one of the basic options that may lead to the recovery of Arab territories occupied through military aggression. Consequently, Jordan accepted Security Council Resolution 242 of November 22, 1967. When the October 1973 war happened, it underlined the importance of continuing work on the political option while in the same time building our intrinsic strength. This war brought about Security Council Resolution 338, which put a stop to military operations and implicitly re-emphasized Security Council Resolution 242.

Based on Security Council Resolution 338, disengagement agreements were concluded between Israel on the one hand and Egypt and Syria on the other. This process completed the Arab circle immediately concerned with the recovery of the occupied lands through political means.

On this basis, Jordan, in cooperation with the Arab states, developed and adopted the concept of forming a unified Arab delegation that would attend an international conference for the purpose of achieving a just and comprehensive peace settlement to the Middle East problem.

In 1974, the Rabat Arab summit conference designated the Palestine Liberation Organization as the sole legitimate representative of the Palestinian people. Jordan went along with the Arab consensus and has been committed to that decision ever since.

The ensuing period saw the disjointment of Arab unity as evidenced by the Camp David accords. Further disintegration in the overall Arab position followed even between those directly affected by the Israeli occupation. All the while,

* Jordanian Cabinet statement.

Jordan kept sounding the alarm on the one hand and persevering in its course of action on the other.

Jordan warned repeatedly of the dangers inherent in the continuation of the no-war, no-peace situation, and of the exploitation by Israel of this situation to perpetuate the status quo by creating new facts in the occupied Arab territories, to realize its declared ambitions, aided by Arab disunity and by its military superiority.

Jordan has also cautioned against letting time pass by without concluding a just and comprehensive peace settlement because time was, and still is, essential to Israel's aim of creating new facts and bringing about a fait accompli.

Sixteen years have passed since the occupation, during which Israel established 146 colonies in the West Bank alone and has illegally expropriated more than 50 percent of that land.

Even today, Israel forges ahead in defiance of all international conventions and of the United Nations resolutions with a systematic policy of evacuating the inhabitants of the West Bank to change the demographic composition of the occupied Arab territories, thus realizing its designs to establish the Zionist state on the whole of Palestine.

From the early days of the occupation, and through awareness of the Zionist aims, Jordan made all these warnings and undertook the task of implementing all policies that may support the steadfastness of the Palestinian people and help them stay in their national soil.

With this objective in mind, we worked incessantly on all levels. Domestically, Jordan provides markets for the industrial and agricultural products of the West Bank and Gaza, and continues to extend support to the existing institutions in the West Bank. Also, we continue to attach great importance to building our intrinsic defense capability in cooperation with other Arab states, through the conviction held by all our nation of the great danger posed by Zionist ambitions, which threaten the Arab world and its future generations.

Within this context Jordan paid particular attention to building its armed forces, looked for new sources of arms within the available financial means and enacted the military service law to mobilize all its national resources for self-defense and for the defense of the Arab world because Jordan remains, by virtue of its geographic location, a constant target for Israeli aggression and the first line of defense on the east flank of the Arab world.

On the Arab level, Jordan sought to provide financial support for the steadfastness of the Palestinian people and formed a joint Jordanian-Palestinian committee, which continues to implement the policy of supporting our people in the occupied lands.

On the international level, Jordan worked to mobilize world opinion to bring pressure to bear on Israel, and in the United Nations, through cooperation with Arab and friendly countries, Jordan succeeded in passing resolutions condemning, isolating and putting pressure on Israel.

All the while, Israel continued with its expansionist colonization program, evicting the Arab inhabitants of Palestine and replacing them by Jewish immigrants. We strive to confront this program, which stands to affect Jordan more than any other country and which threatens Jordan's identity and national security.

In June 1982, Israel launched its aggression on Lebanon, which resulted in that country joining the list of occupied Arab territories. Lebanon was not excluded from the ambitions of Israel, which had already annexed Jerusalem and the Golan Heights, and which works for the de facto annexation of the West Bank and Gaza.

Last September, the United States President Ronald Reagan declared his peace initiative to solve the Middle East crisis, and shortly after, the Fez Arab summit conference resumed its proceedings where the Arab peace plan was formulated. It is evident that both peace proposals were inspired by the provisions of Security Council Resolution 242 and by the United Nations resolutions that followed.

Jordan, as well as other Arab and friendly countries, found that the Reagan plan lacked some principles of the Fez peace plan, but in the same time it contained a number of positive elements. Given the realities of the international situation, on the other hand, the Arab peace plan lacked the mechanism that would enable it to make effective progress. The Reagan plan presented the vehicle that could propel the Fez peace plan forward, and Jordan proceded to explore this possibility.

We believe, and continue to believe, that this aim can be achieved through an agreement between Jordan and the Palestine Liberation Organization on the establishment of a confederal relationship that would govern and regulate the future of the Jordanian and Palestinian peoples. This relationship would express itself, from the moment of its inception, through joint Jordanian-Palestinian action based on the Fez peace plan, Security Council Resolution 242 and the principles of the Reagan initiative. In addition, such a confederal relationship would be sought if only through the faith Arabs have in their joint destiny and in recognition of the bonds that have linked the people of Jordan and Palestine throughout history.

These concepts, and the ideas and assessments that follow from them, formed the subject of intensive discussions held over several meetings between His Majesty King Hussein and PLO chairman Yasir Arafat, as well as between the Government of Jordan and a number of senior members of the PLO, within the framework of a higher committee which was formed for this purpose and which held its deliberations over the five months between October 1982 and the recent convention of the Palestinian National Council in 1982. In addition, a number of prominent Palestinians inside and outside the occupied territories took part in the discussions.

These deliberations resulted in the irrefutable conclusion that Jordan and Palestine are joined by undeniable objective considerations reflected by the common threat against them which united their interests and their goals. There also resulted a joint conviction in the soundness of our approach, and we agreed to form a joint stand capable of pursuing political action, which, with Arab support, can take advantage of the available opportunity to liberate our people, land and, foremost of which, Arab Jerusalem.

Then, upon the request of Mr. Yasir Arafat, we waited to see the results of the Palestinian National Council meeting, where Mr. Arafat assured us he would act to secure the support of the council for the envisaged joint political action, on whose basic elements we agreed, pending their developments in the Palestinian National Council by declaring confederate-union relationship between Jordan and Palestine.

In our latest meeting with Mr. Arafat, held in Amman between March 31 and April 5, we conducted a joint assessment of the realities of the Palestine problem in general, and in particular of the dilemma facing the Palestinian people under occupation.

We also discussed political action in accordance with the Arab and international peace plans, including President Reagan's peace initiative, bearing in mind the resolutions of the PNC. We held intensive talks on the principles and methods, and we reemphasized the importance of a confederal relationship between Jordan and Palestine as being a practical conceptualization from which to work for the implementation of this initiative. We agreed to work together in this delicate and crucial time to form a united Arab stand that would enable us to deal with the practical aspects of these initiatives, in the hope of achieving a just, permanent and comprehensive solution to the Middle East problem, especially the Palestinian problem.

We also agreed to start immediately joint political action on the Arab level to secure Arab support that would contribute enormously to the realization of the common goal of liberating the lands and people under occupation, thus fulfilling our duty to work in all possible ways and to take advantage of every possible opportunity to achieve our aims.

Together with PLO chairman Yasir Arafat, we laid the final draft of our agreement, which required us and Mr. Arafat to make immediate contacts with Arab leaders to inform them of its contents, seeking their blessing and support for the agreement.

The PLO executive committee deliberated on this issue in the course of several meetings, and finally Mr. Arafat decided to discuss the agreement with other PLO leaders outside Jordan and return to Amman after two days to conclude the joint steps necessary for the implementation of the agreement.

Five days later, a delegate was sent by the PLO executive committee chairman to Amman, to convey to us new ideas and to propose a new course of action that differed from our agreement and that did not give priority to saving the land, thus sending us back to where we were in October 1982.

In the light of this, it became evident that we cannot proceed with the course of political action which we had planned together and to which we had agreed in principle and in details, in answer to our historic responsibility to take the opportunities made available by Arab and international initiatives and save our land and people.

In view of the results of the efforts we made with the PLO, and in compliance with the 1974 Rabat summit resolution, and through the strict observance of the independence of the Palestinian decision, we respect the decision of the PLO, it being the sole legitimate representative of the Palestinian people. Accordingly, we leave it to the PLO and the Palestinian people to choose the ways and means for the salvation of themselves and their land, and for the realization of their declared aims in the manner they see fit.

We in Jordan, having refused from the beginning to negotiate on behalf of the Palestinians, will neither act separately nor in lieu of anybody in Middle East peace negotiations.

Jordan will work as a member of the Arab League, in compliance with its resolutions to support the PLO within our capabilities, and in compliance with the requirements of our national security.

Being consistent with ourselves, and faithful to our principles, Arab Jerusalem and holy shrines, we shall continue to provide support for our brothers in the occupied Palestinian territories and make our pledge to them before the Almighty that we shall remain their faithful brothers and side with them in their ordeal.

As for us in Jordan, we are directly affected by the results of the continued occupation of the West Bank and the Gaza Strip through the accelerating colonization program and through the economic pressures systematically being brought on the Palestinian people to force them out of their land.

In the light of these facts, and in the no-war and no-peace situation that prevails, we find ourselves more concerned than anybody else to confront the de facto annexation of the West Bank and Gaza Strip, which forces us to take all steps necessary to safeguard our national security in all its dimensions. Both Jordanians and Palestinians shall remain one family that cares for its national unity to the same extent that it cares to stay on this beloved Arab land.

May God assist us in our aspirations.

The Lebanon-Israel Truce Agreement
(May 17, 1983) *

The government of the Republic of Lebanon and the government of the State of Israel, . . .

Having agreed to declare the termination of the state of war between them,

Desiring to ensure lasting security for both their states and to avoid threats and the use of force between them,

Desiring to establish their mutual relations in the manner provided for in this agreement, . . .

Have agreed to the following provisions:

* Excerpts.

ARTICLE 1

1. The parties agree and undertake to respect the sovereignty, political independence and territorial integrity of each other. They consider the existing international boundary between Lebanon and Israel inviolable.

2. The parties confirm that the state of war between Lebanon and Israel has been terminated and no longer exists.

3. Taking into account the provisions of paragraphs 1 and 2, Israel undertakes to withdraw all its armed forces from Lebanon in accordance with the annex of the present agreement.

ARTICLE 2

The parties, being guided by the principles of the Charter of the United Nations and of international law, undertake to settle their disputes by peaceful means in such a manner as to promote international peace and security and justice.

ARTICLE 3

In order to provide maximum security for Lebanon and Israel, the parties agree to establish and implement security arrangements, including the creation of a security region, as provided for in the annex of the present agreement.

ARTICLE 4

1. The territory of each party will not be used as a base for hostile or terrorist activity against the other party, its territory, or its people.

2. Each party will prevent the existence or organization of irregular forces, armed bands, organizations, bases, offices or infrastructure, the aims and purposes of which include incursions or any act of terrorism into the territory of the other party, or any other activity aimed at threatening or endangering the security of the other party and safety of its people. To this end, all agreements and arrangements enabling the presence and functioning on the territory of either party of elements hostile to the other party are null and void.

3. Without prejudice to the inherent right of self-defense in accordance with international law, each party will refrain:

A. From organizing, instigating, assisting, or participating in threats or acts of belligerency, subversion, or incitement or any aggression directed against the other party, its population or property, both within its territory and originating therefrom, or in the territory of the other party.

B. From using the territory of the other party for conducting a military attack against the territory of a third state.

C. From intervening in the internal or external affairs of the other party.

4. Each party undertakes to ensure that preventive action and due proceedings will be taken against persons or organizations perpetrating acts in violation of this article.

ARTICLE 5

Consistent with the termination of the state of war and within the framework of their constitutional provisions, the parties will abstain from any form of hostile propaganda against each other.

ARTICLE 6

Each party will prevent entry into, deployment in, or passage through its territory, its air space and, subject to the right of innocent passage in accordance with international law, its territorial sea, by military forces, armament, or military equipment of any state hostile to the other party.

ARTICLE 7

Except as provided in the present agreement, nothing will preclude the deployment on Lebanese territory of international forces requested and accepted by the government of Lebanon to assist in maintaining its authority. New contributors to such forces shall be selected from among states having diplomatic relations with both parties to the present agreement.

ARTICLE 8

1. A. Upon entry into force of the present agreement, a Joint Liaison Committee will be established by the parties, in

which the United States of America will be a participant, and will commence its functions. . . .

B. The Joint Liaison Committee will address itself on a continuing basis to the development of mutual relations between Lebanon and Israel, *inter alia* the regulation of the movement of goods, products and persons, communications, etc. . . .

2. During the six-month period after the withdrawal of all Israeli armed forces from Lebanon in accordance with Article 1 of the present agreement and the simultaneous restoration of Lebanese government authority along the international boundary between Lebanon and Israel, and in the light of the termination of the state of war, the parties shall initiate, within the Joint Liaison Committee, *bona fide* negotiations in order to conclude agreements on the movement of goods, products and persons and their implementation on a non-discriminatory basis. . . .

ANNEX
SECURITY ARRANGEMENTS

A. A security region [in southern Lebanon] in which the government of Lebanon undertakes to implement the security arrangements agreed upon in this annex is hereby established. . . .

The Lebanese authorities will enforce special security measures aimed at detecting and preventing hostile activities as well as the introduction into or movement through the security region of unauthorized armed men or military equipment. . . .

B. Lebanese Police . . . may be stationed in the security region without restrictions as to their numbers. These forces and elements will be equipped only with personal and light automatic weapons. . . .

C. Two Lebanese Army brigades may be stationed in the security region. One will be the Lebanese Army territorial brigade. . . .* The other will be a regular Lebanese Army brigade. . . .

D. The existing local units will be integrated as such into the Lebanese Army, in conformity with Lebanese Army regulations. . . .

* Composed of the breakaway force of Major Saad Haddad.

Said Musa: Interview on Internal Dissent
(May 26, 1983)*

. . . Fatah's leadership knows that the Palestinian cause is not an issue of an officer or a group of officers, or an issue of a military group of elements in the arena of conflict in Al-Biqa' rebelling against military orders. Ours is a cry for correcting a mistaken political action that had begun to develop and emerge more clearly following our departure from Beirut. Frankly, there is a political conflict within Fatah that has been going on for years. This conflict has developed into a broad current that believes in political concepts that are committed to Fatah's statutes and political program. . . .

. . . Following our freeze in Beirut, several positive questions evolved. And these should have given us the incentive to stiffen our political stands in order to confront the U.S. imperialist plan and in order for this steadfastness not to become a catalyst for implementing the U.S. plot and program. Following the battle of Beirut, we should have also submitted a struggle plan that commits the Palestinian revolution to confront the U.S. plan on Lebanon's territory by virtue of the fact of the existing occupation and as a field of struggle through alliance with the nationalist movement and the honorable forces who are determined to continue the fight. However, this leadership went to Fez, and we consider that the Fez plan is actually Fahd's plan which stems from Camp David and from UN Resolution 242 despite the inclusion of certain points which at first glance appear positive, such as demanding the establishment of a Palestinian state, the return of refugees, regaining Jerusalem, and eliminating the settlements. But we wonder who is capable of translating this program or that plan. Are Arab summits capable of doing such a thing?

And I answer: No, because from our experience in Lebanon no one moved to provide Beirut's children with a single drink of water. We realize that the establishment of the Palestinian state and the return of the refugees is an issue that requires several wars. When the United States and Israel feel that their interests in the region are threatened, it is only at that moment

* Excerpts from an interview by *Al-Watan* (Kuwait) with Said Musa (Abu Musa), of the anti-Arafat revolt in the PLO.

that our voice as a Palestinian revolution will be heard. Then, the Arab countries can impose their plans, although they are supposed to be on the line of confrontation and in the middle of the conflict and not in a position to make deficient plans. Had these plans been offered by friends or allies or other parties, they could have been accepted, but not from the Arab countries because this is not what is expected of them. However, despite all this we say that whatever the matters may be, there is supposed to be a Palestinian option when there is a state of inability to implement these plans. Our Palestinian option since 1965 has been the option of armed struggle. However, the Palestinian leadership accepted the Arab option and dropped the option of armed struggle. . . .

And as for the Reagan plan, it was proposed on the day on which the last batch left Beirut. We heard the clauses of the plan when we were at sea. Its discussion in the Fatah movement began; we discussed its positive and negative sides. Through a simple political reading of the plan we find that it denies the existence of the Palestinian people and not only the Palestinian question. It also says no to the Palestinian state, no to the PLO, no to Jerusalem and its return, and yes to the settlements and to changing the borders. Despite all this, some voices within Fatah said there were positive points in the plan —that it recognized for the first time that the West Bank and Gaza Strip were under occupation. Is there anything new in this? Is there any justice in this? . . .

After the Reagan plan we plunged into a new whirlpool, the plan for a confederation with Jordan. We began to discuss the details before the state had been established—instead of first establishing the state and then discussing the confederation, which would be a direct result of establishing the state. Without going into all the details of this matter, I say that so far no clear decision has been made on this matter. We have not closed the door on it; it remains unresolved. There should be clear agreement that talks on a confederation are to be held after the establishment of an independent state. . . .

It is not a question of numbers. If it had been so I would have addressed an appeal to all our fedayeen and they would all have joined us. We are an indivisible part of Fatah. We are the conscience of Fatah who have raised their voice and thought aloud, and express the broad faithful base. . . . Therefore, it is necessary to stop and examine what we have achieved. What has this revolution achieved? Is it capable of shouldering the responsibility in confronting these big plans in

light of its current reality or should it rearrange itself in a
proper manner so that it can confront the coming stage? We
say that the . . . National Council when it said yes to many of
the political issues is neither a revolutionary nor a clear act.
Political clarity is the major base. We understand that in the
stages of retreat revolutionary movements adhere more closely
to principles and bases.

What should I say to my father who fought in 1936 before
the occupation of Palestine and the establishment of the Israeli
state? What should I say to those who fought during these
years to prevent the establishment of such a state? Are we
fighting in order to recognize Israel? This is not reasonable,
not reasonable and strange. These issues should be reexplained
and corrected. Lastly, is it fair that the Central Committee
issues decisions to put us under the command of the commander in chief together with Abu Hajim and Al-Haj Isma'il?
Is it fair that it issues decisions to freeze our activity? . . .

Khalid al-Hasan: On the Dissident Rebellion
(May 27, 1983)*

. . . Frankly and without exaggerating or underestimating what
has been described as a rebellion, mutiny, or split within the
Fatah movement, we ask: What did really happen, what were
its causes, and what repercussions is it likely to have?

Answer: The group involved, including Abu Musa, Qadri,
Abu Salih, and others, originally held political views characterized by rejection of the Fez resolutions and other policies. . . . This group, even before Fez, adopted certain political
attitudes based on an idealistic rejection of everything or on
conditional approval of many things. For example, Brother
Abu Salih said that he would support the Fez summit [plan] if
it included setting up a Palestinian state and would oppose it
if it did not. So, fundamentally, this group has been adopting
a certain political attitude for years. We could say that this
attitude began to crystallize after the September events, and it
has been applied to Jordan and to the recent Fez resolutions.
The group included Naji 'Allush, Abu Nidal, and many others.
Some of them left the movement and some continued to work

---

* Excerpts from an interview with Fatah Central Committee member Khalid
al-Hasan in *Al-Hawadith* (London).

within its framework. Even at the recent PNC meetings in Algiers, Abu Musa adopted certain attitudes which stemmed from a comprehensive theory which everyone wished it was possible to implement, even partially. The reason behind the declarations made in Al-Biqa' was certain military organizational decisions made with the approval of the Military Council. They believe that some of these decisions should not have been made, especially the appointment of Abu Hajim as officer in charge of the Al-Biqa' area and Al-Haj Isma'il as officer in charge of the north. Their position developed into a mutiny in the sense that they rejected the new military organizational steps. It was not made on political grounds, although the political aspect later came into it.

As far as discipline is concerned, this matter is serious. Democracy may be required on such matters, but at the level of the Central Committee, not the level of military officers. . . . That is the declared principle of the matter. The other fact is that, very regrettably, Brother Abu Salih overstepped the mark in Fatah's democracy when he extended a hand for funds from a source outside Fatah and cooperated with two Arab states. . . . That money was paid before the PNC conference and it was agreed that five issues would be used to cause a split. They included rejection of the Fez summit, rejection of agreement with Jordan, and rejection of the Reagan initiative. There was no problem there, but to give the dissension a national character they were to use these points and, in the event of failure, they were to raise the issue of the dialogue with Israeli democratic forces. . . .

Another issue had also been raised to cause disunity. That issue was the differences with Syria. . . , I believe that national unity is not unity of the organizations but rather unity of the people behind the leadership and the goals. This does in fact exist because the Palestinian people are united regardless of whether there is a leadership or not. It was the Palestinian people, not an organization or a leadership, who foiled the settlement plots in the fifties. This matter is too great to be undermined. The people are much more united than the organizations. The organizational numbers do not broadly and accurately reflect the real attitudes of the people. One organization or another may have some support here or there, but Abu 'Ammar's leadership is unquestionable and Fatah's political line represents the mainstream. That is why I consider agreement among the organizations to be agreement among the instruments of work—and not national unity because unity is there. Our problem with the unity of the instruments is that some of them are not Palestinian, even though they are identified as such, because they do not take Palestinian orders. National unity or front relations under the National Charter, and in fact under any front regulations anywhere in the world, means agreement on a minimum plan of action with the minority accepting the views of the majority. It is very regrettable that the minority does not accept the opinion of the majority. . . .

A Selective Bibliography

PALESTINE MANDATE

Ibrahim Abu-Lughod. *The Transformation of Palestine*. Evanston, Ill., 1971.

Neil Caplan. *Futile Diplomacy: Early Arab-Zionist Negotiation Attempts, 1913–1931*. Vol. 1. London, 1983.

Michael J. Cohen. *Palestine: Retreat from the Mandate, the Making of British Policy, 1936–1945*. New York, 1978.

————. *Palestine and the Great Powers, 1945–48*. Princeton, 1982.

J. C. Hurewitz. *The Struggle for Palestine*. New York, 1950.

A. W. Kayyoli. *Palestine: A Modern History*. London, 1978.

Ann M. Lesch. *Arab Politics in Palestine, 1917–1939: The Frustration of a National Movement*. Ithaca, N.Y., 1979.

John Marlowe. *The Seat of Pilate: An Account of the Palestine Mandate*. London, 1959.

Y. Porath. *The Emergence of the Palestinian Arab National Movement 1918–1929*. Vol. 1. London, 1974.

————. *The Palestinian Arab National Movement, 1929–1939*. London, 1977.

Christopher Sykes. *Crossroads to Israel*. London, 1965.

ISRAEL AND ZIONISM

David Ben-Gurion. *Rebirth and Destiny of Israel*. New York, 1954.

————. *Years of Challenge*. London, 1963.

Michael Brecher. *Decisions in Israel's Foreign Policy*. New Haven, 1975.

————. *The Foreign Policy System of Israel: Setting, Images, Process*. New Haven, 1972.

Aharon Cohen. *Israel and the Arab World*. Boston, 1976.

Moshe Dayan. *Breakthrough: A Personal Account of the Egypt-Israel Peace Negotiations*. New York, 1981.

Abba Eban. *Abba Eban: An Autobiography*. New York, 1977.

Amos Elon. *Herzl*. New York, 1975.

———. *The Israelis: Founders and Sons*. New York, 1971.

Walter Eytan. *The First Ten Years*. New York, 1958.

Ben Halpern. *The Idea of a Jewish State*. Cambridge, Mass., 1969.

Arthur Hertzberg (ed.). *The Zionist Idea*. New York, 1969.

Walter Laqueur. *A History of Zionism*. New York, 1972.

Ian Lustick. *Arabs in the Jewish State*. Austin, 1980.

Laurence Meyer. *Israel Now: Portrait of a Troubled Land*. New York, 1982.

Howard Penniman. *Israel at the Polls*. Washington, D.C., 1977.

Yoram Peri. *Between Battles and Ballots: Israeli Military in Politics*. Cambridge, England, 1983.

Yitzhak Rabin. *The Rabin Memoirs*. Boston, 1979.

Itamar Rabinovich and Jehuda Reinharz (eds.). *Israel in the Middle East*. New York, 1984.

Bernard Reich. *The Quest for Peace*. New Brunswick, N.J., 1977.

Nadav Safran. *Israel: The Embattled Ally*. Cambridge, Mass., 1978.

Leonard Stein. *The Balfour Declaration*. London, 1961.

David Vital. *The Origins of Zionism*. Oxford, 1975.

Chaim Weizmann: *Trial and Error*. New York, 1949.

THE ARAB WORLD AND ARABISM

Fouad Ajami. *The Arab Predicament*. Cambridge, England, 1981.

George Antonius. *The Arab Awakening*. Philadelphia, 1939; London, 1946.

John Devlin. *Syria: Modern State in an Ancient Land*. Boulder, 1983.

Ismail Fahmy. *Negotiating for Peace in the Middle East*, Baltimore, 1983.

Sami Hadawi. *Bitter Harvest, Palestine 1914–1967*. New York, 1967.

Sylvia Haim (ed.). *Arab Nationalism: An Anthology*. Berkeley, 1962.

Yehoshafat Harkabi. *Arab Attitudes Toward Israel*. Jerusalem, 1976.

Albert Hourani. *Arabic Thought in the Liberal Age, 1798–1939*. Cambridge, England, 1983.

Kemal H. Karpat (ed.). *Political and Social Thought in the Contemporary Middle East*. New York, 1968.

Malcolm Kerr. *The Arab Cold War, 1958–1964*. London, 1965.

Walid Khalidi. *Conflict and Violence in Lebanon*. London, 1983.

Walter Laqueur (ed.). *The Middle East in Transition*. New York, 1958.

Bernard Lewis. *The Middle East and the West*. New York, 1964.

Gamal Abdel Nasser. *The Philosophy of the Revolution*. Cairo, 1964.

H. Z. Nuseibeh. *The Ideas of Arab Nationalism*. Princeton, 1956.

Barry Rubin. *The Arab States and the Palestine Conflict*. Syracuse, N.Y., 1981.

Dankwart Rustow. *Oil and Turmoil*. New York, 1982.

Anwar Al-Sadat. *In Search of Identity*. New York, 1978.

Patrick Seale. *The Struggle for Syria*. New York, 1965.

John Waterbury. *The Egypt of Nasser and Sadat: The Political Economy of Two Regimes*. New York, 1984.

THE PALESTINIANS

John W. Amos II. *Palestinian Resistance: Organization of a Nationalist Movement*. New York, 1980.

Helena Cobban. *The Palestinian Liberation Organization: People, Power, Politics*. New York, 1984.

Abdallah Frangi. *The PLO and Palestine*. London, 1983.

David Gilmour. *The Dispossessed: The Ordeal of the Palestinians, 1917–1980*. London, 1980.

Y. Harkabi. *The Palestine Covenant and Its Meaning*. London, 1981.

Abu Iyad. *My Home, My Land*. New York, 1981.

Joel S. Migdal (ed.). *Palestinian Society and Politics*. Princeton, 1980.

Aaron David Miller. *The PLO and the Politics of Survival*. New York, 1983.

William Quandt, Fuad Jabber, Ann M. Lesch. *The Politics of Palestinian Nationalism*. Berkeley, 1973.

Edward W. Said. *The Question of Palestine*. New York, 1979.

ARAB-ISRAELI WARS

Michael Brecher. *Decisions in Crisis: Israel, 1967 and 1973*. Berkeley, 1980.

E. L. M. Burns. *Between Arab and Israeli*. New York, 1962.

Erskine B. Childers. *The Road to Suez*. London, 1962.

Winston S. Churchill and Randolph S. Churchill. *The Six Day War*. London, 1967.

Moshe Dayan. *Diary of the Sinai Campaign*. Westport, Conn., 1979.

Martin Gilbert. *The Arab-Israeli Conflict: Its History in Maps*. London, 1976.

Mohammed Husanayn Haykal. *The Road to Ramadan*. New York, 1975.

Mark Heller (ed.). *The Middle East Military Balance, 1983*. Boulder, 1984.

Chaim Herzog. *The Arab-Israeli Wars: War and Peace in the Middle East*. New York, 1982.

———. *The War of Atonement*. Boston, 1975.

Fred Khouri. *The Arab-Israeli Dilemma*. Syracuse, N.Y., 1976.

David Kimche and Dan Bawly. *The Sandstorm: The Arab-Israeli War of 1967.* London, 1968.

Jon and David Kimche. *Both Sides of the Hill.* New York, 1960.

Walter Laqueur. *Confrontation: The Middle East War and World Politics.* New York, 1974.

————. *The Road to Jerusalem: The Origins of the Arab-Israeli Conflict.* New York, 1968.

Robert Lieber. *Oil and the Middle East War.* Cambridge, Mass., 1976.

Netanel Lorch. *The Edge of the Sword: Israel's War of Independence, 1947–49.* New York, 1961.

John Norton Moore (ed.). *The Arab-Israeli Conflict: Readings and Documents.* 3 vols. Princeton, 1977.

Itamar Rabinovich. *The War for Lebanon, 1970–1982.* Ithaca, N.Y., 1984.

Alvin Z. Rubinstein (ed.). *The Arab-Israeli Conflict: Perspectives.* New York, 1984.

Nadav Safran. *From War to War: The Arab-Israeli Confrontation, 1948–1967.* New York, 1969.

Hugh Thomas. *Suez Affair.* New York, 1966.

Saadia Tuval. *The Peacemakers: Mediators in the Arab-Israeli Conflict, 1948–1979.* Princeton, 1982.

Ezer Weizman. *The Battle for Peace.* New York, 1981.

Constantine Zurayk. *The Meaning of the Disaster.* Beirut, 1956.

THE GREAT POWERS AND THE CONFLICT

Zbigniew Brzezinski. *Power and Principle: Memoirs of the National Security Adviser, 1977–1981.* New York, 1983.

Robert Freedman. *Soviet Policy Toward the Middle East Since 1970.* New York, 1972.

Galia Golan. *The Soviet Union and the Palestinian Liberation Organization: An Uneasy Alliance.* New York, 1980.

————. *Yom Kippur and After: The Soviet Union in the Middle East Crisis.* New York, 1977.

Matti Golan. *The Secret Conversations of Henry Kissinger.* New York, 1976.

Peter Grose. *Israel in the Mind of America.* New York, 1983.

Henry Kissinger. *White House Years.* New York, 1979.

————. *Years of Upheaval.* New York, 1982.

William Quandt. *Decade of Decisions: American Policy Toward the Arab-Israel Conflict, 1967–1976.* Berkeley, 1977.

E. R. F. Sheehan. *The Arabs, Israelis, and Kissinger.* New York, 1976.

Cyrus Vance. *Hard Choices: Critical Years in American Foreign Policy.* New York, 1983.